Encyclopedia of
Latin American
Politics

Encyclopedia of Latin American Politics

Edited by Diana Kapiszewski
Alexander Kazan, Assistant Editor

Center for Latin American Studies
Georgetown University

ORYX PRESS
Westport, Connecticut • London

The rare Arabian Oryx is believed to have inspired the myth of the unicorn. This desert antelope became virtually extinct in the early 1960s. At that time several groups of international conservationists arranged to have 9 animals sent to the Phoenix Zoo to be the nucleus of a captive breeding herd. Today the Oryx population is over 1,000 and nearly 500 have been returned to reserves in the Middle East.

Library of Congress Cataloging-in-Publication Data

Encyclopedia of Latin American politics / Diana Kapiszewski, editor ; Alexander Kazan, assistant editor.
     p. cm.
    Includes bibliographical references and index.
    ISBN 1-57356-306-4 (alk. paper)
    1. Latin America—Politics and government—Encyclopedias. 2. Politicians—Latin America—Encyclopedias. 3. Latin America—Encyclopedias. I. Kapiszewski, Diana. II. Kazan, Alexander.
    F1410.E56 2002
    320.98'03—dc21   2001036182

British Library Cataloguing in Publication Data is available.

Library of Congress Catalog Card Number: 2001036182
ISBN: 1-57356-306-4

First published in 2002

Oryx Press, 88 Post Road West, Westport, CT 06881
An imprint of Greenwood Publishing Group, Inc.
www.oryxpress.com

Printed in the United States of America

∞™

The paper used in this book complies with the Permanent Paper Standard issued by the National Information Standards Organization (Z39.48–1984).

10 9 8 7 6 5 4 3 2 1

Contents

Preface

Shortly before his death in 1830, Simón Antonio de la Santísima Trinidad **Bolívar y Palacios** (see Colombia) mourned the demise of his dream of a unified Latin America: "America is ungovernable. Those who have served the revolution have plowed the sea." A quick glance at present-day Latin America proves that Bolívar's gloomy prediction was, thankfully, inaccurate. At the beginning of the third millennium, all of the countries of Latin America, save Cuba, are governed by elected leaders. Across the region, democratic institutions are being created, revamped, and strengthened and civil society is becoming more active and engaged in the political process.

This present unifying wave of democratic consolidation notwithstanding, the political histories and realities of the countries of Latin America are extraordinarily diverse, and generally poorly understood. While some perceive Latin America as a region whose countries have been ruled by military dictatorships more often than not, in reality, some countries of the region, such as Chile or Colombia, have extremely strong democratic traditions that rival those of some countries of Western Europe. While others regard Latin America as a very "revolutionary" area, only five Latin American nations have attempted change by revolution in the twentieth century (Mexico 1910–1920; Guatemala, 1944–1954; Bolivia, 1952–1964; Cuba, 1959 to the present; Nicaragua, 1979–1990). While some believe that the hot-blooded Latins are continually going to battle against each other, in truth, international conflict breaks out quite infrequently in the region: there has been just one major international war in the past 100 years, and the region boasts dozens of political pacts, trade groupings, and international organizations.

Perhaps these homogenizing misconceptions about Latin America exist due to the region's complexity, or because Latin America has seldom played an important role in international power politics, and thus has not been considered meritorious of studious analysis. Regardless of the cause, given the many common misconceptions about Latin American politics, a resource is needed to clarify and disaggregate the political histories and political realities of the nations of the region. The *Encyclopedia of Latin American Politics* aspires to be that resource.

Latin America is generally understood to comprise the eighteen Spanish-speaking republics of the Western Hemisphere, together with Portuguese-speaking Brazil and French-speaking Haiti. Thus this volume includes chapters on those twenty nations and, in addition, a chapter on Puerto Rico, a Caribbean island whose current political status is that of a commonwealth of the United States. While the volume includes entries on regional political figures, organizations, dynamics, and events from the 1800s and 1900s, emphasis is placed on the twentieth century. Each chapter includes a country profile listing relevant economic, political, and social data, a brief historical overview, between twenty and forty entries (varying with the size and political complexity of the country), a list of heads of state (from independence to the present), and a bibliography that provides readers with excellent resources for further study.

As the volume's organization by country does not allow for easy inclusion of multilateral agreements, groupings, organizations, or wars, Appendix 1 chronicles the most important of these. In addition, given the significant involvement and influence that the United States has had in regional politics during the twentieth century, Appendix 2 outlines the various approaches to Latin American foreign policy employed by twentieth-century U.S. presidents, and also lists multilateral organizations relevant to the region headquartered in the United States. Finally, a glossary has been added to the Encyclopedia to allow students of the region's politics to familiarize themselves with the political and economic terminology employed throughout the book.

Entries are cross-referenced in three ways to help readers find and make the best use of the wealth of information included in the volume. First, the work is internally cross-referenced through the use of **boldface** type. Upon first mention in an entry, a person, organization, or event that is an Encyclopedia entry is boldfaced; if the entry is located in another chapter or in an appendix, the chapter or appendix in which it can be found is indicated in parentheses. Second, some entries include *see also* listings that direct readers to related entries. Finally, *see* references (consisting of just the name of a person, organization, or event) direct the reader to information included in other entries. These features, plus the index, should help readers easily navigate the volume.

Each entry begins with a brief one-or two-sentence summary highlighting the political significance of the entry. Upon first mention within an entry of any individual who was head of state of a Latin American nation, the dates he held office (or the country in which he held office, if different from the chapter in which he is covered) follow in parentheses. Also, the first time a political party or grouping is mentioned in an entry, the full English translation of its name is given, followed in parentheses by the Spanish, Portuguese, or French name

and usually the acronym by which the party or grouping is known. The first time individuals are mentioned in an entry, their complete name appears. (Complete Spanish and Portuguese surnames often consist of various names.) When mentioned subsequently in that entry, individuals are referred to by the surname by which they were commonly known, which may consist of one or two names.

The *Encyclopedia of Latin American Politics* strives to be a complete and accurate source of basic information on Latin American politics in the last two centuries. The volume attempts to offer clear explanations of the events, individuals, organizations, and dynamics that have shaped the region's past, as well as those that are governing its present, and will affect and guide what will hopefully be its fully democratic future.

Historical Introduction to Latin America

Jeffrey Taggart

Every Latin American country has its own rich and unique history. Nonetheless, the region shares a common cultural heritage, and its countries have experienced similar political and economic trends over the last 500 years. This brief historical overview presents these commonalities and provides a context for the detailed information included in the Encyclopedia. While the introduction necessarily contains generalizations, greater detail about the figures, organizations, events, and dynamics that have shaped each Latin American country's reality can be found in the country chapters and appendices of the Encyclopedia. It is through these that the diversity that characterizes the region comes alive. For the sake of simplicity, the region will be referred to as Latin America, even before its colonization by the European imperial powers.

PRECOLONIAL SPAIN AND LATIN AMERICA

Spain Prior to 1492

Following the Moorish invasion of Spain in A.D. 711, Christians fought to regain control of what would become modern Spain and Portugal (the Iberian Peninsula) from the Moors, followers of Islam from northern Africa. Despite these protracted religious wars, Christians, Muslims, and Jews lived in relative harmony in many parts of the Iberian Peninsula. However, following the final military victory of the Christians over the Moors in 1492, the Catholic Church gained significant authority in Spanish society, and subsequently Christian Courts of Inquisition were held to interrogate people about their religious beliefs. Many who came before these courts were forced to renounce their Muslim or Jewish beliefs or face exile from Spain, or possibly death. This zeal for Christianity and conquest would be carried to the New World by the Spanish *conquistadores* (conquerors).

The initial encounter of European society with Latin America was an accident. At the end of the fifteenth century spices from China and Japan were extremely popular in Europe, prompting Europeans to make periodic voyages by sea to acquire them from those two countries. From Spain, most travelers departed toward the east, continuing around the south of Spain, to the west and around the south of Africa to arrive in China and Japan. Italian explorer Christopher Columbus theorized that the trip would be shorter if he proceeded west from Spain instead, and he appealed to Queen Isabel of Spain for financial support for such a voyage. After weeks at sea, Columbus' crew was at the point of desperation when they spied land on October 12, 1492. While Columbus believed they had reached their planned destination, they had actually arrived on the island subsequently dubbed Hispaniola. Columbus' mistake led to further Spanish exploration, and eventually the establishment of a Spanish empire in this "New World" rich with silver and gold, as well as culture and tradition.

The Encounter of Europeans with Indigenous Peoples of Latin America

In the late fifteenth century, there were countless and diverse indigenous populations living throughout the Americas. The three largest indigenous empires were those of the Aztecs of modern Mexico, the Incas, whose empire dominated much of the Pacific Coast of South America, and the Maya of what is today southern Mexico and Central America.

Aztecs

At the end of the fifteenth century, the Aztec Empire controlled a large territory in the area that is today known as Mexico, having defeated many other indigenous tribes. Members of this advanced society placed great emphasis on religion and had instituted a tribute system whereby conquered tribes regularly paid the Aztecs. Spanish explorer Hernando Cortés reached the center of the Aztec Empire in Tenochtitlán, Mexico, in 1519 and defeated Aztec leader Moctezuma II and his followers with just a small group of soldiers and horses. It is not clear how the Aztecs were so easily defeated; perhaps the horses and the white skin of the Spaniards led Moctezuma to mistake one or more of the men for Quezaltcoatl, the god whose return the Aztecs awaited, or perhaps the Spaniards were able to attract support from regional enemies of the Aztecs. What is certain is that by the beginning of the seventeenth century, Mexico's native population had been devastated, decreasing from 25 million in 1523 to just 1 million in 1605.

Incas

In the early sixteenth century, the Incas were bitterly divided in a civil war between two Inca leaders, Atahualpa and his half-brother Huascar, who competed for control of an immense empire that stretched from Ecuador to the northern half of Chile at its peak. Cortés' conquest of Mexico had opened the floodgates to colonization, and Spaniards hoping to carry out similarly lucrative conquests were attracted to the empire of the Incas because of its wealth of silver and gold. Spaniard Francisco Pizarro arrived there in 1531, and his forces quickly ambushed and captured Atahualpa, holding him for ransom; they subsequently killed Atahualpa despite having received the ransom. Divided and leaderless, the Inca Empire quickly fell under Spanish control.

Maya

Mayan civilization, centered in the southern part of what is today Mexico and in parts of modern Guatemala, Honduras, and El Salvador, boasted a complex social order and many cultural achievements including a written language, astronomical and mathematical discoveries, and the invention of calendars. However, the Maya were already in decline when the Spanish arrived, having been dominated and absorbed by the Toltec Indians of central Mexico, and thus the Spanish *conquistadores* overpowered them with relative ease.

THE COLONIAL ERA

Political Structure of the Spanish Colonies

The Treaty of Tordesillas, signed by Portugal and Spain in 1494, awarded Spain all territory situated to the west of a north-south line drawn through the eastern portion of modern Brazil, and granted Portugal control of the eastern part of the continent. However, the lack of a

Spanish and Portuguese America, 1780

substantial population of Portuguese colonists allowed Spanish colonists to encroach into the Brazilian region.

The Spanish crown administered its colonies through viceroyalties, vast territories ruled by a viceroy who reported directly to the king. While there were initially two viceroyalties, New Spain (today Mexico, Central America, and the Caribbean) and Peru (today Spanish South America), Spain tried to expand the scope and effectiveness of its colonial administration in the late eighteenth century by adding two new viceroyalties, New Granada (modern Ecuador, Colombia, and Venezuela) and La Plata (modern Argentina, Paraguay, and Uruguay). Important checks and balances were placed on the viceroys as the colonial system attempted to centralize authority in the imperial powers. For instance, judges of the *audiencia* could overrule a viceroy, and in an effort to promote loyalty to the crown, *peninsulares* were appointed to hold virtually all of the important positions in the colonial administration. Further, the Catholic Church and the crown retained very close ties (given their shared goal of promoting Christian values), and the crown used the church as its moral authority and as a part of its ruling bureaucracy in the colonies.

Despite these checks and balances, the administration of the colonies through viceroys was bureaucratically cumbersome and logistically difficult given the vast distance and poor communications between the colonies and Spain. While the crown issued many guidelines to protect its interests, these were often ignored by political leaders in the New World who agreed to obey royal orders but often did not actually implement them. As a result, over time, the colonies grew increasingly autonomous and decentralized. In addition, many of the less important political positions, such as seats on the town council, could be legally purchased, which reinforced the interests of the small, minority elite. Away from viceregal capitals, captains-general and presidents ruled as mini-viceroys with great autonomy, and viceroy-deputy kings gained increasing amounts of power, with the smaller areas that they ruled eventually becoming the bases of the region's modern republics.

Economic and Labor Systems

Europeans came to Latin America largely for personal financial gain, having heard tales of the tremendous quantities of gold and silver that existed in the New World. While no *conquistador* ever found the fabled golden city El Dorado in Colombia, vast deposits of precious metals, particularly **silver** (see Bolivia), were found and mined in Mexico and Upper Peru (modern Bolivia). These metals were initially the colonies' primary export to Spain.

As precious metals were not abundant everywhere, the Spanish soon established large-scale plantations to bring them wealth, and perhaps more importantly, status. Initially, the colonists grew the same crops that the indigenous peoples raised, including maize, beans, and potatoes. However, as the Hispanic population grew in the colonies, agricultural production began to reflect European tastes, and started to include products such as wheat, meat, sugar, and wine. Some of the colonists' crops, such as olive oil, were eventually able to compete economically with products cultivated in Spain because of the inexpensive labor force, and thus the lower cost of production in the New World. While manufacturing in the colonies did not develop to a very extensive degree during the colonial period because of the competition from European manufacturers, textiles became an important early manufacture.

As the Spanish could not extract all of the wealth from the colonies themselves, they took advantage of the labor systems that had been established in the most populous parts of Latin America before their arrival to generate a labor pool to work the Spanish mines and plantations in the New World. In the areas where the Inca Empire had previously reigned, the Spanish colonists found an indigenous population that was accustomed to paying tribute either in precious metals or in labor assistance to the Inca leaders through the *mita* system; colonists reinvented and implemented that forced labor system in the silver mines. In areas where agriculture became important, the Spanish employed

the *encomienda* system. These labor and tribute systems in effect enslaved the native population and later the population brought from Africa, and allowed the colonists to extract and generate vast amounts of wealth in the 1600s and 1700s. The crown also benefited, as one-fifth of all riches reaped from the New World by the Spaniards had to be given to the Spanish government as a tax payment known as the *quinto*, or royal fifth.

In addition, in the late 1600s and the 1700s, Jesuit missionaries in the La Plata viceroyalty took a very different approach, organizing the indigenous people on large plantations and educating them in farming, the arts, and literature. These missions, known as *reducciones*, were extremely well organized and operated with economic autonomy, separate from the rest of colonial society. The colonists, fearing that the missions would threaten the colonial economic structure, and jealous of the scarce resources (mainly manual labor) the missions controlled, protested to the Spanish crown, which eventually recalled the Jesuits from the New World in 1767. In the absence of Jesuit guidance, the missions quickly fell into disorganization and ceased to be of economic or social significance.

Social Aspects/Role of Religion

Many of the (often poor) Spaniards who followed Columbus to the New World were able to find wealth and status thanks to the hierarchical society the Spanish created. *Peninsulares* formed the political, economic, and social elite, with creoles just below them. Mestizos occupied the middle strata, and pure indigenous and black slaves occupied the lowest social strata with virtually no political voice. Most officials (who were generally wealthy and powerful) were *peninsulares*. Because the number of white males far exceeded the number of white females, a mixing of the races began, and by the twentieth century, most of the countries in Latin America had populations that were majority mestizo.

Given the previous eight centuries of religious wars in Spain, many of the colonists were also devout Catholics. When they witnessed the vastly different behavior of the indigenous people, noted their inability to speak Spanish, and learned of their religious beliefs, many considered them to be savage and uncivilized. Consequently, churches were often built over temples in an effort to eliminate the indigenous religion and implant the Catholic Church in the sacred space, and some colonists (including some religious clergy) sought to convert the indigenous people to Christianity. While some colonists believed conversion would save the indigenous people morally and religiously, others hoped that they could better control the native peoples through simultaneously imposing Catholicism and repressing native religious practices. Regardless of the motive, conversions carried out by the Spanish were infrequently complete, and the "Christianity" practiced after these conversions was usually a blend of indigenous and Catholic practices. The emphasis on Catholicism would be an important point of contention after Latin America gained independence.

Of course, there were some Spaniards who defended the rights of the indigenous, which caused conflict within the church. Important voices for indigenous rights were Bartolomé de Las Casas, a Franciscan friar in sixteenth-century Mexico, and Antonio Vieira, a Jesuit in seventeenth-century Brazil; those who operated the Jesuit missions mentioned above also tried to improve the lives of the native people. While these individuals devoted many years of their lives to bringing the plight of the native peoples to the attention of the Spanish crown and were able to win some rulings for more humane treatment of the indigenous people, as was often the case with rulings issued in Spain, many colonists officially accepted the ruling but changed their practices very little. Remarkably, in spite of centuries of repression, the influence of these ancient indigenous religions can be seen in Latin American religious practices today, in the many traditions and rituals that are unique to Latin American Catholicism.

During the colonial era, huge numbers of indigenous people were killed; though estimates vary, some indicate that over 90 percent of the indigenous population was wiped out. Many died as a result of direct combat with the Spanish, but many more perished from exposure to European diseases against which they had no immunities, and from being overworked in the mines or on plantations. As a result, the modern populations of many Latin American countries have small percentages of indigenous people; only Peru, Bolivia, Ecuador, Mexico, and Guatemala have substantial indigenous populations. Further, many countries of Latin America became involved in the transatlantic slave trade in order to maintain the labor force needed to keep the colonies economically productive following the exhaustion of the native population. The modern populations of some countries, notably the sugar-producing colonies of the Caribbean and Brazil, include a significant percentage of Africans and mulattos.

INDEPENDENCE

Stirrings of Independence

Many factors combined to encourage the movements for independence in Latin America. Of importance were the American and French revolutions, as well as the European philosophy of Enlightenment. The far-reaching Bourbon Reforms implemented in Spain in the late 1700s provided additional motivation. Initially Spain maintained a very tight economic relationship with its colonies; essentially, the colonies were only permitted to trade through two official Spanish ports, Cádiz and Sevilla, and were not allowed to trade directly with each other or with other nations. As a result, taxes that would have been levied by colonial ports were instead collected by Spanish ports, from which products were redistributed to the colonies or reexported to other nations at much higher prices than the Spanish paid the colonial producers. Economic growth in the colonies was consequently slow, which led to colonial frustration. This was partially relieved by one of the Bourbon Reforms, the 1778 Decree of Free Trade, which allowed trade between colonies and opened all Spanish and American ports to transatlantic trade. The decree led to significant growth in the colonial economy, which inspired a desire among creoles for absolute free trade with other European nations. Other Bourbon Reforms limited the participation of creoles in *audiencias* and senior church positions, and replaced local and corrupt creole *corregidores* (short-term lieutenant governors who to that point had been the only direct representatives of royal administration and justice) with Spanish intendants. Usually *peninsulares*, these new provincial administrators enjoyed broader powers than any who had preceded them. This change, which reduced political participation, also inspired creoles to yearn for independence.

The constitutional crisis brought about by France's invasion of Spain and Napoleon Bonaparte's deposition of Spain's King Ferdinand VII in 1808 added a final impetus. That crisis resulted in the division of the colonists into three major factions: those who wanted to stay loyal to France's Joseph Bonaparte (who had replaced Spain's deposed king), those who wanted to pay continued allegiance to Spain's deposed King Ferdinand, and those who wanted complete independence from any European control. More than any other factor, it was the divisiveness among these three factions and battles between *peninsulares* and creoles over political and economic opportunities that led to the Wars for Independence.

Wars for Independence (1808–1826)

The battles for independence began in earnest in 1808, and though the revolutionary armies scored early victories, by 1815 Spain appeared to have regained control of its colonies. However, the creoles did not give up on winning their independence easily, and General José de **San Martín** (see Argentina) and Simón Antonio de la Santísima Trinidad **Bolívar y Palacios** (see Colombia) provided strong military leadership. Colonial militias that the Spanish had ordered the creoles to create to defend Buenos Aires from British incursions in 1808 formed the foundations of the revolutionary armies that San Martín led across the Andes Mountains. These forces joined with those led by General Bernardo O'Higgins (see Chile) to win a key victory against the Spanish in the Battle of Chacabuco in 1817. By 1819 Bolívar had gained firm control of Venezuela.

The key to defeating the Spanish was winning control of the viceroyalty of Peru, the center of the Spanish American colonies. The turning point came when King Ferdinand gave his support to the Spanish liberal constitution of 1812, which converted the cause of independence from Spain from a radical or liberal cause to a conservative cause against liberalism. This reversal prompted most of the creoles who had been loyal to Spain to support the independence movement, and the patriot armies were soon able to win control of the capital of the viceroyalty of Peru, Lima. Bolívar soon emerged as the undisputed leader of the Spanish American Revolutionary Armies, and he, together with General José de Sucre, fought long wars during which control of territories and cities changed hands numerous times. Eventually, the pair would liberate Venezuela, Colombia, and Ecuador from Spanish control. Despite creole fears of the possible implications of empowering the indigenous populations, Bolívar ultimately attracted many indigenous people to join the independence movement armies, and their participation was crucial to the revolutionaries' eventual victory.

In 1821 General Agustín Cosme Damian **de Iturbide** (see Mexico), the leader of the loyalist troops in Mexico, sensed that colonial independence was inevitable and made a deal with creole patriots for Mexican independence. The area that is today Central America joined Mexico in declaring its independence from Spain in September 1821. Brazilian independence came without violence in 1822 when royal prince Dom **Pedro I** (see Brazil) convoked a constituent assembly in Brazil and declared its independence from Portugal, establishing a constitutional monarchy. Brazil was ruled by an emperor until 1889 and experienced little political, social, or economic change through the end of the nineteenth century.

THE EARLY INDEPENDENCE PERIOD

Political Debates and Evolution

During the early postindependence period, what little political structure had existed under colonial rule soon grew weaker or was discarded, leaving the newly formed states of Latin America with very underdeveloped political institutions. Turbulence and instability, as well as serious political divisions and a lack of formal political organization, thus characterized the postindependence period. Struggles between nations ensued, including the **War of the Peru-Bolivia Confederation** (1836–1839; see Appendix 1), the **War of the Triple Alliance** (or Paraguayan War, 1865–1870; see Appen-

Latin America, 1830

dix 1), and the **War of the Pacific** (1879–1883; see Appendix 1).

Struggles within the young republics arose as well over access to political, social, and economic power. The conflict between liberals and conservatives, debates over the role of the Catholic Church in society, and the growing political involvement of landowning and agrarian elites all marked the second half of the nineteenth century in Latin America. These conflicts over how political and economic power should be controlled and distributed significantly shaped the evolution of the countries of the region in the twentieth century.

Liberals vs. Conservatives

Through the nineteenth century, the national politics of many of the region's countries were dominated by an ideological debate between liberals and conservatives. In many countries, the polemic was reflected in the formation of two major opposing political parties. In general, Latin American conservatives wished to return the Catholic Church to its previous preeminent and privileged status, and supported a central role for the church in the government. Conservatives also wanted to maintain traditional institutions (they supported the military's retention of its special privileges) and preserve the colonial hierarchical society in which white elites enjoyed economic and political well-being, in sharp contrast to the popular masses; they hoped that the church's influence and moral authority could minimize efforts on the part of nonelites to challenge the status quo. In general, the conservatives also supported the establishment of strong centralized states.

By contrast, liberals believed that the Catholic Church should not be involved in politics or government, and held that neither the clergy nor other elites should receive special privileges unavailable to the general population. Liberals believed in the sovereignty of the people and in individual rights and freedoms such as the right to personal security, and freedoms of speech, association, and religion. Liberals tried to create a system of checks and balances so that governments could be restrained and held accountable to their citizens through the periodic election of political leaders. Most liberals supported the idea of decentralized states and federalism.

Liberal/conservative rivalries in the nineteenth century, which often had a destabilizing effect on national politics, resulted in war in some countries. The **War of a Thousand Days** (1899–1902; see Colombia) was one in a long series of bloody disputes between Colombian liberals and conservatives. In Chile, bitter opposition between conservatives and liberals continued through Chile's first century of independence and well into the twentieth century, often leading to civil conflict and war, and in Argentina battles between the **Unitarists and Federalists** (see Argentina) continued until the middle of the 1860s.

Caudillo Rule and the Elite Quest for Power

From independence through the late nineteenth century, the most prevalent type of centralized rule was that of *caudillos*, strongmen who ruled their nations from above through whatever ruthless force was necessary to keep the masses from becoming overly politicized in ways that could threaten the status quo, or the stability or very existence of the nation. In addition to these national *caudillos*, such as Juan Manuel de **Rosas** (see Argentina) and Diego **Portales Palazuelos** (see Chile), during this period, many local *caudillos* continued to exercise control over subnational regions using highly repressive measures. Their strongman tactics, like those of their national counterparts, were usually tolerated in the absence of strong local and national governments in the interest of preventing anarchy.

By the 1880s, however, Latin American elites, especially landowners, began to take a more significant interest in the government and politics of the nations of the region. Their increased involvement, which helped to bring the era of *caudillo* rule to a close by the end of the nineteenth century, usually took one of two forms. In some countries, such as Chile and Argentina, elites, usually supported by the military, took control of national governments, wrote constitutions based on the U.S. or European model, and created strong, exclusive regimes often referred to as oligarchic democracies. In other countries, such as Mexico and Peru, elites exercised indirect political power through designating dictatorial strongmen (often military officers who were rarely elites themselves) to control the nation and maintain law and order. In all cases, the goal of these regimes was the preservation of control and stability.

During the nineteenth century, since small minorities of each country controlled the political system, regimes tended to rise and fall based on the individual appeal of leaders rather than on party affiliation or political issues. As a result, political parties tended to lack importance and political institutions stagnated in their development. The importance of the personal appeal of politicians has continued to characterize Latin American politics in the twentieth century, and partly as a result, the region's democracies and democratic institutions have remained underdeveloped.

Nineteenth-Century Economics

As the nineteenth century wore on, the *encomienda* system was replaced by the hacienda system. Landowning was important for status, and the hacienda was a low-risk investment. These plantations usually yielded one export crop whose production was labor-based (and thus inexpensive given the surplus of cheap labor in the new nations) and required little technology. However, as there were huge inefficiencies on these large plantations and minimal infrastructure (notably poor transportation systems) in these young countries, Latin America enjoyed little economic development or growth in the decades immediately following independence, and the new states were unable to compete effectively in the world economy.

However, the countries of Latin America experienced economic expansion at the end of the nineteenth century when the demand for the region's raw materials increased due to the industrial revolution taking place in North America and Western Europe. Improved roads and transportation systems allowed the countries of the region to meet that higher demand, and the region's products became major exports toward the end of the nineteenth century. The increase in demand for raw materials was fortuitous, as the economies of the region were locked into the production of raw materials for several reasons. The more developed countries of Western Europe and the United States were able to produce higher quality, less expensive consumer goods than were the local economies. Further, while Latin American consumers (mainly elites) desired higher quality imports, the percentage of individuals wealthy enough to buy locally made consumer products was simply too small to support the development of a substantial or competitive local consumer goods industry.

Social Dynamics

Independence from Spain resulted in minimal change in the social and economic structures of the new republics, generating resentment and frustration among marginalized classes, including workers, peasants, and the urban poor. Wealthy whites of Spanish descent remained the political, economic, and social elites of the newly independent ex-colonies, and very little changed for the majority of the region's mixed, black, and indigenous populations. The right to vote in elections was restricted to a very small segment of the population, namely white or mestizo males who owned property; women, indigenous people, black slaves, and nonpropertied whites were all denied the suffrage. The desire for continuity was based on economic interests and fear: many white elites were afraid that involving the indigenous population in the revolutionary process, granting them full participation, or implementing a major change in the social and economic hierarchy might threaten the status quo or inspire indigenous people to rise up in revolts similar to the **1804 Revolution** in Haiti (see Haiti) or the revolt led by Túpac Amaru II in Upper Peru in 1780. While marginalized classes did not play a prominent role in nineteenth-century regional politics, they would achieve greater influence during the early part of the twentieth century as new opportunities for participation arose.

EARLY TWENTIETH-CENTURY POLITICAL AND ECONOMIC DEVELOPMENT

Expanding Political Opportunities

At the beginning of the twentieth century, a number of factors combined to increase political inclusiveness. First, the right to vote in many countries was extended beyond elite males. This was a major development, as in most nations the majority of the populace had long been excluded from any meaningful political participation. In many cases, the expansion of suffrage led to the masses' increased involvement in politics, as well as to the development of professional politicians. Despite these changes, in most countries, indigenous populations and those of African descent remained marginalized from national political systems.

In addition, the export-import boom that lasted from the end of the nineteenth century until 1930, and the economic growth that it engendered, brought greater numbers of people in contact with one another and with new ideas, and led to an increase in the size of the middle class. Both of these factors contributed to expanded political participation. The boom also required countries to expand their labor forces, and the ranks of the working class swelled. Some nations received increasing numbers of immigrant workers, and while many of these immigrants were initially excluded from voting by residency laws, they often brought with them more radical ideologies such as socialism, communism, Marxism, and anarcho-syndicalism; the spread of these ideas led

to increased labor mobilization and the eventual politicization of the labor movement.

All of these dynamics resulted in an increase in the number, importance, and type of political parties in the region. In particular, as a result of the spread of leftist ideology and the politicization of the labor movement, more leftist political parties representing the views of the working classes began to emerge in the 1930s and the decades that followed. These parties, and the trade unionism and the class-based social activism with a leftist orientation that accompanied them, would play a major role in the history and politics of the region in the later twentieth century.

Ironically, the most advanced and successful mobilization of marginalized classes in the early twentieth century—the **Mexican Revolution** (1910–1929)—arose not directly as a result of partisan mobilization, but out of a combination of regime exhaustion and vulnerability, *caudillo* leadership on the regional level, and dissatisfaction with the centralization of political authority toward the end of the thirty-five-year reign of President Porfirio **Díaz** (1876–1880, 1884–1911). The revolution's first decade of armed struggle was followed by another decade of political turmoil, during which the political party that would eventually become the **Institutional Revolutionary Party** (Partido Revolucionario Institucional, PRI), the dominant political force in twentieth-century Mexico, was created.

Export-Led Growth to 1930

As the world's economies expanded and world demand for raw materials grew from the latter half of the nineteenth century forward, the countries of Latin America experienced export-led growth. Different countries produced and exported different products, but the logic was the same across the region: exportation of commodities and importation of relatively more expensive manufactured goods. Argentina used its beef and grain exports to develop into one of the world's strongest economies and most sophisticated cultures at the turn of the twentieth century, and Brazil (which exported sugar, gold, coffee, and rubber), Chile (nitrates and copper), Colombia (coffee), and Cuba (sugar) all experienced economic booms that continued until the effects of the Great Depression were felt in 1930. As had been the case at the end of the nineteenth century, this export-led growth did not foster sustainable economic development or the growth of manufacturing.

POST–WORLD WAR II POLITICS AND POST-DEPRESSION ECONOMICS

It is in the latter half of the twentieth century that the histories of the countries of the region diverge more significantly. Working-class actors responded differently to the expanded political opportunities generated and shaped by different economic outcomes. The economic policies of import substitution industrialization (see below), implemented continent-wide, had varying levels of success, which led to different sets of possibilities for political actors in the different Latin American countries. In terms of politics, the nineteenth-century struggles between liberals and conservatives over social issues like the role of the Catholic Church gave way to more explicit political battles over access to power between leftists (labor unions and communist and socialist parties) and rightists (business and landowning elites and the military). The contested incorporation of some formerly marginalized actors such as labor unions in the early twentieth century did not ameliorate these conflicts, but rather intensified them. These clashes, combined with the political traditions of populism and the continued interference of the United States in hemispheric affairs, significantly influenced the region's subsequent political turbulence.

Leftists, Cold War Politics, and Military Regimes

While leftist involvement in politics grew throughout most of Latin America through the latter part of the twentieth century, it increased to varying degrees, manifested itself in different ways, and engendered different reactions across the region. The rise of populist politicians, the increase in the number and strength of communist and socialist political parties, and the emergence of revolutionary movements led to brutal military regimes in some nations, to protracted civil war in others, and to increased U.S. involvement in many. In other important cases, increased leftist involvement in politics did not lead to considerable domestic turmoil.

Increased Leftist Involvement

The increased inclusiveness of the political sphere that had occurred through the first decades of the twentieth century led to increased political involvement on the part of students, factory workers, the urban poor, and the small but growing professional class. Politicians attempted to appeal to the expanding portion of the population that was politically involved, which resulted in the installation of populist regimes in some countries. These semi-authoritarian administrations usually catered to a particular set of interests, often used repression, and mainly represented the interests of workers and industrialists. Many populist politicians, who depended on personal power and charisma to appeal to and rally diverse groups and retain power, came to power in the mid-twentieth century, including Juan Domingo **Perón** (see Argentina), Getúlio **Vargas** (see Brazil), and Lázaro **Cárdenas** (see Mexico).

The increase in leftist political activity brought a proportionate increase in the size and strength of communist and socialist parties in some Latin American countries. In 1970 the Chilean electorate voted Salvador **Allende Gossens** (see Chile) into office, making him the region's first elected socialist president. In Peru the left-leaning **American Revolutionary Popular Alliance** (Alianza Popular Revolucionaria Americana, APRA; see Peru) gained strength from the 1930s to the 1950s. Leftist parties were seen by most political leaders in Latin America as a threat to the status quo, and many regimes feared that they might incite the masses to rise up in revolt and overthrow governments. To some degree their fear was legitimate as the leftists desired reforms that would have resulted in the redistribution of land and wealth in many countries. Consequently, in numerous countries, communist parties were made illegal for extended periods of time.

The increase in leftist activity and ideology coincided with weak economic growth and limited socioeconomic opportunities for most of the masses, a dynamic that led to the emergence of insurgencies and the upswing in violence that characterized Latin America in the 1970s and 1980s. The brutal **Shining Path** (Sendero Luminoso; see Peru) guerrilla group formed in Peru in 1970 with the goal of wresting power from the elite and military forces, destroying the state, and establishing a communist state based on Maoist principles. In Argentina, the **Montoneros** (see Argentina) carried out urban, guerrilla-like acts of violence to challenge both the government and the military from the mid-1960s through the late 1970s. In Central America, perhaps because the countries of that subregion are smaller and have more rurally based populations or perhaps because they lacked military and economic resources, leftist revolutionaries fought government forces in protracted civil wars in the 1970s and 1980s, specifically in Guatemala, El Salvador, and Nicaragua. The most successful revolutionary movement was the **July 26th Movement** (M-26–7; see Cuba), which triumphed in the **Cuban Revolution of 1959** (see Cuba), bringing Fidel **Castro Ruz** (see Cuba) to power; Castro has used political force to remain Cuba's leader for over forty years.

The U.S. Response: Cold War Politics

The United States became increasingly involved in Latin America during the early twentieth century through the implementation of blanket policies toward the region (see **Roosevelt Corollary to the Monroe Doctrine, Dollar Diplomacy, Missionary Diplomacy,** Appendix 2) and through intervening in and occupying various countries such as the Dominican Republic from 1916 to 1921 (see **United States Occupation,** Dominican Republic) and Nicaragua from 1912 to 1933. However, with the onset of the Cold War, U.S. intervention in Latin America increased dramatically (see **Alliance for Progress,** Appendix 2), complicating the development

Contemporary South America. © 2001 *The Moschovitis Group, Inc.*

and activity of leftist parties in Latin American politics. The United States government shared the fears of many Latin American elites that communists or other leftists would take over their countries and disrupt the capitalist system.

Nowhere was this increased involvement more apparent than in the Central American republics and Cuba. The U.S. Central Intelligence Agency (CIA) helped to arm and support Guatemalan rebels in 1954 to overthrow Guatemalan president Jacobo **Arbenz Guzmán** (see Guatemala), whom it feared was too closely allied with communists. In 1959 the Cold War intensified with the triumph of Fidel Castro's revolution in Cuba and Castro's subsequent alignment with the Soviet Union and support for revolutionary movements and groups in other Latin American countries (see **Bay of Pigs Invasion** and **Cuban Missile Crisis**, Cuba). U.S. president Ronald Reagan intervened extensively in Central America in the 1980s, notably in Nicaragua and El Salvador, where he sent weapons, advisors, and significant financial support for right-leaning regimes as well as rebel forces (see **National Republican Alliance** [Alianza Republicana Nacional, ARENA], El Salvador; **counterrevolutionaries** [contrarevolucionarios, contras], Nicaragua).

The Southern Cone Response: Bureaucratic Authoritarianism

Military regimes ruled in many countries of Latin America in the last half of the twentieth century, and a particular type of regime, dubbed "bureaucratic-authoritarian," evolved in several Southern Cone countries. The goal of these regimes was to contain leftists and leftist violence while stimulating economic growth and development. The military dictatorship headed by Augusto **Pinochet Ugarte** (see Chile) that ruled Chile from 1973 to 1990 committed thousands of human rights violations, but led Chile to experience significant economic success; that country's neoliberal reforms were replicated by civilian administrations throughout the region in the late 1980s and the 1990s. Argentina experienced violent military dictatorships from 1966 to 1970 and from 1976 to 1983, with little economic success. The military regimes that ruled Brazil between 1964 and 1985 relied less on repression than did Chile's, and achieved remarkable (albeit temporary) economic success with the Brazilian **"economic miracle"** (see Brazil).

Exceptions

Other countries experienced neither full-scale revolution, nor intense U.S. intervention, nor a bureaucratic-authoritarian regime during this time period. For example, Colombia's long tradition of formal democratic institutions, including a strong president and two well-established political parties, allowed it to maintain a relatively stable regime structure during the twentieth century despite significant internal turmoil. While a pact formed between the country's major political parties to rotate control of the government in the 1950s helped Colombia to avoid turbulence on the institutional level (see **National Front**, Colombia), the country nonetheless failed to address its economic disparities, which continued to generate unrest on the social level. Similarly, Venezuela avoided violent domestic uprising largely thanks to a political pact among its major political parties (see **Pact of** *Punto Fijo*, Venezuela) and the wealth generated through oil production and export. The monopoly on political power maintained by the authoritarian Mexican PRI allowed it to effectively stifle political opposition without aggressive repression and rule Mexico from 1929 to 2000.

The Rise and Fall of Import Substitution Industrialization and the Debt Crisis

With the onset of the Great Depression in the 1930s, the international demand for raw materials decreased dramatically, and the effect on Latin American economies was severe. The result of this economic downturn was an ideological shift from dependence on international markets and volatile international prices toward increased regional trade and Latin American self-sufficiency. Latin American governments strove for economic independence from the developed countries by producing their own consumer goods for domestic sale or for export to other Latin American countries. This economic policy, advocated by Argentine economist Raúl Prebisch and the **Economic Commission of Latin America and the Caribbean** (ECLAC; see Appendix 1), was known as import substitution industrialization (ISI).

The implementation of ISI policies resulted in increased governmental involvement in the development of national economies, as well as the establishment of large state-owned monopolies. ISI did not succeed in smaller countries but was initially successful in larger countries such as Brazil and Mexico whose domestic populations provided a sufficiently large internal market to support the profitable production and sale of basic consumer goods. However, even in these larger countries ISI was not very successful once production moved to more complex products because this higher level of production required greater capital investments (to develop factories), was dependent on parts only available in other countries, and required a more educated labor force than was available domestically. In addition, even the large countries soon found their national markets too small to support more advanced industrialization. Further, in most cases, governments were subsidizing businesses, and in many countries, governments actually owned and operated businesses at a loss. Finally, as many of these state-owned businesses were monopolies, there was little or no competition in the industries in which they operated, which made them extremely inefficient. There were a few regional efforts at forming trade blocs, but they created little trade (see **Andean Group** and **Central American Common Market** [CACM], Appendix 1).

In the 1960s and 1970s Latin America experienced a significant economic downturn as a result of ISI's failure. Regional governments had large deficits from supporting inefficient state-owned businesses and from the expensive social programs that they implemented in order to retain popularity and power. In an effort to try to cover these large budget deficits, especially in the 1970s and early 1980s, the administrations of many of the region's nations printed money and took out large loans from international lenders. As each successive administration applied short-term strategies to long-term financial problems, the debt situation worsened, in many cases eventually leading to hyperinflation and radically unstable economies.

In 1982 the Mexican government announced that it would be unable to meet its international debt obligations. This default was repeated by several other Latin American nations, resulting in a regional debt crisis. The magnitude of the crisis led to international efforts to forgive some of the loans and to use other methods to reduce some nations' debt burden. The absolutely desperate condition of most of the Latin American economies during this time forced politicians to work with creditor nations to renegotiate their debt, and to give in to the pressures from the International Monetary Fund, the World Bank, and other creditor banks to reorient their economies toward more free-market models.

OPPORTUNITIES AND CHALLENGES IN THE NEW MILLENNIUM

At the beginning of the twenty-first century, a complex set of intertwined dynamics and trends is playing out in Latin America. The process of globalization is gaining momentum in the region, and the nations of Latin America are becoming increasingly involved and invested in the international capitalist system. At the same time, regional economic integration is occurring. The **Southern Cone Common Market** (Mercado Común del Cono Sur, MERCOSUR; see Appendix 1) has emerged as one of the most successful regional trade blocs in the world. Further, all of the nations in the Western Hemisphere except Cuba participated in the **Summits of the Americas** (see Appendix 1) in 1994, 1998, and 2001, at which the region's presidents signed agreements addressing a variety of issues; the most important shared goal is the negotiation of a **Free Trade Area of the Americas** (FTAA; see Appendix 1) by 2005. This willingness to join forces across national borders and share resources and ideas to solve common problems is unprecedented in Latin America. Simultaneously, there has been a rebirth of indigenous pride in some of the countries of the region that has manifested itself in protests against globalization and Western values. The simultaneity of these dynamics has at times led to conflict, as was the case in Chiapas, Mexico, when the **Zapatista National Liberation Army** (Ejército Zapatista de Liberación Nacional, EZLN; see Mexico) began an uprising on January 1, 1994, the very day that the **North American Free Trade Agreement** (NAFTA; see Mexico) went into effect.

Challenges to the Development of Democracy

Along with adjusting to compete in a global economy, perhaps the most important regional dynamic and the biggest remaining regional challenge is democratization. Transitions to democracy occurred in most of the nations of the region during the 1980s and 1990s, except in Cuba, which continued to be ruled by communist leader Fidel Castro in 2001. Democracy returned for different reasons. The end of the Cold War and the end of the communist threat diffused the superpower conflict that had been played out in the Americas during the previous forty years, and diminished superpower influence and intervention. This facilitated the establishment of democracy in some countries, notably in

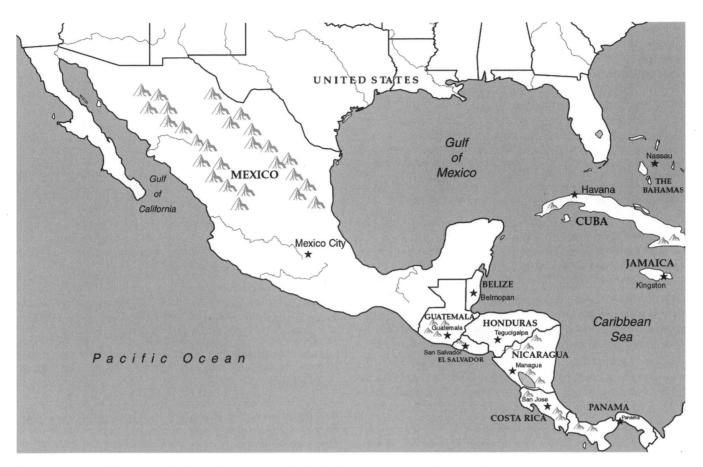

Contemporary Mexico and Central America. © 2001 *The Moschovitis Group, Inc.*

Central America. In other cases, democracy returned when the ruling military regimes lost legitimacy by failing economically and alienating the population through the excessive use of repression and violence. In the case of Argentina, the humiliating defeat in the **Malvinas/Falklands War** (see Argentina) discredited the military and helped lead to civilian rule.

The process of democratic consolidation is a long and difficult one. Some of the countries of the region boast a long democratic tradition and history that can provide a foundation for the kind of consolidated democracy regional leaders are striving to achieve. In Chile for example, democratic elections recently took place in which power peacefully changed hands for the third time since the end of the seventeen-year dictatorship of General Pinochet in 1990. In other countries surprising developments bring even more reason for optimism: in the July 2000 Mexican presidential election, Vicente **Fox Quesada** (see Mexico), who ran on the ticket of the **National Action Party** (Partido Acción Nacional, PAN; see Mexico), became the first opposition president elected in that country since 1929, winning one of the cleanest elections in the nation's history. However, in other cases, such as in most of the Central American republics and in Cuba, there is no strong democratic tradition, and progress toward true democracy is complicated and halting.

The process of democratic consolidation faced—and faces—significant challenges in Latin America. For instance, in countries previously ruled by repressive military regimes and in nations in which significant civil conflict occurred, during the transition to democracy bitter divisions arose over what to do about past human rights abuses. In some countries, governments, or victims or survivors of victims of human rights abuses, attempted to take legal action against the violators (see **Alfonsín Folkes**, Raúl, Argentina); in other countries truth commissions were established in hopes that the populace would be content with the airing of the truth and with reconciliation, and would not desire or demand retribution (see **Agreement for a Firm and Lasting Peace**, Guatemala). In many countries, considerable tensions remain over how to deal with these past abuses (see **Pinochet**, Augusto, Chile). While the future of democracy in some nations could be put in jeopardy if important former military leaders feel too threatened by prosecutorial efforts, for some, unpunished human rights violations call into question the legitimacy and depth of these new democracies.

Another extremely important challenge inherent in the task of democracy-building is the establishment and strengthening of democratic political institutions. Consolidated democracies have strong and vibrant governments with functioning executives, legislatures, and judiciaries that cooperate and act as checks on each other's power. Consolidated democracies also have competitive and strong multiparty systems in which the party is stressed over the candidate, and an active and involved voter population that has faith in the system, considers democracy to be the only political alternative, and fully accepts the rule of law. In consolidated democracies, the government provides and protects individual rights and freedoms. Latin American leaders are trying, slowly but surely, to create and encourage institutions and attitudes such as these.

Another challenge comes from the fact that there is no clear path for democracy in the region. As a result, political regimes of various democratic shades currently exist in Latin America. While some Latin American politicians are striving to implement fully democratic institutions and procedures, other regional leaders have begun to put in place governments and policies that are not wholly democratic in nature. Political protest erupted within and outside Peru when former President Alberto **Fujimori Fujimori** (see Peru) won a controversial third term that appeared to violate the nation's constitution. Further, Venezuela is presently governed by Hugo Rafael **Chávez Frías** (see Venezuela), a populist politician (and former military leader) who wrote a new constitution awarding himself broad powers.

While the revolutionary left has lost relevance in most countries of the region, the ongoing internal conflict that raged throughout the 1990s in nations such as Peru and Guatemala, and that continues strong in Colombia, also presents a significant threat to the growth of democracy. Colombia is embroiled in an intensifying armed struggle among the government, paramilitary forces, and armed rebels (see **April 19th Movement** [Movimiento 19 de Abril, M-19], **Army of National Liberation** [Ejército de Liberación Nacional, ELN], **Revolutionary Armed Forces of Colombia** [Fuerzas Armadas Revolucionarias de Colombia, FARC], Colombia). Mexico experienced its own guerrilla uprising in the mid-1990s led by the EZLN, and that guerrilla force continues strong in its mission to protect and defend the rights of the indigenous population of Mexico.

The involvement of national populations and governments in narcotrafficking remains one of the gravest threats to the development of Latin American democracies in the new millennium. In Colombia, drug cartels in which drug lords wield tremendous political and economic influence (see **Cali Cartel, Medellín Cartel,** Colombia) regularly threaten and kill judges, politicians, and members of the mass media who oppose them, and Mexico's democracy is also threatened by the violence and influence of the drug lords in that country. While the dissolution of the Soviet Union caused a shift in United States foreign policy toward Latin America in the 1990s away from fighting and discrediting communism and toward fighting the spread of drug culti-

vation, production, and dissemination, few U.S. efforts have entailed real cooperation with the region, and most have proven unsuccessful.

Neoliberalism and International Trade

Ultimately, the success of democracy in any country rests upon the will of its citizens to accept and support it; that will often depend fundamentally on citizens' economic situations, which in the long run is determined by the nation's economic health and growth. Neoliberalism has been the primary economic ideology for the region since the late 1980s (though it was implemented in the 1970s by Chilean dictator Pinochet and in the mid-1980s in Bolivia). Neoliberal economic policy promotes the reduction of the role of the state in the economy, encourages fiscal responsibility (including reducing government spending and improving tax collection) to control inflation, and advocates the expansion of trade through the reduction of trade barriers.

The implementation of neoliberal economic policy in Latin America has resulted in the privatization of many state-owned businesses, greater opening of markets to international trade and investment, and dramatically improved macroeconomic stability for most of the region's economies during the 1990s. Strict fiscal discipline by many governments in the region has led to a decrease in overspending (which has consequently helped to prevent high inflation), and many countries have moved toward free market economies and fierce competition. MERCOSUR and the proliferation of regional and intraregional trade agreements have substantially increased trade within Latin America, and today NAFTA is the world's single largest trading bloc. Increased trade and the establishment of trade agreements are also affecting labor standards and environmental policies in Latin America as the countries of the region are exposed to the labor practices, unions, and environmental movements of their international trade partners. The degree of hemispheric integration that occurs in the future will be greatly impacted by regional presidents' success in negotiating the Free Trade Area of the Americas by 2005.

Social Situation

In 2001 the countries of Latin America continue to experience widespread poverty and social dislocation, and the large gap between the rich and the poor persists. After a decade of reform, many of the region's most destitute citizens appear to be worse off, not better. While there were strikes and protests during the 1990s over economic reform in countries such as Bolivia and Ecuador, as well as a more substantial rebellion in Mexico, protest uprisings have not been widespread. One explanation is that international organizations such as the International Monetary Fund and the World Bank, by making aid conditional on the implementation of certain reforms, have taken some of the blame away from national politicians by serving as scapegoats for the establishment of politically unpopular policies. Increasingly democratic political practices and greater individual freedoms in the region may also be contributing to greater tolerance of economic hardship. Finally, today many poor Latin Americans work in the informal sector, as self-employed entrepreneurs, street vendors, subcontractors, or home workers. The resultant disaggregation and fragmentation of the working class in many of the region's countries serve as important obstacles to collective action.

Further, the Latin American left has become far less active and critical than it was for most of the twentieth century due to its loss of political credibility with the fall of the Soviet Union, the economic decline of most communist nations at the end of the 1990s, and the discrediting of the revolutionary model of social change. Given the weakening of the left, Latin America has experienced a shift away from class-based ideological struggles and toward the formation of new social movements based on identity politics. Through the later 1980s and into the 1990s indigenous organizations, women, environmentalists, and other interest groups gained in societal and political influence and became much more prominent and active in traditional politics; in short, the region experienced an unprecedented activation of civil society. In particular, the last decade witnessed a resurgence in ethnic pride and expression as ethnic and indigenous groups, with occasional setbacks, began to express their ethnicity, goals, and beliefs more freely, and started to wield greater influence on national and international politics (see, for instance, **Confederation of Indigenous Nationalities of Ecuador** [Confederación de Nacionalidades Indígenas de Ecuador, CONAIE], Ecuador).

Today the citizens and leaders of the nations of Latin America face many challenges that threaten to prevent the institutionalization and deepening of democracy, challenges that may lead to regional instability if they are not addressed. The most complicated task currently confronting the leaders of the region's countries is the daunting dual undertaking of building and consolidating democracies that will stand strong against external shocks and internal threats, while simultaneously carrying out difficult economic reform that may worsen the lives of a significant portion of these nations' populations before it improves them. Nonetheless, while Latin American countries have experimented with a wide variety of political systems through their histories, today democracy is the regime of choice. There are many reasons to be optimistic that this democratic wave will be a lasting one.

BIBLIOGRAPHY

Print Resources

Collier, David, and Ruth Berins Collier. *Shaping the Political Arena: Critical Junctures, the Labor Movement, and Regime Dynamics in Latin America.* Princeton: Princeton University Press, 1991.

Crow, John A. *The Epic of Latin America.* 4th ed. Berkeley: University of California Press, 1992.

Eckstein, Susan, ed. *Power and Popular Protest: Latin American Social Movements.* Berkeley: University of California Press, 1989.

Guillermoprieto, Alma. *The Heart that Bleeds: Latin America Now.* New York: Alfred A. Knopf, 1994.

LaFeber, Walter. *Inevitable Revolutions: The United States and Central America.* New York: Twayne, 1994.

Lynch, John. *The Spanish American Revolutions, 1808–1826.* 2nd ed. New York: W. W. Norton, 1986.

O'Donnell, Guillermo. *Modernization and Bureaucratic-Authoritarianism: Studies in South American Politics.* Berkeley: Institute of International Studies, University of California, 1979.

Skidmore, Thomas E., and Peter H. Smith. *Modern Latin America.* 4th ed. New York: Oxford University Press, 1997.

Smith, Peter H. *Talons of the Eagle: Dynamics of U.S.–Latin American Relations.* New York: Oxford University Press, 1996.

Winn, Peter. *Americas: The Changing Face of Latin America and the Caribbean.* Updated ed. Berkeley: University of California Press, 1999.

Electronic Resources

Amnesty International
http://www.amnesty.org/
Web site of Amnesty International, a nongovernmental organization that works to protect human rights worldwide. Contains the latest news and information about the human rights situation of countries around the world. Includes a documentation center in Spanish. (In English)

Central Intelligence Agency (CIA) World Factbook
http://www.cia.gov/cia/publications/factbook/index.html
A basic reference containing information on the geography, people, government, economy, communications, transportation, military, and transnational issues for every country in the region (and the world). (In English)

Facultad Latinoamericana de Ciencias Sociales (FLACSO)
http://www.flacso.org/
FLACSO is an influential Latin American think tank that works on sociological, political, and economic issues. Separate FLACSO offices are located in Argentina, Brazil, Chile, Costa Rica, Cuba, the Dominican Republic, Ecuador, El Salvador, Guatemala, and Mexico. (In Spanish)

Human Rights Watch
http://www.igc.org/hrw/

Web site of Human Rights Watch, an organization dedicated to protecting the human rights of individuals all over the world. Contains information on the human rights situation of countries throughout the hemisphere and the world. (In English)

Inter-American Development Bank (IDB)
http://www.iadb.org/exr/ENGLISH/index_english.htm
Contains the Inter-American Development Bank's socioeconomic statistics on land, population, poverty and inequality, the labor force, education, fiscal performance, economic growth, and debt. (In English)

International Monetary Fund (IMF)
http://www.imf.org/
Web site of the IMF, a multilateral organization that provides financial assistance and economic policy guidance to countries throughout the world. Site contains news releases, publications, economic, financial, and development information, statistics, and data on all regional nations, as well as information on internationally recognized standards and codes. (In English)

Internet Resources for Latin America
http://lib.nmsu.edu/subject/bord/laguia/
Assembled by New Mexico State University, this Web site has links to a wealth of sites containing information on Latin America, including sites dealing with border/Latino resources, major Web directories of Latin America, databases, library catalogues, news sources, and other selected organizations. (In English and Spanish)

Latin American Data Base (LADB)
http://ladb.unm.edu/
LADB is the first Internet-based news service in English about Latin America, publishing in depth coverage of Latin American affairs since 1986. (In English and Spanish; subscription-based)

Latin American Network Information Center (LANIC)
http://lanic.utexas.edu/
A very comprehensive source for information on Latin America including well-organized subject and country links. From the University of Texas at Austin. (In English)

Latin American Newsletters
http://www.latinnews.com/
Features real-time newsfeed with major stories from the region. (In English)

Latin Focus
http://www.latin-focus.com/countries/
Contains an overview and description of each Latin American nation's government institutions and political environment, economic and financial information and statistics, and links to government ministries and agencies. (In English)

Latin World
http://www.latinworld.com/
Excellent search engine containing an alphabetical listing of links to Latin American government ministries, political par-

ties, terms, and historical events. (In English, Spanish, and Portuguese)

Library of Congress Country Studies
http://rs6.loc.gov/frd/cs/cotoc.html
Contains the online versions of books previously published in hard copy by the Federal Research Division of the Library of Congress under the Country Studies/Area Handbook Program. Very useful for political and economic history; includes a detailed bibliography. (In English)

Organization of American States (OAS)
http://www.oas.org
Web site of the OAS, a multilateral organization dedicated to increasing inter-American cooperation. Site contains information, documents, and publications related to the organization's activities and regional governance. (In English, Spanish, and Portuguese)

Periódicos y Revistas en Iberoamérica
http://users.erols.com/espana/latinews.htm
Comprehensive list of the newspapers and periodicals of each Latin American country. (In Spanish)

Political Database of the Americas
http://www.georgetown.edu/pdba/
Comprehensive database run as a joint project of Georgetown University and the Organization of American States. Contains information on and links to executive, legislative, and judicial branches of Latin American governments; electoral laws and election results; and other political data for most countries of the region. (In English, Spanish, Portuguese, and French)

Political Resources.net
http://www.politicalresources.net/
Contains many links to sources of information on Latin American politics, including information on Latin American political parties, legislative and executive institutions, laws and legislation, and elections. Also includes links to most countries' constitutions. (In English)

Political Science in Latin America: Web Resources
http://www.lib.berkeley.edu/TeachingLib/Guides/Internet/
LatAmPolSci.html
Assembled by the library at the University of California, Berkeley, this site contains excellent general information regarding how to search the Web for information related to Latin American politics. (In English)

United Nations—Economic Commission for Latin America and the Caribbean (ECLAC)
http://www.eclac.org/
ECLAC (CEPAL in Spanish) is one of the five regional commissions of the United Nations founded to contribute to the economic development of Latin America. Site contains news from Latin America as well as links to many of CEPAL's studies and publications. (In Spanish)

Wilfried Derksen's Elections Around the World
http://www.agora.it/elections/
A comprehensive database of results from elections around the world. Contains results from recent national executive and

legislative elections, as well as explanations of and links to political parties and institutions. (In English)

World Bank
http://www.worldbank.org/

Provides poverty and social statistics for all of the countries of Latin America, and also includes information on key economic indicators and long-term economic trends as well as data on government finance, trade, debt, and resource flows. (In English)

Encyclopedia of
Latin American
Politics

ARGENTINA

COUNTRY PROFILE

Official name	República de Argentina
Capital	Buenos Aires
Type/structure of government	Democratic republic (representative democracy)
Executive	President and vice president elected by popular vote to a four-year term; one consecutive reelection permitted.
Legislative	Bicameral National Congress consists of the Senate with 72 seats (formerly, three members were appointed by each of the provincial legislatures; presently transitioning to a system in which one-third of the members are elected every two years to a six-year term) and the Chamber of Deputies with 257 seats (one-half of the members are elected every two years to four-year terms).
Judicial	Highest court is the Supreme Court of Justice; nine Supreme Court judges are appointed by the president with approval of the Senate.
Major political parties	**Front for the Country in Solidarity** (Frente País Solidario, FREPASO), **Justicialist Party** (Partido Justicialista, PJ; also Peronist Party), **Radical Civic Union** (Unión Cívica Radical, UCR).
Constitution in effect	1994 Constitution (which revised the 1853 Constitution adding 19 new articles, 40 amendments to existing articles, and a chapter on new rights).
Location/geography	South America bordering Chile to the west, the Atlantic Ocean to the east, Uruguay to the northeast, and Brazil, Paraguay, and Bolivia to the north.
Geographic area	2,780,400 sq. km.
Population	36,737,664 (July 1999 est.)*
Ethnic groups	White (of European descent) 85%; mestizo, indigenous or other non-white groups 15%
Religions	Nominally Roman Catholic 90% (less than 20% practicing); Protestant 2%; Jewish 2%; other 6%
Literacy rate	96.2% (1995 est.)
Infant mortality rate	18.41 deaths per 1,000 live births (1999 est.)*
Life expectancy	74.76 years (1999 est.)*
Monetary unit	Argentine peso
Exchange rate	1 U.S. dollar = 1.4 pesos (official rate for external commerce as of January 2002; parallel rate in free market also exists)
Major exports	Cereals, feed, motor vehicles, crude petroleum, steel manufactures
Major imports	Motor vehicles, motor vehicle parts, organic chemicals, telecommunications equipment, plastics
GDP	$374 billion (purchasing power parity) (1998 est.)
GDP growth rate	4.3% (1998 est.)
GDP per capita apart	Purchasing power parity—$10,300 (1998 est.)

*Inter-American Development Bank. *Facing Up to Inequality in Latin America: Economic and Social Progress in Latin America, 1998–99 Report* (Washington, D.C.: Inter-American Development Bank, 1998).

Source: *South America, Central America and the Caribbean, 1999*, 7th ed. (London: Europa Publications, 1998), pp. 49–79.

OVERVIEW

Summary

Argentina is the second largest country in Latin America and the eighth largest in the world. Initially overshadowed by other more mineral-rich areas, Argentina reached its economic peak at the beginning of the twentieth century. Its fertile plains, the pampas, allowed agriculture and cattle ranching to boom. Politically savvy regimes successfully nurtured these resources by incorporating Argentina's active labor and social movements, and by 1930 Argentina had reached levels of social, economic, and political development comparable to those of Canada, Australia, and much of southern Europe. Nonetheless, in one of the most interesting paradoxes of Latin American politics, by the 1970s and 1980s Argentina would be in chaotic disarray. One im-

Argentina. © 1998 The Moschovitis Group, Inc.

portant cause of the country's decline was the disruptive leadership of Argentina's most famous president, Juan Domingo **Perón** (1946–1955, 1973–1974). His presidencies, both divisive and tumultuous, were shadowed by constant military oversight and sporadic intervention. The military ruled Argentina from 1966 to 1973, and again from 1976 until 1983. Although democracy returned to Argentina in 1983, the country continues to struggle to replicate the success it enjoyed in the early twentieth century.

History

Argentina's name is a derivation of the Latin word for silver, a mineral that turned out to be quite scarce in the territory. Because of its lack of precious metals, early in its colonial history Argentina was sparsely populated and of little import to the Spanish crown, compared to silver-rich areas such as Peru and Bolivia. However, the city of Buenos Aires became much more significant in 1776 when it became a viceroyalty, thereby making it a critical port for the Spanish. Argentina eventually generated a great deal of wealth by charging customs duties on supplies and mineral wealth shipped in and out of the colonies through Buenos Ai-

res. Further, as the wars for independence from Spain left much of Argentina relatively unscathed, the country was able to avoid the postwar economic difficulties faced by other liberated republics. Argentina officially declared independence in 1816.

The economic role of the port of Buenos Aires soon proved critical to the economic and political development of the country. Who would control it and how it would be controlled caused great debate between the **Unitarists and Federalists,** whose conflicting views on the development of Argentina would cause national strife long after the country's independence. Whereas the Unitarists, located mostly in Buenos Aires city, supported centralized government, lest they lose control of the port, the Federalists, found in the interior provinces, supported a confederation of provinces and decentralized power and authority. While powerful *caudillo* Juan Manuel de **Rosas** (1829–1833, 1835–1852) used repression to stifle opposition and promote the concept of federalism, his autocratic rule and power unwittingly helped to unify the country. The unification process was not officially institutionalized until 1853, when President Justo José de Urquiza (1852–1860) held a constitutional convention that yielded the 1853 constitution.

The nation's first elected president, Bartolomé **Mitre** (1862–1868), and his successor, Domingo Faustino **Sarmiento** (1868–1874), both liberals, continued the nation's unification. Mitre led his country in an allied effort with Brazil and Uruguay against expansionist Paraguay in the **War of the Triple Alliance** (see Appendix 1), which Paraguay finally lost in 1870. During the presidency of Nicolás Avellaneda (1874–1880), Julio Argentino **Roca** (1880–1886, 1898–1904) led the famous "Conquest of the Desert" in which the Argentines swept the native Indians off the pampas, opening up much more territory on which Argentine ranchers would settle.

At the end of the nineteenth century and during the early part of the twentieth century Argentina's economy soared as grain and beef production combined with substantial foreign investment, particularly from the British. As the economy expanded, European immigrants were welcomed into the country to fill a growing demand for labor. These immigrants brought socialist ideas to Argentine cities, and a new urban working class soon emerged and united, presenting a challenge to the traditional oligarchy of landowners and bankers. Inclusive attempts to expand suffrage to and co-opt this newly mobilized group, such as the Sáenz Peña law of 1912 (named for president Roque **Sáenz Peña** [1910–1913]), created divisions within the political elite. These fissures and the rising tide of popular participation combined to bring an end to the uninterrupted sixty-eight-year string of presidential elections and terms of service with the military ouster of **Radical Civic Union** (Unión Cívica Radical, UCR) president Hipólito **Yrigoyen** (1916–1922, 1928–1930) in 1930. The period from

A 1970 photo of cattle being herded on the Argentine pampas. *Columbus Memorial Library, General Secretariat of the Organization of American States. Reproduced with permission of the Organization of American States.*

1932 to 1943 would subsequently be remembered as the Infamous Decade (*Década Infame*) for a variety of reasons: the traditional oligarchy, backed by the military, resumed control of the country following almost seven decades of civilian rule, and pursued policy programs intended to restore the health of the agricultural export economy (damaged by the global financial depression of 1929) and foment industrialization. Despite their efforts, this eleven-year elite attempt to form a broad national government with the authority and ability to respond to the socioeconomic effects of the world depression was ultimately a failure.

By the end of the Infamous Decade, both the oligarchy and the military were factionalized. Further, the military had proven itself unable to completely squelch the worker movement, and in 1946, with the support of the popular classes, Perón was elected president. The populist Perón is the most significant political figure in Argentine history. During his first term, with the help of his wife María Eva **Duarte de Perón** (Evita), Perón mobilized and solidified the support of the working-class masses. Evita introduced female suffrage, and her dedication to social causes (and her early death in 1952) won her a huge following and the adulation of a significant sector of the Argentine populace, though her detractors were also many. Though Juan Perón was overthrown in a military coup in 1955, his support for unions and the working-class had already made Argentina a land of disparate constituencies with conflicting demands that was extraordinary difficult to rule. In 1966 UCR president Arturo Illia (1963–1966) was removed from power in a repressive coup; the military would rule Argentina for the next seven years. Perón returned from exile in 1973 to briefly serve as president

before dying in office. His third wife and vice president, María Estela **Martínez de Perón** (1974–1976), took office following his death, but was replaced by the dissatisfied military in 1976.

From 1976 until 1983 the country was run by a series of military juntas. Leftist uprisings were crushed by violent police and military repression that resulted in thousands of civilian deaths. This internal violence and repression, later known as the **Dirty War** (1970–1983), further divided the nation. The ruling junta finally returned the country to civilian control after its embarrassing defeat at the hands of the British in the **Malvinas/Falklands War** (1982), which greatly diminished the stature of the military. President Raúl Ricardo **Alfonsín Folkes** (1983–1989) of the UCR was elected president in 1983. Unfortunately, his administration struggled with an economic crisis. Efforts to improve the economy, best exemplified by the **Austral Plan**, failed, damaging the regime's credibility. Alfonsín's aggressive efforts to prosecute military officials for past human rights violations, which led to military uprisings and confrontations, further threatened the newly reestablished democracy.

Peronist party (see **Justicialist Party** [Partido Justicialista, PJ]) candidate Carlos Saúl **Menem** (1989–1999) easily won the 1989 elections and entered office six months earlier than scheduled, as by that time Alfonsín was an ineffective leader. Menem curtailed past human rights prosecutions and issued a general pardon, reducing conflict with the military. In contrast to the populist roots of his Peronist Party, he implemented neoliberal economic policies, which encouraged privatization, liberalized trade, and increased fiscal responsibility, as evidenced by the **Convertibility Plan** implemented by his finance minister, Domingo Cavallo. That plan, which required that each peso in circulation be backed by one dollar in reserves, finally brought inflation under control. Menem's approach to government, however, concerned many; he was often characterized as undemocratic, and his administration was criticized for corruption. For the 1999 presidential election, the **Front for the Country in Solidarity** (Frente País Solidario, FREPASO) coalition formed an alliance (*Alianza*) with the UCR, and presented Fernando **de la Rua** (1999–2001) as its presidential candidate. De la Rua was victorious in the October 1999 contest and took office in December 1999. De la Rua's administration was plagued by a severe economic recession and charges of weak, ineffective leadership, and his *Alianza* coalition was bitterly divided. Due to these dynamics and in the wake of mass antigovernment protests in Buenos Aires in December 2001, de la Rua resigned the presidency late that month. He was eventually succeeded by Peronist Eduardo Duhalde (2002–   ).

ENTRIES

Alfonsín Folkes, Raúl Ricardo (1926–   )

Raúl Ricardo Alfonsín Folkes (1983–1989) was the first civilian president following the military regimes that ruled the country from 1976 to 1983. Alfonsín aggressively prosecuted military officials for past human rights violations (see **Dirty War**) and tried unsuccessfully to revive the Argentine economy.

Raised in Chascomús, Alfonsín was a journalist before entering politics in the 1950s as municipal councillor in Chascomús and later as a **Radical Civic Union** (Unión Cívica Radical, UCR) member of the Buenos Aires province legislature. Alfonsín served in the national Chamber of Deputies during the 1960s and 1970s, becoming a prominent member of the UCR following party leader Ricardo Balbín's death in 1981. Alfonsín surprised many by winning the presidency in 1983 with 51.7 percent of the vote.

Alfonsín immediately used his strong electoral mandate to revoke the broad amnesty for the military that had been issued at the end of the authoritarian regime and appointed a national commission to investigate the thousands of unexplained disappearances during the Dirty War. While the Alfonsín regime prosecuted some military leaders for human rights violations perpetrated during the Dirty War, military pressure (in the form of revolts, protests, and demonstrations) to stem the tide of legal proceedings soon mounted. When Alfonsín began to interpret the mutinies as a threat to democratic rule, in a major reversal he approved the *Ley de Obediencia* and *Ley de Punto Final*. The *Ley de Obediencia* stated that only the most superior officers could be prosecuted for committing human rights abuses, as more junior officers were merely carrying out the orders of a superior and had no ability to avoid carrying them out. The *Ley de Punto Final* created a deadline for filing new human rights cases (two months after the passage of the law).

Alfonsín also faced the challenge of rectifying Argentina's desperate economic situation. With a vast foreign debt, rising unemployment, and spiraling inflation, decisive action was needed. Alfonsín heeded the advice of the International Monetary Fund (IMF) and replaced the peso with a new currency, the austral, simultaneously removing three zeros from the value of the old currency. He also tried to limit inflation by freezing prices and wages and by reducing government spending. The **Austral Plan** was initially effective, but it was difficult to maintain fiscal discipline, and his administration was not blessed with an economic upturn. Eventually public spending rose, and hyperinflation returned.

Peronist Party (see **Justicialist Party**, [Partido Justicialista, PJ]) candidate Carlos Saúl **Menem** (1989–1999) soundly won the May 1989 presidential election. So reduced was Alfonsín's credibility due to the worsening economic crisis that he left office six months before the end of his term, allowing Menem to assume the presidency early and embarrassing his UCR party. However, Alfonsín mounted a political comeback, becoming leader of the UCR and a persistent critic of Fernando **de la Rua** (1999–2001) during the latter's brief presidency.

Austral Plan (1985)

The Austral Plan was an economic plan implemented by the administration of Raúl Ricardo **Alfonsín Folkes** (1983–1989) in June 1985 in an attempt to stabilize the Argentine economy, which was struggling with 30 percent inflation per month. The plan entailed an increase in the prices of public utilities (to reduce the government's losses on these public services), a general price freeze, and the administration's commitment that the Central Bank would not simply create (print) money to fund overspending by the government. The plan represented a final effort to maintain the heterodox, state-oriented economic development model the country had pursued since the 1930s. While it was initially successful (causing prices and interest rates to fall), the plan's success depended on the government's ability and willingness to control public spending and money creation. The government ultimately proved unable to remain disciplined, soon returning to profligate spending and money-printing. Inflation consequently rose to 10 percent per month in 1986–1987, and to an even higher rate in 1988. The public frustration engendered by the administration's failure to keep its promises on economic policy created the political atmosphere necessary for Carlos Saúl **Menem** (1989–1999) to implement the radical **Convertibility Plan** in 1991.

Borges, Jorge Luis (1899–1986)

Renowned and prolific Argentine writer Jorge Luis Borges was born in Buenos Aires and was educated in Switzerland during World War I. He worked on the literary supplement of the daily *Crítica* in the 1930s, and in 1937 began working at the National Library in Buenos Aires. (He was later fired from that job for signing a petition against the Argentine military alliance with the Nazis.) Borges strongly opposed the first administration of Juan Domingo **Perón** (1946–1955, 1973–1974), and his opposition grew even more vehement in 1948 when his sister and mother were arrested for protesting against the new Justicialist (see **Justicialist Party**, Partido Justicialista, PJ) constitution. Borges served as director of the National Library from 1955 to 1973, the years between Perón's two presidencies. Borges' avant-garde poems and tales commented on Argentina's culture and politics and complicated the existing literary dialogue on Argentina's national identity. His work also spoke of universal human conditions, making him one of the foremost figures in Latin American and world literature. Borges published numerous books, essays, and poems, two of the most famous of which are *Ficciones* (1944) and *El Aleph* (1949). Borges won the Formentor Prize (an international publisher's prize) in 1961, which brought him greater international acclaim and prompted the translation of many of his works into different languages. His life and political opinions were of such interest to many that at times they have overshadowed his writings.

Convertibility Plan (1991)

Implemented in March 1991, the Convertibility Plan entailed two phases. The government first made 10,000 australes (Argentina's old currency) equal to one dollar, then replaced the austral by a peso that was equivalent to 10,000 australes, bringing the new exchange rate to one peso for one dollar. Though previous plans to bring hyperinflation under control (including the **Austral Plan**) had failed, after the implementation of the Convertibility Plan, Argentine inflation fell dramatically, approaching annualized single digits in 1994. The plan also established a currency board and made it illegal for the government to have more national currency (pesos) in circulation than the Central Bank had in international reserves (U.S. dollars or gold); the plan thus prevented the government from causing inflation by printing money to pay its international debts.

The Convertibility Plan brought credibility to President Carlos Saúl **Menem's** (1989–1999) administration and fame to its creator, Finance Minister Domingo Cavallo. Convertibility lasted far longer than most anticipated, helping the Argentine peso weather the regional economic downturn caused by the 1994 Mexican peso crisis, and reducing inflation to negligible levels in recent years. The rigid peg to the U.S. dollar contributed to an economic recession in Argentina that began in the late 1990s as a strong dollar reduced Argentina's exports. Unprecedented debate about whether convertibility had outlived its usefulness began in 2001, and Cavallo, who was reappointed finance minister by President Fernando **de la Rua** [1999–2001] in 2001 made several proposals to alter the currency board that same year. Following de la Rua's resignation from the presidency in December 2001 and Eduardo Duhalde's (2002–) assumption of power, convertibility was finally abandoned.

Dirty War (1970–1983)

The Dirty War refers to the violent internal conflict between 1970 and 1983 that pitted the Argentine military against members of the **Montoneros**, the People's Revolutionary Army (Ejército Revolucionario Popular, ERP), and anyone else that it perceived as leftist, socialist, communist, or a threat to the country. Most of those detained, tortured, and "disappeared" by the military were young, usually between twenty and thirty years old. In addition to military and police repression, much of the state-sponsored violence was carried out by right-wing para-police organizations, most notably the Argentine Anti-communist Alliance. Also, during the period, babies were transferred from disappeared leftists to military couples who were not capable of having children. The culture of distrust and fear created by this multipronged assault on Argentine society would have a long-lasting effect on Argentines and Argentina.

A commission appointed by President Raúl Ricardo **Alfonsín Folkes** (1983–1989) to investigate the thousands of unexplained disappearances during the Dirty War published its findings in a book entitled *Nunca Más* (Never Again). The compilation indicated that almost 9,000 Argentine citizens had disappeared and were presumed dead as a result of the actions of the military and its supporters. Ultimately, the perpetrators of the crimes were able to avoid prosecution by way of the *Ley de Obediencia* passed by the Alfonsín administration, and through a pardon issued by President Carlos Saúl **Menem** (1989–1999). However, in 1997 Judge Alfredo Bagnasco decreed that the baby kidnappings were not covered by either of these pieces of legislation. Former junta presidents Generals Jorge Rafael **Videla** (1976–1981) and Reynaldo Benito Antonio Bignone (1982–1983) were arrested in June 1998 and January 1999, respectively, and charged with the systematic theft of infant children of jailed political opponents of the junta. Although it was feared that the military would resist further inquiry into human rights violations, in fact it supported the judge's efforts.

Duarte de Perón, María Eva (also **Evita**) (1919–1952)

María Eva Duarte de Perón (Evita), wife of Juan Domingo **Perón** (1946–1955, 1973–1974) from 1945 until her death in 1952, was a tremendous asset to his presidency and political movement.

Evita was born near Los Toldos into a family of few means. Though her dreams of becoming an actress drew her to Buenos Aires at the age of fifteen, she was never very successful. Following her marriage to Perón in 1945, her life of humble beginnings changed radically as she became actively involved in the political strategy of the Perón administration. Evita worked to bring voting rights to women (legislation to this effect was passed in 1947), and in 1949 she became president of the newly formed feminine branch of the Peronist Party (see **Justicialist Party** [Partido Justicialista, PJ]). She was influential in getting approximately 2.5 million women to vote in the 1951 elections (in which Perón tried unsuccessfully to have her run as his vice presidential candidate, an attempt that was not tolerated by the military), and her efforts yielded the election of twenty-four congresswomen and six women senators.

Evita was the major influence behind the social reforms passed under Perón to help the poor (referred to as the *descamisados* or shirtless ones). She refused to play the traditional role of presidential wife, and her charity work, including her participation with the Foundation of Social Aid, created in 1947, and her other extensive efforts to help Argentina's poor, brought her extreme popularity among the masses while simultaneously offending the elite women of her era. She was also integrally involved with the Department of Labor and Security as well as the nation's most important labor union, the General Confederation of Labor (Confederación General de Trabajo, CGT). Evita installed her friends and supporters in key positions in the CGT leadership and was instrumental in developing the national welfare program.

Her tragic death in 1952 heightened her emotional appeal, virtually lifting her to the status of a martyred saint. Though her outspoken and active participation in politics brought her many critics as well as huge numbers of supporters, she lives on today as an Argentine legend.

Evita. See **Duarte de Perón, María Eva.**

Falklands War. See **Malvinas/Falklands War**

Federalists. See **Unitarists and Federalists**

Front for the Country in Solidarity (Frente País Solidario, FREPASO)

The center-left Front for the Country in Solidarity (Frente País Solidario, FREPASO) coalition originally formed in mid-1993 under the name Broad Front (Frente Grande) with the goals of challenging the dominance of Argentina's traditional parties (the **Justicialist Party** [Partido Justicialista, PJ; also Peronist Party] and the **Radical Civic Union** [Unión Cívica Radical, UCR]),

and offering the possibility of a third significant political party. The disenchantment of growing numbers of voters with the two traditional parties by the 1990s increased the impact of the FREPASO's challenge. FREPASO's main constituents are dissident unions and traditional leftists as well as middle-class Argentines exhausted by the corruption and inefficacy of the two main political organizations. FREPASO's candidate in the May 1995 presidential election, dissident Justicialist José Octavio Bordón, garnered a sizeable 29.2 percent of the vote. For the October 1999 elections, FREPASO formed an alliance (*Alianza*) with the UCR party, and *Alianza* candidate (and UCR member) Fernando **de la Rua** (1999–2001) defeated the Peronist candidate in the presidential race. Despite this victory, the party remains overshadowed by its UCR ally within the *Alianza* coalition. In 2000, tensions flared between FREPASO and the UCR as the country's recession deepened. The resignation of Argentine vice president and FREPASO leader Carlos "Chacho" Alvarez in October 2000 highlighted the growing divisions, as did de la Rua's resignation from the presidency in December 2001.

Galtieri, Leopoldo Fortunato (1926–   )

Military leader and president Leopoldo Fortunato Galtieri (1981–1982) led Argentina into the disastrous **Malvinas/Falklands War** with Great Britain in 1982.

Born in Caseros, Galtieri studied military engineering at the Military Academy, graduating in 1945. In 1958 he became a professor at the Senior War College, and furthered his engineering studies in the United States in 1960. He became commander-in-chief of the Argentine armed forces in December 1979, and was declared president of the country by the military junta in December 1981 due to the illness of President Roberto Eduardo **Viola** (1981–1982).

Simultaneously serving as president and commander-in-chief of the armed forces, Galtieri approved Argentina's military attempt to recover the Falkland Islands (Islas Malvinas) from Great Britain. Argentina's rapid and humiliating defeat in the ensuing war turned public opinion against Galtieri, and resulted in public demonstrations outside the Casa Rosada (the Presidential Palace) and overwhelming criticism from his fellow officers. Galtieri resigned in disgrace in June 1982, and the military junta appointed retired general Reynaldo Benito Antonio Bignone (1982–1983) to replace him as president; Bignone served in a caretaker capacity, holding office through the presidential election of 1983 and until President-Elect (civilian) Raúl Ricardo **Alfonsín Folkes** (1983–1989) assumed the presidency.

Galtieri was prosecuted in 1985 for committing human rights violations as well as for incompetence during the Malvinas/Falklands War. Although he was found not guilty of committing human rights violations, he was sentenced to twelve years in prison following his conviction on the incompetence charge. However, he was released from prison in December 1990 when President Carlos Saúl **Menem** (1989–1999) issued a general amnesty.

Hernández, José (1834–1886)

Poet, legislator, journalist, politician, and soldier José Hernández, born in Buenos Aires province, enlisted in the army at an early age, participating in the wars between the **Unitarists and Federalists**. Hernández believed in the right of the provinces to share power with the domineering federal city. He eventually retired as an assistant captain in 1858 and emigrated to the province of Entre Ríos, where he participated in similar battles and initiated his journalistic career. Hernández, who was well acquainted with the lifestyle of the gaucho (the Argentine equivalent of the cowboy), opposed both Bartolomé **Mitre** (1862–1868) and Domingo Faustino **Sarmiento** (1868–1874), whose own work *Facundo* exalted urban civilization and deplored and ridiculed as barbaric the gaucho way of life. By contrast, in his journalism and political writing Hernández sought to depict favorably the destitute experience of the gaucho and to denounce the injustice inflicted upon this Argentine social stratum, a theme later embodied in the two epic poems *Martín Fierro* (1872) and *La vuelta de Martín Fierro* (The Return of Martín Fierro, 1879). In his ideology and language, Hernández epitomized the interior (i.e., the provinces) of Argentina, and the character Martín Fierro remains the archetypal gaucho, a symbol of the "barbaric" pampas of Argentine society. Hernández later served as a representative and senator from Buenos Aires, and was instrumental in founding the city of La Plata.

Justicialist Party (Partido Justicialista, PJ, also Peronist Party)

Often referred to as the Peronist Party after its founder and most famous member, Juan Domingo **Perón** (1946–1955, 1973–1974), the Justicialist Party (Partido Justicialista, PJ) has been Argentina's dominant political party since 1946.

Perón first formed the Peronist Party in 1946 by bringing together elements of the Labor Party, the Union of Radical Civic Renewal, and the more conservative Independent Centers. According to Perón, *justicialismo* was a mix of democracy and authoritarianism, capitalism and socialism, and individualism and collectivism. During Perón's first presidency the party was hierarchical and acted as an electoral organ and a system of patronage and disciplined control. Associated with the party were a trade union group (the General Confederation of Labor [Confederación General de Trabajo, CGT]) and the Feminist Peronist Party founded by María Eva **Duarte de Perón** (Evita) in 1949. The party was outlawed with Perón's removal from office and his exile from the country by the military in 1955, and disputes within the party continued during Perón's

A 1949 photo of Buenos Aires' Plaza de Mayo, where, during the 1970s and 1980s, *Las Madres de La Plaza de Mayo* marched weekly to protest the disappearance of their children after they were arrested by the Argentine military regime during the Dirty War. *Columbus Memorial Library, General Secretariat of the Organization of American States. Reproduced with permission of the Organization of American States.*

eighteen-year absence. The party existed briefly under the name Popular Union, and then split in 1966 after some members began to advocate an outright rejection of Perón so that the party could be legalized. The mainstream Peronist Party continued under the name PJ.

Argentina's return to democracy in 1983 found the party discredited and factionalized, and as a result, **Radical Civic Union** (Unión Cívica Radical, UCR) leader Raúl Ricardo **Alfonsín Folkes** (1983–1989) won the presidency in 1983. However, his struggles as president, combined with the fact that a more democratic reformist faction gained strength in the Peronist Party, resulted in the election of Peronist Carlos Saúl **Menem** (1989–1999) to the presidency in 1989, and in his reelection in 1995. As Menem's neoliberal program defied traditional Peronism, by 2000 the party was somewhat divided between the neoliberals and those associated with more traditional, working-class Peronism. PJ candidate Eduardo Duhalde (lacking support from several prominent Peronists) lost the October 1999 presidential election to Fernando **de la Rua** (1999–2001), who ran on a combined UCR/**Front for the Country in Solidarity** (Frente País Solidario, FREPASO) ticket. Nonetheless, following de la Rua's resignation in December 2001, Duhalde was eventually elected by the Argentine congress to complete de la Rua's four-year presidential term.

***Ley de Obediencia* and *Ley de Punto Final*.** See Alfonsín Folkes, Raúl Ricardo

Las Madres de La Plaza de Mayo (The Mothers of the Plaza de Mayo)

Las Madres de La Plaza de Mayo was a group of women who marched weekly in front of the Presidential Palace to protest the disappearance of their children in the **Dirty War** carried out by the military between 1970 and 1983, and the government's systematic refusal to share information regarding their whereabouts. Las Madres first appeared as a group on April 30, 1977, when fourteen mothers marched in a deserted plaza. Their demonstration was a daring act since protests were illegal under the military regime. The group was not initially seen as a threat, and the military simply ignored or mocked them, calling them "las locas" (the crazy women). Las Madres did not allow men to march with them, aware of the power of their gender and believing their status as mothers would prevent the government from responding to their protests with violence. Though the police sometimes arrested or prohibited some members from marching, the group continued to grow and meet regularly on Thursdays at 3:30 P.M. in the plaza. Later the military realized the impact of their protests and kidnapped some of these women, but the protests continued. Las Madres were instrumental in raising both national and international awareness of the vast amount of political violence that the military government waged against suspected leftists in Argentina.

Malvinas/Falklands War (1982)

Discovered by the British in 1592, the Falkland Islands (Islas Malvinas), located off the coast of Argentina, were later colonized by the French before being signed over to Spain in 1766. With independence from Spain in 1816, Argentina claimed the islands. However, the British arrived in 1833, drove out the Argentines, and occupied the islands.

Argentine military junta leader Leopoldo Fortunato **Galtieri** (1981–1982) sent 10,000 Argentine troops to the islands on April 2, 1982, in an attempt to retake control and to gain support for Argentina's bureaucratic-authoritarian military regime, whose popularity was waning. The Argentine forces easily subdued the eighty-four British marines and approximately 200 colonists living on the islands. While the Argentine military did not expect Great Britain to react strongly to their invasion of the distant, small, and sparsely populated land, between April and June 1982 the Argentine military was thoroughly routed and humiliated by a much more professional and better-prepared British military. Criticism of the Argentine military's behavior was strong, and some military personnel were convicted and sentenced to prison for their poor decisions in the war. (These individuals were later pardoned by President Carlos Saúl **Menem** [1989–1999].)

The embarrassing defeat contributed to the quick transition to democracy as well as a diminishing role for the military in Argentina; by 1983 the military was no longer seen as a responsible institution of leadership for the nation. Though Argentina restored full diplomatic relations with the United Kingdom under President Menem in February 1990, and though the new Argentine constitution of August 1994 reiterated Argentina's claim to the islands, the Falkland Islands sovereignty issue remains unresolved.

Martínez de Perón, María Estela (also Isabel) (1931–)

María Estela Martínez de Perón (Isabel), the third wife of Juan Domingo **Perón** (1946–1955, 1973–1974), served as vice president from 1973 to 1974, then as president (following Perón's death) from 1974 to 1976. She was Spanish America's first female president.

Isabel was born in La Rioja into a middle-class family. She met Perón in Panama, where he was in exile, eventually marrying him in Spain in 1961. She acted as his emissary three times before the military finally welcomed him back into Argentina in November 1972. In 1973 Juan Perón ran for president with Isabel as his vice presidential candidate. (The military had prevented him from doing this with his former wife, María Eva **Duarte de Perón** [Evita]). The pair won the election with 62 percent of the vote.

By the time Juan Perón took office, the country was gradually sliding toward anarchy and the economic situation was dire. Perón, by that time seventy-eight years old, was unable to manage the divisive situation that his legacy helped to create. He died in July 1974, and Isabel held the presidency for less than two years before the military removed her from office due to widespread social protest and economic problems. Isabel was convicted of corruption and remained under house arrest until 1981, when she returned to Spain.

Menem, Carlos Saúl (1930–)

President Carlos Saúl Menem (1989–1999) brought temporary economic stability to Argentina. However his administration was frequently characterized by corruption and antidemocratic vestiges. Raised in La Rioja province, Menem was the son of Syrian immigrants. From humble beginnings as a truck driver, he became active in the union movement in La Rioja, serving in the provincial legislature, and then as governor for three terms. Menem easily won the May 1989 presidential election on the **Justicialist Party** (Partido Justicialista, PJ, also Peronist Party) ticket, as the administration of Raúl Ricardo **Alfonsín Folkes** (1983–1989) struggled; so weakened was Alfonsín that he resigned six months early and prematurely handed power to Menem.

Although Menem's campaign included traditional populist promises such as wage increases for all, his policies proved much more conservative once he was in office. He implemented a far-reaching neoliberal program of economic stabilization, including the aggressive sale of government-owned businesses (such as the national telephone and national airline companies) to the private sector; these privatizations led to a large reduction in the number of government employees, yielding high levels of unemployment. Menem also sought to improve government finances, and pushed through tax incentives and trade liberalization to stimulate foreign investment in the country. His most significant economic policy was the **Convertibility Plan**, which helped to bring hyperinflation under control; inflation was negligible by the end of the 1990s. Menem's relationship with the military was quite different than Alfonsín's. Soon after taking office, in early 1990, Menem issued pardons for those involved in the military uprisings of 1987 and 1989, an act that signified a victory for the military. A military uprising in December 1990 led Menem to issue pardons to the military junta leaders, assuring them that there would be no further prosecutions for past human rights violations.

Largely because he brought inflation under control, he was reelected with almost 50 percent of the vote in the May 1995 elections. (His reelection was made possible by a revision of the constitution in 1994 that shortened presidential terms from six to four years, but allowed for a president to be reelected once.) During his second term, Menem failed to deepen many of his initial reforms, and ignored others, such as labor reform. He expended great effort simply trying to retain control, and repeatedly showed irritation at the increasing power of others within both his cabinet and the Peronist Party. In 1999 Menem argued in the courts that he should be able to run in the presidential elections of October 1999 since he had only been elected once under the new constitution. Although the courts decided against him, his desire to run for a third term, the high number of presidential decrees he had passed, and widespread allegations of corruption made some question how democratic his administration had been.

Menem's neoliberal, market-based approach contrasted starkly with the Peronists' populist tradition and shifted Argentina's overall political fulcrum rightward to the center. This, in combination with Menem's unwillingness to let go of the political limelight, may have hurt the chances of Eduardo Duhalde, the Peronist candidate in the October 1999 presidential contest. The election was won by Fernando **de la Rua** (1999–2001), who was backed by a coalition of the **Radical Civic Union** (Unión Cívica Radical, UCR) and the **Front for the Country in Solidarity** (Frente País Solidario, FREPASO). In June of 2001, Menem was arrested and subsequently indicted and ordered to stand trial on charges of illegal arms sales during his presidency; though he was placed under house arrest in August, in late November the Argentine Supreme Court quashed the charges against him, and he was released.

Mitre, Bartolomé (1821–1906)

Liberal reformer Bartolomé Mitre (1862–1868) was a well-known historian, journalist, and soldier. His works include *History of Belgrano and Argentine Independence* and *History of San Martín and South American Independence*.

Mitre was a long-standing opponent and critic of Juan Manuel de **Rosas** (*caudillo*, Buenos Aires province, 1829–1852), and was exiled in 1837 to Uruguay, where he worked until 1851. He supported Justo José de Urquiza's (1852–1860) successful attempt to overthrow Rosas in the early 1850s, but disagreed with Urquiza on the issue of the relationship Buenos Aires should retain with the rest of the provinces. This disagreement eventually evolved into armed conflict, with Mitre defeating Urquiza in the Battle of Cepeda in 1859. Mitre became governor of Buenos Aires and finally president of the republic in 1862.

As president, Mitre emphasized developing a national fiscal policy and founded national secondary schools in most of the major cities. Mitre also served as commander-in-chief of the allied forces in the **War of the Triple Alliance** (1865–1870; see Appendix 1) against Paraguay. Mitre used the war to attack *caudillismo* and to quell political conflicts in the interior part of his nation by provoking provincial resistance and subsequently putting it down with tremendous force, thereby asserting the strength of the national government. The war against Paraguay also unified the country against an external threat and brought economic growth to Argentina, particularly from the cattle business and from gold paid by the Brazilian government for Argentine supplies. Largely because of the war, the long-standing divide between the **Unitarists and Federalists** was almost completely resolved in favor of the Unitarists and a more centralized national government.

Mitre left office without attempting to designate his successor, and in 1869 he founded the newspaper *La Nación*, which remains the country's most popular paper today. In 1874 Mitre was stripped of his national senatorial position and temporarily lost his military rank after protesting the victory of Nicolás Avellaneda (1874–1880) in the 1874 presidential election. An active founder of the Civic Union (Unión Cívica, UC) in 1890, Mitre forced a split in that party when he joined Julio Argentino **Roca** (1880–1886; 1898–1904) in supporting Luis Sáenz Peña's (1892–1895) 1892 presidential bid, renouncing his own candidacy; Mitre stayed with the UC while the reformist wing of the party separated to form the **Radical Civic Union** (Unión Cívica Radical, UCR) in 1891. Mitre was elected national senator again in 1894 and retired from politics in 1901.

Montoneros

The Montoneros, named for the bands of *montoneros* (mountaineers) that fought clandestinely in the early nineteenth-century wars for independence, were the best-known group of radical leftist activists tied to the Peronist (see **Justicialist Party** [Partido Justicialista, PJ]) movement. The group carried out urban, guerrilla-like acts of violence to challenge both the government and the military from the mid-1960s until 1982, by which time the military's brutal response had virtually eliminated the group.

The Montoneros emerged in 1964 as an offshoot of the clandestine Peronist Revolutionary Movement (Movimiento Revolucionario Peronista, MRP). Their philosophy was a radicalized, socialist version of Peronism, and they aimed to seize power and implement a revolution similar to that which Fidel **Castro Ruz** (see Cuba) had carried out in Cuba. Members used robberies, kidnappings, and urban insurrections and terrorism to get their message across, and even kidnapped and executed former president Pedro Eugenio Aramburu (1955–1958) for alleged crimes against the Argentine people. The Montoneros reached their high point of influence and terror during the early 1970s, and part of the reason the military accepted the return of Juan Domingo **Perón** (1946–1955, 1973–1974) to the presidency was their hope that he would be able to control this branch of revolutionary Peronism. However, Perón failed to resolve the internal struggle between Peronism's revolutionaries and its democratic reformists.

The group went underground in September 1974. Later that same year, after Perón's death, the government of María Estela **Martínez de Perón** (Isabel, 1974–1976) declared a state of siege with the intent of systematically eradicating any perceived leftist threat. The government's counteroffensive was brutal, lasting throughout the most recent period of authoritarian rule (1976–1983), though the Montoneros and other leftist organizations, such as the People's Revolutionary Army (Ejército Revolucionario Popular, ERP), had been dispersed or simply destroyed as early as 1978. (See **Dirty War** [1970–1983].)

Onganía, Juan Carlos (1914–1995)

Juan Carlos Onganía (1966–1970) was the first of several military junta leaders to apply a top-down bureaucratic-authoritarian approach to economic and political development in Argentina involving deepening industrialization and quashing all dissent. His and similar regimes ultimately failed due to popular resistance to their characteristic repression.

Onganía led a successful coup in July 1966 against President Arturo Illia (1963–1966), took office, and instituted his reforms known as the Argentine Revolution. His administration shut down the Congress, removed opponents from universities, and tried to control Argentine social life. The military allied themselves with foreign investors and technocrats in an effort to stimulate the economy, and implemented a two-year wage freeze (1967–1968) that was made possible by the government's strong repression of strike efforts. In fact, an important part of Onganía's "revolution" was the repression of the labor movement, which had been particularly active since the first presidency of Juan Domingo **Perón** (1946–1955, 1973–1974). The regime succeeded in temporarily dividing organized labor by

Juan Domingo Perón, President of Argentina (1946–1955, 1973–1974). *Columbus Memorial Library, General Secretariat of the Organization of American States. Reproduced with permission of the General Secretariat of the Organization of American States.*

gaining the support of the leader of the General Confederation of Labor (Confederación General de Trabajo, CGT) in the coup effort against Illia. However, Onganía's policies eventually spurred escalating violence, to which he responded with even greater repression. A fearful military finally replaced Onganía with Roberto Marcelo Levingston (1970–1971).

Perón, Juan Domingo (1895–1974)

While Argentine icon Juan Domingo Perón (1946–1955, 1973–1974) lacked a clear political ideology or tradition, his personal charisma united diverse segments of Argentine society, inspiring a populist political movement called Peronism (see **Justicialista Party** [Partido Justicialista, PJ]) that endured more than twenty-five years after his death. Perón had almost as many detractors as followers, and the animosity between Perón and the armed forces, which repeatedly tried to exclude both Perón and his supporters from the political arena, contributed to the legacy of Peronism: the chronically divisive and at times violent nature of Argentine politics.

Perón was born in October 1895 of humble origins in Lobo. He entered the military academy at sixteen, graduating second lieutenant in 1915. His early military career was apolitical; he made captain in 1928, played a minor role in the 1930 revolution carried out by a coalition of military officers and civilian aristocrats, and reached lieutenant colonel in 1936. He spent two years in Italy and Germany, where he was influenced by the ideas of social fascism, subsequently becoming a supporter of the Axis powers. Perón helped plan the June 1943 coup that overthrew President Ramón S. Castillo (1942–1943), and through key military friendships, was subsequently appointed secretary to the minister of war. He later simultaneously served as vice president, minister of war, secretary of labor and social welfare, and head of the Postwar Council, gaining popularity for his social legislation and support of organized labor.

On October 9, 1945, military anti-Peronists took power, arrested Perón, and called for elections. Thousands of supporters protested, forcing his release on October 17. Rather than resume his duties, he initiated a presidential campaign, and succeeded in winning the 1946 election with 54 percent of the vote; the Peronists also won large congressional majorities. In 1949 he amended the constitution to permit his reelection.

Perón's regime reflected the fascist, dictatorial tendencies he had witnessed in Germany and Italy years earlier. He prevented opposition senators from taking office, mobilized Congress to impeach all but one Supreme Court justice, and took control of the media. Perón capitalized on the climate of tension being fomented by the urban working class (which had begun to make repeated demands on the government), allying with trade unions and gaining the popular support of the urban lower class known as the *descamisados* (shirtless ones). His wife María Eva **Duarte de Perón** (Evita) also earned tremendous popularity, helping her husband dramatize his large welfare programs. A nationalist, Perón expropriated the British-owned railways and many public utilities, paid off the national debt, and greatly accelerated industrialization under strong government control, thereby increasing the role of the state in the economy. These policies, however, neglected the agricultural sector, the traditional basis of Argentina's wealth, which led to an increase in rural migration and serious economic imbalances. Real wages decreased and inflation rose as agricultural output fell and demand exceeded supply. By the early 1950s, Argentina was in economic crisis. Eva's untimely death in 1952 deprived Perón of his best link to the Argentine working class.

Perón tried to moderate his policies during his second term in the early 1950s, resisting some workers' wage demands and increasing his support for agriculture. This track soon estranged his earlier supporters, and the military, seeking an end to this divisive chaos, ousted Perón in a 1955 coup, forcing him into exile. To the dismay of the military, Perón maintained political influence during his eighteen years in exile. In an increasingly unstable economic and social context, General Alejandro A. Lanusse (1971–1973) tried to pacify the country by holding national elections and allowing the Peronists to participate. Though Peronist candidate Héctor Cámpora (1973) won the election, he soon resigned to force Perón's return, which came in June 1973. Perón was subsequently elected president in October 1973 with 62 percent of the vote. He accomplished little in his third term, unable to manage the demands of the presidency at the age of seventy-eight, ineffective at controlling the growing guerrilla violence, and incapable of jumpstarting the country's economy, which was suffering from frequent political changes. Perón died on July 1, 1974, bequeathing his third wife, María Estela **Martínez de Perón** (Isabel, 1974–1976), who, as his vice president, succeeded him as president, a nation in turmoil.

Perón, Evita. See **Duarte de Perón, María Eva**

Peronist Party. See **Justicialist Party (Partido Justicialista, PJ)**

Radical Civic Union (Unión Cívica Radical, UCR)

Newly moneyed landowners, old aristocratic families, and successful members of the middle class who yearned for political participation joined forces to create a radical faction within the Civic Union (Unión Cívica, UC) in the late 1880s. A few of the faction's more intransigent members separated from the UC to found the Radical Civic Union (Unión Cívica Radical, UCR) in 1891.

The new party initially resisted participation in the political process (which it considered to be completely corrupt because the oligarchy of landowners, merchants, and bankers consistently rigged elections to remain in power), and tried to gain power through insurrection in 1893, 1896, and 1905, gradually undercutting the stability of the oligarchic order. After their last failed attempt, the party began a campaign to seek out urban and rural middle-class support. The 1912 electoral reform law passed under President Roque **Sáenz Peña** (1910–1913), which expanded suffrage, helped the UCR to extend its support base as the working classes, and in turn middle strata groups, turned to support the party, which granted them a voice. However, the new law also resulted in the mobilization of the working class, to which the party responded with a mixture of co-optation and repression. This dual policy often yielded social explosion and angered the oligarchy, which looked on the inclusion of so many new political actors with indignation. These dynamics gave rise to the coup in 1930 that prematurely ended the second term of Hipólito **Yrigoyen** (1916–1922, 1928–1930).

The UCR maintained a hostile relationship with the conservative administrations of the 1930s and lost a substantial amount of its followers to Juan Domingo

Perón (1946–1955, 1973–1974) in the 1940s, though it again became active following Perón's removal from power in 1955. The division of the Peronists (see **Justicialist Party** [Partido Justicialista, PJ]) following Perón's death and the yielding of power to a military regime in the mid-1970s, as well as the military's loss of legitimacy following its failed attempt at governing the nation, helped UCR candidate Raúl Ricardo **Alfonsín Folkes** (1983–1989) win the presidential election of 1983. Alfonsín's attempts to prosecute past violations of human rights emphasized the party's tradition of fighting corruption and abuse of democratic authority, but his presidency was troubled, and ended prematurely, causing the UCR to lose credibility. As a result, the party spent much of the next decade positioning itself as a viable opposition that could present a more friendly, honest alternative to Carlos Saúl **Menem's** (1989–1999) austere economic policies and shady politics. In 1999 the UCR and the **Front for the Country in Solidarity** (Frente País Solidario, FREPASO) joined forces to support Fernando **de la Rua's** (1999–2001) successful October 1999 presidential bid. De la Rua's term also ended prematurely when he stepped down after only two years in office amidst economic crisis and mass protest. He was eventually replaced by Peronist Eduardo Duhalde.

Roca, Julio Argentino (1843–1914)

As president of Argentina (1880–1886, 1898–1904), Julio Argentino Roca proved a skilled politician whose conquest of the Indians in the southern pampas added a huge expanse of land to the national territory and opened up the pampas for greater economic development, stimulating agriculturally based economic growth toward the end of the nineteenth century.

Born in the northern Tucumán province, Roca studied at the Colegio Nacional de Concepción del Uruguay until age sixteen, and then fought in the army that supported Justo José de Urquiza (1852–1860). Indians controlled much of southern Argentina through the late 1800s, and as late as 1876 they attacked within sixty leagues of the capital. In 1879, as minister of war, Roca launched his very successful "conquest of the desert," leading five columns into the south and quickly killing or driving out the vast majority of the Araucanian and Tehuele tribes. The remaining few were placed on reservations.

This purging of the Indian population brought Roca tremendous support from landowners in the interior, and as a reward for his success against the Indians, President Nicolás Avellaneda (1874–1880) and the National Autonomist Party (Partido Autonomista Nacional, PAN), the only authentic political party at the time, supported him in his successful bid in the 1880 presidential elections. Roca federalized Buenos Aires in 1880, and also carried out various acts of a secular bent, such as permitting civil marriages; these upset the conservative Catholic Church but pleased members of the PAN. During his first term the country enjoyed economic expansion as Argentina became the world leader in corn exports and the second largest exporter of wheat. Foreign capital spurred this economic success, and Roca encouraged European immigration to increase the supply of labor. This influx of money and people along with a surge in cultural arts led many to call Buenos Aires the "Paris of the Americas."

While Roca's successor, Miguel Juárez Celman (1886–1890), ran an extremely authoritarian administration independent of pressure from Roca, Roca served as interior minister under Carlos Pellegrini (1890–1892) and had major influence over the president. He soon became head of the National Senate, and used his power to make Luis Sáenz Peña (1892–1895) the country's next president. While Roca was again very influential in Sáenz Peña's administration, President José E. Uriburu (1895–1898) finally began to resist Roca's efforts to shape policy, prompting Roca to use his political connections to regain the presidency directly in the elections of 1898. His second term as president was much less satisfying due to the mobilization of working-class movements, high foreign debt, and the realization that he could no longer dictate who would be the next president.

Rosas, Juan Manuel de (1793–1877)

Juan Manuel de Rosas was a skilled leader who, as governing *caudillo* of Buenos Aires province from 1829 to 1852, used force to quell his opponents, especially during the latter part of his reign. Though violent, his tactics were effective in unifying Argentina and controlling the anarchy that threatened the young nation.

Rosas was born into one of the best families of La Plata, though he rebelled and left home as a teenager without a single possession. He established a very successful meat-salting plant in 1815, then moved on to ranching, earning the fear and respect of his gaucho workers through his extremely strict discipline and his outstanding ranching skills. He first gained national attention in 1820 when he led his gauchos into battle in Buenos Aires to restore law and order. Nine years later, Rosas was selected by the Buenos Aires legislature to be the governor of Buenos Aires, the only man thought capable of reestablishing order. Though he successfully reinstated order and was very popular, Rosas refused to run again when his three-year term ended. When revolts in the provinces sparked by the imposition of Unitarist (see **Unitarists and Federalists**) demands caused political turmoil and the resignation of the governor of Buenos Aires, the legislature again offered Rosas the position of governor. He accepted after being duly elected and awarded absolute authority.

Rosas, though a self-defined Federalist, united the country under his leadership, gaining control over the interior provinces. While he ruled without extensive abuse of power through 1840, only purging those opposition leaders whom he deemed a threat, he later became ruthless in his efforts to consolidate power and destroy his enemies, using repression, murder, exile and any tactics he thought necessary to strengthen his hold on the country. Other Federalist *caudillos* tried to resist his pressure, but they feared Rosas and soon accepted his hegemony in order to avoid conflict with Buenos Aires. Nonetheless, Rosas was never able to gain tight control over the coastal provinces, which still longed for greater trading rights. In 1851 Brazil and Uruguay supported Entre Ríos provincial *caudillo* Justo José de Urquiza (1852–1860) in his successful attempt to overthrow Rosas, and the next year Rosas left for England, where he lived out the rest of his life. Rosas hungered after power, not money, and he left office a relatively poor man. Urquiza, a Federalist, succeeded Rosas as provisional director in 1852, subsequently serving as president of Argentina from 1854 to 1860.

de la Rua, Fernando (1937–)

Fernando de la Rua (1999–2001) was elected president in October 1999 with approximately 49 percent of the vote. As the candidate of the *Alianza* coalition—which drew support from the **Radical Civic Union** (Unión Cívica Radical, UCR), socialists, and the **Front for the Country in Solidarity** (Frente País Solidario, FREPASO) coalition—de la Rua campaigned on the promise of more socially friendly policies and good governance, pledging to bring an end to the belt-tightening and corruption of the administrations of President Carlos Saúl **Menem** (1989–1999). His term ended prematurely with his resignation in December 2001.

De la Rua was born in September 1937 in the province of Córdoba. He graduated from law school at the University of Córdoba in 1958 and later received the degree of doctor of laws. He joined the UCR during his university years, and served as an advisor to the Ministry of the Interior under President Arturo Illia (1963–1966). He was elected senator for the Federal Capital in April 1973, and served in the Senate and as president of the UCR's Bloc of National Deputies from the early 1980s through the early 1990s. He was elected mayor of Buenos Aires in 1996, and success in that post earned him the UCR/FREPASO nomination for president in late 1998.

De la Rua campaigned on the bedrocks of the Menem economic model—specifically convertibility (see **Convertibility Plan**), fiscal discipline, and openness to foreign investment—but distanced himself from the social costs of this neoliberal program. De la Rua presented a clean image (marking a contrast to Menem's flamboyant and corrupt one) and for many, represented a risk-free change for the better. Consequently, he defeated Eduardo Duhalde, the Peronist candidate, by almost ten percentage points in the October 1999 contest. Inaugurated in December 1999, de la Rua immediately con-

fronted many challenges. His *Alianza* coalition held only a slim majority in the Chamber of Deputies, and he faced a Peronist majority in the Senate; further, two-thirds of the province governorships were in Peronist hands. The economy was struggling by the time de la Rua took office, and battling recession became the biggest challenge facing his administration.

In late 2000, deep divisions began to appear in the *Alianza* coalition, and in early 2001, as the economy continued to flounder, the president was besieged by charges of weak and ineffective leadership. In late December 2001, popular frustration with unemployment and economic recession and decline boiled over, and Buenos Aires erupted in mass protest. On December 20, de la Rua stepped down from the presidency. He was eventually succeeded by Peronist (and unsuccessful 1999 presidential candidate) Eduardo Duhalde (2002–), who was elected by the Argentine congress to finish the remaining two years of de la Rua's term.

Sáenz Peña, Roque (1851–1914)

A member of the upper class, Roque Sáenz Peña studied law at the University of Buenos Aires, and then followed in the footsteps of his father, Luis Sáenz Peña (1892–1895), serving as president from 1910 to 1913. The younger Sáenz Peña is remembered as the last heir of the old oligarchic order, who largely destroyed that political system in order to save it. He is most famous for his support for the electoral reform law of 1912 that took his name. That law, which allowed all males over eighteen to vote and mandated that voting be compulsory and by secret ballot, recognized the growing power of the working class and immigrant groups, and offered them the means to become political actors for the first time. The secret ballot limited electoral corruption, and the law as a whole helped redefine the notion of citizenship in Argentina; prior to its passage, it had been difficult for the majority of immigrants who had arrived in Argentina during the first decade of the twentieth century to fulfill the voting requirements.

San Martín, José de (1778–1850)

José de San Martín is a national hero in Argentina for his roles as a liberator, soldier, and statesman.

Born in the remote area of Misiones, San Martín served in the Spanish army before returning to Buenos Aires in 1812 and joining the revolution for independence. While in January 1814 San Martín was appointed commander of the army of the north in Argentina, after just four months he retired to Córdoba due to poor health. San Martín concluded that the only way to defeat Spain was to win the heart of its empire, Peru. Convinced that attacking from the north would be futile, he planned to cross the Andes, march north through Chile, and attack the Spanish from the south and from the sea. He established his headquarters in Mendoza, where he geared the strong local economy toward raising the money necessary to fund the expedition. A strict disciplinarian with strong organizational skills and planning abilities, he was respected by his troops because of his efforts to safeguard their welfare. In one of the most impressive acts of the independence revolts, in 1817, he crossed the Andes into Chile through Mendoza with 5,000 troops, joined Chilean Bernardo **O'Higgins Riquelme** (see Chile), defeated the Spanish on the plains of Chacabuco, and entered the capital, Santiago, on February 12, 1818. Chile was independent.

On May 14, 1818, San Martín was appointed brigadier general of the Armies of the Fatherland. San Martín departed Valparaíso, Chile, destined for Peru by sea in 1820 with 2,300 Argentines and 2,100 Chileans. Because he was outnumbered by the 23,000-member Spanish royal army, he employed a land and sea blockade of Lima rather than assaulting it directly, hoping to gain the support of Peruvians. Eventually, his plan worked, and he achieved an armistice from the Peruvian viceroy. Peruvian independence was declared on July 28, 1820. San Martín became political and military commander of Peru, preventing Simón Antonio de la Santísima Trinidad **Bolívar y Palacios** (see Colombia) from taking control of the new republic. San Martín immediately abolished forced labor and declared the newborn children of slaves to be free. He also established freedom of the press, ended torture at judicial proceedings, and passed on Lima's reward of 500,000 pesos to twenty of the liberating officers. San Martín sent a contingent of soldiers to help Antonio José de Sucre in the liberation of Guayaquíl.

Both San Martín and Bolívar had a vision for the future form of government for the new nations, but those visions differed: while San Martín favored a constitutional monarchy, Bolívar favored a republic. Nonetheless, they agreed that the new republics should form some kind of federation resembling a United States of South America. However, Bolívar subsequently refused to help San Martín finish the military campaign against the Spanish, and consequently San Martín resigned his post in Peru and returned to Argentina. Upon returning home he found that he was no longer as popular as he had been; he moved to England and then to Brussels before returning to Argentina. Today San Martín is remembered as one of the great liberators in the Spanish American revolutions.

Sarmiento, Domingo Faustino (1811–1888)

Through his work as an author, president (1868–1874), and educator, Domingo Faustino Sarmiento sought to facilitate Argentina's development into a nation characterized by modernization and education.

Born into a poor family, Sarmiento fled to Chile in 1831 to escape the terror of Juan Manuel de **Rosas** (*caudillo*, Buenos Aires province, 1829–1852). In Chile he became a schoolteacher and wrote his famous *Facundo*, a harsh attack on the Rosas dictatorship and a polemical discourse on the glory of civilization and the negative influence of nature and the countryside. He fought with Justo José de Urquiza (1852–1860) in his successful overthrow of Rosas in 1851, and then served as ambassador to the United States for three years before returning home as the elected president of Argentina in 1868. As president, Sarmiento faced daunting challenges, including the **War of the Triple Alliance** (1865–1870; see Appendix 1) and natural disasters. He built schools and promoted education, raising the number of children attending school from 30,000 to 100,000 during his six years in office. Due to his efforts, Argentina's educational system became one of the best in Latin America. He also expanded railroads and roads, improved public health, and modernized the city of Buenos Aires. Immigration also increased under Sarmiento, from 34,000 individuals in his first year to 80,000 in his last year.

Though he ran for president again in 1880 and 1886, he did not win, perhaps due to his intense adulation of the United States. He served in the Senate (1875–1880), as interior minister, and as superintendent of education in the province of Buenos Aires (1879–1882). In addition to founding a newspaper and a journal, he published fifty-two books. Though he was not appreciated by all (some even referred to him as *el loco Sarmiento*, "Sarmiento the crazy one"), today he is remembered and respected as a great leader of Argentina who brought an intellectual, civilian approach to a presidency that had been dominated by military officers.

Unitarists and Federalists

The Unitarists and the Federalists were two opposing political forces that became significant following the Wars of Independence and dominated mid-nineteenth-century Argentine politics. The Unitarist cause was first promoted by Bernardo Rivadavia (de facto governor, Buenos Aires province, 1826–1827). The Unitarists favored a strong, centralized government with complete control over the outlying provinces, and supported liberal European reforms in both economic and religious arenas (which brought them into direct conflict with the more conservative elements of society). Their main base of support came from the capital city, Buenos Aires, and consisted largely of professionals and businessmen.

The Federalists had fought for independence not only from Spain, but from the province of Buenos Aires, which had traditionally exerted a great deal of control and influence over the entire area and the interior; they thus favored a national government that yielded authority to the provinces. Nonetheless, there existed a significant group of Federalists in the capital, led first by Manuel Dorrego, and later by Juan Manuel de **Rosas** (*caudillo*, Buenos Aires province, 1829–1852). The dispute as to the relationship of the national government to the rest of the nation was not resolved until the **War of the Triple Alliance** (1865–1870; see Appendix 1), which President Bartolomé **Mitre** (1862–1868) skillfully used to unite the country and promote the Unitarian interests of a centralized government.

Videla, Jorge Rafael (1925–   )

Jorge Rafael Videla led the military junta that ruled Argentina between 1976 and 1981.

Videla was born in Mercedes in 1925 and was educated at the National Military College. A career officer, he rose through the ranks, becoming chief of the army general staff in 1973 and commander-in-chief of the armed forces two years later. Videla led the junta that took control of the country following the 1976 overthrow of María Estela **Martínez de Perón** (Isabel, 1974–1976). The military, which saw itself as guardians of the nation, justified its seizure of power by pointing to the nation's chaotic political and economic circumstances: urban leftist guerrilla movements (such as the **Montoneros**) had increased the violence of their activities, inflation had risen to 364 percent by 1976, and exports had dropped due to disappointing harvests.

Under Videla, the military quickly implemented the "Process of National Reorganization," a project intended to restructure Argentine society, revitalize the public sector, and rearrange relationships among business, labor, and the state. In implementing their plan, the military penetrated Argentine society as never before, taking control of multiple institutions and abolishing others (such as the General Confederation of Labor [Confederación General de Trabajo, CGT]). The project also involved the use of terror to eradicate urban insurgencies and any other perceived leftist threat; thousands were arrested and murdered, and by 1978 the Montoneros' capacity for creating chaos had been drastically reduced. The siege would subsequently be dubbed the **Dirty War**.

In 1978 Admiral Emilio Massera's faction of the governing junta reinstigated an old dispute with Chile over which country had legal ownership of the Beagle Channel (consisting of three islands in southern Patagonia and access to areas south of the islands) in an attempt to heighten nationalism by focusing the country's attention on the external threat posed by Chile. When Great Britain, which was called in to arbitrate, decided in Chile's favor, Argentina rejected the ruling, and only mediation by the Vatican in December 1978 prevented an outbreak of hostilities. Massera's efforts demonstrated the lengths to which certain elements of the Argentine leadership were willing to go to strengthen the junta's influence over the nation. While Videla retired from the army and the junta in August 1978, he served as president until March 1981, when he was succeeded by Roberto Eduardo **Viola** (1981–1982).

Viola, Roberto Eduardo (1924–1994)

Born in Buenos Aires, Roberto Eduardo Viola (1981–1982) graduated from the military academy in 1944.

From 1967 to 1968 he was Argentina's representative to the **Inter-American Defense Board** (see Appendix 2) in Washington, D.C. By 1975 he was the second most important member of the army, holding the position of chief of the General Staff. His repressive efforts against accused leftists in the **Dirty War** helped him to rise to the position of commander-in-chief of the armed forces in 1978, and in 1981 he was named senior member of the military junta and president. However, his relatively conciliatory policies engendered conservative opposition within the military, which, in addition to his temporary illness and manipulation by General Leopoldo Fortunato **Galtieri** (1982), resulted in Viola's removal from office after less than a year. In 1985, during the presidency of Raúl Ricardo **Alfonsín Folkes** (1983–1989), Viola was sentenced to seventeen years in jail for his participation in the Dirty War. However, in 1990 he was freed from jail when Alfonsín's successor, Carlos Saúl **Menem** (1989–1999), issued a general amnesty.

War of the Triple Alliance (1865–1870). See Appendix 1

Yrigoyen, Hipólito (1852–1933)

The charismatic Hipólito Yrigoyen held office from 1916 to 1922, and again from 1928 until 1930, when he was removed from power by a military coup amid an economic downturn and accusations of corruption. He led the **Radical Civic Union** (Unión Cívica Radical, UCR) and used patronage to run a populist urban political machine.

Yrigoyen, born the son of a blacksmith in the province of Buenos Aires, was charismatic though mysteriously silent as a young man, rarely seeking attention and living humbly in the poorer sections of town. He became police superintendent of Buenos Aires in 1872, won a congressional seat in 1879, and in 1880 was selected as a member of the National Council for Education. He joined the Civic Union (Unión Cívica, UC) in 1890 and participated in the armed overthrow of the regime of Miguel Juárez Celman (1886–1890) that the UC led that same year. He joined the UCR when it split from the UC in 1891, and by 1898 was recognized as the party's leader. While the party, claiming elections were corrupt, continued to attempt revolution, a new electoral law promulgated under President Roque **Sáenz Peña** (1910–1913) gave the party an influx of voters, and Yrigoyen won the presidency in 1916.

Yrigoyen lacked a well-defined political philosophy and relied instead on personalism and patronage to govern. During his first term he devoted much time to restaffing the bureaucracy with his own followers, creating a powerful electoral machine in the process. He sought to include union leaders in his political fold, sporadically supported the striking working classes, and offered discreet backing to the university reform movement, all of which offended the traditional oligarchy and antagonized the military. Despite these tendencies, and although the main ideological position of his party was honesty and inclusion, the president altered provincial election results to his party's benefit and used violence against strikers, allowing conservative volunteer groups to help the army crush the 1919 *Semana Trágica* (Tragic Week) labor riots and employing similar brutality in 1921 against striking rural workers in Patagonia.

At the end of his first term, Yrigoyen was succeeded by Marcelo Torcuato de Alvear (1922–1928), an ally and pupil. Yrigoyen intended to remain influential behind the scenes, but he and Alvear soon parted ways; the UCR suffered from the subsequent power struggle over party leadership. Yrigoyen appeared to win out in 1928 when he showed that he was still capable of mobilizing the party's machinery by returning to the presidency with an overwhelming majority vote. By this time, however, he and the party had alienated most of their former upper-middle-class supporters through their attention to the lower classes. The financial depression of 1929 cost them even more support, as evidenced by the results of the 1930 mid-term elections. Inspired by the party's (and thus Yrigoyen's) diminished backing, the military overthrew the president later in 1930, subsequently banning the political participation of the UCR all together until 1939.

HEADS OF STATE

Bernardo Rivadavia	1826–1827
Vicente López y Planes	1827–1828
Juan Manuel de Rosas, Governor and Captaincy General of the Province of Buenos Aires	1829–1833, 1835–1852
Justo José de Urquiza	1852–1860
Santiago Derquí	1860–1862
Bartolomé Mitre	1862–1868
Domingo Faustino Sarmiento	1868–1874
Nicolás Avellaneda	1874–1880
Julio Argentino Roca	1880–1886
Miguel Juárez Celman	1886–1890
Carlos Pellegrini	1890–1892
Luis Sáenz Peña	1892–1895
José E. Uriburu	1895–1898
Julio Argentino Roca	1898–1904
Manuel Quintana	1904–1906
José Figueroa Alcorta	1906–1910
Roque Sáenz Peña	1910–1913
Victorino de la Plaza	1913–1916
Hipólito Yrigoyen	1916–1922
Marcelo Torcuato de Alvear	1922–1928
Hipólito Yrigoyen	1928–1930
José Félix Uriburu	1930–1932
Augustín P. Justo	1932–1938
Roberto M. Ortíz	1938–1942
Ramón S. Castillo	1942–1943
Arturo Rawson	1943
Pedro P. Ramírez	1943–1944
Edelmiro J. Farrell	1944–1946
Juan Domingo Perón	1946–1955
Eduardo Lonardi	1955
Pedro Eugenio Aramburu	1955–1958
Arturo Frondizi	1958–1962
José María Guido	1962–1963
Arturo Illia	1963–1966
Juan Carlos Onganía	1966–1970
Roberto Marcelo Levingston	1970–1971
Alejandro A. Lanusse	1971–1973
Héctor Cámpora	1973
Juan Domingo Perón	1973–1974
María Estela (Isabel) Martínez de Perón	1974–1976
Jorge Rafael Videla	1976–1981
Roberto Eduardo Viola	1981–1982
Leopoldo Fortunato Galtieri	1982
Reynaldo Benito Antonio Bignone	1982–1983
Raúl Ricardo Alfonsín Folkes	1983–1989
Carlos Saúl Menem	1989–1999
Fernando de la Rua	1999–2001
Adolfo Rodríquez Saa	2001
Eduardo Duhalde	2002–

Source: Thomas E. Skidmore and Peter H. Smith, *Modern Latin America*, 4th ed. (New York: Oxford University Press, 1997).

BIBLIOGRAPHY

Print Resources

Alexander, Robert J. *Juan Domingo Perón: A History*. Boulder: Westview Press, 1979.

Calvert, Susan, and Peter Calvert. *Argentina: Political Culture and Instability*. Worcester, England: Billings and Sons, 1989.

Carranza, Ambrosio Romero, Alberto Rodriquez Varela, and Eduardo Ventura. *Historia Política y Constitucional de la Argentina, Tomo 3, Desde 1868 Hasta 1989*. Buenos Aires: A-Z Editora S.A., 1993.

Crassweller, Robert. *Perón and the Enigmas of Argentina*. New York: W. W. Norton, 1986.

Fraser, Nicolas, and Marysa Navarro. *Evita: The Real Life of Eva Perón*. New York: W. W. Norton, 1996.

Guzmán Bouvard, Marguerite. *Revolutionizing Motherhood: The Mothers of the Plaza de Mayo*. New York: W. W. Norton, 1994.

Hodges, Donald C. *Argentina 1943–1987: The National Rev-

olution and Resistance. Albuquerque: University of New Mexico Press, 1988.

Kirkpatrick, F. A. *A History of the Argentine Republic.* New York: AMS Press, 1969.

Levene, Ricardo. *A History of Argentina.* Translated and edited by William Spence Robertson. Chapel Hill: University of North Carolina Press, 1937.

Lynch, John. *The Spanish American Revolutions: 1808–1826.* 2nd ed. New York: W. W. Norton, 1986.

Rock, David. *Argentina 1516–1982: From Spanish Colonization to the Falklands War.* Berkeley: University of California Press, 1985.

Sabsay, Fernando L. *Ideas y Caudillos.* Buenos Aires: Ediciones Ciudad Argentina, 1997.

Skidmore, Thomas E., and Peter H. Smith. *Modern Latin America.* New York: Oxford University Press, 1997.

Turner, Frederick C., and José Enrique Miguens, eds. *Juan Perón and the Reshaping of Argentina.* Pittsburgh: University of Pittsburgh Press, 1983.

Electronic Resources

Clarín
http://ar.clarin.com/diario/hoy/index_diario.html
The Web version of one of Argentina's premier daily newspapers. Offers comprehensive national and international coverage, with a particularly strong emphasis on national politics and the Argentine economy. (In Spanish)

Cpolítica.com
http://www.cpolitica.com.ar/
Argentine Web site devoted to the study of political science. Contains academic papers, discussion forums, links to academic programs, and numerous reference sources on Argentine politics. (In Spanish)

Latin American Network Information Center (LANIC): Argentina
http://lanic.utexas.edu/la/argentina/
Argentina section of this extensive Web site contains hundreds of links to research resources, cultural centers, economic and business institutions, government agencies, historical sources, magazines and other periodicals, nongovernmental organizations, and grassroots groups. (In English)

Latin Focus: Argentina
http://www.latin-focus.com/countries/argentina.htm
Contains an overview and description of Argentina's government institutions and political environment, economic and financial information and statistics, and links to government ministries and agencies. (In English)

La Nación
http://www.lanacion.com/
The Web version of one of Argentina's premier national daily newspapers. Features comprehensive national and international coverage, with excellent coverage of the national political scene. (In Spanish)

Political Database of the Americas: Argentina
http://www.georgetown.edu/pdba/Countries/argenti.html
Comprehensive database run as a joint project of Georgetown University and the Organization of American States. Section on Argentina contains information on and links to the executive, legislative, and judicial branches of the Argentine government; electoral laws and election results; and other political data. (In English, Spanish, Portuguese, and French)

Political Resources.net: Argentina
http://www.politicalresources.net/argentina.htm
Contains a wealth of links to sources of information on national politics. Includes information on political parties, legislative and executive institutions, laws and legislation, and elections, as well as a link to the constitution. (In English)

Wilfried Derksen's Elections Around the World: Argentina
http://www.agora.it/elections/argentina.htm
Argentina section of a comprehensive database of results from elections around the world. Contains results from recent national executive and legislative elections, as well as explanations of and links to political parties and institutions. (In English)

BOLIVIA

COUNTRY PROFILE

Official name	República de Bolivia
Capital	La Paz
Type/structure of government	Democratic republic
Executive	President (serves as the chief of state, is elected to a five-year term, may not serve consecutive terms); cabinet members are appointed by the president from a list of candidates approved by the Senate.
Legislative	Bicameral congress: Chamber of Senators (27 members, three from each of the nine departments, serve five-year terms); Chamber of Deputies (130 members serve seven-year terms).
Judicial	The Supreme Court heads the judicial branch. Judges are appointed by the Congress and serve ten-year terms.
Major political parties	**Nationalist Revolutionary Movement** (Movimiento Nacional Revolucionario, MNR), **Nationalist Democratic Action** (Acción Democrática Nacionalista, ADN), **Movement of the Revolutionary Left** (Movimiento de la Izquierda Revolucionaria, MIR).
Constitution in effect	1967 (revised in 1994 to reform term lengths and insure human rights).
Location/geography	Located in South America; Bolivia and Paraguay are South America's only two landlocked nations. Surrounded by Peru, Brazil, Paraguay, Argentina, and Chile. Geography varies from high, dry mountains and plateaus to dense tropical rain forest.
Geographic area	1,098,580 sq. km.
Population	7,414,000 (1996)
Ethnic groups	Indigenous (Quechua 30%, Aymara 25%); mestizo 30%; white (of European descent) 15%
Religions	Roman Catholic over 95%
Literacy rate	80% (1998)**
Infant mortality rate	67 deaths per 1,000 live births (1998)**
Life expectancy	62 years (1998)*
Monetary unit	Boliviano
Exchange rate	1 U.S. dollar = 6.1 bolivianos (August 2000)***
Major exports	Metals, natural gas, soybeans, jewelry, wood
Major imports	Capital goods, chemicals, petroleum, food
GDP	$7.4 billion (1998)
GDP growth rate	4.7% (1998)*
GDP per capita	1,000 U.S. dollars (1998)*

*World Bank. *Bolivia at a Glance.* http://wlbn0018.worldbank.org/external/lac/lac.nsf

**U.S. Department of State. http://www.state.gov/r/pa/bgn/

***Latin American Weekly Report. August 22, 2000 (WR-00-33), p. 394.

Source: *CIA World Factbook 1999*, unless noted. http://www.cia.gov/cia/publications/factbook

OVERVIEW

Summary

Bolivia is a multiethnic nation with a rich cultural heritage and vast mineral resources. It is also one of the poorest countries in Latin America, and its socioeconomic situation remained semifeudal well into the twentieth century. Bolivia has one of the most volatile political traditions in Latin America, and has endured an extensive series of interruptions to democratic governance through its history. While Bolivia experienced a social revolution that transformed the country and modernized it extensively in 1952, by the 1960s the country's leaders had lost their reformist impulses, and the democratic governments that have held power since 1982 have been unable or unwilling to pursue a truly reformist agenda. This, together with the international rise in illicit drug demand, has driven a significant percentage of Bolivia's mostly indigenous peasantry into the high-yield cocaine industry previously controlled by the rural elite and the military.

History

After A.D. 100, the high plateau of Bolivia was the center of the Tiwanaku, considered the first great Andean civilization. The Tiwanaku began to decline around

Bolivia. © 1998 The Moschovitis Group, Inc.

1200 as Aymara kingdoms gained influence in the area. The Incas from Peru invaded about two centuries later, introducing Quechua culture and controlling highland Bolivia until the arrival of the Spanish. Francisco Pizarro claimed Peru for the Spanish crown in 1532, and his younger brother Gonzalo Pizarro conquered and annexed highland Bolivia to the Peruvian viceroyalty in 1538. The Spanish established a colonial system based on racism and exploitation whose legacy continues to plague the country into the twenty-first century.

The Spanish crown granted vast areas of land to high government officials and other colonists and allowed them to exact tribute in the form of labor or goods from the indigenous population in return for converting them to Christianity. The Spanish also adapted the *mita* (an Incan forced labor arrangement) to their needs, effectively converting the indigenous population into a slave labor force. Indigenous men toiled under deadly conditions (usually in Bolivia's **silver** mines) for extended periods, which led to the death of hundreds of thousands. The silver extracted from Bolivian mines supported Spain as well as cities in the New World; Potosí, founded in 1545 around the largest mine in the Western Hemisphere, became one of the wealthiest and most populated cities in the New World by the mid-seventeenth century.

Indigenous rebellions during colonial times were common. Túpac Katari sparked the most significant revolt with his brother in 1781 (see *Katarismo*). In 1809 Pedro Domingo Murillo and other revolutionary leaders incited an uprising against the Spanish in the city of

La Paz, ousted the Spanish governors, established a junta, and declared Bolivian independence. However, with little support from the rest of the population and immediate retaliation by the Spanish rulers of the viceroyalty of Peru, the revolutionaries were forced to abandon their plans. Although Bolivian mestizos were the first among their South American counterparts to rebel, their country was the last to declare independence and had to be liberated by forces from Simón Antonio de la Santísima Trinidad **Bolívar y Palacios'** (see Colombia) Gran Colombia. Bolivian nationalists convinced Bolívar not to annex Bolivia to Gran Colombia by naming their country in his honor and offering him the presidency, and Bolivia declared its independence on August 6, 1825.

Bolivia began to lose significant parts of its national territory soon after independence. President Mariano Melgarejo (1864–1871) sold Matto Grosso forest land to Brazil in 1867, and with the truce to the **War of the Pacific** (1879–1884; see Appendix 1), Bolivia lost its Pacific Coast region to Chile, and has been a landlocked nation ever since. The mining industry, already in decline, nearly collapsed in the early part of the century due to a severing of traditional trade routes during the independence period, and economic stagnation persisted between 1825 and 1880. Politically, the early postindependence period was marked by a shift in power away from the colonial silver producers of Potosí, who had dominated the political life of Bolivia for centuries, toward a landed aristocracy and *caudillo* rule.

The conclusion of the War of the Pacific and the **Constitution of 1880** marked the end of *caudillo* rule and the rise of Liberal and Conservative Parties. The Conservatives, who represented the oligarchy and the silver industry, built Bolivia's rail system and maintained power until 1900, losing their dominance with the collapse of the silver market. At the turn of the century, **tin** became Bolivia's primary export and the Liberals gained control of the government, though they were displaced in 1920 when the Republican Party, which emerged out of a schism in the Liberal Party, staged a coup. With the beginning of the Great Depression in 1929 the tin market collapsed and Bolivia was poised to enter the **Chaco War** (1932–1935; see Appendix 1). Following years of heavy losses in the miserable Chaco Boreal, Bolivia ceded the territory to Paraguay.

The loss of additional territory created a sense of discontent among returning soldiers, spurred the growth of leftist parties, and set the stage for the **National Revolution** (1952). This uprising, one of the few successful social revolutions in Latin America, was sparked in 1952 when the military refused to let the **Nationalist Revolutionary Movement** (Movimiento Nacionalista Revolucionario, MNR) take power after its candidate, Víctor **Paz Estenssoro** (1952–1956, 1960–1964, 1985–1989), won the presidential election. Laborers, miners, and peasants took up arms, and after days of fighting the army surrendered. Paz Estenssoro assumed office

A view of the Bolivian Capitol Building as it looked in 1960. *Columbus Memorial Library, General Secretariat of the Organization of American States. Reproduced with permission of the Organization of American States.*

and embarked on a reform program that included nationalizing the tin industry, granting universal suffrage, and declaring major land reform. During his second presidential term, Paz Estenssoro was overthrown by his vice president, General René **Barrientos Ortuño** (1964–1966, 1966–1969), and Alfredo **Ovando Candia** (1964–1966, 1969–1970). Their presidencies began an eighteen-year period of military rule. Popular unrest eventually led to elections following the 1977 resignation of one of the harshest Bolivian military presidents, Hugo **Banzer Suárez** (1971–1977, 1997–2001).

During the politically volatile period between 1978 and 1982, seven military regimes and two civilian administrations led Bolivia. Bolivia returned to civilian rule in 1982, and democratic regimes ruled the country through the 1980s and 1990s, often through political pacts and coalitions. These regimes have implemented harsh economic austerity programs that have led to some improvement in the country's economic situation, but have also left thousands of peasants jobless and forced many into the highly profitable cocaine industry. While it bolsters the economy and provides jobs, the growth of the illegal **drug trade** calls into question the Bolivian state's capacity to maintain order, tears at the

nation's social fabric, and jeopardizes its international relations, especially with the United States.

Hernán **Siles Zuazo** (1956–1960, 1982–1985), facing a chaotic economy and widespread protest, resigned after only three years in office. Paz Estenssoro returned to the presidency for the third time in 1985, and began to dismantle many of the reforms he had implemented as president in 1952, launching his New Economic Policy (Nueva Política Económica, NPE) to fight Bolivia's soaring inflation. Jaime **Paz Zamora** (1989–1993) continued the economic policies of Paz Estenssoro and battled resistance from organized labor and indigenous groups. Paz Zamora was succeeded by Gonzalo **Sánchez de Lozada Bustamente** (1993–1997), who, as minister of planning under Paz Estenssoro, had been the chief architect of the NPE. As president, Sánchez de Lozada Bustamente deepened the economic reforms of his two predecessors, launching a unique privatization scheme known as *capitalización*. He tried to respond to deteriorating social conditions, unemployment, and poverty through his Plan for All (*Plan de Todos*), and oversaw constitutional reforms that expanded the cultural rights of Bolivia's indigenous people, formally recognizing that Bolivia is a multiethnic nation. In 1997 the Bolivian people elected former dictator Hugo Banzer. Banzer pledged to eradicate Bolivia's drug industry by 2002 and, with few exceptions, continued economic liberalization and sought to expand foreign investment in the Bolivian economy. In August 2001, Banzer resigned after being diagnosed with cancer, and Vice President Jorge Quiroga Ramírez (2001–   ) assumed control of the nation.

ENTRIES

Banzer Suárez, Hugo (1926–   )

Hugo Banzer Suárez is one of the central figures in late twentieth-century Bolivian politics. He led a repressive military regime (1971–1977), founded an important center-right political party, and was freely elected to the presidency in 1997, serving until 2001.

Born and raised in Santa Cruz, Banzer attended military school in Bolivia and Argentina. He held the post of minister of education following the 1964 coup led by René **Barrientos Ortuño** (1964–1966, 1966–1969) and Alfredo **Ovando Candia** (1964–1966, 1969–1970), and later served as an attaché to the United States. Though Banzer was exiled in 1971 after a failed coup attempt against President Juan José **Torres González** (1970–1971), a successful coup that same year brought Banzer to the presidency.

Banzer's first term marked a turn away from the goals of the **National Revolution** (1952) and populist military rule, initiating an era of more conservative policies. Banzer suspended civil rights, repressed labor groups, declared the **Movement of the Revolutionary Left** (Movimiento de la Izquierda Revolucionaria, MIR) illegal, imprisoning and exiling its members and leaders, and used military force to crush resistance and to occupy the mines. Banzer's extremely conservative economic policies favored the wealthy over the peasantry and workers, and he ended the government-peasant alliance created by his predecessor Barrientos. Banzer also forged closer ties to foreign countries and multinational corporations. Though the Bolivian economy initially grew during his presidency, it soon faltered due to declining international commodity prices and excess investment and production capacity in the mining and petroleum sectors. Support for Banzer waned, and popular unrest forced him to resign at the end of 1977. Political prisoners were freed, amnesty was granted to exiles, and new elections were scheduled for 1978.

In 1979 Banzer created **Nationalist Democratic Action** (Acción Democrática Nacionalista, ADN) through alliances with important figures in the private sector and the military. Through the 1980s, the center-right party, which supports economic liberalization and socially conservative policies, exerted influence on opposition governments through a series of pacts and co-

Hugo Banzer Suárez, Military Ruler (1971–1977) and President (1997–2001) of Bolivia. *Columbus Memorial Library, General Secretariat of the Organization of American States. Reproduced with permission of the Organization of American States.*

alitions with other parties. While Banzer narrowly lost the presidential election of 1985 to Víctor **Paz Estenssoro** (1952–1956, 1960–1964, 1985–1989) of the **Nationalist Revolutionary Movement** (Movimiento Nacionalista Revolucionario, MNR) (the election was decided in Congress as no candidate secured a majority of the popular vote), ADN supported the MNR government through an informal pact known as the 1985 Pact for Democracy (Pacto por la Democracia). Many of ADN's economic proposals were adopted in Paz Estenssoro's 1985 New Economic Policy (Nueva Política Económica, NPE), an economic stabilization program.

In the 1989 presidential election, neither Banzer, nor Gonzalo **Sánchez de Lozada Bustamente** (1993–1997) of the MNR, nor Jaime **Paz Zamora** (1989–1993) of the MIR won a majority of votes. In the interest of "open dialogue and understanding," the ADN formed a pact (the Patriotic Accord, Acuerdo Patriótico) with the MIR (which Banzer had repressed during his earlier dictatorship) that gave Paz Zamora the presidency and provided Banzer with a role in the government, heading the newly created Political Council of the Patriotic Accord (Consejo Político del Acuerdo Patriótico, COPAP). Banzer was successful in his 1997 bid for the presidency on the ADN ticket. While he faced some opposition (as well as allegations of human rights abuses) due to his actions as a military dictator in the 1970s, the beginning of his presidential term was relatively successful. He promised to eliminate Bolivia's drug industry by the end of his term in 2002, and cooperated with the United States in eradicating coca, though the lack of other viable economic opportunities for coca growers led to occasional confrontations between them and the Bolivian army. Banzer continued with the economic liberalization policies of his predecessor and sought expanded foreign investment in the Bolivian economy. Throughout the first four years of his term, the economy grew at a steady although unspectacular rate. In August 2001, Banzer resigned the presidency after being diagnosed with cancer. Vice President Jorge Quiroga Ramírez (2001–   ) assumed office on August 6, 2001.

Barrientos Ortuño, René (1919–1969)

René Barrientos Ortuño's 1964 coup and subsequent presidency (1964–1966, 1966–1969) ushered in an eighteen-year period of often chaotic and at times brutally repressive military rule.

Barrientos grew up in the Cochabamba Valley speaking Quechua (one of the primary indigenous languages spoken in Bolivia). He attended military school and then held minor state positions. Barrientos participated in the **National Revolution** (1952), supporting the **Nationalist Revolutionary Movement** (Movimiento Nacionalista Revolucionario, MNR), and later served as head of the air force. In the 1964 presidential election, MNR candidate Víctor **Paz Estenssoro** (1952–1956, 1960–1964, 1985–1989) selected Barrientos to be his running mate in an attempt to attract the support of the military. Though Paz Estenssoro won the election, he was overthrown by Barrientos and General Alfredo **Ovando Candia** (1964–1966, 1969–1970) in November 1964. Barrientos and Ovando served as co-presidents and controlled the ruling junta until 1966, when Barrientos was elected president, backed by his Popular Christian Movement (Movimiento Popular Cristiano, MPC) and powerful peasant organizations.

As president, Barrientos traveled through the countryside capitalizing on his ability to speak Quechua to win the support of the peasantry, which following the National Revolution had become one of the most influential sectors of Bolivian society. He also continued the program of land distribution begun a decade earlier. In 1966 Barrientos aligned the peasantry with the military through the Peasant-Military Pact (Pacto Campesino-Militar, PCM); he subsequently used the pact to control the peasantry, agreeing not to threaten their vital interests (especially access to land) in return for their political support, which he consequently attained. Despite his pledges to maintain the goals of the National Revolution (a promise he and Ovando had also used to justify the 1964 coup), Barrientos' government turned against two of the pillars of the revolution, organized labor and the left. His administration oversaw the growth of a wealthy elite, courted foreign investment, and rarely hesitated to use repression to quell strikes,

control the populace, and intimidate political enemies, including workers and mining leaders.

Barrientos died in a helicopter accident in April 1969. Vice President Luis Adolfo Siles Salinas succeeded him, serving as president for only five months before being overthrown by Ovando in September 1969.

Bolivian Workers' Central (Central Obrero Boliviano, COB)

The Bolivian Workers' Central (Central Obrero Boliviano, COB) was created as a national labor federation by miners in late April 1952 in the first days of the **National Revolution** (1952). Though the COB was nominally politically neutral, in reality it was a strong base of support for the **Nationalist Revolutionary Movement** (Movimiento Nacionalista Revolucionario, MNR).

During Víctor **Paz Estenssoro**'s (1952–1956, 1960–1964, 1985–1989) first presidential term, the COB co-governed with the president and the MNR. Many COB leaders held important ministry positions, overseeing peasant affairs, mining, and labor. At first, the MNR leadership resisted many of the COB's demands for reform, such as nationalization of the mines without compensation, the replacement of the army with workers' militias, and radical agrarian reform. But as the pressure from and the influence of the COB grew, the MNR adopted many of the workers' suggested reforms, which radicalized the revolution. While Hernán **Siles Zuazo** (1956–1960, 1982–1985) began his first term repeating this co-governing arrangement, it soon fell apart when COB leader Juan Lechín led miners' strikes against Siles' inflation stabilization plan in 1956. In 1964 the COB completely severed ties with the MNR after Lechín was refused the presidential nomination. MNR candidate Paz Estenssoro won the 1964 presidential election, and the COB supported his almost immediate overthrow by René **Barrientos Ortuño** (1964–1966, 1966–1969) and General Alfredo **Ovando Candia** (1964–1966, 1969–1970). The 1964 coup ushered in two decades of military rule, a period during which the COB suffered repression and internal divisions. Though the COB was driven underground by Barrientos and the first administration of Hugo **Banzer Suárez** (1971–1977, 1997–2001), it supported the regimes of Ovando and Juan José **Torres González** (1970–1971).

The COB reached its greatest influence during the second administration of Siles Zuazo; using massive strikes, the organization protested the president's every attempt to reform the economy. The COB attempted to continue these tactics during Paz Estenssoro's third administration, but received a devastating blow: when the COB went on strike immediately after the August 1985 implementation of Paz Estenssoro's New Economic Policy (Nueva Política Económica, NPE), an orthodox, neoliberal economic stabilization program, Paz Estenssoro declared a state of siege in September 1985. The

COB headquarters was attacked and approximately one hundred of its leaders were arrested and exiled to remote provinces. The NPE resulted in the firing of thousands of miners and the closing of many state mines, which also reduced the influence of the COB, whose key support came from mine workers. Consequently, after 1985, the COB restructured its leadership hierarchy, began to move away from its traditional radical confrontation tactics, and subsequently played a more modest role in national politics. Nonetheless, the COB is still an important voice representing the interests of labor and pushing for policies favoring the poor, often through strikes and demonstrations.

Busch Becerra, Germán (1903–1939)

Germán Busch Becerra, an active military leader and moderate socialist reformer, served as president from 1937 to 1939. He is best known for strongly opposing the **tin** barons, implementing a progressive constitution (1938), and passing Bolivia's first modern labor legislation (1939).

Busch was born in the Beni region to a German doctor and a native Bolivian. He joined the army as a young man and served as an officer in the **Chaco War** (1932–1935; see Appendix 1). Busch also participated in the coups that overthrew presidents Daniel **Salamanca** (1931–1934) and José Luis Tejada Sorzano (1934–1936). These uprisings, born of popular frustration with the incompetence of the old-order politicians and generals (on whom most Bolivians blamed the nation's humiliating defeat in the Chaco War), clearly demonstrated the growing influence of organized labor.

The presidencies of David **Toro** (1936–1937) and Busch began a period of reform during which the traditional political parties were shut out of any role in government as the old liberal order was replaced with an activist state willing to intervene in all aspects of economic and social life. Busch set up a moderate pro-labor welfare state, promulgated the 1938 constitution (a social constitution that severely limited individual property rights in favor of the state), and implemented a modern national labor code in May 1939. Busch also finalized a permanent peace treaty with Paraguay to officially end the Chaco War. Later in his term, Busch's behavior became increasingly erratic, and he ruled by decree. His shocking death by suicide in August 1939 gave him martyr status among the Bolivian left.

Catavi Massacre (1942). See **Tin**

Chaco War (1932–1935). See Appendix 1

Constitution of 1880

In 1880 the Bolivian army was defeated by Chile in the **War of the Pacific** (1879–1884; see Appendix 1). That defeat resulted in Bolivia's loss of access to the sea, an issue that remains important in Bolivia's international affairs. That same year, under the Constitution of 1880, the first truly civilian republican government was established, signaling the end of *caudillo* rule and the beginning of a relatively stable period of Liberal and Conservative party politics.

The main impetus for the new constitution and new political order came from the structural economic changes that had been occurring for the previous thirty years. **Silver** mining had grown and modernized, and the new mining elite began to push for a political system that would serve their interests, and stable governments that could construct the transportation and communication infrastructure they desired to serve the mining industry. Because of Bolivia's relatively sluggish economic development, the transition away from *caudillo* rule occurred later there than in most Latin American nations.

The oligarchic republic established under the Constitution of 1880 served only the elite and was by no means a representative democracy; the vast indigenous majority continued to lack any formal role in Bolivian political life. The Conservatives ruled from 1880 until 1889, when the Liberals seized power. The primary objectives of Bolivia's Conservative Party were the creation of a parliamentary system with a stable civilian president, the construction of modern infrastructure, and the defense of the Catholic Church. While the Liberal Party did not differ significantly on economic issues, it did take a less kindly view of the Catholic Church. While the Conservatives' leaders came from the silver mining elite, the leaders of the Liberal Party tended to be from outside that elite; it is thus no accident that the shift from Conservative to Liberal rule happened at a time when the economy was shifting from silver to **tin** mining.

The period of Conservative and Liberal rule came to an end in the wake of the disastrous **Chaco War** (1932–1935; see Appendix 1). Bolivia's devastating defeat by Paraguay thoroughly discredited the old Conservative-Liberal political, economic, and military elite, effectively preventing them from ever again playing a meaningful role in Bolivian politics. The loss also helped forge a new generation of young military officers and political leaders.

Drug Trade

Third only to Peru and Colombia, Bolivia has become one of the world's largest cultivators of coca, the plant used in the manufacture of cocaine. Consequently, Bolivia receives a significant amount of counter-narcotics aid from the United States.

In the late 1970s and early 1980s, the rural elite and the military controlled the drug trade in Bolivia (most notoriously General Luis **García Meza Tejada**, 1980–1981). However, after Víctor **Paz Estenssoro** (1952–1956, 1960–1964, 1985–1989) implemented his New

Economic Policy (Nueva Política Económica, NPE) in 1985, tens of thousands of miners lost their jobs and peasant families were forced to abandon their land due to cuts in agricultural subsidies. While some moved to urban centers in search of jobs, others migrated to the Bolivian lowlands, especially the Chapare region in the Department of Cochabamba and the Yungas region in the Department of La Paz, where coca is grown and cocaine is processed. This movement, which coincided with the rise in cocaine demand in other countries, occasioned Bolivia's increased involvement in the coca industry. The country has taken various approaches to addressing the problem of illicit coca production since 1982, including crop eradication, interdiction, and crop substitution or other alternative development schemes.

An important law passed under Paz Estenssoro in July 1988 recognized areas of legal coca cultivation for traditional domestic consumption, thus demarcating areas of illegal cultivation where eradication efforts could be focused. Subsequently, President Hugo **Banzer Suárez** (1971–1977, 1997–2001), with the support of the United States, pledged to eliminate illegal coca production in Bolivia by 2002 through his comprehensive Dignity Plan (Plan Dignidad), which combined eradication, interdiction, alternative development, and prevention. Judicial reform meant to weed out corruption that compromised anti drug efforts accompanied the plan, which was initially quite effective; the number of acres eradicated and the amount of drugs seized had both risen significantly by mid-2000.

Nonetheless, eradication efforts, which are concentrated primarily in the Chapare region and to a lesser extent in the Yungas, have faced and continue to face (sometimes violent) opposition, and have often led to charges of human rights abuses. Resistance occurs because growing coca is one of the few livelihoods available for many peasants and thus provides many jobs (supporting some 40,000 households in the Chapare region), because coca plays a traditional role in Andean indigenous culture, and because illicit drug production is a significant source of export earnings, providing much-needed revenue to both peasant producers and the country as a whole. Drug eradication efforts are further challenged by the need to address the social and economic displacements caused by the loss of income as coca production is curtailed.

Flores, Génaro. See *Katarismo*

García Meza Tejada, Luis (1932–   )
General Luis García Meza Tejada's (1980–1981) regime was the most corrupt and inept in the country's history. The regime violently and systematically suppressed any opposition and was blatantly involved in drug smuggling. His brief term thoroughly discredited military governance and marked the end of military rule in late twentieth-century Bolivia.

García Meza was born in 1932 to a military family in La Paz. He quickly rose through the armed forces, and by the late 1970s was head of the Bolivian military. García Meza was named commander of the army in April 1980 by interim president Lydia **Gueiler Tejada** (1979–1980). Inconclusive elections were held in 1980, and through bargaining in the Congress, Hernán **Siles Zuazo** (1956–1960, 1982–1985) was declared president. However, García Meza staged a coup and took the presidency instead, an overthrow that was subsequently dubbed the "cocaine coup."

During his short administration, the press was censored, labor unions shut down, and political opponents imprisoned, exiled, or murdered. García Meza's regime permitted the growth of the illegal drug industry in Bolivia, and the armed forces became directly involved in the burgeoning international cocaine trade. Because of García Meza's obvious ties to cocaine trafficking, international aid was withheld (except by Argentina) and many countries did not recognize the coup government. Thousands of Bolivians, led by student groups, peasant unions, and miners, protested against García Meza's administration. Bolivia's political and economic situation grew steadily worse, and in August 1981 a military junta led by General Celso Torrelio Villa (1981–1982) pushed García Meza out of office. He was later tried by the Supreme Court, and is presently serving a jail sentence in the high-security Chonchocoro Prison in the La Paz district.

Gueiler Tejada, Lydia (1926–   )
An accomplished politician and writer, Lydia Gueiler Tejada (1979–1980) is Bolivia's only female president to date. She held office during the tumultuous demise of military rule in Bolivia.

Gueiler graduated from the American Institute in La Paz, and served as a deputy in Congress and as ambassador to various countries. She came to office following a chaotic series of events. When neither Hernán **Siles Zuazo** (1956–1960, 1982–1985), nor Víctor **Paz Estenssoro** (1952–1956, 1960–1964, 1985–1989), two prominent figures from the **Nationalist Revolutionary Movement** (Movimiento Nacionalista Revolucionario, MNR), received a majority of the popular vote in the presidential election of 1979, the election was sent to the Congress for decision. Unable to choose between the two candidates, Congress settled on declaring an interim government led by Senate president Walter Guevara Arze (1979). With Guevara Arze lacking any support within Congress or the army, and with Bolivia facing a grave economic crisis, Colonel Alberto Natusch Busch (1979) immediately staged a violent coup. Busch's harsh regime faced massive popular resistance, and military leaders soon allowed Congress to name the president of the Chamber of Deputies, Guelier, a member of the MNR, as interim president.

Gueiler's brief presidency, which survived two coup

attempts, was constantly challenged by the army and its unwillingness to give up institutional and political privileges, as well as by a growing economic crisis compounded by Bolivia's huge debt and falling **tin** prices. Another inconclusive election was held in 1980, and though Congress declared Siles Zuazo president, General Luis **García Meza Tejada** (1980–1981) staged a coup and took the presidency instead. Gueiler was exiled but returned to Bolivia following the transition to democracy in 1982.

Katarismo

Katarismo is an Aymara indigenous movement that first emerged in the 1970s, primarily in La Paz, calling for greater legal, cultural, and political rights for Bolivia's indigenous majority. The movement is named for Túpac Katari, who in 1781 instigated a powerful indigenous uprising against the Spanish colonists in the highlands of what is today Bolivia. Túpac Katari's revolution called for Aymara solidarity against both the Spanish and the Quechua (descendants of the Incas, who had conquered the Aymara before the arrival of the Spanish). While Túpac Katari was captured and killed five months into the struggle, the rebellion continued until 1783, and bitter feelings persisted long after the fighting ended. The Bolivian government's denial of the legal, political, and cultural rights of the indigenous majority has continued to exacerbate tensions between Spanish-Bolivians and indigenous Bolivians.

In the wake of the **National Revolution** (1952), the majority indigenous peasantry became a major political force. Their political significance increased under the Peasant-Military Pact (Pacto Campesino-Militar, PCM) established in 1966 by President René **Barrientos Ortuño** (1964–1966, 1966–1969), though Barrientos mainly used the pact to control the peasantry and secure their political support. Nonetheless, through the late 1950s and the 1960s, the Bolivian government, considering native culture an obstacle to modernization, attempted to assimilate and integrate indigenous people into the national mestizo population. Although forced labor arrangements were eliminated and indigenous children were offered public education for the first time, explicit racism and exploitation of the indigenous persisted, and many educated indigenous youth found that they were still unable to secure jobs because of their heritage.

Katarismo emerged among indigenous peasant leaders and Aymara-speaking students and teachers in the La Paz region. Initially the movement's goal was reclaiming indigenous identity and cultural rights, including the right to education in native languages. During the period of military rule (1964–1982), it was an important voice calling for democratic representation and greater political openness. Throughout the late 1970s and the 1980s *katarismo* grew rapidly among peasants and peasant organizations, and the movement's plat-

form expanded to advocate cultural and political rights free from government oppression and manipulation. By the early 1980s the movement was highly politicized, controlled many of the labor federations and peasant unions, and was represented in the **Bolivian Workers' Central** (Central Obrero Boliviano, COB), the national labor federation.

The *katarista* movement produced two important political parties, the Tupac Katari Revolutionary Movement (Movimiento Revolucionario Tupac Katari, MRTK) and the Tupac Katari Indian Movement (Movimiento Indio Tupac Katari, MITKA). While the parties rarely garnered a majority of votes, especially after the 1970s, the movement supported other indigenous groups and brought identity politics and the issue of indigenous cultural rights to the forefront of national politics. Further, the movement's ideas have begun to be integrated into the platforms of other parties. Many of its leaders hold offices in the lower ranks of government, and the movement is a potent force in local politics in the cities of La Paz and El Alto. Gonzalo **Sánchez de Lozada Bustamante** (1993–1997) selected *katarista* Víctor Hugo Cárdenas Conde as his running mate in the 1993 presidential election, and Cárdenas, the first Aymara to attain a high political position, was crucial to Sánchez de Lozada's victory, as he attracted a significant bloc of indigenous votes.

Movement of the Revolutionary Left (Movimiento de la Izquierda Revolucionaria, MIR)

The Movement of the Revolutionary Left (Movimiento de la Izquierda Revolucionaria, MIR) was created by leftist intellectuals in 1971, emerging out of the old left wing of the Bolivian Christian Democrat movement and certain leftist factions of the **Nationalist Revolutionary Movement** (Movimiento Nacionalista Revolucionario, MNR). The MIR supported the traditional Bolivian leftist platform of rights for workers and miners. The party was declared illegal under the military regime of Hugo **Banzer Suárez** (1971–1977, 1997–2001) in the 1970s, and many of its members were imprisoned and its leaders exiled. Though it suffered internal divisions during the transition to democracy in the early 1980s, the MIR was the preeminent party of the left throughout the 1980s and 1990s. One of the party's founders, Jaime **Paz Zamora** (1989–1993), ran for the presidency in 1989 and was eventually declared the winner through an alliance formed between the MIR and its old enemy, Banzer (and his party, **Nationalist Democratic Action** [Acción Democrática Nacionalista, ADN]), marking the first time a member of the MIR held the presidency. Despite the MIR's leftist platform and support, Paz Zamora continued the neoliberal economic policies begun under his predecessor, Víctor **Paz Estenssoro** (1952–1956, 1960–1964, 1985–1989), drawing much criticism from opposition political parties, organized labor, and indigenous groups.

National Revolution (also **1952 Revolution**)

Bolivia's National Revolution of April 1952 stands out as one of Latin America's few successful social revolutions: it permanently changed the political and economic status quo and established organized labor, **tin** miners, and the primarily indigenous peasantry as powerful political forces.

Many scholars believe that the arming of the indigenous peasantry, the complete discrediting of the political, military, and economic leadership of the elite, and the strident nationalism, national discontent, and desire for drastic change that resulted from Bolivia's devastating loss to Paraguay in the **Chaco War** (1932–1935; see Appendix 1) set the stage for the National Revolution and the ascension of leftist political parties. Víctor **Paz Estenssoro** (1952–1956, 1960–1964, 1985–1989), Hernán **Siles Zuazo** (1956–1960, 1982–1985), and other moderately leftist urban intellectuals established the **Nationalist Revolutionary Movement** (Movimiento Nacionalista Revolucionario, MNR) in 1941. Though the party was initially influenced by fascism and economic nationalism and hoped to nationalize the tin mines and other key industries and increase labor organization, by the later 1940s the MNR decided to cast off its fascist tendencies and focus on gaining power.

The MNR won the 1951 presidential election despite the fact that its candidate, Paz Estenssoro, campaigned from exile in Argentina. However, the army refused to allow the MNR to take power, and fighting broke out within days. The MNR, determined to force change even if it meant civil war, was supported by revolutionary forces consisting of a cross-class coalition of peasants, workers (especially miners), the middle class, and progressive factions within the army. On April 9, 1952, after three days of intense fighting in the capital and in the countryside and an estimated 600 deaths, the miners defeated the military, and Paz Estenssoro and Siles Zuazo took office as president and vice president respectively, with strong popular support that would last for more than a decade.

The most dramatic changes took place during Paz Estenssoro's first term. The military was drastically reduced in size in an effort to keep it out of government affairs. Traditional political parties lost their credibility, universal suffrage was granted, and education and social welfare programs were implemented. In 1953 Paz Estenssoro legitimized peasant seizures of large haciendas with a broad land reform act. (Ironically, the distribution of land served to transform the peasantry into a conservative force that no longer desired radical change, fearing such change might cause it to lose the land it had just gained.) Indigenous peoples, who were no longer to be referred to as *indios* (Indians), but rather as *hermanos campesinos* (peasant brothers), were to modernize themselves and assimilate into mestizo culture. Paz Estenssoro also implemented a state-led economic development strategy: the large tin mines owned by *la rosca* (see **Tin**) were nationalized, and the Mining Corporation of Bolivia (Corporación Minera de Bolivia, COMIBOL), the state-controlled tin enterprise, was created, undermining the power of the oligarchy. Mobilized and radicalized tin miners demanded a strong voice in the new government and continued to push for the expansion of social reform for the next four decades.

In 1956 co-revolutionary Siles Zuazo was elected president and soon faced severe inflationary pressures and a faltering economy. With the support of the United States and the International Monetary Fund (IMF), Siles Zuazo adopted an inflation stabilization program. Though the program effectively halted inflation, it required ending many of the social programs implemented in the beginning of the revolution. When Paz Estenssoro returned to the presidency in 1960, he continued the new course begun under Siles Zuazo. In 1964 Paz Estenssoro was overthrown in a coup led by René **Barrientos Ortuño** (1964–1966, 1966–1969), which ushered in nearly two decades of military rule during which many more of the MNR's reforms were reversed and abolished.

Nationalist Democratic Action (Acción Democrática Nacionalista, ADN)

Nationalist Democratic Action (Acción Democrática Nacionalista, ADN) was founded in 1979 by military leader Hugo **Banzer Suárez** (1971–1977, 1997–2001) with the intent of establishing a civilian constituency that would help him legitimately gain office and shield him from some of the accusations of corruption and human rights violations stemming from his previous repressive military regime. The ADN has been one of Bolivia's key political parties, successfully promoting a conservative free market economic agenda and gaining the support of mining entrepreneurs, the politically powerful large-scale farmers of the Santa Cruz lowlands, and many of the technocrats that have played a central role in Bolivian politics since the **National Revolution** (1952).

Through the 1980s, the ADN managed to exert influence in opposition governments through a series of pacts and coalitions with other parties. The ADN supported the **Nationalist Revolutionary Movement** (Movimiento Nacionalista Revolucionario, MNR) government of Víctor **Paz Estenssoro** (1952–1956, 1960–1964, 1985–1989) in the 1980s through the informal 1985 Pact for Democracy (Pacto por la Democracia), and many of ADN's economic proposals were adopted in Paz Estenssoro's 1985 economic stabilization program, the New Economic Policy (Nueva Política Económica, NPE). In 1989 the ADN formed a pact with Jaime **Paz Zamora** (1989–1993) and the **Movement of the Revolutionary Left** (Movimiento de la Izquierda Revolucionaria, MIR) called the Patriotic Accord (Acuerdo Patriótico) that gave Paz Zamora the presidency and offered Banzer a role in the government heading the newly created Political Council of the Patriotic Accord (Consejo Político del Acuerdo Patriótico, COPAP).

Banzer captured the presidency in 1997 on the ADN ticket, and until resigning in 2001 due to poor health, Banzer maintained most of the economic liberalization policies of his predecessor, Gonzalo **Sánchez de Lozada Bustamente** (1993–1997), and also continued democratic reform. The party's platform continues to reflect a right-of-center agenda, supporting economic liberalization and socially conservative policies.

Nationalist Revolutionary Movement (Movimiento Nacionalista Revolucionario, MNR)

Several new political parties grew out of the social ferment that resulted from Bolivia's devastating defeat in the **Chaco War** (1932–1935; see Appendix 1), including three socialist parties and two pro-fascist parties, all responding to middle-class interests. One of those parties, the Nationalist Revolutionary Movement (Movimiento Nacionalista Revolucionario, MNR) was established by Víctor **Paz Estenssoro** (1952–1956, 1960–1964, 1985–1989), Hernán **Siles Zuazo** (1956–1960, 1982–1985), and others in 1941. A decade later, the party would lead Bolivia's watershed **National Revolution** (1952).

The founders of the MNR were moderately leftist urban intellectuals who had played a role in the military socialist regimes of David **Toro** (1936–1937) and Germán **Busch Becerra** (1937–1939). They were also influenced by fascism and economic nationalism, and strongly opposed what they viewed as the **tin** industry's dependence on the United States. The MNR hoped to nationalize the tin mines and other key industries and called for an acceleration in the organization of workers into syndicalist groups. While the MNR did not take a position on the abuse and repression of the peasantry (as did some of the newly emerging parties to the left of the MNR), it did capitalize on popular outrage against the Catavi Massacre (1942) in launching a major attack on the government of *la rosca* (see **Tin**). General Enrique Peñaranda (1940–1943) was overthrown by a military group allied with the MNR in 1943, and Colonel Gualberto Villarroel (1943–1946) became president in a co-governing arrangement with the MNR. Villarroel incorporated the indigenous peasants into the MNR and attempted to implement a reformist, fascist (highly nationalistic) government, relying on violence to suppress opposition. Villarroel was forced to resign in 1946, and when he refused to leave office, he was killed and hung from a lamppost in La Paz by an angry mob. This experience led the MNR to cast off its fascist tendencies, ally itself with the labor leader Juan Lechín, and focus on gaining power.

Though the MNR was not Bolivia's most radical leftist party, the conservative administrations that ruled Bolivia between 1946 and 1952 felt threatened by the MNR and exiled many of its leaders. In 1949, from Argentine exile, the principal leaders of the party attempted to invade Bolivia, foment rebellion, and take over the country, but they were defeated through violent military suppression. While Paz Estenssoro and Siles Zuazo were victorious in their 1952 bids for president and vice president, respectively, the military staged a quick coup and refused to turn over power to the MNR. This inspired even more popular animosity toward the military, which, combined with anger engendered by years of government repression against the middle class, led the population to rise up in protest. A three-day war ensued from which the MNR emerged victorious. Paz Estenssoro, Siles Zuazo, and the MNR implemented many reforms during their twelve years of leadership (1952–1964; see National Revolution).

A 1964 coup led by René **Barrientos Ortuño** (1964–1966, 1966–1969) ushered in nearly two decades of military rule. Under these military dictatorships, the MNR split continually, and in the late 1970s there were approximately thirty factions within the party. Paz Estenssoro even created his own faction, the Historic National Revolutionary Movement (Movimiento Nacional Revolucionario-Histórico, MNR-H), in the early 1980s, but soon reclaimed the party name and successfully ran for president in 1985. His most notable accomplishment during his third term was the implementation of the New Economic Policy (Nueva Política Económica, NPE), an orthodox economic stabilization plan. Paz Estenssoro's willingness to enforce the NPE with authoritarian means and his alliance with Hugo **Banzer Suárez's** (1971–1977, 1997–2001) **Nationalist Democratic Action** (Acción Democrática Nacionalista, ADN) again created fissures within the MNR. The MNR came to power again when Gonzalo **Sánchez de Lozada Bustamente** (1993–1997) was elected president, and continues to play a major role in contemporary Bolivian politics.

Nationalist Revolutionary Movement of the Left (Movimiento Nacionalista Revolucionario Izquierda, MNR-I)
See Siles Zuazo, Hernán

New Economic Policy (Nueva Política Económica, NPE).
See Paz Estenssoro, Víctor

Ovando Candia, Alfredo (1917–1982)
Alfredo Ovando Candia (1964–1966, 1969–1970) led a military coup with then Vice President René **Barrientos Ortuño** (1964–1966, 1966–1969) in 1964 that ousted Víctor **Paz Estenssoro** (1952–1956, 1960–1964, 1985–1989) and ushered in almost two decades of military rule.

Ovando enrolled in the military as a young man and served in the **Chaco War** (1932–1935; see Appendix 1). Following the **National Revolution** (1952), he became army chief of staff, and in 1962, commander-in-chief of the armed forces. Following the 1964 coup, Ovando co-governed with Barrientos, served as head of the armed forces once Barrientos assumed the presidency in 1966, and soon usurped the presidency from Barrientos' vice president, Luis Siles Salinas, upon Barrientos' sudden death in 1969. During his brief presidency, Ovando reversed many of Barrientos' politics and reoriented many of the country's policies toward the fulfillment of the goals of the National Revolution, which had been largely abandoned under Barrientos. Ovando tried to come to terms with the left: he granted the return of civil liberties, legalized the **Bolivian Workers' Central** (Central Obrero Boliviano, COB), the national labor federation, and nationalized Gulf Oil, though he did eventually compensate the U.S.-owned company. However, Ovando was unable to amass popular support or build coherent backing from among political parties or organized labor, and soon also lost the support of the armed forces. As a result, in October 1970 the military replaced Ovando with General Juan José **Torres González** (1970–1971), the last military president to advocate socialist reform.

Pact for Democracy (Pacto por la Democracia) (1985).
See **Nationalist Democratic Action (Acción Democrática Nacionalista, ADN); Nationalist Revolutionary Movement (Movimiento Nacionalista Revolucionario, MNR)**

Paz Estenssoro, Víctor (1907–2001)
Víctor Paz Estenssoro served as president three times (1952–1956, 1960–1964, 1985–1989) and was an important figure in Bolivian politics throughout the second half of the twentieth century.

Paz Estenssoro was born into a wealthy family in southern Bolivia and received his law degree from the Universidad Mayor de San Andrés in La Paz. He held a number of minor state jobs until 1932, when he was conscripted to serve in the **Chaco War** (1932–1935; see Appendix 1). The war left Paz Estenssoro disillusioned with the status quo maintained by the military and the **tin** oligarchy, and in 1941 he helped found the **Nationalist Revolutionary Movement** (Movimiento Nacionalista Revolucionario, MNR). As a congressional deputy, Paz Estenssoro forged alliances with reform-minded military leaders, and as minister of finance to President Gualberto Villarroel (1943–1946), he began to move Bolivia toward a state-led economic program. Paz Estenssoro's six-year self-exile following the overthrow and murder of Villarroel in 1946 halted his direct reform efforts, but he maintained strong ties to the MNR and Bolivian politics. Paz Estenssoro won the 1951 presidential election (on the MNR ticket), and when the military refused to let him assume office, the **National Revolution** (1952) ensued. The revolution brought Paz Estenssoro to power with strong popular support that would last more than ten years.

Víctor Paz Estenssoro, President of Bolivia (1952–1956, 1960–1964, 1985–1989). *Columbus Memorial Library, General Secretariat of the Organization of American States. Reproduced with permission of the Organization of American States.*

Paz Estenssoro handed the reins of power to his co-revolutionary, Vice President Hernán **Siles Zuazo** (1956–1960, 1982–1985), at the end of his first term, and when Paz Estenssoro returned to the presidency in 1960, he continued the new inflation stabilization program Siles Zuazo had begun. This exacerbated divisions within the MNR over the role of the left, notably the **Bolivian Workers' Central** (Central Obrero Boliviano, COB) (led by Juan Lechín and mineworkers in the MNR leadership), which completely severed ties with the MNR in 1964. Paz Estenssoro won the 1964 election, but was almost immediately overthrown by his vice president, General René **Barrientos Ortuño** (1964–1966, 1966–1969), and army commander-in-chief General Alfredo **Ovando Candia** (1964–1966, 1969–1970). Paz Estenssoro fled to Lima but returned seven years later to support Hugo **Banzer Suárez**'s (1971–1977, 1997–2001) coup against Juan José **Torres González** (1970–1971). He was exiled again in 1974, but returned to Bolivia to run in the 1979 presidential election. Neither he nor his opponent, Siles Zuazo, won a majority, and congress declared Walter Guevara Arze (1979) interim president.

Siles Zuazo assumed the presidency in 1982, but in 1985 near political and economic chaos forced him to step down. A presidential election was held in 1985, and when no candidate received a majority of the popular vote, Congress again decided the winner, awarding Paz Estenssoro a third term. To address the economic crisis that gripped the nation (including one of the most extreme episodes of inflation the world has ever seen), in August 1985 Paz Estenssoro launched the New Economic Policy (Nueva Política Económica, NPE), an orthodox neoliberal economic stabilization plan developed by his minister of planning, Gonzalo **Sánchez de Lozada Bustamente** (1993–1997). The NPE initially faced substantial domestic opposition, but Paz Estenssoro secured its passage by an opposition-controlled Congress through the Pact for Democracy (Pacto por la Democracia), an agreement the MNR had made with Banzer's party, **Nationalist Democratic Action** (Acción Democrática Nacionalista, ADN).

The NPE had three main goals: ending inflation in the short term, eliminating the fiscal deficit (through tax reform, devaluing the currency, increasing the rates charged by state-owned enterprises, eliminating government subsidies, freezing all public sector salaries, and implementing fiscal discipline, which implied cutting back social spending) and completely restructuring the Bolivian economy (including replacing the state-led economic development model with a development model based on free markets and private enterprise). The NPE was successful in ending inflation (rates fell dramatically within days of its implementation) and restoring macroeconomic equilibrium. The deficit was reduced, exports rose, and, after an immediate recession, non-inflationary growth returned to the country in 1987. The NPE drew widespread international support and was considered a model of economic reform by many international financial institutions, and its general policies were followed by the subsequent administrations of both Jaime **Paz Zamora** (1989–1993) and Sánchez de Lozada.

However, the NPE's success came at a high social cost, especially for Bolivia's poorest. Thousands of people took to the streets in protest soon after it was implemented, and the COB immediately went on strike, prompting Paz Estenssoro to declare a state of siege in September 1985, wary of the COB's influence. (The COB had effectively thwarted Siles Zuazo's previous attempts at economic reform.) In the years following implementation of the NPE, tens of thousands of state workers lost their jobs, especially within the Mining Corporation of Bolivia (Corporación Minera de Bolivia, COMIBOL), the state-controlled mining enterprise. In addition, poverty increased, and many health and nutrition indicators deteriorated. The policy may also indirectly have led to expanded Bolivian involvement in the international **drug trade**.

Paz Zamora, Jaime (1939–   )

Jaime Paz Zamora, nephew of powerful Bolivian politician Víctor **Paz Estenssoro** (1952–1956, 1960–1964, 1985–1989), was a key figure in late twentieth-century Bolivian politics. He helped found the **Movement of the Revolutionary Left** (Movimiento de la Izquierda Revolucionaria, MIR) and served as president (1989–1993).

Paz Zamora was born in Cochabamba, and though he studied in Belgium to be a priest, his career aspirations soon changed. In 1971 he helped found the MIR. Although he was jailed for planning a coup against the military regime of Hugo **Banzer Suárez** (1971–1977, 1997–2001), he soon escaped and fled to Venezuela, returning to Bolivia in the late 1970s to witness the chaotic transition to democracy in the early 1980s. Paz Zamora served as vice president under Hernán **Siles Zuazo** (1956–1960, 1982–1985) beginning in 1982, but resigned and pulled the MIR out of the government in January 1983. When neither Paz Zamora, running on the MIR ticket, nor Banzer, running on the **Nationalist Democratic Action** (Acción Democrática Nacionalista, ADN) ticket, nor Gonzalo **Sánchez de Lozada Bustamente** (1993–1997), running on the **Nationalist Revolutionary Movement** (Movimiento Nacionalista Revolucionario, MNR) ticket received a majority in the 1989 presidential contest, as mandated by the constitution, it fell to Congress to decide the winner. An ADN/MIR alliance (the Patriotic Accord, Acuerdo Patriótico) formed in the legislature, and the presidency was awarded to Paz Zamora (of the MIR), and the leadership of the newly created Council of the Patriotic Accord (Consejo Político del Acuerdo Patriótico, COPAP) to Banzer (of ADN). While the alliance was surprising due to the repression many MIR leaders had suffered under Banzer's military regime, the two leaders maintained that the pact represented a new phase of open dialogue and understanding.

Although the MIR was the primary party of the left, Paz Zamora continued the neoliberal economic policies begun under Paz Estenssoro. He pursued the privatization of state-owned enterprises, defended the legitimate cultivation of coca (though this policy received little international support), and sought to increase investment in the Bolivian economy. However, economic growth remained relatively slow, and his presidency was beset with problems. His policies were widely criticized by opposition political parties, organized labor, and indigenous groups, and his administration faced widespread charges of corruption. Further, during his term, teachers went on strike to protest low wages, prompting Paz Zamora to declare a state of siege and to arrest hundreds of strikers. In 1993 the MNR's Sánchez de Lozada succeeded Paz Zamora as president.

Peru-Bolivia Confederation. See War of the Peru-Bolivia Confederation (Appendix 1)

La Rosca. See Tin

Salamanca, Daniel (1869–1935)

After taking the presidency in a 1930 revolt, Daniel Salamanca (1931–1934) provoked a full-scale war with Paraguay (see **Chaco War**, 1932–1935; Appendix 1) that resulted in a disastrous loss for Bolivia.

Salamanca, a rural landowner, founded the Republican Party (a splinter group of the Liberal Party) in 1914. The Republicans' philosophy was similar to that of the Liberals, but Salamanca's aims were to guarantee free elections and restrict the power of the president. The Republican Party split into two factions after taking power in 1920, and Salamanca assumed the presidency in 1930 as the leader of a coalition of those factions. Profound economic and social changes were occurring in Bolivia at that time: the mining elite was demanding greater representation, labor and mine workers were calling for a greater political role, and the Great Depression was sending shock waves throughout the economy.

President Salamanca seemed oblivious to these changes, and as the country's economic situation worsened, he began to send Bolivian forces on exploratory missions into the sparsely populated Chaco region (on the border with Paraguay), where oil deposits were known to exist. In late spring 1932, clashes with Paraguay began to escalate in the border region; those conflicts eventually led to full-scale war and eventually to Bolivia's devastating defeat. The Chaco War destroyed the political order that had emerged in 1880 (see **Constitution of 1880**), completely discrediting the political, military, and economic leadership of the elite. Many scholars believe that this disgrace and the resultant emergence of new parties and new movements, in combination with the arming of the indigenous peasantry and the strident nationalism and desire for drastic change that resulted from Bolivia's defeat, set the stage for the ascension of leftist political parties and the **National Revolution** of 1952. Salamanca was overthrown in 1934.

Sánchez de Lozada Bustamente, Gonzalo (1930–)

Gonzalo Sánchez de Lozada Bustamente was the architect of Bolivia's controversial New Economic Policy (Nueva Política Económica, NPE), the orthodox, neoliberal economic plan implemented in 1985 during the presidency of Víctor **Paz Estenssoro** (1952–1956, 1960–1964, 1985–1989). He also served as president (1993–1997), deepening many of the economic reforms begun under Paz Estenssoro.

"Goni," as he is affectionately known in Bolivia, was raised in La Paz and studied philosophy at the University of Chicago. Upon returning to Bolivia, he became a mining industrialist, and eventually owned one of the largest private mining companies in Bolivia, the Mineral Company of the South (Compañía Minera del Sur, COMSUR). He entered politics with the **Nationalist Revolutionary Movement** (Movimiento Nacionalista Revolucionario, MNR), serving as minister of planning under Paz Estenssoro and helping to design and implement Paz Estenssoro's economic reforms. Sánchez de Lozada ran on the MNR ticket in the 1989 presidential election, but eventually lost when Hugo **Banzer Suárez** (1971–1977, 1997–2001) of **Nationalist Democratic Action** (Acción Democrática Nacionalista, ADN) formed a pact with Jaime **Paz Zamora** (1989–1993) of the **Movement of the Revolutionary Left** (Movimiento de la Izquierda Revolucionaria, MIR) that resulted in Paz Zamora's ascension to the presidency.

Sánchez de Lozada, a strong critic of Paz Zamora's administration, won the 1993 presidential election on the MNR ticket with Aymara leader and *katarismo* adherent Víctor Hugo Cárdenas of the Tupac Katari Revolutionary Movement (Movimiento Revolucionario Tupac Katari, MRTK) as his running mate. As president, Sánchez de Lozada deepened the neoliberal economic reforms begun under Paz Estenssoro, notably through a unique privatization program called *capitalización*. He also tried to respond to massive unemployment and widespread poverty through his Plan for All (*Plan de Todos*), which included programs in job creation, health, and education; the plan also included a decentralization law known as the Popular Participation Law (Ley de Participación Popular), which gave increased political power to municipal governments. Sánchez de Lozada also reformed the constitution in 1994 so that it recognized the multicultural and multiethnic nature of the Bolivian nation, and signed important free trade agreements with Mexico and the **Southern Cone Common Market** (Mercado Común del Cono Sur, MERCOSUR; see Appendix 1). While the economy grew moderately throughout his presidency, social problems and persistent poverty continued.

Santa Cruz, Andrés de (1792–1865)

Andrés de Santa Cruz served as Bolivia's first native-born president (1829–1839), gaining tremendous popularity for the political and economic stability established during his administration.

Santa Cruz was born in La Paz of a Spanish father and a Quechua mother. He initially served in the royalist army in Argentina and Peru. However, in 1820, frustrated with the changing policies of the Spanish crown, Santa Cruz switched allegiances and began to fight with the revolutionary army. He served under General José de **San Martín** (see Argentina) in Chile and under General Antonio José de Sucre in Ecuador, and also fought with Simón Antonio de la Santísima Trinidad **Bolívar y Palacios** (see Colombia). In August 1823, Santa Cruz led the liberation of La Paz, but the city was recaptured by royalist troops within months, occasioning the evacuation of Santa Cruz and his army. The royalists were finally definitively defeated in 1824 at the Battle of Ayacucho.

Following Bolivian independence, Santa Cruz held minor government positions in Bolivia. In 1826 he was recalled by Bolívar to serve as Peru's president but was ousted in 1827. In 1829 he was sent to serve as president of Bolivia, where he established political and economic stability by setting up protective tariffs and establishing effective taxes. He also created a rural census, established universities in La Paz and Cochabamba, developed civil and commercial laws based on the Napoleonic Code, and reinstituted indigenous tribute (in exchange for a ten-year guarantee on communal lands) in order to generate revenue for the state. Santa Cruz enjoyed widespread popularity during the first six years of his presidency, especially among the elite. However, following his 1835 invasion and annexation of Peru, war ensued (see **War of the Peru-Bolivia Confederation, 1836–1839**; Appendix 1), and in 1839 Santa Cruz was overthrown by Chilean troops and exiled to Ecuador. Though there were attempts to reinstate him as president of Bolivia, his supporters eventually abandoned him due to intense opposition. Santa Cruz died in France.

Siles Zuazo, Hernán (1914–1996)

Hernán Siles Zuazo served his country twice as president (1956–1960, 1982–1985). Siles Zuazo is considered one of the most important figures in Bolivia's **National Revolution** (1952), and his second presidency initiated Bolivia's transition to democracy following almost two decades of military rule.

Siles Zuazo, the son of Bolivian president Hernando Siles Reyes (1926–1930), grew up in La Paz. In 1941 he helped found the **Nationalist Revolutionary Movement** (Movimiento Nacionalista Revolucionario, MNR) and later commanded revolutionary forces in 1952. He served as vice president during the first administration of Víctor **Paz Estenssoro** (1952–1956, 1960–1964, 1985–1989) and was elected president in 1956. During his first term, the faltering Bolivian economy experienced severe inflationary pressures, and with the support of the United States and the International Monetary Fund (IMF), Siles Zuazo adopted an inflation stabilization program. While the program brought inflation under control, it also halted many of the social programs implemented at the beginning of the National Revolution.

When the military took control of the nation in 1964, Siles Zuazo quickly became an outspoken critic of the authoritarian regime. He fought for the restoration of democracy and never aligned himself with the military, as many other MNR leaders did. As a consequence he suffered harassment from the government and at one point was exiled to Uruguay. In 1972 Siles Zuazo founded the Nationalist Revolutionary Movement of the Left (Movimiento Nacionalista Revolucionario Izquierda, MNR-I), a splinter party of the MNR. He ran for president on the MNR-I ticket in 1978, 1979, and 1980. Though he attained the most votes in each election, he was not permitted to assume the presidency until 1982, after the resignation of military leader General Guido Vildoso Calderón (1982). He came to office supported by a coalition called the Democratic and Popular Union (Unidad Democrática y Popular, UDP), which consisted of his MNR-I, the **Movement of the Revolutionary Left** (Movimiento de la Izquierda Revolucionaria, MIR), and Bolivia's Communist Party.

During his second presidency, Siles Zuazo attempted to set up a democratic populist regime and stabilize the chaotic economy, but his plans were thwarted by military unrest, conservative political opposition, continual squabbling among leftist parties, and the devastating 1983 drought. In addition, the **Bolivian Workers' Central** (Central Obrero Boliviano, COB) protested the president's every attempt to reform the economy, organizing massive strikes. Finally, the Bolivian economy collapsed amid falling mineral production and the Latin American debt crisis. Siles Zuazo twice devalued the peso, and inflation soared as he tried to finance the rapidly increasing fiscal deficit by printing more money. The president was highly criticized, and was even abducted and held captive by a corrupt military official until U.S. ambassador Edwin Corr intervened. Even his vice president, Jaime **Paz Zamora** (1989–1993), turned against him and pulled the MIR out of the government in 1983. When the military threatened a coup in 1984, Siles Zuazo stepped down and allowed for early presidential elections in 1985, and retired to Uruguay. He died eleven years later.

Silver

In 1545 an extraordinary silver deposit was discovered at Potosí in Upper Peru (the area that would later, with independence, become Bolivia). Silver producers dominated political life in the area for the subsequent three centuries. Silver production gradually began to decline in the late 1700s due to the rising costs of imports crucial to mining operations and periodic weaknesses in the international silver market. This decline, combined with the area's relative geographic isolation, made Bolivia one of the poorest republics in Latin America by the time of its independence in the early nineteenth century.

The mining industry collapsed in the early nineteenth century as mines flooded and traditional trade routes were severed in the early years of independence. Mining recuperated in the 1840s, increasing government revenues from mining taxes and decreasing the state's financial dependence on Indian tribute. This brought about a new assault against the indigenous majority: the government sold Indian community land to the highest bidder, reducing communities to haciendas and turning the Indians into serfs. It is estimated that President Mariano Melgarejo (1864–1871) abrogated the land titles of more than 100,000 peasants, about 10 percent of the entire Bolivian population. The new silver oligarchy that took power after 1880 also put Indian lands on the market in an attempt to modernize the agrarian economy, and by the 1920s two-thirds of highland communities had been turned into haciendas.

Bolivia underwent a period of economic prosperity due to silver in the last decades of the nineteenth century, but low silver prices brought about decline and financial crisis by 1892. While Bolivia's economy was revived with the discovery of huge **tin** deposits in the late 1890s, the move from silver to tin undermined the position of the southern elites (residing mainly in Sucre and Potosí) who had benefited most from silver. As a result of the Federalist War (1898–1899), the northern city of La Paz became the de facto capital of the country and the southern regions declined into political and economic marginality from which they have not yet recovered.

Tin

Bolivia's economy was revived with the discovery during the 1890s of huge tin deposits near the old **silver** mines. Tin prices remained high on world markets for decades, and the wealth generated by large-scale tin mining ushered in a period of prosperity. This rapid enrichment, combined with Bolivia's stark socioeconomic inequalities, soon led to serious political upheaval.

While the landed upper classes had been influential in Bolivia since before the country's independence, the tin boom forced them to share power with new mineral entrepreneurs (often referred to as tin barons). This new mixture of powerful economic elites, known as *la rosca*, dominated Bolivia's economy, society, and politics through the first half of the twentieth century. Perhaps the most notorious members of *la rosca* were the three leading mine-owning families who monopolized the tin industry, Aramayo, Patiño, and Hochschild. Unlike their silver predecessors, these new elites did not seek to control the government, but rather encouraged the development of a professional army and a middle class to rationalize the government bureaucracy after decades of neglect. The economic boom thus also led to the expansion and strengthening of several middle-sector groups.

Though competition for the presidency remained intense and at times violent, there was widespread agreement on economic policy. The tin boom ushered in macroeconomic success, and tin wealth financed the modernization of Bolivia, paying for the construction of three new railroad lines (connecting Bolivia to the rest of the world for the first time), a highway system (which helped to integrate larger portions of the country), and many other infrastructure projects. While the boom occasioned the enrichment of the upper classes, its effect on the lower classes was dramatically different. The miners worked unbearably long hours in deplora-

ble, dangerous conditions and were paid barely enough to survive. *La rosca* was thus hated by most Bolivians.

Following Bolivia's overwhelming defeat in the **Chaco War** (1932–1935; see Appendix 1), many people became disillusioned with the established power structure, and began speaking out against members of *la rosca*. In the 1940s, with the support of leftist organizations and despite strong governmental opposition, Bolivian miners began to unionize and hold strikes to demand higher wages and recognition, forcing powerful mining elites and the government to use repression to maintain the status quo. Among those to strike were the miners who worked the Catavi mines, and in December 1942, in the most brutal incident of the period, the army opened fire on the picketing miners, their wives, and their children, massacring hundreds. The massacre attracted national and international attention, and Bolivian leftist organizations, especially the **Nationalist Revolutionary Movement** (Movimiento Nacionalista Revolucionario, MNR), immediately took up the cause and used it to discredit the government and gain support among workers. The MNR's alliance with the tin miners would be pivotal in the success of the **National Revolution** (1952).

The revolutionary government that ruled Bolivia from 1952, headed by Víctor **Paz Estenssoro** (1952–1956, 1960–1964, 1985–1989), outlawed obligatory work and enacted a land reform program that divided up the haciendas in the highlands, ending the domination of *la rosca*. The tin mines were nationalized and placed under the control of a new company, the Mining Corporation of Bolivia (Corporación Minera de Bolivia, COMIBOL), which was controlled by the mine workers' unions until 1960. However, subsequent governments wrested control from the workers, often through violent means, and by 1985 COMIBOL was losing so much money that in his third administration Paz Estenssoro let most of the mine workers go and privatized the company. Today tin is less important than it once was, and no longer represents the majority of export earnings as it did for most of the twentieth century.

Toro, David (1898–1977)

David Toro was born in Sucre. He later joined the military, rising quickly through the ranks. He served in the **Chaco War** (1932–1935; see Appendix 1), aided Germán **Busch Becerra** (1937–1939) in the overthrow of President José Luis Tejada Sorzano (1934–1936) in 1936, and then assumed the presidency. As president from 1936 to 1937, Toro created unions to organize labor and established the Ministry of Labor in recognition of its growing importance. He also granted women equity in all affairs. He nationalized the Bolivian holdings of Standard Oil Company of New Jersey and created a state oil enterprise known as Fiscal Oilfields of Bolivia (Yacimientos Petrolíferos Fiscales de Bolivia, YPFB), enacting the first confiscation without compensation of a major American company in Latin America. In 1937 Toro ceded power to Busch after attempting to raise taxes on **tin** barons. Following his resignation, Toro continued to play a role in politics.

Torres González, Juan José (1921–1976)

Juan José Torres González, who served as president for only ten months (1970–1971), was one of the most radically leftist military rulers in Bolivian history.

Torres was born in Cochabamba and entered the military at a young age. Eventually rising to commander-in-chief of the armed forces, Torres aided in the 1964 overthrow of Víctor **Paz Estenssoro** (1952–1956, 1960–1964, 1985–1989), and assumed the presidency after the overthrow of General Alfredo **Ovando Candia** (1969–1970). Torres, the last military president to advocate socialist reform, deepened and expanded Ovando's policies of land reform, labor empowerment, and industrialization. Torres also rallied against foreign imperialism; he attacked the role of the United States in the country and was the first president to accept Russian and Eastern European aid for the Mining Corporation of Bolivia (Corporación Minera de Bolivia, COMIBOL), the state-controlled mining enterprise.

Torres created the short-lived Popular Assembly in 1970, with which he hoped to replace the legislative branch of the national government. Though the Popular Assembly never obtained full legislative power, garnered popular legitimacy, or passed significant legislation, it did succeed in increasing the gap between conservative factions of the military and radical civilian leaders. It also frightened the right enough to create support for a coup; while the first attempt against Torres' government failed in January 1971, his administration was toppled eight months later, bringing Hugo **Banzer Suárez** (1971–1977, 1997–2001) to the presidency. Torres fled to Argentina, where he was murdered five years later.

Túpac Katari (also Túpac Catari, Julián Apaza) (1750–1781). See *Katarismo*

Villarroel López, Gualberto (1908–1946). See **Nationalist Revolutionary Movement (Movimiento Nacionalista Revolucionario, MNR)**

War of the Pacific (1879–1884). See Appendix 1

HEADS OF STATE

Simón Antonio de la Santísima Trinidad Bolívar y Palacios	1825
Antonio José de Sucre	1825–1828
José María Pérez de Urdininea	1828
José Miguel de Velasco	1828
Pedro Blanco	1828–1829
José Miguel de Velasco	1829
Andrés de Santa Cruz	1829–1839
José Miguel de Velasco	1839–1841
Sebastián Agreda	1841
Mariano Enrique Calvo	1841
José Ballivián	1841–1847
Eusebio Guilarte	1847–1848
José Miguel de Velasco	1848
Manuel Isidoro Belzu	1848–1855
Jorge Córdova	1855–1857
José María Linares	1857–1861
Junta de Gobierno	1861
José María Achá	1861–1864
Mariano Melgarejo	1864–1871
Agustín Morales	1871–1872
Tomás Frías	1872–1873
Adolfo Ballivián	1873–1874
Tomás Frías	1874–1876
Hilarión Daza	1876–1879
Narciso Campero	1880–1884
Gregorio Pacheco	1884–1888
Aniceto Arce	1888–1892
Mariano Baptista	1892–1896
Severo Fernández Alonso	1896–1899
Junta de Gobierno	1899
José Manuel Pando	1899–1904
Ismael Montes	1904–1909
Eliodoro Villazón	1909–1913
Ismael Montes	1913–1917
José Gutiérrez Guerra	1917–1920
Junta de Gobierno	1920–1921
Bautista Saavedra	1921–1925
Felipe Segundo Guzmán	1925–1926
Hernando Siles Reyes	1926–1930
Consejo de Ministros	1930
Carlos Blanco Galindo	1930–1931
Daniel Salamanca	1931–1934
José Luis Tejada Sorzano	1934–1936
David Toro	1936–1937
Germán Busch Becerra	1937–1939
Carlos Quintanilla	1939–1940
Enrique Peñaranda	1940–1943
Gualberto Villarroel	1943–1946
Néstor Guillén	1946
Tomás Monge Gutiérrez	1946–1947
Enrique Hertzog Garaizábal	1947–1949
Mamerto Urriolagoitia	1949–1951
Hugo Ballivián Rojas	1951–1952

Víctor Paz Estenssoro	1952–1956
Hernán Siles Zuazo	1956–1960
Víctor Paz Estenssoro	1960–1964
René Barrientos Ortuño/Alfredo Ovando Candia	1964–1966
René Barrientos Ortuño	1966–1969
Luis Adolfo Siles Salinas	1969
Alfredo Ovando Candia	1969–1970
Guachalla/Sattori/Albarracín	1970
Juan José Torres González	1970–1971
Hugo Banzer Suárez	1971–1977
Juan Pereda Asbún	1978
David Padilla Arancibia	1978–1979
Walter Guevara Arze	1979
Alberto Natusch Busch	1979
Lydia Gueiler Tejada	1979–1980
Luis García Meza Tejada	1980–1981
Torrelio/Bernal/Pammo	1981
Celso Torrelio Villa	1981–1982
Guido Vildoso Calderón	1982
Hernán Siles Zuazo	1982–1985
Víctor Paz Estenssoro	1985–1989
Jaime Paz Zamora	1989–1993
Gonzalo Sánchez de Lozada Bustamante	1993–1997
Hugo Banzer Suárez	1997–2001
Jorge Quiroga Ramírez	2001–

Source: Herbert S. Klein, *Bolivia: The Evolution of a Multi-Ethnic Society*, 2nd ed. (New York: Oxford University Press, 1992).

BIBLIOGRAPHY

Print Resources

Buechler, Hans C., and Judith Maria Buechler. *The Bolivian Aymara*. New York: Holt, Rinehart and Winston, 1971.

Cole, Jeffrey A. *The Potosí Mita, 1573–1700: Compulsory Indian Labor in the Andes*. Stanford: Stanford University Press, 1985.

Conaghan, Catherine, and James Malloy. *Unsetting State-craft: Democracy and Neoliberalism in the Andes*. Pittsburgh: University of Pittsburgh Press, 1994.

Dunkerley, James. *Rebellion in the Veins: Political Struggle in Bolivia, 1952 to 1982*. London: Verso, 1984.

Klein, Herbert S. *Bolivia: The Evolution of a Multi-Ethnic Society*. 2nd Ed. Oxford: Oxford University Press, 1992.

Klein, Herbert S. *Parties and Political Change in Bolivia, 1880–1952*. Cambridge: Cambridge University Press, 1971.

Langer, Erick D. *Economic Change and Rural Resistance in Southern Bolivia, 1880–1930*. Stanford: Stanford University Press, 1989.

Malloy, James. *Bolivia: The Uncompleted Revolution*. Pittsburgh: University of Pittsburgh Press, 1970.

Malloy, James, and Eduardo Gamarra. *Revolution and Reaction: Bolivia 1964–1985*. New Brunswick, NJ: Transaction Books, 1988.

Nash, June C. *We Eat the Mines and the Mines Eat Us: Dependency and Exploitation in Bolivian Tin Mines*. New York: Columbia University Press, 1979.

Rivera Cusicanqui, Silvia. *"Oprimidos Pero No Vencidos": Luchas del Campesinado Aymara-Quechua, 1900–1980*. Geneva: Unrisd, 1986.

Stern, Steve, ed. *Resistance, Rebellion, and Consciousness in the Andean Peasant World: Eighteenth to Twentieth Centuries*. Madison: University of Wisconsin Press, 1987.

Electronic Resources

El Diario
http://www.eldiario.net/
The Web version of one of Bolivia's premier daily newspapers. Offers comprehensive national and international coverage, with an emphasis on Bolivian national politics. (In Spanish)

Latin American Network Information Center (LANIC): Bolivia
http://lanic.utexas.edu/la/sa/bolivia/
Bolivia section of this extensive Web site contains hundreds of links to research resources, cultural centers, economic and business institutions, government agencies, historical sources, magazines and other periodicals, nongovernmental organizations, and grassroots groups. (In English)

Political Database of the Americas: Bolivia
http://www.georgetown.edu/pdba/Countries/bolivia.html
Comprehensive database run as a joint project of Georgetown University and the Organization of American States. Section on Bolivia contains information on and links to the executive, legislative, and judicial branches of the Bolivian government; electoral laws and election results; and other political data. (In English, Spanish, Portuguese, and French)

Political Resources.net: Bolivia
http://www.politicalresources.net/bolivia.htm
Contains a wealth of links to sources of information on national politics. Includes information on political parties, legislative and executive institutions, laws and legislation, and elections, as well as a link to the constitution. (In English)

Wilfried Derksen's Elections Around the World: Bolivia
http://www.agora.it/elections/bolivia.htm
Bolivia section of a comprehensive database of results from elections around the world. Contains results from recent national executive and legislative elections, as well as explanations of and links to political parties and institutions. (In English)

BRAZIL

COUNTRY PROFILE

Official name	República Federativa do Brasil
Capital	Brasília
Type/structure of government	Federal republic
Executive	President directly elected to a four-year term (may be consecutively re-elected); serves as both chief of state and head of the government, and appoints the cabinet.
Legislative	Bicameral National Congress comprising a Federal Senate (81 senators, three from each state or federal district, serve eight-year terms) and a Chamber of Deputies (531 seats; each state's representation is based on its population; deputies serve four-year terms).
Judicial	Highest court is the Supreme Federal Tribune with eleven judges who are appointed by the president and serve for life.
Major political parties	**Brazilian Social Democratic Party** (Partido da Social Democracia Brasileira, PSDB), **Workers' Party** (Partido dos Trabalhadores, PT), and **Brazilian Democratic Movement Party** (Partido do Movimento Democrático Brasileiro, PMDB).
Constitution in effect	1988
Location/geography	Northeast South America bordering every South American nation except Ecuador and Chile; has 2,000 miles of Atlantic coastline and stretches about 3,000 miles into the continent of South America encompassing tropical rainforest (most notably the Amazon), desert areas, and forests.
Geographic area	8,511,965 sq. km.
Population	171,853,126 (July 1999 est.)
Ethnic groups	White (of European descent) 55%; mulatto 38%; black (of African descent) 6%; other 1% (includes Japanese, Arab, and indigenous)
Religions	Roman Catholic 70%; Protestant, various Afro-Brazilian religions 30%
Literacy rate	83.3% (1998)
Infant mortality rate	35.37 deaths per 1,000 live births (1999 est.)
Life expectancy	64.06 years (1998)
Monetary unit	Real (reais, plural)
Exchange rate	1 U.S. dollar = 1.80 reais (August 2000)*
Major exports	Iron ore, soybean bran, orange juice, footwear, coffee, motor vehicle parts
Major imports	Crude oil, capital goods, chemical products
GDP	$1.0352 trillion (1998 est.)
GDP growth rate	.5% (1998)
GDP per capita	$6,100 (1998 est.)

Latin American Weekly Report. August 22, 2000 (WR-00–33), p. 394.

Source: *CIA World Factbook*, unless noted. www.odci.gov/cia/publications/factbook/geos/br.html

OVERVIEW

Summary

Brazil, Latin America's largest country, was Portugal's colonial gem. Millions of Africans were brought to colonial Brazil to work as slaves on sugar plantations, and were replaced later by wage-earning European immigrants, leading to the racial mixing that is still prevalent today. In the past twenty years, Brazil has come to play a key role in the world's economy, but only a small portion of the population has reaped the benefits of its economic success. Millions of people live in poverty, from landless peasants to the many street children that live in Brazil's big cities.

History

Centuries before the arrival of the Europeans, millions of indigenous peoples speaking hundreds of different languages populated the coast and the interior rain forests of what is today Brazil. Upon their arrival, both the Spanish and the Portuguese laid claim to the area known as the "New World." In 1493 the Pope divided the two claims at a meridian 100 leagues west of the Cape Verde Islands, with Spain taking everything 180

Brazil. © 1998 The Moschovitis Group, Inc.

degrees to the west of that point and Portugal taking everything 180 degrees to the east. The Treaty of Tordesillas, signed in 1494, drew a new dividing line between the Spanish and Portuguese claims in the New World 270 leagues west of the original mark, offering Portugal a larger section of the South American continent, whose geography was still unknown to all. In 1500 Pedro Álvares Cabral landed his fleet of thirteen ships and almost 1,500 men on the eastern shores of South America in the area that is today the city of Porto Seguro, Bahia. Cabral claimed the land for Portugal, calling his find "Land of the True Cross" (Terra da Vera Cruz), though people soon began to refer to the territory as Brazil, in reference to the precious brasilwood that was native to the area and valued for its red dye. During the early conquest period, the Portuguese faced constant attempts by the French and the Dutch to seize land along the Atlantic coast, and it soon became clear that the best way to maintain control of the area and its vast natural resources was to colonize it.

The vast territory was difficult to control, however. *Bandeirantes* (bandits), renowned in Brazilian history, made adventurous and often dangerous and destructive treks into the country's interior during the seventeenth and eighteenth centuries in search of runaway slaves, Indians, gold, land, and treasure, with hopes of opening trade routes and claiming Southern American land for Portugal. They pushed the country's boundaries even farther west, and with the crowns of Spain and Portugal intermarried, the Treaty of Madrid (1750) redrew the boundaries established by the Treaty of Tordesillas without war.

A few decades after Cabral's arrival, the Portuguese had begun to cultivate sugarcane in their new colony,

especially in the fertile northeastern area of Bahia and Pernambuco. The Portuguese initially tried to enslave those native peoples who had not been decimated by diseases brought by the Europeans, and later plantation owners increasingly relied on captured Africans to work in their fields and factories; eventually between 3 and 6 million Africans would be forced to make the harrowing journey across the Atlantic Ocean to Brazil to be sold as slaves. Sugar was king for nearly a century and a half before the discovery of gold and diamonds in the interior of Brazil, in what is today the state of Minas Gerais. Small mining towns soon grew into bustling centers of commerce and lawlessness, however, and eventually mining so eclipsed sugar in importance that the capital of Brazil was moved from Salvador, Bahia, to Rio de Janeiro in 1763. In the early nineteenth century, coffee, grown in the southern part of Brazil, especially in São Paulo and Rio de Janeiro, took the place of mining as Brazil's major source of revenue.

Through much of the colonial period, Portugal continually drained its colony of its natural resources and purposefully kept its development in check. During the Napoleonic Wars, in 1807, heir to the Portuguese throne Dom João VI decided to flee to the New World as Napoleon's troops moved closer to Lisbon. With 15,000 of his followers and English protection, Dom João left the Portuguese to the mercy of Napoleon. Upon the royal court's arrival in Rio de Janeiro, Brazil began to change. Its ports were opened to international trade, and aristocratic Portuguese flocked to Rio de Janeiro. When Napoleon was defeated in 1815, Dom João was called back to Portugal by the parliament. However, he refused to go, declaring Rio de Janeiro the capital of Portugal. He became king of Portugal following the death of Queen Maria I in 1816, but remained in Brazil until 1821, when a violent coup forced him out. As he left, he urged his son, Dom **Pedro I** (1822–1831), to take the lead in any independence movement that arose, and to make himself emperor of Brazil. Dom Pedro I declared the country independent in 1822, and both he and his son Dom **Pedro II** (1840–1889) ruled Brazil as emperors. Slavery was abolished in 1888, with the Golden Law (Lei Aurea), and thousands of European immigrants streamed into the country, working in both the country side and the cities. With them came new ideas about government, and in 1889 republican agitators overthrew Dom Pedro II and established the United States of Brazil.

The transition from monarchy was relatively peaceful (with the exception of some bloody skirmishes in the south and the northeast, most notably in the town of **Canudos**), and the provisional government of Marechal Deodoro da Fonseca (1889–1891) promulgated the 1891 Constitution, which was based largely on the U.S. Constitution. At the turn of the century, the rubber boom in the Amazon rain forest was in full swing, *coronelismo* (rule through local bosses or *coronéis*) was

A 1964 photo of government legislative offices in Brasília, which became Brazil's capital in 1960. *Columbus Memorial Library, General Secretariat of the Organization of American States. Reproduced with permission of the Organization of American States.*

rampant in the backlands, and the country lacked national cohesion. Again, dramatic change took only decades. The rubber market went from boom to bust in the 1920s, and in 1930 Getúlio **Vargas** (1930–1945, 1951–1954) and his followers staged a revolution to unite Brazil and empower the working class. Vargas restructured Brazil's economy and foreign affairs, established his Estado Novo in 1937, and proclaimed himself dictator in 1944. Though he was deposed by the increasingly politicized military in 1945, he later returned to the presidency. Following the innovative presidency of Juscelino **Kubitschek de Oliviero** (1956–1961), Jânio da Silva **Quadros** (1961) was elected to govern Brazil. However, he soon resigned, leaving his controversial vice president, João "Jango" Belchoir Marques **Goulart** (1961–1964), to govern. Powerful political connections allowed the liberal Goulart to remain in office despite strong military opposition. With the country on the brink of civil chaos, Goulart continually clashed with the armed forces, and in April 1964 he was overthrown, ushering in twenty-one years of military rule.

These years were marked by a push toward modernization and the expansion of Brazil's exports, economic slumps and astonishing prosperity (see **Economic Miracle**), as well as brutal torture, killings, kidnappings, disappearances, and censorship. Despite the protestations of the hard-line military faction, Ernesto **Geisel** (1974–1979) initiated political liberalization (called *distensão* in Brazil), allowing for some elections and the formation of political parties. His successor, João Baptista de Oliveira **Figueiredo** (1979–1985), pushed the *distensão* to an opening (*abertura*), moving the country closer to democracy.

In 1985 Tancredo de Almeida **Neves**, who had fought against the military dictatorship, won the first presidential elections held since the 1964 coup. However, he died of natural causes before taking office, leaving his vice president, José **Sarney da Costa** (1985–1990), a longtime military supporter, to assume the presidency. Following Sarney, the charismatic Fernando **Collor de Mello** (1990–1992) held office. Despite some success (Collor presided over the 1991 Brazilian accession to the **Southern Cone Common Market** [Mercado Común del Cono Sur, MERCOSUR; see Appendix 1], for instance), Collor was impeached in 1992 amid a corruption scandal, leaving Vice President Itamar Augusto Cauteiro **Franco** (1992–1995) to complete his term. In 1994 Fernando Henrique **Cardoso** (1995–), was elected president, in part due to the success of the economic austerity program he had designed while serving as Franco's minister of finance, which included the introduction of a new currency, the *real*, in 1994. The economy continued to grow and inflation was tamed under Cardoso, and as his first term in office was drawing to a close, he convinced Congress to amend the constitution to allow him to run for a second consecutive presidential term, with the hope of continuing to foster the country's economic growth. Cardoso was victorious in the presidential election of 1998 and skillfully handled Brazil's economic crisis in early 1999. Despite Brazil's successful economic recovery in 1999, the country was plagued by economic problems in 2001 including a severe energy crisis. In addition, the Cardoso administration was accused of being permissive of corruption. Brazilians will head to the polls in late 2002 to elect Cardoso's successor.

ENTRIES

Abertura. See Figueiredo, João Baptista de Oliveira

Alliance for National Renewal (Aliança Renovadora Nacional, ARENA)

The Alliance for National Renewal (Aliança Renovadora Nacional, ARENA) was the official military party created during the 1964 coup that overthrew President João "Jango" Belchoir Marques **Goulart** (1961–1964). Party members instituted a government with a titular president controlled by a twelve-member committee of top military officers called the Establishment (Estado Maior). The president of Brazil served as the president of ARENA and selected all its candidates for political offices. The party's goal was to reform the economy by controlling inflation and strictly supervising the political system.

In 1967 the military formed an official opposition party, the Brazilian Democratic Movement (Movimento Democrático Brasileiro, MDB; see **Brazilian Democratic Movement Party** [Partido do Movimento Democrático Brasileiro, PMDB]), to lend the appearance of legitimacy to the dictatorial government. Nonetheless, ARENA maintained control of the government until the final years of the twenty-one-year period of military rule (1964–1985), winning almost all elections (often by a substantial majority) and holding the presidency and a majority of the seats in both houses of Congress as well as most of Brazil's governorships and mayoralties. By the mid-1970s, dissatisfaction with the military regime began to increase with the decline of Brazil's **economic miracle**, the increasing repression of the government, and international disapproval over rumors of torture. MDB candidates began to defeat their ARENA counterparts, and conservative politicians attempted to disassociate themselves from the military regime.

In 1979 President João Baptista Oliveira **Figueiredo** (1979–1985) ended the exclusive two-party political system and allowed for the organization of other political parties. ARENA reestablished itself as the Social Democracy Party (Partido Democracia Social, PDS), which was defeated in the 1985 presidential elections that returned Brazil to civilian rule following the political opening (*abertura*); conservative politicians maintained a majority in the legislature, however. The party continued to exist into the 1990s, although on a much smaller scale and garnering only a small percentage of votes.

Brasília. See Kubitschek de Oliviero, Juscelino

Brazilian Democratic Movement (Movimento Democrático Brasileiro, MDB).

See Alliance for National Renewal (Aliança Renovadora Nacional, ARENA); Brazilian Democratic Movement Party (Partido do Movimento Democrático Brasileiro, PMDB)

Brazilian Democratic Movement Party (Partido do Movimento Democrático Brasileiro, PMDB)

The Brazilian Democratic Movement (Movimento Democrático Brasileiro, MDB) evolved into the Brazilian Democratic Movement Party (Partido do Movimento Democrático Brasileiro, PMDB) in 1979 in the context of the military regime's political opening (*abertura*).

In 1965, following the military's loss at the polls in the first election after the 1964 coup, President Humberto de Alencar **Castelo Branco** (1964–1967) issued the Second Institutional Acts, a series of repressive laws that included the banning of all political parties. The MDB, which was formed in November 1967 by the military government to lend the appearance of legitimacy to its dictatorial rule, served as the official opposition organization to the military dictatorship's party, the **Alliance for National Renewal** (Aliança Renovadora Nacional, ARENA). However, the MDB, which included opposition politicians of all different backgrounds and platforms, was virtually powerless against ARENA due to restrictions placed upon the MDB by the government, including censorship, and tight control of elections. Nonetheless, members of the MDB such as Tancredo de Almeida **Neves** were integral in Brazil's transition to democracy.

When the military began to withdraw from government and Brazil began to move toward greater democracy in 1979, a multiparty system was reinstated and the MDB became the PMDB. The PMDB maintained many of the MDB's priorities, including pushing for the dismantling of the military government and the lifting of its repressive measures such as censorship and the mandatory carrying of identification documents. Though initially the PMDB was popular due to its stance against the military, as other parties formed following the end of the military regime, the PMDB lost some of its power; a schism in the party's leadership led to the creation of the **Brazilian Social Democratic Party** (Partido da Social Democracia Brasileira, PSDB) in 1988. As of mid-2001, the PMDB held a plurality of seats in the Senate and had the third largest representation in the Chamber of Deputies.

Brazilian Social Democratic Party (Partido da Social Democracia Brasileira, PSDB)

In June 1988, a group of left-wing politicians led by Fernando Henrique **Cardoso** (1995–   ) and José **Sarney da Costa** (1985–1990) left the **Brazilian Democratic Movement Party** (Partido do Movimento Democrático Brasileiro, PMDB) to form the Brazilian Social Democratic Party (Partido da Social Democracia Brasileira,

PSDB) with the goal of ensuring the defense of social democracy and the parliamentary system. Though initially the party had difficulty gaining support (it elected only one governor in the 1990 state elections), it was subsequently more successful. By 2001, the party was well represented in the legislature, with a narrow plurality of seats in the Chamber of Deputies and the third largest contingent in the Senate. The party maintains a centrist stance, with the goal of strengthening the country's democratic process while working to bolster its economy and increase productivity.

Câmara, Dom Helder (1909–1999)

Born in the state of Ceará, Câmara was ordained into the Catholic priesthood at the age of twenty-two. While early on he aligned himself with fascist political organizations, he moved toward a more liberal stance in the 1940s, working for the Brazilian Catholic Action organization. In 1952 he was appointed the auxiliary bishop of Rio de Janeiro, and that same year he helped form the National Conference of Brazilian Bishops (Conferencia Nacional dos Bisopos do Brasil, CNBB). He served as the organization's secretary-general from 1952 through 1964. The CNBB soon became one of the most powerful organizations within the Brazilian Catholic Church, though it came under constant attack from conservatives. Câmara also founded the São Sebastião Crusade, aimed at improving living conditions in Brazil's *favelas* (slums).

In 1964 Câmara was appointed to the archbishopric of Recife and Olinda, the capital of the northeastern state of Pernambuco. That same year the military overthrew President João "Jango" Belchoir Marques **Goulart** (1961–1964), beginning one of the most politically repressive periods in Brazil's history. Câmara denounced the human suffering levied on the Brazilian people and the repression and atrocities committed by the military government (1964–1985) when few had the power or courage to do so. As a result, his rights as a citizen were immediately stripped by the new military government, and he was continually harassed by the regime; many of those who worked with him were tortured, and some were killed for their dissenting ideas. Câmara retired in 1985, when Brazil's transition to democracy seemed to be on solid ground, and subsequently dedicated his life to helping the urban poor.

Campos, Robert. See Economic Miracle

Canudos

Canudos was an alternative folk society created in the early 1890s by impoverished rural workers who suffered at the hands of rich plantation and ranch owners. Located in the state of Bahia, Canudos and its messianic movement were led by Antônio Conselheiro (Anthony the Counselor, born Antonio Vicente Mendes Marciel). Inhabitants of Canudos lived in relative equality,

Fernando Henrique Cardoso, President of Brazil (1995–). *Columbus Memorial Library, General Secretariat of the Organization of American States. Reproduced with permission of the Organization of American States.*

and the town, whose population fluctuated between 5,000 and 32,000 people, offered a sense of security. The movement was not without opposition. Big landowners resented Conselheiro because he drew away employees and made them question their exploitation. The leaders of the new Brazilian republic viewed the movement as an impediment to progress and a threat to civilization along the Brazilian coast. They also believed it to be a religious plot with connections to the Portuguese monarchy because followers believed that God ordained Conselheiro to lead them, and because Conselheiro preached that the end of the monarchy signaled the apocalypse because the emperor had been divinely selected. As Canudos grew and Conselheiro became more popular, elites pushed the government to destroy Canudos. The town weathered three military attacks of increasing strength before succumbing in October 1897 after a six-month assault by 8,000 soldiers, three generals, and the latest military technology. The military, embarrassed by the length of time it took to defeat the inhabitants of Canudos, killed every occupant of the settlement and burned it to the ground. The movement was commemorated in two literary works, Euclydes da Cunha's famous *Os Sertões* (Rebellions in the Backlands, 1902) and Peruvian novelist Mario **Vargas Llosa**'s (see Peru) *La guerra del fin del mundo* (War of the End of the World, 1981).

Cardoso, Fernando Henrique (1931–)

Twice-elected president Fernando Henrique Cardoso's (1995–) economic policies have helped Brazil become and remain a key player in the world economy.

Cardoso was born in Rio de Janeiro and received his degree from the University of São Paulo. He taught political science, and also became a world-renowned sociologist. A Marxist, Cardoso viewed foreign investment as dangerous to national sovereignty and believed that dominant world powers like the United States and Europe had actively kept Latin America underdeveloped to exploit it. He explained those views in the most famous of his books, *Dependency and Development in Latin America* (1969), written with historian Enzo Faletto. Upon the book's publication, Cardoso was exiled by the military government then in power.

As he grew older and obtained more political power, Cardoso's political and economic views changed radically. He was elected senator from São Paulo in 1978 on the ticket of the Brazilian Democratic Movement (Movimento Democrático Brasileiro, MDB), and was reelected on the ticket of the newly formed **Brazilian Democratic Movement Party** (Partido do Movimento Democrático Brasileiro, PMDB). In 1988 he helped found the **Brazilian Social Democratic Party** (Partido da Social Democracia Brasileira, PSDB) and subsequently served as minister of foreign affairs, then minister of finance under President Itamar Augusto Cauteiro **Franco** (1992–1995). As minister of finance, Cardoso courted foreign investment and began to dismantle state-owned companies. He also introduced the Real Plan (*Plan Real*) on July 1, 1994, which replaced Brazil's currency with the *real*, whose value was set to a crawling peg with the U.S. dollar. Inflation dropped from almost 2,500 percent to double digits and real incomes soared.

Riding on the success of the *real* and running on the PSDB ticket, Cardoso defeated Luis Inacio "Lula" da **Silva** of the **Workers' Party** (Partido dos Trabalhadores, PT) in the 1994 presidential election. During his first administration, Cardoso faced difficulty pushing reforms through Congress, and while the economy continued to grow due to the *Real* Plan, little social progress was made as unemployment and extreme poverty rose. In 1997 workers took to the streets to protest Cardoso's policies of economic stringency, which affected them adversely but benefited Brazil's wealthy elite. Further, an international economic crisis began to brew in 1997 when East Asian markets began to fall, and Russia devalued its currency and declared it was unable to pay parts of its domestic and international debt. As his first term came to a close, Cardoso convinced Congress to amend the constitution to allow him to run for a second term, stating that the country's problems could not be solved in one presidential term. Cardoso again defeated Lula in the 1998 presidential elections.

Soon after he began his second term, in mid-January 1999, Brazil was plunged into economic chaos as foreign investors withdrew their capital and reserves sank. On January 15, Brazil was forced to devalue the *real*, abandoning its policy of a pegged exchange rate. Since then, the *real* has been a free-floating currency. Within months Brazil's federal government agreed to an International Monetary Fund (IMF) reform plan that bolstered confidence in the country's economy, and soon foreign capital inflows resumed, rebuilding foreign reserves. Cardoso was praised internationally for his handling of the crisis, which was brought under control by March 1999. However, many of Brazil's laborers and poor question the success of their president's economic programs, which they feel have not addressed the country's socioeconomic disparities.

Castelo Branco, Humberto de Alencar (1900–1967)

As the first president to serve during Brazil's twenty-one-year military dictatorship, Humberto de Alencar Castelo Branco (1964–1967) implemented laws that restricted civil rights and silenced the regime's opponents.

Born in Fortaleza, the capital of the northeastern state of Ceará, Castelo Branco attended military school in Rio Grande do Sul, Rio de Janeiro, and Paris. He fought against Luis Carlos **Prestes** in the Northeast of Brazil, and later worked in the Superior School of War (Escola Superior de Guerra, ESG). Castelo Branco saw the military's mandate as retaining order, and looked down upon the military's extreme right hard-liners (*linha dura*), who pressed for control. Following his unsuccessful attempt to convince President João "Jango" Belchoir Marques **Goulart** (1961–1964) to modify his increasingly radical leftist policies, on April 1, 1964, Castelo Branco led Brazil's armed forces, with the support of the country's elite, middle class, state governors, and opposition politicians, to oust Goulart and assume power. There was little opposition to the coup, except on university campuses and among labor leaders. Unlike past interventions (in 1930, 1945, and 1954), the military planned to remain in power until economic growth had been reinvigorated, inflation tamed, and threats of instability and communism eradicated. Initially, Chamber of Deputies president Raneiri Mazzilli was chosen to serve as president of the country, but within two weeks the military had appointed Castelo Branco to finish out Goulart's term as leader of Brazil. The United States immediately recognized the new government, lending legitimacy to rumors of its complicity in the ouster.

As president, Castelo Branco set out to make good on the promises the military had made during the coup. He conformed Brazilian policies to please the United States, and broke off relations with Cuba and the People's Republic of China, prompting investment and aid from the United States. Nonetheless, his economic austerity policies failed in the short term: inflation increased, wage earners' purchasing power fell, and unemployment rose. Soon after taking office, Castelo Branco implemented the First Institutional Acts, which invested more power in the president, purged the Congress, and stripped the political rights of Brazilian citizens deemed subversive by the government. In addition, Castelo Branco outlawed the Peasant Leagues, encouraged the burning of subversive books, and, just before he was to leave office, canceled scheduled elections for governors and capital city mayors, setting the stage for the continued dominance of the candidates from the **Alliance for National Renewal** (Aliança Renovadora Nacional, ARENA), the official military party.

Though the military suffered a loss at the polls in the 1965 congressional elections, that same year a constitutional amendment was passed that allowed Castelo Branco to rule for fourteen more months. During those months, his administration passed the Second Institutional Acts (1966) which allowed for indirect election of the president and vice president, and abolished all political parties. In 1967 the military created the Brazilian Democratic Movement (Movimento Democrático Brasileiro, MDB; see **Brazilian Democratic Movement Party** [Partido do Movimento Democrático Brasileiro, PMDB]) as a powerless opposition party to offer the government some degree of legitimacy. Later that year, just before yielding the presidency to military hard-liner Artur da **Costa e Silva** (1967–1969), Castelo Branco's administration promulgated a new constitution. Castelo Branco continued exerting some political influence on the military government until his death a few months later in a military accident in Ceará.

Collor de Mello, Fernando Alfonso (1949–   )

Though conservatives hoped to enact economic reforms through the administration of young and energetic President Fernando Alfonso Collor de Mello (1990–1992), Collor's administration crumbled in a corruption scandal within two years of his election.

Born in Rio de Janeiro into a wealthy family, Collor studied at the University of Brasília and the University of Alagôas, receiving a degree in social communications from the former. After graduating, he worked as a reporter. In 1979 the pro-military **Alliance for National Renewal** (Aliança Renovadora Nacional, ARENA) selected him as governor of Maceio. He served for three years before being elected federal deputy on the ticket of the Social Democracy Party (Partido Democracia Social, PDS), the reformed version of ARENA. He served as governor of Alagôas with the **Brazilian Democratic Movement Party** (Partido do Movimento Democrático Brasileiro, PMDB) in the late 1980s, initiating an unrelenting campaign against corruption, sharply criticizing President José **Sarney da Costa** (1985–1990), cutting exorbitant government salaries, and firing almost half of the state's public servants (an action that was later reversed by the state supreme court).

Shunned by the PMDB, Collor began campaigning for the presidency in 1989 with the National Reconstructionist Party (Partido da Reconstrução Nacional, PRN), a self-devised party supported by conservatives.

Promising to make the government more efficient by eliminating corruption and shrinking the bureaucracy, Collor received the most votes among twenty-one presidential candidates in the November 1989 first-round elections, and defeated labor leader Luis Inacio "Lula" da **Silva** in the runoff election. Collor assumed office at the age of forty as Brazil's youngest president. While attempting to lead as a populist, he initiated a program of economic austerity, laid off industry workers, and closed banks for three days and limited withdrawals to the equivalent of $1,200 per month. The $88 billion generated by these measures was reduced to $16 billion because of corruption. He reintroduced the *cruzeiro* as the national currency and tried (unsuccessfully) to fire thousands of civil servants. Despite his efforts, the economy worsened, and striking workers began taking to the streets.

In 1992 Collor began receiving overwhelming negative press. Through a tabloid newspaper, his younger brother accused him of being a cocaine addict, engaging in scandalous behavior, and embezzling millions of dollars from the government. With no support in Congress or in his cabinet, Collor was impeached by the House of Deputies on charges of corruption in October 1992. Collor decided to resign rather than face an impeachment trial, and Vice President Itamar Augusto Cauteiro **Franco** (1992–1995) assumed the presidency. Criminal charges against Collor were later dropped by the Supreme Court due to lack of evidence. Many consider the successful impeachment of Collor a demonstration of the strength of democracy in Brazil.

Conselheiro, Antônio. See **Canudos**

Costa e Silva, Artur da (1902–1969)

The second president to serve following the advent of military rule in Brazil in 1964, Artur da Costa e Silva (1967–1969), a military hard-liner, called for greater military influence over politics, and his administration increased civilian repression. He is credited with helping Brazil achieve its **economic miracle**.

Born in Rio Grande do Sul, Costa e Silva attended military academies, and later served in Italy in World War II with a Brazilian force. He was part of the conspiracy that overthrew President Getúlio **Vargas** (1930–1945, 1951–1954) in 1945, and also aided in the overthrow of President João "Jango" Belchoir Marques **Goulart** (1961–1964) in 1964. In 1966 the legislature, with strong encouragement from the military, selected Costa e Silva to serve as president, succeeding fellow officer Humberto de Alencar **Castelo Branco** (1964–1967). Concerned by Costa e Silva's hard-line tendencies, Castelo Branco promulgated a new constitution just prior to leaving office, and simultaneously the Supreme Court and Congress attempted to assert control over the military-controlled executive.

In response to this, in 1968 Costa e Silva's military

government issued the Third Institutional Acts, which dissolved Congress, suspended elections, decreed media censorship, imprisoned political opponents, and gave the president almost unlimited power. Repression by government police troops, including kidnappings and torture, escalated. The president's economic policies, such as reducing taxes on businesses, courting foreign investment, and obtaining a billion dollar development loan from the World Bank, set in motion Brazil's "economic miracle." Costa e Silva suffered a stroke in 1969, cutting his presidency short. A military junta took power and, defying the constitution, bypassed Vice President Pedro Aleixo and selected Emílio Garrastazú **Médici** (1969–1974) as Costa e Silva's successor. Costa e Silva died soon after.

Delfim Netto, Antônio. See Economic Miracle

Distensão. See Geisel, Ernesto

Economic Miracle (1968–1974)

Brazil's "economic miracle" refers to the high annual rates of economic growth, increased exports, and greater national industrialization the nation enjoyed between 1968 and 1974. The miracle came at the height of the military dictatorship and served to temporarily legitimize its repressive control at home and abroad.

Though the economy initially stagnated under the austerity policies implemented by the military government after the 1964 coup, the dictatorship soon established favorable conditions for the expansion of business by suppressing labor uprisings and courting foreign investment. Exports increased, and inflation began to decrease as foreign capital poured into Brazil. However, few Brazilians saw the benefits, as the domestic market remained small and workers were grossly underpaid. Further, the national government kept tax money that had once been returned to the states to fund development projects. Antônio Delfim Netto, minister of finance under President Emílio Garrastazú **Médici** (1969–1974), was admired by the business community but sharply criticized by social organizations for worsening the plight of the poor while concentrating the benefits of the economic growth in the hands of a few, ignoring basic structural disparities in Brazil. Delfim Netto defended his policies, stating that ensuring the country's long-run prosperity required and justified such short-term failures.

However, in the long run, the economic miracle itself proved a failure. Brazil's growth began to slow in 1974, coinciding with the international oil crisis and a worldwide economic recession, and in the late 1970s inflation started to rise due to federal overspending and dependency on foreign capital. During the following decade, Brazil amassed a huge foreign debt that drained the country's export earnings.

Estado Novo. See Vargas, Getúlio

Figueiredo, João Baptista de Oliveira (1918–1999)

Born in Rio de Janeiro, João Baptista de Oliveira Figueiredo (1979–1985) attended military schools, and rose through the ranks to general. After conspiring in the 1964 overthrow of President João "Jango" Belchoir Marques **Goulart** (1961–1964), he served as chief of the military cabinet, secretary-general of the National Security Council, and head of the National Intelligence Agency (Serviço da Nacional Informação, SNI). After being chosen by the military as the successor to President Ernesto **Geisel** (1974–1979) in 1979, to the dismay of the armed forces, he vowed to continue Geisel's program of reopening Brazil to democracy (distensão). (Trying to present an image of fair governance to the world and cognizant that its reign was coming to an end, the military was not able to simply remove Figueiredo from the post.) Figueiredo gave amnesty to political prisoners and encouraged a multiparty political system to replace the two-party system instituted by the military government. In 1982 he allowed for the first direct election of state governors in more than fifteen years. When Figueiredo's term ended in 1985, he decided to discontinue his involvement in politics.

Franco, Itamar Augusto Cauteiro (1931–)

Itamar Augusto Cauteiro Franco (1992–1995) grew up in Minas Gerais and graduated from college with an engineering degree. He later ran unsuccessfully for a city council seat, and then ran unsuccessfully for deputy mayor. He was elected mayor of Minas Gerais on the ticket of the **Brazilian Democratic Movement Party** (Partido do Movimento Democrático Brasileiro, PMDB) in 1966 and in 1975 was elected to the national Senate. He was the running mate of conservative candidate Fernando Alfonso **Collor de Mello** (1990–1992) in the 1990 presidential elections, and was named interim president after Collor de Mello resigned facing impeachment on charges of corruption. Franco became the president of Brazil in December 1992, vowing to continue Collor's plans of privatizing national businesses, and planning a campaign to alleviate poverty. When the Brazilian currency was devalued to the point that it was nearly worthless, Franco introduced the *Real* Plan, developed by his minister of finance, Fernando Henrique **Cardoso** (1995–), which pegged Brazil's new currency, the *real*, to the American dollar. In the last few months of his term, Franco dealt with widespread political corruption by creating an audit bureau, which saved the government millions of dollars. Franco later served as the governor of Minas Gerais, and in 1999 announced that his state would be unable to pay the debt it owed to the federal government; the press blamed Franco's announcement for causing the economic crisis Brazil suffered that year. In 2001, Franco declared his candidacy for the 2002 presidential election.

Freire, Paulo (1921–1999)

Paulo Freire was a leading Brazilian thinker world-renowned for his educational theories condemning colonialism and his activism for social justice. Freire taught adult literacy in Pernambuco from the late 1940s through the 1950s. By 1959 Freire had completed his Ph.D. and began teaching history and educational philosophy at the University of Recife. He soon gained attention for his revolutionary ideas critiquing the Brazilian educational system's ingrained prejudice and the impossibility for students of low social class to succeed. Freire advocated consciousness-raising (*conscientizão*), which fostered self-respect in students through the learning process. His work in Brazil galvanized sectors of the poor, making them aware of their socioeconomic position with respect to the government and the elite. He led a national literacy campaign under President João "Jango" Belchoir Marques **Goulart** (1961–1964), though he was arrested, jailed, and then exiled by the subsequent military regime. He became a consultant for the World Council of Churches in 1971 and later established the Institute for Cultural Action, which developed experimental teaching following Freire's educational theory in different countries. Considered one of the most innovative and influential educational theorists, Freire wrote a number of books, including *Pedagogy of the Oppressed* (1970) and *Education for the Critical Consciousness* (1973). Freire's work remains relevant in contemporary Brazil.

FUNAI. See National Indian Foundation (Fundação Nacional do Índio)

Geisel, Ernesto (1908–)

Ernesto Geisel (1974–1979) was the fifth general to rule Brazil during its 1964–1985 period of military government. He began the long process that would bring Brazil closer to democracy.

Geisel entered the armed forces at a young age, attending military school in Rio de Janeiro and at the United States Army Command and General Staff College at Fort Leavenworth, Kansas. Later, Geisel served in high positions in the Brazilian military, and also as president of the Brazilian national petroleum company (Petróleo Brasileiro SA, Petrobras). He was selected by the **Alliance for National Renewal** (Aliança Renovadora Nacional, ARENA) and the military high command to serve as president in 1974. When Geisel entered office, the Brazilian **economic miracle** had ended and the country was in financial collapse due to the 1973 oil crisis and an international recession. Geisel continued the military dictatorship's practice of heavy foreign borrowing.

He also initiated the *distensão* (political liberalization), a process through which some of the political re-

strictions imposed by the military were lifted. To the military's dismay, Geisel allowed for some freedom of the press, attempted to reduce police repression, allowed civilian politicians a greater voice, and tried to repair relations with popular organizations that had been alienated by the military regime, such as the Catholic Church and labor. Congressional elections held in 1974 demonstrated the unpopularity of the military regime and ARENA: the opposition movement founded by the military, the Brazilian Democratic Movement (Movimento Democrático Brasileiro, MDB; see **Brazilian Democratic Movement Party** [Partido do Movimento Democrático Brasileiro, PMDB]), won sixteen of twenty-two seats in the Senate. When U.S. President Jimmy Carter criticized Geisel's regime for human rights violations and reduced military aid to Brazil, refusing to reinstate it until the country demonstrated an effort to end human rights abuses, Geisel terminated a twenty-five-year-old military pact with the United States and tried to align Brazil with Japan and West Germany. Geisel selected General João Baptista de Oliveira **Figueiredo** (1979–1985) to succeed him, anticipating he would continue Brazil's democratic opening.

Goulart, João "Jango" Belchoir Marques (1919–1976)

João "Jango" Belchoir Marques Goulart served as president from 1961 to 1964. His overthrow by the military ushered in over two decades of military rule.

Goulart was born in Rio Grande do Sul into a wealthy cattle ranching family with ties to the family of future president Getúlio **Vargas** (1930–1945, 1951–1954). Through business ventures, Goulart soon became a millionaire. He helped Vargas establish the Brazilian Labor Party (Partido Trabalhista Brasileiro, PTB) and served as minister of labor during Vargas' first presidency. However, when he suggested that the minimum wage be doubled, rural landowners and the military sharply resisted and forced Vargas to dismiss Goulart. Later, Goulart served as vice president under both Juscelino **Kubitschek de Oliviero** (1955–1961) and Jânio da Silva **Quadros** (1961). When Quadros suddenly resigned a year into his term, Goulart was the next in line to become president. Though elites and the military both balked, concerned by Goulart's leftist ideology, his supporters threatened a civil war if he did not assume the presidency. Finally, he signed an agreement with the military that severely curbed his power, and assumed office in 1961.

As he took office, inflation was skyrocketing, the economy was stagnant, social tensions were rising, and Congress was sharply divided among twelve political parties. Throughout his presidency, he alienated the military by opposing their will and "mishandling" two military revolts. Goulart used mass demonstrations to frighten his enemies (particularly the military), and some believe he allowed certain problems to worsen to demonstrate to the Brazilian people that the govern-

President of Brazil Juscelino Kubitschek de Oliviero (1956–1961) (holding hat), at dedication day ceremonies in Brasília in 1960. *Columbus Memorial Library, General Secretariat of the Organization of American States. Reproduced with permission of the Organization of American States.*

ment required radical change. He relied heavily on the support of the working classes, but was never able to attract the middle and upper classes to his cause. Though the economy was spiraling out of control, with inflation reaching nearly 100 percent, Brazil received little financial support from the United States, which was alarmed by Goulart's left-wing tendencies.

He became more radical in late 1963 and early 1964; in March 1964 he declared reforms that benefited the working class and the rural poor, including land distribution. Army troops began mobilizing on March 31, and on April 1 Brazil's armed forces, with the support of the country's elite, middle class, and some politicians, ousted Goulart and assumed power, vowing to repair the ailing economy. Goulart fled the country, living in Uruguay and then Argentina before dying of a heart attack in 1976.

Kubitschek de Oliviero, Juscelino (1902–1976)

Innovative president Juscelino Kubitschek de Oliviero (1956–1961) initiated many populist projects during his administration in hopes of uniting Brazil. These initiatives won him widespread support among the populace, but drove up inflation.

Kubitschek was born in Minas Gerais, and attended medical school in the city of Belo Horizonte. In 1934 Kubitschek was elected federal deputy, but had to leave the position following Getúlio **Vargas'** (1930–1945, 1951–1954) self-coup in 1937. Kubitschek was named mayor of Belo Horizonte in 1940, and elected governor of Minas Gerais in 1951. He was elected president of Brazil in 1955 with João "Jango" Belchoir Marques **Goulart** (1961–1964) as his vice president and little

support from the right. Kubitschek promised Brazil "fifty years of progress in five" and set to work implementing extensive plans to develop and modernize the country, including moving the capital from Rio de Janeiro to the interior city of Brasília in the state of Goias, where highways would connect it to all of Brazil's major cities. Capitalizing on the favorable post–World War II economic environment, he encouraged the growth of the automobile, steel, concrete, and energy industries, though his projects drove up inflation.

Unable to run for president again (the Brazilian constitution at that time barred presidents from serving consecutive terms), he subsequently served as a senator from the state of Goias with the hopes of running for president again in 1965. However, following the 1964 coup, his political rights were rescinded by the military and he went into exile, living in the United States and Europe. He returned to Brazil in 1967 and began working as an investment banker. He was killed in a car accident in 1976.

Landless Peasant Movement (Movimento dos Trabalhadores Rurais Sem Terra, MST)

The Landless Peasant Movement (Movimento dos Trabalhadores Rurais Sem Terra, MST) has gained international attention and influence by enhancing the influence of landless peasants on the Brazilian government.

In the late 1970s, peasants in Brazil began to organize to protest the high infant mortality rates they suffered as well as the slavelike work conditions they endured. In 1985 a national congress of peasants met and formed the MST, led by João Pedro Stedile and José Rainha. With the motto "Occupy, Resist, Produce," landless peasants began to usurp unproductive land and form work cooperatives in order to compete against larger farms, later negotiating the redistribution of the land with federal and state authorities. By 1991 the MST had redistributed over a million hectares of land to thousands of landless families. The increasing influence of the landless peasantry sparked retaliation by large landowners. In 1996, nineteen landless peasants were massacred in the state of Pará. The next year, the MST marched on Brasília, demanding justice for the murders and increased land reform. In response, the government established the Ministry of Agrarian Affairs, raised taxes on land that remained unused, and offered credit to new landowners.

The MST's philosophy combines ideas from the **Zapatista National Liberation Army** (Ejército Zapatista de Liberación Nacional, EZLN; see Mexico) and the **Sandinista National Liberation Front** (Frente Sandinista de Liberación Nacional, FSLN; see Nicaragua) with some of the tenets of liberation theology. The movement is organized in nineteen states, not including Amazonas; while it opposes land settlements in the rain forest it has been accused of causing environmental damage through land clearings to prepare for cultivation. Important issues for the MST are the expropriation of lands obtained illegally by multinational corporations, environmental conservation, demarcation of Indian lands, and the prosecution of the murderers of farm workers involved in land conflicts.

Lula. See **Silva, Luis Inacio "Lula" da**

Médici, Emílio Garrastazú (1905–1985)

Emílio Garrastazú Médici (1969–1974) grew up attending military schools and rose quickly through the ranks of the armed forces, leaving the military only briefly to serve as the civilian leader of the National Intelligence Service (Serviçio da Nacional Informação, SNI). Following President Artur da **Costa e Silva**'s (1967–1969) stroke in 1969, the military chose **Alliance for National Renewal** (Aliança Renovadora Nacional, ARENA) candidate Médici to serve as president. Although he promised greater democracy, Médici's administration was marked by further repression and strengthened military rule. Médici maintained the Brazilian **economic miracle** initiated under Costa e Silva by promoting industry through the exploitation of workers. With the expansion of the economy, Médici proposed ambitious projects, including the construction of a 3,250-mile trans-Amazonian highway across Brazil from the Atlantic Coast to the Peruvian border, with which he hoped to encourage immigration into the interior of the country. While Médici allowed for congressional elections in 1970, only the official opposition movement, the Brazilian Democratic Movement (Movimento Democrático Brasileiro, MDB; see **Brazilian Democratic Movement Party** (Partido do Movimento Democrático Brazileiro, PMDB]) was permitted to oppose ARENA, and in anticipation of the elections, the military cracked down on political opponents and arrested about 5,000 people, claiming it needed to do so to maintain economic stability. In 1974 Médici stepped down to allow Ernesto **Geisel** (1974–1979) to take office.

Mendes Filho, Francisco "Chico" Alves (1944–1988)

Francisco "Chico" Alves Mendes Filho grew up helping his father tap rubber, quickly becoming aware of the exploitation of the rubber tappers (*seringueiros*) by merchants and local bosses. Rubber tappers were often given the tools for tapping on credit and were forced to buy goods from the company store, essentially becoming indentured servants to the landowner on whose property they tapped. However, as rubber became less profitable, many landowners began selling their rubber reserves to cattle ranchers, who subsequently often ran the tappers off the land, sometimes killing the tappers and their families. Further, at that time the government was promoting the "opening up" of the rain forest to development projects, such as roads and industries. Cognizant that the fate of the rubber tappers was deeply connected to the rain forest, in 1977 Mendes helped form the Xapuri Rural Workers' Union, which served to unite the often isolated rubber tappers as well as native peoples of the Amazon rain forest against the destruction of the forest. He promoted the idea of extractive reserves, areas of land that would be protected from deforestation and maintained and used for rubber tapping, in the interest of preventing the felling of trees. In 1987, with the help of Brazilian anthropologist Mary Allegretti, Mendes created the National Council of Rubber Tappers (Conselho Nacional de Seringueiros, CNS) to set up cooperatives through which tappers could sell their rubber and buy goods, avoiding exploitation by middle-man merchants. Mendes was assassinated in 1988 by local thugs.

Mendes' efforts brought international attention to the plight of the tappers and the native peoples of the Amazon, spurring the international movement to preserve the world's rain forests and raise awareness of their significance in the maintenance of the planet. He is considered one of Brazil's greatest activists and still serves as an inspiration to rubber tappers in their continuing struggle against the destruction of the rain forest.

Nabuco De Arraju, Joaquim Barretto. See Slavery and Racial Inequality

National Indian Foundation (Fundação Nacional do Índio, FUNAI)

The National Indian Foundation (Fundação Nacional do Índio, FUNAI), established in 1967 to replace the corruption-ridden and ineffectual Indian Protection Service (Serviçio de Proteção ao Índio, SPI), is responsible for protecting indigenous land and culture. However, its efforts have been thwarted by corruption and budget constraints.

The SPI was founded in 1910 by Marechal Cândido Rondon to protect Brazil's indigenous people from massacres and forced land removals, and to support the demarcation of Indian lands. In reality the organization did just the opposite, reducing the Indian population and its access to land. FUNAI was created in 1967 to replace SPI and improve its services. Despite this mandate, FUNAI has also often been accused of corruption, of allowing timber and mining companies to extract resources from "protected" Indian lands, and of assuming a patronizing attitude toward the indigenous. However, the organization is underfunded for its proposed objectives (which had expanded to include the provision of health and education services to the Indians as well as the location of unknown tribes when it replaced SPI). In addition, it faces continual opposition from powerful interest groups and the government.

FUNAI was completely reorganized in 1986 to decentralize its power into five administrative centers (*superintendencias*) in the cities of Curitiba, Cuiabá, Recife, Manaus, and Belém. Further, it was removed from the Ministry of the Interior, where its objectives often clashed with those of the military and the government, and placed in the Ministry of Justice. Despite the creation and reorganization of FUNAI, tensions between native peoples and the government, and between the landless and big landowners, persist. With the recent international focus on the Brazilian rain forest and its people, indigenous groups like the Yanomami and the Kayapo have begun to exert greater pressure on the government and FUNAI to respond to their demands. Further, indigenous congresses have brought together separate native groups to organize around issues of identity, land demarcation, and cultural preservation.

Neves, Tancredo de Almeida (1910–1985)

Despite his sudden death shortly after being elected as the country's first civilian president following twenty-one years of military rule (1964–1985), Tancredo de Almeida Neves remains a symbol of Brazil's return to democracy and the struggle against military repression.

Born in the state of Minas Gerais, Neves received a law degree, and later served as a city council member. When all legislative bodies were dismissed following the 1937 self-coup carried out by President Getúlio **Vargas** (1930–1945, 1951–1954), Neves returned to practicing law. Upon the reinstitution of the legislature in 1947, Neves served as state deputy and then as federal deputy, was elected governor of Minas Gerais in 1960, and subsequently served as prime minister under President João "Jango" Belchoir Marques **Goulart** (1961–1964).

During the military dictatorship, Neves allied himself with the Brazilian Democratic Movement (Movimento Democrático Brasileiro, MDB) in 1966, and was elected to the Senate. When the MDB became a political party, the **Brazilian Democratic Movement Party** (Partido do Movimento Democrático Brasileiro, PMDB), he was elected to serve as its vice president. He was reelected as governor of his home state in 1982. In 1985, with the nation's political *abertura* (opening), Neves (and running mate José **Sarney da Costa** [1985–1990]) defeated the military's candidate for the presidency of Brazil with the Democratic Alliance, a coalition formed by the PMDB and some members of the Social Democracy Party (Partido Democracia Social, PDS; see **Alliance for National Renewal** [Aliança Renovadora Nacional, ARENA]). However, he fell ill days before his inauguration, and died a few months later. Sarney, who had been serving as interim president during Neves' illness, was inaugurated as president later in 1985.

Pedro I (1798–1834)

Although Pedro I (1822–1831) was a member of Portugal's royal court, he was instrumental in obtaining Brazil's independence from the mother country.

Born in Portugal to Dom João VI and Carlota Joaquina, Pedro I came to Brazil with his family at the age of nine, when they fled Portugal during the Napoleonic

Pedro I, Emperor of Brazil (1822–1831). *Columbus Memorial Library, General Secretariat of the Organization of American States. Reproduced with permission of the Organization of American States.*

Wars. When his father returned to Europe almost fourteen years later, he left Pedro I in Brazil to serve as regent, advising him not to resist a Brazilian liberation movement if it should arise, but instead to take part in it and declare himself leader of the new nation. Soon, the Portuguese Parliament ordered that Pedro I return home to finish his education, insisting that he dismantle the Brazilian government that had been constructed under his father. Pedro I refused, issuing his famous "Fico" (I stay). Street demonstrations indicated that he had the support of the people. On September 7, 1822, he declared Brazil independent, and a month later he took the title "Emperor of Brazil." Unlike in all other Latin American countries, in Brazil, independence meant the maintenance of rule by monarch instead of the establishment of a democratic republic. Brazil would not become a republic until 1889 following the ouster of Pedro I's son, **Pedro II**.

In 1824 Pedro I convened an assembly to write a constitution. Unhappy with the results, he dismissed the assembly and drafted his own constitution for the new empire. Considered liberal at the time, it established three branches of government to be moderated by the emperor, in whom almost all power was vested. Nonetheless, Pedro I soon lost control of the government. He relied heavily on the Portuguese monarchists who had remained in Brazil, mismanaged the economy, and lost a portion of Brazilian territory (the Cisplatine Province, what is today Uruguay) to invading forces from Buenos Aires. He tried to end slavery, infuriating large landholders, and his extramarital affairs scandalized the nation. He also drained the Brazilian treasury trying to place his daughter Maria on the Portuguese throne. He grew so unpopular that on April 7, 1831, he heeded the advice of his Imperial Guard and fled Brazil, leaving the throne to his five-year-old son, Pedro II. He returned to Portugal, and died three years later of tuberculosis.

Pedro II (1825–1891)

Dom **Pedro I** fled to Portugal with the rest of his family in 1831, leaving Dom Pedro II the throne when he was only five years old. A regency of varying structure and membership exercised executive power for the subsequent nine years. Although Pedro II was to assume leadership of the country at age eighteen, because of his precocious intelligence and the miserable state of Brazil, he became emperor in 1840, ruling as Brazil's second emperor for the subsequent forty-nine years.

Pedro II was considered a fair and honest ruler. Under his reign, Brazilians enjoyed freedom of the press and free speech, and he granted positions of honor and power to those loyal to him. The **War of the Triple Alliance** (1865–1870; see Appendix 1) demonstrated the country's inefficiency, and he began to update Brazil's communication and transportation systems. He encouraged the building of railroads and the industrialization of the southern state of São Paulo. Considering slavery to be the greatest problem of his time, Pedro II freed his own slaves and worked toward the emancipation of all slaves in Brazil. He supported the 1871 Rio Branco Law, and helped free slaves over the age of sixty-five in 1885. Finally, his daughter Isabel signed the bill that freed all slaves, known as the Golden Law (Lei Aurea), while Pedro II was in Europe in 1888 (see **Slavery and Racial Inequality**).

As Pedro II grew old, Brazilian opposition to rule by the royal family increased; Brazilians were tired of Pedro II's ironclad control over the government and did not want to be ruled by Isabel and her French count husband. As republican opposition grew, the Catholic Church and the military withdrew their support from the emperor. On November 15, 1889, a military coup deposed Pedro II. He fled to Paris, where he died two years later.

Prestes, Luis Carlos (1898–1990)

Throughout his life, Luis Carlos Prestes was a tireless politician, leading Brazil's Communist Party (Partido Comunista Brasileiro, PCB) and speaking out against the government.

Born in Rio Grande do Sul into a poor family, Prestes attended military school in Rio de Janeiro, where he excelled in engineering. He rose to national fame in 1924 when he led a group of 800 rebellious soldiers, known as the Prestes Column, in a two-year, more than 15,000-mile march across Brazil to join a São Paulo column in the state of Paraná in protest of the corrupt rule of President Artur da Silva Bernardes (1922–1926). A charismatic leader, Prestes was dubbed the Knight of Hope (Cavalheiro de Esperança) by his sympathizers and the leftist media. The troops were plagued by malaria and rough terrain as well as by the opposition of the police and loyal federal soldiers throughout their journey, and though they made speeches and held rallies in the countryside, they were unsuccessful in galvanizing the peasantry, probably because of the prevalence of the dynamic of *coronelismo* (rule by local bosses called *coronéis*) and because of their sometimes reckless and destructive behavior.

Although his march set the stage for the Revolution of 1930, Prestes was not included in Getúlio **Vargas'** (1930–1945, 1951–1954) first administration. Prestes traveled to Russia, where he studied communist teachings, then clandestinely returned to Brazil in 1935 and fomented an uprising against Vargas. It failed, and Prestes was captured, sentenced to sixteen years in prison, and jailed, while repression against communism sharply increased. Though in 1940 his sentence increased by forty years for his role in the murder of an alleged police spy in the PCB, Vargas granted an amnesty that released Prestes in 1945. Prestes immediately formed an alliance with Vargas, and merged communist ideas with labor concerns. Prestes was elected senator on the PCB ticket in 1945, though the party was outlawed two years later.

Following the 1964 military coup, Prestes went into hiding, traveling abroad and speaking out against terrorism and guerrilla groups. He returned to Brazil in 1979 when President João Baptista de Oliveira **Figueiredo** (1979–1985) granted amnesty to all political prisoners. Due to his criticism of communist leaders' cooperation with the military government and attempts to legalize their party, he lost his position as secretary-general of the PCB, which he had held for nearly forty years. He spent the rest of his life quietly supporting different politicians.

Quadros, Jânio da Silva (1917–1998)

After being elected in 1960 and assuming office in 1961, Jânio de Silva Quadros mysteriously and abruptly resigned as president, leaving the office to his controversial leftist vice president, João "Jango" Belchoir Marques **Goulart** (1961–1964), and setting the stage for the 1964 military coup.

Quadros was born in the southern state of Mato Grosso. He received a law degree in São Paulo and in 1950 was elected to the state legislature. Three years later he won the mayorship of São Paulo. In 1960 he was elected president of Brazil with the greatest percent of votes in the country's modern history (48 percent), and was the first president to be inaugurated in Brazil's new capital, Brasília. Despite his electoral mandate, Quadros was plagued by political problems even before taking office. His predecessor, Juscelino **Kubitschek de Oliviero** (1956–1961), granted wage increases just as he left office, and upon assuming the presidency, Quadros faced a large foreign debt and rising inflation. He pushed for fiscal austerity and promoted the growth of industry, but his plans for trade with the communist bloc and moderation toward communist Cuba earned him widespread disfavor, especially with the military. As his relations with Congress worsened, Quadros suddenly resigned in frustration in 1961, leaving the presidency to Vice President Goulart.

Most speculate that he left in an attempt to gain a mandate that would give him more power. His plan failed, as Goulart held office until being overthrown by the military three years later. During the subsequent twenty-one years of military rule, Quadros remained at the margins of politics. With the return of civilian rule, he surprised many by winning the 1985 election for mayor of São Paulo.

Real Plan. See Cardoso, Fernando Henrique

Revolution of 1930. See Vargas, Getúlio

Sarney da Costa, José (1930–)

As president of Brazil from 1985 to 1990, José Sarney da Costa unsuccessfully fought inflation, unemployment, and hunger with monetary and fiscal policy, and failed to address government corruption. Nonetheless, he did move Brazil toward democratization.

Born José Ribamar Ferreira Araujo Costa and nicknamed Zé do Sarney as a little boy, Sarney had his name officially changed to José Sarney da Costa in 1965. Trained in law, Sarney began his political career as an alternate federal deputy in 1954, becoming a full deputy two years later. A supporter of the military dictatorship (1964–1985), he was elected governor of Maranhão in 1965 on the **Alliance for National Renewal** (Aliança Renovadora Nacional, ARENA) ticket, and later served in the Senate, again with ARENA. As the military dictatorship came to a close, his alliances shifted toward the left, though he was still identified as a conservative. In 1988 Sarney helped found the **Brazilian Social Democratic Party** (Partido da Social Democracia Brasileira, PSDB), and twice served as its president.

In the first elections following the end of military rule in 1985, Sarney was selected as the running mate of opposition presidential candidate Tancredo de Almeida **Neves**, in an attempt to appeal to conservative factions. However, Neves fell ill days before his inauguration, and Sarney subsequently served as interim president; when Neves soon died, Sarney assumed the presidency, promising to follow the liberal ideas of Neves. Under Sarney, Brazil suffered major inflation, bankruptcy, unemployment, and hunger. To combat this, taxes were raised, a four-year moratorium was imposed on income tax returns, and high interest rates were implemented to impede capital flight. Despite these measures, the economy worsened. In 1987 Brazil suspended payments on all foreign debts, by 1989 inflation was at 1,700

percent, and in 1990 Brazil's foreign debt was U.S. $115 billion. Sarney did little to stop government corruption, while labor unrest and the situation of the poor worsened. The president's few political accomplishments included promulgation of the 1988 constitution (which weakened the executive, strengthened the legislature, and invested more power in the judiciary) and the move toward more open elections.

After his presidency, Sarney was elected senator from the state of Amapá on the **Brazilian Democratic Movement Party** (Partido do Movimento Democrático Brasileiro, PMDB) ticket. In 1994 he tried unsuccessfully to gain the party's presidential nomination.

Sem Terra. See **Landless Peasant Movement (Movimento dos Trabalhadores Rurais Sem Terra, MST)**

Silva, Luis Inacio "Lula" da (1945–)

A prominent leftist political leader in Brazil, Luis Inacio da Silva is an advocate of the working class and a key figure in Brazil's democratization process.

Born in Pernambuco, Lula (as he is known in Brazil) had less than a sixth grade education when he began work as a lathe operator in a factory in São Paulo. He soon gained prominence as a labor leader of the new union (*novo sindicalismo*) movement. From 1978 to 1981 he served as the president of the São Bernardo do Campo Metallurgical Workers Union, leading several strikes. In 1981 Lula helped create the **Workers' Party** (Partido dos Trabalhadores, PT), Latin America's largest leftist party.

Lula advocates higher wages and price controls in support of laborers, and land reform and improved agricultural output for farmers and landless peasants. In 1986 he served as a federal deputy for São Paulo, and two years later helped write Brazil's new constitution. Lula made his first attempt at the presidency in 1989 running with the PT, but was defeated by Fernando Alfonso **Collor de Mello** (1990–1992). He tried again in 1994 and 1998, losing both times by a slim margin to Fernando Henrique **Cardoso** (1995–). Nonetheless, Lula remains an important political figure in Brazil. He recently called for more thorough democratization through the opening of the political process to nonelites and has declared his candidacy for the 2002 presidential election.

Slavery and Racial Inequality

While Brazil's Portuguese colonizers initially tried to force the indigenous peoples who had not been decimated by diseases brought by the Europeans to serve as their labor force, ultimately plantation owners would turn to slaves imported from Africa. Eventually between 3 and 6 million Africans would be forced to make the harrowing journey across the Atlantic Ocean to Brazil to be sold as slaves. Racial inequalities have divided the country since the advent of slavery.

The transition from Indian slave labor to African slave labor began around the mid-1500s. The transformation was slow at the beginning, as the timing was dictated by the initially limited ability of the struggling sugar industry to pay for large numbers of expensive imported slaves. Nonetheless, the advantages of using African slave labor (including the perceived superior physical abilities and productivity of Africans) eventually outweighed the high cost of transportation. Unlike some areas of Spanish America where the Indian majority persisted as a base, or others where Indians were scarce but where the settlers could not afford the alternative of African slaves, in Northeast Brazil the Europeans established a profitable export industry that facilitated the transition to the use of Africans not only as skilled labor and intermediaries, but as the majority work force and base of industry. By the early decades of the seventeenth century, the transition to African labor in the plantation zones of coastal Brazil was complete: Africans had replaced Indians as slaves. African slavery would continue to be an important aspect of Brazilian culture and society through the late nineteenth century.

Brazilian emperor Dom **Pedro II** (1840–1889), who considered slavery to be the greatest problem of his time, freed his own slaves and worked toward the emancipation of all slaves in Brazil. The 1871 Rio Branco Law stated that all children of slaves born subsequent to the law's passage would be free, though they would have to serve their parents' masters until they were twenty-one years old. Leading abolitionist Joaquim Barreto Nabuco De Arraju, who served as president of the Brazilian Anti-Slavery Society (the most important abolitionist organization in the country) in the 1880s, did not sympathize with the suffering of slaves, but believed that slavery was impeding Brazil's progress in the capitalist world. Hoping that the end of slavery would encourage poor European immigrants to come to Brazil, he helped bring the abolitionist cause to Brazil's Parliament and then to the world through international conferences.

In 1885 slaves over the age of sixty-five were freed, and with the signing of the Golden Law (Lei Aurea) on May 13, 1888, by Princess Isabel in the absence of her father, Dom Pedro II, all slaves in Brazil were unconditionally freed (some 500,000 to 700,000 people) without compensation to owners. The law, which followed similar laws in the United States (by twenty-five years) and Great Britain (by eighty years), did little besides legitimize what was already happening: slaves were constantly escaping from plantations, and some owners even had started paying their slaves to stay. Further, it was more economical to hire slaves than to pay for their food and housing. What is more, the law did not include land reform and ultimately many slaves were forced to return to their old masters for work.

The last country in the world to emancipate its slaves, Brazil entered the twentieth century heavily burdened by the legacy of slavery. While former slaves and their descendants were free, these excluded Brazilians enjoyed no rights. As slaves they had stood on the lowest rungs of the social ladder, however once freed, they had no status at all: they became invisible. Until the 1940s, this huge mass of marginalized individuals was barely noticed by Brazilian society and was not recognized under the constitution. Three centuries of slavery generated a mentality of indifference to inequality, violence, and exclusion that went unchecked until the second half of the twentieth century, when a new middle class and the urban masses in general first began to address the issue.

The legacy of slavery is still evident in Brazil today: although half of Brazil's people are white, 69 percent of the poor and destitute are black and mestizo. The marked contrast between the country's black population, most of which lives in *favelas* (slums), and its largely white elite or *moreno* (comparatively light-skinned) elite has encouraged the process of *embranquimento* (whitening): one can "whiten" oneself through one's economic status or job, or may marry a light-skinned person to produce light-skinned offspring. While today many organizations promote solidarity around a shared African heritage that condemns racism, the concept and practice of *embranquimento* has hindered the Afro-Brazilian community's efforts to organize a movement around black pride, as few people wish to identify themselves as "black." Despite this, in recent years, cultural activities based in African traditions have served as focal points around which some groups have organized to promote the cause of blacks in Brazil.

Vargas, Getúlio (1883–1954)

Getúlio Vargas (1930–1945, 1951–1954) dominated Brazilian politics for almost a quarter of a century, serving as both president and dictator, and ending his career with a suicide that he dedicated to the Brazilian people.

Vargas was born in Rio Grande do Sul, and enrolled in the military briefly as a young man. He received a law degree in Porto Alegre, and later worked in the district attorney's office and served in the state's legislature. He was elected to the federal congress in 1922, and four years later was chosen to serve as minister of finance under President Washington Luis Pereira de Sousa (1926–1930). In 1928 Vargas unseated the iron-fisted governor of his home state, and his success as governor led the opposition Liberal Alliance Party to invite Vargas to run on their ticket in the 1930 presidential election. Vargas accepted (though an opposition party had never won the office of president) but lost the election (which many deemed fraudulent given Vargas' strong support among the urban population).

Instead of demanding justice, Vargas simply waited for revolution. A few months later, Rio Grande do Sul, Minas Gerais, and Paraíba (three states that had supported Vargas in his campaign for president) rose up with the support of young military leaders. After three weeks of fighting, the military deposed President Pereira de Sousa, and on November 3, 1930, in an event dubbed the Revolution of 1930, Vargas came to power as interim president, with no specified term and no limits on his power. Vargas upheld the 1891 constitution but dismissed Congress and the state legislatures. These actions met with little protest, as public opinion held that they were necessary and temporary. To garner support for his regime, Vargas enacted labor reform laws and expanded health and educational services; electoral reforms in 1932 allowed working women to vote, lowered the voting age from twenty-one to eighteen, and established the secret ballot. Vargas controlled organized labor through government-sponsored unions that were discouraged from taking political action and striking. He also promoted nationalism, even implementing restrictive immigration laws.

In 1934 Vargas wrote a new constitution giving all women the right to vote and protecting workers. The same year, he was elected to serve a four-year term as president. With the world in the throes of the Great Depression, Vargas tried to jumpstart the Brazilian economy by nationalizing transportation systems and expanding the federal bureaucracy. Following a failed communist revolt in 1935, Vargas tightened his control over Brazilians by suspending civil rights and increasing the power of the police. Two years later, Vargas used the threat of communism to justify a coup, dissolving Congress and proclaiming himself dictator, ushering in his *Estado Novo* (1937–1945). During the *Estado Novo*, which was based on fascist governments in Italy and Portugal, political parties were outlawed, opposition to the regime was suppressed, the press was censored, and the military was used to maintain control. At this time, the German Nazis began looking to Brazil for support and gaining influence in the country. Vargas considered this penetration a threat to national security, and German immigrants in the south of Brazil were persecuted as the Vargas administration put into effect a program of *desgerminasição* or "de-Germanization." German newspapers were prohibited and teachers were required to speak in Portuguese.

Vargas joined the Allied forces during World War II, and even sent Brazilian troops to Italy in 1944. A year later, as the contradictions in Vargas' rule were becoming more evident, he lifted media censorship, reinstated the legality of political parties, and called for new elections. Fearing another coup by Vargas, the military deposed him on October 29, 1945. Vargas lived quietly in Rio Grande do Sul for the next five years, then won the presidential election of 1950. Upon reassuming office, Vargas faced debilitating inflation and a divided Congress. In 1953 he nationalized the oil industry, creating the Brazilian national petroleum company (Petróleo Brasileiro SA, Petrobras). A year later, the media

uncovered deep corruption among Vargas' political cohorts. In August Vargas' bodyguards attempted to murder him, but instead killed an air force major. In the ensuing scandal, the military withdrew support for the president and demanded his resignation. Vargas agreed to step down, and then shot himself, leaving a suicide note to the Brazilian people in which he characterized himself as a sacrifice to their cause. Vice President João Café Filho (1954–1955) finished out Vargas' term.

Workers' Party (Partido dos Trabalhadores, PT)

The Workers' Party (Partido dos Trabalhadores, PT) was established in 1979 and immediately called for direct negotiations between workers and business elites during conflicts, the formation of a ministry of labor, and the unrestricted right to strike. As the party grew, laborers demanded more rights and political power. The metal workers' union, led by the charismatic Luis Inacio "Lula" da **Silva**, was especially vocal in the call for higher wages and improved working conditions. In 1979 there were 113 strikes, involving more than 3 million people across fifteen states. The PT continued to grow stronger through the 1980s, and in 1989 "Lula" made a serious (though unsuccessful) bid for the presidency against Fernando **Collor de Mello** (1990–1992). He tried twice more, in 1994 and 1998, but was defeated both times by Fernando Henrique **Cardoso** (1995–). Important issues for the PT continue to center around labor, the role of the state in the economy, and corruption.

HEADS OF STATE

Pedro I, Emperor of Brazil	1822–1831
Rule by regency	1831–1840
Pedro II, Emperor of Brazil	1840–1889
Marechal Deodoro da Fonseca	1889–1891
Marechal Floriano Peixoto	1891–1894
Prudente José de Morais	1894–1898
Manuel Ferraz Campos Sales	1898–1902
Francisco de Paula Rodrigues Alves	1902–1906
Alfonso Augusto Moreira Pena	1906–1909
Nilo Peçanha	1909–1910
Marechal Hermes da Fonseca	1910–1914
Venceslau Brás Pereira Gomes	1914–1918
Delfim Moreira	1918–1919
Epitácio Pessóa	1919–1922
Artur da Silva Bernardes	1922–1926
Washington Luis Pereira de Sousa	1926–1930
Getúlio Vargas	1930–1945
José Linhares	1945–1946

Marechal Eurico Gaspar Dutra	1946–1951
Getúlio Vargas	1951–1954
João Café Filho	1954–1955
Carlos Luz	1955
Nereu Ramos	1955–1956
Juscelino Kubitschek de Oliviero	1956–1961
Jânio da Silva Quadros	1961
João Belchoir Marques Goulart	1961–1964
Ranieri Mazzili	1964
Humberto de Alencar Castelo Branco	1964–1967
Artur da Costa e Silva	1967–1969
Macio de Souza e Mello	1969
Emílio Garrastazú Médici	1969–1974
Ernesto Geisel	1974–1979
João Baptista de Oliveira Figueiredo	1979–1985
José Sarney da Costa	1985–1990
Fernando Alfonso Collor de Mello	1990–1992
Itamar Augusto Cauteiro Franco	1992–1995
Fernando Henrique Cardoso	1995–

Source: Ronald M. Schneider, *Order and Progress: A Political History of Brazil* (Boulder: Westview Press, 1991).

BIBLIOGRAPHY

Print Resources

Burns, E. Bradford. *A History of Brazil*. New York: Columbia University Press, 1993.

Davis, Shelton H. *Victims of the Miracle: Development and the Indians of Brazil*. New York: Cambridge University Press, 1977.

Haber, Stephen, ed. *How Latin America Fell Behind: Essays on the Economic Histories of Brazil and Mexico*. Stanford: Stanford University Press, 1997.

Jesús, Carolina María de. *Child of the Dark: The Diary of Carolina María de Jesús*. Translated from the Portuguese by David St. Clair. New York: New American Library, 1962.

Levine, Robert M., and John J. Crocitti, eds. *The Brazil Reader*. Durham: Duke University Press, 1999.

Nascimento, Abdias do. *O genocídio do negro brasileiro: Processo de um racismo mascarado*. Rio de Janeiro: Paz e Terra, 1978.

Page, Joseph A. *The Brazilians*. Reading, MA: Addison-Wesley, 1995.

Ramos, Alcida Rita. *Indigenism: Ethnic Politics in Brazil*. Madison: University of Wisconsin Press, 1998.

Russell-Wood, A.J.R. *The Black Man in Slavery and Freedom in Colonial Brazil*. London: Macmillan, 1982.

Schneider, Ronald M. *Order and Progress: A Political History of Brazil*. Boulder: Westview Press, 1991.

Skidmore, Thomas E. *Black into White*. Durham, NC: Duke University Press, 1993.

Stepan, Alfred, ed. *Authoritarian Brazil*. New Haven: Yale University Press, 1973.

Weinstein, Barbara. *For Social Peace in Brazil*. Chapel Hill: University of North Carolina Press, 1996.

Wolfe, Joel W. *Working Women, Working Men: São Paulo and the Rise of Brazil's Industrial Working Class*. Durham, NC: Duke University Press, 1993.

Electronic Resources

Brazil Infonet: Government
http://www.brazilinfo.net/sky3/usbrazi2/public_html/government.html
Government section of broad Web site containing reference information about Brazil and links to numerous Brazilian Web sites. Contains links to Brazilian government Web sites and sources of political, economic, and trade information. (In English)

Brazilian Embassy in Washington Government Directory
http://www.brasilemb.org/informa/iflk01gv.htm
Contains links to nearly every Brazilian government Web site, including legislative, judicial, and executive branch institutions, federal agencies, embassies and consulates, and state governments. (In English)

CNN Brasil
http://www.cnnbrasil.com/
A comprehensive and continuously updated news site with an emphasis on national and international politics. (In Portuguese)

O Estado de São Paulo
http://www.estado.com.br/
The Web version of one of Brazil's premier daily newspapers. Offers comprehensive national and international coverage, emphasizing national politics and the Brazilian economy. (In Portuguese)

Latin American Network Information Center (LANIC): Brazil
http://lanic.utexas.edu/la/brazil/
Brazil section of this extensive Web site contains hundreds of links to research resources, cultural centers, economic and business institutions, government agencies, historical sources, magazines and other periodicals, nongovernmental organizations, and grassroots groups. (In English)

Latin Focus: Brazil
http://www.latin-focus.com/countries/brazil.htm
Contains an overview and description of Brazil's government institutions and political environment, economic and financial information and statistics, and links to government ministries and agencies. (In English)

Political Database of the Americas: Brazil
http://www.georgetown.edu/pdba/Countries/brazil.html
Comprehensive database run as a joint project of Georgetown University and the Organization of American States. Section on Brazil contains information on and links to the executive, legislative, and judicial branches of the Brazilian government; electoral laws and election results; and other political data. (In English, Spanish, Portuguese, and French)

Political Resources.net: Brazil
http://www.politicalresources.net/brazil.htm
Contains a wealth of links to sources of information on national politics. Includes information on political parties, legislative and executive institutions, laws and legislation, and elections, as well as a link to the constitution. (In English)

United States Department of Commerce, International Trade Administration, Brazil Desk
http://www.mac.doc.gov/ola/brazil/index.htm
A U.S. government Web site with a wealth of information on political, economic, and business trends, primarily related to international trade. (In English)

Wilfried Derksen's Elections Around the World: Brazil
http://www.agora.it/elections/brazil.htm
Brazil section of a comprehensive database of results from elections around the world. Contains results from recent national executive and legislative elections, as well as explanations of and links to political parties and institutions. (In English)

CHILE

COUNTRY PROFILE

Official name	República de Chile
Capital	Santiago
Type/structure of government	Democratic unitary republic
Executive	President, elected to six-year, non-renewable term, serves as head of state and head of government, and appoints cabinet members.
Legislative	Bicameral: Senate includes 38 elected members (19 of whom are elected every four years) and 9 appointed members, all of whom serve eight-year terms; former presidents are eligible for lifelong senate positions. Chamber of Deputies includes 120 members who serve four-year terms.
Judicial	Highest court is the Supreme Court, whose 21 judges are appointed by the president and ratified by Congress for lifelong terms.
Major political parties	**Alliance of Democratic Parties** (Concertación de Partidos por la Democracia, CPD; coalition); **Christian Democrat Party** (Partido Demócrata Cristiano, PDC); Independent Democratic Union (Unión Demócrata Independiente, UDI); National Renovation Party (Renovación Nacional, RN).
Constitution in effect	1980 (with reforms in 1989)
Location/geography	Situated on the western portion of the southern half of South America. Borders Pacific Ocean to the west (coastline measures approximately 6,435 km.), Andes Mountains and Argentina to the east, Peru and Bolivia to the north. Atacama Desert in the north, central coast and Andean valleys, wet-forests of Patagonia in the south. Easter Island is a Chilean territory in the South Pacific.
Geographic area	756,945 sq. km.
Population	14.6 million (1997)
Ethnic groups	White (of European descent) 95%; indigenous 3%; other 2%
Religions	Roman Catholic 89%; Protestant 11%
Literacy rate	95% (1998)*
Infant mortality rate	10.02 deaths per 1,000 live births (1998)
Life expectancy	75.46 years (1998)*
Monetary unit	Peso
Exchange rate	1 U.S. dollar = 548.15 pesos (August 2000)***
Major exports	Copper, fishmeal and fish products, wood products, agricultural goods
Major imports	Petroleum, capital goods, agricultural and foodstuffs, textiles, computers, automobiles**
GDP	$77.1 billion (1997)
GDP growth rate	6% (2000 forecast)**
GDP per capita	$4,820 (1997)

*World Bank. *Chile at a Glance.* http://wlbn0018.worldbank.org/external/lac/lac.nsf

**International Monetary Fund. http://www.imf.org/external/country/CHL/index.htm

***Latin American Weekly Report. August 22, 2000 (WR-00-33), p. 394.

Source: *CIA World Factbook*, unless noted. www.odci.gov/cia/publications/factbook/geos/cl.html

OVERVIEW

Summary

Prior to the military coup in 1973, Chile was one of the most stable and enduring democracies in South America. From 1973 to 1990 Chile was ruled by a repressive military dictatorship under which thousands were killed, disappeared, or exiled. The neoliberal economic policies first implemented under the dictatorship and maintained through the transition to democracy have contributed to make Chile's one of the strongest, most dynamic, and fastest growing economies in Latin America. The **Alliance of Democratic Parties** (Concertación de Partidos por la Democracia, CPD), a center-left coalition, brought socialist Ricardo **Lagos** (2000–) to the presidency in 2000. Today Chile strives to consolidate the transition to democracy, maintain strong economic growth (Chile has one of the most vibrant economies in the region), and come to terms with the

Chile. © 1998 The Moschovitis Group, Inc.

social divisions and pain generated by the country's authoritarian interlude.

History

Several indigenous groups inhabited the area now known as Chile before its conquest and colonization by the Spanish, including the Incan Empire in the northern desert region and the nomadic Mapuche tribe in the south. Pedro de Valdivia led the conquest and colonization of Chile in the 1540s, and while colonial Chile provided limited mineral resources to the Spanish crown, it did produce some gold. Agriculture, mining, and ranching were the most prominent economic activities, and, given the trade restrictions imposed by the crown, the colonizers traded with Spain through the viceroyalty of Peru. Though some slaves were brought from Africa, and conquered indigenous people were forced to provide labor as part of the *encomienda* system, the main source of labor in the 1600s and 1700s was poor Spanish settlers. During this time the European and indigenous cultures mixed a great deal.

Following the 1798 Spanish Bourbon Reforms, Chile was declared independent of the Peruvian viceroyalty, and the subsequent Napoleonic invasion of Spain in 1808 threw the colonies into a period of upheaval. On September 18, 1810, a group of creole leaders met in Santiago and declared limited self-government until the Spanish throne was restored. The movement for complete independence continued however; while José Miguel Carrera emerged as a leader of the movement in 1811, Bernardo **O'Higgins Riquelme** (1817–1823)

eventually took over as leader of the revolt, and in February 1817 O'Higgins marched into Santiago, and full independence was declared. O'Higgins became supreme dictator of Chile.

The liberal-minded O'Higgins struggled to gain control and establish a republic, but the Mapuches, the remaining Spaniards, and the powerful Catholic Church, as well as liberal and conservative political factions, all struggled for power. In 1823 O'Higgins stepped down and fled to Peru, and by the 1830s Diego **Portales Palazuelos** and other Conservatives were dominating the Liberals, controlling the country through military might, and reinforcing the power of the church. The country fought a brief civil war in 1851, and following the administration of Conservative Manuel **Montt Torres** (1851–1861) the Liberals gained increasing support and power. The Liberals eventually won out over the Conservatives and continued to control the presidency until 1891. During their time in power they fought and won the **War of the Pacific** (1879–1884; see Appendix 1) against Peru and Bolivia, which expanded Chilean territory by one-third, won Chile new possessions in the nitrate-rich Atacama Desert, and solidified the country's national identity (see **Conservative Party/Liberal Party**).

However, by 1890 Liberal president José Manuel **Balmaceda Fernández**'s (1886–1891) attempts to strengthen the executive branch and weaken the legislature bred congressional opposition, and political and social unrest culminated in the Civil War of 1891 in which Congress (with the support of the navy) battled Balmaceda (to whom the army stayed loyal). The congressionalist forces were victorious. Consequently, the Liberals lost power and the executive branch was forced to restructure Chile from a presidentialist to a parliamentary republic. Initial economic success during the parliamentary period (1891–1924) was accompanied by increased labor activity and union growth, urbanization, European immigration, and the secularization of society. These transformations undermined traditional elite-run politics in Chile and facilitated the development of a number of smaller, more ideologically based parties that challenged the Liberal and Conservative parties and became increasingly adversarial. Arturo **Alessandri Palma** (1920–1924, 1925, 1932–1938) dominated politics for much of this period. Alessandri's first two administrations enacted many social reforms and promulgated the Constitution of 1925, which allowed for more popular political participation and stronger powers for the executive, effectively bringing the parliamentary period to an end.

The Great Depression plunged Chile into a period of economic and political instability, as the price of copper and nitrates, the country's most significant exports, dropped significantly on the world market. World War II brought increasing tensions in the domestic and international political arenas. The Radical Party, Chile's increasingly powerful middle-class party, fell victim to polarization as the presidents of the late 1940s and early 1950s failed to control inflation and other economic problems. The election of Eduardo **Frei Montalva** (1964–1970) ushered in a new period in which the **Christian Democrat Party** (Partido Demócrata Cristiano, PDC) replaced the Radicals as the most powerful party in the political center. Frei Montalva pursued limited land reform and other populist programs, but the pressure to provide more support for the economically disadvantaged Chilean masses and to discontinue favoring large foreign mining companies and landed elites was strong.

Salvador **Allende Gossens** (1970–1973) took office in 1970 as the first democratically elected Marxist leader in the world. He won the election with only 36 percent of the vote, and once in office had very little congressional support and faced severe opposition from the right and the center. Despite those obstacles, his leftist **Popular Unity** (Unidad Popular, UP) coalition sought major economic changes including the nationalization of industries like copper, and helped workers by providing subsidized food and power, and by freezing prices and raising wages. However, when the economy began to collapse with spiraling inflation and very little growth, his administration began to falter. The military plotted against him, and with significant support from the Chilean population and the U.S. government, he was ousted in a bloody coup on September 11, 1973. Allende died in an attack on La Moneda, the presidential palace, during the coup.

The military junta that subsequently took over the government included the heads of the army, the navy, the air force, and the Carabineros, or military police. Augusto **Pinochet Ugarte** (1973–1990), the commander of the army, quickly became the president of the junta. Congress was closed, political parties were banned, and the regime and its representatives engaged in widespread human rights abuses. Pinochet's economic policies were markedly different from those of his predecessors; he privatized almost all companies, dismantled social programs, and increased military spending. By the early 1980s, however, the economy began to show signs of stress, and the resulting recession brought with it political opposition to military rule. Pinochet responded with increased repression. He rewrote the constitution in 1980, and was forced to call for an election when voters indicated that they did not favor an uncontested continuation of his rule in a plebiscite held in 1988. Pinochet's favored candidate, Hernán Büchi, ran against Christian Democrat Patricio **Aylwin Azócar** (1990–1994) in the election of 1989, and Aylwin was victorious, backed by the CPD. A disgraced Pinochet stepped down from the presidency, but maintained his position as head of the armed forces until 1998, when he became senator for life.

Aylwin inherited a thriving economy and a divided society unfamiliar with democracy after seventeen years of dictatorship. The Constitution of 1980 was called a "framework for a democratic transition," but maintained vestiges of authoritarianism. Aylwin maintained most of Pinochet's economic policies, as did his successor, Christian Democrat Eduardo **Frei Ruíz-Tagle** (1994–2000). Both Aylwin and Frei fostered noninflationary economic growth, reduced the debt, attracted foreign investment, and aimed to reduce poverty, and both managed to avoid serious internal conflict and to sustain the transition to democratic institutions in the face of a wary army, an unrepentant Pinochet, and constant threats to stability from the right and left. Aylwin also pursued a policy of investigating the massive human rights abuses that occurred under Pinochet; those issues came to the forefront again in October 1998 with the arrest of Pinochet in Britain on charges that he tortured and killed Chileans and European citizens during his rule. Pinochet was released because of concerns for his health and returned to Chile where he was later judged unfit to stand trial. Ricardo Lagos, the first socialist elected president since Allende, assumed power in March 2000, facing an economic recession brought on by the international financial crisis of the late 1990s, as well as a reopening of social divisions sparked by the return of Pinochet.

ENTRIES

Aguirre Cerda, Pedro (1879–1941)
Pedro Aguirre Cerda, Chile's president from 1938 to 1941, was born in southern Chile in 1879 and graduated from the University of Chile with degrees in education and law. He was elected congressman from San Felipe in 1915 and from Santiago in 1918, and held cabinet positions under the first administration of Arturo **Alessandri Palma** (1920–1924, 1925, 1932–1938). Following his victory in the 1938 presidential election on the Radical Party (Partido Radical, PR) ticket (see **Conservative Party/Liberal Party**), he named cabinet members from the left and center parties, including his own PR. He was the first president to have a truly popular base of support and aimed to implement social welfare programs to benefit workers and reduce poverty. However, he was loathed by Chile's wealthy elite for his promises of agrarian reform and his support for labor. An earthquake in January 1939 that devastated the central region allowed him to convince Congress to increase state involvement in the economy; he subsequently created a state development agency (Corporación de Fomento, CORFO) to foster (protected) industrialization throughout the country. He is also remembered for defining the Chilean borders with Argentina near Antarctica. He died on November 25, 1941, after stepping down from office due to poor health.

Alessandri Palma, Arturo (1868–1950)

Arturo Alessandri Palma served as president of Chile from 1920 to 1924, in 1925, and from 1932 to 1938. Despite the economic depression and congressional disputes that marked his terms in office, he was able to reorganize the nitrate industry and undertake moderate social reforms in agriculture and education.

Alessandri was born in Linares on December 20, 1868, and graduated from the University of Chile in law in 1893. He joined the Liberal Party (see **Conservative Party/Liberal Party**) and began his political career in 1897 as a congressman from Curicó. He held various cabinet offices under Federico **Errázuriz Echaurren** (1896–1901) and Ramón Barros Luco (1910–1915), and was elected senator from Tarapacá in 1915. He was victorious in the presidential elections of 1920 with the support of the Liberal Alliance and the Democratic Party.

During Alessandri's first administration (during Chile's parliamentary period, 1891–1924), political parties in Congress bitterly disputed cabinet assignments and budgetary matters, which prevented Alessandri from paying state employees and implementing his proposed plans for economic and social reform. The economy was in shambles due to a fall in nitrate prices after World War I, and social unrest among workers followed. When the army took partial control in September 1924, Alessandri took a leave of absence, and a junta government seized power. The junta invited Alessandri to return to office in 1925; he agreed and helped map the content and structure of the Constitution of 1925, which reintroduced a presidential republic and curtailed legislative powers.

The years 1924 to 1932 were marked by profound economic and political crises. Alessandri ran for office again in 1932 and was elected to a six-year term. Though Chile suffered a deep depression following the U.S. stock market crash in 1929, Alessandri successfully reduced the fiscal deficit, improved the trade balance, and reduced unemployment. As tensions between political parties in Congress heightened, Alessandri discontinued his alliance with some leftist politicians. He cracked down on striking laborers and the left in 1936, calling a state of siege, closing Congress, and exiling labor leaders. As a result, the parties of the left came together in the Popular Front (Frente Popular) alliance to support Pedro **Aguirre Cerda** (1938–1941) of the Radical Party (Partido Radical, PR) in the next presidential election. Alessandri died in Santiago on August 24, 1950.

Alessandri Rodríguez, Jorge (1896–1986)

As president of Chile from 1958 to 1964, Jorge Alessandri Rodríguez spent much of his term battling inflation and trying to revive a faltering economy.

Alessandri, the son of former President Arturo **Alessandri Palma** (1920–1924, 1925, 1932–1938), was born on May 19, 1896, into an affluent family. The younger Alessandri was trained as an engineer, but served as a congressman from 1926 until 1930. He also held positions in the cabinet of Gabriel **González Videla** (1946–1952) and became a senator in 1956. He defeated Salvador **Allende Gossens** (1970–1973) and Eduardo **Frei Montalva** (1964–1970) in the 1958 presidential election with the support of the Conservative and Liberal Parties (see **Conservative Party/Liberal Party**) as well as part of the Radical Party (Partido Radical, PR). During his administration Alessandri focused on stimulating productivity and economic growth and development through fiscal policy and tax cuts, as well as through implementing industrial and agricultural reforms. The industrial sectors of copper, tin, and steel grew with the help of loans from multinational lenders like the World Bank. He attempted to meet the demands of the working classes by creating massive public works programs. Nonetheless, the country's difficult economic situation and persistent high inflation undermined his success.

Alessandri contested but lost the presidential election of 1970 to socialist candidate Allende. During the dictatorship of Augusto **Pinochet Ugarte** (1973–1990), he was tapped to serve on the panel drafting the **Constitution of 1980**, but stepped down when Pinochet dismissed some of his suggestions as too liberal.

Allende Gossens, Salvador (1908–1973)

The first Marxist in the world to come to power through democratic elections, Salvador Allende Gossens (1970–1973) undertook revolutionary reforms that led to his overthrow in 1973 and the advent of seventeen years of military rule.

Allende was born on June 26, 1908, into an affluent family in the port city of Valparaíso. He served briefly in the military, and then entered medical school in 1926 in Valparaíso. Active in student politics, he was eventually elected president of the Medical Center and also served as its representative to the University Council. Subsequently, Allende became increasingly active in leftist opposition politics. He was involved in demonstrations in 1931 that eventually led to the end of the conservative first regime of Carlos Ibáñez del Campo (1927–1931, 1952–1958), and was imprisoned twice for supporting Marxist ideals and leftist politicians. A vehement supporter of workers' rights, Allende was elected a regional secretary of the Socialist Party (Partido Socialista, PS) in 1936. He served as Valparaíso's representative to the Chamber of Deputies in 1937 and was appointed minister of health in 1938. In 1942 Allende became secretary general of the PS, and subsequently served in the Senate representing various regions on behalf of the PS from 1945 until 1970. Allende was a candidate for the presidency in 1952, 1958, and 1964, representing coalitions of Marxist and non-Marxist leftist parties, placing second in 1958 and 1964.

Salvador Allende Gossens, President of Chile (1970–1973). *Columbus Memorial Library, General Secretariat of the Organization of American States. Reproduced with permission of the Organization of American States.*

In the 1970 presidential election, Allende, the candidate of the **Popular Unity** (Unidad Popular, UP) coalition, won 36 percent of the vote while former president Jorge **Alessandri Rodríguez** (1958–1964) won 35 percent. Congress was given the duty of selecting the new president, as no candidate had achieved a majority, and despite pressure against choosing Allende from the right, parts of the army, conservative parties in Congress, and the United States, Congress named Allende the winner. Following Allende's inauguration in November 1970, he and the UP initiated an economic program that involved greater state control of the economy and the nationalization of many private industries and corporations (including the large copper mines), with the goal of breaking Chile's cycle of dependence on foreign capital and imported industrial goods and creating a more equitable economy not based on the exploitation of Chilean resources. He undertook massive social programs aimed at helping the poor, including educational and public health initiatives. Labor was given concessions, and some private land was expropriated and turned into large collectives for group production. However, the character of the UP, its internal instability, and the lack of cooperation between the UP and the **Christian Democrat Party** (Partido Demócrata Cristiano, PDC), in combination with the rapid deterioration of the economy after 1973, bred opposition and

alarmed the citizenry. In September 1973, the military staged a bloody coup and installed a military government that would rule Chile until 1990. Allende died, most accounts indicate of suicide, on September 11, 1973, during the Chilean armed forces' violent bombing of the presidential palace, La Moneda. (*See also* **Pinochet Ugarte**, Augusto.)

Alliance for Chile (Alianza por Chile)

The Independent Democratic Union (Unión Demócrata Independiente, UDI) and the National Renovation Party (Renovación Nacional, RN) emerged during the period of transition from military rule in 1987 as the two strongest parties of the right. They subsequently formed a center-right alliance, which has contested each legislative election since the return to democracy under a different name: Democracy and Progress (Democracia y Progreso) in 1989, Union for the Progress of Chile (Unión por el Progreso de Chile) in 1993, Union for Chile (Unión por Chile) in 1997, and Alliance for Chile (Alianza por Chile) in 2001. The right alliance has been the main competitor of the center-left coalition, the **Alliance of Democratic Parties** (Concertación de Partidos por la Democracia, CPD) following the transition to democracy.

The UDI, whose roots reach back to the 1960s, formed as an independent organization in 1983 and briefly merged with the RN in 1987 before emerging as an independent political party. UDI leadership is still closely tied to Augusto **Pinochet Ugarte** (1973–1990) in terms of political support and economic policy; the party promotes a free market neoliberal economic model. The UDI suffered a major blow in 1991 when party leader and senator Jaime Guzmán was assassinated by a left-wing extremist group. The UDI is considered more conservative and technocratic than the RN and is thought to have stronger ties to the military.

The center-right RN emerged out of the National Party (Partido Nacional, PN; see **Conservative Party/ Liberal Party**) and the National Work Front (Frente Nacional de Trabajo, FNT) and took over the work that the National Union Movement (Movimiento de Uniones Nacional, MUN) had begun in 1983. The party's philosophy advocates the importance of individual liberties and considers the family as the basic social unit to be nurtured and protected. While originally the RN's ties to the military regime were strong, as the transition to democracy proceeded, the party proposed a renewed separation between the military and the government, as well as a continuation of market-based economic policy.

The Alianza backed the unsuccessful presidential bids of Hernán Büchi in 1989, of Arturo Alessandri Besa in 1993, and of Joaquín Lavín in 1999; Lavín lost a close election to socialist candidate Ricardo **Lagos** (2000–) in the second round of voting in January 2000. However, Lavín was easily elected mayor of Santiago in municipal elections in October 2000, in which the conservative opposition enjoyed its best electoral performance since the return to democracy. The coalition also had a strong showing in the December 2001 legislative elections; following that contest, the UDI held more seats in the lower house than any other party.

Alliance of Democratic Parties (Concertación de Partidos por la Democracia, CPD)

The Alliance of Democratic Parties (Concertación de Partidos por la Democracia, CPD) was formed in 1988 as an eclectic electoral coalition with the common goals of winning a "no" vote in the **Plebiscite of 1988** on the continuation of military rule, and ousting the military regime of Augusto **Pinochet Ugarte** (1973–1990).

The CPD ran a masterful campaign in the 1988 plebiscite, and on October 5, 1988, the "no" vote won with 54 percent of the vote, bringing about the end of the Pinochet regime. The CPD then set its sights on the elections of 1989, drawing up a list of congressional candidates and selecting Patricio **Aylwin Azócar** (1990–1994) of the **Christian Democrat Party** (Partido Demócrata Cristiano, PDC) as the presidential candidate to run against the two parties of the right, the Independent Democratic Union (Unión Demócrata Independiente, UDI) and the National Renovation Party (Renovación Nacional, RN) which had joined together to form the Democracy and Progress coalition, a precursor of the **Alliance for Chile** (Alianza por Chile). In the period leading up to the election the CPD also worked to negotiate amendments to the **Constitution of 1980** that reversed the ban on leftist parties, reduced the number of appointed senators, and changed the composition of the National Security Council. The CPD triumphed in both the presidential and congressional contests of 1989, with Aylwin winning 55 percent of the vote.

The coalition consists of the PDC, the Socialist Party (Partido Socialista, PS), the Party for Democracy (Partido por la Democracia, PPD), and a number of smaller parties. The PS, which was quite radicalized in the 1960s and 1970s, split into two distinct parties in 1979; however, most currents of the party had reunited by 1989 (though strong factions composed of different ideological tendencies still exist). The PS assumed a moderate stance in the 1990s, breaking its traditional ties with the (by this time more radical) **Communist Party of Chile** (Partido Comunista de Chile, PCCh) and allying with the other significant party of the governing left, the PPD. The more moderate PPD was formed out of one of the two strands of the divided PS in 1987 as an "instrumental" organization to contest the 1989 congressional elections. However, the PPD soon grew into a significant party combining a modernizing tendency with political ideas similar to those of the traditional sector of the PS. The relationship between the PS and the PPD is a complex one, and the link between them has grown weaker through the 1990s: though the

parties cooperate, they also compete for electoral support and for the leadership of the governmental left. Further, the PS's and the PPD's fears of being overshadowed by the PDC, the dominant member of the coalition, have been a source of increasing tension within the diverse alliance.

Nonetheless, the CPD has matured into a long-term governing coalition that has eased Chile toward redemocratization, maintaining the market-oriented policies first implemented by the Pinochet government, but broadening these policies to emphasize social justice and shared economic growth. Consistently the strongest electoral force in the country since the return to democracy, the CPD has backed the bid of the winning candidate in each presidential election since 1989, and following the legislative elections of December 2001, maintained a plurality in both houses of Congress.

Aylwin Azócar, Patricio (1918–)

Patricio Aylwin Azócar was the first freely elected president after the dictatorship of Augusto **Pinochet Ugarte** (1973–1990). His role in defeating the dictatorship in the **Plebiscite of 1988**, carefully managing the democratic transition, and broadening market-based reforms to reflect social concerns has been critical to Chile's transition toward a consolidated modern democracy.

Aylwin was born in Viña del Mar in November 1918. He graduated in law from the University of Chile, and later taught there. He became actively involved in politics in the 1940s, and was one of the founders of the **Christian Democratic Party** (Partido Demócrata Cristiano, PDC) in 1957, becoming its president in 1958. From 1958 until the 1973 coup that brought Pinochet to power, Aylwin served as senator, presiding as president of the Senate in 1971. Aylwin remained active in the PDC through the dictatorship, eventually serving as spokesman for, and helping to direct, the "no" campaign against the dictatorship in the Plebiscite of 1988. That effort culminated in the defeat of the military regime and set the stage for the elections of 1989. Running on the ticket of the **Alliance of Democratic Parties** (Concertación de Partidos por la Democracia, CPD), Aylwin won the presidential contest with 55 percent of the vote.

As president, Aylwin created legitimacy for and maintained a consensus for democratic rule. He smoothed over civil-military relations, despite some tense moments, including a 1990 episode in which Pinochet called all troops to their barracks in response to inquiries into a financial scandal involving the military. Aylwin presided over four years of economic growth while simultaneously responding to popular demands for social services by increasing social spending and addressing some of the inequities generated by Chile's austere economic policies.

Aylwin also carefully managed the difficult questions arising from the human rights abuses of the Pinochet years, forming the Commission on Truth and Reconciliation in order to document the human rights abuses perpetrated by the military regime. The commission produced the Rettig Report, named for commission chair Raúl Rettig, which determined that Pinochet's Directorate of National Intelligence (Dirección de Inteligencia Nacional, DINA) had played a major role in the deaths and the systematic torture that occurred during his regime; the report documented 2,279 killings at the hands of the regime (excluding unsolved cases of disappearances). While the constraints posed by the presence of Pinochet and the continued strength of the military (and a 1978 amnesty law passed by the military regime) prevented most individuals involved with the regime's atrocities from being prosecuted, in 1993 former DINA leaders were tried and convicted for their involvement in the 1976 death of Orlando **Letelier del Solar**. Aylwin remained active in politics after the end of his presidential term, and in July 2001, at the age of 84, he assumed the presidency of the PDC.

Balmaceda Fernández, José Manuel (1840–1891)

President José Manuel Balmaceda Fernández (1886–1891) developed the nation's infrastructure and professionalized the military. He was overthrown by congressional forces in a civil war that erupted in 1891.

Born in Santiago on June 19, 1840, Balmaceda was the son of a senator. He served as special assistant to President Manuel **Montt Torres** (1851–1861), served five terms as a congressional deputy from 1864 to 1882, and also served as senator. He helped to ensure Argentine neutrality during the **War of the Pacific** (1879–1884; see Appendix 1) and served in various cabinet positions under the administration of Domingo **Santa María González** (1881–1886). He won the presidential election of 1886 as the candidate of the National Party (Partido Nacional, PN), with the support of the Liberal and Radical Parties (see **Conservative Party/Liberal Party**).

During his administration he improved Chilean infrastructure considerably, developing railway, communication, sanitation, and health systems. In addition to the massive public works schemes he initiated, Balmaceda also modernized the military. However, Congress began to resist these rapid changes and questioned Balmaceda's use of funds, accusing him of overriding the system and being too authoritarian; by late 1889, Balmaceda faced opposition from the National, Radical, and Liberal Parties, and demonstrations against the government escalated throughout 1890. The congressional opposition gained the sympathies of the navy, under the command of Jorge Montt (1891–1896), while the army remained loyal to Balmaceda; that division within the armed forces led to the Civil War of 1891. The navy was able to control the ports and many resources, and in the end was victorious over the forces loyal to Balmaceda. Refusing to resign, Balmaceda took

refuge in the Argentine Embassy until his term expired on September 18, 1891. The following day, still holding to his beliefs, he committed suicide. His presidency is considered the last of the Liberal era (1861–1891).

Bello López, Andrés (1781–1865)

Andrés Bello López was a prominent political and academic figure whose influence reached an entire generation of politicians and literary figures. Born on November 29, 1781, in Caracas, Venezuela, he studied extensively under the tutelage of distinguished national and international scholars and thinkers including Alexander von Humboldt and Simón Antonio de la Santísima Trinidad **Bolívar y Palacios** (see Colombia), and was influenced by the independence sentiments espoused by scholars and activists at the time. He traveled to London to lobby for support for the cause of independence in the Americas in 1810 and stayed there, working as a diplomat and journalist. In 1829 he was invited to Chile by the Chilean Ministry of Foreign Affairs. He collaborated with the Chilean government on a number of projects, helped design the 1833 Constitution, and was elected to the Senate in 1837, serving until 1864. He aided the government in founding the University of Chile in 1842, and held the position of rector for the subsequent twenty-three years, researching and teaching on subjects such as linguistics, law, science, philosophy, and diplomacy. He died in Santiago on October 15, 1865.

Bulnes Prieto, Manuel (1799–1866)

Military leader Manuel Bulnes Prieto served as president from 1841 to 1851. He was instrumental in the development of the country's infrastructure, but lost legitimacy for his authoritarian leanings.

Bulnes was born in Concepción on December 25, 1799. He began his military career at age eleven in the Spanish colonial army, but later joined in the fight for Chilean independence. He was highly regarded for his leadership abilities, eventually rising to the rank of general due to his heroic conduct in the **War of the Peru-Bolivia Confederation** (1836–1839; see Appendix 1). Bulnes was elected president in 1841 and 1846 with the support of the Conservatives.

During his first administration he built infrastructure to facilitate trade and commerce, including ports, roads, and bridges, and witnessed the founding of the University of Chile and the Naval School of Valparaíso. In 1844 he signed a treaty with the government of Spain that formally recognized Chilean independence. He again emphasized infrastructure during his second term, and also oversaw the opening of the National Bureau of Statistics in 1848. He took over the Straits of Magellan from Argentina, creating a territorial dispute that was not settled until 1984. Though Bulnes' stance toward the Liberal opposition was largely conciliatory (leading many prominent Liberal leaders to collaborate with the regime), Liberal opposition to Bulnes' government and his authoritarian tendencies grew throughout the late 1840s, and his legitimacy began to falter. Revolts, led mainly by the Liberals but involving other sectors, culminated in the Civil War of 1851, which broke out at the end of Bulnes' term shortly after the appointment of the authoritarian Manuel **Montt Torres** (1851–1861) as Bulnes' hand-picked successor. The Conservatives survived the challenge as Bulnes, still in command of the army, put down the uprisings and handed power to Montt. Bulnes died in Santiago on October 19, 1866.

Chicago Boys

When Augusto **Pinochet Ugarte** (1973–1990) took control of the nation in 1973, Chile was experiencing severe economic problems due, many believed, to the socialist and populist policies of the two previous presidents, Salvador **Allende Gossens** (1970–1973) and Eduardo **Frei Montalva** (1964–1970). Determined to reinvigorate the economy, Pinochet built an advisory team of technocrats, many from the University of Chicago (subsequently nicknamed the "Chicago Boys") to assist him in developing and implementing an appropriate economic strategy. The Chicago Boys were the main engine behind economic policy from 1973 to 1983.

The Chicago Boys' view of economics was influenced by the orthodox monetarist economics of Milton Friedman, which favored free markets, privatization, and fiscal austerity. With their guidance, the Pinochet government immediately abolished all price controls and devalued the currency. Inflation proved difficult to conquer so in mid-1975 an extreme orthodox "shock treatment" approach was adopted: public spending was slashed, the money supply was cut, and privatization of enterprises that had been nationalized under the Frei Montalva and Allende administrations was accelerated. As expected, the economy went into a deep recession, unemployment and poverty shot up, and social unrest increased, but inflation was controlled. Nonetheless, state intervention in the economy soon increased, and the Chicago Boys' policies were suspended in 1983. The economy eventually recovered, and Chile led the region in economic growth for most of the 1980s.

Many of the Chicago Boys' policies were followed by the administrations of Patricio **Aylwin Azócar** (1990–1994) and Eduardo **Frei Ruíz-Tagle** (1994–2000), who tried to encourage export-oriented growth and scaled back state ownership in industries in order to maintain economic development and thus protect democratic legitimacy and minimize the risk of a return to authoritarian rule. However, as many felt that Chile's economic growth through the 1980s had left too many behind and deepened income inequality, and with the dictatorship and the fear of repression gone, these later regimes simultaneously needed to emphasize poverty re-

duction and targeted social spending in order to meet newly expressed popular demands and to address the health care, nutrition, and education needs of the poor. Despite the need to maintain this balance, Chile's economic growth was the strongest in Latin America for most of the 1990s.

Christian Democrat Party (Partido Demócrata Cristiano, PDC)

The Falangist National Party formed when Eduardo **Frei Montalva** (1964–1970) led a faction of the Conservative Party that challenged the party to include new ideas such as those espoused by socially conscious Catholic Church leaders, to break with the Conservative Party in 1938. The Social Christian Conservative Party (formed in 1949) merged with the Falangist National Party in 1957 to form the Christian Democrat Party (Partido Demócrata Cristiano, PDC).

The ideology of the PDC, which sought to create a "third way" between socialism and unbridled capitalism, was originally guided by modern Catholic social doctrine mainly stemming from two encyclicals, *Rerum Novarum* (1891) and *Quadragesimo Anno* (1931). These ideals were also part of the New Christendom movement, which linked progressive social Catholic doctrine to grassroots popular political movements in an attempt to mobilize the masses and alleviate poverty and despair through political participation.

Frei lost the presidential election of 1958 on the PDC ticket, but ran again in 1964, calling for agrarian reform, nationalization of copper mines, and major social programs, a platform not entirely different from that of his socialist opponent, Salvador **Allende Gossens** (1970–1973). Frei won the election and became the first PDC president of Chile. Though PDC candidate Radomiro Tomic Romero lost the presidential contest of 1970 to socialist candidate Allende, the PDC collaborated with Allende supporters in Congress to pass certain moderate legislation through the first year and a half of Allende's term. However, the party withdrew all congressional support as the Allende administration became more radical, contributing to instability and deadlock. The PDC attempted unsuccessfully to negotiate a peaceful end to the desperate situation before the military coup in September 1973 that initiated seventeen years of dictatorship.

Though the PDC was legally disbanded in 1977 by executive order, it became active in the opposition during the most repressive years of the dictatorship. Upon the reopening of politics after the **Plebiscite of 1988**, the PDC reformed, joining and leading the center-left coalition the **Alliance of Democratic Parties** (Concertación de Partidos por la Democracia, CPD); PDC members of the CPD won the 1989 and 1993 presidential elections. While the CPD chose socialist Ricardo **Lagos** (2000–) as its candidate in the 1999 presidential contest, and though the PDC's vote share shrank in the legislative elections in 1997 and 2001, the PDC remained one of the most important parties in contemporary Chilean politics.

Communist Party of Chile (Partido Comunista de Chile, PCCh)

Formed in 1922 in conjunction with the evolution of the political arm of the labor movement and the Socialist Workers' Party, the Communist Party of Chile (Partido Comunista de Chile, PCCh) has traditionally been one of the largest but least revolutionary communist parties on the South American continent.

The government of Arturo **Alessandri Palma** (1920–1924) increasingly alienated the working class, and the newly formed PCCh quickly gained the support of organized labor, and especially coal miners and nitrate workers. The PCCh moderated its revolutionary position in the 1930s and joined the Popular Front (Frente Popular) alliance, which supported the candidacy of Pedro **Aguirre Cerda** (1938–1941) of the Radical Party (Partido Radical, PR; see **Conservative Party/Liberal Party**) in the 1938 presidential contest. Though three party members were appointed to cabinet posts in the administration of President Gabriel **González Videla** (1946–1952), tensions between the communists and González led to their dismissal, which resulted in massive strikes and the subsequent banning of the PCCh in 1948.

Reinstated in 1958, the party participated in elections at the national and municipal levels, supporting the unsuccessful candidacy of Salvador **Allende Gossens** (1970–1973) in the 1958 presidential election as part of Popular Action (Frente de Acción Popular, FRAP), an alliance of leftist parties created in 1956. The PCCh also supported Allende's 1964 presidential bid, as well as his 1970 candidacy, the latter as part of the **Popular Unity** (Unidad Popular, UP) coalition.

While in general the PCCh played a moderate role in politics prior to 1973, many PCCh members were tortured, exiled, or killed under the dictatorship of Augusto **Pinochet Ugarte** (1973–1990). In 1980, the PCCh abandoned its traditional support for the democratic route, reaffirming its Marxist-Leninist character and calling for armed struggle. In contrast to its previous preeminence among Latin American leftist parties, and due in part to the collapse of communism worldwide, the PCCh emerged from the dictatorial years a severely diminished force. It was excluded from the **Alliance of Democratic Parties** (Concertación de Partidos por la Democracia, CPD) upon its formation, which resulted in its further marginalization by government and Congress. During the 1990s, the PCCh's stance hardened into one of overt opposition, leading some to characterize the party as anti-system. Most consider the party an insignificant force in Chilean national politics.

Conservative Party/Liberal Party

The Conservative Party and the Liberal Party are two of the oldest political parties in Chile. The Conservative Party first formed just following independence, and dominated Chilean politics for the next fifty years. The traditionally elite, oligarchic, aristocratic party protected the rights of landholders and the clergy and believed in close collaboration between the Catholic Church and the state. During the presidency of Manuel **Montt Torres** (1851–1861), certain moderate factions of the party formed coalitions with other groups, and by the end of his presidency, the Conservatives had begun to lose power to the Liberals. Though the two parties coordinated to elect Federico **Errázuriz Zañartu** (1871–1876), and collaborated in subsequent administrations, the Liberal Party, formed in 1857, was the dominant force in Chilean politics during the Liberal era (1861–1891). Though the Liberals believed in creating a secular society, with the Catholic Church playing a minimal role, they tended to be centrists who favored gradual change, especially on the church-state issue. One of the most important Liberal presidents of the era was Errázuriz, who amended the constitution to limit the powers of the presidency and diminish the role of the Catholic Church in everyday life. The Conservatives became a stronger force once again during the parliamentary period (1891–1924).

The parties opposed each other bitterly, and sometimes violently, through Chile's first century of independence and well into the twentieth century, often leading to civil conflict and war. Beyond the issue of the separation of church and state, they were also divided over the issue of federalism. In general, the Conservatives, who were more sympathetic to the colonial legacy, authoritarianism, and a strong executive wanted a strong unitary government, while the Liberals tended to want a federalist state. Despite these differences, both parties represented the interests of the elite, and began to lose relevance in the middle of the twentieth century as structural economic changes led to the emergence of a growing working class and a number of new political parties, particularly on the left. Both parties eventually splintered: the Liberals gave birth to the Radical Party (Partido Radical, PR), and the Conservative Party spun off into the National Party (Partido Nacional, PN), which eventually ended up forming the core of the contemporary National Renovation Party (Renovación Nacional, RN). (See **Alliance for Chile** [Alianza por Chile].)

Constitution of 1980

Drawn up by the regime of Augusto **Pinochet Ugarte** (1973–1990), the Constitution of 1980 placed strong limits on civilian authorities while outlining a controlled transition to democracy to begin in 1988 at the earliest. It forms the basis for Chile's government today.

The charter's most important tenets were the creation

of a strong presidency, the founding of a congress with fairly weak powers (including a senate in which nine of forty-seven members are appointed rather than elected), and the institutionalization of the military's influence in politics. Under the new Constitution, Pinochet would continue to rule until at least 1988, when a second referendum on military rule (the first was held in 1978) would be called (see **Plebiscite of 1988**). The new Constitution also guaranteed Pinochet's position as head of the armed forces until 1998 even if he were to lose the 1988 referendum. Despite the highly technical nature of the document, when Chileans were asked to vote on its adoption on September 11, 1980, 67 percent voted "yes," in part because only the dictatorship could openly campaign. Also, while most pro-democracy forces opposed adoption of the document because of its authoritarian nature, others saw the Constitution as the only way (albeit an imperfect one) to bring about an eventual end to the Pinochet regime. Approval of the Constitution, which went into effect in 1981, lent legal support to the Pinochet regime, leading the dictator to assume that his rule was uncontested by the majority.

The Constitution was amended in 1989 to increase the number of elected senators, reverse the ban on leftist parties, modify the procedure for making amendments, change the composition of the military-dominated National Security Council, and shorten the presidential term for the first new president from eight years to four. (A subsequent reform in 1994 established a six-year presidential term.)

Directorate of National Intelligence (Dirección de Inteligencia Nacional, DINA). See **Pinochet Ugarte, Augusto**

Errázuriz Echaurren, Federico (1850–1901)
The son of President Federico **Errázuriz Zañartu** (1871–1876), Federico Errázuriz Echaurren served as president from 1896 to 1901.

Born in Santiago on November 16, 1850, the younger Errázuriz studied law, and began his political career in 1876 as a congressman, a post he held until 1890. Errázuriz served briefly in the cabinet of President José Manuel **Balmaceda Fernández** (1886–1891), but as political divisions between Congress and the president grew, Errázuriz distanced himself from the administration. The armed forces soon became divided by the political struggle (Errázuriz and the congressional opposition retained the sympathies of the navy, while the army remained loyal to Balmaceda), and civil war broke out in 1891, eventually leading to the overthrow of Balmaceda. Errázuriz later served additional congressional terms, and was elected president in 1896 with the support of a coalition of the Liberal, Conservative, National, and Liberal Coalition Parties (see **Conservative Party/Liberal Party**).

As president, Liberal Party member Errázuriz included Conservative Party members in his cabinet to form a coalition government. This allowed for more stability and compromise, as well as the effective management of growing animosity between Chile and Argentina over their border in the Atacama Desert, in the north of each country. Nonetheless, Liberals and Conservatives in Errázuriz's coalition government remained divided over the role of the Catholic Church in everyday life, particularly in terms of education. Errázuriz left office in 1901 due to a serious illness, transferring power to Aníbal Zañartu, who finished the last few months of his term. Errázuriz died in Valparaíso on June 12, 1901.

Errázuriz Zañartu, Federico (1825–1877)
As president of Chile from 1871 to 1876, Federico Errázuriz Zañartu limited the powers of the presidency as well as those of the Catholic Church.

Born in Santiago on April 25, 1825, to a family of political influence and considerable wealth, Errázuriz graduated in law from the University of Chile in 1846. He held several local and national government posts, serving three times as congressman between 1849 and 1865, and then as senator from 1867 to 1876. He was exiled to Peru in 1859 as a result of his participation in civil uprisings that reflected growing sentiment against Conservative president Manuel **Montt Torres** (1851–1861), but returned to Chile in 1861. He again served in the Senate and was elected president in 1871 with the support of most major parties. Though he was a Liberal, he included Conservatives in his cabinet (see **Conservative Party/Liberal Party**). During his administration he limited the power of the president by amending the constitution to eliminate the possibility of reelection. He also spent large amounts of money improving roads, parks, and schools in Santiago. Errázuriz pushed for a more secular society and attempted to limit the powers of the Catholic Church. Though the end of his term was characterized by economic crisis, he was succeeded by another Liberal, Aníbal **Pinto Garmendia** (1876–1881). Errázuriz died in Santiago on July 20, 1877.

Frei Montalva, Eduardo (1911–1982)
The socially progressive regime of reformer Eduardo Frei Montalva (1964–1970) hastened Chile's industrialization. However, the independent non-coalition political strategy (*partido único*) of the **Christian Democrat Party** (Partido Demócrata Cristiano, PDC) under Frei encouraged political polarization and deadlock.

Born in Santiago on January 16, 1911, Frei studied journalism at the Institute of Humanities and graduated with honors in law from the Catholic University. During his studies he became actively involved in politics through the National Association of Catholic Students and later the Iberoamerican Confederation of University Students. In 1935 he joined the Conservative Party, and in 1938 formed and became president of the splinter

Falangist National Party. He was appointed to serve in President Juan Antonio Ríos' (1942–1946) cabinet, but resigned after one year in protest of police brutality during antigovernment protests. He was elected senator in 1949 and 1957. In the latter year, his Falangist National Party merged with the Social Christian Conservative Party to form the PDC. While Frei lost the 1958 presidential election on the PDC ticket, he won the 1964 contest as the PDC candidate.

Once in office he proposed a wide range of reforms, including agrarian reform, the extension of social programs in education, health, and youth promotion, the granting of new rights to labor, and the nationalization of Chilean copper mines. At the same time he was able to generate significant national reserves and promote industrialization in electronics, automobiles, and several forms of energy. Frei also reestablished official relations with the USSR and several of the Eastern bloc countries, and allowed British arbitration of a territorial dispute with Argentina. Further, his administration witnessed the growth of leftist social movements and political parties ranging from the **Communist Party of Chile** (Partido Comunista de Chile, PCCh) and socialist parties, to the Christian left and other popular religious movements. Frei's accomplishments and the PDC's polarization of the political landscape laid the groundwork for Salvador **Allende Gossens'** (1970–1973) **Popular Unity** (Unidad Popular, UP) government.

Frei Ruíz-Tagle, Eduardo (1942–)

The son of Eduardo **Frei Montalva** (1964–1970), Eduardo Frei Ruíz-Tagle served as president from 1994 to 2000. He worked to attract foreign investment to Chile, maintain a model of export-led growth, and address important human rights issues.

The younger Frei was born on June 24, 1942, in Santiago. He studied civil engineering at the University of Chile, and though he joined the **Christian Democrat Party** (Partido Demócrata Cristiano, PDC) in 1958, he had a successful career in the construction business before becoming active in politics. Frei was a leader in the "no" campaign in the **Plebiscite of 1988**, and in 1989 in the first competitive elections since 1973, Frei was elected senator from Santiago. He became leader of the PDC in 1991, and won the presidential election of 1993 on the ticket of the **Alliance of Democratic Parties** (Concertación de Partidos por la Democracia, CPD).

During his administration, Frei maintained much of the economic policy of his predecessors Augusto **Pinochet Ugarte** (1973–1990) and Patricio **Aylwin Azócar** (1990–1994). He continued to court foreign investors and to foster export-oriented growth, and sought to lower poverty levels in the country. He unsuccessfully pursued membership in the **North America Free Trade Agreement** (NAFTA; see Mexico), and his attempts to modify some of the authoritarian vestiges embedded in the **Constitution of 1980** also failed. While the CPD held a majority in the Chamber of Deputies, the right dominated the Senate, and during Frei's first four years, the nine senators appointed by Pinochet blocked any proposed changes to the Constitution that would have democratized the Senate or diminished the power of the military. Pinochet's assumption of his position as senator for life in 1998 strengthened the power of the right in the Senate and further dampened prospects for changing the institutional framework and democratizing Chile. Nonetheless, in 1995, the Supreme Court upheld the decision to convict former Directorate of National Intelligence (Dirección de Inteligencia Nacional, DINA) leaders for their role in the assassination of Orlando **Letelier del Solar**. Frei remained active in national politics after the end of his presidency, assuming the position of senator-for-life in March 2000.

González Videla, Gabriel (1898–1980)

As the last president from the centrist Radical Party (Partido Radical, PR; see **Conservative Party/Liberal Party**), Gabriel González Videla (1946–1952) and his administration witnessed the growth of left and center-left parties, and faced serious economic problems and labor activism.

Born in La Serena on November 22, 1898, González graduated from the University of Chile in law in 1922. He served as a congressional deputy (1930–1939) and as a senator (1945), and was elected president in 1946. While he initially included Liberals and members of the **Communist Party of Chile** (Partido Comunista de Chile, PCCh) in his cabinet, he asked the communists to resign in April 1945 due to conflicts over economic and labor policy. González then outlawed the PCCh in 1948 in an attempt to control its growing power. While González shared some sympathies with organized labor, he twice used government troops to break strikes and restore order as unrest increased among workers. As economic problems continued and inflation rose, his party began to lose support to center-left parties such as the Falangist National Party and the Social Christian Conservative Party (see **Christian Democrat Party** [Partido Demócrata Cristiano, PDC]). He blamed many of his problems on PCCh agitators, severed diplomatic relations with communist countries, and created a strongly anticommunist government. His government built Chile's first steel mill and smelter, extended social security coverage, and gave women the right to vote (1949). At the end of his term, González withdrew from political life. He died in Santiago on August 22, 1980.

Independent Democratic Union (Unión Demócrata Independiente, UDI). See Alliance for Chile (Alianza por Chile)

Lagos, Ricardo (1939–)

Ricardo Lagos (2000–) is the third president from the **Alliance of Democratic Parties** (Concertación de Partidos por la Democracia, CPD) since the transition to democracy in 1989, and the first socialist to occupy the presidency since Salvador **Allende Gossens** (1970–1973).

Lagos received a law degree from the University of Chile and a Ph.D. in economics from Duke University in the United States. He served as minister of education in the administration of Patricio **Aylwin Azócar** (1990–1994) and as minister of public works under Eduardo **Frei Ruíz-Tagle** (1994–2000). Lagos was an important opposition figure during the military regime of Augusto **Pinochet Ugarte** (1973–1990), serving a short term in jail in 1987 for his activities against the regime. In the unexpectedly competitive 1999 presidential contest, Lagos was opposed by Joaquín Lavín, the candidate of the right. Both candidates emphasized economic growth with increased equity, and both kept their distance from the potentially explosive issue of the arrest and detainment of Pinochet in Britain on charges of human rights abuses. Though the first round of voting in December 1999 was indecisive, Lagos won the second round in January 2000 and was sworn in in March 2000.

Lagos, a moderate, pledged to continue the market-oriented economic policies that had provided the framework for the Chilean economy since the 1970s and that had made Chile a model reformer in the region, optimistically forecasting 6–6½ percent growth in 2000 as the country rebounded from the 1999 recession. Lagos also vowed to increase social spending in such areas as education, health, nutrition, and poverty reduction in order to address some of the social inequities that those economic policies had generated. However, economic recovery was slower than predicted, and by mid-2001, the economy was flagging, unemployment remained high, the peso had plunged to a new low against the dollar, and business confidence in the government was waning; public finances, inflation, and the deficit were well under control, however. Furthermore, while Lagos had initially indicated that he would push for Chile's full membership in the **Southern Cone Common Market** (Mercado Común del Cono Sur, MERCOSUR; see Appendix 1), in November 2000, Chile announced that it had begun free-trade talks with the United States.

Lagos had also hoped to persuade the opposition to agree to modify the **Constitution of 1980**'s undemocratic clauses. However, little progress was made on that front during the first two years of his administration. Nonetheless, since 1999, government-sponsored talks between representatives of the armed forces, human rights lawyers, and church leaders had been progressing regarding atrocities during the Pinochet dictatorship. To encourage officers to provide information regarding the whereabouts of victims of the dictatorship whose bodies were still missing, in June 2000, the Lagos government passed a law guaranteeing those officers anonymity. In January 2001, the armed forces admitted that the bodies of 130 people had been thrown into the sea or into Chilean lakes. The admission marked the first time the army had admitted any wrongdoing under the military regime and represented a step toward closing the debate about the dictatorship.

Letelier del Solar, Orlando (1932–1976)

Born into a wealthy family in Temuco on April 13, 1932, Orlando Letelier del Solar studied law and economics at the University of Chile, and worked at the **Inter-American Development Bank** (IDB; see Appendix 2) in Washington, D.C., during the 1960s. Letelier served as ambassador to the United States and in various cabinet positions under Salvador **Allende Gossens** (1970–1973). Letelier was arrested during the 1973 military coup that brought Augusto **Pinochet Ugarte** (1973–1990) to power, and was subsequently sent into exile. He settled in Washington, D.C., and worked as a lobbyist against U.S. aid to the Pinochet regime. On September 21, 1976, he and his assistant, Ronni Moffitt (a U.S. citizen), were riding in a car in Washington, D.C., when a bomb planted in the car exploded, killing both. Pinochet's Directorate of National Intelligence (Dirección de Inteligencia Nacional, DINA) was held accountable, and five agents were tried and sentenced in U.S. courts, though Chile refused to allow the extradition of others. Despite a 1978 amnesty law, DINA chief Manuel Contreras and his second in command, Pedro Espinoza, were tried in Chile for the murders and sentenced to seven years in prison in 1993. The incident, the trial, and the subsequent appeals highlighted the human rights abuses that had been perpetrated under the Pinochet regime and focused international attention on the impunity with which the Chilean military had acted.

Liberal Party. See Conservative Party/Liberal Party

Montt Torres, Manuel (1809–1880)

Manuel Montt Torres served as Chile's president from 1851 through 1861. Though he fostered modernization, his conservative, authoritarian leadership style cost him legitimacy.

Born in Petorca on September 5, 1809, Montt received a law degree from the University of Chile in 1831 and was immediately appointed vice rector of the National Institute, in which he had formerly been a student. He served in both the Senate and the Chamber of Deputies and held cabinet posts in the administrations of Generals Joaquín Prieto Vial (1831–1841) and Manuel **Bulnes Prieto** (1841–1851). Tensions between Bulnes and the Liberal opposition (see **Conservative Party/ Liberal Party**) were exacerbated by Bulnes' overreaction to a series of minor revolts, and the country exploded into civil war when the authoritarian Montt was appointed president as Bulnes' hand-picked successor. The rebellion was put down by the military (under the command of Bulnes who was still chief of the armed forces), and the Conservative Party retained power.

Despite the turmoil and congressional opposition to the designation of a presidential successor, Montt was inaugurated. He improved social services, education, industrial infrastructure, and rail transportation, investments that paid off as Chile underwent a commercial boom during Montt's first term. However, a large division soon emerged within the Conservative Party (in part because of Montt's handling of church relations), and tensions with the Liberals also continued to grow. Nonetheless, the army stayed loyal to Montt and helped him put down a series of rebellions during his presidency. Montt left discredited, and José Joaquín Pérez (1861–1871) of the National Party (Partido Nacional, PN) won the subsequent presidential election unopposed.

National Renovation Party (Renovación Nacional, RN).
See **Alliance for Chile (Alianza por Chile)**

Neruda, Pablo (1904–1973)
Born Neftalí Ricardo Reyes Basoalto in Parral on July 12, 1904, Neruda studied French and journalism in Temuco and Santiago. As a writer and poet he was successful nationally and internationally, winning numerous prizes including Chile's National Prize for Literature in 1945 and the Nobel Prize for Literature in 1971. His many works of poetry and prose, among them *Crepusculario* (1923), *Veinte Poemas de Amor y una Canción Desesperada* (1924), *Canto General* (1950), and *Aún* (1969), were influenced by his political philosophy and participation in the **Communist Party of Chile** (Partido Comunista de Chile, PCCh). Beginning in 1927, this influential leftist political figure served in a series of different diplomatic posts in foreign nations and was elected senator from Tarapacá and Antofagasta in 1945 for the PCCh. He was exiled by president Gabriel **González Videla** (1946–1952) in 1949, and after living briefly in Europe and traveling to various Eastern bloc countries, he returned to Chile. He ran as the PCCh candidate for president in the 1969 election, but dropped out before the elections to support Salvador **Allende Gossens** (1970–1973) and the **Popular Unity** (Unidad Popular, UP) coalition. He served as ambassador to France under Allende, resigning for health reasons. He returned to Chile in 1972 and, symbolically, died at his home on Isla Negra on September 23, 1973, just after the military coup that brought Augusto **Pinochet Ugarte** (1973–1990) to power.

O'Higgins Riquelme, Bernardo (1778–1842)
Bernardo O'Higgins Riquelme, who is remembered as the father of Chilean independence, served as the first president of Chile (1817–1823).

O'Higgins was born on August 21, 1778, in Chillán into a political family. He attended school in Lima, Peru, Chillán, and finally in London, where he studied with Francisco de Miranda, a scholar who inspired O'Higgins with the ideals of freedom and liberty. Upon his return to Chile in 1802, O'Higgins inherited his family's estate in the southern part of the country and became a successful and wealthy landowner and businessman.

His political involvement in the Chilean independence movement began in 1811 when he and José Miguel Carrera Verdugo began to conspire to overthrow the Spanish colonial government and establish an independent republic. While O'Higgins and Carrera soon separated forces, with O'Higgins replacing Carrera as commander of the Chilean army in 1814, increasing Spanish control of the area forced O'Higgins and Carrera to join forces once again. When O'Higgins and Carrera were exiled to Argentina after the Spanish won the Battle of Rancagua in October 1814, O'Higgins and Argentine leader José de **San Martín** (see Argentina) joined forces, temporarily pushing Carrera further into Argentina, and crossing the Andes Mountains together to defeat the Spanish at Chacabuco in February 1817.

Within a week O'Higgins marched into Santiago and was appointed leader of the republic, with the title of supreme dictator. O'Higgins emphasized the security of the republic during his first few years in office, working to form an armed naval force that would become one of the best in the region, and struggling to control the country, deal with the remaining loyal Spanish forces and rebellious indigenous groups, and contain the effects of the disorder and military problems in neighboring Argentina and Peru. His opposition, which included those sympathetic to Carrera, political conservatives, the Catholic Church, and the wealthy classes, began to plot uprisings against him, and by 1823 his regime was falling. He resigned and went into exile in Peru, where he died on October 24, 1842. He is remembered for his implementation of liberal ideals, particularly the separation of church and state.

Party for Democracy (Partido por la Democracia, PPD).
See **Alliance of Democratic Parties (Concertación de Partidos por la Democracia, CPD)**

Pinochet Ugarte, Augusto (1915–)
As dictator of Chile from 1973 to 1990, Augusto Pinochet Ugarte maintained control of the nation through repressive iron-fisted rule, while implementing economic reforms that would strengthen the economy and make Chile a model of neoliberal economic reform.

Born in Valparaíso in November 1915, Pinochet graduated from the prestigious Military School in 1936, and then taught classes there and in Ecuador. By 1970 he had risen to army division general, and in 1972 was named commander-in-chief of the army during the turbulent socialist administration of Salvador **Allende Gossens** (1970–1973). While the anti-Marxist Pinochet was

Chilean dictator Augusto Pinochet Ugarte (1973–1990), (seated, with legs crossed). *Columbus Memorial Library, General Secretariat of the Organization of American States. Reproduced with permission of the Organization of American States.*

dismayed at the country's political and economic situation, he was reluctant to join with the leaders of the other branches of the armed forces in the planning and execution of the military coup that took place on September 11, 1973. Nonetheless, Pinochet soon emerged as the leader of the junta that took control of the country after the coup (which included the heads of the army, the air force, the navy, and the Carabineros, the military police force), and in 1974 he was named president by the provisional military government.

Pinochet's biggest priority was improving the nation's economic situation. He and his advisors, the **"Chicago Boys,"** reoriented the economy along free market lines by privatizing businesses and encouraging growth in the export sector. Pinochet retained absolute control of the nation, ruling through violent repression of civil society and political groups. The Congress had been dissolved just following the coup, and Pinochet assigned members of the military hierarchy to oversee the functioning of schools, universities, and public offices at all levels.

The Directorate of National Intelligence (Dirección de Inteligencia Nacional, DINA), led by General Manuel Contreras, organized and carried out Chile's internal war against political adversaries and so-called subversives, specifically targeting socialists and other leftist groups (which were officially banned in 1977). The organization worked in secret, using torture, assassination, and "disappearing" people (suddenly kidnapping people who often were never heard from again) to intimidate and stamp out political opposition. In coordination with Argentine, Bolivian, Brazilian, Uruguayan, and U.S. security forces, the Chilean military

also engaged in terrorist activities in other countries. The most dramatic examples were the murder of General Carlos Prat and his wife in Buenos Aires, Argentina, in 1974, the attempted assassination of politician Bernardo Leighton in Italy in 1975, and the assassination of former Allende cabinet minister Orlando **Letelier del Solar** in 1976. Through these cases, the human rights abuses committed by the DINA became well known, and Pinochet received strong criticism from the international community for his regime's prolonged and systematic abuse of human rights. The DINA was disbanded under international and domestic pressure in 1977 and replaced by the National Information Center (Centro Nacional de Información, CNI).

In the late 1970s Pinochet put conservative members of the judiciary to work writing a new constitution (see **Constitution of 1980**). In January 1978 Chilean voters were asked to express their support of Pinochet's defense of the fatherland and the legitimacy of his government by voting "yes" (an expression of support for the regime) or "no" (indicating a lack of support for the regime) in a national plebiscite; the vote was fraudulently carried out, and the "yes" vote won, effectively legitimizing Pinochet's regime. That same year, Pinochet's government passed an amnesty law that prohibited the prosecution of crimes committed by agents of the state (effectively preventing cases of human rights abuses from subsequently being taken up by the courts). A plebiscite on the new Constitution was held in 1980, and the populace approved the document, though again there were charges of electoral fraud from many sources. The new Constitution guaranteed Pinochet an eight-year term, and in 1988 voters returned to the polls to express their preference on the continuation of military rule (see **Plebiscite of 1988**). To his surprise, Pinochet lost the 1988 plebiscite, forcing him to call a presidential election for 1989. Hernán Büchi, the Pinochet-supported candidate, lost that contest to Patricio **Aylwin Azócar** (1990–1994) a member of the **Christian Democrat Party** (Partido Demócrata Cristiano, PDC) running on the ticket of the **Alliance of Democratic Parties** (Concertación de Partidos por la Democracia, CPD).

In accordance with the Constitution, Pinochet remained commander-in-chief of the army during and after the transition to democracy. He used this position to remind the government that the military remained an autonomous political force to be reckoned with; in December 1990 he called all troops to the barracks in response to congressional inquiries into financial scandals involving the military (and his family), and in May 1993 he had the Ministry of Defense surrounded by soldiers, ordering his generals to report in full battle dress.

In October 1998, just after becoming senator-for-life, Pinochet was unexpectedly arrested while visiting London for medical treatment. Early in 1999, a British high court ruled that the former Chilean dictator could be extradited to Spain to face probable charges of murder, torture, and hostage-taking. This event triggered an emotional debate around the world regarding the nature of authoritarian rule and human rights, and divided the Chilean government and population between those who supported the former leader and current senator, and those who advocated his extradition to and trial in Spain. However, after months of negotiations among the Chilean government (which claimed that Pinochet had diplomatic immunity) and the British and Spanish governments, and under a barrage of legal and diplomatic pressure, in December 1999, Britain ordered Pinochet released based on medical reports claiming that he was not fit—because of age and health—to face trial.

When Pinochet arrived back in Chile in March 2000, he was greeted not only by buoyant celebration on the part of the military high command, but also by a series of lawsuits. Over the previous two years, almost sixty cases had been filed against him in Chile relating to atrocities during his dictatorship. Subsequently, prosecutors in the most advanced of the lawsuits filed a petition with the Santiago Appeals Court to revoke the immunity from prosecution that Pinochet enjoyed as senator-for-life. The Appeals Court ruled against the general in May 2000, and Chile's Supreme Court upheld the decision in August 2000. Medical tests to determine whether Pinochet was fit to stand trial were subsequently ordered, and in January 2001, the former dictator underwent psychological testing. Later that month, a Chilean judge formally charged Pinochet with

kidnapping and murder, and the ailing and isolated general was placed under house arrest. However, an appeal was requested, and in July 2001, the Santiago Appeals Court ruled that Pinochet was mentally unfit for trial. While the ruling applied to only one case, it was expected to be applied more widely and was interpreted as signaling that the former dictator was unlikely to face trial in more than 300 other cases that had been brought against him in Chile. Despite its anticlimactic conclusion, the Pinochet case nudged forward Chile's transition to democracy.

Plebiscite of 1988

The **Constitution of 1980** drawn up by the regime of Augusto **Pinochet Ugarte** (1973–1990) provided for a vote in 1988 to decide on the future political direction of the country. On October 5, 1988, Chilean citizens voted in a yes/no plebiscite that was basically a referendum on military rule: if the voters favored the "yes" vote then Pinochet would stay in office, uncontested, for another eight years. If the "no" vote won, congressional and presidential elections would be called the following year. The 1988 plebiscite began the democratic transition in Chile.

A slight political opening preceded the plebiscite. In 1987 non-Marxist political parties were allowed to formally organize and register, and eventually coalitions began to form among right, center, and left parties on either the "yes" or "no" side. However, the "yes" campaign had more funding and the advantage of the military regime's unquestioned support, and Pinochet could easily intimidate the media. In fact, severe restrictions were placed on the "no" campaign's attempts to organize and on its use of the media until international pressure forced the regime to open access to the media for the opposition and clarify the legal and logistical framework of the vote. Given the charges of fraud in previous plebiscites (1978, 1980), the opposition questioned the legitimacy of the event, and some groups decided to boycott the plebiscite entirely. Voter registration began early in 1987. Many voters feared that the election would be filmed by hidden cameras in order to identify and persecute anyone opposing the military regime, and opposition leaders worried that if they won, the military would react and reassume power. Despite these concerns, the "no" forces won with 54 percent of the vote; only 43 percent of voters voted "yes," an outcome that allegedly surprised Pinochet, who had assumed an easy victory. The success behind the "no" was partially due to a broad-based effort by the registered political parties, which, despite many ideological differences, joined forces to lead a masterfully strategized campaign in support of the "no" vote. Pinochet agreed to follow the constitutional framework and allow for elections in 1989.

Popular Unity (Unidad Popular, UP)

Popular Unity (Unidad Popular, UP) was a coalition of political parties originally formed in October 1969 by the **Communist Party of Chile** (Partido Comunista de Chile, PCCh), the Socialist Party (Partido Socialista, PS), the Radical Party (Partido Radical, PR; see **Conservative Party/Liberal Party**), the Popular Unitary Action Movement (Movimiento de Acción Popular Unitaria, MAPU), and the Independent Popular Action Party (Acción Popular Independiente, API) (and later joined by the Christian left and the Leftist Radical Party, Partido de Izquierda Radical, PIR) in support of the candidacy of Salvador **Allende Gossens** (1970–1973) in the presidential election of 1970.

The coalition's goal was to achieve social change, combat the exploitation of workers, peasants, and other marginalized sectors of Chilean society, and make structural changes to the political and economic systems that allowed for such exploitation. The UP proposed the formulation of a new constitution that would allow for massive popular participation through reorganization of state structures, including a new legislature called the Popular Assembly. The UP sought to reform Chile's capitalist system, moving toward a state-run socialist planned economy, with nationalized public services, natural resources, and industries. While the UP lacked the congressional support necessary to legislate such significant reforms, Allende's regime had some significant policy successes. However, extremist factions within the UP, and within the revolutionary-militant left, were at odds with Allende and the more moderate sectors of the coalition with regard to formulation and implementation of policy. This instability within the UP, the threat posed by its revolutionary leanings, and the lack of cooperation between the UP and the **Christian Democrat Party** (Partido Demócrata Cristiano, PDC) led to political deadlock in Congress, and to a major crisis of government by the end of 1972. By August 1973, the coalition ceased to function. Certain sectors of the armed forces mobilized against Allende and the UP, ousting them from power in a military coup on September 11, 1973.

Portales Palazuelos, Diego (1793–1837)

Though he never served as president of the nation, Diego Portales Palazuelos was an influential figure in Chilean politics, and for two decades used his keen negotiating skills to maintain conservative control of the Chilean political scene.

Portales was born on June 15, 1793, in Santiago into a prestigious and wealthy family. Trained in commerce, he opened a company that was given a monopoly on the sale of liquor and tobacco, among other goods, by the government of Ramón Freire Serrano (1823–1826). Portales joined the Pelucón Party (which eventually became the Conservative Party; see **Conservative Party/Liberal Party**) in 1830 and was very active in Conservative politics. After civil war (1829–1830) led to a Conservative victory over the Liberals, Portales held various cabinet posts under President José Tomás Ovalle Bezanilla (1830–1831), and later became governor of Valparaíso. Portales believed in a strong, centralized government, and supported the Constitution of 1833, a presidentialist constitution giving the executive broad powers that would not break down until 1891. As minister of the interior under Joaquín Prieto Vial (1831–1841), Portales declared war on the Peru-Bolivia Confederation (see **War of the Peru-Bolivia Confederation** [1836–1839]; Appendix 1) in December 1836, and led Chile to a victory that established its naval domination of the Pacific Coast. Despite this external military victory, domestic strife continued as Liberals and Conservatives struggled for control of the nation. Portales was killed in the Mutiny of Quillota on July 6, 1837.

Santa María González, Domingo (1825–1889)

President Domingo Santa María González (1881–1886) was born in Santiago on August 4, 1825. He studied law at the University of Chile, graduating in 1847. He was a member of the Liberal Party and participated in the Civil War of 1851. He served as a judge on the Supreme Court, diplomat, and cabinet member under Aníbal Pinto Garmendia (1876–1881). His successful presidential bid in 1881 was supported by the Liberal, Radical, and National Parties (see **Conservative Party/Liberal Party**). As president, Santa María oversaw the resolution of the **War of the Pacific** (1879–1884; see Appendix 1), which resulted in a large and economically profitable territorial addition to Chile. However, tensions between supporters of the Catholic Church and their opponents reached a high point during his rule, as Santa María fought to reduce the power of the church, passing legislation that secularized Chilean life and denied the church its monopoly over birth registration, marriage, and cemeteries. As was the case through the 1800s, Liberal/Conservative tensions ran very high during his administration, and partisan disputes in Congress, combined with disagreements between Congress and the president, contributed to the eventual inauguration of the Parliamentary Republic in the 1890s, during which more powers were shared between the executive and legislative branches of government.

Socialist Party (Partido Socialista, PS). See Alliance of Democratic Parties (Concertación de Partidos por la Democracia, CPD)

Vicariate of Solidarity (Vicaría de la Solidaridad)

The Vicariate of Solidarity (Vicaría de la Solidaridad) has its roots in the popular religious movements surrounding the liberation theology movement that grew in Latin America in the late 1960s. One month after the September 1973 coup that ousted the government of

Salvador **Allende Gossens** (1970–1973), Cardinal Raúl Silva Henríquez and other religious leaders founded the Peace Committee to aid victims of repression and monitor human rights abuses. Though the organization was forced to close two years later, Silva founded the Vicariate in January 1976, which continued to provide legal aid and comfort to victims, monitor human rights abuses, and attempt to protect victims of the regime. It criticized the abuse of power and economic policy of the regime of Augusto **Pinochet Ugarte** (1973–1990), eliciting a negative response from the government. While the regime believed that church activities should be religious, not political, the important role the Catholic Church had traditionally played in Chilean politics and cultural life gave it legitimacy that other organizations lacked, in the eyes of both the public and the government. Through its negotiations with the Pinochet administration, the church became one of the only viable avenues of opposition under the repressive regime. The Vicariate closed in December 1992.

HEADS OF STATE

Bernardo O'Higgins Riquelme	1817–1823
Ramón Freire Serrano	1823–1826
Francisco Ruíz Tagle	1826–1829
Junta	1829–1830
Francisco Ruíz Tagle	1830
José Tomás Ovalle Bezanilla	1830–1831
Joaquín Prieto Vial	1831–1841
Manuel Bulnes Prieto	1841–1851
Manuel Montt Torres	1851–1861
José Joaquín Pérez	1861–1871
Federico Errázuriz Zañartu	1871–1876
Aníbal Pinto Garmendia	1876–1881
Domingo Santa María González	1881–1886
José Manuel Balmaceda Fernández	1886–1891
Junta	1891
Jorge Montt	1891–1896
Federico Errázuriz Echaurren	1896–1901
Germán Riesco	1901–1906
Pedro Montt	1906–1910
Ramón Barros Luco	1910–1915
Juan Luis Sanfuentes	1915–1920
Arturo Alessandri Palma	1920–1924
Luis Altamirano	1924–1925
Emilio Bello Codesido (part of a junta)	1925
Arturo Alessandri Palma (recalled by military junta)	1925
Luis Barros Borgaño	1925
Emiliano Figueroa Larraín	1925–1927

Carlos Ibáñez del Campo	1927–1931
Pedro Opazo Letelier	1931
Juan Esteban Montero	1931
Manuel Trucco Franzini	1931
Juan Esteban Montero	1931–1932
Junta	1932
Arturo Alessandri Palma	1932–1938
Pedro Aguirre Cerda	1938–1941
Jerónimo Méndez Arancibia	1941–1942
Juan Antonio Ríos	1942–1946
Alfredo Duhalde	1946
Gabriel González Videla	1946–1952
Carlos Ibáñez del Campo	1952–1958
Jorge Alessandri Rodríguez	1958–1964
Eduardo Frei Montalva	1964–1970
Salvador Allende Gossens	1970–1973
Augusto Pinochet Ugarte	1973–1990
Patricio Aylwin Azócar	1990–1994
Eduardo Frei Ruíz-Tagle	1994–2000
Ricardo Lagos	2000–

Sources: Simon Collier and William F. Sater, *A History of Chile, 1808–1994* (Cambridge: Cambridge University Press, 1996); Dieter Nohlen, *Enciclopedia Electoral Latinoamericana y del Caribe* (San José, Costa Rica: Instituto Interamericano de Derechos Humanos, 1993).

BIBLIOGRAPHY

Print Resources

Bauer, Arnold. *Chilean Rural Society from the Spanish Conquest to 1930*. Cambridge: Cambridge University Press, 1975.

Bethel, Leslie, ed. *Chile since Independence*. Cambridge: Cambridge University Press, 1993.

Collier, Simon, and William F. Sater. *A History of Chile, 1808–1994*. Cambridge: Cambridge University Press, 1996.

Edwards, Sebastián, and Alejandra Cox-Edwards. *Monetarism and Liberalization: The Chilean Experiment*. Chicago: University of Chicago Press, 1991.

O'Brien, Thomas. *The Nitrate Industry and Chile's Crucial Transformation, 1870–1891*. New York: New York University Press, 1982.

Pocock, H.R.S. *The Conquest of Chile*. New York: Stein and Day, 1967.

Scully, Timothy. *Rethinking the Center: Parties and Politics in Nineteenth and Twentieth Century Chile*. Stanford: Stanford University Press, 1992.

Siavelis, Peter. *The President and Congress in Post-Authoritarian Chile: Institutional Constraints to Democratic Consolidation*. University Park: Pennsylvania State University Press, 2000.

Spooner, Helen. *Soldiers in a Narrow Land: The Pinochet*

Regime in Chile. Berkeley: University of California Press, 1994.

Valenzuela, Arturo. *The Breakdown of Democratic Regimes: Chile.* Baltimore: Johns Hopkins University Press, 1978.

Valenzuela, J. Samuel, and Arturo Valenzuela, eds. *Military Rule in Chile: Dictatorship and Oppositions.* Baltimore: Johns Hopkins University Press, 1986.

Winn, Peter. *Weavers of Revolution: The Yarur Workers and Chile's Road to Socialism.* Oxford: Oxford University Press, 1986.

Electronic Resources

Latin American Network Information Center (LANIC): Chile
http://lanic.utexas.edu/la/chile/
Chile section of this extensive Web site contains hundreds of links to research resources, cultural centers, economic and business institutions, government agencies, historical sources, magazines and other periodicals, nongovernmental organizations, and grassroots groups. (In English)

Latin Focus: Chile
http://www.latin-focus.com/countries/chile.htm
Contains an overview and description of Chile's government institutions and political environment, economic and financial information and statistics, and links to government ministries and agencies. (In English)

El Mercurio
http://www.emol.com/
Web version of Chile's premier national daily newspaper. Contains international and national coverage of political, economic, and cultural affairs. (In Spanish)

Political Database of the Americas: Chile
http://www.georgetown.edu/pdba/Countries/chile.html
Comprehensive database run as a joint project of Georgetown University and the Organization of American States. Section on Chile contains information on and links to the executive, legislative, and judicial branches of the Chilean government; electoral laws and election results; and other political data. (In English, Spanish, Portuguese, and French)

Political Resources.net: Chile
http://www.politicalresources.net/chile.htm
Contains a wealth of links to sources of information on national politics. Includes information on political parties, legislative and executive institutions, laws and legislation, and elections, as well as a link to the constitution. (In English)

Spotlight on Chile
http://www.localaccess.com/chappell/chile/
Educational Web site with research resources and links to additional sites covering cultural, political, and historical information. Government section contains a detailed description of the legislative, executive, and judicial branches of the Chilean government. (In English)

Wilfried Derksen's Elections Around the World: Chile
http://www.agora.it/elections/chile.htm
Chile section of a comprehensive database of results from elections around the world. Contains results from recent national executive and legislative elections, as well as explanations of and links to political parties and institutions. (In English)

COLOMBIA

COUNTRY PROFILE

Official name	República de Colombia
Capital	Santa Fé de Bogotá
Type/structure of government	Democratic republic
Executive	President elected to four-year non-renewable term.
Legislative	Bicameral legislature made up of a Senate (102 members elected in a single nationwide district) and an Assembly (161 members elected in multimember districts).
Judicial	Supreme Court, Constitutional Court, and Council of State.
Major political parties	**Colombian Conservative Party** (Partido Conservador Colombiano, PCC) **and Liberal Party** (Partido Liberal, PL).
Constitution in effect	1991 (with reforms in 1997)
Location/geography	Located in northern South America; has coastline on both the Caribbean Sea and the Pacific Ocean and shares borders with Panama, Ecuador, Peru, Brazil, and Venezuela; many mountainous and central highland regions; rain forest in the Amazonian and Orinocan River basins.
Geographic area	1.1 million sq. km.
Population	39,309,000 (July 1999)*
Ethnic groups	Mestizo 58%; white (of European descent) 20%; mulatto 14%; black (of African descent) 4%; mixed black/indigenous 3%; indigenous 1%*
Religions	Roman Catholic 95%; other 5%
Literacy rate	95% (1997 estimate)**
Infant mortality rate	24.3 deaths per 1,000 live births (1999)*
Life expectancy	70.48 years (1999 estimate)*
Monetary unit	Peso
Exchange rate	1 U.S. dollar = 2,185 pesos (August 2000)****
Major exports	Petroleum, coffee, coal, emeralds, cut flowers
Major imports	Parts, machinery, industrial and technological goods
GDP	$66.1 billion (1998)**
GDP growth rate	.2% (1998); −4.5 (1999); 3.0 (projected 2000)***
GDP per capita	$1,620 (1998)**

*CIA Factbook. http://www.odci.gov/cia/publications/factbook/co.html

**InterAmerican Development Bank. http://www.iadb.org/int/sta/ENGLISH/brptnet/english/colbrpt.htm

***Ministerio de Hacienda, República de Colombia. http://www.minhacienda.gov.co/

****Latin American Weekly Report, August 22, 2000 (WR-00-33), p. 394.

OVERVIEW

Summary

Colombia is unique in Latin America in terms of both its stability and its instability. It has one of the longest traditions of democracy in the region, and until recently had one of the best economic records, with over sixty consecutive years of positive economic growth since the 1930s. Colombia's remarkable level of violence belies this stable image, however. Beset by a variety of societal problems including insurgent movements, drug trafficking and corruption, and deep political cleavages that have divided the country since the middle of the nineteenth century, Colombia has one of the highest per capita homicide rates in the Western Hemisphere and in recent years has gained the reputation as one of the most violent countries in the world, with a murder rate ten times that of the United States. Over 26,000 murders occurred during 1997, and while the rate subsequently fluctuated, it remained extremely high. Efforts at resolving this combination of intertwined crises have been halting, and Colombia's historical reputation for stability has faded in recent years.

History

Pre-Columbian Colombia was populated by a variety of indigenous groups, including members of the Chibcha, Arawak, and Carib groupings. The Spanish first sighted the Guajira Peninsula in 1500, and shortly

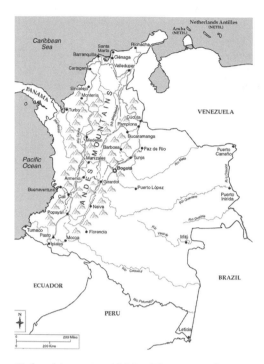

Colombia. © 1998 The Moschovitis
Group, Inc.

thereafter made their initial attempt at colonization near where present-day Colombia borders Panama. The first main city, Santa Marta, was founded on the Caribbean Coast in 1526, and Cartagena was founded in 1533. Santa Fé de Bogotá was founded in 1538 and selected as the capital of New Granada (a colonial administrative division that included contemporary Colombia). In 1539 the Spanish crown claimed control over the territory and turned it over to a series of governors. Gold was found on the slopes of one of three Andean mountain ranges, and many mines were opened and worked by forced labor extracted from the indigenous population and by slaves brought from Africa. The Spanish also dedicated themselves to farming and raising livestock. However, due to New Granada's difficult geographical terrain, the lack of infrastructure, and the wide variety of groups that populated it, the region was neither a center of economic dynamism, nor a unified entity at any point during the pre-independence period.

Calls for independence began to emerge as a result of a growing rivalry between creoles and *peninsulares* centered on discrimination in economic matters as well as over appointments to administrative positions. The opportunity to break away from Spain arose with its conquest by Napoleon in 1808, and a junta of creoles replaced the viceroy of Bogotá in July 1810, swearing their allegiance to the deposed Spanish king, Ferdinand VII. Similar juntas arose in many other cities, reflecting New Granada's disunity. A loose confederation arose under the name of the United Provinces of New Granada and independence was declared in 1813. None-

theless, six years of fighting ensued. Finally, in August 1819, an army of Venezuelans led by Simón Antonio de la Santísima Trinidad **Bolívar y Palacios** (1819–1830) defeated the Spanish army at the Battle of Boyacá. Modern Venezuela, Colombia, Ecuador, and Panama were united under Bolívar's leadership as Gran Colombia.

Though Bolívar was named the first president of the republic, he soon departed to continue liberating the continent from Spanish rule, leaving Vice President Francisco de Paula Santander executive power. Bolívar returned to Bogotá in 1826, and when Venezuela and Ecuador separated themselves from Gran Colombia shortly thereafter, Bolívar began to focus on Colombia. Santander and Bolívar had different visions for the nation. Bolívar favored a strong centralized government and close ties between the state and the Catholic Church, policies that would later be reflected in the platform of the Colombian Conservative Party. Santander favored a decentralized government, expanded suffrage, and state rather than church control of education, beliefs that would influence the development of the Liberal Party (See **Colombian Conservative Party** [Partido Colombiano Conservador, PCC] **and Liberal Party** [Partido Liberal, PL].) Bolívar exiled himself in 1830 due to his failing health and weakening power.

Political parties began to emerge in Colombia in the 1840s, as did political conflict; struggles over power and ideology between the PL and the PCC burst into episodic violence throughout Colombia's subsequent history. The War of the Supremes (1839–1841), the first in a long series of armed political struggles, was followed by many other clashes in the latter half of the 1800s centered on the church's level of involvement with the state. While the Constitution of 1863 championed Liberal values, causing uproar among Conservatives, a new constitution was promulgated in 1886 that did away with many Liberal policies, creating a highly centralized government and reinstating the close ties between the state and the Catholic Church. Colombia developed a significant export trade in coffee in the late 1880s, but by the mid-1890s the price of coffee in world markets crashed and the economy went into a severe recession. These economic difficulties, combined with the vehement repression of Liberals in the wake of their negative reaction to the Constitution of 1886, led to the outbreak of the **War of a Thousand Days** (1899–1902). The conflict, which quickly gained momentum and was powered by guerrilla forces, left 100,000 dead and carved the country's political divisions much deeper. Less than a year after the end of the conflict, the Colombian region of Panama declared its independence (see **independence from Colombia**, Panama), with the support of the United States.

The hegemony of the PCC continued into the twentieth century. In 1904 General Rafael **Reyes** (1904–1909) won the presidency in an election that was con-

In 1961, U.S. President John F. Kennedy and Colombian President Alberto Lleras Camargo (1958–1962) (right) inaugurate the first school to be built in Colombia under the Alliance for Progress program. *Columbus Memorial Library, General Secretariat of the Organization of American States. Reproduced with permission of the Organization of American States.*

sidered fraudulent by many. Though Reyes dismissed the Congress and took control of the government and all executive powers in 1905, he upheld many Conservative beliefs and policies. At the end of the 1920s, however, labor strikes in the countryside led to massive repression and arrests. Conservative dominance slipped, and the PL returned to power in 1930. While governing, the Liberals grew stronger and introduced labor and social reforms. However, the PL was deeply divided by the presidential election of 1946, in which the outspoken populist leader Jorge Eliécer **Gaitán** split the Liberal vote with another candidate, allowing Conservative Mariano Ospina Pérez (1946–1950) to win the presidency.

Violence broke out when power shifted back to the PCC, and organizations that previously had enjoyed the backing of the government were denied access to power. Rural areas became inflamed in violence first, initiating a period of civil unrest that would later be known as *La Violencia*. The assassination of the popular Gaitán in 1948 in Bogotá sparked days of streets riots known as the *Bogotazo*, and led to a dramatic escalation of the rural violence that endured for another ten years. Following various unsuccessful attempts by the administrations of Ospina Pérez and Laureano **Gómez** (1950–1953) to stop the violence, General Gustavo **Rojas Pinilla** (1953–1957) took control of the government in a bloodless coup in 1953. All but one faction of the PL and PCC supported the coup, trusting that the military would be better equipped to quell the violence and restore social order. Though for a brief period under Rojas Pinilla the violence declined significantly, the fragile

peace did not hold, and by the mid-1950s violence again began to escalate; 200,000 lives would be lost before the violence finally ended in the early 1960s.

In 1957, realizing that something had to be done to mend the country's extreme political divisions, the PCC and PL agreed upon a strategy known as the **National Front** (Frente Nacional), which was ratified in a constitutional plebiscite. Through that pact, Colombia's two traditional political parties agreed to alternate the presidency and established a 50–50 power-sharing arrangement throughout the executive, legislative, and judicial branches of government. The pact, which excluded the participation of all other political parties, was in force during the next sixteen years. It led to a dramatic transformation of the nation's political culture, easing tensions between Liberals and Conservatives and bringing about a major reduction in the partisan violence; however, it simultaneously sewed new discord between those who were included in the National Front and those who felt excluded. Insurgent movements with roots in the earlier violence as well as new ones inspired by the **Cuban Revolution of 1959** (see Cuba) took up arms in the 1960s. Most prominent among these were the communist **Revolutionary Armed Forces of Colombia** (Fuerzas Armadas Revolucionarias de Colombia, FARC), founded by former liberal and communist guerrillas, and the **Army of National Liberation** (Ejército de Liberación Nacional, ELN), founded by Colombian students in Havana.

The 1970s saw the emergence of a number of new guerrilla groups, including the urban-based **April 19th Movement** (Movimiento 19 de Abril, M-19), which held that democratic participation in Colombia was impossible and carried out spectacular "armed propaganda" actions in the name of the nation's poor and excluded. In the 1980s the government also began to face the challenges of the growing drug trade (see **Drugs**): by the end of the decade, Colombia had become the world's largest supplier of cocaine, and a major supplier of heroin. Drug cartels began to impact Colombian politics, injecting millions of dollars into the economy and encouraging a new brand of violence. Soon a third player, right-wing death squads or paramilitaries, emerged in the struggle (see **United Self-Defense Forces of Colombia** [Autodefensas Unidas de Colombia, AUC]). Though in some cases these were created by the state, they often seemed immune to government control.

Today guerrillas, paramilitaries, and the Colombian armed forces compete for control and influence throughout rural Colombia. Colombian democracy and political control are significantly undermined by the many insurgent factions and nonpolitical players who occupy the political arena. Attempts for peace in the 1990s, including promising negotiations between the government of President Andrés **Pastrana** (1998–) and the FARC, and government pledges to rein in the paramilitary forces, have been frustrated. In an effort to mitigate growing instability in Colombia and spillover into neighboring countries, in 1999 the United States began working with the Colombian government to create *Plan Colombia*, a four-year development program that focuses on the peace process and counternarcotics strategies. Despite support for an end to the violence in Colombia from the United States, the European Union, and other Latin American countries, Colombia has yet to find peace.

ENTRIES

April 19th Movement (Movimiento 19 de Abril, M-19)

The April 19th Movement (Movimiento 19 de Abril, M-19) formed in the early 1970s and was active from 1974 to 1990. Although this guerrilla group was an offshoot of the **National Popular Alliance** (Alianza Nacional Popular, ANAPO), that party denied any relations with the M-19. The M-19 took its name from the date of the 1970 presidential election, in which it believed its candidate, General Gustavo **Rojas Pinilla** (1953–1957), was fraudulently denied the presidency.

Led by urban professionals and focused on Colombia's urban areas, the M-19 followed the ideas of Jaime Bateman Cayon, who hoped to mold the movement into a political and military organization with a nationalist ideology similar to that espoused by Simón Antonio de la Santísima Trinidad **Bolívar y Palacios** (1819–1830) 150 years before. The group's goals were to crit-icize the means and methods of traditional politics, destroy the credibility of the government, and galvanize popular support. Its actions were typically dramatic. In 1979, for instance, the M-19 broke into a military base and stole 5,000 weapons, and in February 1980 the group took over the embassy of the Dominican Republic, holding fourteen ambassadors hostage. In November 1985, the M-19 attacked the Palace of Justice and took more than 400 hostages in an attempt to force President Belisario **Betancur Cuartas** (1982–1986) to reopen negotiations on an agenda that included demands for extensive structural reforms. Betancur refused to negotiate with the guerrillas, and the national army raided the palace, resulting in a brutal battle in which 106 people died, including eleven Supreme Court justices and an estimated thirty guerrillas.

In March 1990 the M-19 surrendered their arms and formed the M-19 Democratic Alliance (Alianza Democrática/M-19, AD/M-19), a political party. Though the group's leader, former guerrilla Carlo Pizarro Leongómez, was assassinated while campaigning in the 1990 presidential election, his replacement, former guerrilla Antonio Navarro Wolf, gained 12.5 percent of the votes, a remarkable achievement for a third party in Colombia. Later that year, the AD/M-19 received 30 percent of the vote in special elections for a constituent assembly. Despite these successes, the new party could not sustain its support at the polls. In the 1994 presidential election, the AD/M-19 candidate got only 2 percent of the vote, and the party achieved no representation in the legislature.

Army of National Liberation (Ejército de Liberación Nacional, ELN)

One of the most prominent guerrilla groups in Colombia, the Army of National Liberation (Ejército de Liberación Nacional, ELN) has made a significant impact on Colombian politics.

The ELN was created in the 1960s by a group of Colombian students who had visited Cuba and been inspired by Fidel **Castro Ruz** (see Cuba). The group carried out its goal (the "conquest of power for the popular classes") through direct guerrilla attacks on the Colombian government and on projects that benefited the government. The group captured national attention in January 1966 when Father Camilo Torres Restrepo, a prominent and outspoken leftist Catholic priest, was killed in an ELN battle only a few weeks after joining the movement. Though the group was severely damaged by a government attack in 1973, it reorganized and revitalized during the 1980s and staged several attacks on Colombian infrastructure. The ELN also targeted Colombian oil production centers; protection money from oil companies (along with ransom from kidnapping) forms a major portion of the group's income.

Since the early 1990s the ELN has been calling for reforms, including protection of human rights, social and economic justice, and a redefinition of the role of the military in the country. When the government began drafting a new constitution in 1991, the ELN and another guerrilla group, the **Revolutionary Armed Forces of Colombia** (Fuerzas Armadas Revolucionarias de Colombia, FARC), joined forces to launch a new attack on the government to protest their exclusion from the constitutional reform process.

The ELN's strategy mixes violence and kidnappings with negotiation with the government: in 1998 the group reached a preliminary accord with the government of Ernesto **Samper Pizano** (1994–1998) that called for a Constituent Assembly to be formed in order to discuss transformations of Colombian politics and society. Subsequent negotiations soon collapsed. Though the ELN was initially marginalized by the peace process forwarded by the government of Andrés **Pastrana** (1998–   ), in July 2000 negotiations with the guerrilla group were renewed. In April 2001, the government agreed to create a demilitarized zone (*zona de despeje*) for the ELN. However, government efforts to fulfill that commitment were frustrated by the continued presence of the **United Self-Defense Forces of Colombia** (Autodefensas Unidas de Colombia, AUC), a paramilitary force, in the area; the AUC violently opposes the creation of such a zone. As a consequence of the administration's inability to deliver on its promise, the ELN continues to question the government's strength and commitment to the peace process.

Barco Vargas, Virgilio (1921–1998)

The administration of Virgilio Barco Vargas (1986–1990) was riddled with problems due to the increase in violence (see *La Violencia*) by Colombian guerrilla groups and drug cartels (see **Drugs**) and the emergence of paramilitary groups.

Educated in the United States and in Colombia, Barco served in several different cabinet posts in the 1960s, and also served as the appointed mayor of Bogotá (1966–1969) and as ambassador to the United States. In his campaign for president as the Liberal Party (Partido Liberal, PL) candidate in 1986, Barco promised to use his technocratic background and style to break down the bipartisan blockages that were legacies of the **National Front** (Frente Nacional) political arrangement. Barco won the presidency in a landslide victory, and formed the first non-bipartisan government since 1958. The government was strongly opposed by Colombian Conservative Party leaders who were excluded from power. (See **Colombian Conservative Party** [Partido Conservador Colombiano, PCC] **and Liberal Party** [Partido Liberal, PL].)

Although the economy stayed stable throughout Barco's four years in office, this success was overshadowed by an upswing in guerrilla and drug-related violence. While Barco was willing to negotiate with the guerrillas, unlike his predecessor Belisario **Betancur**

Cuartas (1982–1986), he refused to discuss substantive reforms with insurgent groups. Under Barco, kidnappings by both drug cartels and guerrilla groups became commonplace, and right-wing death squads emerged in the countryside. While these paramilitary groups supposedly protected citizens, their presence resulted in an increase in murders. Barco's continued refusal to negotiate with any of these groups on anything more than unilateral cease-fires and guerrilla disarmament led to popular frustration.

Shortly before Barco left office, however, the **April 19th Movement** (Movimiento 19 de Abril, M-19) unexpectedly accepted his severe negotiating rules, turned in its weapons, and created a legitimate political party, the M-19 Democratic Alliance (Alianza Democrática/ M-19, AD/M-19). This, along with administrative reforms that streamlined Colombian bureaucracy, are Barco's legacy. After leaving office, he served as ambassador to Great Britain and later returned to private life in Bogotá.

Bateman Cayon, Jaime. See April 19th Movement (Movimiento 19 de Abril, M-19)

Betancur Cuartas, Belisario (1923–   )

Belisario Betancur Cuartas (1982–1986) is noted for beginning open dialogue with guerrilla groups, and for the increase in guerrilla and drug-related violence (see **Drugs**) that occurred during his administration.

A progressive publisher who rose from a lower-middle-class background, Betancur served as minister of labor in 1963, then ran unsuccessfully for president in 1970 and 1978 on the ticket of the Colombian Conservative Party (see **Colombian Conservative Party** [Partido Conservador Colombiano, PCC] **and Liberal Party** [Partido Liberal PL]). To support his 1982 presidential bid, Betancur created an alliance between PCC liberals who had distanced themselves from the party, and the **National Popular Alliance** (Alianza Nacional Popular, ANAPO). Thanks to that alliance and the increasing violence the country had begun to experience during the presidency of liberal Julio César **Turbay Ayala** (1978–1982), Betancur won the presidency. To combat the increase in guerrilla violence, President Betancur strove to include the guerrillas in mainstream politics, engaging each of the different groups in highly publicized peace talks and negotiations. In 1984 he signed the La Uribe agreement that created a bilateral cease-fire between the **Revolutionary Armed Forces of Colombia** (Fuerzas Armadas Revolucionarias de Colombia, FARC) and the Colombian military and set an agenda for negotiations on political and social reforms. Similar cease-fire agreements were soon signed with four other guerrilla movements, including the Maoist Popular Liberation Army (Ejército Popular de Liberación, EPL) and the **April 19th Movement** (Movimiento 19 de Abril, M-19).

However, guerrilla leaders soon became dissatisfied

with Betancur's unwillingness or inability to implement the reforms they most wanted, such as land reform and economic change. Tensions climaxed in 1985 when members of the M-19 occupied the Palace of Justice, taking more than 400 people hostage; Betancur refused to negotiate and permitted the Colombian army to counterattack the palace, resulting in the death of over a hundred people. The remainder of Betancur's administration was tainted by this highly controversial action. Betancur's main accomplishments include the initiation of a peace process that endured in different manifestations long after his presidency, his active role in the **Contadora Process** (see Appendix 1) to bring peace to Central America, and the implementation of massive literacy programs and the introduction of the popular election of mayors in Colombia.

Bogotazo (1948). See **Gaitán, Jorge Eliécer**

Bolívar y Palacios, Simón Antonio de la Santísima Trinidad (1783–1830)

A native of Venezuela, Simón Antonio de la Santísima Trinidad Bolívar y Palacios (1819–1830) is regarded as the liberator of most of the countries of the Andean region of South America.

By the time Bolívar had reached his mid-twenties, he was already involved in South America's first movements toward independence from Spain. Bolívar supported a junta led by the more radical Francisco Miranda that declared itself the true government of Venezuela in 1810, leading Miranda's army in battles against royalist and Spanish forces. Though a declaration of independence was issued in 1811, in 1812 the royalists recaptured the government, and Bolívar fled to New Granada (current-day Colombia). There he penned the Cartagena Manifesto, in which he called upon citizens of New Granada to support an independent Venezuela. In August 1813 Bolívar and 600 supporters marched on the Venezuelan capital of Caracas, defeated the royalists, and declared it liberated from Spain. However, this victory was short-lived: a group of mountain herdsmen from the inland regions of Venezuela soon swept Bolívar out of Caracas, forcing him to flee in defeat.

By the end of 1814, Bolívar was forced back into exile in New Granada. He soon traveled to Jamaica, where he composed the most famous of his political writings, the Jamaica Letter (*Carta de Jamaica*), a call for unity in support of the cause of independence in Latin America that argued that Latin America was under threat, and therefore should choose a more centralized form of government over (what he considered to be a weaker) representative democracy. While in 1815 a Spanish army of 10,000 landed in Venezuela and swept through New Granada, reasserting Spanish authority in a brutal campaign, at the end of 1816 Bolívar reinitiated the fight for independence, returning to Venezuela and teaming up with José Antonio Páez. In 1819 Venezuelan independence was declared. Bolívar called for elections and was soon ratified as the leader of the country, though the Spanish had not yet been expelled. Bolívar left the governance of Venezuela in the hands of Páez, led an army to New Granada, won the decisive Battle of Boyacá in August 1819, occupied Bogotá, and declared independence for New Granada that same month. Bolívar soon departed, leaving native Francisco de Paula Santander in charge of the newly independent region. The viceroyalty of Quito (present-day Ecuador) was liberated in 1822, and later that year Bolívar proclaimed Venezuela, New Granada, and Quito to be Gran Colombia (Republic of Greater Colombia). Reluctantly, Bolívar agreed to serve as the republic's first president, with Santander as the vice president. However, Bolívar soon left his presidential post and continued his mission to liberate the rest of the continent, giving Santander executive power.

In 1823 and 1824 Bolívar fought in and freed Peru and Upper Peru (the area that is today Bolivia). Both new nations adopted constitutions that were similar to Bolívar's original ideas of an elite centralized republic operating under rules of strict morality, documents that are the origin of much conservative political thought in Colombia (see **Colombian Conservative Party** [Partido Conservador Colombiano, PCC] **and Liberal Party** [Partido Liberal, PL] and throughout Latin America. Bolívar called for a congress of all Spanish American nations in 1826, hoping to gather momentum for the formation of a unified Latin America that would bring the region to maturity and convert it into a powerful player on the international stage. However, Bolívar's hoped-for Pan-American alliance did not come to fruition, as Spanish America was geographically divided, suffering economically from the decade of warfare with Spain, and fraught with personal rivalries and regionalism. Its leaders, only four of whom attended the congress, were not interested in forfeiting authority over their personal fiefdoms. As Bolívar's power and popularity began to dwindle, Gran Colombia began to disintegrate. With the end of the war for independence and the disappearance of a common external enemy, factionalization had increased, and ultimately the geographic distances and the economic and social differences among the included countries were too great for the union to last. Bolívar retook control of Gran Colombia in 1826, retracting many of the republic's progressive policies. Soon after, Páez led a successful rebellion in Venezuela. Guayaquil and Quito revolted in 1827, and other rebellions occurred in parts of Colombia shortly thereafter. In 1830 both Ecuador and Venezuela withdrew from the union. Distraught, ailing, and weak, Bolívar stepped down in 1830, and the republic collapsed that same year. He attempted to flee, but died, discredited for his dictatorial actions, before he was able to board a boat. Nonetheless, Bolívar is still considered a hero and is revered throughout Latin America, and many politicians and political groups throughout the region trace their heritage to him.

Cali Cartel

Based in the city of Cali, the Cali Cartel, once one of the most important drug trafficking cartels in Colombia, became involved in drug transshipment in the mid-1970s, and dominated the drug trade throughout the 1980s. Unlike its main competitor, the **Medellín Cartel**, the Cali Cartel limited its acts of violence and concentrated on increasing its business and profits throughout the world. When the Medellín Cartel came under serious scrutiny from Colombian and U.S. authorities beginning in 1982, the Cali Cartel gained in strength and market share. Further, the death of Medellín Cartel leader Pablo **Escobar** in 1993 allowed the Cali Cartel to take over the Medellín Cartel's market share and become an even more powerful group in the international arena; the cartel was once considered by some one of the most sophisticated business networks in Latin America. In the late 1990s, with the aid of the U.S. government, Colombian authorities cracked down on the Cali Cartel. By 2000 the large Colombian cartels had been replaced by scores of smaller cartels known as *cartelitos* ("little cartels") and much of their international trafficking had been taken over by powerful Mexican cartels. (See also **Drugs**.)

Colombian Conservative Party (Partido Conservador Colombiano, PCC) and Liberal Party (Partido Liberal, PL)

The Colombian Conservative Party (Partido Conservador Colombiano, PCC), founded in 1849, and the Liberal Party (Partido Liberal, PL), formed in the 1840s, are two of the oldest parties in Latin America. They have dominated Colombian politics, alternating power, since their inception; the PCC is a key force in contemporary politics, and the PL remains the largest political party with the most elected officeholders in contemporary Colombia.

Original PCC doctrine called for a strong relationship between the government and the Catholic Church and for the centralization of power, and the PCC has traditionally enjoyed more support in rural areas. The PL has historically supported the decentralization of political power and the separation of church and state; its traditional power base has been the urban areas of Colombia due in part to its encouragement of industrialization and support of labor. The PL alternated the presidency with the PCC for most of the nineteenth century, though the PCC dominated politics from 1886 to 1930 in a period of "conservative hegemony." Disputes between the PL and the PCC simmered throughout the century, generating outbursts such as the War of the Supremes (1839–1841) and the **War of a Thousand Days** (1899–1902).

Though strong popular identification with the mul-

ticlass PCC persisted through the twentieth century, and while the party continued to organize, mobilize, and represent large sectors of society throughout the country, the PL was the stronger party for most of the 1900s. While the ideological differences between Liberals and Conservatives faded in the twentieth century, party identity in Colombia remained strong through the 1960s, and the divisions and rivalry between the PCC and the PL continued to cause violence and civil strife. In an attempt to quell *La Violencia* of the 1940s and 1950s, the PL and the PCC negotiated the **National Front** (Frente Nacional) pact in 1957, a power-sharing agreement that guaranteed each party an equal role in government and excluded other parties. Many PL supporters and organizers were marginalized by the party's focus on power-sharing, which led to clientelism and corruption. Attempts to reform the PL led by Luis Carlos **Galán** collapsed with his assassination in 1989.

By the 1990s, both the PL and the PCC were splintering, creating a chaotic atmosphere during elections. The new electoral system that emerged from the 1991 constitutional reform encouraged politicians to create their own organizations for mobilizing support, rather than remaining beholden to national parties. The resultant fracturing of the party system weakened the traditional parties' power base and challenged their dominance. The PL was further discredited during the administration of Ernesto **Samper Pizano** (1994–1998) when revelations emerged that his campaign had received funds from the **Cali Cartel**. While the PCC won the subsequent presidential election, third-party candidate Noemí Sanín gained 27 percent of the vote and nearly qualified for the second round, further demonstrating the weakening of traditional parties. Nonetheless, both PL and PCC candidates will vie for votes in the 2002 presidential election.

Drugs (Illegal Narcotics)

Colombia is involved in the production and refinement of drugs, and the export of drugs to the United States and Europe and increasingly to other areas of the world. A significant quantity of marijuana is grown in the country, heroin production increased in the 1990s, and an estimated 90 percent of the world's cocaine supply is Colombian in origin. The trade of illegal narcotics affects Colombia in many ways, contributing to a national climate of violence and lawlessness and complicating the country's relations with the United States.

The entry of Colombia as a major player in the international drug market began in the late 1970s when U.S. pressure on Mexico to crack down on marijuana production led to a shift of production to Colombia. Marijuana smuggling soon led to the development of cocaine smuggling as a side business. Until the 1980s production of the coca crop took place mainly in Bolivia and Peru, while refinement and transshipment, the stages with higher profits, took place in Colombia. Through the 1980s, the Latin American debt crisis and the resultant rise of the informal economy led to a boom in the production of both coca and cocaine. Coca production shifted to Colombia during the 1990s following crackdowns by a series of Bolivian governments and by Peruvian President Alberto **Fujimori Fujimori** (see Peru).

Beginning in the early 1980s, drug producers and smugglers began to band together into cartels in order to reduce costs and combat threats from guerrillas and the Colombian government, supported by the U.S. Drug Enforcement Agency (DEA). The most powerful of these were the **Cali Cartel** and the **Medellín Cartel**, which dominated the drug trade throughout the 1980s. These groups, particularly the Medellín Cartel, responded to government actions against them by murdering officials. They reacted to guerrilla threats by forming or hiring paramilitary groups to attack guerrillas and to defend cartel leaders and their sources of income. The resultant massive escalation of violence throughout the 1980s and 1990s, in combination with the giant profits from the illegal trade of drugs, soon began to pose a threat to the stability of the Colombian state, corrupting politics, the judiciary, and much of the economy.

The Colombian government responded with several different tactics. In 1978 the administration of Julio César **Turbay Ayala** (1978–1982) and the United States signed a far-reaching extradition treaty that allowed Colombians to be extradited, prosecuted, and incarcerated in the United States (where prosecution was more severe). This led to increased violence by the cartels, which prompted increased pressure by the Colombian government, resulting in a marked and unprecedented increase in urban terrorism and high-level assassinations. Extradition was reversed under President César **Gaviria Trujillo** (1990–1994) in 1991, and a new law was promulgated that allowed drug bosses to confess to lesser crimes and serve short jail terms (in luxurious conditions). This led to the collapse of some cartels. Though allegations emerged in 1994 that President Ernesto **Samper Pizano** (1994–1998) had accepted $6 million in campaign funds from the Cali Cartel, his administration was quite successful at cracking down on the production and refinement of cocaine in Colombia. At the beginning of his administration, President Andrés **Pastrana** (1998–   ) focused on achieving peace with the guerrilla groups that dominate much of the Colombian countryside; some believed that the change in focus led to an increase in drug production. In 2000 the United States Congress approved a $1.3 billion aid package, *Plan Colombia*. The principal aim of the program was to help Colombia crack down on the production of coca and cocaine.

Colombia's drug crisis complicates and exacerbates all of the economic, political, and social challenges the country faces. The drug trade has challenged the legitimacy of the state, increased financial support to perpetrators of violence on all sides of the conflict sweeping Colombia, and complicated Colombia's relations with its neighbors and the United States. Despite a variety of attempts to reduce the power of this illegal enterprise, it remains an important element in Colombia's social crisis.

Escobar, Pablo (1949–1993)

Pablo Escobar grew up in Medellín, and became involved in large-scale cocaine trafficking in the 1970s. He soon became one of the leaders of the **Medellín Cartel**, one of Colombia's main cocaine cartels, gaining fortune and fame. He was elected as an alternative representative to Congress in 1982, providing him with immunity from prosecution, but resigned in 1983 when Justice Minister Rodrigo Lara Bonilla began investigating him and the Medellín Cartel. (The Medellín Cartel assassinated Lara Bonilla in 1984.) In 1991 Escobar entered into negotiations with the government of César **Gaviria Trujillo** (1990–1994), and soon surrendered to Colombian authorities with promises of a reduced sentence and new constitutional guarantees against his extradition. He was incarcerated right outside of Medellín in his hometown of Envigado; his "jail cell" was thousands of square feet, and was furnished with a waterbed, hot tub, fax machines, and computers. With access to his colleagues, Escobar continued running the cartel from prison. Escobar escaped in July 1992, prompting Colombian authorities and the U.S. Drug Enforcement Administration (DEA) to initiate what would become a year and a half long manhunt. In December 1993, Colombian authorities determined Escobar's whereabouts through a cellular phone call he placed, and went to arrest him. Escobar and his bodyguard were both killed in the subsequent shoot-out. The Colombian government received international praise for its determination to combat narcotrafficking and the violence associated with it.

Gaitán, Jorge Eliécer (1898–1948)

The 1948 assassination of Jorge Eliécer Gaitán, an energetic Liberal, sparked nationwide political protests and violence, known as the *Bogotazo*, which served as both a symbol and an accelerator of the conflict that swept through Colombia during the period, known as *La Violencia*.

Always bright and outspoken, Gaitán studied law in Colombia and Italy. He returned to Colombia in 1928 and toured the country speaking out against injustices. He was soon elected to Congress, and in 1931 was elected president of the legislature. However, Gaitán's Liberal Party (see **Colombian Conservative Party** [Partido Conservador Colombiano, PCC] **and Liberal Party** [Partido Liberal, PL]) colleagues grew frustrated by his deviation from main party lines and platforms, and Gaitán grew frustrated by the confines of the party. In 1933 he formed his own party, the National Revolutionary Union (Unión Nacional Revolucionaria, UNR), which was entirely devoted to popular causes such as land reform and labor laws. It failed to gain much momentum, and Gaitán returned to the PL in 1935. He was reelected to the legislature, appointed mayor of Bogotá in 1936, and held several cabinet posts in different Liberal administrations in the early 1940s.

Gaitán ran for president in 1946, but as he had to split party support with another PL candidate, a Conservative was elected. Gaitán was slated to be the single Liberal candidate running in the 1950 presidential election, and due to his popularity, was considered the favorite. However, he was assassinated on April 9, 1948, by Juan Roa Sierra, a drifter with no association with politics. In the wake of the murder, the city of Bogotá erupted in violence, looting, and rioting, an event that would subsequently be known as the *Bogotazo*; the violence soon spread to other cities and continued for days. Surrounded by many conspiracy theories (many believed Gaitán's murder was a plot of the PCC), Gaitán's death raised questions about Colombia's potential for change and peace that still resonate today.

Galán, Luis Carlos (1943–1989)

The assassination at the peak of his career of Luis Carlos Galán, a leader in the Liberal Party (see **Colombian Conservative Party** [Partido Conservador Colombiano, PCC] **and Liberal Party** [Partido Liberal, PL]) reflected the turbulent politics of the time.

Galán began his political career as a young teen, protesting against the presidency of General Gustavo **Rojas Pinilla** (1953–1957). He wrote as a journalist with the popular newspaper *El Tiempo* and then at age twenty-seven was named minister of education by President Misael Pastrana (1970–1974). In 1972 he was named ambassador to Rome, and in 1974 was appointed the representative to the Food and Agriculture Organization of the United Nations. He returned to Colombia in 1976 and joined former president Carlos Lleras Restrepo (1966–1970) at his political magazine, *Nueva Frontera*, which Lleras Restrepo used to promote his political beliefs and to criticize political leaders and their policies. Galán was elected to the Senate in 1978.

In 1979 Galán and several other PL leaders broke with the party and founded the New Liberalism movement, which sought to make politicians and the government more accountable to the Colombian population. Galán thought the government should be more actively involved in the evolution of Colombia's cities, the integration of the entire national territory, and the growth and guidance of the Colombian economy. He also wanted to make the Congress more transparent through such acts as regulating and publicizing each candidate's financial resources and reducing corruption and clientelism. His ideas and polished style brought his move-

ment a significant following, and by 1982 New Liberalism had six senators and nine assemblymen.

In the late 1980s Galán turned his attention and energy to fighting narcotrafficking in Colombia (see **Drugs**), thereby putting his life in danger, as during that period drug cartels were focusing on eliminating anyone who threatened their power. Galán was nominated to be the PL candidate in the 1990 presidential elections, and was considered the front-runner. However, in what many consider a tragedy in Colombian politics, Galán was assassinated by the **Medellín Cartel** in August 1989 in the middle of a massive campaign rally. Many consider the 1991 Constitution promulgated under President César **Gaviria Trujillo** (1990–1994) Galán's legacy, since calls for it emerged in the aftermath of his death.

García Márquez, Gabriel (1928–)

Awarded the Nobel Prize for literature in 1982, Gabriel García Márquez is one of the most profound and respected writers in Latin American history. His works, which combine fantasy and reality, are some of the seminal pieces in the genre of magical realism.

García Márquez was born in 1928 in Aracataca, Colombia. Though he enrolled in law school, after two years he took a position at the newspaper *El Universal*, and then moved to another paper, *El Espectador*. In the second half of the 1950s, García Márquez, still a journalist, began to focus on writing novels and became involved in politics. He was sent to cover the **Cuban Revolution of 1959** (see Cuba), and in Cuba he developed what would become a lasting relationship with Fidel **Castro Ruz** (see Cuba). Though García Márquez briefly directed Castro's newly developed news agency, *Prensa Latina*, from New York, pressure from the U.S. government and the **Cuban exile community** (see Cuba) (both of which were overtly concerned by García Márquez's leftist leanings), splits with the Cuban government over the content and direction of the magazine, and García Márquez's growing frustration with the lack of success of his fictional writing soon prompted him to move his family to Mexico City and devote himself to his own writing. Finally, in 1967, his novel *One Hundred Years of Solitude* was an overnight success, winning numerous awards.

With his newfound acclaim, García Márquez became more involved in politics throughout Latin America. He supported leftist leaders like Castro and Omar **Torrijos Herrera** (see Panama), and championed causes such as freeing political prisoners. These leanings brought him under close scrutiny by the United States and Colombia. The Colombian government even accused him of financing the **April 19th Movement** (Movimiento 19 de Abril, M-19), and President Belisario **Betancur Cuartas** (1982–1986) involved him as a mediator in negotiations with the group. The publication of *Love in the Time of Cholera* in 1986 brought the author interna-

César Gaviria Trujillo, President of Colombia (1990–1994) and Secretary General of the Organization of American States (1994–   ). *Columbus Memorial Library, General Secretariat of the Organization of American States. Reproduced with permission of the Organization of American States.*

tional accolades once again. In a departure from his traditional genre (fiction), in 1997 he published the nonfiction work *News of the Kidnapping*, which documented the horrible realities of Colombia's political struggles with narcotrafficking (see **Drugs**) and guerrilla groups. These and other works secured García Márquez's place in Latin American literary history.

Though García Márquez was also an important symbol and leader of the left in Colombian politics, in 1994 he organized a group of intellectuals that publicly distanced themselves from the guerrillas and their indiscriminate violence.

Gaviria Trujillo, César (1947–   )

César Gaviria Trujillo led Colombia from 1990 to 1994, a politically tumultuous period. Gaviria's hard policies on drug trafficking (see **Drugs**) and guerrilla movements brought him global recognition.

Gaviria began his political career at an early age, serving as the appointed mayor of his hometown, Pereira, in 1974. He served as vice minister of development under President Julio César **Turbay Ayala** (1978–1982), and became increasingly involved with the leadership of the Liberal Party (see **Colombian Conservative Party** [Partido Conservador Colombiano, PCC] **and Liberal Party,** [Partido Liberal, PL]). He was appointed minister of the treasury and later minister of transpor-

tation by President Virgilio **Barco Vargas** (1986–1990), and was asked by the PL leadership to head the 1990 presidential campaign of PL candidate Luis Carlos **Galán**. When Galán was assassinated by the **Medellín Cartel** in August 1989, Gaviria was chosen to replace him as the PL candidate, and was elected with 47 percent of the vote. Gaviria faced a nation riddled with problems: guerrilla groups were rising up against the government, drug cartels were carrying out highly publicized acts of violence, and the country had begun to receive international criticism for its inability to control its domestic problems, especially the production of illegal narcotics, which an increasing number of countries were importing.

In 1991 Gaviria led the country through a constitutional reform process mandated by a plebiscite on constitutional reform held concurrently with the 1990 elections. That process was seen as an instrument for peace, particularly with the **April 19th Movement** (Movimiento 19 de Abril, M-19), which participated heavily in the process. However, the large-scale military offensives the government simultaneously carried out against the **Revolutionary Armed Forces of Colombia** (Fuerzas Armadas Revolucionarias de Colombia, FARC) and the **Army of National Liberation** (Ejército Nacional de Liberación, ELN) sparked major attacks by the FARC and ELN against state forces. The increased violence led to another round of negotiations with these guerrilla groups, but those negotiations collapsed, leading to a reescalation of the armed conflict that tainted the social renewal aspect of the constitutional reform process. Nevertheless, the new constitution, which opened the political system to the participation of new political parties and groupings, was an important step for dissident and guerrilla groups.

Gaviria also worked to boost Colombia's foreign trade and to improve foreign relations. The president received international praise in 1991 when his government negotiated the surrender of Medellín Cartel leader Pablo **Escobar**. Though crisis soon followed when Escobar escaped in July 1992, Gaviria's government redeemed itself when it killed Escobar in December 1993. To many abroad, this demonstrated Gaviria's commitment to fighting drugs as well as his leadership ability.

Upon completing his presidential term, Gaviria was elected secretary general of the **Organization of American States** (OAS; see Appendix 2), and was reelected to another five-year term as secretary general in 1999.

Gómez, Laureano (1889–1965)

Laureano Gómez, a strong leader of the Colombian Conservative Party (see **Colombian Conservative Party** [Partido Conservador Colombiano, PCC] **and Liberal Party** [Partido Liberal, PL]), served as president from 1950 to 1953, one of the bloodiest periods of the nation's history. During those years, Liberals and Conservatives indiscriminately killed each other, with members of one party often cleansing entire towns of the other party.

Gómez was involved in politics from an early age, leading fellow students to protest the dictatorship of Rafael **Reyes** (1904–1909). He was elected to the legislature in 1911, climbed the ranks of the PCC, and soon became an outspoken leader. When the party lost control of the presidency in 1930, Gómez, who believed that Conservatives had become apathetic during the party's long stretch of dominance since 1886, saw the defeat as an opportunity for the party to revitalize and reinvent itself. He and others used the break to guide the party back to its conservative roots, realigning it with the Catholic Church and promoting strong state control.

In 1949 Gómez was elected president on the PCC ticket; the PL abstained from participating in the election in the tumultuous period following the assassination of Liberal leader Jorge Eliécer **Gaitán** and the dramatic escalation of *La Violencia*. However, just as Gómez settled into office and his plans to create a corporatist-style state with a strong executive gained momentum, his health began to falter. In 1951 he suffered a stroke and had to cede power to Vice President Roberto Urdaneta Arbeláez while he recovered. In 1953 Gómez was overthrown by General Gustavo **Rojas Pinilla** (1953–1957), who forced Gómez into exile. In 1957 Gómez represented the PCC in negotiations with the PL that led to the **National Front** (Frente Nacional), a pact to stop *La Violencia*.

Liberal Party (Partido Liberal, PL). See Colombian Conservative Party (Partido Conservador Colombiano, PCC) and Liberal Party (Partido Liberal, PL)

López Pumarejo, Alfonso (1886–1956)
Regarded as one of the most influential Colombian presidents of the twentieth century, Alfonso López Pumarejo spearheaded initiatives that modernized and liberalized Colombian social and economic policy during his two presidential terms (1934–1938, 1942–1945).

Born into a wealthy family, López was a successful banker until 1924, when he decided to dedicate himself to politics. In 1925 he was elected to Congress, and in 1929 he gained national attention at the Liberal Party (see **Colombian Conservative Party [Partido Conservador Colombiano, PCC] and Liberal Party [Partido Liberal, PL]**) convention, where he enthusiastically shared his vision for the future of the party. President Enrique Olaya Herrera (1930–1934) appointed López ambassador to the United States, and shortly thereafter López became the president of the PL. He rejuvenated and energized the party, and in 1933 was nominated by the PL to run as its candidate in the 1934 presidential election, which he won.

Once in office, López passed several packages of legislation that addressed Colombia's economic problems, labor issues, and social welfare. Colombia was still recovering from the effects of the Great Depression, and López and his colleagues worked to ensure that the country would be protected from economic downturn. In an effort to incorporate labor and the poor into the PL and to stem rising social unrest, he supported labor in disputes, incorporated the working class into politics, carried out moderate agrarian reform, and addressed problems of poverty and inequality. The constitutional reform that López guided enshrined liberal principles such as the removal of the church from public education and the introduction of universal male suffrage.

Though López was reelected in 1942, by that time the PL was suffering from internal divisions, while the PCC had revitalized. His attempts to continue his reforms were hamstrung by wartime economic problems (including shortages, reduced exports, and reduced government earnings due to declines in tariff collections) and blocked by PCC opposition. Though a military coup against the president in 1944 was unsuccessful, he was forced to resign in 1945. However, he remained active in politics after his resignation, serving as the Colombian delegate to the newly founded United Nations in 1947 and later as ambassador to Great Britain.

Medellín Cartel
Based in Medellín and formerly run by Pablo **Escobar** and Fabio and Jorge Ochoa, this alliance of drug traffickers (see **Drugs**), which formed in the 1970s, is credited with revolutionizing the drug trade by pioneering the delivery of large shipments to the United States and then to Europe. This innovation allowed the group to expand exponentially, and by the mid-1980s the leaders of the Medellín Cartel were billionaires and the cartel was responsible for up to two-thirds of all of the cocaine flowing out of the country. The cartel effectively dominated the Colombian drug trade through the 1980s.

The Medellín Cartel was committed to influencing Colombian politics. Following the signing of an extradition treaty between the United States and Colombia in 1978, the cartel initiated a campaign of violence and terrorist attacks against the government with the goals of blocking investigation of the cartel and overturning the extradition treaty. In 1984 the cartel assassinated Justice Minister Rodrigo Lara Bonilla (who had been investigating Escobar), and in 1988 the cartel kidnapped and later killed Attorney General Carlos Mauro Hoyas. Through the 1980s, the cartel also targeted and murdered thousands of leaders and members of the Patriotic Union (Unión Patriótica, UP) political party (see **Revolutionary Armed Forces of Colombia [Fuerzas Armadas Revolucionarias de Colombia, FARC]**). Prior to the 1990 presidential election, four candidates were killed by the narco-traffickers including popular politician and presidential favorite Luís Carlos **Galán**; his murder occasioned a reescalation of the war between the government and the cartel at the end of the term of President Virgilio **Barco Vargas** (1986–1990).

The 1990 peace proposal between the cartel and the government of César **Gaviria Trujillo** (1990–1994), brokered by Jorge Ochoa, led to the surrender of Escobar and other leaders. The 1978 extradition treaty had been found unconstitutional in 1986, and the promise of nonextradition was formalized in the 1991 constitution (though the provision was reformed under U.S. pressure in 1997). Following Escobar's murder by the Colombian government in December 1993 and the removal of other leaders, and given the shift of the drug trade from Colombia to Mexico, the cartel lost a substantial amount of power through the 1990s. (See also **Cali Cartel**.)

Mosquera, Tomás C. de (1798–1878)

Tomás C. de Mosquera served as president of Colombia on four different occasions (1845–1849, 1861–1862, 1863–1864, 1866–1867). A member of neither of the country's main political parties (see **Colombian Conservative Party** [Partido Conservador Colombiano, PCC] **and Liberal Party** [Partido Liberal, PL]), the moderate Mosquera supported both parties during various internal conflicts.

Mosquera's career began in the republican army of Simón Antonio de la Santísima Trinidad **Bolívar y Palacios** (1819–1830) in 1814. He rose quickly through the military ranks, became a general in 1829, and subsequently served in various diplomatic posts. In 1840 he became secretary of war under PCC president José Ignacio de Márquez (1837–1841), and led the victorious army in the War of the Supremes (1839–1841).

During his first presidential term, Mosquera guided the beginning of Colombia's economic and political transformation, which included the opening of the nation's economy to trade (led by a booming tobacco industry) and the initiation of liberal reforms (such as the subordination of the church to the laws of the state). Mosquera lived in the United States for several years after his first term, but returned to Colombia to join the ultimately successful fight against the military government of José María Melo (1854). Mosquera served in the Assembly and then the Senate from 1855 to 1857, and as president of the Congress, participated in the writing of a new federalist constitution. When conflict between Liberals and Conservatives over the implementation of the new Constitution led to war, Mosquera led the Liberal secession of several states from the union. Mosquera served as president of the separatist faction (1861–1862), leading the eventually victorious Liberals in their struggle for control of Colombia, and then served as the nation's provisional president (1863–1864), finally implementing the new constitution.

Mosquera became president for the fourth time in 1866. He focused his efforts on stamping out corruption in the government, and was forced to close Congress in order to overcome opposition to his investigation. He was overthrown in 1867, judged by the Senate, and sentenced to three years of exile. He returned to the Senate in 1876 and served until shortly before his death two years later.

National Front (Frente Nacional)

By 1956 almost 200,000 Colombians had died as a result of *La Violencia*. Although during his presidency General Gustavo **Rojas Pinilla** (1953–1957) had begun to quell the violence through a strong military presence, it was obvious that the bitter rivalry between the nation's two main political parties (see **Colombian Conservative Party** [Partido Conservativo Colombiano, PCC] **and Liberal Party** [Partido Liberal, PL]) would continue to cause turmoil. In an effort to halt the unrest, the PL and the PCC compromised: through discussions led by PL leader Alberto Lleras Camargo (1958–1962) and PCC leader Laureano **Gómez** (1950–1953), an agreement was formulated (and approved in a plebiscite in 1957) that instated a sixteen-year period of collaborative power-sharing to restore oligarchical hegemony, end traditional political divisions and quash internal hostilities, reunify the republic, modernize the economy, and consolidate the attitudes and practices requisite to constructive partisan competition.

Specifically, the National Front agreement called for the presidency to alternate between the PL and PCC for the subsequent sixteen years, mandated that the PL and the PCC would have equal representation in the presidential cabinet, the Congress, and the judicial system, and instructed that a two-thirds majority would be necessary to pass any legislation through the Assembly. The agreement also allowed the parties to remove Rojas Pinilla. The first sixteen years of the pact saw Colombia prosper economically in a climate of relative political peace. Pleased with the results of the power-sharing arrangement, Colombia's leaders continued to carry out the edicts enshrined in the pact for several administrations after 1974. The administration of Virgilio **Barco Vargas** (1986–1990) was the first to break with the pact; Barco avoided forming a bipartisan government with equal representation of both parties by reinterpreting the wording of the pact to suggest that each party be represented based on the vote share that it received.

In sum, the National Front pact brought an end to the violence of the 1950s and created an environment for economic growth; the Colombian economy was the most stable in the region from the late 1950s to the mid-1990s. However, the National Front's climate of consensus also led to accusations of collusion between the PL and the PCC and to popular disillusionment with the country's two traditional parties, as evidenced by the high abstention rates in recent presidential elections.

The pact also denied important actors access to power, which led to polarization and caused other players to turn to nondemocratic means of gaining power; the pact is blamed by many members of the political and academic communities for contributing to the violence that afflicts Colombia today.

National Popular Alliance (Alianza Nacional Popular, ANAPO)

A marginal political party in Colombia in the late twentieth century, the National Popular Alliance (Alianza Nacional Popular ANAPO) was originally formed by General Gustavo **Rojas Pinilla** (1953–1957) after his 1957 overthrow to embody his political platform, aid him in gathering momentum and supporters in a more legitimate format, and facilitate his reentry into mainstream politics. A reflection of Rojas Pinilla's inchoate political beliefs, ANAPO's political platform was unclear and consciously modeled after the Peronist movement (see **Justicialist Party** [Partido Justicialista, PJ], Argentina). The party sought the support of lower-class urban sectors, the same group to which Jorge Eliécer **Gaitán** had made his successful appeal in the late 1940s. The party soon gained the backing of those disillusioned with Colombia's two traditional parties, and won one-fifth of the congressional seats in 1966. Rojas Pinilla ran for the presidency on the ANAPO ticket in 1970 and was narrowly defeated, many claim through fraud (see **April 19th Movement** [Movimiento 19 de Abril, M-19]).

Rojas Pinilla's daughter, María Eugenia Rojas de Morena Días, ran on the party's ticket in the 1974 presidential contest, finishing third, significantly behind the candidates of Colombia's two traditional parties. The party had no significant electoral success subsequent to that election, as it began to falter after the death of Rojas Pinilla in 1975. Both Rojas Pinilla's daughter and his grandson, Samuel Moreno, led the party after his death. In 1982 the party did not present its own candidate for president, but rather supported conservative candidate Belisario **Betancur Cuartas** (1982–1986).

Núñez, Rafael Wencesclao (d. 1894)

Rafael Wencesclao Núñez served as president from 1880 to 1882 and from 1884 to 1894, presiding over the rise of the Colombian Conservative Party (see **Colombian Conservative Party** [Partido Conservador Colombiano, PCC] **and Liberal Party** [Partido Liberal, PL]).

While Núñez entered the political arena in the 1850s as a member of the PL, he soon distanced himself from the party, concerned with strengthening central authority over the weak federalist system, and convinced that the state should ally with the church in order to take advantage of its vast power. Elected for the first time in 1880, Núñez sought to reform the federalist Constitution of 1863, but was blocked by the requirement that reforms be unanimously approved by all states; his term

ended uneventfully in 1882. He was reelected in 1884, but his opposition immediately revolted against him.

Using this pretext to declare the 1863 Constitution lapsed, Núñez set out to write a new document, which was completed in 1886 and remained in effect (with many amendments) until 1991. The centralist document, which allowed the president to name mayors and governors and offered the party in power the opportunity to exclude its opponents nationwide, aroused the enmity of the PL (which saw Núñez as a repressive figure who was excluding them through excessive centralization of power) and fueled political violence (see *La Violencia*). In other attempts to institutionalize the centralization of power during his term, Núñez created a national bank through which leaders could guide the economy and strengthened the power of the executive. He also empowered the church, restoring the strength it had enjoyed prior to the era of liberal reform and allowing it to play a role in education and to own property. Though Núñez presided over a boom in coffee exports, the economic upswing was offset by his inflationary monetary policies. Núñez remained the titular president of Colombia until 1894, but spent the later years of his term ruling from his home in Cartagena, leaving the day-to-day management of government to his aides. He died in 1894 and was succeeded by Miguel Antonio Caro (1894–1898).

Pastrana, Andrés (1954–)

Andrés Pastrana, the son of former president Misael Pastrana (1970–1974), became president of Colombia in 1998 at a crucial juncture in Colombian politics. His election was a victory for the Colombian Conservative Party (see **Colombian Conservative Party** [Partido Conservador Colombiano, PCC] **and Liberal Party** [Partido Liberal, PL]) as it ended the PL's twelve-year hold on the presidency.

Born in Bogotá, Pastrana studied law there and international affairs at Harvard University. He returned to Colombia in 1978 and soon became involved in local politics. Though he rejected President Belisario **Betancur Cuartas'** (1982–1986) offer of the mayorship of Bogotá in 1982, he ran for and won the post in the 1988 election, becoming Bogotá's first directly elected mayor (despite being kidnapped by members of the **Medellín Cartel** and held captive for a week during his campaign). Though his term was uneventful, his administration was noted for its clean politics.

Pastrana was later elected senator, but soon resigned so that he could run for president in the 1994 election. The race between Pastrana and PL candidate Ernesto **Samper Pizano** (1994–1998) was the closest in Colombian history. Following his loss to Samper, Pastrana released recorded telephone calls between Samper and cartel leaders in which Samper solicited political contributions. This revelation, which set Samper's administration off on a tumultuous course, brought Pastrana a great deal of criticism, and he dropped out of the public eye, resurfacing just in time to be nominated as the PCC candidate in the 1998 presidential election. Pastrana received backing from many prominent Colombian business leaders, as he promised to revitalize the Colombian economy. Pastrana also pledged to end Colombia's civil conflicts, which had become reinflamed under Samper, and opened conversations with members of the **Revolutionary Armed Forces of Colombia** (Fuerzas Armadas Revolucionarias de Colombia, FARC) even before taking office.

Pastrana began formal peace negotiations after his accession to office and, in a drastic move, accepted a proposal from the FARC that called for a demilitarized zone (*zona de despeje*, an area about the size of Switzerland within the boundaries of the Colombian state that the group would control while negotiations were carried out). Pastrana hoped to demonstrate his commitment to bring peace to Colombia by agreeing to this demand. Though there was little progress toward peace during the first years of his term, and though negotiations repeatedly stalled while violence by guerrilla groups and paramilitaries continued to escalate, Pastrana agreed to create a demilitarized zone for the **Army of National Liberation** (Ejército Nacional de Liberación, ELN) in 2000. The Colombian economy also deteriorated during the first half of Pastrana's term. In an effort to facilitate the consolidation of peaceful democracy in Colombia, Pastrana attempted a variety of institutional reforms. Many of his proposals were blocked by the legislature, prompting Pastrana to threaten to follow the example of some of his contemporaries and close Congress. Though he had taken no steps in this direction by the end of 2001, with a faltering economy and no clear, demonstrable progress toward peace, Pastrana had lost a great deal of popular support, as well as momentum for reform in Colombia.

Plan Colombia

Working closely with U.S. President Bill Clinton and his administration, the government of President Andrés **Pastrana** (1998–) formulated *Plan Colombia*, an elaborate proposal to help guide peace negotiations with Colombia's two main guerrilla groups (the **Revolutionary Armed Forces of Colombia** [Fuerzas Armadas Revolucionarias de Colombia, FARC] and the **Army of National Liberation** [Ejército de Liberación Nacional, ELN]), and to facilitate efforts to combat **drug** production and trafficking in Colombia. The United States pledged a $1.3 billion aid package to support the plan, and the U.S. Congress approved the package in 2000; the European Union promised its support for the plan almost simultaneously. While *Plan Colombia* included other components (such as strategies to stimulate economic development, strengthen civil society, and promote human rights), the coca eradication efforts and military buildup that the plan anticipated were to re-

ceive the largest portion of funding. *Plan Colombia* was criticized by some of Colombia's neighbors that remained wary of U.S. intervention in Latin America and feared that coca eradication in Colombia would spill over to their countries; Venezuelan President Hugo **Chávez Frías** (see Venezuela) was a particularly vocal critic. *Plan Colombia*, the most costly U.S. aid package for the region in recent years, became one of the main topics at the Quebec **Summit of the Americas** (see Appendix 1) in April 2001. Amid such scrutiny, Clinton's successor, U.S. President George W. Bush, attempted to recast *Plan Colombia* as a broader "Andean Initiative" that would also provide funding for other countries in the Andean region.

Revolutionary Armed Forces of Colombia (Fuerzas Armadas Revolucionarias de Colombia, FARC)

The Revolutionary Armed Forces of Colombia (Fuerzas Armadas Revolucionarias de Colombia, FARC) which grew out of the communist movement in the early 1960s, was founded in 1964 in the aftermath of the turbulent period known as *La Violencia*. One of the strongest and best-supported guerrilla groups in Colombia, the FARC has gained control of significant portions of the countryside. The group has a rural base, and a majority of its supporters and fighters are peasants.

The FARC and the government of Belisario **Betancur Cuartas** (1982–1986) negotiated and signed the La Uribe agreement in 1984, which called for a cease-fire and established a schedule for future negotiations. Guerrilla action subsided briefly, and the FARC formed a legal political party, the Patriotic Union (Unión Patriótica, UP), hoping to pursue its beliefs through traditional political means while continuing its military strategy. After initial success, the UP suffered persecution at the hands of paramilitary groups; in subsequent years, thousands of its members were assassinated, including two presidential candidates.

At least in part as a result of the failure of its political efforts, through the late 1980s and 1990s, the FARC carried out hundreds of kidnappings a year, targeting political leaders and wealthy individuals. These crimes produced income for the FARC and demonstrated the group's disdain for the moneyed elite, which it blames for the dynamic of economic and political exclusion in Colombia. In the 1990s the corruption of Colombian leaders and government corroboration with cocaine cartels helped the FARC gain more support in rural areas where peasants sought leadership and defense. The Colombian government continually engaged the FARC in talks, and President Andrés **Pastrana** (1998–) even turned over control of a portion of Colombia's territory to the FARC. Though the Pastrana government and the guerrillas subsequently agreed on a twelve-point negotiating agenda and began formal talks, and despite international and domestic support for the peace process, by 2001 no significant progress had been made toward a final peace settlement. (See also **Gavriria Trujillo,** César; **Army of National Liberation** [Ejército de Liberación Nacional, ELN]).

Reyes, Rafael (1849–1921)

A leader of the Colombian Conservative Party (see **Colombian Conservative Party** [Partido Conservador Colombiano, PCC] **and Liberal Party** [Partido Liberal, PL]), Rafael Reyes (1904–1909) served as president of Colombia in the wake of the violence of the **War of a Thousand Days** (1899–1902).

Reyes, who was a businessman and explorer in the 1860s, joined the military in 1884 and served as a member of the group that authored a new constitution in 1886 in an environment of strengthening conservatism. He was elected senator from Cauca in 1890, was named minister of government in 1895, and represented the Colombian government and business concerns in Paris from 1896 to 1900. He returned to Colombia after the War of a Thousand Days and found the country transformed by the wave of violence that had swept it. In the new context, Reyes' political views, based on the typical late nineteenth-century positivist ideals of progress and grand public works, found support.

He was elected president in 1904 in an election that the PL boycotted. His technocratic rule was complemented by the many dictatorial powers that he added to the office of the presidency and by the creation of the secret police. He strayed from strict party politics, allowing the PL back into government (lifting the ban put in place after the War of a Thousand Days) and jailing anyone who opposed him from both political parties, which cost him PCC support. He presided over the 1905 assembly that reformed the constitution and many of Colombia's political institutions to emphasize centralization, strengthened and modernized the military, and developed industry and a modern economy.

Reyes' handling of the issue of Panama (see **Panama Canal,** Panama) led to popular discontent, and his dictatorial practices eventually alienated both the PL and the PCC. The two parties eventually united in the "Republican Union," pressuring Reyes to resign in 1909. General José Marcelo Holguín (1909) succeeded Reyes, and Reyes spent much of the remainder of his life in voluntary exile.

Rojas Pinilla, Gustavo (1900–1975)

Serving as president from 1953 to 1957, General Gustavo Rojas Pinilla tried to restore order to Colombia during a turbulent period known as *La Violencia*. Although he was initially popular, his ineffective economic policies cost him public support.

Rojas Pinilla joined the Colombian military academy as a teen. He later studied engineering in the United States, but returned to Colombia and rejoined the army in 1932, quickly rose in the military ranks, and was appointed lieutenant general by 1949. At that time, the country was suffering serious civil strife that neither of the traditional political parties (see **Colombian Conservative Party** [Partido Conservador Colombiano, PCC] **and Liberal Party** [Partido Liberal, PL]) had been able to stop or control. In 1953 Rojas Pinilla led a bloodless coup that overthrew President Laureano **Gómez** (1950–1953). Initially, Rojas Pinilla enjoyed tremendous popular support as well as the backing of both parties, as the nation put their faith in his ability to end *La Violencia*.

With the help of the military and through an amnesty and rehabilitation program, Rojas Pinilla's administration was initially quite successful at curbing the violence. However, Rojas Pinilla proved ineffectual at performing the other functions of the executive, such as guiding the economy. His often disastrous policies did not align with either PL or PCC beliefs, and in 1957 PL and PCC leaders negotiated the **National Front** (Frente Nacional) pact (which would allow them to govern without instigating another wave of politically motivated violence) and pushed Rojas Pinilla from office.

Hoping to continue his political career, but alienated from both parties, Rojas Pinilla formed his own party in 1961, the **National Popular Alliance** (Alianza Nacional Popular, ANAPO). Rojas ran for president on the ANAPO ticket in 1970, campaigning on a populist platform promising change for Colombians. He narrowly lost; many believe that he was denied victory through fraud (see **April 19th Movement** [Movimiento 19 de Abril, M-19]). ANAPO continued on, but lost steam after Rojas Pinilla's death in 1975.

Samper Pizano, Ernesto (1950–)

Ernesto Samper Pizano (1994–1998) won the presidency by the smallest margin in Colombian history. Although initially popular, his administration was plagued with scandal both within Colombia and internationally.

Educated as an economist, Samper was initially a professor before becoming involved in politics as a member of the Liberal Party (see **Colombian Conservative Party** [Partido Conservador Colombiano, PCC] **and Liberal Party** [Partido Liberal, PL]). Samper sat on the Bogotá city council from 1984 to 1986, and was elected to the Senate in 1987. President César **Gaviria Trujillo** (1990–1994) appointed Samper minister of development and then later ambassador to Spain.

In his 1994 campaign for the presidency, Samper promised to combat narcotrafficking (see **Drugs**) and to encourage discussions of Colombia's entry into the **North American Free Trade Agreement** (NAFTA; see Mexico). The race for the presidency was close, and Samper defeated his opponent, Conservative Andrés **Pastrana** (1998–), by less than 160,000 votes. However, shortly after his victory, accusations surfaced that he had accepted millions of dollars from the **Cali Cartel** in exchange for the implementation of lenient drug policies once he assumed the presidency. Samper immediately denied those accusations and demanded that the police thoroughly investigate. Congressional investigations began in 1996, and though Congress cleared Samper of all charges, the damage to his credibility and his administration had already been done. Several members of his government resigned or were imprisoned, and guerrilla groups, such as the **Revolutionary Armed Forces of Colombia** (Fuerzas Armadas Revolucionarias de Colombia, FARC), began new campaigns. The United States was particularly skeptical of Samper.

Samper's crisis of legitimacy and governance was compounded by several critical errors. For instance, while attempting to negotiate with the FARC and other guerrilla groups, Samper also created state-supported rural security cooperatives (known as Convivir) that quickly allied themselves with paramilitary groups and began to attack perceived guerrilla supporters, escalating conflict and violence. At the same time, Colombia experienced its first economic crisis in the postwar era. Though the Cali Cartel was basically dismantled and its key members imprisoned under Samper, the government's overall record in terms of its antidrug efforts was checkered. Further, at the end of Samper's presidency, the PL, the government, and indeed the entire political system were widely discredited. Samper admitted shortly after leaving office in 1998 that cartel money had, without his knowledge, entered his campaign treasury.

Torres Restrepo, Camilo (1929–1966). See **Army of National Liberation (Ejército de Liberación Nacional, ELN)**

Turbay Ayala, Julio César (1916–)
President Julio César Turbay Ayala (1978–1982) held office at the beginning of a period of civil strife brought on by insurgent groups and the growing power of drug lords (see **Drugs**). By 1978 Colombians were disillusioned with the **National Front** (Frente Nacional) and national politics, as evidenced by the fact that only 41 percent of the population voted in the 1978 election. Turbay was elected on an ideologically vague platform, and it soon became obvious that his main interest was in strengthening the Liberal Party (see **Colombian Conservative Party** [Partido Conservador Colombiano, PCC] **and Liberal Party** [Partido Liberal, PL]) organization rather than in effecting any programmatic changes. This led to attacks from within the party. Turbay also alienated the opposition PCC by reinterpreting the National Front agreement and reducing the PCC's representation in his administration.

As soon as Turbay assumed office in late 1978, guerrilla groups carried out an assassination attempt. When the **April 19th Movement** (Movimiento 19 de Abril, M-19) stole thousands of weapons from a military arsenal in 1979, the lapse in security was blamed on the pres-

ident, and he was harshly criticized. Turbay faltered again the following year when the M-19 occupied the embassy of the Dominican Republic for almost two months. In reaction to the M-19's activities, Turbay gave the military relative freedom to crack down on the violence. This policy also brought criticism, as the military began carrying out random arrests and mistreating prisoners.

Although the country suffered neither major economic decline nor government breakdown during Turbay's presidency, he was never able to win over the population. In addition, the failures of the state and the National Front compromise began to gain importance under Turbay, with their effects becoming critical under the administrations of his successors Belisario **Betancur Cuartas** (1982–1986) and Virgilio **Barco Vargas** (1986–1990). Turbay continued to be a target for drug cartel leaders even after he left office, and in the late 1980s, his daughter was kidnapped by associates of the **Medellín Cartel** and later killed.

United Self-Defense Forces of Colombia (Autodefensas Unidas de Colombia, AUC)
By the end of the 1980s, former military officers joined forces to create paramilitary forces in Colombia. Their intent was to protect the Colombian citizenry from the violent assaults of the two main guerrilla groups, the **Revolutionary Armed Forces of Colombia** (Fuerzas Armadas Revolucionarias de Colombia, FARC) and the **Army of National Liberation** (Ejército de Liberación Nacional, ELN). Subsequently, however, the paramilitaries became a third power contending for control of Colombian land and politics. In the late 1990s and early 2000s, the United Self-Defense Forces of Colombia (Autodefensas Unidas de Colombia, AUC) was accused of massacring entire villages in an effort to purge guerrilla sympathizers and to assert its presence in certain areas of the country. In 2000, following U.S. congressional approval of *Plan Colombia* (which included a U.S. aid package for Colombia totaling $1.3 billion), the United States and the European Union began to demand that President Andrés **Pastrana** (1998–) crack down on the paramilitaries and denounce any collusion between the Colombian military and the AUC. The capture of sixty AUC fighters by the Colombian military in 2001 appeared to demonstrate that the military had begun to sever all ties to the paramilitaries; after the capture, AUC leader Carlos Castaño resigned from his position. By mid-2001, the government refused to recognize the AUC as a political force. Further the FARC remained adamant that it would withdraw from any peace process with the government if the AUC were offered a place at the negotiating table.

La Violencia
La Violencia refers to the turbulent period of civil strife that began in 1946 and continued through the early

1960s, during which hundreds of thousands of Colombian lives were lost.

Sparked by political divisions between Colombia's two main political parties (see **Colombian Conservative Party** [Partido Conservador Colombiano, PCC] **and Liberal Party** [Partido Liberal, PL]), violence initially erupted primarily in rural areas, but escalated and temporarily spread to Colombia's urban areas following the assassination of PL leader Jose Eliécer **Gaitán** in 1948. Although President Mariano Ospina Pérez (1946–1950) was able to contain the violence within a few days in the urban areas, his methods of containment and his vicious police forces sparked more protest. Violence in rural areas escalated through the following years; by 1953, over 100,000 people had died and all PCC and PL efforts to calm the unrest had failed. General Gustavo **Rojas Pinilla** (1953–1957) took power in a bloodless coup in 1953, and was initially able to subdue the conflict. However, the violence soon began to escalate again, and after three years of military rule, the PL and the PCC negotiated the **National Front** (Frente Nacional) pact aimed at ending this disruptive period in Colombian history. Sporadic violence continued into the mid-1960s, and it was not until the presidency of Carlos Lleras Restrepo (1966–1970) that Colombian politics began to be reenergized.

The long-term implications of *La Violencia* are numerous. The principal insurgent group active today, the **Revolutionary Armed Forces of Colombia** (Fuerzas Armadas Revolucionarias de Colombia, FARC), has roots in this period, and many of the social issues that sparked the violence, particularly land conflicts, remain factors in the strife that continues today. Colombia's contemporary multifaceted violence has contributed to both internal and international migration. Over 1 million rural residents have moved to urban areas in the last five years, and many members of Colombia's middle and upper classes have left the country, slowing economic development and destroying the political center. In addition to political violence, high rates of nonpolitical violence have plagued Colombia. Social cleansing, kidnapping for ransom, and other crimes thrive in a nation in which the rule of the law is so weak. Although elections take place regularly, the extent of the violence calls into question the ability of the government to control its population.

War of a Thousand Days (1899–1902)

The War of a Thousand Days was one in a long series of bloody disputes between the **Colombian Conservative Party** (Partido Conservador Colombiano, PCC) **and Liberal Party** (Partido Liberal, PL). A previous conflict, the 1860–1862 Federal War, had resulted in a Liberal victory, enhancing that party's advocacy of states' rights and anticlericalism. However, the pendulum swung back to the Conservatives under Rafael Wencesclao **Núñez** (1880–1882, 1884–1894), who did away with

many of the Liberal policies of the mid-1800s, creating a highly centralized government and reinstating close ties between the state and the Catholic Church. Liberals reacted but were vehemently repressed, which led to the outbreak of the War of a Thousand Days in 1899. Although initially relatively tame, the conflict soon gained momentum, powered by guerrilla forces, and by 1902, 100,000 people had died. The war left Colombia under Conservative domination as it entered the twentieth century, and carved the country's political divisions even deeper. It also distracted the government sufficiently so that Panama was able to claim independence without much of a fight less than a year later, further shattering both the economy and national morale.

HEADS OF STATE

José Miguel Pey De Andrade	1810–1811
Jorge Tadeo Lozano de Peralta González-Manrique	1811
Antonio Nariño y Alvarez Del Casal	1811–1812, 1812–1813
José Camilo Clemente Torres y Tenorio	1813–1814, 1815–1816
Series of presidents during struggle for independence	1816–1819
Simón Antonio de la Santísima Trinidad Bolívar y Palacios	1819–1830
Joaquín Mariano Mosquera	1830
Rafael Urdaneta	1830–1831
Francisco de Paula Santander	1831–1837
José Ignacio de Márquez	1837–1841
Pedro Alcántara Herrán	1841–1845
Tomás C. de Mosquera	1845–1849
José Hilario López	1849–1853
José María Obando	1853–1854
José María Melo	1854
Manuel María Mallarino	1854–1857
Mariano Ospina Rodríguez	1857–1861
Tomás C. de Mosquera	1861–1864
Manuel Murillo Toro	1864–1866
Tomás C. de Mosquera	1866–1867
José Santos Gutiérrez	1868–1870
Manuel Murillo Toro	1871–1874
Santiago Pérez	1874–1876
José Bonifacio Aquileo Parra	1876–1878
Julián Trujillo	1878–1880
Rafael Wencesclao Núñez	1880–1882
Francisco Javier Zaldúa	1882–1884
Rafael Wencesclao Núñez	1884–1894
Miguel Antonio Caro	1894–1898

Manuel Antonio Sanclemente	1898–1900
José Manuel Marroquín	1900–1904
Rafael Reyes	1904–1909
José Marcelo Holguín	1909
Carlos Eugenio Restrepo	1910–1914
José Vincente Concha	1914–1918
Marco Fidel Suárez	1918–1921
Pedro Nel Ospina	1922–1926
Miguel Adabia Méndez	1926–1930
Enrique Olaya Herrera	1930–1934
Alfonso López Pumarejo	1934–1938
Eduardo Santos Montejo	1938–1942
Alfonso López Pumarejo	1942–1945
Mariano Ospina Pérez	1946–1950
Laureano Gómez	1950–1953
Gustavo Rojas Pinilla	1953–1957
Gabriel París Gordillo	1957–1958
Alberto Lleras Camargo	1958–1962
Guillermo León Valencia	1962–1966
Carlos Lleras Restrepo	1966–1970
Misael Pastrana	1970–1974
Alfonso López Michelsen	1974–1978
Julio César Turbay Ayala	1978–1982
Belisario Betancur Cuartas	1982–1986
Virgilio Barco Vargas	1986–1990
César Gaviria Trujillo	1990–1994
Ernesto Samper Pizano	1994–1998
Andrés Pastrana	1998–

Source: Gran Enciclopedia de Colombia, vol. 7 (Bogotá: Círculo de Lectores, 1993), pp. 181–84.

BIBLIOGRAPHY

Print Resources

Bergquist, Charles W. *Coffee and Conflict in Colombia, 1886–1910*. Durham, NC: Duke University Press, 1978.

Bergquist, Charles, Ricardo Peñaranda, and Gonzalo Sánchez, eds. *Violence in Colombia: The Contemporary Crisis in Historical Perspective*. Wilmington, DE: SR Books, 1992.

Berry, A., et al., eds. *Politics of Compromise: Coalition Government in Colombia*. New Brunswick, NJ: Transaction Books, 1980.

Bushnell, David. *The Making of Modern Colombia: A Nation in Spite of Itself*. Berkeley: University of California Press, 1993.

Carrigan, Ana. *The Palace of Justice: A Colombian Tragedy*. New York: Four Walls Eight Windows, 1993.

Chernick, Marc. "Negotiating Peace amid Multiple Forms of Violence: The Protracted Search for a Settlement to the Armed Conflicts in Colombia." In Cynthia Arnson, ed., *Comparative Peace Processes in Latin America*. Washing-

ton, DC: Woodrow Wilson Press and Stanford University Press, 1999.

Dix, Robert. *The Politics of Colombia*. New York: Praeger, 1987.

Giraldo, Javier. *Colombia: The Genocidal Democracy*. New York: Common Courage Press, 1996.

Hartlyn, Jonathan. *The Politics of Coalition Rule in Colombia*. Cambridge: Cambridge University Press, 1988.

Kline, Harvey F. *Colombia: Democracy under Assault*. Boulder: Westview Press, 1995.

MacDonald, Scott B. *Dancing on a Volcano: The Latin American Drug Trade*. New York: Praeger, 1988.

Mirajes, Augusto. *The Liberator*. Trans. John Fisher. Caracas: North American Association of Venezuela, 1983.

Pearce, Jenny. *Colombia: Inside the Labyrinth*. London: Latin American Bureau, 1990.

Wilde, Alexander. "Conversations among Gentlemen: Oligarchical Democracy in Colombia." In Juan Linz and Alfred Stepan, eds., *The Breakdown of Democratic Regimes: Latin America*. Baltimore: Johns Hopkins University Press, 1978, pp. 28–81.

Electronic Resources

Amnesty International: Colombia
http://www.amnestyusa.org/countries/colombia/
The Web site of this respected international human rights organization contains information about the armed conflict in Colombia, including news items, opinion pieces, and general information about the hostilities between Colombia's government, guerrilla organizations, and paramilitary groups. (In English)

Colombia Human Rights Network Home Page
http://www.igc.org/colhrnet/
Contains information on what U.S. human rights groups are doing to support the peace process in Colombia and in Washington, D.C. (In English)

Foreign Policy in Focus
http://www.foreignpolicy-infocus.org/colombia.html
A collection of briefs and very current information on Colombia, focusing mainly on the issues of violence and drugs, published by the Interhemispheric Resource Center. Includes recommendations for changes in U.S. policy and lists of contacts in the Washington, D.C. NGO community. (In English)

Latin American Network Information Center (LANIC): Colombia
http://www.lanic.utexas.edu/la/colombia/
Colombia section of this extensive Web site contains hundreds of links to research resources, cultural centers, economic and business institutions, government agencies, historical sources, magazines and other periodicals, nongovernmental organizations, and grassroots groups, as well as many other organizations. (In English)

Latin Focus: Colombia
http://www.latin-focus.com/countries/colombia.htm
Contains an overview and description of Colombia's government institutions and political environment, economic and fi-

nancial information and statistics, and links to government ministries and agencies. (In English)

Political Database of the Americas: Colombia
http://www.georgetown.edu/pdba/Countries/colombia.html
Comprehensive database run as a joint project of Georgetown University and the Organization of American States. Section on Colombia contains information on and links to the executive, legislative, and judicial branches of the Colombian government; electoral laws and election results; and other political data. (In English, Spanish, Portuguese, and French)

Political Resources.net: Colombia
http://www.politicalresources.net/colombia.htm
Contains a wealth of links to sources of information on national politics in Colombia. Includes information on political parties, legislative and executive institutions, laws and legislation, and elections. (In English)

Revista Cambio
http://www.revistacambio.com/web/home.php
Web version of the magazine published by Nobel laureate Gabriel García Márquez. Includes current events, political commentary, and investigative reporting. (In Spanish)

Revista Semana
www.semana.com.co
A weekly news magazine with commentary pieces by many columnists as well as interviews and investigative reporting on corruption, the peace process, organized crime, drugs, paramilitaries, and many other subjects relevant to Colombian politics. (In Spanish)

El Tiempo
http://eltiempo.terra.com.co/
The Web version of one of Colombia's best newspapers for political and economic news. Contains comprehensive national and international coverage, with a particularly strong emphasis on national politics and economics. Includes searchable archives. (In Spanish)

Wilfried Derksen's Elections Around the World: Colombia
http://www.agora.it/elections/colombia.htm
Colombia section of a comprehensive database of results from elections around the world. Contains results from recent national executive and legislative elections, as well as explanations of and links to political parties and institutions. (In English)

COSTA RICA

COUNTRY PROFILE

Official name	República de Costa Rica
Capital	San José
Type/structure of government	Democratic republic
Executive	Includes the president (who is elected by popular vote to a four-year term and may not be reelected); two vice presidents and a cabinet appointed by the president.
Legislative	57-member unicameral National Assembly; deputies are elected to four-year terms and may be reelected after a one-term absence.
Judicial	Highest court is the Supreme Court; includes 22 magistrates who are appointed to renewable eight-year terms by the legislature.
Supreme Electoral Tribunal	Known as the "fourth power," this independent tribunal governs all aspects of the electoral process; consists of three magistrates elected by the legislature for staggered six-year terms.
Major political parties	**National Liberation Party** (Partido Liberación Nacional, PLN); **Social Christian Unity Party** (Partido Unidad Social Cristiano, PUSC).
Constitution in effect	1949
Location/geography	Small nation in Central America, bordering Panama to the south, Nicaragua to the north, the Pacific Ocean to the west, and the Caribbean Sea to the east; includes four mountain ranges, numerous volcanoes, and a tropical rain forest.
Geographic area	51,032 sq. km.
Population	3.7 million (1999 est.)
Ethnic groups	Mestizo 96%; black (of African descent) 2%; indigenous 1%; Chinese 1%
Religions	Roman Catholic 85%; Evangelical 15%*
Literacy rate	94.8% (1995)*
Infant mortality rate	13 deaths per 1,000 live births (1999 est.)
Life expectancy	76.04 years (1999 est.)
Monetary unit	Colón
Exchange rate	1 U.S. dollar = 306.30 colones (August 2000)**
Major exports	Bananas, coffee, textiles, sugar, manufactured products
Major imports	Raw materials, consumer goods, capital equipment, petroleum
GDP	$24 billion (1998 est. purchasing power parity)
GDP growth rate	5.5% (1998 est.)
GDP per capita (year)	$6,700 (1998 est. purchasing power parity)

*United States Department of State Country Reports. http://www.state.gov/www.background_notes/costa_rica_1196_bgn.html

**Latin American Weekly Report*, August 22, 2000 (WR-00-33), p. 394.

Source: CIA World Factbook, unless otherwise noted. http://www.cia.gov/cia/publications/factbook/index.html.

OVERVIEW

Summary

Costa Rica is known throughout Latin America and the world for its democratic stability and tradition of political participation and social justice, characteristics that distinguish the small nation from its Central American neighbors. Costa Rica's role as an international peacekeeper is frequently praised, as are its economy and **education system**; many consider Costa Rica the most developed Central American nation. Though the country has confronted the same economic challenges that most Latin American nations have faced, Costa Rica's political stability has allowed it to capitalize on two late twentieth-century phenomena to its economic benefit. The increased popularity of ecological tourism has facilitated Costa Rica's development into a hot spot for adventure-seeking tourists. Further, in the wake of the technological revolution, the Costa Rican government has successfully solicited high-tech companies to invest in the country.

Costa Rica. © 1998 The Moschovitis Group, Inc.

History

In 1502, during Christopher Columbus' fourth and final trip to the New World, he landed in the area that is today Costa Rica, naming it "Rich Coast," perhaps due to native tales of gold, or perhaps because of the lush and diverse landscape. The native Indian tribes he encountered, including the Boruca, the Chorotega, and the Huetar, were soon killed by disease spread by the Spanish colonists, who began to settle in Costa Rica in 1522. In 1564 the first permanent city, Cartago, was founded, and the colonists began to settle in the central plateau. Despite the tales of riches, hardly any gold or minerals were found in the area, and agriculture became the economic mainstay. Colonists began to set up small independent farms, and these, together with the absence of grand slaveholding plantations and Costa Rica's relative isolation from the main population and power centers of Mexico and the Andean region, contributed to the equality that developed in Costa Rica.

Costa Rica gained independence from Spain in 1821 and established itself as an autonomous nation in 1838, after the failure of the **United Provinces of Central America** (see Appendix 1). Costa Ricans unified to protect and develop a sovereign nation, rather than battling each other for control of the new country. The fact that Costa Rica's first leader, Juan Mora Fernández (1824–1833), retained office for nine years is a clear indication of the relative tranquility of the time. Braulio Carrillo Colina (1835–1837, 1838–1842), attempted to consolidate the Costa Rican state, establishing San José as the capital and officially withdrawing Costa Rica from the Central American Federation. Costa Rica also soon began to take advantage of its fertile land and trade internationally, exporting many of its agricultural products. Carrillo encouraged coffee cultivation by giving young trees to peasant farmers to grow, and coffee subsequently became one of Costa Rica's most profitable exports. While the economic primacy of coffee created an oligarchy (see **Coffee Oligarchy**) that profited from the success of the crop, unlike similar oligarchies that formed in other Latin American countries, the coffee elite in Costa Rica was a heterogeneous group that included individuals from diverse backgrounds. Further, the coffee elite did not exploit the peasant producers; due to Costa Rica's shortage of labor, the relationship between elites and peasants was more of a partnership. This tradition foreshadowed the social democratic values that would characterize modern Costa Rica.

During the 1850s Costa Rica was involved in several armed confrontations with neighboring Nicaragua, primarily due to the aggression of U.S. adventurer and Nicaraguan president William **Walker** (see Nicaragua). After these violent conflicts, the country was struck with a cholera epidemic that claimed up to 10 percent of its population. Stability did not return to Costa Rica until the presidency of Tomás **Guardia Gutiérrez** (1870–1882) in 1870. Though Guardia's governing style was more authoritarian and his ideas and ideology more conservative than those of his liberal predecessors, he is praised for building the country's railroad, which encouraged economic advancement and allowed Costa Rica to add banana production to its agricultural portfolio. Today, bananas and coffee are the country's top exports, and the descendants of the foreign laborers who were brought into Costa Rica from Jamaica and the West Indies to help build the railroad now constitute the majority of the country's non-mestizo population. At the end of the nineteenth century the country implemented a policy that many believe is the crux of its successful development: free and mandatory public education. Introduced during the presidency of Bernardo Soto Alfaro (1885–1889), this commitment to literacy and education continued throughout the twentieth century.

Two men dominated Costa Rican politics during the first half of the 1900s: Cleto González Víquez (1906–1910, 1912–1914, 1928–1932) and Ricardo **Jiménez Oreamuno** (1910–1912, 1924–1928, 1932–1936). Both men continued and enriched Costa Rica's democratic traditions, making civil rights, education, and economic development the priorities of their administrations. Concern grew at the beginning of the twentieth century over the influence of foreign companies in Costa Rica. In particular, the U.S.-based United Fruit Company (see **Keith**, Minor Cooper) held significant portions of land; many believed that the company enjoyed undue influence over the elite, and some criticized it for operating with little concern for the working classes. In 1931 the Costa Rican **Communist Party** (Partido Comunista, PC) was formed, a reflection of a global trend as well as concern within Costa Rica for labor rights.

While political parties continued to pass progressive social legislation, political concerns, tensions, and conflicts deepened during the 1940s. The abundance of social legislation left the elite classes feeling that the government was not being fiscally prudent. At the same time, the middle classes rejected the administration of conservative Rafael Ángel **Calderón Guardia** (1940–1944), whom they viewed as one of the elite. When the legislature agreed to annul the results of the 1948 presidential election (on the conservative government's request, as it appeared that conservative candidate Calderón had lost), civil war broke out (see **Revolution of 1948**). A peace treaty was negotiated in April 1948, with the liberal opposition agreeing to uphold the conservatives' policies as long as the liberal candidate and winner of the 1948 election, Otilio Ulate Blanco (1949–1953), was able to take office. During the subsequent eighteen months, the country was ruled by a junta led by José **Figueres Ferrer** (1948–1949, 1953–1958, 1970–1974) that rewrote the constitution (see **Constitution of 1949**) and abolished the armed forces (see **Military**). Ulate Blanco's government was also essentially run by a coalition led by Figueres.

Liberal leaders in the second half of the twentieth century continued to develop Costa Rica's economy and infrastructure. The 1963 creation of the **Central American Common Market** (CACM; see Appendix 1) opened up new markets for Costa Rica though the collapse of the CACM during the 1980s adversely affected Costa Rica's economy. President Rodrigo **Carazo Odio** (1978–1982) declared a moratorium on debt payments (1981), and suffered immense criticism for his handling of the Costa Rican economy and the nation's foreign debt. Despite these economic challenges, Costa Rica managed to avoid the political turbulence that occurred in other Central American nations during the 1980s, and was even called upon to be a mediator of regional conflicts; President Oscar **Arias Sánchez** (1986–1990) was awarded the Nobel Peace Prize for his involvement in the development of the Central American peace accords (see **Esquipulas Accords**, Appendix 1). In 1998 Costa Rica elected its thirty-fifth president, Miguel Ángel Rodríguez Echeverría (1998–), who pledged to lower inflation and to privatize some state-owned industries. The next presidential elections are scheduled to take place in 2002.

ENTRIES

Arias Sánchez, Oscar (1941–)

Oscar Arias Sánchez, the youngest president ever elected in Costa Rica, headed the nation from 1986 to 1990. Arias' most notable accomplishments as president

Oscar Arias Sánchez, President of Costa Rica (1986–1990), delivering a speech in 1987. *Columbus Memorial Library, General Secretariat of the Organization of American States. Reproduced with permission of the Organization of American States.*

were his efforts to aid Costa Rica's neighbors in negotiating settlements to end their internal conflicts and bring peace to the Central American region. He was awarded the Nobel Peace Prize in 1987.

Educated at the University of Costa Rica and then in England, Arias served on the faculty of the University of Costa Rica in the early 1970s. He held a cabinet post during the third administration of President José **Figueres Ferrer** (1948–1949, 1953–1958, 1970–1974) and became active in the **National Liberation Party** (Partido de Liberación Nacional, PLN). From 1975 to 1979 he served as secretary for international affairs, was subsequently elected to the National Assembly, and then served in the cabinet of President Luis Alberto Monge Alvarez (1982–1986). Arias ran as the PLN candidate for president in 1986, defeating Rafael Ángel Calderón Fournier (1990–1994).

During Arias' presidency, the Costa Rican economy was on the upswing, in part due to an increase in exports such as coffee and bananas. Arias reaffirmed Costa Rica's traditions of neutrality and demilitarization, and also initiated a program to build more low-income housing. In an effort to foment regional peace and stability and to help Costa Rica's neighbors quell the severe civil conflict they were experiencing, Arias pulled together the leaders of Honduras, El Salvador, Guatemala, and Nicaragua in 1987 and proposed an intraregional plan of cooperation. The plan, known as Esquipulas II (see **Esquipulas Accords**, Appendix 1), called on these countries to initiate a cease-fire, begin talks with opposition organizations, and stop supporting any counterrevolutionary groups; the accord also prohibited the use of one country's land as a staging ground for aggression against another country. Signed in August 1987, the plan was particularly effective for Nicaragua, and Arias organized the first meeting between Nicaraguan officials and the Nicaraguan **coun-**

terrevolutionaries (contrarevolucionarios, contras; see Nicaragua) soon after Esquipulas II was signed.

After leaving office in 1990, Arias continued to be a global advocate for peace and human rights, and also remained involved in Costa Rican politics as an active member of the PLN.

Calderón Guardia, Rafael Ángel (1900–1970)

Despite his conservative background, Rafael Ángel Calderón Guardia (1940–1944) implemented major social reforms during his presidency, prompting accusations that he had socialist or communist tendencies.

Educated as a doctor in Belgium, Calderón began his political career at the local level as a councilman for the capital city of San José, where he had been practicing medicine. In 1934 he was elected to the National Assembly, and in his second term was elected president of the Assembly. In 1939 the National Republican Party (Partido Republicano Nacional, PRN) nominated him as its presidential candidate, and Calderón won the election with the support of the **Communist Party** (Partido Comunista, PC). Calderón's medical background and social Christian upbringing heightened his awareness of the plight of the poor and the underprivileged and influenced his policymaking, and he firmly believed that class conflict would emerge if social equality were not made an immediate goal. Consequently, one of his first initiatives as president was major social reform, including reopening the University of Costa Rica, creating a social security system (the first in Central America), and implementing a labor code. His mainly upper-class critics accused him of economic imprudence, not considering the interests of his peers (the oligarchy), and being too socialist in his policies.

Calderón sought reelection in 1948, but lost the contest to Otilio Ulate Blanco (1949–1953), a liberal journalist. When the conservative government declared fraud and demanded that the vote be nullified, and Congress agreed to anul the results of the contest, political chaos swept the country. José **Figueres Ferrer** (1948–1949, 1953–1958, 1970–1974) initiated an armed movement to reinstitute the results of the election, and that movement soon escalated into the **Revolution of 1948**, a brief but bloody civil war that pitted pro-government forces led by Calderón and the communists against Figueres' insurgents. After a month of fighting, Calderón went into exile in Nicaragua, leaving Figueres to assume control of the country. Calderón unsuccessfully attempted to invade Costa Rica to defeat Figueres twice more, once later in 1948 and again in 1955.

Finally, in 1958 Calderón returned to Costa Rica peacefully and was elected to Congress. Encouraged by his political success, Calderón ran for president in 1962, but lost again. In the last years of his life he served as ambassador to Mexico. His political ideologies live on today in the **Social Christian Unity Party** (Partido Unidad Social Cristiano, PUSC). The party's first president was Calderón's son, Rafael Ángel Calderón Fournier (1990–1994).

Carazo Odio, Rodrigo (1926–   )

As president from 1978 to 1982, Rodrigo Carazo Odio governed during a time of serious economic decline that resulted from the failure of the import substitution industrialization development strategy that Costa Rica had followed for the previous three decades. Unable to alleviate Costa Rica's financial crisis, Carazo focused on Nicaragua's internal conflict.

Carazo began his political career as a protégé of José **Figueres Ferrer** (1948–1949, 1953–1958, 1970–1974), serving in his cabinet during his second administration. In 1970 Carazo was defeated by Figueres in a presidential primary for the nomination of the **National Liberation Party** (Partido Liberación Nacional, PLN). Carazo was elected president in 1978 as the candidate of the Unity (Unidad) coalition; his campaign was anticommunist, and strongly criticized the tumultuous politics the Central American region was experiencing.

At the beginning of his presidency, Carazo continued Costa Rica's tradition of peace by founding the University for Peace under the auspices of the United Nations. He subsequently became deeply entrenched in the affairs of neighboring Nicaragua. Although he had spoken out against the rebels (see **Sandinista National Liberation Front** [Frente Sandinista de Liberación Nacional, FSLN], Nicaragua) that were battling the regime of Nicaraguan leader Anastasio **Somoza Debayle** (see Nicaragua) during his campaign, once elected in 1978, Carazo expressed sympathy for their cause. His opinions wavered, however, when Somoza sent troops to the Costa Rican border, and Carazo offered to act as mediator between Somoza and the rebels. Somoza was removed from office in 1979, and in 1980 a group of Somoza sympathizers attacked a radio station outside the Costa Rican capital of San José, the first in a series of bombing incidents.

High oil prices and falling coffee prices, as well as the disintegration of the **Central American Common Market** (CACM; see Appendix 1), challenged Carazo's economic policies throughout his time in office. Many believed that he focused on the conflict in Nicaragua to distract attention from the faltering economy. During his presidency, Costa Rica's foreign debt more than tripled, and his administration suspended debt payments to the International Monetary Fund (IMF) and other creditors.

Central American Common Market (CACM). See Appendix 1

Coffee Oligarchy

Coffee cultivation was introduced in 1805, and coffee soon surpassed all other crops in terms of profitability. Costa Rica began to export coffee in the 1820s, and by

1843 England was the leading consumer of the country's coffee. President Braulio Carrillo Colina (1835–1837, 1838–1842) recognized the economic potential of coffee and offered incentives, such as free land, to those who would agree to grow the crop. Carrillo also made sure that Costa Rica's infrastructure was ready to handle this booming new product. In part because coffee was grown in the Central Valley, where most of the population resided, the social benefits of the crop were widely distributed, and coffee's success facilitated the emergence of a middle class.

The success of the crop also spawned a new social class known as the "coffee barons." These elites, who had secured large portions of land during the country's fight for independence from Spain, began to grow and sell coffee and reap tremendous profits with little regulation or interference from the government, which was also profiting from the boom. The barons used their influence to ensure that economic policies would continue to favor trade, and that taxes on exports would be low. They also acted as middlemen, purchasing coffee from smaller farmers and marketing it abroad. The coffee barons subscribed to a liberal doctrine that encouraged the development of democracy in the country as well as the expansion of general education (see **education system**) and public works programs. While political leaders were almost always members of this new social class, the relatively open system of government prevented the coffee barons from completely excluding the lower classes from the political system; in contrast with the rest of Central America, the Costa Rican coffee oligarchy was not deeply segregated from the rest of society.

Coffee made up 90 percent of Costa Rica's export earnings by 1890, continued to be an important product in the twentieth century, and is still a pivotal crop today; consequently, the Costa Rican economy has continued to depend on the rise and fall of international coffee prices. The coffee barons remained very influential in Costa Rican politics until the **Revolution of 1948.**

Communist Party (Partido Comunista, PC)

The Communist Party (Partido Comunista, PC) was founded in 1931 by law student Manuel Mora Valverde and changed its name to the Popular Vanguard Party (Partido Vanguardia Popular, PVP) in 1943 in order to gain support from noncommunist workers. The PC, one of the first Costa Rican parties to organize around a programmatic platform, had the backing of labor and the rural poor. The peak of the party's influence came during the period before and during the **Revolution of 1948.** In 1940 the PC joined forces with the oligarchic National Republican Party (Partido Republicano Nacional, PRN) to elect Rafael Ángel **Calderón Guardia** (1940–1944). The Catholic Church supported the PC/PVP during Calderón's administration, and the PVP supported the election of Teodoro Picado Michalski

(1944–1948). The growing strength of the alliance of the PVP, the PRN, and the Catholic Church was unsettling to many of Costa Rica's political elite. Following the Revolution of 1948, in part due to the domestic political struggle, and in part due to the growing influence of the United States in the Cold War atmosphere, the PVP was outlawed in 1949 (see **Constitution of 1949**); the party regained its legal status in 1975. Although not powerful today, the PVP greatly influenced twentieth-century Costa Rican politics.

Constitution of 1949

The Constitution of 1949, which arose from the electoral conflicts of 1948 and the consequent **Revolution of 1948**, is the charter under which Costa Rica is governed today. One of the major goals of the Constitution was to dilute the power of the executive and award more autonomy to the legislative and judicial branches of government: the Constitution originally prohibited the president from running for immediate reelection, and in 1969 was amended to completely prohibit presidential reelection. The new Constitution also established the Supreme Electoral Tribunal, a body with significant independence and responsibility that is the equivalent of a fourth branch of government. Furthermore the charter awarded many national agencies (banking, health, and insurance) more autonomy, distancing them from electoral politics and protecting them from partisan debate. The Constitution established the public regulation of private property. The document also called for the armed forces to be replaced by a national police force; this deemphasis on armed strength is atypical of the countries of Central America. The constitution awarded women and blacks the right to vote, and removed literacy as a requirement for suffrage. The perseverance of this document is unusual in Latin America, where constitutions are frequently short-lived, and reflects the stability of Costa Rican politics.

Education System

Free and mandatory primary education (which begins at age six and lasts for six years) was introduced in 1869. The subsequent expansion of general education in the country's urban centers allowed Costa Ricans to become aware of their rights and more informed about politics. In 1940 the University of Costa Rica was organized. It was the most advanced institution of higher education in Central America, and many of Costa Rica's political leaders began their careers as university professors. The **Constitution of 1949** made secondary education free and required that no less than 6 percent of the gross national product be reserved for education. (This expenditure is facilitated by the fact that Costa Rica has no standing army, and thus spends far less on defense than most Central American nations.) During the presidency of Otilio Ulate Blanco (1949–1953), a particularly high percentage of Costa Rica's budget was

Costa Rica has long been known for the quality of its education system. In this 1968 photo, Costa Rica students are given a tour of the National Museum. *Columbus Memorial Library, General Secretariat of the Organization of American States. Reproduced with permission of the Organization of American States.*

spent on education. As a result, today's population is the most literate in Central America, and the nation's education system is often hailed as the best in the subregion. President Miguel Ángel Rodríguez Echeverría (1998–   ) hoped to introduce computer technology to Costa Rica's students to maintain the high level of training and education of the country's workforce. Many have attributed Costa Rica's political stability and strong development to its education system and educated populace.

Figueres Ferrer, José (1906–1990)

A key figure in the **Revolution of 1948**, José Figueres Ferrer was president from 1948 to 1949 (guiding the writing of the **Constitution of 1949**) and subsequently served two terms as president, from 1953 to 1958, and from 1970 to 1974. Figueres developed Costa Rica's infrastructure, denounced the autocratic presidents in other Central American republics, and created controversy by supporting the Soviet Union.

The son of Spanish immigrants, Figueres attended the Massachusetts Institute of Technology in the United States, but returned to Costa Rica before graduating to set up a farm and a small factory. He was expelled from Costa Rica in 1942 for accusing the administration of President Rafael Ángel **Calderón Guardia** (1940–1944) of exhibiting communist tendencies and of fiscal irresponsibility. While living in exile in Mexico, Figueres became acquainted with other Latin American leaders who shared his political ideologies and who also opposed Calderón's leftist leanings. After two years in exile, Figueres returned to Costa Rica, where he won support and respect for speaking out against Calderón and what many considered to be the president's auto-

cratic tendencies. When Calderón lost the 1948 presidential election and the government of Teodoro Picado Michalski (1944–1948) consequently contested the election results, Figueres led an armed movement against the pro-government forces of Calderón and the communists that evolved into Costa Rica's brief civil war (see Revolution of 1948).

Figueres' rebels defeated Calderón's troops, and a junta led by Figueres ruled the country for the next eighteen months. During the junta's tenure, Figueres implemented a number of important social democratic policies, including nationalizing the banking system and imposing a tax on the wealthy. He also held elections for a Constituent Assembly and guided the process of rewriting the country's constitution; when the new charter was promulgated in 1949, Figueres ceded power to Otilio Ulate Blanco (1949–1953), who had won the previous year's elections. However, Figueres quickly became disenchanted with Ulate, finding him too moderate. Figueres formed a new party, the **National Liberation Party** (Partido Liberación Nacional, PLN), to forward his goals for Costa Rica. He ran for president on the PLN ticket in 1953 and won.

As president, Figueres created national services to provide health care, insurance, and telephone service, worked to expand the public school system, and created agencies to encourage and fund agriculture and business. He spoke out against other Central American leaders and their autocratic ways and discouraged the United States from supporting such leaders. In addition, he renegotiated Costa Rica's contract with the U.S.-based United Fruit Company (see **Keith**, Minor Cooper), increasing the tax on their profits and gaining control over public services in the banana regions. Through the 1960s, Figueres was active in the PLN and the international arena, promoting Latin American democracy and development.

Figueres was reelected in 1970. While his establishment of trade and diplomatic relations with the Soviet Union caused an uproar both domestically and abroad, and though he also faced accusations that he was beholden to United States investors, this second full presidential term and the subsequent success of PLN presidential candidates confirmed the party's longevity and power in Costa Rican politics. Figueres encouraged employment, decreased the country's dependence on coffee as the main export, and nationalized the Northern Railway, Minor Cooper Keith's original line.

Figueres later broke away from the PLN and refused to campaign for PLN candidate Luis Alberto Monge Álvarez (1982–1986) in the 1978 presidential election, an act that many believed contributed to Monge's defeat in that contest.

Guardia Gutiérrez, Tomás (1831–1882)

During his presidency from 1870 to 1882, Guardia Gutiérrez worked to democratize Costa Rica and pushed to build a railroad that would help develop export industries such as coffee and bananas.

Unlike many political leaders of the time, Guardia was not a member of the **coffee oligarchy**; he rose to power as a result of his contribution to the defeat of U.S. adventurer and Nicaraguan president William **Walker** (see Nicaragua). Guardia overthrew Jesús de Jiménez Zamora (1863–1866, 1868–1870) and assumed the presidency in 1870, pledging to reduce the power of the coffee oligarchy. Guardia championed the effort to rewrite the constitution in 1871. The new charter created a powerful executive branch, though it barred presidents from seeking successive terms; many of its tenets are present in the current constitution (see **Constitution of 1949**). While Guardia stepped down briefly in 1872, he returned to office later that year and remained president until 1876. Though an election was held in 1876, Guardia soon dismissed the president-elect and reassumed the position.

During his tenure, Guardia engaged in many autocratic practices, including the prohibition of open political debate. While he broke the power of the coffee oligarchy, he replaced that powerful sector with his own family and circle of friends. He also strengthened the legislative and judicial branches of the government, and, at the behest of his wife, abolished the death penalty. He aggressively pursued the expansion of public works and infrastructure, such as sanitation and education, helped develop export industries, and pushed for the building of a railroad through Costa Rica, which aided the export of agricultural goods. However, Guardia borrowed a large amount of money from British banks, accruing a large debt that had to be renegotiated several times and put a significant strain on the economy. The U.S.-based United Fruit Company (see **Keith**, Minor Cooper) later traded this debt for thousands of acres of Costa Rican land. Guardia ruled until his death in 1882.

Jiménez Oreamuno, Ricardo (1859–1945)

Ricardo Jiménez Oreamuno (1910–1912, 1924–1928, 1932–1936) was a leader in liberal politics in the early twentieth century.

Jiménez was born in the town of Cartago and earned a law degree in 1884 from the University of Santo Tomás. He became involved in politics soon after completing his education and in 1886 he wrote an essay known as the *Colegio de Cartago*, which focused on the separation of church and state and strongly criticized Jesuit control of schools in Costa Rica. His essay became the benchmark for liberal thought at the time, and Jiménez became a leading liberal voice in Costa Rican politics. In 1886 he was awarded a cabinet post, and in 1890 was appointed president of the Supreme Court. However, he resigned in 1892 to protest the dictatorship of José Joaquín Rodríguez Zeledón (1890–1894).

In 1906 he was elected to Congress, where he spoke out against the U.S.-based United Fruit Company (see **Keith**, Minor Cooper) and the government's preferential treatment of the firm. Elected president in 1910, Jiménez fought for a constitutional amendment that would allow for the direct election of the president, and the amendment was approved in 1913. He also helped reduce public debt. During his second term he created a government insurance agency. During his third administration, Jiménez struggled to alleviate the effects of the Great Depression on Costa Rica. He enacted the first minimum wage law and regulated coffee production in order to control falling prices. In 1935 the United Fruit Company gave Jiménez a quarter of a million acres of land to redistribute to the landless as smallholdings. He is remembered for his liberal idealism and social legislation.

Keith, Minor Cooper (1840–1929)

U.S. entrepreneur Minor Cooper Keith founded the successful Tropical Trading and Transport Company, and later created the behemoth United Fruit Company.

Born in New York, Keith went to Costa Rica in the 1870s at the request of his uncle, Henry C. Meiggs, a railroad magnate in Peru, who asked that he oversee the building of a railroad along the Caribbean coast in Costa Rica. (The Costa Rican government had contracted the construction negotiating land grants along the railroad as a form of payment.) Keith was quick to realize the great potential of Costa Rica's fertile land, and while building the railroad, he planted bananas on the land grants. He began exporting the bananas in 1878, and his Tropical Trading and Transport Company soon became a huge success.

When Costa Rica turned to Keith for assistance in alleviating its foreign debt in 1884 (the Costa Rican government owed the British millions of dollars), Keith traded Costa Rica's debt with the British for 800,000 acres of land, approximately 7 percent of Costa Rica. Keith used the land he gained through the arrangement to expand his agricultural business, and in 1889 his company merged with the Boston Fruit Company. The resulting company, the United Fruit Company, continued to dominate the Costa Rican economy—and other economies of Central America—long after Keith sold his shares. Later in life Keith invested in Costa Rican museums and continued to live in the country.

Military

Costa Rica has never had a high level of militarization, in contrast to other Central American nations in which the military has historically shaped politics. The Costa Rican Constitution of 1871 stated that the military was to be subordinate to civil authority. Following the **Revolution of 1948**, on December 1, 1948, José **Figueres Ferrer** (1948–1949, 1953–1958, 1970–1974) abolished the Costa Rican military, an act that was formalized in the **Constitution of 1949**. This decision, motivated by Figueres' desire to return to the peaceful tradition of Costa Rica's past after the recent revolution, occasioned no public protest. The army was replaced by the Guardia Civil (Civil Guard), a national police force responsible for keeping internal order, not fighting external wars. The old military barracks were converted into an art museum, and the Ministry of Defense became the Ministry of Education. Costa Rica was the first country in the world to abolish its national army.

Though the fact that Costa Rica lacks a true military earned it the nickname the "Switzerland of Central America," increasing militarization occurred in the late twentieth century, partially in response to Costa Rican concerns about the **Sandinista National Liberation Front** (Frente Sandinista de Liberación Nacional, FSLN; see Nicaragua) regime that ruled Nicaragua through the 1980s. The Guardia Civil was unable to adequately protect Costa Rica's border against the encroachments of Nicaragua, and the country consequently accepted training from the United States and agreed to professionalize the Guardia Civil and expand the military in return for financial aid during the debt crisis. However, President Oscar **Arias Sánchez** (1986–1990) reemphasized Costa Rica's traditional neutral position and put a halt to professionalization. Today there are at least nine different police agencies, including the Guardia Civil, a rural guard, and border troops. Yet each section remains decentralized, small, and unlikely to influence politics.

Mora Porrás, Juan Rafael (1814–1860)

Juan Rafael Mora Porrás (1849–1859) established the University of Santo Tomás and the first archdiocese in Costa Rica during his first term in office. During his second term, he gained popularity by successfully leading the country in fending off the attacks of Nicaraguan president William **Walker** (see Nicaragua), organizing 9,000 troops to defend the Costa Rican border with Nicaragua. However, his valiant efforts against Walker were soon overshadowed by a series of missteps. His creation of a state bank in 1858, the Banco de Medina, was highly criticized by commercial coffee growers who feared that the institution would favor smaller farms and believed that it was just a front for Mora to gain more control over the economy. His administration also infuriated the Catholic Church by refusing to recognize the newly created archdiocese of Costa Rica, and by expelling an archbishop who was vehemently defending his family members in disputes with the president. When Mora threatened to auction off state lands that poor Costa Ricans were renting from the government, mass protests ensued, and he was soon removed from office by the military and replaced by Jose María Montealegre Fernández (1859–1863), his brother-in-law. Following an unsuccessful attempt to overthrow the

government through armed attack in 1860, he was executed.

National Liberation Party (Partido Liberación Nacional, PLN)

Founded by José **Figueres Ferrer** (1948–1949, 1953–1958, 1970–1974) in 1951, the National Liberation Party (Partido Liberación Nacional, PLN), one of the most prominent political parties in Costa Rica, dominated the National Assembly for most of the second half of the twentieth century. Officially the PLN is a social democratic party, but since the 1980s it has adhered to the neoliberal economic policies advocated by the U.S. government and international financial institutions such as the International Monetary Fund (IMF) and the World Bank.

The PLN began as a multiclass party. Despite belonging to the Socialist International, it lacked a working-class base, and drew its major support from the rural areas and the middle class. The PLN advocated a welfare state policy and created many civil service jobs. Figueres was the first PLN candidate to be elected president, and Oscar **Arias Sánchez** (1986–1990) was also elected on the PLN ticket. In recent years the party has suffered internal conflict over its incorporation of more modern economic policies. Constituents have charged that the party no longer cares about the poor, and voters turned against the PLN in the 1990 presidential election, and again in 1998. Nonetheless, the PLN remains one of Costa Rica's leading political parties and continues to project itself as concerned with social welfare and as a party of the people. It also prides itself on having many women in its upper leadership.

Popular Vanguard Party (Partido Vanguardia Popular, PVP). See Communist Party (Partido Comunista, PC)

Revolution of 1948

The Revolution of 1948 was a six-week struggle for succession that ensued when the conservatives lost control of the presidency.

During the last years of the administration of conservative president Teodoro Picado Michalski (1944–1948), political tensions ran high as the liberals pulled together a unified and strong opposition. The views and practices of the dominant political parties were increasingly divergent, and the resulting ideological conflict culminated in street protests and occasional violence. In the 1948 presidential election, the liberals supported Otilio Ulate Blanco (1949–1953), while the conservatives pushed for their leader, Rafael Ángel **Calderón Guardia** (1940–1944). When the election results indicated that Ulate was victorious, the government and its conservative supporters charged fraud and demanded that the results be annulled. The legislature, which had a conservative majority, granted the request and an-

Soldiers prepare to leave for the front during the brief civil war known as the Revolution of 1948. *Columbus Memorial Library, General Secretariat of the Organization of American States. Reproduced with permission of the Organization of American States.*

nulled the election in February 1948. Violence soon broke out.

José **Figueres Ferrer** (1948–1949, 1953–1958, 1970–1974), an outspoken liberal, took charge of the campaign to reinstitute the election results, assembling a liberal army and seizing some cities in southern Costa Rica in March 1948. Though President Picado, who was still in power, initially did not think the threat was serious, after some bloody battles in which more than 1,000 people were killed, Picado and his peers began negotiations with the liberals. The crisis was resolved through the Mexican Embassy Pact of April 1948, in which the liberals agreed to uphold the conservatives' policies as long as the liberals were able to take control of the executive branch, as the original 1948 election results had dictated. The Founding Junta of the Second Republic, led by Figueres, ruled Costa Rica for eighteen months following the resolution of the conflict, and power was not handed to Ulate until November 1949.

Social Christian Unity Party (Partido Unidad Social Cristiano, PUSC)

Formed in 1977, the Social Christian Unity Party (Partido Unidad Social Cristiano, PUSC) is an alliance of four conservative parties that banded together to oppose the liberal **National Liberation Party** (Partido Liberación Nacional, PLN). During the last two decades of the twentieth century, the PUSC alternated power with the PLN, though throughout the 1980s, the PUSC grew and the PLN declined. Headed by Rafael Ángel Calderón Fournier (1990–1994), the PUSC embodies many of the political beliefs of Calderón Fournier's father, Rafael Ángel **Calderón Guardia** (1940–1944). The party caters to business and to the elite sectors of the population and aspires to completely restructure Costa Rica's financial system. It supports fiscally conservative policies, while also encouraging free markets. Under

PUSC leadership, Costa Rica has projected itself as a marketplace for high-tech companies.

HEADS OF STATE

Juan Mora Fernández	1824–1833
José Rafael Gallegos y Alvarado	1833–1835
Braulio Carrillo Colina	1835–1837
Joaquín Mora Fernández	1837
Manuel Aguilar Chacón	1837–1838
Braulio Carrillo Colina	1838–1842
Manuel Antonio Bonilla Nava	1842
Francisco Morazán Quesada	1842
Antonio Pino Suárez	1842
José María Alfaro Zamora	1842–1844
Francisco María Oreamuno Bonilla	1844
Rafael Moya Murillo	1844–1845
José María Alfaro Zamora	1845–1847
José María Castro Madríz	1847–1849
Miguel Mora Porrás	1849
Juan Rafael Mora Porrás	1849–1859
José María Montealegre Fernández	1859–1863
Jesús de Jiménez Zamora	1863–1866
José María Castro Madríz	1866–1868
Jesús de Jiménez Zamora	1868–1870
Bruno Carranza Ramírez	1870
Tomás Guardia Gutiérrez	1870–1882
Próspero Fernández Oreamuno	1882–1885
Bernardo Soto Alfaro	1885–1889
Carlos Durán Cartín	1889–1890
José Joaquín Rodríguez Zeledón	1890–1894
Rafael Yglesias Castro	1894–1902
Ascensión Esquivel Ibarra	1902–1906
Cleto González Víquez	1906–1910
Ricardo Jiménez Oreamuno	1910–1912
Cleto González Víquez	1912–1914
Alfredo Gonzáles Flores	1914–1917
Federico Tinoco Granados	1917–1919
Julio Acosta García	1919
Juan Bautista Quirós Segura	1919
Julio Acosta García	1920–1924
Ricardo Jiménez Oreamuno	1924–1928
Cleto González Víquez	1928–1932
Ricardo Jiménez Oreamuno	1932–1936
León Cortes Castro	1936–1940
Rafael Ángel Calderón Guardia	1940–1944
Teodoro Picado Michalski	1944–1948
Santos León Herrera	1948

José Figueres Ferrer	1948–1949
Otilio Ulate Blanco	1949–1953
José Figueres Ferrer	1953–1958
Mario Echandi Jiménez	1958–1962
Francisco José Orlich Bolmarich	1962–1966
José Joaquín Trejos Fernández	1966–1970
José Figueres Ferrer	1970–1974
Daniel Oduber Quiros	1974–1978
Rodrigo Carazo Odio	1978–1982
Luis Alberto Monge Álvarez	1982–1986
Oscar Arias Sánchez	1986–1990
Rafael Angel Calderón Fournier	1990–1994
José María Figueres Olsen	1994–1998
Miguel Ángel Rodríguez Echeverría	1998–

Sources: Theodore S. Creedman, *Historical Dictionary of Costa Rica* (Metuchen, NJ: Scarecrow Press, 1991); Pedro Rafael Gutierrez and Guillermo Malavassi V., eds., *Diccionario Biográfico de Costa Rica* (San José, Costa Rica: Universidad Autónoma de Centroamérica, 1993); Thomas E. Skidmore and Peter H. Smith, *Modern Latin America*, 4th ed. (New York: Oxford University Press, 1992).

BIBLIOGRAPHY

Print Resources

Ameringer, Charles D. *Don Pepe: A Political Biography of José Figueres of Costa Rica*. Albuquerque: University of New Mexico Press, 1978.

Barry, Tom. *Costa Rica: A Country Guide*. Albuquerque: Inter-Hemispheric Education Resource Center, 1989.

Bell, John Patrick. *Crisis in Costa Rica: The 1948 Revolution*. Austin: University of Texas Press, 1971.

Biesanz, Richard, Karen Zubris Biesanz, and Mavis Hiltunen Biesanz. *The Costa Ricans*. Englewood Cliffs, NJ: Prentice-Hall, 1982.

Bird, Leonard. *Costa Rica: The Unarmed Democracy*. London: Sheppard Press, 1984.

Blachman, Morris J., William M. LeoGrande, and Kenneth E. Sharpe, eds. *Confronting Revolution: Security Through Diplomacy in Central America*. New York: Pantheon Books, 1986.

Edelman, Marc, and Joanne Kenen, eds. *The Costa Rica Reader*. New York: Grove Weidenfeld, 1989.

Sick, Deborah. *Farmers of the Golden Bean: Costa Rican Households and the Global Coffee Economy*. DeKalb: Northern Illinois University Press, 1999.

Wilson, Bruce M. *Costa Rica: Politics, Economics and Democracy*. Boulder: Lynne Rienner, 1998.

Woodward, Ralph Lee, Jr. *Central America: A Nation Divided*. New York: Oxford University Press, 1976.

Electronic Resources

Latin American Network Information Center (LANIC): Costa Rica
http://lanic.utexas.edu/la/ca/cr/
Costa Rica section of this extensive Web site contains hundreds of links to research resources, cultural centers, economic and business institutions, government agencies, historical sources, magazines and other periodicals, nongovernmental organizations, and grassroots groups. (In English)

La Nación Digital
http://www.nacion.co.cr/
The Web version of one of Costa Rica's major daily newspapers. Offers comprehensive national and international coverage, with a particularly strong emphasis on the Costa Rican economy and national politics. (In Spanish)

Political Database of the Americas: Costa Rica
http://www.georgetown.edu/pdba/Countries/costa.html
Comprehensive database run as a joint project of Georgetown University and the Organization of American States. Section on Costa Rica contains information on and links to the executive, legislative, and judicial branches of the Costa Rican government and other political data. (In English, Spanish, Portuguese, and French)

Political Resources.net: Costa Rica
http://www.politicalresources.net/costa.htm
Contains a wealth of links to sources of information about national politics. Includes information on political parties, legislative and executive institutions, laws and legislation, and elections, as well as a link to the constitution. (In English)

Tico Times
http://www.ticotimes.net/
Web version of Central America's largest English-language newspaper. Contains political, economic, and cultural information about all of Central America, with a strong emphasis on Costa Rica. (In English)

Wilfried Derksen's Elections Around the World: Costa Rica
http://www.agora.it/elections/costarica.htm
Costa Rica section of a comprehensive database of results from elections around the world. Contains results from recent national executive and legislative elections, as well as explanations of and links to political parties and institutions. (In English)

CUBA

COUNTRY PROFILE

Official name	Cuba
Capital	La Habana
Type/structure of government	One-party state
Executive	Includes the Council of Ministers and the Council of State. The councils are appointed by the legislative branch. The Executive Committee consists of the president, the first vice president, and the vice presidents of the Council of Ministers. The president of the Council of Ministers and Council of State is both chief of state and head of government.
Legislative	National Assembly of People's Power consists of 601 members elected by direct ballot to five-year terms.
Judicial	The highest court, the People's Supreme Court, consists of a president, a vice president, and other judges elected by the National Assembly of People's Power.
Major political parties	The **Communist Party of Cuba** (Partido Comunista Cubano, PCC) is the only legal political party. It controls the island's social organizations (such as neighborhood associations called Committees for the Defense of the Revolution).
Constitution in effect	1976; revised extensively 1992
Location/geography	Largest island in the Western Antilles, 90 miles off the coast of Florida. Terrain varies from flat, rolling hills to mountainous regions in the southwest.
Geographic area	110,860 sq. km.
Population	11,096,395 (1999 estimate)
Ethnic groups	Mulatto 51%; white (of European descent) 37%; black (of African descent) 11%; Chinese 1%
Religions	Since the revisions of the constitution in 1992, Cuba is considered secular. The majority of the population is Roman Catholic; Protestants, Jehovah's Witnesses, Jews, and Santería adherents are also represented.
Literacy rate	95.7% (1995 estimate)
Infant mortality rate	7.81 deaths per 1,000 live births (1999 estimate)
Life expectancy	75.78 years (1999 estimate)
Monetary unit	Cuban peso (U.S. dollars legal and circulating freely since 1993)
Exchange rate	1 U.S. dollar = 1 Cuban peso at official rate 1 U.S. dollar = 22 Cuban pesos at unofficial rate (August 2000)**
Major exports	Sugar, tobacco, nickel, citrus, coffee, seafood, and medical products
Major imports	Petroleum, food, machines, and chemicals
GDP	$17.3 billion (1998 estimate, purchasing power parity)*
GDP growth rate	6.2% (1999 estimate)**
GDP per capita	$1,560 (1998 estimate)*

*CIA World Factbook 1999. http://www.cia.gov/cia/publications/factbook/geo's/cu.html

**Latin American Weekly Report. August 22, 2000 (WR-00-33), p. 94.

Source: U.S. Department of State, Bureau of Inter-American Affairs. Background Notes—Cuba. http://www.state.gov/www/regions/wha/cuba/country-info.html

OVERVIEW

Summary

Cuba's history is marked by the legacy of Spanish colonial rule, which lasted through the nineteenth century, as well as by repeated United States intervention in the late nineteenth and through the twentieth centuries. The island's ongoing quest for self-determination and deep sense of nationalism led to the **Cuban Revolution of 1959,** and remained pillars of the revolutionary government that took power under the leadership of Fidel **Castro Ruz** (1959–   ). Shortly after the revolution, which became an important symbol of freedom and anti-imperialism in the region, Cuba emerged as the only communist country in the Western Hemisphere, and at the height of the Cold War, Cuba turned to the Soviet Union for political and economic support; Cuba consequently became embroiled in the geopolitical struggles between the world's superpowers. The collapse of the Soviet Union in 1991 left the centrally planned Cuban

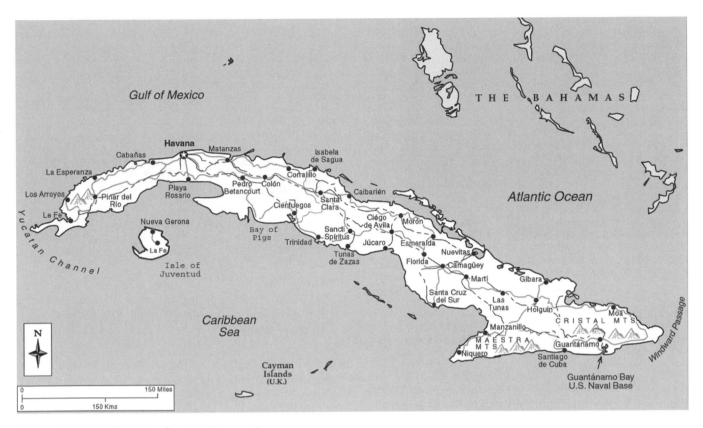

Cuba. © 1998 The Moschovitis Group, Inc.

economy in crisis and recession. Out of necessity Cuba began to open up to international trade after a long period of isolationism, and the Cuban economy has grown slowly but steadily in recent years. The Cuban political landscape, however, remains unchanged despite pressure from the United States. Castro and the **Cuban Communist Party** (Partido Comunista Cubano, PCC) continue to dominate the country's politics to this day.

History

Christopher Columbus landed on what is now Cuba in October 1492. The Spanish crown named the island Fernandina and appointed Diego Velázquez as governor in 1510. The *encomienda* system was implemented under his rule, and those it enslaved became the labor force for agricultural and mining industries that developed through the sixteenth, seventeenth, and eighteenth centuries. When the indigenous population was exhausted, the slave trade brought Africans to work the island's farms and mines.

Cuba's proximity to the United States and protracted Spanish colonization shaped both its political and economic development. The United States' influence on the island increased beginning in the early nineteenth century, during which some sectors within Cuba supported U.S. annexation or purchase of Cuba, while others favored gaining independence from Spain and establishing a republic. As the nineteenth century progressed,

however, Cuban nationalist sentiments also increased. In 1868 a group of rebels led by Carlos Manuel **de Céspedes** launched the first serious revolt against the Spanish, which escalated into the **Ten Years War** (1868–1878). The war ended with the signing of the Pact of Zanjón, which granted slightly more political freedom to the island while still preserving Spanish rule.

Rebellions continued in the following years, and while their leaders (such as José Julian **Martí y Pérez**, Antonio **Maceo**, and Máximo **Gómez y Báez**) were exiled, they continued formulating plans to overthrow the colonial government from abroad. The **Cuban Revolutionary Party** (Partido Revolucionario Cubano, PRC) began a major revolt in 1895; this uprising escalated into a war when the United States entered the struggle following the sinking of a U.S. battleship, the *Maine*, in Havana's harbor on February 15, 1898. The **Spanish American War** (1895–1898; see Appendix 1) continued until the signing of the Treaty of Paris on December 10, 1898. The treaty placed Cuba under the trusteeship of the United States, and the United States appointed John Rutter Brooke as the first military governor. Official Cuban independence came on May 20, 1902, when the United States gave control of the island to the first elected president, Tomás **Estrada Palma** (1902–1906). Cuba was the last of the Spanish colonies in Latin America to gain independence, which earned it the title "The Ever Faithful Island."

For the first few years of the Cuban republic, the liberal and conservative factions challenged one another

This plaza in Old Havana across from the former Capitol Building ("El Capitolio") is a remnant of Cuba's Spanish colonial past. *Photograph by Meghann Curtis.*

Known now as "El Capitolio," this building served as Cuba's capitol in the early twentieth century until the Cuban Revolution of 1959. *Photograph by Meghann Curtis.*

for power. Internal disputes were frequently settled by U.S. intervention, as provided for by the **Platt Amendment** (1901) to the Cuban Constitution, which granted the United States privileges and influence over Cuban political and military matters. During the early part of the twentieth century, the new nation struggled economically as the price of **sugar** (the island's main export) rose and then dramatically dropped in world markets following World War I. Politically, the island suffered under the administration of military strongman Gerardo **Machado y Morales** (1925–1933) and then experienced a short-lived experiment with socialist idealism under Ramón **Grau San Martín** (1933–1934, 1944–1948). The governments of Carlos **Mendieta y Montefur** (1934–1935), José A. Barnet y Vinegeras (1935–1936), Miguel Mariano Gómez y Arias (1936), and Federico **Laredo Brú** (1936–1940) were controlled from behind the scenes by General Fulgencio **Batista y Zaldívar** (1940–1944, 1952–1958). Following Batista's forceful power grab in 1952 in the face of an election he feared he would lose, he ruled as dictator until 1958, implementing policies that favored U.S. economic interests, and violently suppressing social and political opposition.

The **July 26th Movement** (M-26–7), led by Castro, challenged Batista's dominance for most of the 1950s. The group, which included Ernesto "Ché" **Guevara**, Raúl **Castro Ruz**, and Camilo **Cienfuegos**, was supported by middle-class moderates, sectors of the military, and the Cuban masses, who had grown weary of Batista's repression and the economic and political control of the United States. The Cuban Revolution triumphed on January 1, 1959. Fidel Castro took control of the country, creating and implementing a series of cultural and social programs that improved education and basic social services (such as health care), increased the Cuban literacy rate, and eradicated several major

epidemic diseases. Castro centralized the economy, implemented significant land reform, encouraged industrialization, and nationalized large plantations and sugar industries. Many Cubans welcomed these reforms, but many foreign investors and members of the wealthy Cuban elite, who were stripped of their assets in Cuba, quickly fled the country.

Many nations broke diplomatic ties with Cuba during the 1960s, including the United States in 1961. In April 1961 a group of Cuban exiles supported and trained by the U.S. Central Intelligence Agency (CIA) participated in the **Bay of Pigs Invasion**, an unsuccessful attempt to oust the Castro regime. By the end of 1961, Castro declared Cuba a Marxist-Leninist socialist state and began aligning the island with the Soviet Union. In the context of the Cold War, the United States perceived Cuba as a major security threat, and relations between the two countries worsened steadily through the 1960s. The United States established a trade embargo on all goods to and from Cuba in 1962, and in October of that year, Cuba found itself in the middle of the **Cuban Missile Crisis**, a nuclear standoff between the United States and the Soviet Union prompted by the latter's installation of missiles on Cuban soil. The **Organization of American States** (OAS; see Appendix 2) expelled Cuba in 1962. Cuba's relations with many countries around the globe became increasingly tense as it began to actively support guerrilla movements in Latin American and African countries in an attempt to ignite revolutionary internationalism.

The 1970s were years of relative success for the Cuban economic system and the revolutionary government that was institutionalized under the Constitution of 1976. The 1970s were also marked by Cuba's military involvement in revolutionary movements in Angola and

A view of Havana's Plaza de la Revolución. *Photograph by Meghann Curtis.*

Ethiopia. However, the closed political system, repression of anything "counterrevolutionary," and economic difficulties late in the decade drove many Cubans into exile. In 1980 the **Mariel boatlift** brought more than 120,000 Cubans to the United States in the first legally sanctioned exodus under the Castro regime. Further, isolation from former trade partners had resulted in Cuba's dependence on trade and economic support from the USSR, and the withdrawal of Soviet subsidies that began in 1989 devastated the Cuban economy. In 1990 Cuba entered a period of austerity referred to by the government as a "Special Period in a Time of Peace" and by the time the Soviet Union fell in 1991, Cuba was experiencing severe economic crisis.

In the early 1990s, the government reformed the constitution to allow for some changes to the economic system, including foreign investment and trade, limited private enterprise for Cubans, and the circulation of foreign currencies. The economic adjustments and increased remittances from the **Cuban exile community** helped to keep Cuba afloat even as the United States' economic embargo strengthened during this period. But the small economic openings did not mean political openings; the Castro government refused to abandon the political model or to open the political system to dissidents who oppose the PCC.

The future of Cuba depends on Castro's ability to successfully confront the various internal and external challenges that his regime will face in the near term (including growing economic inequalities, political dissent, and criticism from the international community for alleged human rights violations), as well as his ability to foment continued economic growth. Further, while Castro has managed to carry Cuba into the twenty-first century, serious questions about a post-Castro period have arisen on and off the island. The survival of the Cuban revolution will hinge on the strength of a successor to Castro, the organization of a transition government and its ability to continue to resist pressure from the United States and the exile community, and the willingness of the Cuban people to support *"Fidelismo"* without Fidel.

ENTRIES

Authentic Party (Partido Auténtico, PA)

The Authentic Party (Partido Auténtico, PA) was created in 1934 by student leaders and opponents of the regime of Gerardo **Machado y Morales** (1925–1933). The party's specific goals were the recognition and protection of civil rights, the improvement of education, and more domestic control of the economy.

The party supported President Ramón **Grau San Martín** (1933–1934, 1944–1948), who took power following the overthrow of Carlos Manuel **de Céspedes y de Quesada** (1933) and the subsequent brief rule and dissolution of the five-man junta known as the Pentarchy (1933). When Grau was deposed in 1934 by the forces of Fulgencio **Batista y Zaldívar** (1940–1944, 1952–1958) after less than one year in office, the PA transformed into a major opposition force. The party supported Grau again in the presidential election of 1944, and Grau's win marked the party's first electoral victory.

However, while president, Grau failed to accomplish the idealistic social reforms that the PA's original leadership had envisioned. Further, the corruption of Grau's administration was well known and spurred some members to split from the PA to form the Orthodox Party (Partido Ortodoxo, PO) in 1947; that party subsequently provided opposition to the ruling PA administrations and the Batista regime. PA candidate Carlos Prío Socarrás (1948–1952) was victorious in the 1948 presidential elections. Although he was considered a progressive, socially compassionate leader, accusations of nepotism and corruption plagued his political career. The party grew weaker and finally was outlawed by the Constitution of 1976 and the Penal Code, which together make illegal virtually any form of political activity outside the purview of the **Communist Party of Cuba** (Partido Comunista Cubano, PCC).

Autonomous Party (Partido Autonomista, PA); also Liberal Party (Partido Liberal, PL)

One of the first political parties in Cuba, the Autonomous Party (Partido Autonomista, PA) was created by reform-minded Cubans early in the struggle for Cuban independence, after the end of the **Ten Years War** (1868–1878) when the Spanish first allowed active political parties. The party's leadership wanted increased civil rights and a more powerful Cuban government under Spanish rule, and did not originally seek Cuban independence. The Spanish soon agreed to give Cubans a degree of control over politics on the island, allowing the PA and other parties to vie for power; however, the Spanish still largely controlled Cuban politics. Party members continued their opposition to Spanish dominance and began to support the idea of complete independence. They gained an advantage over their political rivals just before the **Spanish American War** (1895–1898; see Appendix 1) and eventually took the side of those fighting for the end of colonial rule.

Batista y Zaldívar, Fulgencio (1901–1973)

Military strongman Fulgencio Batista y Zaldívar served as president of Cuba from 1940 to 1944, and ruled the country as a dictator between 1952 and 1958.

Born in the Oriente province in January 1901 into a family of poor workers, Batista received his early education with Quaker missionaries. He later joined the army and quickly ascended the military ranks. In 1933 he joined forces with the civilian and military factions that ousted President Carlos Manuel **de Céspedes y de Quesada** (1933). From that point, Batista retained an extremely important position in the Cuban political and military spheres, facilitating many politicians' success or failure simply by pledging or denying his own support. As president in the 1940s, he ushered in a series of social welfare programs and allowed for the diversification of the political arena. He developed strong alliances with the United States government and U.S. businesses, which he maintained over the course of his leadership. In 1944 his political rival Ramón **Grau de San Martín** (1933–1934, 1944–1948) was elected president. Batista left Cuba and lived in Florida until 1948, when he was elected senator from the Santa Clara province.

In 1952 Batista was again a candidate for the Cuban presidency. Fearing he would lose the election, in March 1952 he overthrew the government of Carlos Prío Socarrás (1948–1952) and took control of Cuba, dissolving the Congress and suspending the Constitution of 1940. Batista suppressed all political opposition through intimidation, torture, and terror. He granted the United States major concessions in the **sugar** industry and facilitated the U.S. military presence on the island. He alienated the population through the use of severe repression, through neglect of the country's education and health systems, and through ignoring the economic needs of the people. Opposition grew, and in 1953 Fidel **Castro Ruz** (1959–   ) and a group of rebels attacked the Moncada army barracks to protest the Batista dictatorship (see **July 26th Movement**, M-26–7). The attack was put down, and Castro was sentenced to a fifteen-year prison term (though he was released in 1955). In 1957 another group of rebels attacked the presidential palace in a failed attempt to assassinate Batista.

The dictator was ousted in 1958 when Castro and his July 26th Movement joined forces with student and other opposition groups, including sectors of the armed forces. Batista fled to the Dominican Republic and eventually to Spain. He died in Madrid in 1973 after publishing a number of books about Cuba and his role in Cuban politics.

Bay of Pigs Invasion (1961)

On April 17, 1961, a group of 1,300 U.S.-backed Cuban exiles trained by the U.S. Central Intelligence Agency (CIA) attacked Cuba at the Bahía de Cochinos (Bay of Pigs) in an unsuccessful attempt to overthrow the regime of Fidel **Castro Ruz** (1959–   ). The exiles (see **Cuban Exile Community**) involved in the invasion had fled Cuba in the wake of the **Cuban Revolution of 1959**, outraged by their loss of power, wealth, and freedom, and specifically by the land appropriations that had been carried out by the revolutionary government. The group, which had the tentative support of U.S. president John F. Kennedy, hoped to launch a military strike, which they assumed would be supported by opposition groups in Havana and throughout the island, with the ultimate goal of destabilizing the Castro regime.

Instead, the 1,300 troops who landed in the isolated, swampy Bay of Pigs were defeated, and almost all were captured by the Cuban military. Their attempt failed for a number of reasons. The majority of their weapons never arrived, and Kennedy unexpectedly withdrew his direct support for the invasion by refusing to commit the military aid that was planned in conjunction with the invasion. In addition, the United States and the Cuban exiles overestimated the degree of opposition to Castro within Cuba. The prisoners were eventually released in exchange for over fifty tons of material aid from the United States, including clothing and medicine.

The invasion worsened U.S.-Cuban relations and strengthened anti-American sentiment on the island. The victory against the invaders strengthened Castro's support in Cuba, and Castro declared Cuba a Marxist-Leninist state in the days following the invasion. The United States, humiliated by its involvement in the event, became even more adamant about destabilizing the Castro regime and ridding the hemisphere of communist influences.

Castro Ruz, Fidel (1926–   )

Fidel Castro Ruz, leader of the **July 26th Movement** (M-26-7) that overthrew dictator Fulgencio **Batista y Zaldívar** (1940–1944, 1952–1958) in the **Cuban Revolution of 1959**, has led Cuba since the triumph of the revolution. He holds the most important positions within the government: he is president of the Council of State and president of the Council of Ministers, chair of the Communist Party, and commander-in-chief of the Revolutionary Armed Forces. Revolutionary turned totalitarian socialist leader, Castro has become world famous for his charismatic leadership, powerful personality, dynamic speaking abilities, communist ideology, and defiant stance against the United States.

Castro was born in the Oriente province on August 13, 1926. His father was a wealthy landowner who migrated to Cuba from Galicia, Spain, and his mother was a native Cuban. Castro studied law at the University of Havana from 1945 to 1950 and became politically active during that period. He joined the Orthodox Party (Partido Ortodoxo, PO; see **Authentic Party** [Partido Auténtico, PA]), was involved in a failed attempt to overthrow Dominican leader Rafael Leonidas **Trujillo y Molina** (see Dominican Republic) in 1947, and participated in the *Bogotazo* (see **Gaitán, Jorge Eliécer**, Colombia) in 1948.

Castro militantly opposed the Batista dictatorship and on July 26, 1953, he took part in an unsuccessful attack on the Moncada army barracks (see July 26th Movement), which led to a fifteen-year prison sentence and converted him into a national hero. Castro and his brother Raúl **Castro Ruz** were released from prison by Batista in 1955 under a general amnesty. They immediately went to Mexico and began training and planning further attempts to overthrow the Batista regime. During this time, Castro met Ernesto "Ché" **Guevara**, whose ideas about guerrilla warfare and revolutionary movements influenced Castro heavily. Together they formed the July 26th Movement, naming it after the date of the attack on the Moncada barracks.

In December 1956, Castro and fifty-two co-conspirators sailed to Cuba in a yacht called the *Granma* to stage another attack on the island. Following the unsuccessful assault, Castro and the twelve surviving members of the movement headed to the Sierra Maestra in the Oriente province, which became the focal point of their armed revolutionary movement against the Batista regime. From this location, Castro organized secret military training and orchestrated a propaganda campaign that contributed to the destabilization of the Batista regime. Many Cubans (particularly members of the middle and lower classes) took up arms in support of the revolutionary movement, swayed by the nationalist and anti-imperialist flavor of Castro's moderate discourse and by his promises of a more open democracy and improvements in public welfare.

Batista fled Cuba in December 1958, and the July 26th Movement, with Castro as its central figure, triumphed on January 1, 1959. The first appointed president of the regime (Manuel Urrutia Lleó, 1959) was quickly deposed, and Castro became the premier in less than two months, though it was not until 1961 that he officially declared himself a Marxist-Leninist. Castro consolidated and centralized power in the years following the revolution: he nationalized land holdings and industries from wealthy members of society, built schools for the poor, supported literacy campaigns, and created a health care system for all Cubans. While Castro's policies alienated the wealthy Cuban elite and encouraged many to flee the island, they appealed to a large portion of the population. By emphasizing ethical values and the image of the "New Cuban Man" who was committed to the improvement of the entire society, Castro gathered support for his brand of Cuban nationalism, often referred to as *Fidelismo*.

At the height of the Cold War, Castro became embroiled in geopolitics and actively supported revolutionary movements throughout the Third World. In light of that support, and the fact that his politics and ideology flew in the face of capitalism and democracy, Cuba became the target of U.S. political and economic sanctions, and Castro himself became the target of U.S.-backed assassination attempts in the 1960s. Castro aligned his regime with the Soviet Union and forged relationships with Soviet leaders Nikita Khrushchev and Leonid Brezhnev as well as many leaders of the Third World. In 1979, Castro gained international prestige when he was named president of the Non-Aligned Movement (a multilateral initiative of Third World Nations during the Cold War). In the 1980s Castro heavily influenced Nicaragua's revolutionary government led by Daniel José **Ortega Saavedra** (see Nicaragua).

Despite the withdrawal of Soviet subsidies in 1989 and the collapse of the Soviet Union and the Eastern Bloc in the early 1990s, Castro refused to abandon the essential tenets of the Cuban revolution and communism. He was forced to open the economy to some foreign investment and private enterprise so that the Cuban people could survive the austere conditions on the island; however, he retained tight control over the political landscape. In an effort to maintain prominence on the world stage, Castro received Pope John Paul II during the Pope's visit to Cuba in January 1998 and forged a close alliance with Venezuelan president Hugo **Chávez Frías** (see Venezuela); his relationship with the United States remained antagonistic. As Castro turned 75 in August 2001, friends and foes of the Castro regime raised questions about a post-Castro period in Cuba, the survival of the Cuban revolution, and the future for *"Fidelismo"* without Fidel.

Castro Ruz, Raúl (1931–   )

Raúl Castro Ruz, brother of Fidel **Castro Ruz** (1959–   ), has served as minister of the Revolutionary Armed Forces since 1959, and as first vice president of the Council of Ministers and first vice president of the Council of State since 1976. He would assume power in the event of Fidel Castro's death.

Castro was born in the Oriente province in June 1931. His father was a wealthy landowner who migrated to Cuba from Galicia, Spain, and his mother was a native Cuban. Castro studied at the University of Havana, where he became involved with the Youth of the **Communist Party of Cuba** (Partido Comunista Cubano, PCC) and grew increasingly interested in Marxist ideology. Opposed to the repressive regime of Fulgencio **Batista y Zaldívar** (1940–1944, 1952–1958), he participated in the attack on the Moncada army barracks in 1953, helped train the **July 26th Movement** (M-26–7) in Mexico, participated in the *Granma* expedition in 1956, and was involved in the guerrilla warfare that led to the triumph of the **Cuban Revolution of 1959**. Having proved his abilities as a military leader during the revolution, he was named minister of the Revolutionary Armed Forces of Cuba following the death of Camilo **Cienfuegos** in 1959. Castro was one of the early proponents of aligning with the Soviet Union and declaring Cuba a Marxist-Leninist state.

de Céspedes, Carlos Manuel (1819–1874)

Carlos Manuel de Céspedes became a national political hero as a result of his efforts to establish Cuban independence from Spain in the nineteenth century. Born into a wealthy family in the Oriente province, de Céspedes studied law at the universities of Barcelona and Madrid. Soon thereafter he became active in the cause for Cuban independence from Spain and was arrested by the Spanish government for his activities. In 1868 he announced the *Grito de Yara*, a proclamation that declared Cuban independence from Spain and began the **Ten Years War** (1868–1878). During the war, Cuban rebels established a "government of the rebellion," and de Céspedes was elected its first president in 1869. He soon grew authoritarian; criticism of his regime escalated, and he was removed from office and replaced by Salvador Cisneros Betancourt. De Céspedes was killed by Spanish troops in February 1874, and his son Carlos Manuel **de Céspedes y de Quesada** (1933) continued his legacy of political activism in Cuba.

de Céspedes y de Quesada, Carlos Manuel (1871–1939)

Carlos Manuel de Céspedes y de Quesada, son of Carlos Manuel **de Céspedes**, served briefly as president of Cuba following the overthrow of Gerardo **Machado y Morales** (1925–1933). De Céspedes y de Quesada was born in New York (where his family spent time during the **Ten Years War**, 1868–1878, in which his father fought and died) in August 1871, and studied and lived in Europe and Venezuela for much of his youth. He eventually went to Cuba and earned a law degree from the University of Havana in 1901. He was soon elected as a congressman and later obtained cabinet and foreign service positions under leaders Alfredo **Zayas y Alfonso** (1921–1925) and Machado y Morales. He was appointed president of Cuba by forces that opposed Machado y Morales in 1933. While de Céspedes y de Quesada maintained good relations with the United States, he ignored the interests of militant student and labor groups and failed to gain public support. In less than a month, he was deposed by Fulgencio **Batista y Zaldívar** (1940–1944, 1952–1958) and his supporters, who put a five-man group at the head of the government (the Pentarchy, 1933). This group quickly dissolved due to internal disputes and was succeeded by one of its members, Ramón **Grau San Martín** (1933–1934, 1944–1948). De Céspedes y de Quesada died in Havana in 1939.

Cienfuegos, Camilo (1931–1959)

Camilo Cienfuegos was the guerrilla military leader of the **July 26th Movement** (M-26–7) and briefly served as minister of the Revolutionary Armed Forces of Cuba in 1959.

Born to a poor family in the province of Havana, Cienfuegos received very little formal education as a child but was instructed by a family friend who was an outspoken communist. Later, as an artist and political activist, Cienfuegos protested against authoritarianism, corruption, and imperialism and joined forces with antifascist movements. He worked in the United States from 1951 through 1955, when he returned to Cuba to fight against the repressive regime of Fulgencio **Batista y Zaldívar** (1940–1944, 1952–1958). He soon joined Fidel **Castro Ruz**, Raúl **Castro Ruz**, Ernesto "Ché" **Guevara**, and other Cuban dissidents in Mexico and returned with them when they invaded the island in an attempt to overthrow Batista in 1956 (see *Granma*). One of only twelve survivors of that failed expedition, Cienfuegos subsequently trained with the rebels in the Sierra Maestra, serving as a military leader.

When the rebels triumphed on January 1, 1959 (see **Cuban Revolution of 1959**), Cuba's provisional president surrendered to Ché Guevara and Cienfuegos at Fort La Cabaña, and Cienfuegos took charge of the army. He was killed in a mysterious plane crash in October of that year and is considered a martyr of the revolution.

Communist Party of Cuba (Partido Comunista Cubano, PCC); also Popular Socialist Party (Partido Socialista Popular, PSP)

Originally supported by unions, the working class, students, and educators, the Cuban Communist Party (Partido Comunista Cubano, PCC) slowly broadened its ideological affiliations through the early part of the twentieth century, even briefly forming a tactical alliance with the military and Fulgencio **Batista y Zaldívar** (1940–1944, 1952–1958).

Julio Antonio Mella formed the earliest communist party on the island in 1925. The party posed a major challenge to the dictatorship of Gerardo **Machado y Morales** (1925–1933), spawning small revolutionary terrorist groups and calling strikes that paralyzed the country. The party, which changed its name to the Popular Socialist Party (Partido Socialista Popular, PSP) during the Batista regime, was heavily involved with the movements that eventually destabilized that regime, though Fidel **Castro Ruz** (1959–) and the **July 26th Movement** (M-26-7) were not initially affiliated directly with the party.

Once the **Cuban Revolution of 1959** triumphed, Castro did not immediately incorporate the PSP or communist ideology into his government. Nonetheless, following the **Bay of Pigs Invasion** (1961), Castro declared the Cuban Revolution to be Marxist-Leninist. The PSP subsequently merged with other groups to form the Integrated Revolutionary Organization (Organización Revolucionaria Integral, ORI) in 1961, which was renamed the PCC in 1965. The only legal political party existing in Cuba since 1976, the PCC dominates the media, controls most sectors of society, and facilitates the mobilization of the population in the interests of the

Cuban Revolution. The PCC has created smaller organizations for particular interests (women's groups, youth groups, neighborhood committees, etc.) in order to channel public participation through the official political party. Fidel Castro is the head of the PCC.

Cuban Exile Community

Since the victory of the **Cuban Revolution of 1959**, many Cubans have left the island for the United States, Spain, and Latin America. The term "Cuban exile community" usually refers to the group residing in Miami, Florida, which remains virulently opposed to the regime of Fidel **Castro Ruz** (1959–).

Those who opposed the **July 26th Movement** (M-26-7), including some who had been involved in the regime of Fulgencio **Batista y Zaldívar** (1940–1944, 1952–1958), were the first to flee the island. Moderates of the upper and middle classes, many of whom had supported the July 26th Movement initially, began leaving Cuba by the end of 1959 and continued to depart into the early 1960s as Castro's policies became increasingly radical. Socialist-style reforms including land and property appropriation and nationalization by the government especially angered the wealthy Cuban elite. In subsequent years, thousands of Cubans fled the country seeking political asylum from Castro's communist regime in the United States and other nations.

In an early and unsuccessful attempt to thwart Castro's power in Cuba, a group of Cuban exiles trained by the U.S. Central Intelligence Agency (CIA) launched the **Bay of Pigs Invasion** in 1961. Throughout the 1960s and 1970s many Cubans took to the Florida Strait in small boats and rafts destined for the United States. The **Mariel boatlift**, the first legally sanctioned mass migration from Cuba, brought more than 120,000 Cubans to the United States between April and September 1980. Another mass migration led to migration talks between Cuba and the United States in 1994. A controversial migration case arose in late 1999 over whether a six-year-old boy, Elián González, one of only three Cubans to survive the shipwreck of a vessel taking them from Cuba to Florida, should be placed with his relatives in Miami or returned to his father in Cuba. After months of tension between Cuba and the United States, the U.S. Justice Department finally rejected demands from the exile community for the boy's naturalization and reunited him with his Cuban father in 2000.

The Cuban American population in Miami (as well as that in New Jersey) has become a strong economic and political force in the United States, a successful business enclave, a strong, traditionally conservative voting bloc, and a significant lobbying group. Cuban Americans founded the Cuban American National Foundation (CANF) in 1980; led for many years by "strongman" Jorge Más Canosa and headed more recently by his son Jorge Más Santos, CANF has worked to bring down the Castro regime by vigorously supporting the United States trade embargo against Cuba and funding political dissidents on the island. Radio Martí, a radio station based in Miami that also broadcasts in Cuba, receives strong support from the exile community and has long been a point of contention between Cuba and the United States due to its efforts to diminish support for Castro in Cuba. Brothers to the Rescue is another Cuban American group formed to help Cuban nationals on the island and to weaken the Castro regime. Tensions between the U.S. and Cuban governments flared in February 1996 when Cubans shot down a Brothers to the Rescue aircraft that supposedly had flown illegally into Cuban airspace. The controversy led U.S. president Bill Clinton to sign the Helms-Burton Act of March 1996, the harshest version of the U.S. economic embargo that seeks to punish foreign firms doing business with Cuba. While the administrations of U.S. presidents Clinton and George W. Bush waived many of the articles in the Helms-Burton Act, the exile community continued to push for full application of the law.

Cuban Missile Crisis (1962)

The Cuban Missile Crisis began when the United States discovered Soviet nuclear capacity weapons on Cuba through U-2 spy plane photography in 1962. In October of that year, Cuba found itself in the middle of a standoff between the United States and the Soviet Union. U.S. President John F. Kennedy ordered the Soviets to remove the missiles on October 22. They did not, and by October 24 the United States established a naval blockade around Cuba in order to intercept any incoming weaponry. In the following two weeks, Kennedy and Soviet premier Nikita Khrushchev negotiated an end to the nuclear crisis: the Soviets agreed to remove the weapons if the United States agreed not to invade Cuba. Fidel **Castro Ruz** (1959–   ) was outraged that the Soviets struck such a deal with the Americans without consulting him. He refused to allow United Nations weapons inspectors onto the island and accused Khrushchev of giving in to the United States. Although U.S.-Soviet relations improved slightly following the incident, Cuban-Soviet relations were strained while Cuban-U.S. relations continued to be tense but militarily nonconfrontational.

Cuban Revolution of 1959

The Cuban Revolution led by Fidel **Castro Ruz** (1959–   ) and the **July 26th Movement** (M-26-7) overthrew dictator Fulgencio **Batista y Zaldívar** (1940–1944, 1952–1958) and triumphed on January 1, 1959. The period since the 1959 victory is also referred to as the Cuban Revolution by Castro and the Cuban population, who hold that the revolution continues to evolve. Castro has led the nation without pause since 1959, with varying degrees of internal and external criticism and support.

An obelisk commemorating the Cuban Revolution stands in the center of Havana's Plaza de la Revolución. The word on the wall below, "unidos," means "united." *Photograph by Meghann Curtis.*

The revolution that overthrew Batista grew out of societal tensions over Cuba's long history of political and economic dependence, initially on Spain and later on the United States. By the mid-twentieth century, many Cubans had begun to detest the political elite and their economic ties to the United States as well as the widening gap between the rich and the poor on the island. The Batista-led coup in 1952 and the subsequent corruption and brutal repression of the Batista dictatorship further infuriated many sectors of Cuban society.

Castro and other young activists began to oppose the Batista regime during their years at the University of Havana, and soon began to launch assaults on the dictator. Castro and others unsuccessfully attacked the Moncada army barracks on July 26, 1953. Following the failed *Granma* expedition in 1956, the leaders of the July 26th Movement (Fidel and Raúl **Castro Ruz**, Ernesto "Ché" **Guevara**, and Camilo **Cienfuegos**) organized a guerrilla army in the eastern Sierra Maestra. From there, Castro launched publicity campaigns against Batista, and took advantage of the activism of various sectors of Cuban society to organize a strategic military campaign that mobilized the opposition into secretive military cadres that were responsible for taking over certain areas of the island. The July 26th Movement capitalized on labor unions' strikes and protests against Batista, communicated with the urban sector to win over moderates and the middle class in the cities, and joined the Federation of University Students in their attack on the presidential palace in 1957.

When Bastista resigned and fled the country (December 31, 1958), Castro and other leaders of the July 26th Movement marched triumphantly into Havana and quickly began to organize a new government. While Manuel Urrutia Lleó (1959) was appointed the revolution's first president, Castro and other less moderate leaders, including members of the **Communist Party of Cuba** (Partido Comunista Cubano, PCC), soon began to push for drastic social reforms. Urrutia was forced to resign after a few months in office, and Castro took over as premier, appointing Osvaldo Dorticós Torrado (1959) as president. The leadership of the Cuban Revolution became increasingly authoritarian, and its reforms increasingly severe and socialist in nature, which angered and alienated the upper and middle classes and alarmed the United States government, which feared the threat of communism on the island. Opposition on the part of the United States and Cuban exiles escalated, culminating in the unsuccessful **Bay of Pigs Invasion** in 1961.

By the end of 1961, Castro declared Cuba a Marxist-Leninist state and aligned it with the Soviet Union, gaining that country's economic and political support. Tensions mounted as Cuba began supporting revolutionary movements in various Latin American countries, including Bolivia, Grenada, Nicaragua, El Salvador, and Chile. The **Organization of American States** (OAS; see Appendix 2) expelled Cuba in 1962. Undaunted, Cuba continued its foreign policy of revolutionary internationalism in the 1970s, sending military troops to support revolutionary movements in Angola and Ethiopia.

The Castro regime used Cuban nationalism to keep the revolution alive over the decades. Events like the "Ten Million Ton **Sugar** Harvest Campaign" in 1970 and the many anti-American rallies that were held in Havana were all efforts to reenergize the social revolution. In addition, the government actively sought to channel all facets of Cuban life through the PCC. Dissidents of the revolution were kept in check with threats of being charged and imprisoned for "counterrevolutionary" activity, and the government established neighborhood surveillance committees, known as Committees for the Defense of the Revolution, throughout the island to sustain revolutionary fervor and maintain control over the people. Over the years, Cuba continued to reform its health care and education systems (eventually succeeding in providing both services to all Cubans), carried out literacy campaigns and land appropriations, instituted policies that sought to eradicate gender, racial, and class discrimination on the island, and also reformed its military.

The gains of the revolution were undermined by continuous economic hardship that began in the 1970s when the sugar harvest failed to produce expected revenues. The withdrawal of Soviet subsidies initiated in 1989 devastated the Cuban economy, leading to a period of austerity that Castro dubbed the "Special Period in a Time of Peace." The subsequent fall of the Soviet Union, and the continued U.S. embargo significantly affected the Cuban economy in the early 1990s: the standard of living dropped, official unemployment and second economy activity rose, and the country suffered shortages of supplies and foreign reserves and a deficit in the current account balance. In view of the crisis, the Castro government implemented economic reforms to stave off recession: it passed a new foreign investment law in 1992 that made business conditions more attractive and resulted in an influx of foreign investment, allowed for some private enterprise activity, encouraged and expanded the tourism industry, and legalized the circulation of foreign currencies in 1993.

As a result of these reforms as well as the expansion of trade with new partners, the Cuban economy began to see positive annual growth after 1995. However, by the turn of the century, growth rates had not increased fast enough to allow the populace to achieve its pre-1989 standard of living. The country's economic challenges caused many Cubans to doubt the efficacy of the revolution, but reforms and continued rallying cries from the Castro regime helped the Cuban revolution to survive the crisis. While there is little indication that Cuba will transition fully to a free market economy or to a representative democracy in the near future, the survival of the revolution and its communist policies in a post-Castro period remains in question.

Cuban Revolutionary Party (Partido Revolucionario Cubano, PRC)

The Cuban Revolutionary Party (Partido Revolucionario Cubano, PRC) was formed by José Julian **Martí y Pérez**, who had been exiled from Cuba by the Spanish due to his opposition to continued colonial rule. The group strove for complete Cuban independence.

From their exile base in the United States, Martí and his counterparts organized financial and political support for their effort. They sailed to Cuba in 1895, proclaimed the *Grito de Baire* (which called for Cuban independence from Spain and an end to imperialism on the island), and began to fight for independence. Martí was killed early in the fighting, which continued under the leadership of fellow PRC members Antonio **Maceo** and Máximo **Gómez y Báez**. The independence movement was successful only after the United States intervened to support the PRC against Spain (see **Spanish American War**, 1895–1898; Appendix 1). The party dissolved following the end of the war.

Estrada Palma, Tomás (1835–1908)

Tomás Estrada Palma served as the first president of the Republic of Cuba from 1902 to 1906.

Born in the Oriente province in July 1835, Estrada studied law and philosophy at the University of Havana and the University of Seville, Spain. One of the military leaders in the early Cuban struggle for independence (see **Ten Years War**, 1868–1878), Estrada was elected president by the provisional government set up by the rebels in 1876. The Spanish arrested him in 1877, and he was held in Spanish prisons until the Pact of Zanjón (Pacto de Zanjón) between the Spanish and the rebel leaders ended the war. Upon his release, he traveled through Europe, Latin America, and the United States, and began working with José Julian **Martí y Pérez** and the **Cuban Revolutionary Party** (Partido Revolucionario Cubano, PRC).

During the **Spanish American War** (1895–1898; see Appendix 1), Estrada gained a reputation as an honest and trustworthy politician and administrator. Following the establishment of full Cuban independence in 1902, Estrada was elected the first president of the Republic of Cuba. He promoted the development of public education and responsible fiscal spending. However, during the latter part of his first term, he was accused of corruption and criticized for the close political and economic ties he maintained with the United States. He ran for reelection in 1906 as the candidate of the newly founded Conservative Republican Party. The opposition Liberal Party withdrew from the election, charging Estrada with fraud, and he was reelected but lacked public support. Rebellions led by the Liberal Party sprang up across the island later in 1906. Estrada called for U.S. intervention, as was possible under the **Platt Amendment** (1901) to the Cuban Constitution, and resigned from office, dying two years later. The United States remained in control of the presidency until 1909.

García Menocal y Deop, Mario (1866–1941)

Mario García Menocal y Deop was president of Cuba from 1913 to 1921. Born in the Matanzas province in December 1866, García Menocal spent parts of his youth in the United States and Mexico. He studied at the University of Maryland and earned a degree in engineering from Cornell University. He returned to Cuba in 1891 and worked as an engineer in the **sugar** industry and served as major general in the army during the struggle for independence. He was elected president in 1913 and successfully implemented social welfare programs in public health and education. He upheld the interests of U.S. businessmen and supported the U.S. in World War I. The wartime increase in sugar prices brought prosperity for the Cuban sugar industry, and García Menocal was reelected in 1917. However, his second administration was accused of fraud and corruption, and following his second term he returned to work in the sugar industry, though he remained active

in politics. He was a leader of the movement that opposed the regime of Gerardo **Machado y Morales** (1925–1933) and participated in the Constitutional Assembly that drafted the Constitution of 1940.

Gómez y Báez, Máximo (1836–1905)

Máximo Gómez y Báez was a hero of the Cuban war for independence.

Born in the Dominican Republic into a middle-class family, Gómez y Báez moved to Cuba in 1865 and fought with Carlos Manuel **de Céspedes** in the **Ten Years War** (1868–1878). He proved a capable military leader and earned the rank of general; he then worked closely with Antonio **Maceo** to liberate the western provinces from the Spaniards. Though Gómez y Báez favored the emancipation of slaves and the founding of a Cuban Republic, he supported the Pact of Zanjón (Pacto de Zanjón) between the Spanish and rebel leaders, which ended the Ten Years War without emancipation or independence.

Gómez y Báez later joined forces with José Julian **Martí y Pérez** and Maceo in the United States. Though Gómez y Báez quarreled with them over the relative importance to the independence movement of the military campaign versus the political struggle, the three collaborated on the 1895 invasion of Cuba that began the conflict that would escalate into the **Spanish American War** (1895–1898, see Appendix 1). Gómez y Báez took over military control of the movement when Martí was killed in 1895, and he encouraged Cubans to fight against the Spanish with weapons as well as economic measures such as halting **sugar** harvesting and production. Following the war, Gómez y Báez was asked to run for the presidency, but he declined, saying that a political career did not suit military leaders.

Gómez y Gómez, José Miguel (1874–1921)

José Miguel Gómez y Gómez was president of Cuba from 1909 to 1913 following United States occupation of the island (1906–1909). Born in the Las Villas province in July 1874, Gómez y Gómez fought in the Cuban war for independence (see **Spanish American War**, 1895–1898, Appendix 1). He later became active in politics with the Conservative Party and was elected to Congress in 1901. He switched to the Liberal Party and ran against Tomás **Estrada Palma** (1902–1906) in the presidential elections of 1906. Though Estrada was reelected, soon thereafter Gómez y Gómez accused the president of corruption and election tampering and organized insurrections against him, prompting Estrada to call in United States troops, and resign later in 1906. The United States occupied the island until 1909, when Gómez y Gómez was elected president. During his administration Gómez y Gómez focused on public education and increased military expenditures and was accused of irresponsible management of public funds.

He remained active in Cuban political life after leaving office in 1913.

Granma

The yacht the *Granma* (its name a Spanish misspelling of the English word "grandma") carried Fidel **Castro Ruz** (1959–), Raúl **Castro Ruz**, Camilo **Cienfuegos**, Ernesto "Ché" **Guevara**, and fifty-two other members of the **July 26th Movement** (M-26-7) from Mexico to Cuba on their mission to overthrow Fulgencio **Batista y Zaldívar** (1940–1944, 1952–1958). The *Granma* landed on Cuba on December 2, 1956, beginning the July 26th Movement assault on Batista's armed forces. Though the expedition failed, the few surviving members of the movement continued training in the Sierra Maestra and eventually triumphed over Batista. Today, *Granma* is the name of one of Cuba's fourteen provinces as well as the name of the daily newspaper of the **Communist Party of Cuba** (Partido Comunista Cubano, PCC).

Grau San Martín, Ramón (1882–1969)

Ramón Grau San Martín served as president of Cuba between 1933 and 1934 and between 1944 and 1948.

Grau earned a medical degree from the University of Havana and later taught physiology. He led a movement of socially committed, revolutionary students who sought to end elite rule and extend political power to marginalized groups during the administration of Gerardo **Machado y Morales** (1925–1933). Grau was exiled by Machado to the United States for his political activities, but soon returned to Cuba to lead opposition groups that were instrumental in the overthrow of Presidents Machado and Carlos Manuel **de Céspedes y de Quesada** (1933). Grau was a member of the five-man junta (Pentarchy, 1933) that succeeded de Céspedes y de Quesada and assumed the presidency upon its dissolution.

During his first administration, Grau gave women the right to vote, improved public services, and provided for agrarian reform. While his political philosophy was moderate, based on nationalism and nonradical socialism, his idealism and anti-imperialism alarmed the United States, which feared he would threaten U.S. investments in the Cuban **sugar** industry. Forces led by Fulgencio **Batista y Zaldívar** (1940–1944, 1952–1958) overthrew Grau in 1934 and placed Carlos **Mendieta y Montefur** (1934–1935) in the presidency.

Grau's second presidential term was more successful. He sought significant social reform and also strove to lessen Cuba's economic dependence on the United States. After leaving the presidency, he remained active in politics and was an outspoken opponent of the Batista regime. He retired in Havana after the triumph of the **Cuban Revolution of 1959**.

The image of Ernesto "Ché" Guevara appears on the Ministry of Defense building in Havana. The phrase below the image, "Hasta la Victoria Siempre," means "Until Victory Always." *Photograph by Meghann Curtis.*

Guevara, Ernesto "Ché" (1928–1967)

Ernesto "Ché" Guevara is a hero in Cuba and throughout Latin America for his role in revolutionary movements, including the **Cuban Revolution of 1959**.

Born in June 1928 in Rosario, Argentina, Guevara studied medicine, became a physician in 1953, and traveled throughout Latin America. He witnessed the Guatemalan socialist experiment carried out by the government of Jacobo **Arbenz Guzmán** (see Guatemala), and observed Arbenz's overthrow by right-wing factions supported by the U.S. Central Intelligence Agency (CIA) in 1954. From Guatemala, Guevara traveled to Mexico, where he met Fidel **Castro Ruz** (1959–) and other Cuban exiles who were plotting to overthrow the regime of Fulgencio **Batista y Zaldívar** (1940–1944, 1952–1958). Guevara became a key strategist in Castro's **July 26th Movement** (M-26-7), helping the group plan the rural guerrilla insurrection and urban propaganda campaign it would use to bring down Batista. In 1960 Guevara published his book *Guerrilla Warfare*, outlining his main tactics, including his *foco* theory, which posited that subjective factors were more important than objective factors in the success of revolutionary movements.

After the triumph of the Cuban Revolution on January 1, 1959, Guevara became a central part of the revolutionary government. He advised Castro on economic, industrial, and agricultural policy and promoted Cuban foreign relations with other developing nations with revolutionary movements. In 1965 Guevara traveled to Bolivia, where he planned to work with clandestine revolutionary groups. However, his groups suffered serious losses in combat with Bolivian military forces, and Guevara was captured and killed by the Bolivian military in October 1967.

Guevara is memorialized in Cuba as one of the heroes of the revolution and a champion of Marxist ideals. His theory of the "new Cuban man" is still popular in Cuba today. He remains a symbol of revolutionary hope and victory in Cuba and around the world.

July 26th Movement (M-26–7)

The nationalistic and anti-imperialist July 26th Movement, initiated by Fidel **Castro Ruz** (1959–) in opposition to the regime of Fulgencio **Batista y Zaldívar** (1940–1944, 1952–1958), is named for the date in 1953 when Castro led an unsuccessful attack on the Moncada army barracks.

Following the Moncada attack, Castro was imprisoned and exiled to Mexico. There the July 26th Movement formed and grew, as Castro, brother Raúl **Castro Ruz**, Ernesto "Ché" **Guevara**, and Camilo **Cienfuegos** prepared for armed struggle against Batista, designed a guerrilla war strategy and developed the revolutionary ideals and symbolism that became the **Cuban Revolution of 1959**. The movement suffered in the 1956 battle that followed a failed invasion of the island (see *Granma*), and its surviving twelve members fled to the Sierra Maestra. There they began to mobilize the Cuban masses, organize politically, and train militarily with the continuing goal of overthrowing the Batista regime. They worked with both moderate and revolutionary groups, eventually recruiting support throughout the cities and the countryside. They used various propaganda campaigns to target marginalized peasants and workers as well as sectors of the middle class that were tired of the brutal and corrupt dictatorship. Batista's regime fell in late December 1958, and the July 26th Movement marched into Havana on January 1, 1959. The movement, the Popular Socialist Party (Partido Socialista Popular, PSP), and other groups eventually merged to form the **Communist Party of Cuba** (Partido Comunista Cubano, PCC).

Laredo Brú, Federico (1875–1946)

Federico Laredo Brú was president of Cuba from 1936 to 1940. Born in April 1875 in the Las Villas province, Laredo began his military career during the war of independence from Spain (see **Spanish American War**, 1895–1898, Appendix 1). In 1923 he led an uprising against President Alfredo **Zayas y Alfonso** (1921–1925). He served as vice president under Miguel Mariano Gómez y Arias (1936) and was appointed president when Gómez y Arias was impeached by Congress in 1936. Laredo was supported by the military, and Fulgencio **Batista y Zaldívar** (1940–1944, 1952–1958) controlled Cuba from behind the scenes throughout Laredo's years in office. During his tenure, Laredo invested in the modernization and reformation of the **sugar** industry. He also maintained a friendly relationship with the United States, implementing a higher debt ceiling for Cubans who sought funds from the United States and

strengthening the economic ties between the two countries. In 1940 Laredo called for a Constituent Assembly (over which Carlos Prío Socarrás [1948–1952] presided), and pushed for the new charter to include an increased emphasis on civil rights and social welfare. The Constitution of 1940 was completed shortly before Laredo left office.

Liberal Party. See Autonomous Party (Partido Autonomista, PA)

Maceo, Antonio (1845–1896)

Antonio Maceo is famous for his role as part of the liberating army during the **Ten Years War** (1868–1878) and for his heroic performance in the **Spanish American War** (1895–1898; see Appendix 1). He is remembered as a hero of Cuban independence and is a role model for Cubans of African descent.

Born in Santiago de Cuba in June 1845, Maceo was the son of a Venezuelan immigrant and a freed Cuban slave. He enlisted in the rebel forces during the Ten Years War, and thanks to his strong leadership skills and strategic abilities, he advanced to the rank of general. Many feared that Maceo would lead the rebels to form a free black republic at the end of the war, but Maceo preferred to found a republic for all Cubans. He opposed the Pact of Zanjón (Pacto de Zanjón) that the Spanish and the rebel leaders signed to end the Ten Years War, as it allowed for neither independence nor emancipation, and continued fighting for independence from Spain and freedom for slaves.

Maceo fled Cuba when the battle became futile and eventually worked with José Julian **Martí y Pérez**, Máximo **Gómez y Báez**, and the **Cuban Revolutionary Party** (Partido Revolucionario Cubano, PRC) in the United States. Together these leaders planned an attack on Cuba for February 1895. Maceo returned to Cuba just after the war for independence had begun, and when Martí was killed early in the fighting, Maceo and Gómez y Báez carried on the movement for the island's autonomy. Maceo was killed in December 1896 when the Spanish ambushed his battalion.

Machado y Morales, Gerardo (1871–1939)

Gerardo Machado y Morales was president from 1925 to 1933; his regime grew increasingly authoritarian during his time in office.

Born on September 28, 1871, in the Las Villas province, Machado advanced through the military ranks during the **Spanish American War** (1895–1898; see Appendix 1). Following the war, he held several political positions and was elected president on the Liberal Party ticket, taking office in 1925. During his first term he attempted to revive the Cuban economy through a program he called "regeneration." While Machado remained wary of Cuba's political and economic dependence on the United States, he cooperated with the U.S. government and U.S. businesses.

In 1928 he stood for reelection and was able to win by garnering support from the three main political parties, Liberal, Conservative, and Popular. During his second term, he attempted to control the **sugar** industry, and his regime became increasingly repressive as Cuban economic conditions worsened during the Great Depression. He used the military to control striking workers, rebellious students, and general opposition to his rule. In response to United States criticism of his ability to manage the political situation and provide for stability, Machado became more nationalistic and authoritarian.

Soon political opposition began to manifest itself in new ways. Women's groups, student associations, revolutionary groups, unions, and professionals organized to overthrow Machado's government. As the situation became more heated, several of these opposition groups began using extreme violence, which Machado met with increasing military force and repression. In August 1933 the armed forces joined the opposition and deposed Machado. Fearful of United States intervention, they installed Carlos Manuel **de Céspedes y de Quesada** (1933). Machado died in exile in 1939.

Mariel Boatlift (1980)

The Mariel boatlift refers to the mass migration of over 120,000 Cubans to the United States from the Cuban port of Mariel between April and September 1980.

Early in 1980, six Cubans broke into the Peruvian Embassy in hopes of securing political asylum in Peru. The Cuban government sent the police force to the embassy and opened dialogue with several other Latin American countries regarding asylum and exit visas for political dissidents on the island. When President Fidel **Castro Ruz** (1959–   ) withdrew the Cuban police force from the Peruvian Embassy, over 10,000 Cubans crowded onto the grounds in hopes of getting asylum. When U.S. president Jimmy Carter denounced Castro's treatment of political opponents, Castro responded by announcing that those who wished to could come to the port of Mariel in small boats to pick up friends and family members and take them to the United States. He added the condition that they also take those whom he saw as "socially undesirable."

Between April and September 1980, more than one hundred thousand Cubans were picked up at Mariel and taken to southern Florida. The United States was faced with the task of housing and assimilating this huge influx of people, which included those whose emigration Castro had encouraged, mainly criminals, homosexuals, and mentally retarded persons. The United States risked losing face if it did not accept all of the immigrants, which it did for a time. The exodus finally ended when the United States announced in September 1980 that it could not accommodate more immigrants.

The image of José Martí adorns the public library building in Havana. *Photograph by Meghann Curtis.*

Many perceived the affair as an embarrassment to the United States and a success for Castro.

Martí y Pérez, José Julian (1853–1895)

José Julian Martí y Pérez was one of Cuba's most important literary figures. Martí became a national hero during the island's struggle for independence, and a point of reference for all Latin Americans who fought injustice and imperialism.

Martí was born in Havana on January 28, 1853, to a poor family of Spanish immigrants. As a young student he wrote on freedom, anti-imperialism, and Cuban independence. In 1869 he was arrested and sentenced to six years of hard labor for criticizing the Spanish colonial government, and in 1871 was exiled to Spain. He studied at universities in Madrid and Zaragoza and continued to write about Spanish rule in the Americas. Throughout the rest of the 1870s, Martí traveled through Latin America, France, and the United States, sometimes working as a teacher and journalist. His mastery of the Modernist literary style won him international acclaim, and his essays on justice, love, and anti-imperialism were also very well received in Latin America and around the world.

In 1892 he formed the **Cuban Revolutionary Party** (Partido Revolucionario Cubano, PRC) with other Cuban exiles in the United States. They mobilized support and gathered resources with the intention of overthrowing the Spanish government in Cuba and establishing a new republic. Martí, in collaboration with generals Antonio **Maceo** and Máximo **Gómez y Báez**, led a force that invaded Cuba in 1895, proclaimed the

Grito de Baire and Cuban independence, and thus began the conflict that would eventually escalate into the **Spanish American War** (1895–1898; see Appendix 1). Martí was killed in battle in May 1895.

Mendieta y Montefur, Carlos (1873–1960)

Carlos Mendieta y Montefur was president of Cuba from 1934 to 1935. Born in the Las Villas province in November 1873, he began his military career during the **Spanish American War** (1895–1898; see Appendix 1). After independence he was active in politics, organizing the Republican Conservative Party and serving as a congressman and governor of his home province. His presidency and those of his successors Miguel Mariano Gómez y Arias (1936) and Federico **Laredo Brú** (1936–1940) were considered puppet governments for Fulgencio **Batista y Zaldívar** (1940–1944, 1952–1958), who controlled much of the political sphere from behind the scenes during all three administrations. Mendieta's most significant action while in office was the abrogation of the **Platt Amendment** (1901) in May 1934, officially ending the right of the United States to intervene in Cuban politics. In 1935 his regime collapsed, and he resigned. José A. Barnet y Vinageras (1935–1936) became provisional president, but held office for only five months before stepping down to allow for the inauguration of Gómez y Arias in May 1936.

Orthodox Party (Partido Ortodoxo, PO); also Cuban People's Party (Partido Popular Cubano, PPC). See Authentic Party (Partido Auténtico, PA)

Platt Amendment (1901–1934)

The Platt Amendment was a clause added to the Cuban Constitution of 1901 that allowed for limited Cuban independence and awarded the United States special privileges and influence in Cuban political and military matters. After the liberation of Cuba from Spanish colonial rule in the **Spanish American War** (1895–1898; see Appendix 1), the United States maintained Cuba as a protected territory, assisting in the elaboration of political institutions and establishing military bases. In 1901 the United States agreed to withdraw troops from the island on the condition that the Platt Amendment, named after U.S. senator Orville H. Platt, be added to the Cuban Constitution. The amendment, originally attached to and passed with the U.S. Army appropriations bill of March 1901, limited the amount of foreign debt that Cuba could incur, restricted Cuba from entering into treaties with other countries, and legalized United States intervention in Cuban domestic politics. It also established the Guantánamo Bay base as a legal U.S. military outlet until such time as both Cuba and the United States would agree to its removal. The United States used these privileges to intervene in Cuba on several occasions during the early years of the republic. The Platt Amendment was revoked formally in May

1934, but the United States remained interested and involved in many aspects of the Cuban economy and state.

Popular Socialist Party. See Communist Party of Cuba (Partido Comunista Cubano, PCC)

Spanish American War (1895–1898). See Appendix 1

Sugar

Sugarcane production and the sugar refining industry have been linked to wealth and power in Cuba since the Spanish colonial period.

During the colonial period, sugar brought wealth to Cuba and to the Spanish crown, and inserted the island into the world economy. Wealthy Spaniards and creoles controlled the sugar industry, and initially, sugar production relied on a work force made up of the indigenous population. Once that population had been exhausted, African slaves were brought to the island to produce the precious commodity. Cuba became an even larger producer of sugar after the **1804 Revolution** in Haiti (see Haiti), when much of the industry moved to Cuba.

In the early years of Cuban independence, many politicians and powerful members of the elite, including President Mario **García Menocal y Deop** (1913–1921), were directly connected to the sugar industry. The United States also invested in the industry prior to the **Cuban Revolution of 1959**. Despite the wealth that sugar brought to the island, many people, including Fidel **Castro Ruz** (1959–), were dissatisfied with Cuba's dependence on sugar as an export commodity.

After the revolution, the Castro government nationalized the sugar industry and tried to break Cuban dependency on sugar production by encouraging industrialization. However, inefficiencies in other industries led Cuba back to "king sugar." In 1970 Castro led the "Ten Million Ton Harvest Campaign" that attempted to incorporate the entire Cuban population in the production of sugar, at the expense of other modes of production. The attempt fell short of its goal, and the Labor Ministry reported that productivity among sugar workers was so low that the cost of the 1970 harvest was three times higher than its value on the world market. Subsequently, Cuba counted on Soviet subsidies to support the industry until the USSR began to withdraw those subsidies in 1989.

While today the Cuban economy is still very dependent on this historic single crop, it also relies heavily on revenues from the island's lucrative tourist industry.

Ten Years War (1868–1878)

The Ten Years War represents Cuba's first serious (though failed) attempt to gain independence from Spain. The war broke out in the Oriente province in 1868 when Carlos Manuel **de Céspedes**, fellow creoles, and freed slaves declared the *Grito de Yara*, calling for universal male suffrage, the gradual liberation of slaves, and Cuban independence from Spanish rule. The war effort was complicated by disagreements among the creole population over the emancipation of slaves and whether the ultimate goal of the uprising should be the foundation of a Cuban republic or annexation by the United States.

After ten years of fighting and severe destruction to the **sugar** industry, the peace treaty that ended the war, the Pact of Zanjón (Pacto de Zanjón), was signed by the Spanish and rebel leaders. The Spanish remained in control of Cuba but granted Cubans additional political rights, including the right to form political parties. The slaves who fought with the rebels were freed under the pact, and the Spanish government promised gradual emancipation of the remaining slave population. Many rebel leaders protested the signing of the treaty because their original goals of full independence and emancipation were not met, and they continued to fight for Cuban independence (see **Gómez y Báez**, Máximo; **Maceo**, Antonio; **Martí y Pérez**, José Julian).

Zayas y Alfonso, Alfredo (1861–1934)

Alfredo Zayas y Alfonso was president of Cuba from 1921 to 1925.

Born in the Havana province in February 1861, Zayas was the first non-military president of Cuba. He received a law degree from the University of Havana in 1883 and pursued a career as a journalist and historian. He worked with José Julian **Martí y Pérez** and the **Cuban Revolutionary Party** (Partido Revolucionario Cubano, PRC) prior to the **Spanish American War** (1895–1898; see Appendix 1), but was arrested by the Spanish in 1896 when they discovered his writings in support of Cuban independence.

Jailed in exile for the remainder of the war, Zayas y Alfonso returned to the island after 1898 and held positions in the government installed by the United States, under whose trusteeship Cuba remained until 1902. He worked in the state legal system as both a judge and a prosecutor, and served as a senator from the Havana province and as mayor of Havana. Zayas y Alfonso served as vice president to President José Miguel **Gómez y Gómez** (1909–1913), and won the presidency in 1921 on the **Autonomous Party** (Partido Autonomista, PA) ticket. During his presidency, he secured the legal title to the Isle of Pines, a territory disputed by Cuba and the United States. Accusations of heavy-handed power and corruption marred his regime's reputation, and he left politics after the end of his term in 1925.

HEADS OF STATE

Tomás Estrada Palma	1902–1906
William H. Taft	1906
Charles E. Magoon	1906–1909
José Miguel Gómez y Gómez	1909–1913
Mario García Menocal y Deop	1913–1921
Alfredo Zayas y Alfonso	1921–1925
Gerardo Machado y Morales	1925–1933
Alberto Herrera French	1933
Carlos Manuel de Céspedes y de Quesada	1933
Pentarchy (Pentarquía)	1933
Ramón Grau San Martín	1933–1934
Carlos Hevía de los Reyes Gavilán	1934
Carlos Mendieta y Montefur	1934–1935
José A. Barnet y Vinageras	1935–1936
Miguel Mariano Gómez y Arias	1936
Federico Laredo Brú	1936–1940
Fulgencio Batista y Zaldívar	1940–1944
Ramón Grau San Martín	1944–1948
Carlos Prío Socarrás	1948–1952
Fulgencio Batista y Zaldívar	1952–1958
Andrés Rivero Agüero	1959
Manuel Urrutia Lleó	1959
Osvaldo Dorticós Torrado	1959
Fidel Castro Ruz	1959–

Source: Thomas E. Skidmore and Peter H. Smith, *Modern Latin America*, 4th ed. (New York: Oxford University Press, 1997).

BIBLIOGRAPHY

Print Resources

Baloyra, Enrique A., and James A. Morris, eds. *Conflict and Change in Cuba*. Albuquerque: University of New Mexico Press, 1993.

Castañeda, Jorge. *Compañero: The Life and Death of Ché Guevara*. Vancouver: Vintage Books, 1998.

Castro, Fidel. *Political, Social, and Economic Thought of Fidel Castro*. Havana: Editorial Lenox, 1959.

Dominguez, Jorge I. *Cuba: Order and Revolution*. Cambridge, MA: Harvard University Press, 1978.

———. *To Make a World Safe for Revolution: Cuba's Foreign Policy*. Cambridge, MA: Harvard University Press, 1989.

Guevara, Ernesto. *Ché: Selected Works of Ernesto Guevara*. Cambridge, MA: MIT Press, 1969.

Horowitz, Irving Louis, and Jaime Suchlicki, eds. *Cuban Communism*. New Brunswick, NJ: Transaction, 1998.

Ibarra, Jorge. *Prologue to Revolution: Cuba, 1898–1958*. Boulder: Lynne Rienner, 1998.

Patterson, Thomas G. *Contesting Castro: The U.S. and the Triumph of the Cuban Revolution*. New York: Oxford University Press, 1994.

Pérez, Louis A., Jr. *Cuba: Between Reform and Revolution*. New York: Oxford University Press, 1995.

Szulc, Tad. *Fidel: A Critical Portrait*. London: Avon Books, 2000.

Thomas, Hugh. *Cuba: The Pursuit of Freedom*. New York: Harper and Row, 1971.

Electronic Resources

Casa de las Américas
http://patriagrande.net/cuba/
Presents a nonpartisan look at Cuban history, government, political figures, culture, and current events. (In Spanish)

Cuba Political Data
http://www.cubapolidata.com/gpc/gpc.html
Private Web site containing comprehensive news, analysis, and information about politics in Cuba. Contains a vast archive of resources on government institutions, policy, leaders, and other political actors. Also has links to government documents, including electoral laws and the constitution. (In English)

Cuban American National Foundation (CANF)
http://www.canfnet.org/
Web site of a nonprofit U.S. organization dedicated to supporting democracy, freedom, and economic prosperity in Cuba. (In English and Spanish)

Cubaweb
http://www.cubaweb.cu/
Offers detailed information about the country's current events, government, economy, geography, demography, and social services. (In Spanish)

Department of State: US and Cuba
http://www.state.gov/www/regions/wha/cuba/index.html
U.S. government Web site on U.S.-Cuban relations. Contains a variety of sections detailing U.S. policy toward Cuba, fact sheets on the country, and economic and business information. (In English)

Granma Internacional Digital
http://www.granma.cu/

The Web version of Cuba's official state newspaper. Presents the official government view on Cuban politics, economics, and international relations. (In Spanish, English, French, Portuguese, and German)

Latin American Network Information Center (LANIC): Cuba
http://lanic.utexas.edu/la/cb/cuba/
Cuba section of this extensive Web site contains hundreds of links to research resources, cultural centers, economic and business institutions, government agencies, historical sources, magazines and other periodicals, nongovernmental organizations, and grassroots groups. (In English)

Political Database of the Americas: Cuba
http://www.georgetown.edu/pdba/Countries/cuba.html
Comprehensive database run as a joint project of Georgetown University and the Organization of American States. Section on Cuba contains information on and links to the executive, legislative, and judicial branches of the Cuban government; electoral laws and election results; and other political data. (In English, Spanish, Portuguese, and French)

Political Resources.net: Cuba
http://www.politicalresources.net/cuba.htm
Contains a wealth of links to sources of information on national politics. Includes information on political parties, legislative and executive institutions, laws and legislation, and elections, as well as a link to the constitution. (In English)

Republic of Cuba
http://www.cubagob.cu/
Government of Cuba's Web site. Provides news and information from the ministries of foreign affairs, of the economy, and of social services. (In Spanish)

Wilfried Derksen's Elections Around the World: Cuba
http://www.agora.it/elections/cuba.htm
Cuba section of a comprehensive database of results from elections around the world. Contains results from recent national executive and legislative elections, as well as explanations of and links to political parties and institutions. (In English)

DOMINICAN REPUBLIC

COUNTRY PROFILE

Official name	República Dominicana
Capital	Santo Domingo
Type/structure of government	Democratic republic
Executive	President and vice president elected together to serve four-year terms with no consecutive reelection permitted; cabinet selected by the president. President is chief of state and head of the armed forces and appoints governors for each of the 29 provinces.
Legislative	Bicameral National Congress: Senate (currently 30 members) and Chamber of Deputies (currently 120 members); all members are popularly elected to serve four-year terms.
Judicial	Highest court is Supreme Court of Justice, which includes sixteen judges appointed by the National Council of the Magistrate, is composed of members of the legislative and executive branches, and is directed by the president.
Major political parties	**Dominican Liberation Party** (Partido de la Liberación Dominicana, PLD); **Social Christian Reformist Party** (Partido Reformista Social Cristiano, PRSC); **Dominican Revolutionary Party** (Partido Revolucionario Dominicano, PRD).
Constitution in effect	Proclaimed in 1966; amended in 1994.
Location/geography	Occupies the eastern two-thirds of the island of Hispaniola (remaining third is occupied by Haiti), located between the Caribbean Sea and the North Atlantic Ocean. Topography is mostly mountainous.
Geographic area	48,730 sq. km.
Population	8,129,734 (July 1999 est.)
Ethnic groups	Mixed white/indigenous/black 73%; white (of European descent) 16%; black (of African descent) 11%
Religions	Roman Catholic 95%
Literacy rate	82.1% of total population (1995)
Infant mortality rate	42.52 deaths per 1,000 live births (1999 est.)
Life expectancy	70.07 years (1999 est.)
Monetary unit	Dominican peso
Exchange rate	1 U.S. dollar = 16.24 pesos (August 2000)*
Major exports	Apparel, shoes, leather goods, ferronickel, sugar, gold, coffee, cocoa
Major imports	Foodstuffs, petroleum, cotton and fabrics, chemicals and pharmaceuticals
GDP	$39.8 billion (purchasing power parity, 1998 est.)
GDP (real) growth rate	8.3% (1999 est.)
GDP per capita	$5,000 (purchasing power parity, 1998 est.)

Latin American Weekly Report. August 22, 2000 (WR-00-33). p. 394.

Source: *CIA World Factbook 1999*, unless otherwise noted. http://www.cia.gov/cia/publications/factbook/geos/dr.html

OVERVIEW

Summary

After gaining independence from Spain in the early 1820s, the Dominican Republic experienced frequent foreign occupation and intervention, beginning with the **Haitian occupation** (1822–1844) and the **Spanish Annexation** (1861–1865) in the nineteenth century, and extending into the twentieth century (see **United States occupation** [1916–1924] and **Civil War and United States intervention** [1965]). Strongman rule involving personalism, militarism, and social and economic elitism characterizes the history of the Dominican Republic, as personified by the repressive regimes led by Rafael Leonidas **Trujillo y Molina** (dictator/de facto head of state 1930–1961) and the continued conservative rule of Trujillo disciple Joaquín **Balaguer** (who served as president for twenty-four years between 1960 and 1996). Though the base of democracy is growing in the Dominican Republic with the development of literacy, political parties, interest groups, and a larger

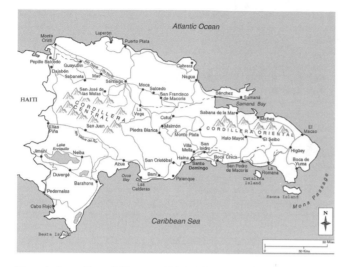

Dominican Republic. © *1998 The Moschovitis Group, Inc.*

middle class, authoritarian impulses remain a source of potential danger, particularly in times of economic distress.

History

Before Christopher Columbus arrived on the island of Hispaniola in 1492, the Caribs, a people that apparently migrated to the Antilles from the South American mainland, were battling the native Taino and Arawak peoples. Through Spanish colonization, the imposition of forced labor, and the spread of European diseases, the Caribs, Arawak, and Taino were virtually eliminated. Throughout the colonial period, both the native populations and slaves brought from Africa were excluded politically and economically.

While for the first half-century of Spanish rule (circa 1500–1550) the colonies on the island flourished, over the next three centuries the Spanish focused their energy, attention, and finances on their other colonies in the New World. Consequently, the colonies of Hispaniola degenerated economically, and were often raided by other foreign powers. In 1697 the Spanish ceded the western third of Hispaniola to the French in the Treaty of Ryswick; this cession divided Hispaniola into Saint-Domingue (as the French called their colony, today Haiti) and Santo Domingo (now the Dominican Republic) for the first time. In 1795, as a result of its defeat in European wars, Spain ceded the rest of the island to France as well. Following a violent slave revolt (see **1804 Revolution**, Haiti), Saint-Domingue gained independence from the French, becoming the Republic of Haiti in 1804. The revolting slaves swept into the eastern half of the island as well, but Spain regained control of Santo Domingo in 1809. Nonetheless, in 1822 the Haitians liberated the eastern half of the island from Spain, and retained control for the subsequent twenty-

two years in what is known as the Haitian occupation. In 1844 the Dominican Republic finally gained independence under the leadership of Juan Pablo **Duarte**.

Beginning in 1844, the tradition of *caudillo* rule took root as General Pedro Santana Familias (1844–1848, 1853–1856, 1858–1861) and Coronel Buenaventura **Báez** (1849–1853, 1856–1857, 1865–1866, 1868–1874, 1876–1878) competed for power, alternating political control of the country for more than thirty years. Both looked to foreign powers to protect and assure the governability of the Dominican Republic. When Santana voluntarily placed the country under Spanish rule in 1861, the Dominican people immediately rebelled, conducting insurrections known as the War of Restoration (1861–1865) until 1865, when the republic regained independence. Following this second independence, the Dominican Republic experienced a prolonged period of political and economic instability and deterioration, as the next half century brought a chain of short-lived administrations and rapid changes in political power, a trend broken only by the twelve-year dictatorship of General Ulises **Heureaux** (1882–1884, 1887–1899).

In light of the domestic civil unrest brought about by the plunder and mismanagement of the nation's treasury, and the large external debt that the country was steadily accruing, the United States military occupied the Dominican Republic from 1916 until 1924. The U.S. forces quelled civil unrest and established a customs receivership to enforce collection of the Dominican Republic's overdue debt. By the mid-1920s the Dominican Republic appeared to be on the road to democracy. However, Commander Rafael **Trujillo** emerged from the Dominican army created by the United States during the occupation to interrupt that tentative progress, assuming power in 1930 via a coup d'état. Trujillo ruled the Dominican Republic as a brutal dictator (at times through puppet presidents) until his assassination in 1961. Juan **Bosch Gaviño** (1963) of the **Dominican Revolutionary Party** (Partido Revolucionario Dominicano, PRD) was elected in 1962 but was overthrown by the military after only seven months. A three-man junta ran the country until 1965, when supporters of Bosch, including members of a military garrison, conducted a coup that was followed immediately by another attempted coup, leading to a brief civil war. This unrest resulted in a second intervention by U.S. troops (1965) and the subsequent installation of an **Organization of American States** (OAS; see Appendix 2) peace force in order to restore democracy.

Following this second U.S. intervention, Joaquín Balaguer, a strong supporter of Trujillo, was elected president successively in 1966, 1970, and 1974. Balaguer carried on Trujillo's tradition of repression and political manipulation. He was finally defeated by Silvestre Antonio **Guzmán Fernández** (1978–1982) of the PRD in a more participatory election in 1978, and the 1982 election of another PRD president, Salvador **Jorge Blanco** (1982–1986), seemed to promise a continuation of this shift toward democracy. However, a 1984 riot in protest of the country's excessively high inflation rate that resulted in sixty civilian deaths, coupled with the country's economic problems and a general lack of unity in the PRD, occasioned the reelection of Balaguer in 1986, 1990, and 1994 on the ticket of the **Social Christian Reformist Party** (Partido Reformista Social Cristiano, PRSC). While Balaguer pursued rapid economic growth by encouraging increased foreign investment and implementing a comprehensive public works program, great political pressure against the president led to the passing of a constitutional amendment that shortened Balaguer's last term to two years, called for 1996 elections, and outlawed consecutive presidential reelection.

The election of 1996 was the first in thirty years in which neither Balaguer nor perennial candidate Bosch ran for president. Leonel Antonio **Fernández Reyna** (1996–2000) of the **Dominican Liberation Party** (Partido de la Liberación Dominicana, PLD) won the 1996 presidential race. Fernández lacked a majority in Congress, which complicated the passage and implementation of many of his proposed reforms, and thus his record was mixed. While he was able to curb inflation and expand the economy, growth occurred only in specific sectors; the illegal drug trade flourished, agriculture stagnated, and while unemployment fell slightly and social spending increased, poor Dominicans did not feel the benefits of growth. In addition, a violent hurricane in October 1998 (George) did substantial damage to the nation's infrastructure, handicapping agricultural production.

Frustrated by endemic poverty, a high percentage of Dominicans turned out for the May 16, 2000 presidential election to choose among three candidates with markedly opposing strategies to help the poor: free-market advocate Danilo Medina of the governing PLD; left-leaning populist Hipólito Mejía (2000–   ) of the PRD; and the ninety-three-year-old Balaguer, running on the PRSC ticket and seeking an eighth term as president. Mejía garnered 49.87 percent of the vote in the first round; when second-place finisher Medina, who was some 25 percentage points behind Mejía, declined to participate in a second round (which could have been held, as no candidate had won an absolute majority in the first round), Mejía was declared the victor.

Mejía and the Dominican Republic face significant challenges in terms of economic development and political stability. The country remains extremely poor and unstable economically, and remittances from the United States are still a major source of hard currency. Conflict and tension continue to characterize the country's relationship with Haiti because of migration issues stemming from Haiti's extreme poverty relative to that of the Dominican Republic. The country's economic development and political future are, in large part, tied to the will and ability of its three major political parties to work together to keep the Dominican Republic moving in a democratic direction and to legislate and implement effective economic policy.

ENTRIES

Báez, Buenaventura (1812–1884)

Coronel Buenaventura Báez (1849–1853, 1856–1857, 1865–1866, 1868–1874, 1876–1878), alternated *caudillo* control of the Dominican Republic with General Pedro Santana Familias (1844–1848, 1853–1856, 1858–1861) for almost thirty years.

The son of a wealthy landowner and a slave, Báez began his political career representing his home province of Azua in the Haitian Congress and Constituent Assembly during the **Haitian occupation** (1822–1844) of the Dominican Republic, in which the Haitians attempted to unify the island of Hispaniola under the rule of their president, Jean-Pierre **Boyer** (see Haiti). Báez initially distrusted Dominican attempts to gain independence from Haiti, doubting that the Dominican Republic was strong enough to succeed on its own or independently repel a French attempt to regain both former colonies. He therefore attempted to establish a protectorate relationship of some kind with France, Britain, Spain, and the United States, but was never successful.

Báez assumed the presidency for the first time in 1849. Although Santana had commanded him in the army and helped him rise to the presidency, Báez quickly alienated Santana, replacing Santana's supporters (Santanistas) in the government with his own supporters (Baecistas) and pardoning opponents of Santana. Consequently, when Santana won the presidency in 1853, he exiled Báez, citing Báez's actions during the Haitian occupation as a threat to national security (despite the fact that Báez had subsequently repelled numerous Haitian attacks as president).

Santana resigned in 1856 following his unpopular negotiations with the United States over the commercial use of a small plot of Dominican land. Santana's vice president, Manuel de Regla Mota, soon stepped aside to allow Báez (next in the chain of succession) to assume the presidency. Báez quickly exiled Santana and once again installed his own Baecistas in place of Santanistas in the government. Báez also soon began to print large amounts of currency, quickly making Dominican money nearly worthless. Farmers in Cibao, angry that their crops were being bought with nearly valueless money, rose up against Báez, and their rebellion, in tandem with other political and economic problems caused by Báez's money-printing, pushed Báez from power in 1857. A provisional government was established with Santana at the helm.

After the **Spanish Annexation** (1861–1865), Báez returned to power, but his ruthless efforts to stop his opponents and his negotiations with the United States to sell the Samana Peninsula again led to revolt in Cibao, and his exile. While his supporters, still powerful, succeeded in restoring him to the presidency in May 1868, he became increasingly irrational and violent, and even tried to sell the entire country to the United States. Again, revolutionary forces removed him from power and exiled him from the country. Baecistas returned him to the island for a final term of office in 1876, but rebels again deposed him after only two years. Báez left as his legacy a country rife with conflict and lacking unity where foreign involvement seemed welcome, setting the stage for the dictatorship of Ulises **Heureaux** (1882–1884, 1887–1899) and for the **United States occupation** (1916–1924).

Balaguer, Joaquín (1907–   )

Joaquín Balaguer served as president seven times between 1960 and 1996. Emulating Rafael Leonidas **Trujillo y Molina** (dictator/de facto head of state 1930–1961), Balaguer maintained economic strength through conservative fiscal policy and retained control and power through the brutality of his National Police. Balaguer and Trujillo are two of the most influential figures in twentieth-century Dominican politics.

Balaguer was born in Villa Bisonó and was an author and a lawyer as well as an important political figure. Balaguer helped Trujillo to take power in 1930, and subsequently held a variety of posts during Trujillo's thirty-one-year reign, serving as ambassador, minister of foreign affairs, minister of education, and vice president (1957–1960); he even served as president (1960–1962) under Trujillo's de facto leadership (until the dictator's death in 1961). Nonetheless, he staunchly opposed the continuation of political leadership by the Trujillo dynasty.

Balaguer's significance in Dominican politics increased after Trujillo's death, and following a series of military juntas, a brief civil war, and U.S. occupation (see **Civil War and United States Intervention** [1965]), Balaguer was elected president in 1966 on the ticket of the Reformist Party (Partido Reformista, PR). Repression against electoral opponent Juan **Bosch Gaviño** (1963) and his supporters greatly facilitated Balaguer's victory in 1966; Balaguer was reelected in 1970 and 1974 in large part because the main opposition party, the **Dominican Revolutionary Party** (Partido Revolucionario Dominicano, PRD), terrorized by Balaguer's repressive National Police and bands of thugs organized by the police, boycotted the elections. Between 1966 and 1978, the Dominican Republic received large amounts of U.S. aid, and high world sugar prices fueled a strong Dominican economy; the country experienced record growth during late 1960s and early 1970s. While this resulted in popularity for Balaguer, that popularity

soon waned due to the political repression of his regime as well as an economic downturn brought about by high oil prices and a sharp fall in sugar prices at the end of the 1970s. Two PRD members, Silvestre Antonio **Guzmán Fernández** (1978–1982) and Salvador **Jorge Blanco** (1982–1986), won the next two presidential elections.

However, severe economic problems in the early 1980s encouraged the populace to turn once again to Balaguer, whom they reelected in 1986, 1990, and 1994. Balaguer's strategic creation of a unified political party to support his candidacy, the **Social Christian Reformist Party** (Partido Reformista Social Cristiano, PRSC, an alliance of Balaguer's PR and the original PRSC), facilitated these electoral successes, affording him the political backing of unions, students, and peasant organizations. From 1986 to 1994 Balaguer maintained popularity by implementing conservative economic policies to satisfy the wealthy, and by giving enough government jobs and land to the poor to retain their support. Balaguer also simultaneously maintained positive relations with the United States while establishing better relations with Cuba, and prevented the military from uniting against him by changing military assignments often and rewarding those in the military who supported him.

Though he was elected to a four-year term in 1994, complaints of electoral fraud soon became widespread. Public opinion and pressure from the legislature resulted in the passage of an extraordinary constitutional amendment that shortened Balaguer's term to two years, called for 1996 elections, and outlawed consecutive presidential reelection, effectively barring Balaguer from running in the 1996 contest. While Balaguer did run once again in the May 2000 presidential election, he was overwhelmingly defeated by Hipólito Mejía (2000–   ) of the PRD.

Bosch Gaviño, Juan (1909–   )

Elected in 1962 in the first free and fair election following the 1961 assassination of dictator Rafael Leonidas **Trujillo y Molina** (dictator/de facto head of state 1930–1961), Juan Bosch Gaviño served as president for only seven months before being ousted by a military coup. He subsequently became the perennial opposition candidate in national elections, repeatedly losing to Trujillo's disciple, Joaquín **Balaguer** (1960–1962, 1966–1978, 1986–1996).

Bosch was born in La Vega in 1909. Before launching his political career, he was a sociologist, historian, and novelist. Suppression of his work and a year spent in jail (1934–1935) on conspiracy charges inspired him to become active politically. Bosch lived in self-induced exile in various Latin American countries from 1938 to 1956. His true political involvement began while he was living in Cuba, where he helped to found the **Dominican Revolutionary Party** (Partido Revolucionario Dominicano, PRD) in 1939, and participated in the planning of Cayo Confite, a failed attempt in 1947 (inspired by Fidel **Castro Ruz**; see Cuba) to overthrow Trujillo in an invasion launched from Cayo Confite off the coast of Cuba, and worked as secretary for Cuban president Carlos Prío Socarrás from 1948 to 1952.

Following his victory in the 1962 presidential election, Bosch sought to confiscate and redistribute Trujillo's landownings as part of a program of agrarian reform. However, his efforts at improving the lot of the masses worried traditional elites, who saw his innovations as dangerously akin to similar actions taken in Castro's Cuba. As a result, he was removed by the military (backed by conservative businessmen, the Catholic Church, and landowners) after holding office for only seven months and exiled to Puerto Rico, where he lived from 1963 to 1966. His supporters continued to promote him, hoping that he would return to the Dominican Republic and lead them in an uprising against the new government, an unpopular three-man civilian junta led by Donald Reid Cabral (1963–1965). In 1965 Bosch supporters participated in a coup, which began the **Civil War** that resulted in U.S. military intervention.

In 1966, running again on the PRD ticket, Bosch opposed but lost to Balaguer of the Reformist Party (Partido Reformista, PR), the predecessor of today's **Social Christian Reformist Party** (Partido Reformista Social Cristiano, PRSC). Bosch left the PRD in order to found the **Dominican Liberation Party** (Partido de la Liberación Dominicana, PLD) in 1973. Bosch lost the 1990 presidential election to Balaguer in a very tight race, and subsequently accused Balaguer of fraud. Bosch will be remembered as a great author as well as a longtime opposition candidate in Dominican politics.

Civil War and United States Intervention (1965)

U.S. president Lyndon B. Johnson sent marines to the Dominican Republic in 1965 to support conservative forces and stabilize the nation, which was experiencing significant political turmoil.

Shortly after the 1961 assassination of long time dictator Rafael Leonidas **Trujillo y Molina** (dictator/de facto head of state 1930–1961), Juan **Bosch Gaviño** (1963) came to power. Bosch led the nation for only seven months before a coup d'état brought a three-person civilian junta led by Donald Reid Cabral (1963–1965) to power. The junta gained neither the support of the country's conservative groups nor that of the backers of exiled President Bosch, and in April 1965 a group of Bosch supporters, including civilians, members of the military, members of the **Dominican Revolutionary Party** (Partido Revolucionario Dominicano, PRD), and members of a group who called themselves the constitutionalists (in reference to their support of the 1963 Constitution), staged a coup and appointed Rafael Molina Urena as president until Bosch could return to the country to assume the presidency. The following day,

The Costa Rican National Guard arrives in the Dominican Republic to help maintain order during the civil unrest of 1965. *Columbus Memorial Library, General Secretariat of the Organization of American States. Reproduced with permission of the Organization of American States.*

army general Elías Wessin y Wessin (1965) led a conservative group of military known as loyalists in an attempted coup against the constitutionalists. Despite the loyalists' military strength, the constitutionalists held their ground and appeared close to victory.

Alarmed, U.S. president Johnson sent U.S. Marines to the island to restore order. Johnson, believing that the constitutionalists were communists, and hoping to avoid Bosch's return to power, instructed the U.S. forces to support Wessin y Wessin. Mexico and Chile protested this violation of Roosevelt's **Good Neighbor Policy** (see Appendix 2) of nonintervention. The **Organization of American States** (OAS; see Appendix 2) eventually sent a peace force to the Dominican Republic; the OAS troops supported the U.S. Marine presence, which ultimately reached 20,000 troops. Violent episodes continued between loyalists and constitutionalists through late 1965, and U.S. troops were not completely withdrawn until presidential elections were held in 1966.

Dominican Liberation Party (Partido de la Liberación Dominicana, PLD)

Juan **Bosch Gaviño** (1963) founded the Dominican Liberation Party (Partido de la Liberación Dominicana, PLD) in 1973 as a more radical alternative to the **Dominican Revolutionary Party** (Partido Revolucionario Dominicano, PRD). The party has been secondary in importance to the PRD and the **Social Christian Re-**

formist Party (Partido Reformista Social Cristiano, PRSC).

The PLD initially promoted a strong anti-U.S. approach, maintained close ties to the Soviet Union (and later to Russia) and Cuba, and supported the creation of a "revolutionary dictatorship" (though it later disavowed these ideas). It gained popularity in the 1980s as a result of the Dominican Republic's increasing economic and political problems. The PLD became the chief opponent of the Reformist Party (Partido Reformista, PR, which later became the PRSC) when the PRD divided into two factions in the late 1980s. Leonel Antonio **Fernández Reyna** (1996–2000) replaced Bosch as president of the party in 1995 and was elected president of the country on the PLD ticket the following year (with the support of the PRSC), defeating PRD candidate José Francisco **Peña Gómez** in a very close race.

When Fernández entered office, his PLD held only one Senate seat and thirteen seats in the Chamber of Deputies, and faced strong opposition from the PRD. In addition, the PRSC quickly came to feel that its support for Fernández in the 1996 elections was not being reciprocated, and withdrew congressional backing. This, in conjunction with the legislature's institutional weakness, complicated the passage and implementation of Fernández and the PLD's desired programs. Although the 1998 mid-term elections resulted in the election of PLD members to four Senate seats and forty-nine seats in the Chamber of Deputies, the PRD maintained a congressional majority.

Dominican Revolutionary Party (Partido Revolucionario Dominicano, PRD)

The Dominican Revolutionary Party (Partido Revolucionario Dominicano, PRD) was formed in 1939 by a group of Dominicans exiled for their political opposition to Rafael Leonidas **Trujillo y Molina** (dictator/de facto head of state 1930–1961). The PRD has been the Dominican Republic's best-organized party, and has espoused the most consistent ideology, centered around the promotion of democracy and nationalism.

After consistently opposing Trujillo's dictatorship for over two decades, the party finally gained representation in the government with the election of party cofounder Juan **Bosch Gaviño** (1963) to the presidency in 1962. Bosch was soon overthrown, and subsequent escalating political turmoil finally led to the outbreak of **civil war and United States intervention**, and new elections in June 1966. Bosch was defeated in that election, and the PRD boycotted national elections for the next twelve years due to the repression unleashed on the opposition by President Joaquín **Balaguer** (1960–1962, 1966–1978, 1986–1996).

In 1973 Bosch left the PRD to form his own party, the more radical **Dominican Liberation Party** (Partido de la Liberación Dominicana, PLD), and José Francisco **Peña Gómez** took control of the PRD. While two PRD candidates, Silvestre Antonio **Guzmán Fernández** (1978–1982) and Salvador **Jorge Blanco** (1982–1986), were consecutively elected president, economic difficulties prevented them from successfully implementing their social programs. Following the PRD's loss of control of the presidency in 1986, it divided into two factions: a right-leaning faction led by Jacobo Majluta Azar (1982), and a left-leaning faction led by Peña Gómez. These internal divisions greatly weakened the party, resulting in its failure to elect another Dominican president until PRD candidate Hipólito Mejía's (2000–) victory in the May 2000 presidential election.

Duarte, Juan Pablo (1813–1876)

Juan Pablo Duarte's efforts to free his country from the **Haitian occupation** (1822–1844) and later from **Spanish Annexation** (1861–1865) earned him the title "Father of Dominican Independence." The Haitian occupation was an attempt to unify the island of Hispaniola under the rule of Haitian president Jean-Pierre **Boyer** (see Haiti). Duarte was one of the founding members of *La Trinitaria*, a secret organization formed in 1838 to remove the Haitians from power. Though the group was ultimately successful, Duarte was exiled before Haitian president Boyer was removed. After the transition to Dominican rule, Duarte returned to the Dominican Republic, but his idealism put him at odds with General Pedro Santana Familias (1844–1848, 1853–1856, 1858–1861; see **Baez** Buenaventura), and he was soon exiled again. Duarte returned again briefly to the Dominican Republic, but was exiled a third time in 1865 after he led his countrymen in protest against the Spanish Annexation. Despite spending over twenty-five years of his life in exile, Duarte is considered a national hero.

Fernández Reyna, Leonel Antonio (1953–)

Leonel Antonio Fernández Reyna, of the minority **Dominican Liberation Party** (Partido de la Liberación Dominicana, PLD), was president from 1996 to 2000. Fernández replaced longtime PLD leader Juan **Bosch Gaviño** (1963) in 1995 as head of the party. In 1996 Fernández was elected president by a slim margin over **Dominican Revolutionary Party** (Partido Revolucionario Dominicano, PRD) opposition candidate José Francisco **Peña Gómez** in the second round of voting. His victory was in part due to the support of Joaquín **Balaguer** (1960–1962, 1966–1978, 1986–1996) and the **Social Christian Reformist Party** (Partido Reformista Social Cristiano, PRSC). For the first two years of Fernández's presidency, the PLD enjoyed very little congressional support, which hindered Fernandez's ability to carry out his political agenda. Nonetheless, Fernández focused on improving fiscal discipline and increasing the effectiveness of tax collection. He also took a strong stance on relations with Haiti; shortly after assuming office, he deported 15,000 Haitians, prompting a deterioration of island relations. While Fernández visited Haiti in 1998 (the first visit by a Dominican president in sixty-two years) in an effort to ease tensions between the two countries, relations remain strained.

The PLD more than doubled its congressional seats in the legislative election of 1998. However, before Fernández could capitalize on that increased legislative support, Hurricane George hit the island in October 1998, causing widespread damage and occasioning the expenditure of a huge amount of government resources. By 2000 Fernández's record was mixed: he had been able to curb inflation, and under his leadership the country's economy had experienced significant growth (7.3 percent in 1998, 8.3 percent in 1999, and an estimated 12 percent in 2000). However, growth occurred only in specific sectors (tourism, telecommunications, and construction), and the illegal drug trade continued to flourish, while agriculture was stagnant. Public investment went toward a few big projects in the cities, and though unemployment fell slightly and social spending increased, poor Dominicans did not feel the benefits of growth. Fernández was succeeded by Hipólito Mejía (2000–) of the PRD.

Guzmán Fernández, Silvestre Antonio (1911–1982)
Silvestre Antonio Guzmán Fernández, president from 1978 to 1982, pursued a reform agenda in a less aggressive manner than some members of the **Dominican Revolutionary Party** (Partido Revolucionario Dominicano, PRD) would have liked.

Guzmán was born in 1911 in the northern city of La Vega. As a teenager he held a management position with the Curaçao Trading Company, and by 1940 he was a wealthy cattle rancher. After the 1961 death of Rafael Leonidas **Trujillo y Molina** (dictator/de facto head of state 1930–1961), Guzmán joined the liberal PRD and rose through the ranks of the party under the direction of its founder, Juan **Bosch Gaviño** (1963). The PRD boycotted the 1970 and 1974 elections to protest the fraud and violence of President Joaquín **Balaguer** (1960–1962, 1966–1978, 1986–1996), and Bosch left the PRD to form the **Dominican Liberation Party** (Partido de la Liberación Dominicana, PLD) in 1973.

Bosch's departure made way for Guzmán to run on the PRD ticket in the 1978 presidential election, which he won by promising to reduce federal expenditures on the expensive public works projects of the Balaguer administration. However, the dominance of Balaguer's **Social Christian Reformist Party** (Partido Reformista Social Cristiano, PRSC) in the Senate (due to a questionable counting method employed by the Central Electoral Board to tally the votes of the 1978 congressional election) made implementing the policies he had promised nearly impossible. Guzmán's attempts to effect change were also hindered by increasing oil prices (one of the country's leading imports) and falling sugar prices (one of the country's main exports). Guzmán was

forced to impose austerity policies to combat the country's economic problems, thus decreasing his popularity. Despite these challenges, Guzmán made a valuable contribution to the development of a truly democratic state by depoliticizing the military through promoting younger, more apolitical officers, removing or demoting those officers who were more politically active, institutionalizing a course of study for officers, and enlisting soldiers who recognized the importance of a nonpolitical, professional military in a democratic state.

Guzmán committed suicide in 1982, forty-three days before the end of his term, leaving Vice President Jacobo Majluta Azar to serve the remainder of his time in office. Though Guzmán had promoted Majluta as the PRD candidate for the 1982 presidential election, the PRD chose the more liberal Salvador **Jorge Blanco** (1982–1986) as its candidate. Jorge Blanco was victorious and, despite a contrasting ideology, carried on Guzmán's democratic legacy.

Haitian Massacre (1937)
Rafael Leonidas **Trujillo y Molina** (dictator/de facto head of state 1930–1961) ordered the execution of all Haitians in the Dominican Republic in 1937, prompting an international outcry and highlighting the strained relations between the two nations. Complaining that the border areas between the Dominican Republic and Haiti were dominated by Haitians who were not involved in the Dominican economy, Trujillo ordered all Haitians who were residing on Dominican soil to be killed in early October 1937. In compliance, the Dominican army murdered between 18,000 and 25,000 Haitians. Trujillo tried to create the impression that Dominican peasants had risen up against Haitian cattle thieves; his government never admitted that it had blatantly carried out the genocide of thousands of Haitians. The reaction throughout the Americas was very negative, and international pressure led the Trujillo government to agree to pay the Haitian government $750,000 in compensation for damages and injuries caused by what the Trujillo government called "frontier conflicts." Secretly, Trujillo sent a special envoy to Port-au-Prince to bribe Haitian officials to reduce the total compensation from $750,000 to $525,000.

In the end, Trujillo got his wish: the border areas that had long been under Haitian control were reincorporated into the Dominican Republic through a process termed Dominicanization, and eventually made economically productive. The repopulation of those border areas with native Dominicans and the strong presence of the Catholic Church in the country helped Trujillo perpetuate the myth that he was the protector of the Hispanic and Catholic heritage of the Dominican Republic. The event clearly demonstrated the continued presence of the racial and economic tensions that had traditionally complicated relations between the two countries.

Haitian Occupation (1822–1844)

Haitians attempted to unify the island of Hispaniola under the rule of Haitian president Jean-Pierre **Boyer** (see Haiti), occupying the Dominican Republic from 1822 until 1844.

In the early 1800s, anxious to gain independence from France as Haiti had done in 1804 (see **1804 Revolution**, Haiti) and, after 1809, independence from Spain, Dominicans were considering movements to join Gran Colombia (see **Bolívar y Palacios**, Simón Antonio de la Santísima Trinidad, Colombia) or Haiti. Both Haitians and Dominicans believed unification of the island could be a source of strength and independence from colonial powers. On November 15, 1821, the Dominican pro-Haitian political party in two Dominican border towns declared independence from Spain, asking to be protected by Haitian laws and requesting Haitian arms to defend themselves. On November 30, 1821, troops led by Dominican José Núñez de Cáceres gained control of the Spanish colony, proclaiming it the Independent State of Spanish Haiti. While Núñez de Cáceres envisioned the state as a part of Gran Colombia, a letter from Haitian president Boyer outlining why establishing separate states on the island was impractical, the manifest support of the Dominican mulatto population for unification with Haiti, and the dissatisfaction of wealthy Dominicans with independence from Spain convinced Núñez de Cáceres to accept unification with Haiti in 1822.

Under Haitian president Boyer, Haitians and Dominicans focused on increasing the island's economic strength and creating a unified nation. Ironically, the push for prosperity that had motivated unification also caused its downfall. Various laws implemented by Boyer, including his "Rural Code" (a collection of decrees made in 1826 that sought to increase the productiveness of the land), were immediately unpopular with Dominicans, in part because they were at odds with Spanish systems to which Dominicans were accustomed. When Boyer refused to repeal an unpopular 1835 law requiring import duties to be paid in foreign currency, the former Spanish colony reached its boiling point.

While differences in viewpoint on agricultural and economic policy were important to the eventual dissolution of the union, intolerance of fundamental societal and cultural differences, given the areas' differing colonial heritages (Haiti had mainly been a French colony and the Dominican Republic mainly a Spanish one), were even more crucial. Some Dominican historians have even portrayed the occupation as culturally abusive, noting that Boyer placed Haitians in higher administrative positions, severed ties between the Catholic Church in the unified state and Rome, destroyed Hispanic culture, and closed the main Dominican university.

In July 1838 in Santo Domingo, Juan Pablo **Duarte**, who had seen his father's business ruined under Haitian rule, began to assemble a group to oppose the Haitian occupation and its economic impositions. The group, which eventually became known as *La Trinitaria*, was ultimately successful, and Boyer was ousted from office in 1843. His ouster left Haiti in a state of civil war, and an army under the leadership of General Pedro Santana Familias (1844–1848, 1853–1856, 1858–1861; see **Báez**, Buenaventura) liberated the Dominican Republic from Haiti in 1844.

Heureaux, Ulises (1844–1899)

Ulises Heureaux, of mixed racial descent, led the country from 1882 to 1884 and from 1887 to 1899, despite the racial prejudice of the time. He quickly evolved into a dictator, creating a police state and enforcing economic policy that ultimately proved destructive to the Dominican economy.

Heureaux rose from humble beginnings as the illegitimate son of a Haitian father and a mother from St. Thomas, and experienced the racial prejudice of the late nineteenth-century Dominican Republic from an early age. Heureaux joined a revolt against Spain in the 1860s, quickly distinguished himself in the military, and eventually rose to attain the influential position of interior minister under President Fernando Arturo de Meriño (1880–1882). In September 1882, amid chaos, de Meriño relinquished power to Heureaux. During Heureaux's subsequent two-year term as president, the Dominican Republic enjoyed relative political stability. While Heureaux wanted to rule the country, he did not want to serve as president, and so threw his support to Francisco Gregorio Billini (1884–1885) in the presidential election of 1884, assuming that Billini would serve as his puppet if elected.

Billini won the 1884 presidential contest but rejected attempts by Heureaux to dictate his actions. This resistance prompted Heureaux to spread scandalous political rumors that led to Billini's resignation in May 1885. Power was transferred to Vice President Alejandro Woss y Gil (1885–1887), who proved more willing to serve as Heureaux's puppet. Heureaux became the commander of the national army and placed his supporters in key positions in Woss y Gil's administration. With the support of the Blue Party, a liberal party from Cibao in the North, and with obvious electoral fraud, Heureaux won the 1886 presidential election.

Following a brief armed rebellion by the opposition, Heureaux took office in early 1887. Elections were held again in 1888, and Heureaux was opposed by Gregorio Luperón. Despite the strong support of liberals from Luperón's Blue Party, Luperón eventually realized that victory was impossible given Heureaux's corrupt practices, and fled the island. Consequently, Heureaux easily won the election and soon consolidated a dictatorship: he created a police state, amended the constitution to abolish direct elections and establish an electoral college system, created a strong power base (incorporating members of both major parties), established a network of secret police and informants, and restricted the press.

Under Heureaux's leadership, the Dominican foreign debt rose substantially due to his large infrastructure projects and other presidential extravagancies. Even with considerable growth in agriculture, particularly in the sugar industry, the country went bankrupt due to Heureaux's disastrous economic decisions. Heureaux responded in 1897 by printing large amounts of money, which soon caused the nation's currency to become practically worthless. Heureaux's mismanagement of the country's finances was a major factor leading to the eight-year **United States occupation** (1916–1924).

An organization called the Young Revolutionary Junta eventually emerged in opposition to Heureaux's dictatorial ways. One of the group's members, Ramón Cáceres Vásquez, shot and killed the president in 1899, ending the twelve-year Heureaux dictatorship and bringing Vice President Wenceslao Figuereo (1899) to the presidency.

Jorge Blanco, Salvador (1926–)

Salvador Jorge Blanco (1982–1986) was the second consecutive **Dominican Revolutionary Party** (Partido Revolucionario Dominicano, PRD) president. Though his moderate social democratic ideology contrasted with that of his predecessor, the more conservative Silvestre Antonio **Guzmán Fernández** (1978–1982), Jorge Blanco's government continued the respect for civil liberties and human rights that had characterized the previous administration, a policy that distinguished his presidency. Jorge Blanco also promised to bring "economic democracy" to the country, but his term in office coincided with a worldwide economic recession that significantly increased the price of oil (one of the country's chief imports) and severely constricted export markets for Dominican products (especially in Europe and the United States). This made Jorge Blanco's reform policies impossible to implement and forced him to impose austerity measures, including a reduction in government services. These policies, which were in strong contrast to the president's campaign ideology, were especially hard on the poor and resulted in anger and violent protests, culminating with riots in 1985. Nonetheless, Jorge Blanco's balanced economic austerity program helped to stabilize the nation's economy at least marginally before he yielded the presidency to Joaquín **Balaguer** (1960–1962, 1966–1978, 1986–1996) in the 1986 elections.

In 1987, the Balaguer administration formally accused Jorge Blanco of illegal enrichment and other crimes while in office, and condemned him to twenty years in prison in August 1991. However, he never served this sentence and continued to be active in the PRD leadership. In May 2000, following the election of PRD candidate Hipólito Mejía (2000–) to the presidency, the sentence was annulled by the Santo Domingo Court of Appeals. However, shortly thereafter it was announced that Jorge Blanco and ten of his collaborators would again be tried for presumed corruption.

Peña Gómez, José Francisco (1937–1998)

José Francisco Peña Gómez was the leader of the **Dominican Revolutionary Party** (Partido Revolucionario Dominicano, PRD) for more than thirty years. Throughout his political career, Peña Gómez supported liberal ideas, appealing to the urban poor.

Both of Peña Gómez's parents were killed in the **Haitian Massacre** in 1937 shortly after his birth. Despite this tragedy, he went on to study law, and was later recruited by the PRD. A skilled and charismatic speaker, he rose quickly in the party after receiving political training in Peru and Venezuela. Among his major accomplishments were the important contacts he made for the party within the military, and his successful reorganization of the party after Juan **Bosch Gaviño** (1963), one of the PRD's founders, was forced from office in 1963. After Bosch ran a half-hearted campaign on the PRD ticket and subsequently lost the presidential election of 1966, Bosch and Peña Gómez came into conflict over the future of the party. Though Peña Gómez resigned as secretary general of the PRD in 1973, when Bosch left the party to form the more radical **Dominican Liberation Party** (Partido de la Liberación Dominicana, PLD) later that year, Peña Gómez reassumed leadership of the party. He served as mayor of Santo Domingo from 1978 to 1982.

Peña Gómez was to be the running mate of Jacobo Majluta Azar (1982) on the PRD ticket in the presidential election of 1986, a contest the party was likely to win following their electoral victories in 1978 and 1982. However, due to intense rivalry between Peña Gómez and Majluta, Peña Gómez withdrew. He competed for the presidency on the PRD ticket in the elections of 1990 and 1994, but lost both contests to **Social Christian Reformist Party** (Partido Reformista Social Cristiano, PRSC) candidate Joaquín **Balaguer** (1960–1962, 1966–1978, 1986–1996). The issue of Peña Gómez's nationality (he is of Haitian descent) hurt his candidacy in both contests.

Santana Familias, Pedro (1801–1964). See Báez, Buenaventura; Haitian Occupation (1822–1844); Spanish Annexation (1861–1865)

Social Christian Reformist Party (Partido Reformista Social Cristiano, PRSC)

The Social Christian Reformist Party (Partido Reformista Social Cristiano, PRSC), dominated for more than fifty years by Joaquín **Balaguer** (1960–1962, 1966–1978, 1986–1996), lacked a consistent political ideology but garnered support by offering jobs to its backers in return for their votes and political support.

The contemporary PRSC has its roots in the Reformist Party (Partido Reformista, PR). As leader of the PR, Balaguer won the presidential elections of 1966, 1970, and 1974, but lost the elections of 1978 and 1982 to **Dominican Revolutionary Party** (Partido Revolucionario Dominicano, PRD) candidates Silvestre Antonio **Guzmán Fernández** (1978–1982) and Salvador **Jorge Blanco** (1982–1986), respectively. Frustrated with his lack of electoral success, Balaguer joined his PR with the PRSC, to form a larger party that kept the latter name. This strategic alliance gave Balaguer the support of unions, students, and peasant organizations, and helped him to win the presidential elections of 1986, 1990, and 1994.

In the late 1980s and early 1990s, Balaguer and the conservative PRSC implemented neoliberal economic reforms, but did little to encourage democratic political development in the Dominican Republic. The PRSC remains one of the dominant political parties in the country today. However, it is considered a personalistic party, inextricably linked to Balaguer. The party's future will depend on who replaces the aging Balaguer as party leader following his resignation or death.

Spanish Annexation (1861–1865)

In 1861 President Pedro Santana Familias (1844–1848, 1853–1856, 1858–1861; see **Báez**, Buenaventura) invited Spain to annex the Dominican Republic. Dominicans immediately rose up in a series of revolts that eventually culminated in the War of Restoration (1863–1865) through which the country regained its independence in 1865.

Ongoing conflicts with and invasions from neighboring Haiti (see **Haitian occupation** [1822–1844]), in addition to fear that economic and political problems could make the Dominican Republic ungovernable, motivated Presidents Santana and Báez (1849–1853, 1856–1857, 1865–1866, 1868–1874, 1876–1878) to seek to quell domestic political strife through establishing a protectorate relationship with powerful foreign nations. After several failed attempts to attract the United States, France, or Spain to annex the country, Santana was finally able to arrange for annexation by Spain in 1861. Spain's leader, General Leopoldo O'Donnell, was interested in gaining new land, and was reassured that the United States would not use force to back up the **Monroe Doctrine** (see Appendix 2), as the U.S. was preoccupied by the civil war being waged in the United States in the early 1860s.

However, it soon became clear that the majority of Dominicans opposed annexation: the first revolts against the Spanish occurred just two months after the initiation of Spanish control, and Santana quashed major rebellions in May and June 1861. Beyond frustration with the loss of independence and the imposition of foreign policy and leadership that annexation implied, Dominicans were enraged by the high taxes, strict religious reform, and restricted trade the Spanish imposed. High inflation and racial tensions only exacerbated the situation. Ironically, even Santana soon grew frustrated with the Spanish and the restrictions to his power that their leadership brought, and resigned his Spanish-granted position of captain general in 1862.

Alarmed by the resistance, the Spanish declared a state of siege in 1863, which unwittingly fueled the rebels and led to the consolidation of the rebellions. Though Dominican troops remained loyal to Spain, the rebels succeeded in establishing a provisional government in the north of the Dominican Republic in September 1863 under the leadership of General José Antonio Salcedo Ramírez. The provisional government soon declared an Act of Independence that eventually led to the outbreak of the War of Restoration. Santana lost his remaining support, and the provisional government declared that he should pay for his treason with death; Santana allegedly committed suicide in June 1864. The provisional government held a national convention, adopted a new constitution, and elected Pedro Antonio Pimentel Chamorro president in February 1865, further consolidating the strength of the opposition.

Given Spanish casualties in battle, Spanish deaths from disease, the end of the Civil War in the United States, and the spreading and strengthening of the insurrection, the Spaniards soon realized that the situation was out of their control. In March 1865, the queen of Spain repealed the annexation of Santo Domingo and withdrew Spanish troops from the island. Two political parties subsequently were formed in the Dominican Republic, the liberal Blue Party, dominated by residents of Cibao, and the more conservative Red Party, based in the South. The Spanish Annexation and consequent strife left the country less centralized both politically and militarily, robbed the political arena of democratic tradition, and resulted in great political instability.

Trujillo y Molina, Rafael Leonidas (1891–1961)

Rafael Leonidas Trujillo y Molina ruled the Dominican Republic as dictator, and, when not directly in power, as de facto head of state from 1930 until his assassination in 1961.

Born in San Cristobal, Trujillo worked as a security guard and as a telegraph operator before joining the U.S.-created National Guard in 1918 (see **United States occupation** [1916–1924]). Trujillo rose rapidly within the organization, and when U.S. troops withdrew in 1924 and the National Guard became the Dominican National Police, Trujillo was named chief of police. In 1928 this police force was transformed into the National Armed Forces, and he became commander in chief of the military. With the support of the United States, he became president in 1930.

Trujillo used coercion and violence to control the Dominican people, closing down any political party, news

Rafael Leonidas Trujillo y Molina (wearing sash) led the Dominican Republic as dictator or de facto head of state from 1930 to 1961. *Columbus Memorial Library, General Secretariat of the Organization of American States. Reproduced with permission of the Organization of American States.*

organization, or labor union that opposed him. He modernized the country, developing a paved road system, building new factories, and encouraging the utilization of agricultural machinery. He also amassed a huge personal fortune that some estimate at $800 million. He tried to "whiten" the population by killing an estimated 25,000 Haitians living in the Dominican Republic in the **Haitian Massacre** (1937), and by encouraging the immigration of whites from Europe and Asia. In 1938 he arranged the electoral victory of Jacinto Bienvenido Peynado (1938–1940), but remained in complete control of the country from behind the scenes.

Trujillo initially gained U.S. support by making payments on the debt the Dominican Republic owed to the United States, and subsequently maintained a very close relationship with the United States, which strengthened his control of the country. The two nations signed the Trujillo-Hull Treaty in 1940, which called for the United States to stop collecting Dominican customs duties (which it had done since its 1916–1924 occupation). In an effort to garner stronger U.S. support, Trujillo supported the United States in World War II and became violently anticommunist in 1947. However, in the following years, the Dominican Republic became increasingly isolated politically and Trujillo increasingly paranoid about foreign powers.

Soon after the **Cuban Revolution of 1959** (see Cuba), Venezuela and Cuba supported a group of anti-Trujillo Dominican exiles that invaded the Dominican Republic. Most were killed or captured in the effort. Trujillo responded by bombing the car of Venezuelan president Rómulo **Betancourt** (see Venezuela), wounding but not killing the president. In response, the **Organization of American States** (OAS; see Appendix 2) imposed economic sanctions on the Dominican Republic, and the United States implemented a special tax on sugar, one

of the country's most important exports. The assassination attempt as well as its ramifications caused domestic outrage against Trujillo and the atrocious acts of his secret police. Furthering his downfall, the United States soon withdrew its support of Trujillo's presidency, no longer willing to tolerate his autocratic and repressive rule. Trujillo was assassinated in 1961, and many believe that the United States supplied the arms used by his enemies to carry out his murder.

United States Occupation (1916–1924)

U.S. president Woodrow Wilson sent the U.S. marines to the Dominican Republic in 1916 to quell domestic unrest. The eight-year U.S. occupation resulted in increased order and the development of infrastructure, but also created an environment conducive to the subsequent rise of dictators and strongmen.

After the assassination of President Ramón Cáceres (1906–1911) in 1911, the Dominican Republic found itself in a state of fiscal and political chaos, and the United States became increasingly involved in internal Dominican affairs and in encouraging economic and political stability in the country. U.S. involvement was not only motivated by a desire to aid the country and encourage peace in the Americas, but was also linked to U.S. pursuit of its own economic interests: by 1911, the United States had become the chief importer of Dominican products and the chief source of Dominican imports. Thus, economic and political instability in the Dominican Republic posed a threat to the economic interests of the United States.

In 1914 the United States threatened to send in the military if the Dominican Republic did not elect a president. Dominicans elected Juan Isidro Jiménes (1899–1902, 1903–1904, 1914–1916) that same year. However, Jiménes did not stabilize or democratize the nation but instead continued the tradition of strongman rule, appointing prominent members of various political factions to positions in his government in order to broaden his support. He later rejected a U.S. proposal for the development of a national guard controlled directly by the U.S. military, and proved reluctant to agree to U.S. control over the appointment of the director of public works. Despite these efforts to consolidate power, Jiménes remained weak. As a result, in 1916 secretary of war Desiderio Arias took control of the armed forces and the Congress.

Concerned by this turn of events, frustrated by Jiménes' reluctance to cooperate, and convinced that the Dominican Republic would not achieve stability on its own, U.S. president Woodrow Wilson sent the U.S. marines into the country in 1916. While the Dominican Congress selected Francisco Henríquez y Carvajal (1916) to assume the presidency, the United States refused to recognize the new president until its earlier demand that the U.S. military develop and control a national guard, and that the U.S. manage the country's public works were met. Henríquez resisted, eventually accepting U.S. control of public works but refusing to yield leadership of the armed forces, though the national guard was eventually established.

During the occupation, U.S. Marines restored order throughout most of the nation, and public works projects greatly improved the country's infrastructure. The nation's budget was balanced, and economic growth ensued. In addition, the country's foreign debt was reduced when the United States established a customs receivership to enforce collection of the Dominican Republic's overdue debt to foreign nations. At the same time, however, the United States' thorough control of the nation and the establishment of the national guard made the country susceptible to strongman rule following the withdrawal of U.S. troops. Also, many Dominicans resented the power wielded by the U.S. forces and their frequent abuse of authority, and felt that this rule by foreigners, some of whom seemed to have no interest in the republic and could not even speak Spanish, was an unnecessary infringement on national sovereignty.

Opposition to the U.S. military presence was initially weak, in large part due to the improvement of the Dominican economic situation that resulted from the soaring of profits from the export of sugar and other commodities during World War I. However, when sugar prices plummeted at the end of the war, anti-American sentiment grew stronger. Opposition groups such as the peasant guerrilla group known as the *gavilleros* began to actively resist the U.S. presence. By the early 1920s the United States wanted to remove its military forces, but even this proved contentious: while the United States hoped to pull out its troops with certain conditions, Dominicans favored an unconditional withdrawal. When U.S. forces finally withdrew in 1924, the Dominican Republic remained a U.S. protectorate: the United States retained the right to intervene when necessary and the right to control the Dominican customs house. Through the signing of the Trujillo-Hull Treaty in 1940 (see **Trujillo y Molina**, Rafael Leonidas), the Dominican Republic regained control of its customs house.

War of Restoration (1863–1865). See **Spanish Annexation**

HEADS OF STATE

Pedro Santana Familias	1844–1848
Manuel Jiménes	1848–1849
Santiago Espaillat	1849
Buenaventura Báez	1849–1853
Pedro Santana Familias	1853–1856
Manuel de Regla Mota	1856
Buenaventura Báez	1856–1857
José Desiderio Valverde (ruled in Santo Domingo; there was another leader in Santiago during the same period)	1857–1858
Pedro Santana Familias	1858–1861
Spanish Rule	1861–1865
José María Cabral	1865
Buenaventura Báez	1865–1866
Triumvirate: Gregorio Luperón, Pedro Antonio Pimentel, and Federico de Jesús García	1866
José María Cabral	1866–1868
Buenaventura Báez	1868–1874
Ignacio María González	1874–1876
Ulises Francisco Espaillat	1876
Ignacio María González	1876
Buenaventura Báez	1876–1878
Jacinto de Castro	1878
Cesáreo Guillermo	1878–1879
Gregorio Luperón	1879
Fernando Arturo de Meriño	1880–1882
Ulises Heureaux	1882–1884
Francisco Gregorio Billini	1884–1885
Alejandro Woss y Gil	1885–1887
Ulises Heureaux	1887–1899
Wenceslao Figuereo	1899
Juan Isidro Jiménes	1899–1902
Horacio Vásquez	1902–1903
Alejandro Woss y Gil	1903
Juan Isidro Jiménes	1903–1904
Carlos P. Morales	1904–1906
Ramón Cáceres	1906–1911
Eladio Victoria	1911–1912
Adolfo Nouel y Bobadilla	1912–1913
José Bordas y Valdés	1913–1914
Ramón Báez	1914
Juan Isidro Jiménes	1914–1916
Consejo de Secretarios de Estado	1916
Francisco Henríquez y Carvajal	1916
Admiral Knapps et al. (United States occupation)	1916–1922
Juan Bautista Vicini Burgos	1922–1924
Horacio Vázquez	1924–1930
Rafael Estrella Ureña	1930
Rafael Leonidas Trujillo y Molina	1930–1938
Jacinto Bienvenido Peynado	1938–1940
Manuel de Jesús Troncoso de la Concha	1940–1942
Rafael Leonidas Trujillo y Molina	1942–1952
Héctor Bienvenido Trujillo y Molina	1952–1960
Joaquín Balaguer	1960–1962
Consejo de Estado	1962–1963

Juan Bosch Gaviño	1963
Emilio de los Santos	1963
Donald Reid Cabral	1963–1965
Elías Wessin y Wessin	1965
Antonio Imbert Barreras	1965
Francicso Camaño Deño	1965
Héctor García Godoyy Cáceres	1965–1966
Joaquín Balaguer	1966–1978
Silvestre Antonio Guzmán Fernández	1978–1982
Jacobo Majluta Azar	1982
Salvador Jorge Blanco	1982–1986
Joaquín Balaguer	1986–1996
Leonel Antonio Fernández Reyna	1996–2000
Hipólito Mejía	2000–

Source: Diccionario Enciclopédico Dominicano 1998 (Santo Domingo: Enciclocomputos, S.A., 1998).

BIBLIOGRAPHY

Print Resources

Atkins, G. Pope, and Larman C. Wilson. *The United States and the Trujillo Regime.* New Brunswick, NJ: Rutgers University Press, 1972.

Bell, Ian. *The Dominican Republic.* Boulder: Westview Press, 1981.

Black, Jan Knippers. *The Dominican Republic: Politics and Development in an Unsovereign State.* Boston: Allen and Unwin, 1986.

Calder, Bruce. *The Impact of Intervention: The Dominican Republic During the U.S. Marine Occupation of 1916–1924.* Austin: University of Texas Press, 1984.

Campillo Pérez, Julio G. *Historia Electoral Dominicana 1848–1986.* Santo Domingo: Junta Central Electoral, 1986.

Crassweller, Robert D. *Trujillo: The Life and Times of a Caribbean Dictator.* New York: Macmillan, 1966.

Haggerty, Richard A. *Dominican Republic and Haiti Country Studies.* Washington, DC: Library of Congress, 1991.

Hartlyn, Jonathan. *The Struggle for Democratic Politics in the Dominican Republic.* Chapel Hill: University of North Carolina Press, 1988.

Jiménez Polanco, Jacqueline. *Los Partidos Políticos en la República Dominicana.* Santo Domingo: Actividad Electoral y Desarrollo Organizativo, 1999.

Kumar, U. Shiv. *Intervention in Latin America: Dominican Crisis and the OAS.* New York: Advent, 1987.

Moya Pons, Frank. *The Dominican Republic: A National History.* Princeton: Markus Wiener, 1998.

Wiarda, Howard J., and Michael J. Kryzanek. *The Dominican Republic: A Caribbean Crucible.* Oxford: Westview Press, 1992.

Wucker, Michele. *Why the Cocks Fight: Dominicans, Haitians, and the Struggle for Hispaniola.* New York: Hill and Wang, 1999.

Electronic Resources

Dominican Experience
http://chat.carleton.ca/~rmckenzi/experience.html
A Web site about the politics and culture of the Dominican Republic created and administered by students. Contains extensive links to news sources and information on the country's political and economic institutions. (In English)

Latin American Network Information Center (LANIC): Dominican Republic
http://lanic.utexas.edu/la/cb/dr/
Dominican Republic section of this extensive Web site contains hundreds of links to research resources, cultural centers, economic and business institutions, government agencies, historical sources, magazines and other periodicals, nongovernmental organizations, and grassroots groups, as well as many other subjects. (In English)

Political Database of the Americas: Dominican Republic
http://www.georgetown.edu/pdba/Countries/domrep.html
Comprehensive database run as a joint project of Georgetown University and the Organization of American States. Section on the Dominican Republic contains information on and links to the executive, legislative, and judicial branches of the Dominican government; electoral laws and election results; and other political data. (In English, Spanish, Portuguese, and French)

Political Resources.net: Dominican Republic
http://www.politicalresources.net/dominican_r.htm
Contains a wealth of links to sources of information on national politics. Includes information on political parties, legislative and executive institutions, laws and legislation, and elections, as well as a link to the constitution. (In English)

Ultima Hora
http://www.ultimahora.com.do/
The Web version of one of the Dominican Republic's major daily newspapers, offering comprehensive national coverage. (In Spanish)

Wilfried Derksen's Elections Around the World: Dominican Republic
http://www.agora.it/elections/domincanrepublic.htm
Dominican Republic section of a comprehensive database of results from elections around the world. Contains results from recent national executive and legislative elections, as well as explanations of and links to political parties and institutions. (In English)

ECUADOR

COUNTRY PROFILE

Official name	República del Ecuador
Capital	Quito
Type/structure of government	Democratic presidential republic
Executive	President is elected to a four-year term and may not be consecutively reelected; cabinet appointed by the president.
Legislative	Unicameral National Congress consisting of 12 nationally elected representatives who serve four-year terms, and 65 provincially elected representatives who serve two-year terms.
Judicial	The highest court is the Supreme Court; justices are selected by the Congress and serve life terms.
Major political parties	Traditionally: **Conservative Party** (Partido Conservador, PC); **Radical Liberal Party** (Partido Liberal Radical, PLR); the last two decades of the twentieth century witnessed a proliferation of small parties.
Constitution in effect	1998
Location/geography	Northwest South America bordering Peru (to the south), Colombia (to the northeast), and the Pacific Ocean (to the northwest). Geography includes highlands, jungles, and coastline.
Geographic area	283,560 sq. km.
Population	12.1 million (1997)
Ethnic groups	Mestizo 65%; indigenous 25%; other 10%
Religions	Roman Catholic 95%; Protestant and other 5%
Literacy rate	90.1% (1995)*
Infant mortality rate	30.69 deaths per 1,000 live births (1999)*
Life expectancy	72 years (1999)
Monetary unit	Sucre
Exchange rate	1 U.S. dollar = 25,000 sucres (August 2000)**
Major exports	Petroleum, bananas, cacao, shrimp, coffee
Major imports	Machinery, chemical products
GDP	$58.7 billion (1998 est.)* (purchasing power parity)
GDP growth rate	1% (1998 est.)*
GDP per capita	$4,800 (1998 est.)* (purchasing power parity)

*CIA World Factbook 1999.
http://www.cia.gov/cia/publications/factbook/geos/ec.html
**Latin American Weekly Report, August 22, 2000 (WR-00-33), p. 394.

Source: U.S. State Department Background Notes. http://www.state.gov/www/background_notes/ecuador_0010_bgn.htm.

OVERVIEW

Summary

Historically, regionalism has guided politics in the small but heterogeneous nation of Ecuador, as the geographical cleavage between the mountains (known as the Sierra) and the coastal areas (known as the Costa) overlapped with the political cleavage between the conservatives, centered in Quito in the Sierra, and the liberals, centered in Guayaquil in the Costa. Personalism has also dominated Ecuadorian politics; leaders have garnered support based on personality rather than governing ability or ideology, and parties and factions have risen and fallen around candidates and contemporary issues, rather than around more stable, long-term agendas. Further, Ecuador has been extremely vulnerable to fluctuations in the world market for its exports throughout its history, which has created a pattern of politically influential economic booms and busts. Indigenous and colonial traditions remain alive (though not central) in Ecuador, and toward the end of the twentieth century, the historically marginalized indigenous population began to organize and assert its power in the political arena. The result of all of these dynamics has been political instability throughout Ecuador's history.

History

Prior to the arrival of the Spanish, in the early fifteenth century, the area that is today Ecuador was divided into

Ecuador. © 1998 The Moschovitis Group, Inc.

An early twentieth-century view of the room in Quito where the Ecuadorian Declaration of Independence was signed in the early 1800s. *Columbus Memorial Library, General Secretariat of the Organization of American States. Reproduced with permission of the Organization of American States.*

warring states, which came to be dominated by the Inca Empire in the late fifteenth and early sixteenth centuries. The Inca had limited cultural impact but did spread the Quechua language throughout the area. A territorial dispute between Inca leaders Huascar and Atahuallpa led to a civil war that coincided with the arrival of Francisco Pizarro and the Spanish in 1532, facilitating the Spaniards' defeat of the empire. The Spanish first established colonies in the Sierra, which boasted a large indigenous population. Large estates were granted to colonists by the Spanish crown and were worked by indigenous people. Subsequently, a textile industry began to develop, and the Spanish established factories that enslaved indigenous peoples and heavily taxed the indigenous communities. The Costa remained relatively unpopulated and unproductive during this period of colonization, slowly developing a racially and culturally mixed population. By the end of the seventeenth century, the textile industry was in decline as the market became more competitive and the native population decreased, making labor scarce.

The Ecuadorian uprising against Spanish rule began in Quito around 1809 and culminated in 1822 when the troops of Simón Antonio de la Santísima Trinidad **Bolívar y Palacios** (see Colombia) and Antonio José de Sucre helped Ecuadorian rebels win independence in the Battle of Pinchincha. During the subsequent eight years, Ecuador, along with Colombia and Venezuela, formed the confederation of Gran Colombia, an amalgam of newly independent states led by Bolívar. In 1830 Ecuador broke from this group and became a sovereign nation.

Ecuador's early history as an independent nation was dominated by General Juan José **Flores** (1830–1834, 1839–1845). Flores used the armed forces to maintain power, thus beginning a tradition of military involvement in national politics. Subsequently, under the leadership of José María **Urbina** (1851–1856) of the Liberal Party (see **Radical Liberal Party** [Partido Liberal Radical, PLR]), a variety of anticlerical and social reforms were implemented, including the abolition of slavery. The staunchly pro-Catholic Gabriel **García Moreno** (1859–1865, 1869–1875) governed the country with an iron fist, and the **Conservative Party** (Partido Conservador, PC) formed out of his followers. Though García Moreno was assassinated in 1875, the Conservatives were able to retain power until the Liberal opposition, led by General José Eloy **Alfaro Delgado** (1895–1901, 1906–1911), defeated the Conservatives in the Revolution of 1895.

The Liberals remained in control of the country through the early 1940s. Focused on secularizing Ecuador, the Liberals introduced many anticlerical reforms. Nonetheless, there was some continuity with the earlier Conservative period as Alfaro continued the tradition of *caudillo* rule, and other leaders carried on García Moreno's infrastructure projects. Land reform was never conducted, and the indigenous populations remained impoverished. The PLR began to lose its grip on power beginning in the early 1930s with the Great Depression, during which the *sucre* (the nation's currency) drastically dropped in value; however, the price of raw materials produced in Ecuador increased during World War II, resulting in an improvement in Ecuador's economic situation. In 1941 Peru invaded Ecuador (see **Peru/Ecuador Border Conflict**, Appendix 1). The 1942 Rio Protocol, the treaty that (temporarily) resolved the conflict, awarded most of the disputed territory to Peru. This led to popular discontent with President Carlos

Alberto Arroyo del Río (1940–1944), prompting his overthrow and the end of Liberal dominance.

After World War II, Ecuador experienced a long period of constitutional rule with free elections and only two interludes of military government (1963–1966 and 1972–1979). The dominant force in the period was *caudillo* leader José María **Velasco Ibarra** (1934–1935, 1944–1947, 1952–1956, 1960–1961, 1968–1972), who was popular among the masses but accomplished little while in office, acting fairly erratically and proving unable to garner the support of any permanent political institution. Following Velasco's final fall from power in 1972, the armed forces ruled the country until 1979 (see **Constitution of 1979**). During this period of military rule, oil booms brought increased wealth to the middle class, but simultaneously caused inflation. Though infrastructure improvement projects were introduced, social reforms to distribute the increased wealth were never implemented, and the gap between the rich and the poor (particularly indigenous groups) increased dramatically.

Since the early 1980s, political leaders have tried to balance implementing social reforms in an attempt to decrease inequality with implementing economic austerity measures in an attempt to achieve stability. Attempts by President Jaime Roldós Aguilera (1979–1981) of the Social Christian Party (Partido Social Cristiano, PSC) and President Osvaldo Hurtado Larrea (1981–1984) of the Christian Democrats to achieve greater equality were unsuccessful. While President León **Febres-Cordero Ribadeneyra** (1984–1988) tried to promote development by expanding Ecuador's participation in the international market and attracting foreign investment, falling oil prices thwarted his economic strategy. Rodrigo **Borja Cevallos** (1988–1992) of the **Democratic Left** (Izquierda Democrática, ID) won the election of 1988 by promising socialist reforms, but was forced by economic circumstances to implement free-market policies. Borja's successor, Sixto **Durán-Ballén Cordovez** (1992–1996), was also unsuccessful in his attempts to implement economic reforms and achieve economic and political stability.

Frustrated by the lack of progress toward development and stability, in 1996 the Ecuadorian people elected populist candidate Abdala **Bucaram Ortiz** (1996–1997), known as "el Loco" (the crazy one). Bucaram implemented extremely austere economic measures and led a corrupt administration that only resulted in further instability. In 1997 Congress declared Bucaram mentally unfit to govern, and placed Fabian **Alarcón** (1997–1998) in the presidency, and Jamil **Mahuad Witt** (1998–2000) was elected in 1998. Mahuad attempted to stabilize the economy through the implementation of austerity measures, and proposed the dollarization of the economy, hoping to eliminate the instability caused by the falling value of the *sucre*. However, in 1999, GDP declined by 7.3% and the government defaulted on its foreign debt. Meanwhile, the indigenous groups that had been organizing and uniting under the **Confederation of Indigenous Nationalities of Ecuador** (Confederación de Nacionalidades Indígenas del Ecuador, CONAIE) throughout the end of the twentieth century began to actively protest the national government, which for decades had implemented austerity measures that had pushed them further into poverty and systematically ignored their calls for **land reform** and equality. The military, claiming it feared a "social explosion," removed Mahuad from office, installing Vice President Gustavo **Noboa Bajarano** (2000–) as the new president in January 2000. Noboa, in an attempt to improve the country's disastrous economic situation, continued Mahuad's austerity measures and implemented dollarization in his first few months in office. Under his leadership, the economy slowly began to recover and stabilize in 2001; the country's fiscal position strengthened, and authorities projected that Ecuador would meet or exceed its 2001 targets for growth and inflation reduction.

ENTRIES

Alarcón, Fabian (1948–)

Fabian Alarcón (1997–1998) served as president of the National Congress before assuming the presidency of the nation after President Abdala **Bucaram Ortiz** (1996–1997) was declared unfit to govern. Alarcón's brief term as president was plagued by accusations of corruption.

Alarcón began his political career in 1970 when he was elected to the city council of Quito, Ecuador's capitol. In 1972 he formed his own political party, the Radical Alfarista Front (Frente Radical Alfarista, FRA), hoping to emulate the earlier success of liberal opposition leader José Eloy **Alfaro Delgado** (1895–1901, 1906–1911). Alarcón established himself politically by holding a broad array of government positions, including positions in the National Congress, by the early 1990s. Nonetheless, Alarcón never articulated strong political views, and was regarded by many as a political chameleon who adapted easily to a variety of circumstances and situations, quickly making alliances across party lines.

As president of the National Congress, Alarcón spoke out against President Bucaram in the late 1990s, reiterating the widespread allegations of corruption that had been made against him, and criticizing his history of conflict with Congress and other political institutions and his adoption of unpopular economic measures. In February 1997 the National Congress voted Bucaram out of office on the grounds of mental instability, temporarily placed Bucaram's vice president, Rosalia Arteaga, in the presidency, and elected Alarcón as president. When Alarcón tried to take office, however, Arteaga attempted to maintain the presidency, backed by the armed forces; she held office for only two days before the constitutional amendment denying the vice president immediate succession was enforced.

Alarcón took office on February 11, 1997, and general elections were planned for the following year. During his eighteen-month presidency, Alarcón put the military in charge of the customs system, which had become plagued with corruption, and reinstated the civil employees who had been fired by the Bucaram administration. He also formed a Constituent Assembly, which completed writing a new constitution in June 1998. Elections were held in May 1998, and Jamil **Mahuad Witt** (1998–2000) succeeded Alarcón as president of Ecuador in August 1998; the new constitution went into effect the day he took office.

Alfaro Delgado, José Eloy (1842–1912)

José Eloy Alfaro Delgado led the Liberals to victory over the Conservatives in the 1895 Revolution and served as president of Ecuador from 1895 to 1901 and from 1906 to 1911. His authoritarian regime belied his liberal ideology.

Alfaro was born in Montecristi, Manabí. A leader in the Liberal revolts of 1865 and 1871 against the ultra-conservative dictatorship of Gabriel **García Moreno** (1859–1865, 1869–1875), Alfaro fled to Panama after the second of these rebellions failed. He became a successful businessman, and financed continued Liberal revolts from Panama, soon gaining a reputation in Ecuador as a revolutionary. In 1895 Alfaro returned to Ecuador to lead the Liberal forces, now officially consolidated as the **Radical Liberal Party** (Partido Liberal Radical, PLR), to victory against the Conservative regime. That same year, Alfaro penned a new constitution and was installed by the military as president of Ecuador. One year later, Alfaro was elected constitutional president.

Alfaro's administrations passed many liberal and secular reforms, including relaxing control of the press, removing the church from public education, implementing civil marriage and burial, allowing freedom of religion, abolishing the church's tithe, and confiscating large church-owned estates. Alfaro also continued García Moreno's railroad program, and the Quito-Guayaquil railroad was completed in 1908. Nonetheless, Alfaro also continued the legacy of strongman military rule in Ecuador, as it was a coup that brought him to power for his second term. In addition, indigenous people and peasants remained untouched by Alfaro's liberal policies, which did not include **land reform**, and land remained unequally distributed in the Andes and on the coast, perpetuating an unfair balance of power within the population. Some also criticized Alfaro's government for its affinity for the United States and for allowing the pursuit of U.S. economic interests

This illustration depicts the events of January 1912, when a lynch mob broke into a Quito jail and seized former President José Eloy Alfaro Delgado (1895–1901, 1906–1911) (top figure) and his chief lieutenants. As shown in the center drawing, the mob dragged the men through the streets and then burned their bodies. *Columbus Memorial Library, General Secretariat of the Organization of American States. Reproduced with permission of the Organization of American States.*

on Ecuadorian soil through such projects as building the railroad.

Alfaro's *caudillo* tendencies, his failure to evenly distribute wealth and power, and his catering to U.S. interests led to his overthrow in 1911 by a coalition of Conservatives and dissident Liberals. Alfaro moved to Panama; when he returned to Ecuador three months later liberal leaders soon had him arrested. On January 28, 1912, a lynch mob broke into the jail in Quito where Alfaro and his lieutenants were being detained, dragged the prisoners through the streets, and burned their bodies.

Bolívar y Palacios, Simón Antonio de la Santísima Trinidad. See Colombia

Borja Cevallos, Rodrigo (1935–   )

While Rodrigo Borja Cevallos (1988–1992) won the presidency in 1988 as the leader of the **Democratic Left**

(Izquierda Democrática, ID), the unfavorable economic conditions that the country faced during his term in office forced him to implement more conservative, neoliberal policies that contrasted with his socialist ideals.

Borja was born in Quito and later graduated with distinction from the Universidad Central law school in 1960. He was elected to Congress in 1962. Center-left in political leaning, advocating European socialist ideals, he soon asserted himself as a leader in the **Radical Liberal Party** (Partido Liberal Radical, PLR), and then led other young PLR members in establishing ID in 1977. In 1978 Borja ran for president in the first electoral contest after an extended period of military rule (see **Constitution of 1979**); though he lost the election, his campaign helped to establish ID as Ecuador's first political party with mass-based appeal. He ran again without success in the 1984 presidential contest, but was finally successful in the 1988 presidential contest.

Though Borja was committed to introducing social reforms such as improvements in human rights, the severe economic crisis that gripped Ecuador when Borja assumed office compelled him to betray his social democratic beliefs. Instead of funding social programs and increasing government subsidies, Borja was forced to implement neoliberal policies such as cutting off subsidies and advocating a free market in order to combat inflation and economic recession, both of which were exacerbated by the low oil prices of the day. The failure of these policies hurt the president's and ID's popularity, and in the 1990 legislative elections, ID lost its congressional majority. Borja, who was succeeded by Sixto **Durán-Ballén Cordovez** (1992–1996), continued to be an active leader in ID after the end of his presidential term.

Bucaram Ortiz, Abdala (1952–)

Abdala Bucaram Ortiz, known as "el Loco" (the crazy one), served as Ecuador's president for only six months (1996–1997) before being impeached by Congress, which found him mentally unfit to govern.

Bucaram's interest in politics was triggered by the political success of his uncle, Asaad Bucaram Elmhalin, who was preparing to run for president in 1972 (an election he was favored to win) when the military staged a coup and took power. The younger Bucaram first held public office in the early 1980s in Guayaquil, where he served as police commissioner. Although he lowered the crime rate, many believed that he supported extortion activities. When Bucaram's brother-in-law, former president Jaime Roldós Aguilera (1979–1981), was killed in 1982, Bucaram founded a political party, the Ecuadorian Roldosist Party (Partido Roldosista Ecuatoriano, PRE), to continue Roldós Aguilera's political vision. Bucaram was elected mayor of Guayaquil in 1984 on the PRE ticket, but left office one year later when his criticism of the Ecuadorian army put him at odds with the military. Bucaram left Ecuador and was soon arrested in Panama on charges of cocaine possession. Never convicted, Bucaram maintained that he was set up by political opponents.

He returned to Ecuador in 1987, and ran unsuccessfully for president in 1988 and again in 1992. Bucaram ran yet again for president in 1996, carrying out a very nontraditional campaign that included touring the country with a rock band and singing before his political speeches, often dressed in costumes. Although he was a quirky candidate, the substance of Bucaram's message resonated with Ecuadorians, especially those looking for an expansion of social programs for the lower classes. Bucaram came in second in the first round of elections, and won the runoff in July 1996 by a surprisingly large margin.

Upon assuming the presidency, Bucaram began to implement policies that even his most ardent supporters questioned. Some of his bizarre decrees included the imposition of a 1000 percent tax on liquor and cigarettes; these were quickly reduced to 63 percent and 700 percent, respectively. He also proposed a plan for a "real economy" with drastic cuts to electricity, transit, and cooking gas subsidies in addition to dollarization. Bucaram's administration was rife with corruption, which, combined with his personal antics, alienated almost everyone. Congress impeached him on February 6, 1997, finding him mentally unfit to govern, mainly as a result of his inappropriate behavior and his unconventional economic policies. He was replaced by Congress president Fabian **Alarcón** (1997–1998).

Bucaram soon went into exile in Panama, which granted him political asylum. Though he was commanded by Congress to return to Ecuador to stand trial for treason after he made negative remarks about the military while in exile, in 2001, Bucaram remained in Panama, frequently criticizing the current Ecuadorian government and announcing his plans to return to office.

Confederation of Indigenous Nationalities of Ecuador (Confederación de Nacionalidades Indígenas del Ecuador, CONAIE)

The main mission of the Confederation of Indigenous Nationalities of Ecuador (Confederación de Nacionalidades Indígenas del Ecuador, CONAIE), formed in 1980 and representing an estimated 70 percent of all indigenous peoples in Ecuador, is to coordinate and promote the demands of Ecuador's various indigenous populations, which make up 45 percent of the country's population.

Indigenous movements in Ecuador gained momentum toward the end of the twentieth century as indigenous leaders, frustrated with traditional political parties that ignored many of their basic needs, began to look for alternative means to achieve their goals. CONAIE developed from the union of the regional associations of the Sierra and the Confederation of Indigenous Nationalities of the Ecuadorian Amazon (Confederación de Nacionalidades Indígenas de la Amazonia Ecuatoriana, CONFENIAE). The group's specific concerns include racial discrimination, **land reform**, environmental protection, the resolution of border conflicts, bilingual education, and the inclusion of indigenous populations in the political process.

CONAIE gained prominence and legitimacy in 1990 when it staged a massive uprising that included blocking roads, boycotting commercial centers, and even taking hostages. The success of the uprising resulted in more government attention for the organization, and increased domestic and international support. In the mid-1990s, the Pachakutik–New Country Party (Movimiento Pachakutik–Nuevo País, MP-NP) was formed by indigenous citizens as CONAIE's representative political party. MP-NP quickly gained popularity, winning substantial seats in Congress in the 1998 elections.

At the end of 1999 and the beginning of 2000, CONAIE staged a series of protests, in conjunction with the military, against President Jamil **Mahuad Witt** (1998–2000), forcing him out of office. Though the military initially replaced Mahuad with a three-man junta consisting of former Supreme Court justice Carlos Solórzano, indigenous leader Antonio Vargas, and General Carlos Mendoza, under strong international pressure the military soon removed the junta, and Vice President Gustavo **Noboa Bajarano** (2000–   ) assumed the presidency.

Conservative Party (Partido Conservador, PC)

Traditionally one of the two dominant parties in Ecuador, the Conservative Party (Partido Conservador, PC) was formed in the 1860s by a group of followers of Gabriel **García Moreno** (1859–1865, 1869–1875). The rightist PC promoted close cooperation between church and state, a strong, centralized government, and private property. Formally established in 1883, the party was particularly popular in the Sierra, enjoying its strongest support in Quito and Cuenca.

The PC maintained political power until 1895, when José Eloy **Alfaro Delgado** (1895–1901, 1906–1911) seized the presidency in a civil war. After Alfaro's coup, the PC steadily lost power to the **Radical Liberal Party** (Partido Liberal Radical, PLR), which dominated the political scene between 1895 and 1944. While the PC remained significant in Ecuadorian politics as late as the presidency of Camilo **Ponce Enríquez** (1956–1960), the party lost influence when its most progressive members left to form Popular Democracy (Democracia Popular, DP) in 1964. The party was further damaged by the introduction of universal suffrage in the **Constitution of 1979**, as the political preferences of those who gained the vote leaned left, offsetting the strength of the PC's supporters. While the party was able to join rightist coalitions to win ten congressional seats in 1978 and two congressional seats in 1984, by the 1990s the PC had

lost all its seats in the National Congress, and subsequently played an insignificant role in Ecuadorian politics.

Constitution of 1979

The Constitution of 1979, the seventeenth constitution in the history of Ecuador but the first to impact the popular masses, marked the transition from an extended authoritarian interlude to a period of democratization and brought a new stability to Ecuadorian politics.

When the military ousted Guillermo **Rodríguez Lara** (1972–1976) from the presidency in 1976 and installed a military triumvirate to lead the country, the introduction of a new constitution that would return Ecuador to civilian rule was at the top of the new government's agenda. A bloody 1975 failed coup attempt by the military had revealed weaknesses within the armed forces to the public, and the military hoped that a new constitution and the reestablishment of civilian rule would eliminate or at least hide the institution's debilities. The resultant constitution did in fact anticipate and encourage an unprecedented degree of democratization.

The Constitution of 1979 allowed for a considerable amount of state intervention and provided the citizenry with many new economic and social rights, creating a far more progressive government than had previous constitutions. In addition, the constitution granted citizenship and suffrage to all Ecuadorians over eighteen years of age and required candidates in popular elections to affiliate with a legally recognized party. The constitution attempted to check the power of the executive by requiring the election of the president and vice president in the same contest and prohibiting either from seeking a successive term, by strengthening the independence of the judiciary, and by awarding Congress the ability to elect a new vice president if the incumbent were to resign. However, the document also allowed the president to declare a state of national emergency and to finance the public debt without prior legislative authorization, and extended the presidential term to five years.

The Constitution of 1979 was amended in 1984 and 1986, and in the wake of the political unrest of the late 1990s, a new constitution was introduced in 1998.

Democratic Alliance of Ecuador (Alianza Democrática del Ecuador, ADE)

The Democratic Alliance of Ecuador (Alianza Democrática del Ecuador, ADE) formed in the 1940s in opposition to President Carlos Alberto Arroyo del Río's (1940–1944) signing of the Rio Protocol in 1942 that temporarily resolved the **Peru/Ecuador Border Conflict** (see Appendix 1). ADE consisted of an unlikely coalition of socialists, independents, conservatives, and communists who joined forces with the military to support José María **Velasco Ibarra** (1934–1935, 1944–1947,

1952–1956, 1960–1961, 1968–1972) in his efforts to remove Arroyo del Río from office.

Arroyo's signing of the Rio Protocol was seen as a breach of national pride in Ecuador, and his apparent ties with the U.S. government caused further resentment among the Ecuadorians. At the same time, persistent inflation steadily diminished the purchasing power of salaried workers, occasioning further dissatisfaction with the president. Following an ADE-sponsored uprising against Arroyo's police in May 1944 in Guayaquil, Arroyo finally realized the extent of his unpopularity and resigned. The military handed power to ADE, which named Velasco president. Velasco proved a popular choice, returning to Quito from exile in Colombia to crowds of cheering supporters. However, Velasco did not live up to his popularity and was voted out of office in 1947.

As ADE was initially established specifically for the purpose of deposing Arroyo, the alliance faded after its successful removal of the president in 1944. Though ADE attempted to revitalize its membership in 1964, rallying to remove the military government of Ramón Castro Jijón (1963–1966), the coalition lost any strength it had regained when Velasco established his own party later in the 1960s, and finally dissolved completely with Velasco's fall from power in 1972.

Democratic Left (Izquierda Democrática, ID)

The Democratic Left (Izquierda Democrática, ID), which formed in 1977, has philosophical and organizational links to European socialists and social democrats. Its power base lies among teachers, government workers, and professionals, in the more prosperous parts of the Sierra. Supporters of ID advocate social reform, including improvements in human rights and increased funding for government social programs. When ID leader Rodrigo **Borja Cevallos** (1988–1992) ran for president in 1978 on this platform, ID became the first party in Ecuadorian history to enjoy true mass appeal. Though Borja lost the 1978 presidential contest, ID grew rapidly in the 1980s. Consequently, Borja was victorious in the 1988 elections, in which ID also gained a significant number of congressional seats. While the government that Borja subsequently led was committed to increasing the protection of human rights, it failed to implement other social reforms that ID had promised because of ongoing economic problems. Instead, the new government carried out more neoliberal economic reforms, notably opening Ecuador to foreign trade. In 1990 opposition parties gained control of Congress, and through the 1990s, ID began to lose the political strength it had quickly gained through the 1980s.

Durán-Ballén Cordovez, Sixto (1921–)

During Sixto Durán-Ballén Cordovez's tumultuous presidential term (1992–1996), he implemented strict economic policies that incited opposition on the part of the general public and the legislature.

The son of an Ecuadorian diplomat, Durán-Ballén was born in the United States but grew up in Guayaquil. He studied urban architecture at Columbia University, then returned to Ecuador and became minister of public works in 1951. He established himself politically through the 1970s and was elected mayor of Quito, and then ran unsuccessfully for president in 1978 and 1988. Originally a member of the Social Christian Party (Partido Social Cristiano, PSC), Durán-Ballén left the party in 1992 when it chose a younger nominee for the presidency. He formed his own party, the center-right Republican United Party (Partido de Unidad Republicana, PUR), which carried him to victory over several other candidates, including Jaime Nebot Saadi, the candidate backed by the **Democratic Left** (Izquierda Democrática, ID), in the 1992 presidential race. Central to Durán-Ballén's campaign were promises of free-market reform to lower inflation and foster growth in export industries.

Immediately following his inauguration in August 1992, Durán-Ballén pledged to introduce a series of economic policies including budget cuts and measures to control inflation, occasioning public protest. During the summer of 1993, Durán-Ballén broke away from the PUR when the resignation of his minister of energy (due to a disagreement over the implications of Durán-Ballén's proposed tax hikes on **petroleum**) led to a crisis of support in his cabinet. His struggle for support continued when the PSC won a significant number of new seats in the midterm legislative elections of 1994, which delivered a Congress in which only twelve out of seventy-seven members supported Durán-Ballén's presidency. Opposition from other parties within the legislature and Durán-Ballén's constant clashes with National Congress president Samuel Belletini over economic strategy made it almost impossible for the president to pursue any of his more controversial reforms. Durán-Ballén was succeeded in August 1996 by Abdala **Bucaram Ortiz** (1996–1997).

Febres-Cordero Ribadeneyra, León (1931–)

León Febres-Cordero Ribadeneyra (1984–1988) was an unpopular and ineffective president. Failed economic programs, political violence, and authoritarianism characterized his term in office.

Trained as an engineer, Febres-Cordero began his career in politics in the 1960s, serving as a deputy in the Constituent Assembly and as president of the Congressional Economic and Financial Commission from 1968 to 1970. Politically conservative, Febres-Cordero served as primary spokesman for the right-leaning parties, such as the **Conservative Party** (Partido Conservador, PC) and the Social Christian Party (Partido Social Cristiano, PSC), which spoke out against the military regimes that governed Ecuador from 1972 to 1979. He reentered

Congress in 1979 as a PSC deputy and criticized the subsequent administrations of Jaime Roldós Aguilero (1979–1981) and Osvaldo Hurtado Larrea (1981–1984) while supporting conservative business interests.

In 1984 he won the presidential election as the candidate of the National Reconstruction Front (Frente de Reconstrucción Nacional, FRN), a conservative coalition, running on a populist platform and advocating free-market reforms; many attributed his success to popular dissatisfaction with the unsuccessful economic policies of his predecessors, which advocated more state intervention in the economy and more redistribution. He entered office facing a suffering economy and congressional opposition (only sixteen of the seventy-seven deputies were of a party that supported his candidacy). Febres-Cordero believed that the rewards of participating in the free market and attracting foreign investment would reach all levels of society eventually without social legislation. However, his programs, such as reducing government regulation, freeing exchange rates, and encouraging foreign investment, did little to improve Ecuador's economic situation, which was made worse by faltering oil prices. Increasing criticism, opposition, and political violence marked his tenure, as Febres-Cordero's authoritarian style alienated other political parties and the general public. Febres-Cordero left office in 1988 and was succeeded by Rodrigo **Borja Cevallos** (1988–1992) of the **Democratic Left** (Izquierda Democrática, ID).

Flores, Juan José (1800–1864)

As Ecuador's first (and third) president, Juan José Flores (1830–1834, 1839–1845) established a tradition of personalistic rule and strong military influence in government.

Flores was born in Venezuela in 1800. As a teenager, he joined the Spanish army, and was captured by the forces of Simón Antonio de la Santísima Trinidad **Bolívar y Palacios** (see Colombia). Flores soon began to voluntarily support Bolívar's cause, rising to the rank of colonel in Bolívar's army, and becoming governor of Pasto province in Colombia by the time he was twenty-three. Bolívar later appointed Flores governor of Ecuador during Ecuador's association with Gran Colombia. Despite his humble background and lack of education, Flores gained the acceptance of the upper class.

When Gran Colombia dissolved in 1830, Flores convened an assembly that declared Ecuador's independence, and named himself president of the new nation. It soon appeared that Flores was primarily interested in maintaining his own power as president; he failed to attend to important domestic matters and expended a majority of federal funds on the military. When four liberal intellectuals who opposed Flores were killed in 1833, the public associated the crimes with his administration (though Flores was not involved in the murders), and criticism of his regime heightened substantially.

In 1834 Flores' opponents attempted to install José Vicente Rocafuerte (1834–1839) as president through armed rebellion. Though the rebellion failed, Flores sponsored Rocafuerte as a presidential candidate in the subsequent election, and successfully co-opted the new president, Flores retained the post of head of the army during Rocafuerte's term in office, then returned to the presidency in 1839. He remained president until 1845, when he was forced into exile. He returned to Ecuador in 1860 to help end a civil conflict, and subsequently supported Conservative leader Gabriel **García Moreno's** (1859–1865, 1869–1875) successful presidential bid in 1861.

García Moreno, Gabriel (1821–1875)

As president from 1859 to 1865 and 1869 to 1875, Gabriel García Moreno created a theocratic state, centralized authority under a new constitution, and introduced widespread education and infrastructure programs. After his death, Conservatives hailed García Moreno as Ecuador's great nation builder, while Liberals denounced him as a tyrant.

García Moreno was born in 1821 in Guayaquil to a Conservative and religious family. As a university student in Europe, he focused on civil and religious law, but also studied sciences and mathematics. García Moreno taught chemistry at the University of Quito after his studies, but was drawn into politics in 1851 when his passionate religious beliefs led him to defend the Jesuits, whom the Liberal government of General José María **Urbina** (1851–1856) had expelled from Ecuador (see **Radical Liberal Party** [Partido Liberal Radical, PLR]).

García Moreno was exiled from Ecuador for his actions, but returned in 1856, welcomed by all except the Liberals. His pro-church ideology assisted him in becoming mayor of Quito, senator, and rector of the central University of Quito. He was appointed provisional president in 1859, and was formally elected president in 1861. García Moreno believed that the order and hierarchy of Catholicism could unify Ecuador after the chaos and instability of the 1850s. He imposed moral conduct on Ecuadorians, and made religion central to both of the constitutions promulgated during his term in office: the Constitution of 1861 named Catholicism as the official religion in Ecuador, and the Constitution of 1869 made Roman Catholicism a prerequisite for citizenship (in addition to making the presidential term six years and allowing unlimited reelection). During the García Moreno regimes, the Pope appointed ecclesiastical officers, officially giving the Catholic Church power within the government.

García Moreno also implemented many improvements in education and infrastructure that helped build national unity and helped Ecuador become integrated into the world economy: new schools were established from the primary to the polytechnic training levels, roads were constructed, and the first portion of the railroad was built. Despite these successes, García Moreno's rule, especially its violence and antiliberalism, was highly criticized by many, and in 1875 four Liberals assassinated García Moreno as he exited the cathedral in Quito. His death left the nation divided between Conservatives and Liberals, a situation that continued until the liberals took control in 1895.

Huasipungo System

Initiated during the colonial era and most commonly used in the rural mountain areas of Ecuador, the *Huasipungo* system of labor required poor indigenous farmers to work on the haciendas of wealthy landowners. In return, these farmers were allowed to use a small plot of land to plant their own subsistence crops. Although there were a number of variations on the *Huasipungo* system, in most cases a poor farmer had to donate four days of work per week to the landowner as rent for his individual plot. Generally the wealthy landowner also required domestic help, which was usually provided by the wife of the indigenous farmer. *Huasipungueros* (or those who offered labor through the *Huasipungo* system) also had to participate in collective work parties during the planting and harvesting seasons. The system lasted into the 1960s, and was only officially outlawed by the Agrarian Reform Law of 1964. Even after the passage of this law (and the later de facto demise of the *Huasipungo* system) and the ratification of **land reform** laws in the 1960s and 1970s, the Ecuadorian peasantry continued to be exploited and extremely poor, and most Ecuadorian peasants still only owned small plots of land. In the late twentieth century, indigenous groups such as the **Confederation of Indigenous Nationalities of Ecuador** (Confederación de Nacionalidades Indígenas del Ecuador, CONAIE) began to press for further reforms in order to achieve fairer land distribution, among other goals.

Land Reform

Ecuador's traditional and current inequitable distribution of land, and the abject poverty that much of its indigenous population endures today, stem from the essentially feudal land system used by the Spanish colonizers (the *encomienda* system), which in Ecuador evolved into the *Huasipungo* system. While the various land reform laws that were passed in Ecuador since the mid-twentieth century provided indigenous populations with some additional freedom, they did little to improve the severe poverty those populations suffer.

Beginning in 1936, pressure from abroad, from domestic humanitarian and liberal groups, and from large landowners on the coast who needed additional cheap labor, forced the government to legislate land reform. Though fifteen agrarian reform measures that released

indigenous people from the *Huasipungo* system and provided them with land were passed between 1936 and 1964, much of the provincial elite refused to enforce the new laws. The military government led by Ramón Castro Jijón (1963–1966) implemented the Idle Lands and Settlement Act in 1964. Designed to end the traditional hacienda system that had existed since colonial times, the law modified the land tenure system, outlawing absentee ownership, limiting the legal size of individual holdings, and setting a minimum amount of land to be granted in the redistribution. It also created the autonomous Ecuadorian Institute for Agrarian Reform and Colonization (Instituto Ecuatoriano de Reforma Agraria y Colonización, IERAC) to oversee the administration and enforcement of agrarian reform. However, the law, which was part of a larger effort to modernize Ecuador, brought little real change.

In the early 1970s the law was revised to require that all land with absentee landlords be sold to the tenants and that squatters be permitted to acquire title to land they had worked for three years. Political opposition, however, prevented IERAC from effectively implementing the land reform act by minimizing government funding and prohibiting the active encouragement of expropriation. In addition, amendments exempting efficiently run farms were passed. In the end, landowners kept the more fertile land for themselves. The land that *was* granted to indigenous people was often low-quality land on mountainsides, and indigenous people were rarely offered government assistance to improve the productivity of their land.

Ecuadorian agrarian reform left the country's agriculture quite underdeveloped, and despite some positive changes, did not significantly reduce the influence of the traditional landowning class. By 2000 a relatively small number of people remained in control of Ecuadorian land, and the indigenous masses continued to live in poverty. However, indigenous groups such as the **Confederation of Indigenous Nationalities of Ecuador** (Confederación de Nacionalidades Indígenas del Ecuador, CONAIE) had begun to organize and fight for more equitable and effective land reform.

Mahuad Witt, Jamil (1949–)

Jamil Mahuad Witt served as president of Ecuador from 1998 to 2000, promoting dollarization as a means to stabilize the economy. In 2000 the armed forces, in tandem with a significant subset of the indigenous population, rebelled against Mahuad's government, deposing him.

Born in the town of Loja, Mahuad graduated from Ecuador's Catholic University with a degree in political science in 1973, earned a law degree there in 1979, and graduated from Harvard University with a master's degree in public administration in 1989. He worked in banking for five years and was very active in the Catholic Church, serving as a professor in the Catholic University in Quito. He began his political career as minister of work and human resources under President Osvaldo Hurtado Larrea (1981–1984), and subsequently served various terms in the National Congress representing the Pinchincha province. Mahuad contested and lost the 1988 presidential election, but was elected mayor of Quito in 1992, and was reelected in 1996.

By the May 1998 presidential election, the Ecuadorian people were disenchanted with politics after the inept rule (and consequent deposition) of President Abdala **Bucaram Ortiz** (1996–1997) and the continued corruption and inefficiency that characterized the term of interim president Fabian **Alarcón** (1997–1998). Consequently, they elected Mahuad, as he promised to return the nation to order after years of political and economic chaos. His reputation as an effective administrator and an honest public servant, as well as his pledges to improve health care and education and to reduce crime, won him enough votes to narrowly defeat his opponent, Alvaro Noboa Ponton, who was backed by the populist Ecuadorian Roldosist Party (Partido Roldosista Ecuatoriano, PRE), the party former president Bucaram had founded in honor of President Jaime Roldós Aguilera (1979–1981).

Despite his promises to restore order and end corruption in Ecuadorian government, Mahuad's cabinet was tarnished by numerous accusations of corruption, and his presidency was plagued by serious economic problems, particularly relating to the *sucre* (the nation's currency), which lost much of its value under his neoliberal policies. The resulting economic strife led to indigenous protests and strikes that only further strained the national economy. In a desperate effort to curb the devaluation of the *sucre* and to gain credibility, Mahuad proposed dollarization of the national currency in early January 2000, and implemented a number of unpopular economic austerity measures, including privatizing state industries, drastically increasing taxes, freezing bank accounts, and firing public employees. Such extreme measures led to considerable social unrest and forced Mahuad to declare a nationwide state of siege, initiating the most intense police-military operation in Ecuador's history.

On January 22, 2000, an unlikely combination of indigenous groups and the military ousted his government. (Some believed that the military co-opted the indigenous population into participating in the overthrow of Mahuad in hopes of preventing a social explosion.) The armed forces replaced Mahuad with a three-man junta consisting of former Supreme Court justice Carlos Solórzano, indigenous leader Antonio Vargas, and General Carlos Mendoza. Under strong international pressure, however, the military soon removed the junta and decreed that Vice President Gustavo **Noboa Bajarano** (2000–) would be president.

Noboa Bajarano, Gustavo (1937–)
Gustavo Noboa Bajarano (2000–) was installed as president of Ecuador after a coup jointly conducted by the military and indigenous organizations in January 2000 overthrew President Jamil **Mahuad Witt** (1998–2000).

Noboa was born in Guayaquil in 1937. He earned a degree in Political and Social Sciences from the Catholic University of Guayaquil and was awarded a doctorate in law from the same university in 1965. He began to teach in that university's Faculty of Jurisprudence and Social and Political Sciences beginning in 1966, and subsequently served as the dean of that faculty (1969–1972, 1978–1980), and as rector of the university (1986–1991, 1991–1996). Noboa was also involved in the business world and successfully established close links to the powerful businessmen of Guayaquil, Ecuador's main commercial center. In addition, he held diplomatic posts, serving on an Ecuadorian delegation sent to negotiate the contentious Amazon border territory with Peru and Brazil. His political career began in 1983 when he became governor of the province of Guayas, and he also held various posts under the administration of Sixto **Durán-Ballén Cordovez** (1992–1996), though he declined Durán-Ballén's offers to serve as his vice president or as a minister in his cabinet. Nonetheless, he accepted Mahuad's offer to be his running mate in the 1998 presidential election, which Mahuad won.

However, Mahuad failed to achieve the stability he had promised during his campaign, and in January 2000, the military, in coordination with indigenous organizations, overthrew Mahuad, eventually placing Noboa in the presidency. Despite the new president's populist appeal, the international community, the military, and the Ecuadorian people were skeptical of Noboa's center-right government during his first months in office. However, his administration was supported by the right-wing Social Christian Party (Partido Social Cristiano, PSC) and more hesitantly by the Ecuadorian Roldosist Party (Partido Roldosista Ecuatoriano, PRE). The new president also enjoyed the backing of the business community, which supported his proposal to continue with structural, modernizing economic reforms. Nonetheless, many difficulties faced Noboa: Ecuador was experiencing a deep recession and very high unemployment (17%). Further, 62% of the population was living under the poverty line, and the country boasted the highest inflation rate in the Americas (55%). This perilous situation had begun to generate an exodus in which hundreds of thousands of Ecuadorians of all social classes abandoned the country destined for Europe.

Despite these challenges, in March 2000 the dollarization project that had been proposed by Noboa's predecessor became law, and in September of that year, the rapidly fluctuating *sucre* (which had been the nation's currency for the previous 116 years) was replaced with the stable U.S. dollar; Noboa hoped this measure would control the instability of the Ecuadorian economy. Under Noboa, Ecuador also received substantial loans from such organizations as the International Monetary Fund (IMF) and the **Inter-American Development Bank** (IDB; see Appendix 2), intended to aid the country in rebuilding its economy. While the interminable price readjustments and the illiquidity of dollars combined to reactivate indigenous protest at the beginning of February 2001 obligating Noboa to declare a state of emergency, Noboa and Antonio Vargas, president of the **Confederation of Indigenous Nationalities of Ecuador** (Confederación de Nacionalidades Indígenas del Ecuador, CONAIE) came to an agreement within a few days. Under Noboa's tutelage, the Ecuadorian economy had slowly begun to recover and stabilize by the end of 2001.

Petroleum

The petroleum industry has been at the center of the Ecuadorian economy since the mid-1970s. Since that time, the country has struggled to find an efficient way to pump the vast reserves out of the Amazon, and has proven unable to find a way to refine even half of its petroleum. These problems have prevented Ecuador from realizing its full potential in terms of oil exports and economic gain from its oil reserves.

While petroleum reserves were originally found on the western coast near Guayaquil in the early 1900s, the discovery by two U.S. oil companies (Texaco and Gulf Oil) of rich oil fields in the eastern part of Ecuador in 1967 and the subsequent influx of other companies finally brought the petroleum industry to the political and economic forefront. During the twenty years that followed the discovery of the eastern oil fields, more than fifty new wells began producing commercial quantities of crude petroleum, mostly in the eastern part of the country. Foreign investment consequently increased markedly. However, in 1987 a strong earthquake disconnected the Amazonian pipeline. Though a temporary pipeline was constructed to Peru, Ecuador's oil profits dropped dramatically until repairs could be made.

Foreign companies have long owned and controlled petroleum production and refining in Ecuador. However, in 1989, the national oil company, Petroecuador, gained control of the Trans-Ecuadorian Pipeline, and in the 1990s Petroecuador continued its efforts to gain more control over the petroleum industry. As 2000 approached, a new, larger pipeline from the Oriente Province was being constructed, promising increased production. Price fluctuations in the international market for petroleum drastically affect the country, and managing the economy during times of fluctuation has become a central political challenge. Economic management may become more difficult should Ecuador continue to increase national control of the oil industry. Further, as Ecuador's petroleum industry expands, a politically significant choice may have to be made between producing more oil through national industries, or through an increase in foreign investment, implying the further penetration of international corporations.

Ponce Enríquez, Camilo (1912–1976)

Camilo Ponce Enríquez held office from 1956 to 1960 despite the opposition of the powerful José María **Velasco Ibarra** (1934–1935, 1944–1947, 1952–1956, 1960–1961, 1968–1972), who had originally supported him.

Born into a wealthy family, Ponce received his law degree from the Central University in Quito soon after beginning his career in politics. In 1951 he founded the conservative Social Christian Movement (Movimiento Social Cristiano, MSC), which formed his main base of support throughout most of his career. Ponce served in President Velasco's cabinet during his third administration, and in 1956 was named the presidential candidate of the **Conservative Party** (Partido Conservador, PC). He won the 1956 presidential election by only 3,000 votes.

With such a close victory, the election was disputed, and Ponce spent most of his time in office trying to gain legitimacy and support. Even though Velasco and the PC had supported Ponce in the election, Velasco soon became the new president's principal opponent. In order to maintain power despite Velasco's opposition, Ponce included Liberals as well as members of the PC and the MSC in his cabinet. While he failed to implement the reforms he had promised during the election, Ponce did manage to maintain political stability during his term despite a worsening economic situation. (In an unlucky twist, during Ponce's administration the banana boom that had fostered economic stability during the previous decade of constitutional rule came to an end, leading to a decrease in export prices, increasing unemployment, dissatisfaction on the part of the working class, and even some rioting in 1959.)

In the 1960 elections, popular discontent with Ponce's rule, and Velasco's personalistic appeal, led to a landslide victory for Velasco. Ponce, enraged by Velasco's vicious campaign tactics, resigned on his last day in office rather than handing over the presidency to Velasco. Ponce ran for reelection in 1968 but lost in a close race with Velasco.

Radical Liberal Party (Partido Liberal Radical, PLR)

The Liberal Party (Partido Liberal, PL) controlled Ecuador through the 1850s, yielding power to the **Conservative Party** (Partido Conservador, PC) in 1860. The Radical Liberal Party (Partido Liberal Radical, PLR), which came into existence during the latter part of the nineteenth century in response to the conservatism of President Gabriel **García Moreno** (1859–1865, 1869–

1875), dominated politics from 1895 until the mid-1940s. Defeat and capitulation to Peru in the 1941 **Peru/Ecuador Border Conflict** (see Appendix 1) led the military to oust the Liberals from power in 1944.

Ecuadorian Liberals were slow to organize a political structure. Throughout the 1880s, the PL remained divided between the civilist faction comprising intellectuals who opposed the Conservative government through the press and legislature, and a more radical faction led by José Eloy **Alfaro Delgado** (1895–1901, 1906–1911). Following an unsuccessful attempt by the radical faction to overthrow the Conservative government in 1884, that faction was temporarily defeated in 1887, and the civilist faction again took the lead within the party, holding an official party assembly in Quito in 1890. Factionalism continued within the party until Liberal opposition to Conservative rule became so strong that Alfaro was able to consolidate the Liberal factions to form the PLR in 1895.

The PLR took control of Ecuadorian politics shortly after consolidating, and remained dominant until 1944, although it began to decline after surviving a coup attempt in 1925 perpetrated by a group calling for an end to the nation's Liberal-Conservative divide. The PLR's traditional power base was the Costa, though it won a significant following in Quito in the 1960s. Traditionally, the PLR called for secularization of the country and decentralization. PLR supporters did not believe that Catholicism should be imposed on all citizens and instead supported a greater separation between the church and state. During its forty years of domination, the PLR reversed many of the laws that had been passed to incorporate the Catholic Church into the politics of Ecuador. However, the party became more conservative when its liberal stance on the principal issues for which it stood, church-state relations, public education, and external trade, became less popular. After the 1920s, the PLR's platform included agrarian reform. Though the PLR traditionally aligned itself with the armed forces and commercial interests, which offered the party significant financial support, the military distanced itself from the party after 1942 since affiliation with a political party impaired its legitimacy.

Carlos Alberto Arroyo del Río (1940–1944), who was deposed in 1944, was the last PLR president. The PLR's importance declined in the 1950s, and the national election held in 1968 was the last in which the party played a significant role; in that presidential contest, PLR candidate Andrés Córdova lost to José María **Velasco Ibarra** (1934–1935, 1944–1947, 1952–1956, 1960–1961, 1968–1972). Further, the party lost the support of many of its younger followers when they formed the **Democratic Left** (Izquierda Democrática, ID) in 1977. Although the party has tried to form coalitions with other parties, it has ceased to be powerful in national politics.

Rodríguez Lara, Guillermo (1923–1988)

Guillermo Rodríguez Lara (1972–1976) was a career military officer who assumed the presidency when the military took control of the government in hopes of reforming and modernizing the nation.

Born to a humble family in Pujilí, Rodríguez Lara had a very successful thirty-three-year career in the military. He studied military tactics in the United States, Colombia, and Argentina, served as the director of the Army War Academy, and briefly held the post of commanding general of the army in April 1971. Rodríguez Lara became head of state following the 1972 military coup that removed José María **Velasco Ibarra** (1934–1935, 1944–1947, 1952–1956, 1960–1961, 1968–1972) from the presidency. The military overthrew Velasco in order to assure their stake in revenues that would soon enter the country under a 1964 **petroleum** concession and in order to prevent Asaad Bucaram Elmhalim, the favorite in the upcoming 1972 election, from becoming president. The military felt that Bucaram would be dangerous and unpredictable as president, especially with the extra income expected from the petroleum concessions.

Rodríguez Lara intended to implement socioeconomic reforms and modernization policies similar to those being implemented by the progressive military regime in neighboring Peru (see **Velasco Alvarado**, Juan, Peru) but faced resistance from the more conservative elements of the military. Specifically, the right wing of the military opposed his plans to nationalize the petroleum industry as well as his proposals for agrarian and tax reform. Despite the resultant political paralysis, under Rodríguez Lara the major oil refinery and petrochemical complex in Esmeraldas were constructed, highway and electrification projects were completed, and state capitalist enterprises, particularly the Ecuadorian State Petroleum Corporation (Corporación Estatal Petrolera Ecuatoriana, CEPE), were developed.

Given that Rodríguez Lara's public support was weak, the traditional wing of the military was able to force him to resign in 1976. He was replaced by a three-man junta that served until democracy was restored with the **Constitution of 1979**.

Urbina, José María (1808–1891)

During José María Urbina's presidency (1851–1856) and during the subsequent decade, Urbina represented the Liberal (see **Radical Liberal Party** [Partido Radical Liberal, PLR]) opposition to Gabriel **García Moreno** (1859–1865, 1869–1875), the leader of the **Conservative Party** (Partido Conservador, PC). This rivalry defined and represents the ideological dichotomy that continues to split Ecuador in the twenty-first century.

Born in Ambato in 1808, Urbina attended Naval School at Guayaquil, leaving before graduating to participate in military actions. He rose rapidly through the ranks of the military, soon becoming aide-de-camp to

President Juan José **Flores** (1830–1834, 1839–1845). In 1837 his political prestige suffered a major setback, however, when he was caught plotting against the government of President José Vicente Rocafuerte (1834–1839) while on a diplomatic mission in Bogotá. He was banished from the country but returned two years later and was appointed governor of Manabí for his loyalty to Flores. Nonetheless, in 1845 Urbina joined a rebel group to overthrow Flores, and was appointed chief of the general staff under provisional president Vicente Ramón Roca (1845–1849). His political and military power, augmented substantially by his new position, allowed him to conduct another coup in 1851 and assume the leadership of the nation. He was elected president in 1852 under a new constitution, and controlled Ecuadorian politics for the rest of the decade.

Urbina's Liberal government was dominated by the executive branch. In one of his administration's most significant actions, during the first week following his coup, Urbina freed the slaves, displaying the social concern for the masses that characterized the Liberals. Soon thereafter he successfully resisted an invasion by Flores from Peru. During his four-year constitutional term, he passed various Liberal anticlerical reforms, in overt defiance of the theocratic tendencies of his Conservative political rival, García Moreno. These included severing ties with the Vatican and expelling the Jesuits from the nation. Urbina also unsuccessfully sought to establish a U.S. protectorate over Ecuador during his presidency. Though his term expired in 1856, Urbina continued to dominate Ecuadorian politics from 1856 to 1859 by controlling the administration of his successor and lifelong friend, President Francisco Robles (1856–1859). During this time, Urbina continued to advocate Liberal social reforms; for instance, he encouraged Robles to end three centuries of required annual payments of tribute by the Indian population, thus initiating a Liberal tradition of advocating for Ecuador's nonwhite population.

In 1859 a Peruvian attack at Guayaquil resulted in the collapse of the Robles government. Urbina went into exile in Peru, where he plotted his return to power in Ecuador. He returned in 1876, helping to bring Ignacio de Veintemilla (1876–1883) to power during a period of Conservatism. Unexpectedly, Veintemilla evolved into a military dictator, and in part as a result of that reversal, Urbina's influence slowly diminished. He died in Guayaquil in 1891 in relative obscurity.

Velasco Ibarra, José María (1893–1979)

José María Velasco Ibarra served as president on five different occasions, from 1934 to 1935, 1944 to 1947, 1952 to 1956, 1960 to 1961, and 1968 to 1972. All but one of these terms ended with his forceful removal from office. He was a personalistic leader who openly criticized political parties, weakened the party system, and contributed to political volatility. However his five terms in office helped to eliminate the political dominance of the corrupt Liberals and increase national unity.

Velasco was born into a wealthy family in 1893. He was educated in law in Paris, and then returned to Quito as a professor at the Central University. Velasco entered politics at an early age, holding various administrative posts and, through his column in *El Comercio*, the principal newspaper of Quito, speaking out against electoral fraud and in favor of effective democracy. In 1932 he was elected to Congress as a Liberal, but often voted with the Conservative minority. Velasco was elected speaker of the National Congress in 1933, and from that post led the fight against Juan de Dios Martínez Mera (1932–1933), whom many believed had reached the presidency through electoral fraud. Congress voted Martínez out of office, and within a year Velasco was elected president with both Liberal and Conservative support. Velasco quickly became frustrated by the barriers to legislation and democracy posed by the Quito oligarchy, and attempted to rule by dictatorial decree. The military, dissatisfied with his administrative style, forcefully removed him from office after only eleven months.

Despite his forced ouster, Velasco remained popular with the public, and when the political scene again became turbulent in the mid-1940s, the populace turned to him. In 1944 he returned from exile in Colombia to assume the presidency after the military removed President Carlos Alberto Arroyo del Río (1940–1944). Velasco immediately condemned the corrupt government of Arroyo and pledged to restore order. Under pressure from Liberals, Velasco's administration promulgated a new constitution in 1945 that introduced reforms that checked the power of the executive in relation to Congress. The new charter left Velasco extremely dissatisfied, and in 1946 he dissolved the Constituent Assembly so that a new body could be elected. The new, more Conservative assembly drafted a document more to Velasco's liking, as it placed power back in his hands. Despite his resultant latitude to administer and govern unchecked, Velasco failed to address the country's economic problems, instead funding the often unsuccessful schemes of his colleagues. As Velasco neglected the economy, inflation increased, the national standard of living decreased dramatically, and foreign reserves fell to dangerously low levels. By 1947 the economy reached a breaking point, and Velasco was again removed from office.

Though Ecuadorian politics remained unstable after Velasco's second exit, by 1952 the political arena had settled down somewhat and Velasco again ran for the presidency. His populist tendencies helped him appeal to and gain the support of civil groups, which brought him electoral victory again in 1952. Upon assuming office, he pledged to increase social spending and public works. A stable economy helped him fulfill his promises. Though Velasco had come to power through the support of the Guayaquil-based Concentration of Popular Forces (Concentración de Fuerzas Populares, CFP), he arrested and deported the CFP boss, Carlos Guevara Moreno, and other party leaders after he became president. Though this resulted in the loss of his political support base, he still managed to stay in office for the entire term. During this third administration, Velasco quashed opposition through violent suppression of students, labor unions, and the press.

In 1960 Velasco made a fourth bid for the presidency and was once again victorious. He again faced a period of economic instability, however, with rising unemployment and falling export prices, and again committed to serving Ecuador's poor even though the country's economy could not support wide-ranging social spending. The economy continued to weaken, and Velasco's opponents grew weary of his inability to remedy Ecuador's problems. Congress was clearly anti-Velasco, as was his vice president, and in 1961 he was once again removed from office. A period of heightened political instability ensued, punctuated by the passage of a new constitution in 1967.

In 1968 Velasco won his fifth presidency, with less than one-third of the popular vote. Velasco lacked majority support in Congress, and his vice president, Jorge Zavala Baquerizo, soon became one of his strongest critics. His economic policies (such as devaluing the *sucre*) were immensely unpopular. He lost even more support as he began to campaign for the removal of the 1967 Constitution, which he believed made the executive too weak to be effective. After alienating all of his allies, Velasco was removed from office by the military in 1972, marking the beginning of a seven-year period of military rule. Many believe that his final ouster was not so much a reflection of dissatisfaction with Velasco but rather of the military's and the elite's dislike for his presumed successor, Asaad Bucaram Elmhalim. Velasco went into exile and returned in 1979 a month before his death.

HEADS OF STATE

Juan José Flores	1830–1834
José Vicente Rocafuerte	1834–1839
Juan José Flores	1839–1845
José Joaquín de Olmedo	1845
Vicente Ramón Roca	1845–1849
Manuel de Ascásubi	1849–1850
Diego Noboa y Areta	1850–1851
José María Urbina	1851–1856
Francisco Robles	1856–1859
Gabriel García Moreno	1859–1865
Jerónimo Carrión	1865–1867
Pedro José de Arteta y Calisto	1867–1868
Francisco Javier Espinoza	1868–1869
Gabriel García Moreno	1869–1875
Francisco Javier León	1875
Antonio Borrero y Cortázar	1875–1876
Ignacio de Veintemilla	1876–1883
José María Plácido Caamaño y Cornejo	1883–1888
Antonio Flores Jijón	1888–1892
Luis Cordero Crespo	1892–1895
Vicente Lucio Salazar	1895
José Eloy Alfaro Delgado	1895–1901
Leónidas Plaza Gutiérrez	1901–1905
Lizardo García	1905–1906
José Eloy Alfaro Delgado	1906–1911
Carlos Freile Zaldumbide	1911–1912
Francisco Andrade Marín	1912
Leónidas Plaza Gutiérrez	1912–1916
Alfredo Baquerizo Moreno	1916–1920
José Luis Tamayo	1920–1924
Gonzalo S. Córdova	1924–1925
Provisional Government Junta	1925–1926
Isidro Ayora	1926–1931
Luis Larrea Alba	1931
Alfredo Baquerizo Moreno	1931–1932
Alberto Guerrero Martínez	1932
Juan de Dios Martínez Mera	1932–1933
Abelardo Montalvo	1933–1934
José María Velasco Ibarra	1934–1935
Federico Páez Chiriboga	1935–1937
Gil Alberto Enríquez Gallo	1937–1938
Manuel María Borrero González	1938
Aurelio Mosquera Narváez	1938–1939
Andrés Fernández de Córdova Nieto	1939–1940
Carlos Alberto Arroyo del Río	1940–1944
José María Velasco Ibarra	1944–1947
Carlos Julio Aroseamena Tola	1947–1948
Galo Plaza Lasso	1948–1952
José María Velasco Ibarra	1952–1956
Camilo Ponce Enríquez	1956–1960
José María Velasco Ibarra	1960–1961
Carlos Julio Arosemena Monroy	1961–1963
Ramón Castro Jijón	1963–1966
Clemente Yerovi Indaburu	1966
Otto Arosemena Gómez	1966–1968
José María Velasco Ibarra	1968–1972
Guillermo Rodríguez Lara	1972–1976
Alfredo Ernesto Poveda Burbano	1976–1979
Jaime Roldós Aguilera	1979–1981
Osvaldo Hurtado Larrea	1981–1984

León Febres-Cordero Ribadeneyra	1984–1988
Rodrigo Borja Cevallos	1988–1992
Sixto Durán-Ballén Cordovez	1992–1996
Abdala Bucaram Ortiz	1996–1997
Fabian Alarcón	1997–1998
Jamil Mahuad Witt	1998–2000
Gustavo Noboa Bajarano	2000–

Source: *Rulers*. http://rulers.org/rule.htm#ecuador

BIBLIOGRAPHY

Print Resources

Andrade, Roberto. *Historia del Ecuador*. Quito: Corporación Editora Nacional, 1982–1984.

Bretón, Víctor. *Capitalismo, reforma agraria y organización comunal en los Andes: Una introducción al caso ecuatoriano*. Lleida, Spain: Ediciones de la Universidad de Lleida, 1997.

Hanratty, Dennis M., ed. *Ecuador: A Country Study*. Washington, DC: Headquarters, Department of the Army, 1991.

Hey, Jeanne A. K. *Theories of Dependent Foreign Policy and the Case of Ecuador in the 1980s*. Athens: Ohio University Center for International Studies, 1995.

Hidrobo Estrada, Jorge. *Power and Industrialization in Ecuador*. Boulder: Westview Press, 1992.

Isaacs, Anita. *Military Rule and Transition in Ecuador, 1972–1992*. Pittsburgh: University of Pittsburgh Press, 1993.

Reyes, Oscar Efrén. *Breve historia general del Ecuador*. Quito: Fray Jodoco Ricke, 1967.

Selverston, Melina H. "The Politics of Culture: Indigenous Peoples and the State in Ecuador." In *Indigenous Peoples and Democracy in Latin America*. New York: St. Martin's Press, 1995.

Torre, Carlos de la. *La seducción velasquista*. Quito: Ediciones Libri Mundi, 1993.

Vargas, José María. *Historia del Ecuador, siglo XVI*. Quito: Centro de Publicaciones, Pontificia Universidad Católica del Ecuador, 1977.

———. *Historia del Ecuador, siglo XVII*. Quito: Centro de Publicaciones, Pontificia Universidad Católica del Ecuador, 1977.

Villacrés Moscoso, Jorge W. *Historia diplomática de la República del Ecuador*. Guayaquil: Universidad de Guayaquil, 1967.

Wood, Bryce. *Aggression and History: The Case of Ecuador and Peru*. Ann Arbor: University Microfilms International, 1978.

Electronic Resources

Hoy Online
http://www.hoy.com.ec/
The Web version of one of Ecuador's major daily newspapers. Offers comprehensive national coverage, with a particularly strong emphasis on the economy and national politics. (In Spanish)

Latin American Network Information Center (LANIC): Ecuador
http://lanic.utexas.edu/la/ecuador/
Ecuador section of this extensive Web site contains hundreds of links to research resources, cultural centers, economic and business institutions, government agencies, historical sources, magazines and other periodicals, nongovernmental organizations, and grassroots groups, as well as many other subjects. (In English)

Political Database of the Americas: Ecuador
http://www.georgetown.edu/pdba/Countries/ecuador.html
Comprehensive database run as a joint project of Georgetown University and the Organization of American States. Section on Ecuador contains information on and links to the executive, legislative, and judicial branches of the Ecuadorian government; electoral laws and election results; and other political data. (In English, Spanish, Portuguese, and French)

Political Resources.net: Ecuador
http://www.politicalresources.net/ecuador.htm
Contains a wealth of links to sources of information on national politics. Includes information on political parties, legislative and executive institutions, laws and legislation, and elections, as well as a link to the constitution. (In English)

Wilfried Derksen's Elections Around the World: Ecuador
http://www.agora.it/elections/ecuador.htm
Ecuador section of a comprehensive database of results from elections around the world. Contains results from recent national executive and legislative elections, as well as explanations of and links to political parties and institutions. (In English)

EL SALVADOR

COUNTRY PROFILE

Official name	República de El Salvador
Capital	San Salvador
Type/structure of government	Democratic republic
Executive	President elected to a five-year term; reelection not permitted
Legislative	Unicameral Legislative Assembly with 60 seats (20 free nationwide seats, and 40 seats to which members are elected every three years in each of the country's fourteen departments).
Judicial	Highest court is the Supreme Court of Justice, composed of magistrates elected to fixed terms by the majority political party in the Legislative Assembly.
Major political parties	**National Republican Alliance** (Alianza Republicana Nacional, ARENA); **Partido Farabundo Martí National Liberation Front** (Frente Farabundo Martí para la Liberación Nacional, FMLN).
Constitution in effect	1983
Location/geography	Central America, bordering Honduras to the northeast, Guatemala to the northwest, and the Pacific Ocean to the south; volcanic terrain with fertile coast.
Geographic area	21,720 sq. km.
Population	5,839,079 (July 1999 est.)
Ethnic groups	Mestizo 94%; indigenous 5% white (of European descent) 1%
Religions	Roman Catholic 75%; extensive activity by Protestant groups throughout the country with an estimated 1 million Protestant evangelicals by the end of 1992.
Literacy rate	71.5% (1995 est.)
Infant mortality rate	28.38 deaths per 1,000 live births (1999 est.)
Life expectancy	70 years (1999 est.)
Monetary unit	Colón
Exchange rate	1 U.S. dollar = 8.71 colones (August 2000)**
Major exports	Coffee, sugar, shrimp, textiles
Major imports	Raw materials, consumer goods, capital goods, fuels
GDP	$7,663 million (1997)*
GDP growth rate	4.0% (1997)*
GDP per capita	1,293 (1997)*

*Inter-American Development Bank. *Facing Up to Inequality in Latin America: Economic and Social Progress in Latin America, 1998–99 Report.* Washington, DC. Inter-American Development Bank, 1998.

**Latin American Weekly Report.* August 22, 2000 (WR-00-33), p. 394.

Source: U.S. Library of Congress. *El Salvador: A Country Study.* http://lcweb2.loc.gov/frd/cs/svtoc.html

OVERVIEW

Summary

El Salvador, 200 miles long and 50 miles wide, is the smallest and most densely populated nation in Latin America. Its history and culture are rooted in the country's role as an agricultural exporter and its colonial legacy of gross disparities between the wealthy elite and the poor majority. In the past twenty years, El Salvador has been shaken by political chaos, civil war, foreign intervention, natural disasters, and worsening poverty. Half of the nation's population lives in poverty, and El Salvador is one of the world's most underdeveloped countries. In early 2001, El Salvador was rocked by a series of devastating earthquakes.

History

Around the year 1000, the Olmecs settled in what is today El Salvador. Five hundred years later, three major indigenous groups, the Maya, the Lenca, and the Pipil, populated the region. Following the arrival of the Spanish colonizers in the New World, in 1525, Pedro de Alvarado, who had served under Spanish explorer Hernán Cortés in Mexico, led an expedition into Pipil territory and established the Spanish city of San Salvador near the indigenous city of Cuzcatlán. A century later, an estimated 80 percent of the native population had been decimated by disease, slavery, and warfare.

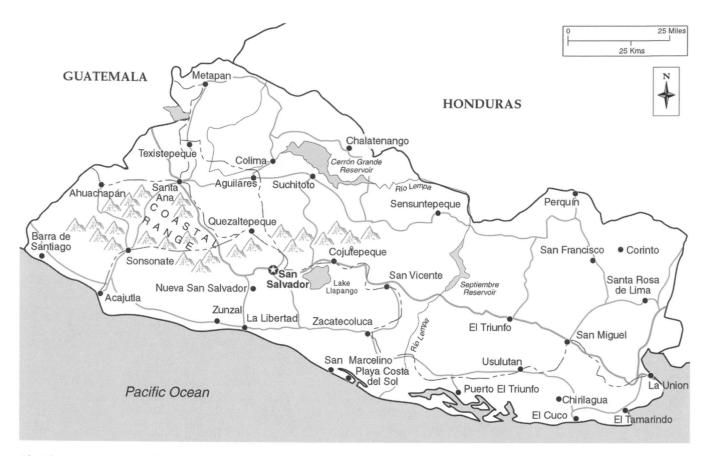

El Salvador. © 1998 The Moschovitis Group, Inc.

During the colonial period, El Salvador was ruled by the Spanish crown through the Kingdom of Guatemala. The area began to prosper agriculturally due to its fertile volcanic soil, and most of El Salvador's colonizers were farmers. Cacao, the first major crop, was cultivated by Indian slave labor to enrich a wealthy minority. This early period would set a precedent for El Salvador's economic dependence on agricultural export commodities, as well as for socioeconomic relations, which would continue to be characterized by a small fraction of the population amassing great fortunes through the exploitation of the peasantry. By the 1600s indigo had replaced cacao as the country's main export; it would continue to play a key role in the economy for the next three centuries, until coffee replaced it as El Salvador's chief agricultural export.

With Mexico's independence from Spain in 1821, Central America came under the rule of its northern neighbor, only to declare its independence two years later as the **United Provinces of Central America** (see Appendix 1). Although El Salvador sought to break away from that union, complete independence was thwarted by a Mexican-Guatemalan alliance. The United Provinces first began to disintegrate in the late 1830s and by 1840 El Salvador had declared its independence (though an independent republic was not fully established until 1856). In contrast to conservative Gua-

temala, liberals controlled El Salvador's government and its army for the rest of the century. Despite five coups, two presidential executions, and many insurrections by the increasingly disenfranchised poor, reforms enacted in the late 1800s, including the construction of commercial infrastructure and the usurpation of indigenous lands, furthered the privileged position of the elite. As coffee became the leading export, a small oligarchy of wealthy planters—often referred to as El Salvador's legendary "fourteen families"—gained political prominence, backed by an increasingly powerful military.

In spite of the privileged position of the elite, El Salvador was considered Central America's most progressive nation by the turn of the century. However, with the Great Depression, the coffee market fell, shattering the country's economy. Worker unrest grew rampant, and labor leaders such as Alberto Masferrer and Agustín **Farabundo Martí** began calling for political and economic reform. In 1931 Labor Party (Partido Laborista, PL) candidate Arturo **Araujo** (1931) was elected president, only to be overthrown less than a year later by the military, with the support of the reactionary oligarchy, and replaced by his vice president, General Maximiliano **Hernández Martínez** (1931–1934, 1935–1944). Incited by Farabundo Martí and the communists, the peasantry rose up in protest. The new govern-

This photo from the 1960s shows Salvadoran farmers transplanting coffee plant seedlings. *Columbus Memorial Library, General Secretariat of the Organization of American States. Reproduced with permission of the Organization of American States.*

ment responded mercilessly, killing between 10,000 and 30,000 people in a tragic event remembered today as *La Matanza* (The Slaughter [1932]). In 1944 Hernández Martínez was finally overthrown by young military officers, workers, and students, including future president José Napoleón **Duarte Fuentes** (1984–1989). El Salvador subsequently experienced significant political unrest; coups were common and the military often ruled the nation.

Despite the diversification of the economy in the 1950s, the emergence of a small middle class, and the creation of the **Central American Common Market** (CACM; see Appendix 1) in 1960, the country's population growth soon outpaced economic growth. El Salvador could not produce enough food to feed its people; one result was the migration of many Salvadorans to neighboring Honduras, a dynamic over which conflict flared between the two nations in 1969 (see **Soccer War**, Appendix 1). Tensions also erupted into war between the Salvadoran government and a small but formidable guerrilla army, the **Farabundo Martí National Liberation Front** (Frente Farabundo Martí para la Liberación Nacional, FMLN). El Salvador was rav-

aged by the **civil war of the 1980s** beginning with a military coup in 1979 and continuing until the **Chapultepec Accords** of 1992.

The U.S. administrations of Presidents Ronald Reagan and George Bush, fearing that the victory of the **Sandinista National Liberation Front** (Frente Sandinista de Liberación Nacional, FSLN; see Nicaragua) in neighboring Nicaragua in 1979 would spread communism throughout Central America, supported El Salvador's military and the ultraconservative political party, the **National Republican Alliance** (Alianza Republicana Nacional, ARENA) in spite of the kidnappings, rapes, tortures, and murders of guerrillas and civilians with which it was associated. Atrocities included the 1980 assassination of Archbishop Oscar Arnulfo **Romero**, the rape and murder of three U.S. nuns and a lay worker by Salvadoran guardsmen that same year, the 1981 massacre of approximately 900 villagers in El Mozote, Morazán, and in 1989, the murder of six Jesuit priests and two civilians at the University of Central America in San Salvador.

Though civilian rule returned to El Salvador in the mid-1980s with the election of Duarte, it was not until the 1990s that the nation was truly free of significant

This photo from 1969 shows Salvadoran government troops marching in a demonstration of strength after the war with neighboring Honduras. *Columbus Memorial Library, General Secretariat of the Organization of American States. Reproduced with permission of the Organization of American States.*

military influence in its government. By 2001 power had changed hands peacefully between democratic regimes three times, and the country had experienced more than a decade of almost unprecedented constitutional continuity under governments led by the ARENA party. Further, in 1992 the national government and the FMLN guerrillas signed the Chapultepec Accords, officially ending Salvador's long civil conflict. Nonetheless, El Salvador still has not recovered from its devastating civil war, in which more than 70,000 were killed, and which led nearly a million people to flee the country. Exacerbating the country's and its population's precarious economic situation, in the fall of 1998, Hurricane Mitch blasted through the region, causing billions of dollars in damage and killing hundreds of people. By 2000 crime rates were higher than they were during the civil war of the 1980s and deep socioeconomic disparities persisted, fueling continued immigration to the United States. In early 2001, El Salvador was hit again by natural disaster. A series of strong earthquakes rattled the country in January and February 2001, destroying or damaging some 350,000 homes (nearly one-fourth of the country's housing) and killing more than 1,500 people.

ENTRIES

Araujo, Arturo (1877–1967)
Arturo Araujo (1931) served briefly as president of El Salvador; he was the country's first elected head of state following decades of appointed presidents.

Araujo was born into El Salvador's powerful oligarchy and earned an engineering degree in England. Strongly pro-union, he later helped form the Labor Party (Partido Laborista, PL). He ran unsuccessfully for president in 1919, and in 1922 failed in an attempt to take power through force. Araujo contested and won the 1931 presidential election on the ticket of the PL, basing his platform on the program of equity, education, and social development laid out in the work *Vital Minimum* by the famous Salvadoran author and labor leader Alberto Masferrer. Araujo's supporters hoped that he would lead the country toward a social democracy, promoting land reform and improved health and education services. Workers and peasants rallied to his cause, while the ruling oligarchy refused to support his administration. After only ten months in office, Araujo was ousted in a coup staged by young conservative military officers on December 2, 1931, in response to his allowing the Communist Party to participate in the municipal elections scheduled for later that month. His vice president, General Maximiliano **Hernández Martínez** (1931–1934, 1935–1944), assumed the presidency.

Arce, Manuel José (1787–1847)
Manuel José Arce served as president of the **United Provinces of Central America** (see Appendix 1) from 1825 to 1828. Although he was born in El Salvador, Arce allied himself with conservative Guatemalans, eroding his support at home and eventually undermining his power.

Arce was the nephew of powerful priest Father José Delgado, who played a central role in the 1823 declaration of Central America's independence from Spain and Mexico. Arce attended university briefly in Guatemala, and later became an influential landowner. He was imprisoned for five years after participating in the 1811 and 1814 independence revolts, and fled to the United States after attempting unsuccessfully to defend El Salvador from Mexican annexation in 1821.

Arce returned to El Salvador in 1823 following Central American independence and served on the ruling junta of the United Provinces of Central America. In 1825 he was elected president of the federation, which included El Salvador, Guatemala, Honduras, Nicaragua, and Costa Rica. Constant infighting marked the union, and he soon sided with conservative factions from Guatemala, alienating Salvadoran liberals. Arce later angered another faction when he advocated powerful central government instead of strong state governments. Arce left the presidency of the joint republic in 1828, and the following year the liberals took power in El Salvador. Arce was forced into exile in Mexico and was forbidden to return to El Salvador until 1844.

Calderón Sol, Armando (1948–)
Armando Calderón Sol (1994–1999), a member of the right wing **National Republican Alliance** (Alianza Republicana Nacional, ARENA) since its 1981 creation, was a close friend of its controversial founder, Roberto **D'Aubuisson**. Calderón Sol rose to national prominence as mayor of San Salvador, a post to which he was elected in 1988 and reelected in 1991. He won ARENA's presidential bid for the 1994 election because it was believed that he could hold together the moderate and extreme factions of the party, and he was subsequently victorious in the election. Soon after he assumed office however, the party's internal disputes worsened as corruption scandals perpetrated by the administration of his predecessor, Alfredo Félix **Cristiani Burkard** (1989–1994), emerged. Calderón Sol enacted neoliberal economic reforms, including the privatization of state-owned enterprises. In 1995 he joined with smaller left-of-center political parties in a reform pact; however, the other parties soon withdrew from the agreement after the president failed to enact social, health, or worker protection laws. Calderón Sol also alienated parts of the military by not following through on pay compensation promised to soldiers in the **Chaputlepec Accords** that ended the country's **civil war of the 1980s**. Protests by workers and prisoners also disrupted his administration. Calderón Sol yielded the presidency to fellow ARENA member Francisco Guillermo **Flores Pérez** (1999–) in 1999.

Chapultepec Accords (1992)
After more than a decade of warfare, in which an estimated 75,000 Salvadorans lost their lives, the conservative Salvadoran government controlled by the **National Republican Alliance** (Alianza Republicana Nacional, ARENA), and the leftist **Farabundo Martí National Liberation Front** (Frente Farabundo Martí para la Liberación Nacional, FMLN) guerrilla army agreed to negotiate peace with the aid of the United Nations. The FMLN and the government signed the Chapultepec Accords on January 11, 1992, at Chapultepec Castle in Mexico City. Through the accords, the FMLN agreed to lay down its weapons and recognize the ARENA government and the 1983 Constitution in exchange for its acceptance as a political party, the passage of certain constitutional amendments, a reduction in the size of the military, electoral reform, and a commitment on the part of the government to create a more open and democratic political environment. Both sides agreed to the creation of truth and human rights commissions to investigate the atrocities perpetrated during the war, as well as a special human rights institution (the National Council for the Defense of Human Rights). The formal cease-fire went into effect on February 1, 1992, and the war officially ended on December 15, 1992.

Christian Democrat Party (Partido Demócrata Cristiano, PDC)
The Christian Democrat Party (Partido Demócrata Cristiano, PDC) was founded in 1960, and in 1962 became the first opposition party to gain seats in the Legislative Assembly since the 1931 communist-peasant uprising that resulted in an army massacre known as *La Matanza* (the Slaughter [1932]).

With close ties to Christian Democrat parties in other countries, El Salvador's PDC aimed to enact moderate social reforms without causing class violence. Following its initial electoral victory in 1962, the PDC became a major political party in El Salvador. However, the PDC suffered serious setbacks in the 1970s as the military expanded its power. In the 1972 presidential election, PDC candidate José Napoleón **Duarte Fuentes** (1984–1989) won a plurality of the votes, but the military fraudulently awarded the office to Arturo Armando **Molina Barraza** (1972–1977). Similarly, in the 1977 contest, victorious PDC candidate Colonel Ernesto Claramount was denied the presidency by the military, which again awarded the office to their candidate, Carlos Humberto **Romero Mena** (1977–1979). Following Romero's ouster in 1979, successive civilian-military juntas governed the country. The PDC was represented in each junta and promised to institute social and economic reforms to lessen the gap between the nation's wealthy few and its poor majority, especially land reform, the creation of peasant cooperatives, and the nationalization of some industries, including banking.

Though the PDC positioned itself as a moderate alternative to the radical **National Republican Alliance** (Alianza Republicana Nacional, ARENA) in the 1980s, the party was influenced by the military and worked closely with U.S. presidents Ronald Reagan and George Bush. By the late 1980s, the PDC was weakened by corruption, its leadership was faltering, and it had proven unable to institute the reforms it promised in 1979. ARENA took advantage of this, winning the Legislative Assembly elections in 1988 and controlling Congress through 1997, and winning the presidency in 1989, 1994, and 1999. This, along with the institutionalization of the **Farabundo Martí National Liberation Front** (Frente Farabundo Martí para la Liberación Nacional, FMLN) as an official party in 1992, marked the end of the PDC's centrality in Salvadoran politics.

Civil War of the 1980s

Since El Salvador's birth as a nation, the country's elite have often used violence against the large peasantry, carrying out many land seizures and continually engaging in general intimidation. El Salvador's poor have historically suffered among the highest malnutrition, infant mortality, and illiteracy rates in the Western Hemisphere. Centuries of mistreatment and turmoil finally exploded in a protracted and devastating conflict in the 1980s, during which the leftist guerrilla group the **Farabundo Martí National Liberation Front** (Frente Farabundo Martí para la Liberación Nacional, FMLN) sought popular revolution, battling the national government for more than a decade. An estimated 75,000 people were killed in the bloody clash.

Following the fraudulent election of Arturo Armando **Molina Barraza** (1972–1977) and Carlos Humberto **Romero Mena** (1977–1979) to the presidency, small but growing popular organizations began rallying against the corrupt government through demonstrations and strikes. In response, these presidents used repression to maintain control. In October 1979, as human rights violations worsened and the economy lagged, a group of junior officers overthrew Romero and set up a governing junta known as the Fifteenth of October Movement (Movimiento 15 de Octubre). While initially reformist in nature, conservative elements soon gained control of the junta and blocked its proposed reforms. On January 11, 1980, when demonstrators took to the streets demanding agrarian reform and nationalization of certain industries, the military and the police opened fire.

The FMLN was established as a coalition of guerrilla groups in May 1980. The civil war broke out in January 1981 with a failed FMLN attack against the government known as the "final offensive," and fighting continued throughout the rest of the decade. In 1989, as more conservative factions in the government gained control, the FMLN launched another major offensive, in an unsuccessful attempt to rally support among the populace. Despite initial victories, the uprising was put down within three weeks. The failure of this offensive prompted the FMLN to increase its engagement in the peace negotiation process, which had been faltering since 1981.

The United States played a major role in El Salvador's civil war. Through the late 1970s and the 1980s, U.S. policy toward and influence in the country was motivated by two contradictory priorities. Under President Jimmy Carter, U.S. policy emphasized human rights (see **Carter Doctrine**, Appendix 2), and the United States tried to curb the gross and escalating human rights abuses in the country through decreasing military assistance and sanctions. Under Presidents Ronald Reagan and George Bush, however, the United States perceived El Salvador as a pivotal point in stopping the spread of communism in the hemisphere, and awarded increased economic and military aid to El Salvador's government (see **Reagan Doctrine**, Appendix 2).

The war ended with the signing of the **Chapultepec Accords** in Mexico in 1992 as the government and the FMLN agreed to move the dispute from the battleground to the political arena.

Cristiani Burkard, Alfredo Félix (1947–)

A moderate conservative and a successful businessman, Alfredo Félix Cristiani Burkard was chosen as the presidential candidate of the **National Republican Alliance** (Alianza Republicana Nacional, ARENA) in 1989 in an attempt to modify the party's radical right-wing reputation. He won the election and served as president from 1989 to 1994.

Cristiani was born into a wealthy coffee family and graduated from the American School in San Salvador and from Georgetown University in Washington, D.C. Before moving into politics, Cristiani served as president of the Salvadoran Coffee Exporters' Association and was a leading industrialist. He married into one of El Salvador's fabled "fourteen families," increasing his wealth and prestige. Cristiani represented the moderate faction of ARENA and presented a more reputable image than party leader Roberto **D'Aubuisson**, who had connections to death squads and paramilitary groups. Consequently, in 1984 D'Aubuisson began grooming Cristiani to serve as the party's leader and presidential candidate.

Following Cristiani's victory in the March 1989 presidential elections, the leftist **Farabundo Martí National Liberation Front** (Frente Farabundo Martí para la Liberación Nacional, FMLN) guerrilla group, which for most of the decade had been involved in a civil war with the government, launched a series of attacks in which the attorney general and the minister of the presidency were assassinated. In response, right-wing groups killed union members and FMLN supporters. The murder of six Jesuit priests in November 1989 shortly after Cristiani assumed office shocked the world, and Cristiani's administration was perceived as ineffective in finding the perpetrators of the murders, due to links between the military and the right-wing groups considered responsible for the crimes.

However, Cristiani demonstrated his desire for peace in 1992 with his participation in the negotiation of the peace accords with the FMLN that ended El Salvador's civil war (see **Chapultepec Accords**). Nevertheless, his administration was unable to implement several key aspects of the accords, including prosecuting human rights offenders to the fullest extent and removing certain officers from the armed forces. El Salvador's economy improved under Cristiani, and in 1994, following the end of Cristiani's term, power was transferred peacefully, through elections, to ARENA President-Elect Armando **Calderón Sol** (1994–1999), suggesting that democracy might also be taking hold in the war-torn country.

D'Aubuisson, Roberto (1943–1992)

In 1981 Major Roberto D'Aubuisson founded the **National Republican Alliance** (Alianza Republicana Nacional, ARENA), the key political party in El Salvador during the 1980s and 1990s. Throughout his lifetime, D'Aubuisson was associated with radical conservatism, harsh repression, human rights violations, and death squads targeting the country's leftist insurgency. His calls for oppression, which incited his supporters and provoked his enemies, played an integral role in the violence of the **civil war of the 1980s.**

D'Aubuisson began his career as an intelligence officer, working for the **National Democrat Organization** (Organización Demócrata Nacional, ORDEN), a government-operated paramilitary group used to quell political unrest. He was expelled from the armed forces for his brutal tactics following the 1979 coup that unseated Carlos Humberto **Romero Mena** (1977–1979). D'Aubuisson soon gained national notoriety for his fierce, macho image and heated television appearances, during which he often showed photographs and documents of alleged leftists, advising them to modify their behavior or face serious consequences; many of these alleged subversives were later murdered by death squads. In 1980 D'Aubuisson was arrested for planning a coup against the junta in power led by José Napoleón **Duarte Fuentes** (who would later serve as president,

1984–1989) but he was released days later. After his arrest documents linking him to the assassination of Archbishop Oscar Arnulfo **Romero** were discovered.

In 1981 D'Aubuisson created ARENA, an extreme right-wing political party that quickly gained influence and popularity. In 1982, D'Aubuisson vowed that if he were elected provisional president of the country, the guerrilla group, the **Farabundo Martí National Liberation Front** (Frente Farabundo Martí para la Liberación Nacional, FMLN), would be destroyed within three months. Only pressure from the United States, which feared that D'Aubuisson's extremist attitude would cast a negative light on the Salvadoran government (which the U.S. was supporting with millions of dollars of aid), prevented D'Aubuisson from becoming the country's provisional leader.

D'Aubuisson ran for president against **Christian Democrat Party** (Partido Demócrata Cristiano, PDC) candidate Duarte in the 1984 elections, but was defeated in a runoff. The United States encouraged him to slowly withdraw from the political stage. He stepped down as the head of ARENA in 1988, making way for Alfredo Félix **Crisitiani Burkard** (1989–1994), whom he had groomed politically, to assume a more central position in the party. D'Aubuisson died of cancer in 1992.

Duarte Fuentes, José Napoleón (1925–1990)

José Napoleón Duarte Fuentes represented the moderate left in El Salvador's national political arena for much of the second half of the twentieth century. As president from 1984 to 1989, he was heavily influenced by the United States, the Salvadoran military, and the country's more conservative factions.

Duarte was born into a wealthy family, and as a young man participated in the student movement that helped overthrow dictator Maximiliano **Hernández Martínez** (1931–1934, 1935–1944) in 1944. Duarte graduated from the University of Notre Dame in the United States with a degree in civil engineering. He helped found the **Christian Democrat Party** (Partido Demócrata Cristiano, PDC) in 1960, and was elected mayor of San Salvador in 1964 on the PDC ticket. In his six years as mayor of the capital, he increased revenues by taxing the rich and improved the city's infrastructure. Duarte was favored to win the 1972 presidential election (again on the PDC ticket), and he received a plurality of votes; nonetheless, he was denied the position when the military rigged the elections and installed their own candidate, Arturo Armando **Molina Barraza** (1972–1977), as president. After an attempted coup led by young military officers later that year, Duarte was captured by the government and exiled to Venezuela.

Following the 1979 coup that ousted Carlos Humberto **Romero Mena** (1977–1979), Duarte returned to El Salvador and served on the juntas that ruled the country from 1979 to 1982. After campaigning on the PDC ticket and receiving $1 million in support from the United States, Duarte was elected president in 1984, defeating Roberto **D'Aubuisson**, the candidate of the **National Republican Alliance** (Alianza Republicana Nacional, ARENA). Many hoped that his election would bring an end to the **civil war of the 1980s** and were encouraged when Duarte met with **Farabundo Martí National Liberation Front** (Frente Farabundo Martí para la Liberación Nacional, FMLN) leaders soon after his election. However, Duarte soon came to be regarded as a puppet of the military and the United States.

No important reforms were implemented during Duarte's administration. Corruption increased and the size and influence of the army escalated dramatically. After his daughter was kidnapped in 1985 by the guerrilla forces, Duarte freed a number of rebel prisoners in exchange for her release, drawing sharp criticism from the right. In 1989 Duarte yielded power to President-Elect Alfredo Félix **Cristiani Burkard** (1989–1994) of the ARENA party. Duarte died of cancer in 1990.

Farabundo Martí, Agustín (1893–1932)

Agustín Farabundo Martí was a leading social activist in the early twentieth century. He founded the Communist Party of El Salvador in 1930. Guerrilla forces struggling against repressive national governments later in the twentieth century would adopt his name.

Farabundo Martí enrolled in the National University of El Salvador's law school in 1914, but never graduated because he was arrested and exiled to Guatemala for his leftist political activism. He returned to El Salvador when the Guatemalan government forced all foreign leftists out of the country, and was soon arrested again for his political activities. He was released after a hunger strike. In 1928 he left for Nicaragua to join General Augusto César **Sandino Calderón** (see Nicaragua) in his armed opposition to the occupation of that country by the United States. Subsequently exiled from Nicaragua, Farabundo Martí returned to El Salvador and founded the Communist Party of El Salvador. Enraged when General Maximiliano **Hernández Martínez** (1931–1934, 1935–1944) was named dictator of El Salvador following the coup that unseated Arturo **Araujo** (1931) in 1931, Farabundo Martí led an unsuccessful peasant revolt in January 1932. The revolt ended in a bloody massacre known as *La Mantanza* (The Slaughter [1932]), carried out by the government troops. Martí was captured and killed in the massacre. His revolutionary spirit lives on in the guerrilla army turned political party that bears his name, the **Farabundo Martí National Liberation Front** (Frente Farabundo Martí para la Liberación Nacional, FMLN).

Farabundo Martí National Liberation Front (Frente Farabundo Martí para la Liberación Nacional, FMLN)

Named in homage to martyred communist leader Agustín **Farabundo Martí**, the Farabundo Martí National Liberation Front (Frente Farabundo Martí para la Liberación Nacional, FMLN) was created to join five groups as an armed front to battle the Salvadoran government and its repressive military and paramilitary groups (see **civil war of the 1980s**). While there were often ideological and tactical disagreements between the separate organizations, the FMLN proved to be a powerful force.

On January 10, 1981, the united FMLN launched its first major offensive, which was intended to instigate a national insurrection, but instead ended in defeat. The FMLN persisted and eventually occupied much of northern El Salvador. The guerrillas' subsequent attacks focused on weakening El Salvador's economy by destroying critical infrastructure like bridges, telephone lines, and roads. The FMLN's Radio Venceremos played a decisive role in the group's rise to influence as an effective propaganda tool.

While the FMLN received support from the Nicaraguan **Sandinista National Liberation Front** (Frente Sandinista de Liberación Nacional [FSLN]; see Nicaragua), Cuba, and the USSR, the United States supported the Salvadoran government's war effort against the FMLN, providing weaponry and funding. By 1985 approximately 8,000 FMLN members faced over 50,000 government military troops. Nonetheless, it is widely believed that the FMLN would have defeated the Salvadoran government had the United States not provided critical support. In 1989, while planning a major armed offensive, the FMLN began advocating a "democratic revolution" and a peaceful settlement to the conflict. The government ignored the group's proposal, and that same year the Salvadoran military bombed the National Federation of Salvadoran Workers, leaving ten people dead. The FMLN responded with the major offensive it had been planning, during which hundreds of FMLN guerrillas were killed.

Demobilization of the FMLN began in 1991 with the encouragement of the United Nations, and in 1992 the official peace agreement, the **Chapultepec Accords**, was signed. Later that year, the FMLN became a political party, and was soon second in national representation to the **National Republican Alliance** (Alianza Republicana Nacional, ARENA) despite the loss of some of its founding members. In 1997 Héctor Silva secured the mayorship of San Salvador on an FMLN-led coalition ticket, and by 2000 the FMLN controlled about one-third of the national Congress. (ARENA controlled another third and various smaller political parties the last third.)

Flores Pérez, Francisco Guillermo (1959–)

In 1999, at the age of thirty-nine, Francisco Guillermo Flores Pérez became the youngest president in the history of El Salvador. He had held a leading position in El Salvador's Congress before his election as the country's leader.

Flores graduated from Amherst College in Massachusetts with a degree in political science and spent a year at Harvard University before returning to El Salvador. After a brief stint teaching philosophy, he was elected to the Legislative Assembly on the **National Republican Alliance** (Alianza Republicana Nacional, ARENA) ticket, and served as president of the Assembly during his second term as congressman. ARENA chose Flores as its candidate for the 1999 presidential election in part because he had no connections to the violence and **civil war of the 1980s**, and in part because he represented a more moderate faction of the right-wing party. Nonetheless, during the campaign, Flores' opponent, **Farabundo Martí National Liberation Front** (Frente Farabundo Martí para la Liberación Nacional, FMLN) candidate Facundo Guardado (a former peasant who fought as a guerrilla leader in the nation's civil war), assured the country that Flores represented the same exploitative factions that had traditionally held power in El Salvador.

With a voter turnout of only 35 percent, Flores won the 1999 presidential election. Upon assuming office, Flores declared that he would appoint a diverse cabinet, and then proceeded to fill his cabinet with ARENA technocrats who had been schooled abroad. Though he made little progress in terms of economic or political reform in the first years of his presidency, Flores successfully organized disaster relief efforts after a series of strong earthquakes rocked El Salvador in early 2001.

Hernández Martínez, Maximiliano (1882–1966)

Renowned for his use of violent repression, Maximiliano Hernández Martínez held the presidency from 1931 to 1934, and again from 1935 to 1944. He served in support of El Salvador's elite, but was removed from office by the very same factions whose interests he had spent his career protecting.

Hernández Martínez began his career in military school in Guatemala, entered the Salvadoran army in 1903, and then fought against Guatemala when unrest broke out between the two countries in 1906. After losing the 1930 presidential election to Arturo **Araujo** (1931), Hernández Martínez became his vice president. In 1931 a group of young military officers toppled Araujo's weak administration in a coup in which it was widely speculated that Hernández Martínez played a role. He was jailed, but was soon released and appointed leader of El Salvador later that year. In January 1932 peasants and rural workers rose up to protest his appointment, incited by the Communist Party and led by Agustín **Farabundo Martí**. Hernández Martínez ordered his troops to quell the unrest, and tens of thousands of people were subsequently massacred in an event that is remembered as *La Matanza* (The Slaughter [1932]).

Hernández Martínez used violent repression throughout his time in power, justifying the use of force by labeling his victims communists. In 1934 he resigned so

that he could run for the presidency the following year, and he was elected president in 1935. As president, he centralized political power in the executive branch, increased the size and influence of the army, replaced civilian officials with military officers, and nationalized utility companies. He also created the Pro-Patria Party, which he used as a tool to retain control. Despite Hernández Martínez's repression, a number of coup attempts were made against his regime, all of which he survived. Hernández Martínez originally formed close ties with the Axis powers during World War II and supported Spanish dictator General Francisco Franco; however, when these relations proved detrimental to El Salvador's economy by threatening trade with the United States, the president began to support the Allied powers.

In the 1940s Hernández Martínez adopted strange and occult practices, holding séances and attempting to use magic to resolve national dilemmas. People began to refer to him as "El Brujo" (The Witch) and began losing confidence in his ability to lead. In 1944, following a failed coup attempt that left 200 people dead, students, young army officers, and workers went on strike for days, paralyzing the city of San Salvador and finally forcing Hernández Martínez to resign. The subsequent administration of Andrés Ignacio Menéndez (1934–1935, 1944) reinstated freedom of the press and granted political prisoners and exiles amnesty before being toppled by a coup within months.

Hernández Martínez moved to Honduras and became a farmer. An employee killed him during an argument in 1966. His spirit lived on among certain right-wing factions, and a right-wing death squad bore his name in the 1980s.

La Matanza (The Slaughter) (1932)

In January 1932, one month after Maximiliano **Hernández Martínez** (1931–1934, 1935–1944) was appointed head of El Salvador by the military, rebel leaders, including Communist Party founder Agustín **Farabundo Martí**, led El Salvador's peasantry and coffee-pickers in a revolt to demand the improvement of worsening socioeconomic conditions. Armed with machetes and farm tools, the rebels were no match for the government's violent response. Within three days tens of thousands of rebels were massacred by the army and vigilante groups, Farabundo Martí and other communist leaders were executed, and many indigenous communities were effectively exterminated.

La Matanza was the result of years of rising tensions between the wealthy oligarchy, supported by the military, and agricultural laborers allied with the peasantry. Since the late 1920s, communist and labor leaders had become increasingly influential. Labor unrest had expanded, and the oligarchy had grown fearful and reactionary and had increasingly relied on the military to protect its assets and maintain the status quo. *La Matanza*, remembered as one of the most brutal acts in a long history of government repression, serves as a milestone in Salvadoran history, marking the advent of harsh military rule, and the end of labor organization and popular uprisings in the country for the subsequent four decades.

Molina Barraza, Arturo Armando (1927–   )

Arturo Armando Molina Barraza's repressive administration (1972–1977) set the stage for the brutal government response to the popular uprisings of the 1980s.

Following family tradition, Molina attended military school and soon rose through the ranks of the armed forces to become an officer. In 1972 President Fidel Sánchez Hernández (1967–1972) selected Molina to contest that year's presidential election on the ticket of the **National Conciliation Party** (Partido de Conciliación Nacional, PCN). Opposing Molina was José Napoleón **Duarte Fuentes** (1984–1989), who ran with a coalition that included the **Christian Democrat Party** (Partido Demócrata Cristiano, PDC) and other left-of-center parties. Molina was announced the winner of the obviously rigged election, during which there was a media blackout as Duarte began to take a strong lead.

Because of the blatant electoral fraud that brought Molina to power, his administration met with resistance and faced demonstrations, especially by students. Within weeks of his inauguration, the president closed the national university and arrested 800 people. In 1975, after peaceful protests arose over the Miss Universe pageant to be held in San Salvador, twelve people were killed by the military and twenty disappeared. That same year, the oligarchy easily blocked an attempt on the part of the government to pass an agrarian reform measure that was backed with money from the U.S. Agency for International Development (USAID). In response, workers and peasants began to organize and demand their basic rights, and guerrilla groups formed to protect them against the repression of the military and the oligarchy.

Molina selected Carlos Humberto **Romero Mena** (1977–1979) to run as the PCN candidate in the presidential election of 1977; Romero won the contest through obvious electoral fraud.

National Conciliation Party (Partido de Conciliación Nacional, PCN)

The National Conciliation Party (Partido de Conciliación Nacional, PCN), founded in 1961, served as the military's official political party in the 1960s and 1970s, protecting the interests of the armed forces in national politics. The PCN controlled the presidency from 1962 to 1979 through the administrations of Julio Adalberto Rivera Carballo (1962–1967), Fidel Sánchez Hernández (1967–1972), Arturo Armando **Molina Barraza** (1972–1977), and Carlos Humberto **Romero Mena** (1977–1979).

The party initially advocated a reformist and mod-

ernizing agenda, while opposing communism and supporting the foreign policy of the United States. Later, as it lost members to more conservative parties, the PCN became more extreme. In the 1970s the PCN was only able to win elections through blatant fraud. With the creation of the **National Republican Alliance** (Alianza Republicana Nacional, ARENA) in 1981, the PCN lost much of its support, but continued to win some seats in the Legislative Assembly. After the 1982 elections, it worked with ARENA to maintain a right-wing majority in the Assembly. Though the party was subsequently plagued by scandal, it continued to exist, winning fourteen seats in the Legislative Assembly in the 2000 elections.

National Democrat Organization (Organización Demócrata Nacional, ORDEN)

The National Democrat Organization (Organización Demócrata Nacional, ORDEN), whose acronym means "order" in Spanish, was a large and influential paramilitary unit created in 1964 to control peasant and labor unrest and suppress political dissidents, especially communists.

José Alberto Medrano founded ORDEN in 1964 in reaction to the increasing influence and rise to power of the **Christian Democrat Party** (Partido Demócrata Cristiano, PDC). ORDEN members (normally ex-military officers and landowners) acted with almost complete impunity. It is estimated that at its peak, ORDEN had between 100,000 and 150,000 members (though far fewer were probably active in the group). ORDEN members were targeted by guerrilla troops in retaliation for their violence against leftist political organizers. Founder Medrano directed the organization until a power struggle in 1979 led to his ouster. The group then came under the control of President Carlos Humberto **Romero Mena** (1977–1979), whose administration devoted forty people to coordinating its activities. After a coup in 1979, the ruling junta officially dissolved ORDEN. However, the organization continued to exist, and Roberto **D'Aubuisson** worked with Medrano to harness its network of support to create the right-wing **National Republican Alliance** (Alianza Republicana Nacional, ARENA) in 1981.

National Republican Alliance (Alianza Republicana Nacional, ARENA)

Founded in 1981 by Roberto **D'Aubuisson**, the National Republican Alliance (Alianza Republicana Nacional, ARENA) is a highly nationalistic right-wing political party staunchly opposed to communism, left-wing politics, and land reform. Throughout the **civil war of the 1980s**, the party, with the support of El Salvador's small but powerful oligarchy, maintained its own death squad to intimidate political dissidents, and retained connections to military and paramilitary organizations, such as the **National Democrat Organization** (Organización Demócrata Nacional, ORDEN).

Early in its existence, ARENA prided itself on its nearly fascist nationalism, and consequently appealed mainly to conservative extremists. While the **Christian Democrat Party** (Partido Demócrata Cristiano, PDC) received more votes than did ARENA in the first elections that ARENA contested, for the Legislative Assembly in 1982, ARENA managed to secure a majority by creating a coalition with other right-wing parties, including the **National Conciliation Party** (Partido de Conciliación Nacional, PCN).

After its defeat in the 1984 presidential election, the party began to tame its image, including pushing leader D'Aubuisson to the sidelines. It simultaneously began to attract people who were frustrated with the PDC's apparent inability to repair the country's faltering economy or negotiate a peace settlement with the guerrilla army, the **Farabundo Martí National Liberation Front** (Frente Farabundo Martí para la Liberación Nacional, FMLN). This broadened appeal, coupled with the weakening of the PDC's leadership, guaranteed ARENA's success in the 1988 congressional elections and its continued control of the Legislative Assembly. ARENA controlled the presidency through the 1990s (electing Alfredo Félix **Cristiani Burkard** [1989–1994], Armando **Calderón Sol** [1994–1999], and Francisco Guillermo **Flores Pérez** [1999–   ]) and also controlled both the Legislative Assembly and the Supreme Court until 1997. By 2000 ARENA held about one-third of the seats in the Legislative Assembly, with the FMLN holding another third, and smaller political parties making up the last third.

ARENA worked closely with the FMLN to draw up the **Chapultepec Accords** of 1992 to bring an end to El Salvador's civil war, and by the early 2000s, ARENA supporters included more moderate conservatives and business interests as well as nationalist extremists.

Osorio Hernández, Oscar (1910–1969)

Oscar Osorio Hernández served as president from 1950 to 1956, ruling through an odd mixture of reforms and repression.

Following a military education, Osorio was active in the opposition movement, playing a key role in several political demonstrations in the early 1940s. In 1945 he was exiled to Mexico for his participation in a failed coup. He soon returned and led a successful uprising against the corruption-riddled administration of President Salvador Castañeda Castro (1945–1948) in 1948, supported by young officers angered by the lack of upward mobility in the military's ranks. Osorio led the junta (Consejo de Gobierno Revolucionario [1948–1952]) that ruled following the coup, and subsequently organized the Revolutionary Party of Democratic Unification (Partido Revolucionario de Unificación Democrática, PRUD), based on the model of Mexico's **Institutional Revolutionary Party** (Partido Revolucionario Institucional, PRI; see Mexico).

Osorio contested the presidential election of 1950 on the PRUD ticket, winning easily. Within a month he drafted a new constitution, and then implemented a program he called a "controlled revolution," which aimed to strengthen the middle class through moderate reforms without radically disrupting the position of the upper class. Osorio built public housing, legalized labor unions, created a social security system, and encouraged industry and trade. His reforms were most helpful to urban laborers, who were given the right to strike, while rural workers were not. His regime also restricted the organizing of other political parties (facilitating the PRUD's maintenance of political control) and squelched political dissent, especially in the universities. So effective was his repression of political opponents that all parties other than the PRUD withdrew their candidates from the 1955 presidential election.

Though Osorio wished to choose a civilian leader to assume the presidency after he left office, the military pressured him into selecting army officer José María Lemus López (1956–1960) as his successor. Three years later, Osorio broke from the PRUD to create a new political party, the Revolutionary Party of Authentic Unification (Partido Revolucionario de Unificación Auténtica, PRUA).

Romero, Oscar Arnulfo (1917–1980)

Following his assassination in 1980, as the **civil war of the 1980s** escalated, Archbishop Oscar Arnulfo Romero became a martyr and a powerful symbol in the struggle for justice in El Salvador. Shortly before his death, Romero was nominated for the Nobel Peace Prize.

Born in the town of San Miguel, Romero attended the National Seminary in 1937, and afterwards studied in Rome at the Gregorian University. He was ordained a priest in 1942 and returned to El Salvador during World War II. In the late 1960s he was appointed to the National Bishops' Conference, subsequently held other prestigious positions, and was appointed archbishop of San Salvador in 1977. Considered an ally of the conservative oligarchy and the military, he was selected by the church because it believed that he would uphold the status quo. To that point, he had advised fellow priests to stay out of politics and had rejected the doctrine of liberation theology.

However, continued persecution of the clergy, including kidnappings and murder, drove Romero to become one of the most outspoken critics of the government. Three weeks after his appointment as archbishop, Romero was devastated by the assassination of Father Rutilo Grande. When his outrage and protests were met with the expulsion of a number of priests and greater repression, Romero retaliated by refusing to attend President Carlos Humberto **Romero Mena**'s (1977–1979) inauguration, a great offense. Archbishop Romero preached against the violence committed by both the army and the **Farabundo Martí National Liberation Front** (Frente Farabundo Martí para la Liberación Nacional, FMLN), and he criticized the oligarchy for its role in El Salvador's civil war. Broadcast over the radio, his sermons and weekly interviews were heard all over the country. He refused to be intimidated by pressure to quiet him, and spoke out frequently against the United States for fueling the war.

To the alarm and disbelief of the Salvadoran population, Romero was assassinated on March 24, 1980, while delivering a sermon during a mass in a Salvadoran church. It is widely thought that Roberto **D'Aubuisson**, a conservative radical politician with connections to death squads, played a role in the shooting. The day before the murder, Romero had petitioned young soldiers to lay down their weapons and disobey orders to torture and kill. Four days after the assassination, more than 100,000 people gathered to pay homage to Romero as random gunfire rained down upon them. While Romero's successor, Arturo Rivera y Damas, tried to continue the work of the murdered archbishop, the Salvadoran church strove to ensure that he did not offend the government.

Romero Mena, Carlos Humberto (1924–   )

Taking power after the controversial presidential election of 1977, Carlos Humberto Romero Mena attempted to control the populace through repression, but was pushed out of office in 1979 as the country's economy deteriorated.

Romero Mena began his career attending military schools and rose through the ranks of the armed forces, eventually serving as minister of defense under Arturo Armando **Molina Barraza** (1972–1977). Molina selected Romero Mena to run as the candidate of the **National Conciliation Party** (Partido de Conciliación Nacional, PCN) in the 1977 presidential election and, like Molina, Romero Mena came to power through obvious electoral fraud: the PCN stuffed ballot boxes, military officials voted more than once, and ballots in support of Romero Mena were cast in the name of dead people. Protesters, including **Christian Democrat Party** (Partido Demócrata Cristiano, PDC) candidate Ernesto Claramount, gathered in the Plaza Libertad (Liberty Plaza) in San Salvador and refused to leave until the fraudulent elections were annulled. The army attacked and dispersed the group of protesters, killing many.

When Romero Mena took office, he vowed to end human rights violations, but only really effected change in the capital. In 1977 Romero Mena passed a law prohibiting public gatherings and the publication of information that criticized the government. Crimes against the clergy increased under Romero Mena, often pitting him against San Salvador's Archbishop Oscar Arnulfo **Romero**, a critic of the repressive government. The sit-

uation worsened as coffee prices dropped, causing economic decline, and armed opposition groups began to take action against the government and military repression.

Romero Mena tried to reverse his stance in 1979, calling for agrarian reform, reinstating civil laws, and forcing a hated army official into retirement. However, the effort attracted Romero Mena no support from the lower or middle classes, and alienated the oligarchy. Inspired by the victory of the **Sandinista National Liberation Front** (Frente Sandinista de Liberación Nacional, FSLN; see Nicaragua) in neighboring Nicaragua, Salvadoran protesters took to the streets to demonstrate their opposition to the Romero Mena regime. Condemned both at home and abroad, Romero Mena was overthrown on October 15, 1979, and left El Salvador, ending his involvement in politics.

Soccer War. See Appendix 1

HEADS OF STATE

Pedro Barriere	1821
José Matías Delgado	1821–1823
Mariano Prado	1823–1824
Juan Manuel Rodríguez	1824
Mariano Prado	1824
Juan Vicente Villacorta	1824–1826
Mariano Prado	1826–1829
José María Cornejo	1829–1832
José Francisco Morazán	1832
Joaquín de San Martín	1832
Mariano Prado	1832–1833
Joaquín de San Martín	1833–1834
Carlos Salazar	1834
José Gregorio Salazar	1834
Joaquín Escolán y Balibrera	1834
José María Silva	1834–1835
Nicolás Espinosa	1835
Francisco Gómez Elizondo	1835–1836
Diego Vigil	1836–1838
Timoteo Menéndez	1838–1839
Antonio José Cañas	1839
José Francisco Morazán	1839–1840
José María Silva	1840
Antonio José Cañas	1840–1841
Juan Lindo	1841–1842
José Escolástico Marín	1842
Juan José Guzmán	1842–1844
Francisco Malespín	1844–1845
Joaquín Eufrasio Guzmán	1845–1846

Eugenio Aguilar	1846–1848
Doroteo Vasconcelos	1848–1851
Francisco Dueñas	1851–1854
José María San Martín	1854–1856
Rafael Campo	1856–1858
Gerardo Barrios	1858
Miguel Santín del Castillo	1858–1859
Gerardo Barrios	1859–1863
Francisco Dueñas	1863–1871
Mariscal Santiago González	1871–1876
Andrés Valle	1876
Rafael Zaldívar	1876–1885
José Rosales	1885
Fernando Figueroa	1885
Francisco Menéndez	1885–1890
Carlos Ezeta	1890–1894
Rafael Antonio Gutiérrez	1894–1898
Tomás Regalado	1898–1903
Pedro José Escalón	1903–1907
Fernando Figueroa	1907–1911
Manuel Enrique Araujo	1911–1913
Carlos Meléndez	1913–1914
Alfonso Quiñónez Molina	1914–1915
Carlos Meléndez	1915–1918
Alfonso Quiñónez Molina	1918–1919
Jorge Meléndez	1919–1923
Alfonso Quiñónez Molina	1923–1927
Pio Romero Bosque	1927–1931
Arturo Araujo	1931
Directorio Cívico	1931
Maximiliano Hernández Martínez	1931–1934
Andrés Ignacio Menéndez	1934–1935
Maximiliano Hernández Martínez	1935–1944
Andrés Ignacio Menéndez	1944
Osmin Aguirre y Salinas	1944–1945
Salvador Castañeda Castro	1945–1948
Consejo de Gobierno Revolucionario	1948–1950
Óscar Osorio Hernández	1950–1956
José María Lemus López	1956–1960
Junta de Gobierno de El Salvador	1960–1961
Directorio Cívico Militar de El Salvador	1961–1962
Eusebio Rodolfo Cordón Cea	1962
Julio Adalberto Rivera Carballo	1962–1967
Fidel Sánchez Hernández	1967–1972
Arturo Armando Molina Barraza	1972–1977
Carlos Humberto Romero Mena	1977–1979
Primera Junta Revolucionaria de Gobierno	1979–1980
Segunda Junta Revolucionaria de Gobierno	1980
Tercera Junta Revolucionaria de Gobierno	1980–1982
Alvaro Alfredo Magaña Borja	1982–1984
José Napoleón Duarte Fuentes	1984–1989
Alfredo Félix Cristiani Burkard	1989–1994
Armando Calderón Sol	1994–1999
Francisco Guillermo Flores Pérez	1999–

Source: Rulers. http://www.rulers.org/rule.html#el_salvador

BIBLIOGRAPHY

Print Resources

Anderson, Thomas P. *Politics in Central America.* New York: Praeger, 1982.

Baloyra, Enrique. *El Salvador in Transition.* Chapel Hill: University of North Carolina Press, 1982.

Barry, Tom. *Central America Inside Out.* New York: Grove Weidenfeld, 1991.

Berryman, Philip. *Stubborn Hope: Religion, Politics and Revolution in Central America.* New York: Orbis/The New Press, 1994.

Didion, Joan. *Salvador.* New York: Simon and Schuster, 1982.

Dunkerley, James. *Power in the Isthmus: A Political History of Central America.* London: Verso Books, 1988.

Montgomery, Tommie Sue. *Revolution in El Salvador.* Boulder: Westview Press, 1982.

Murray, Kevin, with Tom Barry. *Inside El Salvador.* Albuquerque: Resource Center Press, 1995.

Russell, Philip L. *El Salvador in Crisis.* Austin, TX: Colorado River Press, 1984.

Woodward, Ralph Lee. *Central America: A Nation Divided.* Oxford: Oxford University Press, 1985.

Electronic Resources

El Diario de Hoy
http://www.elsalvador.com/noticias/index.html
The Web version of one of El Salvador's premier daily newspapers. Offers comprehensive national and international coverage, with a particularly strong emphasis on national politics and the national economy. (In Spanish)

History of El Salvador
http://www.emulateme.com/history/elhist.htm
This Web site provides a comprehensive yet relatively concise political history of El Salvador from the Spanish Conquest, through independence, to the present. (In English)

Latin American Network Information Center (LANIC): El Salvador
http://lanic.utexas.edu/la/ca/salvador/
El Salvador section of this extensive Web site contains hundreds of links to research resources, cultural centers, economic and business institutions, government agencies, historical sources, magazines and other periodicals, nongovernmental organizations, and grassroots groups, as well as many other subjects. (In English)

Political Database of the Americas: El Salvador
http://www.georgetown.edu/pdba/Countries/elsalvad.html
Comprehensive database run as a joint project of Georgetown University and the Organization of American States. Section on El Salvador contains information on and links to the executive, legislative, and judicial branches of the Salvadoran government; electoral laws and election results; and other political data. (In English, Spanish, Portuguese, and French)

Political Resources.net: El Salvador
http://www.politicalresources.net/el_salvador.htm
El Salvador section of a Web site containing a wealth of links to sources of information about national politics. Includes information on political parties, legislative and executive institutions, laws and legislation, and elections, as well as a link to the constitution. (In English)

Wilfried Derksen's Elections Around the World: El Salvador
http://www.agora.it/elections/elsalvador.htm
El Salvador section of a comprehensive database of results from elections around the world. Contains results from recent national executive and legislative elections, as well as explanations of and links to political parties and institutions. (In English)

GUATEMALA

COUNTRY PROFILE

Official name	República de Guatemala
Capital	Guatemala City
Type/structure of government	Democratic republic
Executive	President elected to four-year non-renewable term.
Legislative	Unicameral Congress (113 seats); members are elected to serve four-year terms by popular vote.
Judicial	Highest court is Supreme Court of Justice, composed of 13 justices serving concurrent five-year terms.
Major political parties	Guatemalan Republican Front (Frente Republicano Guatemalteco, FRG), the National Advancement Party (Partido de Avanzada Nacional, PAN), and the New Guatemala Democratic Front (Frente Democrático Nueva Guatemala, FDNG).
Constitution in effect	Enacted January 1986
Location/geography	Central America, bordering Mexico to the north, Belize to the east, and Honduras and El Salvador in the south. Coastline on both the Caribbean and the Pacific; central and northern areas are mountainous; coastal plain in the west; tropical rain forest in department of El Petén.
Geographic area	108,890 sq. km.
Population	12,335,580 (July 1999 est.)
Ethnic groups	Mestizo 56%; indigenous 44%
Religions	Roman Catholic, Protestant, and traditional Mayan
Literacy rate	55.6% (1999)
Infant mortality rate	46.15 deaths per 1,000 live births (1999 est.)
Life expectancy	66.45 years (1999 est.)
Monetary unit	Quetzal
Exchange rate	1 U.S. dollar = 7.79 quetzales (GTQ) (August 2000)*
Major exports	Coffee, sugar, bananas, cardamom, and petroleum
Major imports	Fuel and petroleum products, machinery, grain, fertilizers, motor vehicles
GDP	$18.9 billion (1998)
GDP growth rate	4.6% (1998)
GDP per capita	$1,017 (1998)

Latin American Weekly Report, August 22, 2000 (WR-00-33), p. 394.

Sources: Statistics and Quantitative Analysis Unit, Inter-American Development Bank. http://www.iadb.org/int/sta/ENGLISH/brptnet/english/gtmbrpt.htm; World Bank, *Guatemala at a Glance*. http://www.worldbank. org/data/countrydata/aag/gtm_aag.pdf; *CIA World Factbook*. http://www.cia.gov/cia/publications/factbook/geos/gt.html; Embassy of Guatemala in the United States. http://www.guatemala-embassy.org.

OVERVIEW

Summary

Much of Guatemala's history has been marked by internal struggles, which have often been violent. Thirty-six years of armed conflict in the twentieth century ended with the signing of the comprehensive **Agreement for a Firm and Lasting Peace** by the Guatemalan government and the **Guatemalan National Revolutionary Unit** (Unidad Revolucionaria Nacional Guatemalteca, URNG) in December 1996. The accords serve as a plan for the country's development with particular attention to improving human rights policy toward the rural indigenous population. The current economic and social situation in Guatemala is dire for a majority of the population: 75 percent of the population lives below the national poverty line, malnutrition levels are high, and violence and human rights abuses remain rampant.

History

Mayan and Aztec civilizations existed in Guatemala before the arrival of Spanish forces led by Pedro de Alvarado in 1523, and they maintained a considerable presence during the subsequent long period of stable colonial rule. The Kingdom of Guatemala joined Mex-

Guatemala. © *1998 The Moschovitis Group, Inc.*

ico in declaring its independence from Spain on September 15, 1821. Agustín Cosme Damian de **Iturbide**'s (see Mexico) Mexican Empire then invaded and held Guatemala until 1823, when a congress of the Central American provinces met and established the **United Provinces of Central America** (see Appendix 1). Guatemala remained a part of the United Provinces of Central America until the federation began to dissolve in 1838. In 1839 a conservative faction in Guatemala declared its independence from the Central American union.

Between 1839 and 1944, control of Guatemala shifted back and forth between the Conservative and Liberal parties. While Conservative Mariano Rivera Paz (1839–1844) stood as the nation's first leader, Conservative José Rafael **Carrera** (1844–1848, 1852–1865) actually led the country from 1839. Carrera restored power to the landed elite, the church, and the army, and in March 1847 eliminated all final ties with the Central American union and established the Republic of Guatemala, the first Central American state to do so. General Vicente Cerna (1865–1871) continued Carrera's Conservative government policies. Justo Rufino **Barrios** (1873–1885) was the first in a series of Liberal dictators. Barrios encouraged economic growth and foreign investment, and curtailed the power of the Catholic Church. Economic development led to the establishment of a new coffee elite, a loss in power for the merchant class, and the unchecked exploitation of the indigenous population.

The Barrios dictatorship's repression and generation of personal wealth established a pattern that was followed by future Liberal governments, including those of General Manuel Lisandro Barillas (1885–1892), José María Reyna Barrios (1892–1898), and Manuel Estrada Cabrera (1898–1920). Under Cabrera, whose repressive twenty-two-year rule became the longest uninterrupted presidential term in Guatemalan history, the Liberal focus on economic development continued, while the idealism behind it disappeared. Foreign investment led to the expansion of railroads and the establishment of banana plantations by the United States–based United Fruit Company (see **Keith**, Minor Cooper Costa Rica). Cabrera was overthrown and eventually replaced by Liberal Party generals José María Orellana (1921–1926) and Lázaro T. Chacón (1926–1930), who established more open and democratic regimes; uneven economic growth continued and elite-military alliances were formed so that both could maintain their power in the government. General Jorge **Ubico y Castañeda** (1931–1944), who controlled the country through the military and his alliance with the United Fruit Company, took a strong stance against communism, purged many leftist unions and political parties, and reduced indigenous sovereignty.

When Ubico was overthrown in 1944, power was remanded to a military junta, from among whose members Congress chose General Federico Ponce Vaides (1944) to be provisional president. Ponce Vaides could not control the rising opposition and was deposed in what is now referred to as the October Revolution, led by Major Francisco Javier Arana, Captain Jacobo **Arbenz Guzmán** (1951–1954), and a civilian, Jorge Toriello Garrido. The three led the nation from 1944 to 1945, when Juan José **Arévalo Bermejo** (1945–1951) took office. Arévalo challenged the power of the coffee and military elites, isolated the church, increased political participation, and renewed labor organizations, political parties, and constitutional government. Fierce rivals Arana and Arbenz were the leading candidates for the presidential election to be held in 1950. However, Arana was assassinated in July 1949, and Arbenz went on to defeat Miguel **Ydígoras Fuentes** (1958–1963). As president, Arbenz moved Arévalo's "revolution" even more toward the left, leading to his overthrow in 1954 by a Guatemalan force headed by Carlos **Castillo Armas** (1954–1957) and led covertly by the U.S. Central Intelligence Agency (CIA).

Over the next thirty years the military dominated politics, and Guatemala's long civil war devastated the country. Military repression of the indigenous population and guerrillas heightened, right-wing death squads terrorized the countryside, and guerrilla groups increased their violence against the government. As the military moved into lands inhabited by the Indians, and human rights abuses against the indigenous population intensified, indigenous groups had three choices: be killed by the army, join the guerrillas, or flee Guatemala. Refugee camps sprang up in Chiapas, Mexico, and in other neighboring areas, and in the 1970s two new guerrilla groups emerged, the **Guerrilla Army of the Poor** (Ejército Guerrillero de los Pobres, EGP) and the **Revolutionary Organization of the People in Arms** (Organización Revolucionaria del Pueblo en Armas, ORPA). As the war against the guerrillas intensified, leftist groups united to form the URNG, in 1982.

The administration of Marco Vinicio **Cerezo Arévalo** (1986–1991) faced many challenges. The economy needed to be jumpstarted, the military appeased, guerrilla activity quelled, and Guatemala's reputation in the eyes of the world improved. Commissions and councils arose to address human rights violations, and peace talks were held with the URNG, yet no resolution was reached, and the terror persisted. The election of Jorge Antonio **Serrano Elías** (1991–1993) marked the first time in Guatemalan history that a civilian succeeded a civilian, and Serrano tried to establish firm civilian control over the government. However, in 1992 he and the URNG came to an impasse during the peace negotiations, and in May 1993 Serrano dissolved Congress and the Supreme Court and stated that he would rule by decree. He was removed from office by the military seven days later. Congress returned and held elections immediately, and Ramiro **de León Carpio** (1993–1996) was elected to complete Serrano's term. De León was popular at the onset of his term, but lost support as the problems of poverty and corruption proved insurmountable. Nonetheless, the United Nations Verification Mission in Guatemala (Misión de Verificación de las Naciones Unidas en Guatemala, MINUGUA) was established in September 1994 to supervise the implementation of a human rights accord signed in March of that year.

The main challenge facing the administration of Alvaro Enrique **Arzú Irigoyen** (1996–2000) was insuring military support for the Agreement for a Firm and Lasting Peace signed by the government of Guatemala and the URNG in December 1996; the eleven accords included in the agreement ended the thirty-six-year-old civil war and provided for changes that would make the military and intelligence services subordinate to elected officials. While Arzú developed a program of economic modernization and state reform crucial to the implementation of the peace accords, he faced endless obstacles. First, Guatemalan voters rejected a package of constitutional reforms designed to help institutionalize the peace process in a national referendum in May 1999. Also, right-wing groups within the armed forces and the landed elite opposed the proposed social and political reforms, and continuing social problems also inhibited progress. Finally, a demobilized URNG moved to form a political party, dissatisfied with the government's social and economic policy. Alfonso Antonio **Portillo Cabrera** (2000–), a member of the right-wing Guatemalan Republican Front (Frente Republicano Guatemalteco, FRG), drew on popular dissatisfaction with the state of the economy and increasing lawlessness to win the 1999 presidential election. Once in office, Portillo undertook civil-military reforms to decrease the autonomy of the armed forces.

ENTRIES

Agreement for a Firm and Lasting Peace (1996)

The Agreement for a Firm and Lasting Peace, which ended Guatemala's civil war, was signed on December 29, 1996, by the government of Alvaro Enrique **Arzú Irigoyen** (1996–2000) and the **Guatemalan National Revolutionary Unit** (Unidad Revolucionaria Nacional Guatemalteca, URNG) following a protracted peace process begun in 1990. The agreement, intended to promote democratization and social and economic development in Guatemala, implemented eleven peace accords created between 1994 and 1996, including the following:

1. The "Human Rights Accord" (March 29, 1994), signed by representatives from Guatemala and the United Nations, contained general commitments regarding the protection of human rights in Guatemala. The United Nations agreed to provide the appropriate international verification mechanisms for the agreement to succeed, and organized the United Nations Verification Mission in Guatemala (Misión de Verificación de las Naciones Unidas en Guatemala, MINUGUA) to oversee compliance with the agreement.

2. The "Resettlement Agreement of the Population Groups Uprooted by the Armed Conflict" (June 17, 1994) sought to promote reconciliation, peace, and tolerance by reintegrating the uprooted population and ensuring civil rights and fundamental freedoms.

3. The "Agreement on the Establishment of the Historical Clarification Commission" (June 23, 1994) created a body (unofficially named the "Guatemalan Truth Commission") charged with providing a comprehensive report on human rights violations perpetrated during the thirty-six years of armed conflict. The commission began investigating via testimonies and interviews on July 31, 1997, and issued its final report on February 25, 1999.

4. The "Indigenous Peoples' Rights Accord" (March 31, 1995) acknowledged the contributions of the indigenous community, and called for an end to discrimination against indigenous groups, their incorporation into the national sphere, and respect for their identity and rights (especially territorial), as well as more decentralization in education, health, and cultural services.

5. The "Agreement on Social and Economic Aspects and Agrarian Reform" (May 6, 1996) called for increased democratization and participatory, social, agricultural, and rural development as well as modernization of government services and fiscal policy.

On May 16, 1999, a national referendum was held on a congressionally approved package of fifty constitutional reforms designed to help institutionalize the peace process and correct the underlying causes of the war by recognizing Mayan languages and legal rights and overhauling the executive, legislative, and judicial branches of the federal government. Despite the progress that the signing of the above agreements signaled, Guatemalans rejected the reform package. In fact, over 80 percent of eligible voters did not cast a ballot, suggesting a low level of popular trust and confidence in Guatemala's government and institutions. This blow to the peace process also highlighted serious flaws in the electoral registry (as many as one in three voters were not registered) and voting procedures. Many attributed the rejection to the strong "no" campaign led by right-wing political and business organizations that played on voters' fears and deep-rooted racism. As key aspects of the peace accords required significant constitutional and legislative change, the "no" vote seriously hampered implementation of the accords.

Arana, Francisco Javier. See **Arbenz Guzmán, Jacobo**

Arbenz Guzmán, Jacobo (1913–1971)

The agrarian reforms implemented by Jacobo Arbenz Guzmán during his presidency (1951–1954) dissatisfied the upper and middle classes and created concerns in the United States about the spread of communism and the loss of U.S.-owned business assets in Guatemala. A Guatemalan opposition force trained by the U.S. Central Intelligence Agency (CIA) overthrew Arbenz in 1954.

Arbenz was born in Quezaltenango to a Guatemalan mother and a Swiss immigrant father and completed military school in 1935 at the Escuela Politécnica. He participated in the 1944 overthrow of Jorge **Ubico y Castañeda** (1931–1944) and subsequently played an important role, along with Francisco Javier Arana's elite military corps, the Guardia del Honor (Honor Guard) in deposing General Federico Ponce Vaides (1944) in the October Revolution of 1944. Arana, Arbenz, and Jorge Toriello Garrido then formed a junta to oversee the smooth transition to a democratic government; elections held in December 1944 brought Juan José **Arévalo Bermejo** (1945–1951) to power. Arbenz served as minister of defense under Arévalo, and though he met with political opposition from Arana, who was then serving as chief of the armed forces, Arbenz managed to block potential rebellion by arming students and workers. While Arbenz, Arana, and Miguel **Ydígoras Fuentes** (1958–1963) all planned to contest the 1950 presidential election, Arana's assassination in 1949 cleared the way for Arbenz's victory, with the support of the military, peasants, trade unions, the left, and the center.

As president, Arbenz sought to continue the revolution that Arévalo had begun by redistributing capital

Jacobo Arbenz Guzmán, President of Guatemala (1951–1954). *Columbus Memorial Library, General Secretariat of the Organization of American States. Reproduced with permission of the Organization of American States.*

away from foreign ownership and into the hands of Guatemalans. He supported the agrarian reform initiatives of the National Farmworkers Confederation of Guatemala (Confederación Nacional de Campesinos Guatemaltecos, CNCG) and enacted Decree 900, which expanded domestic purchasing power, awarded 1.5 million acres of land to approximately 100,000 peasants, and called for the government to issue $8 million in bonds for the land. The U.S.-based United Fruit Company (see **Keith, Minor Cooper, Costa Rica**), which owned part of the land, claimed that it was not sufficiently reimbursed, and the upper- and middle-class Guatemalans who had originally supported the revolution also opposed the agrarian reform law.

Fearing the possible spread through Central America of what it saw as the regime's communist tendencies, the U.S. CIA provided opposition leaders Carlos **Castillo Armas** (1954–1957) and Ydígoras Fuentes with arms and sanctuary in Honduras, and encouraged their actions to destabilize the Arbenz regime. Though the Guatemalan government requested that the United Nations (UN) declare the activity of the United States aggressive and that it take action to stop the attacks, the case was removed from the UN Security Council, remanded to the **Organization of American States** (OAS; see Appendix 2), and never acted upon. Castillo Armas and other Guatemalan political dissidents overthrew Arbenz in June 1954 and Castillo Armas took control of the country. Arbenz went into exile in various countries, eventually dying in Mexico.

Arévalo Bermejo, Juan José (1904–1990)

As Guatemala's controversial president from 1945 to 1951, Juan José Arévalo Bermejo attempted to stabilize democracy, increase social welfare, and implement economic development.

Arévalo was born in Taxisco, Santa Rosa, received his doctorate in education from the Universidad de la Plata in Argentina, served in a mid-level position within the Guatemalan Ministry of Education, and later completed a doctorate in philosophy while in voluntary exile in Argentina during the presidency of Jorge **Ubico y Castañeda** (1931–1944). The leaders of the 1944 October Revolution that overthrew Ubico's successor, General Federico Ponce Vaides (1944), brought Arévalo back from Argentina to run in the December 1944 presidential contest, which he won with 85 percent of the vote.

As president, Arévalo sought to promote economic development while maintaining economic nationalism, to stabilize democracy while increasing political participation, and to improve social welfare while advancing industrialization. His administration established a relationship with the Soviet Union (1945), passed a social security law that assured workers' compensation, maternity benefits, and health care (1946), and enacted a labor law that legalized collective bargaining and the right to strike and imposed a minimum wage (1947). His administration also oversaw the building of hospitals and clinics, increased access to credit for small producers, and created a national bank and planning office. In 1949 Congress passed a law that allowed the poor to rent unused land on large estates, and also began to redistribute land that had been confiscated from German owners during World War II. Arévalo's administration lost legitimacy as it leaned increasingly left, and also suffered criticism for its alleged involvement in the 1949 assassination of presidential hopeful Francisco Javier Arana. Arévalo dealt with twenty coup attempts, and left Guatemala at the end of his presidency.

In 1962 Arévalo announced from Mexico that he would again run for president, and returned to Guatemala in March 1963 to aid in the overthrow of Miguel **Ydígoras Fuentes** (1958–1963). A military government took control following the coup, preventing Arévalo's possible reelection. He was appointed ambassador to France in 1970, but was relieved of his position in 1972. Arévalo wrote several books on political philosophy and returned to Guatemala in the 1980s, where he lived until his death in 1990.

Arzú Irigoyen, Alvaro Enrique (1946–   )

Alvaro Enrique Arzú Irigoyen was president of Guatemala from 1996 to 2000. His most important contribution was overseeing the institutionalization of Guatemala's peace accords.

Before entering politics, Arzú was a businessman in the tourism, commercial, and industrial sectors. He directed the Guatemalan Institute of Tourism (Instituto Guatemalteco de Turismo, INGUAT) from 1978 to 1981. Arzú was elected mayor of Guatemala City in 1982, but was prevented from assuming the position (due to a military coup) until 1986; he held the post until 1990. In 1989 Arzú founded the National Advancement Party (Partido de Avanzada Nacional, PAN), a business-oriented party seen as a modernizing force in Guatemalan politics, and served as its secretary-general beginning in 1991. Arzú lost the presidential election of 1990 to Jorge Antonio **Serrano Elías** (1991–1993), under whom he served as minister of foreign relations in 1991. The pro-business, conservative Arzú ran once again in the 1995 presidential election as the candidate of the National Alliance (Alianza Nacional), a coalition of **Guatemalan Christian Democracy** (Democracia Cristiana Guatemalteca, DCG), the Social Democratic Party (Partido Democracia Social, PDS), and the National Center Union (Unión del Centro Nacional, UCN), and narrowly defeated Alfonso Antonio **Portillo Cabrera** (2000–   ) of the Guatemalan Republican Front (Frente Republicano Guatemalteco, FRG) in the January 1996 runoff election, winning 51.2 percent of the votes.

Arzú's biggest accomplishment was the December 29, 1996 signing of the **Agreement for a Firm and Lasting Peace** between the Guatemalan government and the **Guatemalan National Revolutionary Unit** (Unidad Revolucionaria Nacional Guatemalteca, URNG). Arzú also developed a program of economic modernization and state reform crucial to the implementation of the peace accords, particularly the ones on socioeconomic and agrarian reform. Nonetheless, his government faced multiple challenges. Right-wing groups within the armed forces and the landed elite opposed the proposed social and political reforms, and a package of reforms was also rejected in a national referendum in May 1999; these obstacles limited the government's efforts to meet the demands of the indigenous population. Further demobilized URNG moved to form a political party to express its dissatisfaction with the government's social policy, privatization, utility rate increases, and the lifting of price controls on basic food products.

Asturias, Miguel Ángel (1899–1974)

Miguel Ángel Asturias, winner of the 1967 Nobel Prize for literature, is considered Guatemala's greatest twentieth-century writer.

Asturias was born in the district of La Parroquia in Guatemala City. He received a law degree from the University of San Carlos, emerging as a student leader in the movement to overthrow Manuel Estrada Cabrera (1898–1920). He never practiced law, but wrote for many years as a correspondent for *El Imparcial*, a leading Guatemalan newspaper. Following the overthrow of dictator General Jorge **Ubico y Castañeda** (1931–1944), Asturias went to Mexico, where he published *El señor presidente*, his most famous work, which deals with Latin American dictatorship. President Juan José **Arévalo Bermejo** (1945–1951) named Asturias the cultural attaché in Mexico, ambassador to Argentina (where he published another well-known novel, *Hombres de maíz*, in 1949), and ambassador to El Salvador. Asturias returned to Guatemala following the coup that deposed Jacobo **Arbenz Guzmán** (1951–1954) and later served as ambassador to France when his friend Julio César **Méndez Montenegro** (1966–1970) was elected president of Guatemala. Asturias won the Lenin Peace Prize in 1966 and the Nobel Prize for literature in 1967. With the election of Carlos Arana Osorio (1970–1974) to the presidency, Asturias resigned as ambassador. He died four years later in Madrid and was buried in Paris.

Barrios, Justo Rufino (1835–1885)

The Liberal dictatorship of Justo Rufino Barrios (1873–1885) modernized Guatemala and established the predominance of a coffee elite, serving as the model for subsequent Liberal regimes.

Born July 19, 1835, Barrios was raised by a landowning family in San Lorenzo, in the department of San Marcos. He attended university in Guatemala City, where he was influenced by Liberal ideas. Barrios subsequently built a ranch on the Mexican-Guatemalan border from which he launched numerous revolts against Conservative president General Vicente Cerna (1865–1871). In 1869 he joined the Liberal movement and organized a rebel force in Chiapas, Mexico. Along with Miguel García Granados (1871–1872) he overthrew Cerna's regime in 1871; subsequently García Granados assumed the presidency and Barrios served as the commander of the Los Altos district. Angered by the slow pace of García Granados' reforms, Barrios led an army to Guatemala City and forced him to resign in 1872. Barrios was victorious in the presidential election of 1873 and led the country as dictator for the subsequent twelve years.

Barrios' progressive regime was based on Liberal ideals that would dominate Guatemalan politics for decades. Known as "the Reformer," Barrios initiated sweeping change, ridding the government of its Conservative opposition and greatly centralizing the power of the state. Barrios attacked the traditional influence of the Catholic Church by expelling the Jesuits, expropriating church property, guaranteeing religious freedom, permitting civil licenses for marriage, secularizing the University of San Carlos, and legalizing divorce. While he promoted and enlarged the public education system, his academic reforms only truly benefited the middle and upper classes of society. Barrios laid the foundation for an export-led model of growth. He encouraged foreign immigration and investment (leading to foreign ownership of the railroads and telegraph services) and facilitated the economic and political dominance of the coffee-growing elite. His policies helped initiate a tremendous increase in coffee exports, but hurt indigenous communities by eroding land rights and creating a system of enforced labor based on debt peonage. Barrios repeatedly intervened in neighboring countries' affairs, and was killed in battle after his forces invaded El Salvador in 1885.

Carrera, José Rafael (1814–1865)

José Rafael Carrera (1844–1848, 1852–1865) rose from poverty to become the president of Guatemala at a critical time in the country's history. He was instrumental in establishing the Republic of Guatemala.

Carrera was born into a lower-class family in Guatemala City and entered the Central American federal army as a drummer at age twelve. He rose in the ranks of the army during the Central American civil wars of 1826–1829 (see **United Provinces of Central America,** Appendix 1), and embraced the ideology of the army's dominant Conservative elements. Liberal forces led by Honduran general Francisco **Morazán** (see Honduras) defeated the Conservative forces in 1829, bringing Morazán to the head of the Central American Federation. Mariano Gálvez (1831–1838) assumed the governorship of Guatemala in 1831, implementing a number of comprehensive Liberal reforms, enacting anticlerical legislation, and initiating an ambitious campaign to modernize Guatemala's economy by increasing agricultural exports. By the mid-1830s, Carrera became the leader of peasants and landowners in opposition to Morazán and Gálvez. In June 1837 Carrera led a successful rural uprising that eventually took Guatemala City, resulting in the establishment of a more Conservative government. War broke out again in March 1838, and that same year each of the states of the federation was declared to be sovereign. In April 1839 Carrera took the Guatemalan capital once again and another Conservative government was formed. Finally, in March 1840 Carrera defeated Morazán in Guatemala City.

Carrera became president of Guatemala in December 1844, and in March 1847 established the Republic of Guatemala, thereby eliminating all ties with the Central American union. Liberal opposition and rebel activity in eastern Guatemala led to his resignation and exile to Mexico in August 1848. When the new Liberal government failed to solve Guatemala's problems, Carrera returned in March 1849 as head of an "army of restoration," and was named commander of the Guatemalan army five months later. The army carried out actions against rebels in Guatemala and also confronted Liberal attempts to restore the Central American union; with the assistance of staunch ally General Vicente Cerna (1865–1871) Carrera was victorious in a battle at San José la Arada in February 1851, a triumph that helped guarantee Carrera's military dominance in Central America.

Carrera assumed the Guatemalan presidency again in November 1852 and became president for life in October 1854. During this second stint as the country's leader, Carrera intervened throughout Central America to assure the continuation of Conservative rule in the region and also achieved economic growth and stability for Guatemala. While his political dictatorship benefited mainly the Guatemala City elite, Carrera did protect the rural Indian populations, prevent additional exploitation of their land, and incorporate them into the military and political leadership. His most lasting legacy was establishing the military as the leading political institution in the nation. In April 1865 Carrera endorsed Cerna to be his successor; Carrera died shortly thereafter, and Cerna won the subsequent presidential election in a close race. Cerna continued Carrera's Conservative policies, passed a new monetary law to appease mounting opposition to his regime in 1870 and improved the nation's infrastructure (building a port on the Pacific Coast, introducing the telegraph, and initiating some improvements to the road and highway systems). However, his regime faced growing opposition from Liberal elements and the coffee-growing elite, and forces led by Miguel García Granados (1871–1872) and Justo Rufino **Barrios** (1873–1885) deposed Cerna in June 1871.

Castillo Armas, Carlos (1914–1957)

Carlos Castillo Armas (1954–1957) came to power via the U.S.-backed coup that overthrew Jacobo **Arbenz Guzmán** (1951–1954). Castillo Armas quickly dismantled the reforms that had been enacted over the previous ten years following the October Revolution (1944).

Born in Escuintla, Castillo Armas later joined the military and rose to become a colonel and head of the military academy in 1947. The assassination of Francisco Javier Arana (who was to be a candidate in the presidential election of 1950) in 1949 enraged Castillo Armas and motivated him to take drastic steps, in particular against Arbenz, the winner of the contest. Although he was jailed and sentenced to death after leading an attack on a military base in 1949, Castillo Armas escaped in June 1951 by tunneling out of the prison. He and other Guatemalan political dissidents established the National Liberation Movement (Movimiento de Liberación Nacional, MLN) in the early 1950s and, with the support of the U.S. Central Intelligence Agency (CIA), successfully overthrew Arbenz in July 1954. Castillo Armas was chosen to head the five-man governing junta that subsequently took control of the country, and in October 1954 he ran unopposed in a national plebiscite and was elected president.

Castillo Armas effectively dismantled the programs and institutions that had been created by the regimes of Juan José **Arévalo Bermejo** and Arbenz. He banned all existing political parties, peasant organizations, and labor federations, retracted Arbenz's agrarian reform law, allowed Catholic religious instruction in public schools, and excluded illiterates from the electorate. Castillo Armas encouraged foreign investment in the economy and acquired loans and credits from the United States. His administration was brought to an unexpected and sudden halt when he was assassinated in July 1957, allegedly by one of his bodyguards, and perhaps in connection with a power struggle within his party, the National Democratic Movement.

Cerezo Arévalo, Marco Vinicio (1942–)

As the first elected civilian president in Guatemala following sixteen years of military rule, Marco Vinicio Cerezo Arévalo (1986–1991) attempted unsuccessfully to bring peace to Guatemala.

Born into a politically influential family, Cerezo received a law degree from the University of San Carlos and continued his studies at Loyola University, and in Chile, West Germany, Italy, and Venezuela. Cerezo became politically active when Jacobo **Arbenz Guzmán** (1951–1954) was overthrown, joining **Guatemalan Christian Democracy** (Democracia Cristiana Guatemalteca, DCG) and eventually becoming secretary-general of the party. He survived many assassination attempts throughout his political career and was an outspoken critic of the army and of the death squad violence of the 1970s and 1980s. He was elected president in 1986, with military support, on a platform of bringing peace to Guatemala.

The Cerezo administration faced a number of challenges, including an insurgent left, a violent military lacking any civilian control, a failing economy, and a mobilized peasantry. Though Cerezo's neoliberal economic program helped improve the national economy, the standard of living deteriorated for most of the population. The country weathered a series of massive strikes in 1987, 1988, and 1989, and Cerezo survived coup attempts in 1988 and 1989. Though he participated in the regional peace process and signed the **Esquipulas Accords** (see Appendix 1) in 1987, Cerezo failed to make significant domestic progress on human rights or on bringing lasting peace to Guatemala. As his term came to an end, the army continued dominant, the insurgent left remained active, and human rights violations persisted. Cerezo was also accused of corruption and drug trafficking, allegations that hurt the DCG candidate in the 1991 presidential race and facilitated the victory of Jorge Antonio **Serrano Elías** (1991–1993) of the Movement of Mutual Action (Movimiento de Acción Solidaria, MAS).

Cerna, General Vicente. See **Carrera, José Rafael**

A monument commemorating Manuel Estrada Cabrera, who ruled Guatemala from 1898 to 1920. *Columbus Memorial Library, General Secretariat of the Organization of American States. Reproduced with permission of the Organization of American States.*

Committee for Campesino Unity (Comité Unidad Campesina, CUC). See Menchú Tum, Rigoberta

Estrada Cabrera, Manuel (1857–1924)

Manuel Estrada Cabrera served as minister of the interior and justice and as first designate (vice president) under President José María Reyna Barrios (1892–1898) and then ruled Guatemala for twenty-two years (1898–1920). Mindful of nurturing and maintaining the support of the Conservative elite and dedicated to order and progress, Estrada Cabrera fostered the creation of an economy based on large landed estates, forced labor, exports, and centralized political power. He delegated little power and cultivated the support of the army and other officials by granting them favors. The growing middle class, student, and labor sectors were denied any access to political power or expression. In late 1917 and 1918, general discontent with Estrada Cabrera was further fueled by a series of earthquakes that destroyed Guatemala City. Cabrera's lack of response to the crisis led all of the capital city's major actors (students, the Catholic Church, the middle class, organized labor, the military, and the elite) to join in supporting a new coalition, the Unionist Party, to oppose the dictator. Estrada Cabrera's inability to adapt to the changing political and social situation led to his overthrow in 1920.

Gálvez, Mariano. See Carrera, José Rafael

Guatemalan Christian Democracy (Democracia Cristiana Guatemalteca, DCG)

Guatemalan Christian Democracy (Democracia Cristiana Guatemalteca, DCG) arose in August 1959 from the Movement of National Strengthening of Christianity (Movimiento de Afirmacia Nacional de la Cristianidad, MANC), a pro-church organization that emerged during the presidency of Jacobo **Arbenz Guzmán** (1951–1954). The DCG formed as a middle-class party committed to anticommunism and opposing organized labor, and through the 1980s, the party fielded military candidates with progressive platforms. While the DCG initiated a move to the right in the mid-1970s, compared with the repressive military regimes that ruled the country, the DCG appeared to be a progressive party. Nonetheless, neither DCG president Marco Vinicio **Cerezo Arévalo** (1986–1991) nor his successor, Jorge Antonio **Serrano Elías** (1991–1993), was able to effectively curb human rights violations and abuses, which increased after 1989. In the 1995 elections the party collaborated with the National Center Union (Unión del Centro Nacional, UCN) and the Social Democratic Party (Partido Democracia Social, PDS) to form the National Alliance (Alianza Nacional), which won four seats in the 1995 legislative elections. The party has since diminished in importance; during the 1999 elections, it elected only two members to Congress.

Guatemalan Labor Party (Partido Guatemalteco del Trabajo, PGT)

The Guatemalan Labor Party (Partido Guatemalteco del Trabajo, PGT) was founded as the Guatemalan Communist Party, but eliminated "communist" from its name and became the PGT in 1952. Banned after the overthrow of Jacobo **Arbenz Guzmán** (1951–1954) in 1954, the PGT began to operate clandestinely and supported guerrilla movements and armed struggle in the 1960s and 1970s. The party was perceived as a threat to Guatemala's traditional elite, although its membership never exceeded 4,000 people and its candidates never won more than four of the fifty-six existing congressional seats. The party encouraged agrarian reform and supported labor organizations. The PGT eventually joined forces with one faction of the Revolutionary Movement of November 13th (Movimiento Revolucionario del 13 de Noviembre de 1960, MR-13) to form the **Rebel Armed Forces** (Fuerzas Armadas Rebeldes, FAR) in 1965. When the FAR and the PGT broke apart in January 1968, the PGT created its own armed branch, the Revolutionary Armed Forces (Fuerzas Armadas Revolucionarias, PGT-FAR). Many leaders of the PGT-FAR were captured and murdered by the army. As the PGT moved away from guerrilla warfare, its ranks split. The PGT and three other rebel groups then formed the **Guatemalan National Revolutionary Unit** (Unidad Revolucionaria Nacional Guatemalteca, URNG) in January 1982.

Guatemalan National Revolutionary Unit (Unidad Revolucionaria Nacional Guatemalteca, URNG)

The Guatemalan National Revolutionary Unit (Unidad Revolucionaria Nacional Guatemalteca, URNG) was created in January 1982 as a coalition of four Guatemalan leftist rebel movements unified against the government: the **Guatemalan Labor Party** (Partido Guatemalteco del Trabajo, PGT), the **Revolutionary Organization of the People in Arms** (Organización Revolucionaria del Pueblo en Armas, ORPA), the **Guerrilla Army of the Poor** (Ejército Guerrillero de los Pobres, EGP), and the **Rebel Armed Forces** (Fuerzas Armadas Rebeldes, FAR). These four movements maintained their distinct philosophies and operated in separate regions until their true fusion in 1985. In 1991 the Urban Revolutionary Command (Comando Urbano Revolucionario, CUR) joined the URNG.

Ideologically, the URNG was primarily Marxist-Leninist, with some elements of liberation theology and social democracy. Its objectives included eliminating repression, guaranteeing all citizens human rights and government representation, providing necessities to the poor, decreasing the concentration of power in the hands of the wealthy, establishing equality among cultural and ethnic groups, and promoting a foreign policy of nonalignment and international cooperation. Presidents Marco Vinicio **Cerezo Arévalo** (1986–1991), Jorge Antonio **Serrano Elías** (1991–1993), and Ramiro de León Carpio (1993–1996) all engaged in peace talks with the guerrillas, but progress was halting.

The URNG called for a two-week cease-fire prior to the 1995 presidential election, in which it supported the social democratic New Guatemala Democratic Front (Frente Democrático Nueva Guatemala, FDNG), a party created by Indians, labor leaders, and human rights activists. The party's participation in the election marked the first time that the left had taken part in national elections since Guatemala's return to democracy in 1985. The FDNG candidate came in a distant third despite an intimidation campaign against party members. While some believed the party's link to the URNG eroded some support among more moderate-left social democrats, the FDNG denied claims that it had direct ties to the guerrilla forces.

The URNG signed the comprehensive **Agreement for a Firm and Lasting Peace** with the Guatemalan government of Alvaro Enrique **Arzú Irigoyen** (1996–2000) on December 29, 1996. While a demobilized URNG formed a political party, by 2000 the URNG was no longer a major force in Guatemalan politics.

Guatemalan Republican Front (Frente Republicano Guatemalteco, FRG). See Ríos Montt, José Efraín

Guerrilla Army of the Poor (Ejército Guerrillero de los Pobres, EGP)

The Marxist-leaning Guerrilla Army of the Poor (Ejército Guerrillero de los Pobres, EGP) was formed in 1972 by a group of dissidents from the **Rebel Armed Forces** (Fuerzas Armadas Rebeldes, FAR) in the Ixcán region of the Quiché highlands. The objective of the EGP, led by Rolando Morán (a.k.a. Ricardo Ramírez) and Mario Payeras (a.k.a. Benedicto), was to launch a prolonged anti-imperialist, anticapitalist agrarian revolution. Its strategy was to mobilize the support of rural, often primarily indigenous, communities through popular education and promises of land reform. The EGP gained a political and military presence in the late 1970s, becoming Guatemala's largest guerrilla organization by 1981, but barely survived the government's intense counterinsurgency campaigns of the 1980s, which involved eradicating the indigenous populations supporting the guerrilla groups and repressing all popular organizations and development groups. The EGP joined the **Guatemalan National Revolutionary Unit** (Unidad Revolucionaria Nacional Guatemalteca, URNG) in 1982, though it continued its military campaign. In 1993 the EGP was implicated in the murder of President Ramiro **de León Carpio**'s (1993–1996) cousin, two-time presidential candidate Jorge Carpio Nicolle.

de León Carpio, Ramiro (1942–   )

Ramiro de León Carpio (1993–1996) was elected president after the military removed Jorge Antonio **Serrano Elías** (1991–1993) from office.

De León was an active student leader during his university career. He presided over the Constituent Assembly that ended thirty-one years of continuous military rule in 1985, and ran unsuccessfully as the vice presidential candidate of the center-right Democratic Center Union (Unión del Centro Democrático, UCD) in the election of 1985. He served as human rights ombudsman under Serrano Elías, and was viewed by many as a moral leader and a staunch defender of human rights.

Though he was initially popular as president, de León's administration soon began to suffer criticism for its inability to combat Guatemala's intractable problems, including poverty and state corruption. With the help of the Catholic Church, in 1993 the president and Congress signed an agreement to reform forty-three articles of the constitution, and to elect a special interim Congress to serve until the November 1995 general elections. This plan was ratified by a referendum in January 1994. Though a conclusive peace agreement with the **Guatemalan National Revolutionary Unit** (Unidad Revolucionaria Nacional Guatemalteca, URNG) was never reached under de León, the United Nations Verification Mission in Guatemala (Misión de Verificación de las Naciones Unidas en Guatemala, MINUGUA) was established in September 1994 to supervise the implementation of the human rights accord signed in March of that year. De León followed a neoliberal economic model and sought to deepen trade relations with the other Central American nations.

Menchú Tum, Rigoberta (1959–)

Rigoberta Menchú Tum won the Nobel Peace Prize in 1992 for her efforts to achieve peace and expand indigenous rights in Guatemala.

Born in Chimel to Maya peasants, Menchú was self-educated. During the 1970s, the government began to confiscate land in the highlands of El Quiché, a primarily Mayan region. Menchú and her family became involved with the Committee for Campesino Unity (Comité Unidad Campesina, CUC), a peasant organization that emerged in April 1978 to organize temporary and permanent laborers on agribusiness plantations and small farmers in the rural highlands. On January 31, 1980, a group of CUC members including *campesinos*, students, and trade unionists peacefully occupied the Spanish Embassy to draw attention to the ongoing massacres in the western highlands. Government forces burned down the embassy, killing almost everyone inside, including Menchú's father, Vicente Menchú. The CUC was soon forced underground, and would not reemerge until January 1989.

Menchú helped found the United Representation of the Guatemalan Opposition (Representación Unida de la Oposición Guatemalteca, RUOG). She began her most active work with that organization in the highlands in the late 1970s when she armed inhabitants with rocks and machetes to repel the government's heightened repression against guerrilla groups. Though she was forced into exile in 1981, Menchú continued to fight for peace and the rights of the indigenous people of Guatemala from abroad, speaking in international fora and participating in many United Nations working groups. She first gained international prominence with the 1984 book *I, Rigoberta Menchú: An Indian Woman in Guatemala*, which details many of the atrocities committed by the Guatemalan army. (While some question the accuracy of the book in describing events, others defend it, arguing that it is a politically motivated text that cannot be judged on strictly objective criteria.) Among many awards, Menchú has won the 1990 UNESCO Education for Peace Prize, the 1991 French Committee for the Defense of Freedoms and Human Rights Prize, and the 1992 Nobel Peace Prize. Menchú continues her efforts to speak out against human rights violations committed in Guatemala.

Méndez Montenegro, Julio César (1915–1996)

Julio César Méndez Montenegro (1966–1970) is remembered for his scorched earth rural pacification campaigns and the emergence of paramilitary death squads during his administration.

Born in Guatemala City, Méndez left his legal studies at the University of San Carlos to take part in the 1944 October Revolution. He served as the first president of the Liberating Popular Front (Frente Popular Libertador, FPL), which supported Juan José **Arévalo Bermejo** (1945–1951) for president in 1945. Méndez then returned to school, graduated in 1945, and taught at the National University until 1965, eventually becoming dean of the law school. Though he won the presidential election of 1966 on the ticket of the Revolutionary Party (Partido Revolucionario, PR), he did not receive an absolute majority of votes, forcing him to bargain with the military and legislative supporters to secure congressional approval of his presidency.

In a drastic reversal of his initial political leanings, Méndez's administration carried out rural campaigns against left-wing guerrilla insurgencies, and during his presidency military-supported antiguerrilla terrorist groups also emerged. *Mano Blanca* ("White Hand"), a right-wing death squad created by landowners and politicians associated with the National Liberation Movement (Movimiento de Liberación Nacional, MLN), rationalized its terrorist actions as a necessary way to end communist subversion, and received support from the military and the police in torturing, killing, and kidnapping its opponents. *Mano Blanca* disappeared in the early 1970s when the military cut ties with the MLN. *Ojo Por Ojo* ("Eye for an Eye"), supported by wealthy landowners and the military, began to form in the 1960s, and formally began operations in April 1970 to combat the success of guerrilla movements in eastern Guatemala and carry out attacks on leftist sympathizers at the University of San Carlos in Guatemala City.

Despite the violence that occurred during his presidency, Méndez oversaw significant economic development projects and passed certain reform measures. Schools, hospitals, port facilities, and a hydroelectric plant were constructed, and the railroad was nationalized. Méndez's efforts proved futile in the areas of agrarian and tax reform. After his term as president ended, Méndez returned to the legal profession and taught at the University of San Carlos.

National Advancement Party (Partido de Avanzada Nacional, PAN). See Arzú Irigoyen, Alvaro Enrique; Portillo Cabrera, Alfonso Antonio

New Guatemala Democratic Front (Frente Democrático Nueva Guatemala, FDNG). See Guatemalan National Revolutionary Unit (Unidad Revolucionaria Nacional Guatemalteca, URNG)

October Revolution (1944). See Arbenz Guzmán, Jacobo and Arévalo Bermejo, Juan José

Portillo Cabrera, Alfonso Antonio (1951–)

Alfonso Antonio Portillo Cabrera, the candidate of the Guatemalan Republican Front (Frente Republicano Guatemalteco, FRG), won the November 1999 presidential elections.

Born on September 24, 1951 to a schoolteacher, Portillo originally was a supporter of the leftist rebels during the Guatemalan civil war. During fifteen years of exile in Mexico, Portillo received a law degree from the Autonomous University of Guerrero and a doctorate in economics from the National Autonomous University of Mexico. He served as a legislator in the Guatemalan Congress representing **Guatemalan Christian Democracy** (Democracia Cristiana Guatemalteca, DCG) from 1991 to 1996, and from 1992 to 1994 he served as leader of the DCG. However, in 1995 Portillo switched parties and ran as the presidential candidate of the right-wing FRG (the party of former dictator José Efraín **Ríos Montt** [1982–1983]), but lost in the runoff to Alvaro Enrique **Arzú Irigoyen** (1996–2000).

Portillo spent the next four years distancing himself from Ríos Montt and reaching out to the population. His party publicly advertised the fact that Portillo had killed two Mexicans in a fight in 1982 and evaded justice in a somewhat ironic effort to support his image as a tough candidate prepared to fight for law and order in a country troubled by increasing crime and violence. Portillo defeated Óscar Berger Perdomo of the National Advancement Party (Partido de Avanzada Nacional, PAN) in the second round of the 1999 presidential election. However, the PAN retained the second-largest bloc in Congress, attaining thirty-seven seats. Portillo promised to reform civil-military relations, and in March 2000 forced twenty-two generals linked to the military's abusive past to retire, subsequently cajoling the newly promoted military authorities into accepting civilian authority. The biggest challenge Portillo faced in the first half of his term was balancing the demands for implementing human rights reforms issued by the international foreign aid community with the army's insistence on autonomy.

Rebel Armed Forces (Fuerzas Armadas Rebeldes, FAR)

The Rebel Armed Forces (Fuerzas Armadas Rebeldes, FAR) grew out of the Revolutionary Movement of November 13th (Movimiento Revolucionario del 13 de Noviembre de 1960, MR-13). MR-13, created in 1962 by Marco Antonio Yon Sosa and Luis Agosto Turcios Lima, carried out military and social action among the peasantry, attacks on police stations, bank robberies, and kidnappings. When MR-13 moved ideologically from a nationalist, anti-imperialist orientation to embrace Marxism, divisions began to emerge within the group. In 1965 Turcios Lima officially dissociated himself from MR-13 and joined with members of the **Guatemalan Labor Party** (Partido Guatemalteco del Trabajo, PGT) to form the FAR.

The FAR, which advocated communist revolution through guerrilla warfare, began operating in the eastern regions of Izabal and Zacapa and later in Guatemala City, the highlands, El Petén, and northern Alta Verapaz. The death of Turcios Lima in a car accident in 1966 and the army's counterinsurgency campaign caused the loss of two FAR fronts. In 1968 the FAR formally separated from the PGT. MR-13, which had

continued to operate as a guerrilla group under Yon Sosa after Turcios' departure, rejoined the FAR after Yon Sosa was killed by the Mexican army in Chiapas in 1970. Nonetheless, the FAR never regained its dominance, as new guerrilla groups were more effective at organizing the country's indigenous population. The FAR joined the **Guatemalan National Revolutionary Unit** (Unidad Revolucionaria Nacional Guatemalteca, URNG) in 1982 and was the group most resistant to concessions in the peace process, though it eventually did adopt the URNG's emphasis on democratic political participation. The FAR is no longer a dominant political force in part because many of the issues for which it fought were officially settled by the 1996 **Agreement for a Firm and Lasting Peace**.

Revolutionary Movement of November 13th (Movimiento Revolucionario del 13 de Noviembre de 1960, MR-13). See Rebel Armed Forces (Fuerzas Armadas Rebeldes, FAR)

Revolutionary Organization of the People in Arms (Organización Revolucionaria del Pueblo en Armas, ORPA)

The Revolutionary Organization of the People in Arms (Organización Revolucionaria del Pueblo en Armas, ORPA), a leftist guerrilla group, was created in 1972 in Mexico by Rodrigo Asturias Amado, son of Miguel Ángel **Asturias**. The group, which incorporated many former members of the **Rebel Armed Forces** (Fuerzas Armadas Rebeldes, FAR), operated mostly in the departments of Sololá, Quetzaltenango, San Marcos, and Suchitepequez. While it embraced Marxism, Leninism, Maoism, and the ideas of José Carlos **Mariátegui** (see Peru), ORPA was the least ideological and most practical of the Guatemalan guerrilla groups. The organization incorporated the indigenous communities and developed a strong local base in rural areas. Its predominantly indigenous forces believed they were carrying out not only a class-based socialist revolution, but also a revolution of Indians against the Spanish. After recognizing the need for support from the intellectual and professional community, ORPA organized within the urban labor movement but never joined a political front organization, believing that military action was the only way to end the struggle. ORPA grew slowly during the 1970s until the Guatemalan government heightened its antiguerrilla campaigns in the early 1980s. Despite its initial tenets regarding politics, in 1982, ORPA joined the **Guatemalan National Revolutionary Unit** (Unidad Revolucionaria Nacional Guatemalteca, URNG) to negotiate for a peaceful resolution to Guatemala's decades-long civil war.

Ríos Montt, José Efraín (1926–)

The repressive regime of José Efraín Ríos Montt (1982–1983) focused on counterinsurgency to combat guerrilla organizations.

Ríos Montt joined the army in 1943 and rose through the ranks, eventually becoming a general. After training in counterinsurgency at U.S. military schools, Ríos Montt became army chief of staff under President Carlos Arana Osorio (1970–1974). He lost the 1974 presidential election to Kjell Laugerud (1974–1978), but following a military coup that ousted President Fernando Romeo Lucas García (1978–1982), the military named Ríos Montt as one member of the three-man junta it installed to govern Guatemala. Ríos Montt soon dismissed the other two members and declared himself president of the republic. At the beginning of his rule, much of the western highlands were controlled by or sympathetic to guerrilla forces. Ríos Montt placed Guatemala under a state of siege from July 1982 to March 1983 and conducted a large counterinsurgency campaign to drive the rebels from the highlands. During this period of intense repression and human rights abuses, all union and political activity was banned, the press was censored, and the military had the authority to arrest citizens and deny them judicial rights. Though the campaign reduced the power of the insurgents, many civilian lives were lost and many Guatemalans were forced into exile by the violence. In August 1983 Ríos Montt was overthrown in a military coup led by his minister of defense, Oscar Humberto Mejía Victores (1983–1986).

Prior to the November 1990 presidential election, Ríos Montt formed the right-wing Guatemalan Republican Front (Frente Republicano Guatemalteco, FRG). Though he was favored to win the election, he was unable to run because of a constitutional provision preventing former coup leaders from contesting presidential elections. Nonetheless, the FRG acquired eleven seats in the 1990 legislative elections. In the 1994 elections, Ríos Montt was elected to the legislature and the FRG gained a majority representation in Congress. In December 1994, Ríos Montt was elected president of Congress, a post in which he continued to serve after the 1999 elections. At the beginning of 2000, the Spanish National Court was investigating genocide charges against Ríos Montt in connection with the deaths of thirty-seven people (including Rigoberta **Menchú Tum**'s father) in the Spanish Embassy fire of 1982.

Serrano Elías, Jorge Antonio (1945–   )

As president from 1991 to 1993, Jorge Antonio Serrano Elías attempted to unite various factions, including the military and the private sector, to improve Guatemala's economic and political situation.

Born in Guatemala City and educated at the University of San Carlos and Stanford University, Serrano entered politics during the administration of José Efraín **Ríos Montt** (1982–1983) as president of the Council of State. He then formed the Movement of Mutual Action (Movimiento de Acción Solidaria, MAS) and finished third out of eight candidates in the 1985 presidential election. When it became clear that Ríos Montt would be ineligible to enter the presidential race in 1990, support for Serrano increased, and he defeated National Center Union (Unión del Centro Nacional, UCN) candidate Jorge Carpio Nicolle in the January 1991 runoff election. Serrano vowed to join together government, labor, and business for the country's benefit and also strove to remain at peace with the military. His government implemented a neoliberal economic platform oriented toward the private sector. Rising social unrest caused Serrano to dismiss the constitution on May 25, 1993, in an attempt to regain control. Seven days later, he was removed from office by the military, which charged him with corruption. Congress elected Ramiro de León Carpio (1993–1996) to complete his term.

Ubico y Castañeda, Jorge (1878–1946)

As president of Guatemala from 1931 to 1944, Jorge Ubico y Castañeda maintained centralized control of government and developed the nation's infrastructure.

Born in Guatemala City to a diplomat father, Ubico was educated in the United States and in the military academy in Guatemala. He joined the military in 1897 and rose to the rank of colonel by the age of twenty-eight. Ubico became chief of staff in 1920, played a role in deposing President Carlos Herrera (1920–1921) in 1921, and served as minister of war under President José María Orellana (1921–1926). Ubico ran for president in 1922 and 1926, and finally came to power in 1931 after winning that year's presidential contest. Under his rule, authority was concentrated in a strong presidency, military leaders held key government positions and Ubico's Progressive Party controlled the legislature. He used harsh methods to monitor and control the population of Guatemala, censor the press, and repress all political opposition. With the help of constitutional amendments, he was twice reelected through plebiscites.

During the Great Depression, Ubico promoted economic stabilization through frugal fiscal policies. Infrastructure was Ubico's greatest legacy to Guatemala: he built sewers, stadiums, government buildings, parks, public bathhouses, an aqueduct, and roads. Ubico sought to restore agricultural productivity through cultivating unused land and incorporating the Indians into the national economy. He also wished to promote Guatemalan dominance in Central America, spread the ideals of liberalism in nearby nations, and maintain stability in the region. The Ubico regime was overthrown in the 1944 October Revolution (see **Arévalo Bermejo, Juan José**) by a group that included military officers and student strikers. Ubico went into exile in the United States and later died in New Orleans.

United Nations Verification Mission in Guatemala (Misión de Verificación de las Naciones Unidas en Guatemala, MINUGUA) (1994). See **Agreement for a Firm and Lasting Peace**

United States Intervention (1954). See **Arbenz Guzmán, Jacobo**

Ydígoras Fuentes, Miguel (1895–1982)

The regime of Miguel Ydígoras Fuentes (1958–1963) was marked by a mix of nationalistic populism and conservative economic policy.

Born in Pueblo Nuevo, Retalhuleu, to a family of Basque ancestry, Ydígoras Fuentes later served in the military, holding the post of departmental governor in Retalhuleu, El Petén, San Marcos, and Jalapa (1922–1939). His support for the 1944 October Revolution that deposed Jorge **Ubico y Castañeda** (1931–1944) earned him the position of ambassador to Great Britain in the subsequent regime. Though Ydígoras was a candidate in the 1950 presidential election, he went into exile in El Salvador during the months preceding the contest, and lost the race to Jacobo **Arbenz Guzmán** (1951–1954). Ydígoras helped to arrange the U.S.-supported overthrow of Arbenz in 1954, and when President Carlos **Castillo Armas** (1954–1957) was assassinated in July 1957, Ydígoras Fuentes reorganized his political party to campaign for the presidency later that year. Ydígoras lost the highly disputed election and consequently organized huge street demonstrations that resulted in the nullification of the election results. In January 1958 he defeated Colonel José Luis Cruz Salazar in what was viewed as a fair election, and assumed the presidency.

During Ydígoras Fuentes' populist, nationalistic reign, he employed conservative economic policy, implemented an industrial incentives law, a law guarding foreign investment, an agrarian reform law, and an income tax law, and supported the creation of the **Central American Common Market** (CACM, see Appendix 1). In March 1962 rumors of corruption and incompetence, along with student protests, led Ydígoras Fuentes to install a military cabinet to maintain control. The military changed loyalties and deposed Ydígoras in a coup led by defense minister Colonel Alfredo Enrique Peralta Azurdia (1963–1966) in March 1963. Ydígoras went to Nicaragua, Costa Rica, and El Salvador for some time after the coup, but returned to Guatemala when Carlos Arana Osorio (1970–1974) offered amnesty to all exiled ex-presidents. Ydígoras Fuentes served as ambassador in various administrations, and continued to comment in the press about Guatemalan affairs.

HEADS OF STATE

Mariano Rivera Paz	1839–1844
José Rafael Carrera	1844–1848
Juan Antonio Martínez	1848
José Bernardo Escobar	1848
Mariano Paredes	1849–1851
José Rafael Carrera	1852–1865
Pedro de Aycinena	1865
Vicente Cerna	1865–1871
Miguel García Granados	1871–1872
Justo Rufino Barrios	1873–1885
Alejandro Sinibaldi	1885
Manuel Lisandro Barillas	1885–1892
José María Reyna Barrios	1892–1898
Manuel Estrada Cabrera	1898–1920
Carlos Herrera	1920–1921
José María Orellana	1921–1926
Lázaro T. Chacón	1926–1930
Baudillio Palma	1930
Manuel Orellana	1930–1931
José María Reyna Andrada	1931
Jorge Ubico y Castañeda	1931–1944
Federico Ponce Vaides	1944
Triumvirate: Francisco Javier Arana, Jacobo Arbenz Guzmán; Jorge Toriello Garrido	1944–1945
Juan José Arévalo Bermejo	1945–1951
Jacobo Arbenz Guzmán	1951–1954
Carlos Castillo Armas	1954–1957
Luis Arturo González López	1957
Guillermo Flores Avendano	1957–1958
Miguel Ydígoras Fuentes	1958–1963
Alfredo Enrique Peralta Azurdia	1963–1966
Julio César Méndez Montenegro	1966–1970
Carlos Arana Osorio	1970–1974
Kjell Laugerud	1974–1978
Fernando Romeo Lucas García	1978–1982
José Efraín Ríos Montt	1982–1983
Oscar Humberto Mejía Victores	1983–1986
Marco Vinicio Cerezo Arévalo	1986–1991
Jorge Antonio Serrano Elías	1991–1993
Ramiro de León Carpio	1993–1996
Alvaro Enrique Arzú Irigoyen	1996–2000
Alfonso Antonio Portillo Cabrera	2000–

Sources: Thomas E. Skidmore and Peter H. Smith. *Modern Latin America*, 4th ed. (New York: Oxford University Press, 1997); *Guatemala News Watch*. http://www.quetzalnet.com/newswatch/

BIBLIOGRAPHY

Print Resources

Barry, Tom. *Guatemala: A Country Guide*. Albuquerque, NM: Inter-Hemispheric Education Resource Center, 1989.

Cullather, Nick. *Secret History: The CIA's Classified Account *of Its Operations in Guatemala.* Stanford: Stanford University Press, 1999.

Dominguez, Jorge I., and Mark Lindenburg, eds. *Democratic Transitions in Central America.* Gainesville: University Press of Florida, 1997.

Dosal, Paul J. *Doing Business with the Dictators: A Political History of United Fruit in Guatemala, 1899–1944.* Wilmington, DE: Scholarly Resources, 1993.

Gleijeses, Piero. *Shattered Hope: The Guatemalan Revolution and the United States, 1944–1954.* Princeton: Princeton University Press, 1991.

Goulding, Marrack, and Susanne Jonas. *Of Centaurs and Doves: Guatemala's Peace Process.* Boulder: Westview Press, 2000.

Gross, Liza. *Handbook of Leftist Guerrilla Groups in Latin America and the Caribbean.* Boulder: Westview Press, 1995.

Handy, Jim. *Gift of the Devil: A History of Guatemala.* Boston: South End Press, 1984.

Menchú, Rigoberta. *I, Rigoberta Menchú: An Indian Woman in Guatemala.* London: Verso, 1984.

Moore, Richard E. *Historical Dictionary of Guatemala.* Metuchen, NJ: Scarecrow Press, 1973.

South America, Central America, and the Caribbean 1999. London, UK: Europa Publications, 1998.

Weaver, Frederick Stirton. *Inside the Volcano: The History and Political Economy of Central America.* Boulder: Westview Press, 1994.

Electronic Resources

Center for Guatemalan Studies
http://www.c.net.gt/ceg
The Web site of this nonpolitical organization contains information on social, economic, and political issues. (In Spanish).

Guatemala Daily
http://www.guatemaladaily.com
Produced by WorldNews.com, this site includes links to newspapers, guides, and directories, contains articles about Guatemala, and acts as a clearinghouse for all articles written about Guatemala in English-speaking news sources. (In English and Spanish)

Guatemalan News Watch (GNW)
http://www.quetzalnet.com/newswatch/default.html
GNW is a monthly publication released by the Guatemalan Development Foundation (FUNDESA) that provides information on Guatemalan current events. The Web form of the journal covers the years since 1996. (In English)

Guatemalan Peace Process
http://www.c-r.org/acc–guat/Contents.htm
This Web site, run by an international nongovernmental organization oriented toward conflict resolution, contains a database of resources on Guatemala's peace process. Includes the full texts of the primary documents related to the peace process, profiles of the main actors, and historical articles about Guatemala's civil war and peace settlement. (In English)

La Hora
http://www.lahora.com.gt/
Web site of a major Guatemalan daily newspaper. (In Spanish)

Latin American Network Information Center (LANIC): Guatemala
http://www.lanic.utexas.edu/la/ca/guatemala/
Guatemala section of this extensive Web site contains hundreds of links to research resources, cultural centers, economic and business institutions, government agencies, historical sources, magazines and other periodicals, nongovernmental organizations, and grassroots groups, as well as many other subjects. (In English)

Misión de Verificación de las Naciones Unidas en Guatemala
http://www.minugua.guate.net/
The United Nations' official Web site of the Guatemalan peace process. Contains historical documents and other information about Guatemala's civil war and peace process. (In Spanish)

Political Database of the Americas: Guatemala
http://www.georgetown.edu/pdba/Countries/guate.html
Comprehensive database run as a joint project of Georgetown University and the Organization of American States. Section on Guatemala contains information on and links to the executive, legislative, and judicial branches of the Guatemalan government; electoral laws and election results; and other political data. (In English, Spanish, Portuguese, and French)

Political Resources.net: Guatemala
http://www.politicalresources.net/guatemala.htm
Guatemala section of a Web site containing a wealth of links to sources of information on national politics. Includes information on political parties, legislative and executive institutions, laws and legislation, and elections, as well as a link to the constitution. (In English)

Prensa Libre
http://www.prensalibre.com/
The Web version of one of Guatemala's major daily newspapers. Offers comprehensive national and international coverage, including coverage of the national political scene. (In Spanish)

Wilfried Derksen's Elections Around the World: Guatemala
http://www.agora.it/elections/guatemala.htm
Guatemala section of a comprehensive database of results from elections around the world. Contains results from recent national executive and legislative elections, as well as explanations of and links to political parties and institutions. (In English)

HAITI

COUNTRY PROFILE

Official name	République d'Haiti
Capital	Port-au-Prince
Type/structure of government	Republic
Executive	President is directly elected to four-year term and leads the Senate; prime minister is appointed by the president with the approval of the parliament and leads the government; secretary of state; cabinet.
Legislative	Elected bicameral parliament (National Assembly, Assemblée Nationale) consisting of a Senate with 27 seats and a Chamber of Deputies with 83 seats.
Judicial	Highest court is the Supreme Court (Court of Cassations), appointed by the president with the approval of the parliament.
Major political parties	Many small, weakly supported political parties exist; most prominent are Organization of People in Struggle (Organisation du Peuple en Lutte, OPL) and Lavalas Family (Famni Lavalas, FL; a remnant of the **Lavalas** political movement).
Constitution in effect	1987
Location/geography	Occupies western third of island of Hispaniola (remaining two-thirds is occupied by the Dominican Republic), located between the Caribbean Sea and the North Atlantic Ocean; coastal plains with a mountainous interior.
Geographic area	27,750 sq. km.
Population	6,884,264 (June 1999 est.)
Ethnic groups	Black (of African descent) 95%; mulatto 5%
Religions	Roman Catholic 80%; Protestant 10%; Voodou prevalent
Literacy rate	45% (1999 est.)
Infant mortality rate	97.64 deaths per 1,000 live births (1999 est.)
Life expectancy	51.65 years (1999 est.)
Monetary unit	Gourde
Exchange rate	1 U.S. dollar = 20.249 gourdes (August 2000)*
Major exports	Coffee, cacao, sugar, meat, sisal, bauxite, light industrial goods, handicrafts
Major imports	Rice, wheat flour, motor vehicles, soybean oil, machinery, sugar, petroleum
GDP	$8.9 billion (1998 est.)
GDP growth rate	3% (1998 est.)
GDP per capita	$1,300 (1998 est.)

Latin American Weekly Report, August 22, 2000 (WR-00-33), p. 394.

Source: CIA World Factbook, unless otherwise noted. http://www.cia.gov/cia/publications/factbook/geos/ha.html

OVERVIEW

Summary

Situated on the western third of the island of Hispaniola in the Caribbean Sea, Haiti has had a tumultuous history that has left it one of the poorest countries in the world. The majority of its population is a largely black peasantry, while a small minority of Haitians are members of the rich, overwhelmingly mulatto elite. Haiti's culture is a mix of European customs dominated by African traditions. Today, as a young democracy, Haiti is attempting to control violence and instability by bolstering its economy through foreign aid, developing infrastructure, and opening up markets. However, as Haiti's history demonstrates, violence has traditionally been the most effective means to bring about change in the small island nation.

History

In 1492 Christopher Columbus landed on the island called Ayiti ("mountainous land") by its indigenous inhabitants, the Taino and the Carib. Claiming it for the Spanish crown, Columbus named the island Hispaniola. In 1593 the first Africans were brought to Hispaniola to work as slaves on the island's plantations, taking the place of the native peoples, who had been decimated under brutal Spanish treatment. The Spanish largely ne-

Haiti. © 1998 *The Moschovitis Group, Inc.*

A peasant cutting sugarcane, long an important crop in Haiti. *Columbus Memorial Library, General Secretariat of the Organization of American States. Reproduced with permission of the Organization of American States.*

glected the area, and the French began to encroach upon it, especially French pirates, who used it as a base for their attacks. In 1697 the Spanish and French signed the Treaty of Ryswick, under which the western third of Hispaniola was ceded by the Spanish to the French. The French called their colony Saint-Domingue.

Saint-Domingue became one of the most prosperous colonies in the New World, producing sugar, cacao, coffee, indigo, and cotton through the efforts of the hundreds of thousands of African slaves who worked the plantations, few of whom had been born on the island. By the late eighteenth century, slaves (estimated at between 500,000 and 700,000) vastly outnumbered whites. Led by François Dominique Toussaint L'Ouverture (and inspired, ironically, by the ideas of the French Revolution), slave rebellions intensified in the early 1790s, setting in motion a twelve-year process of liberation that resulted in the massive slaughter of whites, the end of slavery (abolished in 1794 by the French), and Saint-Domingue's independence from Napoleon Bonaparte's France in 1804. Haiti, as the African slaves who took control of the western third of the island renamed it, thus became the first black republic of the New World and the second colony in the Americas to gain its independence.

Jean-Jacques **Dessalines** (1804–1806), commander of the revolutionary forces, assumed control of the nation, and soon crowned himself emperor. He ruled with an iron fist, killing as many whites as possible. He failed to unify the revolutionary forces however, and after his death the country was divided between the north and south; Henri **Christophe** (1807–1820) ruled the northern half of the country and Alexandre Sabés **Pétion** (1807–1818) the southern. Upon Pétion's death in 1818, Jean-Pierre **Boyer** (1818–1843) took his place as president, and upon Christophe's death in 1820, Boyer

reunited the country. Haitians attempted to unify the island of Hispaniola under Boyer's rule, occupying the eastern two thirds from 1822 until 1844. Boyer was overthrown by a coup in 1843, and his ouster left Haiti in a state of civil war, facilitating the Dominican Republic's attainment of independence from Haiti in 1844.

The years from 1843 to 1915, which witnessed the installation and overthrow of twenty-two dictators, were marked by greed, corruption, and violence. Fearing threats of European invasion of the Western Hemisphere and suspecting that the weak and destabilized nation might be a target for foreign attack, the United States sent troops to Haiti in 1915 (see **United States Intervention** [1915–1934]), and subsequently occupied the country for nineteen years. While marine brigadier general John H. Russell oversaw the election of a series of puppet presidents, it was actually he and the U.S. troops who controlled the country. Though resistance to the U.S. presence increased among black peasants between 1918 and 1920, all uprisings were eventually suppressed, resulting in the death of approximately 3,000 Haitians. The presence of white Americans helped spawn the **Négritude** movement, which encouraged Haitian nationalism and pride in the country's African heritage.

The United States pulled out of Haiti in 1934, a year now hailed as that of the country's second liberation. A period of relative calm followed as Haiti was ruled by a string of civilian administrations, juntas, and military governments. The 1957 election of François **Duvalier**, commonly known as "Papa Doc" (1957–1971), would end that calm: proclaiming himself president for life, Duvalier maintained control through violence and repression, using his **Tontons Macoute**, a paramilitary force, to dispense his will through brutal torture and

A 1980 photo of the Government Palace in Haiti. *Columbus Memorial Library, General Secretariat of the Organization of American States. Reproduced with permission of the Organization of American States.*

murder. Upon his death in 1971, he bequeathed his position to his son, Jean-Claude **Duvalier**, known as "Baby Doc" (1971–1986). Under the second Duvalier dictatorship, Haiti maintained a semblance of stability. However, in 1986 riots broke out in protest of the overly luxurious lifestyle of the first family, which contrasted sharply with the poverty suffered by the rest of the country. Duvalier was evacuated to France and a military regime was installed. While a new constitution was drafted in 1987, most presidents elected under that new constitution averaged only eight-month terms before being overthrown. During the 1980s, massive numbers of refugees fled Haiti, destined for the United States and the Bahamas. U.S. policy on the treatment and handling of the often poor, sick, and uneducated refugees has been discriminatory and inconsistent.

Hope for the country came in 1990 with the election of Jean-Bertrand **Aristide** (1991, 1994–1996, 2001–). Shortly after his inauguration, however, Aristide was ousted by a military coup. Between 300 and 500 Haitians were killed in the days immediately following the coup, and an estimated 3,000 people were murdered during the three-year military regime that the coup brought to power. In 1994, after much international negotiation, many threats of U.S. invasion, and the eventual dispatching of an occupation force consisting of 20,000 U.S. troops, military leader Raoul **Cédras** resigned and Aristide was reinstalled as president. In 1995, despite Aristide's attempts to remain in power, René **Préval** (1996–2001) was elected president. Préval soon began the process of privatizing badly run state industries and initiating other reforms so that Haiti could qualify for foreign loans. Months-long bickering with Congress, though, tied up foreign aid that would have benefited the country. Despite increasing violence in the streets between Aristide supporters and oppo-

nents, on November 30, 1997, the three-year mandate keeping United Nations (UN) peacekeeping troops in Haiti expired, and they withdrew. The 5,200-member Haitian police team formed and trained under UN and U.S. auspices could not contain the growing violence, and, in fact, contributed to it, killing many people.

Reports of corruption and human rights violations by the Haitian police force continued in 2001. Due to high unemployment, persistent poverty, and the country's location between Colombia and the United States, Haiti has also become an important transit point in the international drug trade. Approximately one-third of all drugs arriving in the United States pass though Haiti, and the southern portion of the small island nation is controlled by drug lords. Also, continued immigration battles with the Dominican Republic have strained Haitian relations with its island neighbor. The country's political outlook is also bleak. Following Préval's dissolution of the Senate in early 1999, more than 10,000 government posts went vacant for longer than sixteen months as elections for those positions were repeatedly postponed. Haiti finally held local and parliamentary elections on May 21, 2000, and while the contest initially revived a bit of hope for democracy, soon afterwards reports of vote-counting irregularities for Senate seats surfaced, a recount was called for, several members of the electoral council resigned, and runoffs scheduled for June 25 were postponed. Presidential elections were held in late November 2000. Aristide was victorious, garnering a reported 92 percent of the vote, partly because all of the country's major opposition parties boycotted the balloting. Aristide's party, Lavalas Family (Famni Lavalas, FL; see **Lavalas**) also took all nine contested Senate seats; in late 2001, FL held all but one seat in the Senate and 80 percent of the Chamber of Deputies. An agreement on re-running the disputed May 2000 legislative elections was finally reached in August 2001.

ENTRIES

1804 Revolution

Haiti's independence movement, the world's only successful slave rebellion, led to the creation of the world's first black republic. Haiti, as the slaves who took control of the former French colony of Saint-Domingue renamed it, was the second colony in the Americas to gain independence. The rebellion remains a source of pride for Haitians, and those who fought for the country's independence are considered among Haiti's greatest heroes.

In 1593 the first Africans were imported to Hispaniola to work as slaves on the island's plantations, taking the place of the native peoples, who had been decimated under brutal Spanish treatment. Europeans clashed violently with the African slaves on the western third of the island (the French colony of Saint-Domingue). Major slave uprisings began in the 1750s, and by the early 1790s the hundreds of thousands of African slaves who had been brought to Saint-Domingue began to threaten the precarious power of the colony's French rulers who numbered only approximately 40,000. As chaos spread across the colony, Spanish and British forces descended upon Saint-Domingue in hopes of seizing it for themselves. While many blacks joined the Spanish army in an attempt to thwart the French, the French abolition of slavery in 1794 prompted some black soldiers to switch allegiances and join the French army.

The French retained their hold on Saint-Domingue, and François Dominique Toussaint **L'Ouverture**, who had led the French troops in battle, was named governor of the colony. However, when L'Ouverture began to dismantle French power in hopes of liberating Saint-Domingue from France in the early 1800s, Napoleon Bonaparte sent French troops back to the island in 1802. L'Ouverture held off the French for a few months, and then suddenly surrendered. The French captured L'Ouverture and exiled him to France, where he soon died, but black commanders, including Jean-Jacques **Dessalines** (1804–1806) and Henri **Christophe** (1807–1820), soon reinitiated the independence struggle. Preoccupied with a war against Britain, French troops withdrew within a year. On January 1, 1804, Dessalines declared Haiti independent, though no foreign country would recognize the new republic. Though its leaders remained extremely wary of another foreign invasion, Haiti was never again a colony of Europe.

Aristide, Jean-Bertrand (1953–   )

Jean-Bertrand Aristide, Haiti's youngest president, led the nation briefly in 1991, again from 1994 to 1996, and was reelected in 2000. In the 1990s, Aristide was the country's hope for change, as his presidency followed more than three decades of tyrannical and corrupt rule under François **Duvalier** (1957–1971) and Jean-Claude **Duvalier** (1971–1986). Aristide's reelection in 2000 suggested that Haitians still considered the charismatic former priest their best hope for the future.

Aristide was born and raised among peasants in a small village in the southwest of Haiti. He earned a bachelor's degree in psychology from the National University of Haiti and a master's degree in biblical theology from the University of Montreal. Aristide returned to Haiti and became a priest in Port-au-Prince's slum district, preaching against the elite as well as the Duvalier dictatorships and their **Tontons Macoute**. He was asked to leave the clergy in the mid-1980s as his political opposition to the second Duvalier regime intensified.

Aristide ran for president in the 1990 election on a platform of "transparency, participation, and justice," promising to devote himself to the plight of the poor

and to eradicate vestiges of the Duvalier dictatorships if elected. His presidential bid, and his political movement, **Lavalas**, ignited the poor Haitian masses, and voter turnout was overwhelming. Aristide received almost 70 percent of votes cast, winning the presidency in the face of strong opposition from the army, the Catholic Church, and the remaining Tontons Macoute. The military did not support his presidency and the elites feared his influence, so Aristide assumed office under the protection of sixty Swiss guards. He immediately dismissed almost all high-ranking army officials and began making overtures to the poor, including taxing the rich, raising the minimum wage, and separating the police and military.

On September 30, 1991, within months of his inauguration, Aristide was overthrown in a coup led by Brigadier General Raoul **Cédras**. The coup leaders tried to justify their actions by falsely accusing Aristide of disregarding the 1987 Constitution and persecuting political opponents, despite the fact that human rights violations had decreased since he had assumed office. Thousands of people were killed in the coup, which left the country engulfed in violence. The United States, Canada, France, and Venezuela intervened to prevent the assassination of Aristide, who initially found sanctuary in Venezuela and then moved to Washington, D.C. Aristide remained active and visible while in the United States, campaigning for his return to elected office.

Though Cédras signed an agreement (known as the Governors Island Accords) in 1993 that ensured Aristide's return to power, he later refused to honor it. In 1994 U.S. president Bill Clinton threatened to invade Haiti if Aristide were not allowed to return to the presidency. However, as troops were readied, a team of U.S. diplomats came to a compromise with Haiti's military leaders, who withdrew from power and were flown to safety. In September 1994, in an effort called Operation Uphold Democracy, more than 20,000 U.S. troops were sent to Haiti to ensure Aristide's reinstallation, help build infrastructure, and control violence throughout the country, as much of the military remained intact and armed. Modifying his former radicalism to appease business interests and the elite, Aristide appointed Smark Michele as prime minister, and together they planned the election of a new legislature. Simultaneously, violence against Aristide's opponents increased, and most believed that the president was somehow inspiring the brutality. In the 1995 presidential election, which he attempted to cancel several times, Aristide lost the presidency to René **Préval** (1996–2001) in a bitter battle.

Aristide continued to play an integral role in Haitian politics and was reelected to the presidency in November 2000 in a contest that was marred by intimidation, violence, and low voter turnout, and that the nation's main opposition parties boycotted. Aristide assumed office in February 2001 facing a dire domestic situation (including slowing economic growth, rising inflation, and a worsening budget deficit) and the dual challenge of cutting spending while improving health, education, and infrastructure, which continued to deteriorate due to faltering efforts toward economic restructuring or privatization. Aristide survived what appeared to be an attempted coup in December 2001, though questions were raised regarding whether the Aristide government had staged the event.

Avril, Prosper (1937–)

Colonel Prosper Avril, one of Haiti's most powerful and feared leaders, worked behind the scenes of every Haitian regime from 1957 through 1988, and then held office himself from September 1988 through March 1990.

Avril served as a key advisor to dictator François **Duvalier** (1957–1971) and then controlled the presidency of his son, Jean-Claude **Duvalier** (1971–1986). Following the younger Duvalier's ouster, Avril served on the National Council of Government (Conseil National de Gouvernement, CNG, 1986–1988), until popular protest forced him out of the junta. Avril served as the head of the Presidential Guard under Leslie François Manigat (1988) and Henri **Namphy** (1988). Frustrated by Namphy's heavy-handed and disastrous rule, Avril ousted him after only four months and assumed power in September 1988.

Avril immediately amazed and confused the populace by purging fifty-seven top officers from the army and lessening the power of the paramilitary force, the **Tontons Macoute**. While the U.S. Congress and State Department initially supported Avril's regime, within a year the United States was forced to cut back on aid due to increasing popular unrest in the country, persistent reports of human rights violations, and Avril's connections to international drug trafficking networks. Elites and the middle class began to lose faith in their leader, and by 1990 Avril maintained power only through military force. Following Avril's imposition of a violent state of siege, increasingly influential Haitian political groups forced him from his post and the country in March 1990.

Avril fled to Florida, and Ertha Pascal-Trouillot (1990–1991), the first female member of the Haitian Supreme Court, proved to be the only member of the Court both willing to serve as provisional president and eligible to do so under the 1987 Constitution. She assumed the presidency in 1990, and despite one coup attempt, maintained control over the country as it prepared for the election that brought Jean-Bertrand **Aristide** (1991, 1994–1996, 2001–) to power for the first time. Avril was arrested in May 2001 on charges of torture and human rights violations committed while he led the nation between 1988 and 1990.

Boyer, Jean-Pierre (1776–1850)

Jean-Pierre Boyer served as president of Haiti from 1818 to 1843, when he was unseated by a revolt inspired by the corruption of his regime.

Following the death of Emperor Jean-Jacques **Dessalines** (1804–1806), Haiti was divided in half by vying political factions led by Alexandre Sabés **Pétion** (who led the southern half of the nation, 1807–1818) and Henri **Christophe** (who led the northern half, 1807–1820). Boyer took Pétion's place after Pétion's death in 1818, and following the suicide of Christophe, Haiti was reunited under the presidency of Boyer in 1820.

Concerned by the potential for invasion by the French, whose colonial leadership the nation had recently escaped, Boyer bargained for French recognition in return for a 150 million franc indemnity and low tariffs for French goods. In order to pay the indemnity, Boyer borrowed heavily from foreigners and taxed Haitians. While Boyer repressed voodou in favor of Catholicism and attempted to revive the plantation economy, the land reform begun under Pétion continued, as families divided small plots among their heirs. In an attempt to stave off economic decline, in 1826 Boyer mandated the *Code Rural*, under which peasants were forced to work on large plantations.

In perhaps the greatest victory of Boyer's administration, in 1822 Haitian forces conquered and occupied Santo Domingo (today the Dominican Republic), which had just gained independence from Spain. A group that opposed Boyer's corruption, as well as the **Haitian occupation** (see Dominican Republic) of Santo Domingo, began to form in late 1838, and succeeded in ousting Boyer from office in 1843. Boyer fled to Jamaica and later to Paris. His ouster left Haiti in a state of civil war, and Haitian troops withdrew from Santo Domingo in 1844.

Cacos War (1918–1920). See United States Intervention

Cédras, Raoul (1949–)

As commander-in-chief of the army during the first administration of President Jean-Bertrand **Aristide** (1991, 1994–1996, 2001–), Raoul Cédras was a leader of the 1991 coup that overthrew Aristide. Cédras ruled Haiti behind puppet presidents for two years, before being forced to flee the country as the United States military prepared to invade.

Cédras was born into a prominent family that supported the dictatorships of François **Duvalier** (1957–1971) and Jean-Claude **Duvalier** (1971–1986). He joined the military and rose quickly through the ranks. At the beginning of his first administration, Aristide trusted Cédras as an advisor and appointed him as commander-in-chief of the army. Nonetheless, on the night of September 30, 1991, Cédras and Police Chief Michele François, with the support of the mulatto elite, participated in a coup that overthrew Aristide. The coup, which was staged to protect the status quo and Haitian business interests, including the massive drug trafficking networks that had been put in place by former military leaders Henri **Namphy** (1988) and Prosper **Avril** (1988–1990), resulted in the death of thousands, as coup supporters attacked and killed unarmed citizens in an effort to prevent popular uprisings. Cédras promoted himself to lieutenant general and ruled Haiti for the next two years behind puppet presidents Joseph C. Nerette (1991–1992) and Marc Louis Bazin (1992–1993). Those regimes came under harsh international scrutiny for human rights abuses, especially those inflicted by the paramilitary **Front for the Advancement and Progress of Haiti** (Front pour l'Avencement et le Progrès d'Haiti, FRAPH).

In June 1993 Cédras and Aristide signed the Governors Island Accords, which called for the return of Aristide to the presidency of Haiti and the resignation of Cédras, and granted amnesty to Cédras. The accords also lifted the United Nations and **Organization of American States** (OAS; see Appendix 2) trade embargo that had been placed on Haiti. Aware that it was very unlikely that the Haitian parliament, whose upper house was largely pro-Aristide, would grant him amnesty, Cédras immediately violated the accords by refusing to resign. Instead, he began to campaign through the countryside in anticipation of the upcoming presidential election, demonstrating his intention to remain in power until that election.

Though international pressure for Cédras' resignation and a return to democracy mounted through 1994, Haitian military leaders ignored sanctions and warnings, driving the United States to threaten armed intervention in the fall of 1994. In a final effort to avoid conflict, former U.S. president Jimmy Carter, former chairman of the U.S. Joint Chiefs of Staff Colin Powell, and U.S. senator Sam Nunn traveled to Haiti to negotiate a settlement with Cédras. Although he was initially defiant, the dispatching of airplanes from the United States finally made the threat real for the military leader. Cédras signed an agreement, promising to leave office and the country, leading to jubilant rioting in Haiti. Cédras fled to Panama, and Emile Jonassaint, chief justice of the Haitian Supreme Court, briefly served as provisional president until Aristide reassumed office in late 1994.

Christophe, Henri (also King Henri I) (1767–1820)

After the assassination of Jean-Jacques **Dessalines** (1804–1806), a struggle for power between Henri Christophe and Alexandre Sabés **Pétion** (1807–1818) split Haiti between the north and south. Christophe ruled the northern half of the divided country from 1807 until his death in 1820.

Christophe was born a slave in Grenada, and later was sold to a Haitian owner. He participated in the historic Haitian slave rebellions of the early nineteenth century (see **1804 Revolution**) that led to Haiti's independence, fighting under François Dominique Toussaint **L'Ouverture**. In 1807 he was offered a weakened presidential office by the mulatto elite. Enraged by this attempt to dilute his power, Christophe tried to capture Port-au-Prince, but was defeated by troops led by Pétion. Christophe retreated to the northern half of the nation and established a base from which to govern that half of Haiti, effectively dividing the country in two. He maintained tight control, employing a system of forced labor known as the *fermage* and enforcing extremely strict laws that attempted to legislate integrity among the population under his control. Christophe also established a sound currency, the *gourde* (which is still used today), and made education mandatory.

Many people attempted to flee to the south, which Pétion ruled much less harshly, and Christophe carefully guarded the makeshift border. On March 28, 1811, Christophe crowned himself King Henri I. In a new constitution, he created a nobility and generously parceled out land and serfs to those it included. Christophe feared invasion, and as his rule became increasingly tyrannical, factions within his army began plotting his overthrow. In 1820 an aging Christophe killed himself as the countryside rose up in revolt.

Dessalines, Jean-Jacques (also Emperor Jacques I) (1758–1806)

In 1804 Jean-Jacques Dessalines declared the independence from France of the French colony of Saint-Domingue and created the new nation of Haiti, which he ruled until 1806. Because of his intense belief in the strength of blacks against the imperialism of whites, he is considered by some the father of **Négritude**.

Dessalines was raised a slave in northern Haiti, suffering hardships at the hands of whites and mulattos that would shape the ferocity of his rule almost half a century later. As an illiterate runaway slave, he joined the **1804 Revolution** that was under way led by François Dominique Toussaint **L'Ouverture**, and served as a lieutenant in his army. Dessalines also collected usurped plantations, garnering a huge income. He was later sent to the south of Haiti to serve as occupational governor. During his rule, he is said to have murdered hundreds of mulattos and whites.

On January 1, 1804, Dessalines declared Saint-Domingue's independence from France, and named the new country Haiti. He created Haiti's blue and red flag by tearing the white stripe out of the French flag, an action that symbolized the end of European (white) influence. Six months into his rule he crowned himself Emperor Jacques I. He ruled with an iron fist, forcing blacks back into harsh labor on the plantations, augmenting his army, and slaughtering whites, while alienating the mulatto elite. Dessalines promulgated a new constitution in 1805 that gave him absolute power. In 1806 he was assassinated by his own troops in Port-au-Prince in retaliation against his tyrannical rule.

François Duvalier, known as "Papa Doc," ruled Haiti between 1957 and 1971. *Columbus Memorial Library, General Secretariat of the Organization of American States. Reproduced with permission of the Organization of American States.*

Duvalier, François (also "Papa Doc") (1907–1971)

François Duvalier (commonly known as "Papa Doc") ruled Haiti from 1957 until his death in 1971, when he bequeathed his status as "president for life" to his son Jean-Claude **Duvalier** (1971–1986). The elder Duvalier used brutality and terrorism to maintain control, creating the **Tontons Macoute,** a paramilitary force, to silence his enemies and intimidate the populace.

Born in Port-au-Prince, François Duvalier earned a doctorate from L'Ecole de Médicine, and subsequently became increasingly involved in politics, working on the public health campaign of President Dumarsais Estimé (1946–1950) and serving briefly as her undersecretary of labor. He was also involved in the **Négritude** movement that sought to recognize and celebrate the black experience in Haiti. A 1950 coup brought to office the antithesis of that movement, Paul Eugène Magloire (1950–1956). A member of the black elite, Magloire enjoyed the support of the Catholic Church and the United States government, and promoted modernization, offering foreign investors the best land for their agro-export businesses and often pushing Haitian peasants from their subsistence plots. In response, with the support of the Noiriste Party, the black middle class, and the poor masses, Duvalier was elected president in 1957. Once in office, he repeatedly appealed to Haiti's black population, alienating many educated mulattos

and forcing many skilled professionals out of the country.

His regime became increasingly tyrannical and personalistic. He continually offered government offices to his supporters, and used his Tontons Macoute progressively more to enforce loyalty, control his opposition, and terrorize the masses while simultaneously diminishing the power of the official military. He dismantled foreign control of the church, legitimized voodou by making it a central aspect of his regime, and appointed Haitian clergy, a move for which he was excommunicated by the Vatican. He lessened some of the power of the elites, which satisfied the middle class; nonetheless, during his administration the standard of living dropped as the population grew and land division continued. Thousands of Haitians left the country during his years in power.

In 1961 he claimed to have been reelected to the presidency, and in 1963 proclaimed his rule a dictatorship. That same year, U.S. president John F. Kennedy cut off aid to Haiti, prompting Duvalier to reinforce the themes of Négritude and nationalism. In 1964 Duvalier held a rigged plebiscite that decreed him president for life. He died in 1971, after ruling Haiti for fourteen years, bequeathing his presidency for life to his only son, Jean-Claude Duvalier.

Duvalier, Jean-Claude (also "Baby Doc") (1951–)

As president of Haiti from 1971 to 1986, Jean-Claude Duvalier established a regime that was less violent though more corrupt than that of his father and predecessor, François **Duvalier** (1957–1971).

Schooled in Haiti, the younger Duvalier had little success as a law student. He was bequeathed and assumed the position of "president for life" at the age of twenty upon the death of his father, President François Duvalier. While during his first year in office the younger Duvalier left decisions to a cabinet previously appointed by his father, Duvalier soon became increasingly active in governing the nation, promoting economic stabilization through foreign investment and promising reform in order to receive international aid. New investments brought about 80,000 jobs to Haiti. While Haiti received an extraordinary amount of foreign aid during Duvalier's regime, much of it was embezzled by government officials.

Though Duvalier brought some political stability to the country, his 1980 marriage to Michèle Bennett (a member of the mulatto elite) and his transformation of Michèle's father into one of the richest coffee barons in the country upset that nascent stability. The growing black middle class resented the return of mulatto influence (and the threat of their dominance) in the government, and Michèle Bennett's extravagance and the obvious luxury of her lifestyle infuriated the poor, and polarized Haiti's rich elite and impoverished masses.

From 1984 to 1986 the country was racked with

food riots, which were supported by liberation theologians and some parts of the Catholic Church. The unarmed demonstrations were often quashed with military repression. Duvalier attempted to control the country through violence, but by 1986 the countryside was beyond the government's control. Duvalier and his wife fled to France, the only country that would accept them, taking with them millions of dollars from Haiti's Central Bank. In a subsequent event remembered today as the *dechoukaj*, or "uprooting," rioters in Haiti sought to destroy everything related to the twenty-nine-year Duvalier dictatorship.

Estimé, Dumarsais. See Négritude

Front for the Advancement and Progress of Haiti (Front pour l'Avencement et le Progrès d'Haiti, FRAPH)

Formed in 1993, the Front for the Advancement and Progress of Haiti (Front pour l'Avencement et le Progrès d'Haiti, FRAPH), its name a homonym for the Creole word "to hit," was a right-wing civilian paramilitary group that violently suppressed supporters of former president Jean-Bertrand **Aristide** (1991, 1994–1996, 2001–) after his overthrow in 1991. Following Aristide's overthrow, Colonel John Patrick Coins of the United States encouraged the creation of a group that could counter Aristide's wide base of support. Haitian Emmanuel "Toto" Constant created the FRAPH for that purpose. Controlled by police chief Michel François, the organization held violent demonstrations, kidnapped political adversaries' children, and used village massacres, rape, and public beatings as weapons of terror, all with the implicit consent of the police and the military-led government. For instance, in September 1994, following a mass commemorating the third anniversary of Aristide's overthrow, thousands of people poured out of churches and into the streets in a show of support for Aristide. The demonstrators soon clashed violently with the FRAPH, and several people were killed. The U.S. military responded by raiding the FRAPH headquarters in Port-au-Prince, arresting thirty-five members of the organization, and confiscating weapons. The United States turned the building over to the people, who quickly destroyed it in vengeance.

Upon Aristide's reinstallation as president in 1994, his administration initiated investigations of certain members of the FRAPH for their involvement in human rights abuses. President René **Préval** (1996–2001) continued the investigations, though only one person had been tried and convicted by early 2000.

Lavalas

This political movement was created and popularized by President Jean-Bertrand **Aristide** (1991, 1994–1996, 2001—) in the early 1990s. Though the objective of the movement was to support the will of the Haitian people, it has also faced charges of corruption and political bullying.

The broad-based, loosely structured Lavalas movement grew out of a speech given by Aristide on the eve of his presidential election in 1990 in which he compared the changes that would occur in Haiti if he were elected president to a *lavalas*, the Creole word for a debris-clearing flood that follows a rainstorm. With foundations in ecclesiastical base communities, the movement incorporated urban and rural groups including the highly active Papaye Peasant Movement (Mouvman Peyizan Papaye, MMP), and successfully united the poor.

Its original objectives were to dismantle the vestiges of the dictatorship of Jean-Claude **Duvalier** (1971–1986) and prepare the country for democracy. The movement persisted despite violent repression during the period of military rule that followed Aristide's 1991 overthrow, and after Aristide's return in 1994, Lavalas sponsored a number of political candidates in different parties. René **Préval** (1996–2001) was elected to the presidency in 1995 on the Lavalas ticket, defeating Aristide, who had formed his own party, Lavalas Family (Famni Lavalas, FL), following a disagreement within Lavalas over an economic stabilization plan proposed by the International Monetary Fund (IMF) that Aristide believed compromised the will of the people.

Despite bitter government infighting, and charges of massive electoral fraud, harassment, and intimidation by opposition politicians against Aristide's supporters in the FL, the results of the local and parliamentary elections held in May 2000 suggested that Aristide and the FL continued to enjoy great popular support; those results were challenged by opposition forces. Aristide was victorious in the November 2000 presidential election, and the FL took all nine Senate seats contested in the concurrent legislative elections, giving the party all but one seat in the Senate. It also holds 80 percent of the Chamber of Deputies.

Lavalas Family (Famni Lavalas, FL). See Lavalas

Lescot, Élie. See Vincent, Sténio Joseph

L'Ouverture, François Dominique Toussaint (1743–1803)

François Dominique Toussaint L'Ouverture, the leader of the slave rebellion (1794–1802; see **1804 Revolution**) that liberated Saint-Domingue (modern Haiti) from French rule, is one of the greatest heroes of Haitian history.

L'Ouverture was born a slave on a Haitian plantation. He spent most of his life working in the privileged post of coachman, and also learned to read. In 1790 he joined the Spanish army positioned on the island of Hispaniola to challenge French ownership of Saint-Domingue, and quickly rose to third in command,

François Dominique Toussaint L'Ouverture was the leader of a slave rebellion that liberated Saint-Domingue (modern Haiti) from French rule in 1804. *Columbus Memorial Library, General Secretariat of the Organization of American States. Reproduced with permission of the Organization of American States.*

creating an army of over 4,000 blacks. After three years, he defected to the French forces (which included many former slaves), eventually leading them against the British, who threatened the island. From that position of leadership, L'Ouverture attempted to maintain large plantations to preserve Haiti's economy, parceled out vast plots of land to his favored generals, enforced the *fermage* (obligatory labor on the plantations), and invited plantation owners back to Haiti, fearing that the island's economy would crumble if the plantation system broke down. L'Ouverture also suppressed voodou in favor of Catholicism.

The French were eventually victorious in repelling the Spanish and British forces, and L'Ouverture was appointed governor of Saint-Domingue. However, hoping to liberate Saint-Domingue from France, L'Ouverture soon began to dismantle the French control structure, sending home the remaining French officials, declaring himself governor-general for life in 1801, and introducing a new constitution. In response, Napoleon sent French troops back to the island. L'Ouverture held off the French for a few months, and then suddenly surrendered. The French told L'Ouverture that he would be allowed to retire, but instead captured him and exiled

him to France, where he died two years later, sick from the freezing cold of his mountaintop prison. Furious at this betrayal, black commanders reinitiated the independence struggle. Preoccupied with a war against Britain, French troops withdrew within a year, and Haiti declared independence on January 1, 1804.

Magloire, Paul Eugène. See **Duvalier, François**

Manigat, Leslie. See **Namphy, Henri**

Namphy, Henri (1932–   )

General Henri Namphy, who ruled Haiti from June to September 1988, is remembered as one of the most brutal and heavy-handed rulers in the country's history.

Namphy headed the six-man junta known as the National Council of Government (Conseil National de Gouvernement, CNG, 1986–1988) that came to power following the downfall of the Duvalier dynasty (see **Duvalier**, François [1957–1971] and **Duvalier**, Jean-Claude [1971–1986]). While the CNG claimed that the government was civilian, most believed that it was firmly controlled by the military. To legitimize itself, the CNG held elections in November 1987. Many candidates campaigned hoping the contest would be free and fair, but as voters lined up on election day outside the Ecole Argentine in Port-au-Prince, armed thugs linked to Namphy raided the building, massacring at least seventeen people. Many considered the incident more violent than anything perpetrated by the Duvaliers. Namphy canceled the election results and attempted to rule as head of the CNG, but international pressure forced him to again hold elections.

Almost all the previous candidates refused to run in the highly fraudulent February 1988 contest, and less than a quarter of the population voted. The dubious honor of president was awarded to Leslie François Manigat (1988). Manigat appointed a cabinet of Duvalierists (supporters of the Duvalier dictatorships) despite the country's continuing rancor for them, and headed an administration deemed illegitimate by most, that Namphy appeared to control from behind the scenes. When Manigat tried to undermine Namphy by forcing the general to retire and then having him arrested in June 1988, Namphy ousted Manigat two days later, exiling him to the Dominican Republic.

Namphy took over as chief of state and abandoned all democratic pretenses. During his four months in power, Haiti's link to the international drug trade was established and strengthened; an estimated $700 million of drug money passed through the country every month during his regime. Human rights violations and violence against political dissidents and slum-dwellers soared. One of the regime's most violent acts occurred in September 1988: as outspoken anti-Duvalierist Jean-Bertrand **Aristide** (1991, 1994–1996, 2001—) said mass in his St. Jean-Bosco church, paramilitary troops and a gang of mercenaries invaded the building, slaughtering more than twelve of the Haitians and foreign journalists in attendance, wounding more than eighty more, and burning the church to the ground.

Namphy's obvious connections to the attack and his vicious autocratic rule prompted Colonel Prosper **Avril** (1988–1990), a prominent force behind the scenes of Namphy's regime, along with a group of minor officers, to overthrow the dictator. Namphy went into exile in the Dominican Republic.

National Council of Government (Conseil National de Gouvernement, CNG). See **Avril, Prosper; Namphy, Henri**

Négritude (also Noirisme)

Négritude is an ideology encouraging black pride and emphasizing African tradition. Many Haitian intellectuals and politicians, including François **Duvalier** (1957–1971), have aligned themselves with the movement that espouses it.

Race has played a major role in Haitian history, from the first slave rebellions leading to Haitian independence (see **1804 Revolution**) to the ongoing power struggles between blacks and mulattos. Racial tensions were exacerbated by the **United States intervention** (1915–1934) in Haiti, as the United States worked predominantly with the mulatto class, and as it was mostly white American soldiers who were sent to police the majority black Haitian population. The 1937 massacre of migrant Haitians by Dominican dictator Rafael Leonidas **Trujillo y Molina** (see Dominican Republic; see also **Haitian Massacre**, Dominican Republic) prompted even greater resentment of whites by blacks in Haiti.

Inspired by Jean Price-Mars' 1928 book, *Ainsi Parla l'Oncle* (*So Spoke the Uncle*), Duvalier and his associates formed the Griot movement to forward the cause of Négritude in Haiti. They practiced voodou and other African traditions, encouraged Haitians to abandon European-based culture, and advocated social justice. They formed the Noiriste Party and backed the election of Dumarsais Estimé (1946–1950), who granted labor the right to organize, implemented an income tax, allowed greater freedom of speech, and offered vaccinations to Haitians. Estimé was overthrown by a military coup in 1950 led by Paul Eugène Magloire (1950–1956), a member of the mulatto elite whose ideals were anathema to those of the movement.

Seven years later, the movement brought Duvalier to the presidency. Though Duvalier demonstrated his alliance with the poor masses and reevaluated Haitian history emphasizing its African heritage, his administration is remembered more for its brutality than for its

espousal of Négritude or its forwarding of the Noiriste Party.

Pascal-Trouillot, Ertha. See **Avril, Prosper**

Pétion, Alexandre Sabés (1770–1818)

In 1806, after the death of Jean-Jacques **Dessalines** (1804–1806), a power struggle erupted between Alexandre Sabés Pétion and Henri **Christophe** (northern Haitian ruler, 1807–1820) that divided Haiti into northern and southern regions. Pétion ruled the southern half of Haiti from 1807 to 1818.

Born into a wealthy family in Port-au-Prince, Pétion joined the French colonial army at the age of eighteen and rose to the rank of captain within three years. Fighting under François Dominique Toussaint **L'Ouverture** and Dessalines, Pétion proved to be a skilled soldier. Soon after his 1807 assumption of the presidency of the southern half of Haiti, Pétion dissolved what he considered to be the overly powerful Senate. While Pétion envisioned the country as a republic ruled by an oligarchy of mulattos, he did break up some of the large plantation estates and distribute them to black war veterans. He also ended the *fermage*, a system of forced labor that had been used during the rebellions that preceded the **1804 Revolution**.

Pétion's land reform measures won him widespread popularity, but caused economic problems as land that had once been devoted to export crops began to be used for subsistence farming on small family plots. Nonetheless, Pétion was reelected in 1811 and 1815. Upon Pétion's death in 1818, Jean-Pierre **Boyer** (1818–1843) assumed power in the south and later reunified Haiti.

Préval, René (1943–   )

Despite his campaign promises of reform and growth, René Préval's administration (1996–2001) was characterized by persistent political infighting and dire economic problems.

Préval was born in Port-au-Prince and received a degree in agronomy from the College of Gembloux in Belgium. In 1963 persecution by the regime of François **Duvalier** (1957–1971) forced Préval's family into exile. Préval returned to Haiti in 1975, and after the fall of Jean-Claude **Duvalier** (1971–1986), became active in political and social organizations. He aided in Jean-Bertrand **Aristide's** (1991, 1994–1996, 2001—) election to the presidency in 1991 and served as his prime minister until Aristide's 1991 ouster. Préval lived in exile in Washington, D.C., from 1992 to 1994. He defeated Aristide in the 1995 presidential contest, running on a **Lavalas** movement party ticket. The United States sent a security team to Haiti to guard the new president because the Haitian security forces were largely still loyal to Aristide. Street violence increased after Préval assumed office, and the president and his family were targeted by armed thugs.

Préval tried to activate Haiti's economy and implement the required reforms so that the nation could qualify for loans from the International Monetary Fund (IMF) through opening its markets (simultaneously offering domestic rewards) and privatizing inefficient state industries (concurrently granting small plots of land to landless peasants). The reforms, whose application Aristide had staunchly opposed, were unpopular with some sectors of the populace. In 1996 the U.S. troops that had been stationed in Haiti in 1994 to facilitate the reinstallation of Aristide were replaced by the 500-member U.S. Support Group in Haiti. Over the next four years, the group built miles of roads, wells for drinking water, and schools, treated thousands of Haitians for medical problems, and trained 250 Haitians to provide medical care. They also helped train the civilian police force, though that force continued to disregard and violate human rights. The last of these U.S. troops withdrew in January 2000.

Despite U.S. expenditure of more than $2 billion in military and economic aid, the Haitian economy never fully recovered from the international economic sanctions that had been applied to the country between 1991 and 1994 (see **Cédras, Raoul**), and remained in a shambles during Préval's administration. Further, legislative elections in which voters were to choose a third of the Senate, originally scheduled for April 1997, were postponed repeatedly, as were local contests. Prime Minister Rosny Smarth resigned in October 1997, disgusted by the government's inability to resolve the situation, and the opposition-controlled parliament repeatedly blocked Préval's nominations for prime minister, causing a two-year power struggle that tied up hundreds of millions of dollars of international aid and loans from donors (including the World Bank and the **Inter-American Development Bank** [IDB; see Appendix 2]). In January 1999 Préval installed Prime Minister Jacques-Edouard Alexis and appointed a new cabinet without the approval of Congress. When Congress objected, Préval dissolved the legislature (stating that parliament members' terms had expired) and subsequently ruled by decree. Violent street riots ensued, and opposition politicians, human rights organizations, and other countries sharply condemned the president's actions.

While parliamentary and local elections were eventually held in May 2000, the Senate contest was marred by reports of vote-counting irregularities, and a second round of voting scheduled for June 2000 was soon postponed. Presidential elections were held in November 2000, and Aristide was again victorious, garnering 92 percent of the vote in a contest boycotted by all of Haiti's major opposition parties, and marred by intimidation and violence.

Refugees

Between the 1970s and the 1990s, thousands of Haitians left their island home in small makeshift boats or crammed aboard larger cargo craft destined for the United States or the Bahamas. Propelled by Haiti's hopeless economic conditions, the continued threat of violence there, and hopes of finding safe haven or work elsewhere, these illegal immigrants often paid thousands of dollars to make the harrowing journey.

In 1981 about 8,000 Haitians attempted to enter the United States. That same year, U.S. president Ronald Reagan drew up an interdiction agreement with the government of Jean-Claude **Duvalier** (1971–1986) that called for the return of all Haitians intercepted on the high seas (with only cursory attempts to determine whether they faced political persecution at home) and granted the U.S. Coast Guard the ability to search boats in Haitian ports to detect potential illegal immigrants. The next year, fewer than 150 Haitians were intercepted as illegal immigrants. During the 1980s, many Haitians who were intercepted were quarantined at Guantanamo Bay, Cuba, sometimes for longer than a year. Human rights organizations criticized the conditions at Guantanamo Bay and the repressive treatment of the refugees by the U.S. military and the U.S. Immigration and Naturalization Service (INS). Other Haitians who were intercepted at sea were returned to Haiti because they were not considered political refugees. Although the United States promised to check up on repatriated refugees, many were arrested, beaten, and even murdered by Haitian police upon their return to Haiti.

Following the bloody ouster of Jean-Bertrand **Aristide** (1991, 1994–1996, 2001–) and the takeover by Raoul **Cédras** in 1991, the number of refugees at Guantanamo Bay increased, though U.S. president George Bush continued Reagan's policy of repatriation. By 1992 about 38,000 Haitians had fled the country, leading Bush to declare that all Haitians who were intercepted at sea would be returned to Haiti without exception. To counter that policy, during the U.S. presidential campaign in 1992, Democratic Party candidate Bill Clinton promised to offer immediate though temporary asylum to all Haitian refugees if he were elected. However, Clinton renounced his promise shortly after his election, stating that he would continue the Bush administration's policy. Following the 1994 U.S. intervention and the reinstallation of Aristide to the presidency, the United States stated that since Haiti now had a stable democracy, the United States would accept no refugees.

In 1997 an inter-governmental agreement was reached that granted Cuban and Central American immigrants special protection and offered them almost two years to apply for permanent U.S. residency. Haitian immigrants were not included in the agreement, and groups such as the National Association for the Advancement of Colored People (NAACP), the Southern Christian Leadership Conference, and the National Coalition for Haitian Refugees protested. In response, the United States promised to grant 50,000 Haitian refugees nine months to apply for permanent residency. Today about a million Haitians live in the United States, mostly in New York City and Miami, Florida, and send between $300 million to $1 billion back to Haiti annually.

Russell, John H. R. See United States Intervention

Tontons Macoute (Tonton-Makout in Creole) (also Volunteers for National Security [Voluntaires de la Securité National, VSN])

The Tontons Macoute were a paramilitary group used by President François **Duvalier** (1957–1971) and his son Jean-Claude **Duvalier** (1971–1986) to terrorize their enemies and intimidate Haitians into submission. The name of the paramilitary group comes from a Haitian folktale character who kidnaps bad children in a knapsack and eats them alive. The Tontons Macoute wore sunglasses, dressed in jeans, and tied red bandanas around their necks, personifying the voodou deity of farming. Members were mostly from the middle class, and it was rumored that they were trained by Rafael Leonidas **Trujillo y Molina** (see Dominican Republic). The Tontons Macoute received no salary, but were allowed to keep any money or goods they ransacked or extorted from their victims.

The elder Duvalier initially used the Tontons Macoute to subdue his political enemies, and later employed the group to enforce general repression throughout Haiti. While at first the dictator denied the group's existence, he attempted to legitimize it in 1962 by folding it into the Volunteers for National Security (Voluntaires de la Securité National, VSN), an army made up mostly of peasants. However, most Tontons Macoute did not officially join the VSN.

At its height in the mid-1980s the organization included approximately 9,000 members. However, under the younger Duvalier, the division between the Tontons Macoute and the army blurred. After the fall of the Duvalier dynasty, vengeance was sought against the Tontons Macoute in the *dechoukaj* (uprooting) of all things Duvalier. Violence was perpetrated against many lower-class members of the group, while middle-class soldiers escaped. In the late 1990s many former Tontons Macoute still roamed the streets of Haiti armed, contributing to the devastating violence that continues to disrupt life in the country.

United States Intervention (1915–1934)

In 1915 riots broke out in Haiti, and France threatened to invade the island to collect debts. Invoking the **Monroe Doctrine** (see Appendix 2), the United States sent marine forces to Port-au-Prince in July 1915 to restore order.

During the intervention, Brigadier General John H. Russell of the U.S. Marines controlled Haiti, overseeing the election of a series of puppet presidents while revoking freedom of speech and other rights. Little was done to improve education or diversify the economy, although U.S. investment in Haiti skyrocketed. In 1917 Franklin D. Roosevelt (then U.S. assistant secretary of the navy) drafted a new constitution for Haiti that put the country under U.S. control and allowed foreign ownership of Haitian land. U.S. Marines also trained a new army, the Haitian Guard (Garde d'Haiti), and U.S. troops placed Haitians in labor corvees and forced them to construct roads, bridges, sewage systems, and hospitals, and to install telephone and electric wires. Rural blacks led by Charlemagne Péraulte tried unsuccessfully to end the corvee system through a rebellion known as the War of the Cacos (1918–1920); approximately 3,000 Haitians died when U.S. troops crushed the rebellion. The presence of white U.S. soldiers and the U.S. restoration of mulatto businessmen and politicians to power heightened nationalism and racial awareness, and contributed to the development of **Négritude**, an African pride movement.

While it was agreed in 1930 that the United States would withdraw from Haiti, four years of negotiations followed the agreement, and it was not until 1934 that Haitian president Sténio Joseph **Vincent** (1930–1941) finally convinced U.S. president Franklin D. Roosevelt to pull the U.S. troops out. Many credit the intervention with uniting the Haitian people in a common cause: to rid the country of the U.S. troops.

Vincent, Sténio Joseph (1874–1959)

President Sténio Joseph Vincent (1930–1941) presided over the 1934 withdrawal of U.S. Marines after the **United States intervention** (1915–1934). He considered himself Haiti's second liberator and encouraged a sense of nationalism in Haitians.

After serving as mayor of Port-au-Prince, Vincent won the presidency in 1930, enjoying widespread support across class and color boundaries. As part of the mulatto elite, he was suspicious of the Haitian Guard (Garde d'Haiti), the mostly black army created and trained by the U.S. Marines during their occupation of Haiti. Upon assuming office, he rewrote the constitution, taking power from the legislature and investing it in the executive. In 1934, after years of negotiation between Haiti and the United States, Vincent convinced U.S. president Franklin D. Roosevelt to withdraw the remaining U.S. troops from Haiti. Reelected in 1934, Vincent extended his second term from four to six years through questionable means and then expelled the Senate. In 1937 Vincent drew major criticism from blacks when he offered no retaliation after Dominican dictator Rafael Leonidas **Trujillo y Molina** (see Dominican Republic) ordered his army to round up migrant Haitians and massacre them leading to the death of between 18,000 and 25,000 Haitians (see **Haitian Massacre**, Dominican Republic). Vincent conceded office when his second term ended in 1941 without further attempt to extend his rule, aware of his unpopularity among black Haitians.

Vincent was succeeded by Élie Lescot (1941–1946), who also favored the mulatto elite over poor blacks; the two leaders' attitudes hastened the racial consciousness-raising that was occurring among the black population (see **Négritude**). Lescot aligned his policies closely with U.S. interests, courted foreign business, and (using World War II as an excuse) implemented harsh domestic policies, suspending the constitution and confiscating the lands of Germans and Italians on the island. He resigned in January 1946 amid riots and general chaos.

HEADS OF STATE

Jean-Jacques Dessalines	1804
Jacques I (Dessalines)	1804–1806
Henri Christophe (Northern Haiti)	1807–1811
Henri I (Northern Haiti)	1811–1820
Alexandre Sabés Pétion (Southern Haiti)	1807–1818
Jean-Pierre Boyer	1818–1843
Rule by Executive Council	1843
Rivière Hérard	1843–1844
Philippe Guerrier	1844–1845
Louis Pierrot	1845–1846
Jean Baptiste Riché	1846–1847
Faustin Soulouque	1847–1849
Faustin I	1849–1859
Fabre Geffrard	1859–1867
Sylvain Salnave	1867–1869
Rule by Executive Council	1869–1870
Nissage Saget	1870–1874
Michel Domingue	1874–1876
Boisrond-Canal	1876–1879
Lysius Félicité Salomon	1879–1888
Rule by Executive Council	1888
François Denys Légitime	1888–1889
Rule by Executive Council	1889
Florvil Hyppolite	1889–1896
Tirésias Simon Sam	1896–1902
Rule by Executive Council	1902
Nord Alexis	1902–1908
Antoine Simon	1908–1911
Cincinnatus Leconte	1911–1912
Tancrède Auguste	1912–1913
Michel Oreste	1913–1914
Oreste Zamor	1914
Davilmar Théodore	1914–1915
Vilbrun Guillaume Sam	1915
Sudre Dartiguenave	1915–1922
Louis Borno	1922–1930
Louis Eugène Roy	1930
Sténio Joseph Vincent	1930–1941
Élie Lescot	1941–1946
Rule by Executive Military Government	1946
Dumarsais Estimé	1946–1950
Rule by Junta	1950
Paul Eugène Magloire	1950–1956
Nemours Pierre-Louis	1956–1957
Franck Sylvain	1957
Rule by Executive Council	1957
Daniel Fignolé	1957
Rule by Military Council	1957
François Duvalier	1957–1971
Jean-Claude Duvalier	1971–1986
Rule by CNG: National Council of Government (Conseil National de Gouvernement)	1986–1988
Leslie François Manigat	1988
Henri Namphy	1988
Prosper Avril	1988–1990
Hérard Abraham	1990
Ertha Pascal-Trouillot	1990–1991
Jean-Bertrand Arisitide	1991
Joseph C. Nerette	1991–1992
Marc Louis Bazin	1992–1993
Jean-Bertrand Aristide	1994–1996
René Préval	1996–2001
Jean-Bertrand Aristide	2001–

Source: Patricia Schutt-Ainé, *Haiti, A Basic Reference Book: General Information on Haiti* (Miami: Librairie au Service de la Culture, 1994).

BIBLIOGRAPHY

Print Resources

Aristide, Jean-Bertrand, with Christophe Wargny. *Aristide: An Autobiography.* Translated by Linda M. Maloney. Maryknoll, NY: Orbis Books, 1993.

Danticat, Edwidge. *The Farming of Bones.* New York: Soho Press, 1998.

Diederich, Bernard. *Papa Doc—Haiti and Its Dictator.* New York: Harmondsworth, Penguin, 1972.

James, C.L.R. *The Black Jacobins: Toussaint L'Ouverture and the San Domingo Revolution.* New York: Vintage Books, 1963.

Lundahl, Mats. *Peasants and Poverty: A Study of Haiti*. New York: St. Martin's Press, 1979.

MacFadyen, Deidre, and Pierre LaRamée, with Mark Fried and Fred Rosen, eds. *Haiti: Dangerous Crossroads*. Boston: South End Press (for the North American Congress on Latin America), 1995.

Nicholls, David. *From Dessalines to Duvalier: Race Colour, and National Independence in Haiti*. Cambridge: Cambridge University Press, 1979.

Plummer, Brenda Gayle. *Haiti and the United States: The Psychological Moment*. Athens: University of Georgia Press, 1992.

Price-Mars, Jean. *So Spoke the Uncle*. (Translated by Magadline W. Shannon). Washington, DC: Three Continents Press, 1983.

Ridgeway, James, ed. *The Haiti Files: Decoding the Crisis*. Washington, DC: Essential Books, 1994.

Schmidt, Hans. *The Occupation of Haiti, 1915–1934*. New Brunswick, NJ: Rutgers University Press, 1971.

Shacochis, Bob. *The Immaculate Invasion*. New York: Viking, 1999

Trouillot, Michel-Rolph. *Haiti, State Against Nation: The Origins and Legacy of Duvalierism*. New York: Monthly Review Press, 1990.

Wilentz, Amy. *The Rainy Season: Haiti since Duvalier*. New York: Simon and Schuster, 1989.

Electronic Resources

Haiti Info
http://www.haiti-info.com/
Offers comprehensive national and international news coverage, with an emphasis on Haitian politics and economics. (In French)

infohaiti.com
http://www.theworldpress.com/ru/newspap/haiti/info.htm
Offers comprehensive national and international news coverage, with an emphasis on Haitian politics and economics. (In French)

Latin American Network Information Center (LANIC): Haiti
http://lanic.utexas.edu/la/cb/haiti/
Haiti section of this extensive Web site contains hundreds of links to research resources, cultural centers, economic and business institutions, government agencies, historical sources, magazines and other periodicals, nongovernmental organizations, and grassroots groups. (In English)

Political Database of the Americas: Haiti
http://www.georgetown.edu/pdba/Countries/haiti.html
Comprehensive database run as a joint project of Georgetown University and the Organization of American States. Section on Haiti contains information on and links to the executive, legislative, and judicial branches of the Haitian government; electoral laws and election results; and other political data. (In English, Spanish, Portuguese, and French)

Political Resources.net: Haiti
http://www.politicalresources.net/haiti.htm
Haiti section of a Web Site containing a wealth of links to sources of information about national politics. Includes information on political parties, legislative and executive institutions, laws and legislation, and elections, as well as a link to the constitution. (In English)

Wilfried Derksen's Elections Around the World: Haiti
http://www.agora.it/elections/haiti.htm
Haiti section of a comprehensive database of results from elections around the world. Contains results from recent national executive and legislative elections, as well as explanations of and links to political parties and institutions. (In English)

HONDURAS

COUNTRY PROFILE

Official name	República de Honduras
Capital	Tegucigalpa
Type/structure of government	Democratic (presidential) republic
Executive	President elected by direct and universal vote to four-year nonrenewable term; cabinet appointed by the president.
Legislative	Unicameral Congress (National Assembly) with 128 popularly elected members.
Judicial	The highest court is the Supreme Court of Justices, composed of nine judges and seven alternates elected by Congress to four-year terms.
Major political parties	**Honduran Liberal Party** (Partido Liberal Hondureño, PLH) and **Honduran National Party** (Partido Nacional Hondureño, PNH); many small parties exist but play a minor role in government.
Constitution in effect	1982
Location/geography	Bounded on the north and east by the Caribbean Sea, on the southeast by Nicaragua, on the southwest by the Pacific Ocean and El Salvador, and on the west by Guatemala. Mostly mountains in interior, narrow coastal plains.
Geographic area	112,492 sq. km.
Population	6.25 million (2000 est.)
Ethnic groups	Mestizo 90%; indigenous 7%; black (of African descent) 2%; white (of European descent) 1%
Religions	Roman Catholic 93%; Protestant minority
Literacy rate	71% (1998)
Infant mortality rate	36 deaths per 1,000 live births (1998)
Life expectancy	69 years (1998)
Monetary unit	Lempira
Exchange rate	1 U.S. dollar = 14.7318 lempiras (August 2000)*
Major exports	Coffee, bananas, shrimp and lobster, minerals, meat, lumber
Major imports	Machinery and transport equipment, industrial raw materials, chemical products, manufactured goods, fuel and oil, foodstuffs
GDP	$5.3 billion (1998)
GDP growth rate	3% (1998)
GDP per capita	$730 (1998)

Latin American Weekly Report, August 22, 2000 (WR-00-33), p. 394.

Sources: *CIA World Factbook 1999*. http://www.cia.gov/cia/publications/factbook/geos/ho.html; *Honduras at a Glance*, World Bank. http://wbln0018.worldbank.org/External/lac/lac.nsf/countries/Honduras

OVERVIEW

Summary

Honduras, one of the largest Central American republics, is among the poorest countries in the Western Hemisphere, suffering from high unemployment and a large external debt. Honduras' chief agricultural exports are subject to dramatic price fluctuations, adding to economic insecurity. The United States is the country's main export market and import supplier, and Honduras relies heavily on the international community for economic aid. In the mid- to late 1990s, the government made strides toward economic stability, including lowering the inflation rate, but foreign debt continues to be a heavy burden. The country has suffered authoritarian rule and political instability throughout its history. While Honduras did not experience severe civil conflict in the 1970s and 1980s as did several of its Central American neighbors, military involvement in politics has been perpetuated by regional political turmoil.

History

Prior to the arrival of the Spanish in the 1500s, the Mayan civilization occupied a large portion of the western part of the area that is today Honduras. The Maya were the most advanced of the indigenous civilizations that populated the area, and at their peak controlled parts of modern Mexico, Guatemala, Honduras, and El Salvador. While this sophisticated civilization had al-

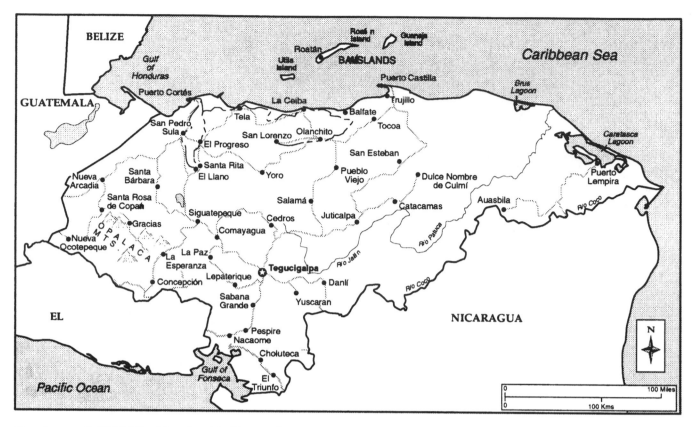

Honduras. © *1998 The Moschovitis Group, Inc.*

ready declined by the time the Spanish reached what is today Central America, the resistance efforts of a Lenca Indian named Lempira inspired a major indigenous revolt in 1537, which marked the most aggressive challenge that the Spanish faced from the indigenous population during their conquest of the area. The modern Honduran monetary unit is the lempira, named after this national hero. The present-day descendants of the Maya make up only a small percentage of the country's population, and Western clothing and the Spanish language have replaced their native dress and idiom.

Like most countries of Central America, Honduras joined Mexico in declaring its independence from Spain, without much warfare, on September 15, 1821. Agustín Cosme Damian de **Iturbide**'s (see Mexico) Mexican empire then ruled Honduras until 1823, when a congress of the Central American provinces met and established the **United Provinces of Central America** (see Appendix 1). Conflict within the union soon arose, however, leading to bloody civil wars between 1826 and 1829. Francisco **Morazán** (1827–1828, 1829, 1830) led Liberal forces to victory and served as president of the federation until it began to dissolve in the late 1830s. In 1838 Honduras became a sovereign nation.

For most of the period from 1840 to the 1870s a series of Conservative dictatorships, notably those of Francisco Ferrera (1833–1834, 1841–1844), Juan Lindo (1848–1852), and J. Santos Guardiola (1862),

ruled the republic. Elections meant little and revolutions were frequent. Central American states often intervened in each other's affairs during the period, and it was with the support of Liberal Guatemalan president Justo Rufino **Barrios** (see Guatemala) that Liberals José Trinidad Cabañas (1852–1855), Marco Aurelio Soto (1876–1883), and Luis Bográn Barahona (1883–1891) ruled Honduras. The transfer of the capital from Conservative Comayagua to Liberal Tegucigalpa in 1880 reflected both the triumph of the Liberals and the renewed emphasis on mining, which the government stimulated by attracting foreign investment. U.S. mining companies played a major role in late nineteenth-century Honduran economic growth, although Honduras remained the least developed country in Central America. Liberal dictators also dominated the state in the early twentieth century, beginning to emphasize modernization and exports.

In the early twentieth century U.S. fruit companies with operations in Honduras, notably United Fruit (see **Keith**, Minor Cooper, Costa Rica), Standard Fruit and Cuyamel, rapidly made bananas the principal export of the country as they competed ruthlessly for favorable concessions from the Liberal governments. The economic and political influence of the United States in Honduran affairs increased with the rise of the **banana industry**. When President Miguel R. Dávila (1907–1911) tried to halt the land concessions given to these companies in 1910, he was overthrown by a group of

A view of Tegucigalpa, the capital of Honduras. *Columbus Memorial Library, General Secretariat of the Organization of American States. Reproduced with permission of the Organization of American States.*

U.S. adventurers, who eventually replaced him with Manuel Bonilla (1903–1907, 1912–1913). The fruit companies gave Honduras a major export commodity, developed its Caribbean ports, and indirectly facilitated the growth of the Honduran city of San Pedro Sula into the major population center on the Central American Caribbean plain. However, they contributed little to the general development of the country.

Dictator Tiburcio **Carías Andino** (1933–1948) strengthened the military at the expense of democracy and greatly improved the country's infrastructure with roads and air service to remote areas. Carías selected his successor, Juan Manuel Gálvez (1949–1954), who allowed greater expression by the opposition **Honduran Liberal Party** (Partido Liberal Hondureño, PLH). After 1948 the military and the landholding elite governed the country and resisted political, social, or economic modernization. When no candidate received a majority of the vote in the presidential election of 1954, congressional leader Julio Lozano Díaz (1954–1957) assumed the presidency and created a government with the support of the three candidates. Lozano Díaz was forced out by the military in 1957 when it became clear that he had no intention of leaving office. A Constituent Assembly elected Ramón Villeda Morales (1957–1963) president in 1957. He led the country into the **Central American Common Market** (CACM, see Appendix 1), initiated programs for agrarian reform and education, and tried

to implement the U.S. assistance program, the **Alliance for Progress** (see Appendix 2).

His policies, combined with apprehension over the rise of communism in Cuba, brought about a coup led by Colonel Oswaldo **López Arellano** (1963–1971, 1972–1975) in 1963. Under López Arellano, the fragile Honduran economy was further weakened by a brief but costly war with El Salvador in 1969 (see **Soccer War**, Appendix 1). The final blow for López Arellano was the exposure in 1974 of a $250,000 bribe paid to government officials by United Brands (successor to United Fruit). The army helped Colonel Juan Alberto Melgar Castro (1975–1978) take power in 1975, but he was ousted in 1978 in another coup, led by General Policarpo Paz García (1978–1982). Paz García made some progress toward constitutional government, and the military returned official control to civilian leaders via elections in 1982.

The central problem for Honduras in the late 1970s and the 1980s was political instability in neighboring countries, specifically the civil wars taking place in Nicaragua, El Salvador, and Guatemala. Liberal presidents Robert **Suazo Córdova** (1982–1986) and José Simón **Azcona Hoyo** (1986–1990) operated under the watchful eye of the Honduran generals and were greatly influenced by the military and the United States. During the 1980s there were numerous human rights violations against leftists in Honduras. The 1990s brought greater peace to the region, particularly by the middle of the decade, when all three civil wars had ended. President Rafael Leonardo **Callejas Romero** (1990–1994) of the **Honduran National Party** (Partido Nacional Hondureño, PNH) implemented unpopular neoliberal economic policies, which, in tandem with charges of corruption against his administration, enabled the PLH to win the 1994 and 1998 presidential elections. Further, in the 1990s, there was a move away from excessive military intervention in civilian politics, especially by president Carlos Roberto **Reina Idiáques** (1994–1998). Reina strengthened civilian control by removing the police from under the jurisdiction of the military and putting the armed forces under a civilian defense minister beginning in 1999.

The country entered the new millennium under the administration of President Carlos Roberto **Flores Facussé** (1998–2002), a newspaper publisher and former president of the Honduran Congress. His biggest challenge was reconstructing the economy and national infrastructure, which were devastated when **Hurricane Mitch** slammed through Honduras in October 1998. The hurricane, which killed an estimated 5,500–7,000 people, resulted in the loss of as much as 70 percent of the nation's crops, and caused damage to roads and other infrastructure that was expected to cost billions of dollars to repair. Some observers believed that the storm set the nation's development back by decades. Flores remained popular as the country tried to address its serious problems. Presidential and legislative elections were held in November 2001, and Ricardo Maduro Joest (2002–) of the PNH assumed the presidency in early 2002, marking the fifth consecutive time that power had peacefully and constitutionally changed hands since Honduras' transition to democracy in 1982.

ENTRIES

Alvarez Martínez, Gustavo Adolfo (1937–1989)
General Gustavo Adolfo Alvarez Martínez was head of the Honduran armed forces from 1982 to 1984.

Alvarez was born in Tegucigalpa in 1937 and studied military affairs in Honduras, Argentina, Guatemala, Peru, and the United States. He graduated from Peru's School of War (Escuela de Guerra) in 1972. In 1978 he became commander of the Fourth Infantry Battalion in La Ceiba, Honduras. Virulently anticommunist, Alvarez led a group of officers known as the "iron circle" that controlled the military in the early 1980s. As head of the Honduran armed forces, he established great individual control of the military, as well as political influence, and he was the major force behind the increase in violent repression against the left in the 1980s. He strongly supported U.S. president Ronald Reagan's anticommunist policies in the country and in Central America; for instance, he allowed Salvadoran troops to train on Honduran territory at Puerto Castilla on the North Coast during the Salvadoran **civil war of the 1980s** (see El Salvador).

His concentration of personal power led to his replacement by General Walter López Reyes. Exiled to Costa Rica, he later lived in Miami before returning to Honduras, where he was assassinated by leftists known as the Cinchonero Popular Liberation Movement (Movimiento Popular de Liberación Cinchonero, MPLC; see **Guerrilla Groups**) on January 25, 1989.

Azcona Hoyo, José Simón (1927–)
Under the administration of José Simón Azcona Hoyo (1986–1990), a member of the **Honduran Liberal Party** (Partido Liberal Hondureño, PLH), the Honduran military and the United States continued to play a significant role in dictating national policy.

Born in the North Coast city of La Ceiba in 1927, Azcona graduated from the National University in 1970. An active member of the PLH, he was elected to the party's Central Executive Council (Consejo Central Ejecutivo) in 1977 and in 1979 became the chair of organization and campaigning of the council. He supported Roberto **Suazo Cordova**'s (1982–1986) presidential candidacy in 1982, but later withdrew his backing after not being reelected to the presidency of the PLH Central Executive Council.

Due to reforms in the electoral law (which mandated that the presidency was not awarded to the individual who received the highest number of popular votes, but rather to the candidate of the political party that won the most votes), Azcona won the December 1985 presidential elections despite having received fewer popular votes than Rafael Leonardo **Callejas Romero** (1990–1994), the candidate of the **Honduran National Party** (Partido Nacional Hondureño, PNH). Once in office, Azcona continued his predecessor's tendency of yielding to the interests of the military as well as the Cold War geopolitics of the United States. With Nicaragua and El Salvador embroiled in civil wars, the United States (which was involved in both conflicts) sent large amounts of military aid to Honduras during Azcona's term and used joint exercises with the Honduran military to fight leftists both within and outside of the country.

Honduras' economic and social crisis deepened during Azcona's presidency. Divisions within the PLH and disagreements between the PLH-controlled executive and the legislature limited his power. Honduras' external debt increased during his term in office and the currency was devalued, benefiting the national exporting sector, whose members had become influential by the end of the 1980s.

Banana Industry
Bananas have long been one of Honduras' most important exports, and have played a key role in the Honduran economy throughout the twentieth century. The U.S.-based United Fruit Company (see **Keith**, Minor Cooper, Costa Rica) came to Honduras in the early 1900s and set up banana plantations along the North Coast. Two of its centers of production were in the Sula Valley near San Pedro Sula and the beach resort town of Tela.

After suffering poor treatment and exploitation at the hands of foreign banana companies (which enjoyed the support of the military and the government of Honduras) for five decades, Honduran workers finally carried out a general strike in 1954. Though the strike hindered the banana companies' production, the companies had enough financial assets to wait out the strike. Eventually the poor workers had no other option but to return to work, though they did win some concessions. The strike marked the start of what would become a substantial labor movement in Honduras that would eventually successfully promote labor reform. The banana companies had less influence during the second administration of Oswaldo **López Arellano** (1963–1971, 1972–1975) and had to resort to bribes to see their desired policies implemented. United Brands (formerly United Fruit) offered a $1.25 million bribe to Honduran minister of the economy Abraham Bennaton Ramos and another to López Arellano to remove a recently imposed tax on bananas. Once the bribes had been uncovered, popular outrage over the payoffs led to a renewed sense of nationalism and anti-imperialism as well as the end of López Arellano's regime in early 1975.

The banana companies operating in Honduras have been repeatedly criticized for exploiting workers and monopolizing the country's most fertile lands, leaving these areas unavailable for Hondurans to cultivate. Despite this criticism, the country's North Coast has generally enjoyed a higher standard of living than the rest of the country because of the jobs created by the banana companies located there. In addition, the companies have been controversial due to the power they have historically wielded in local and national politics. Although their influence has diminished, bananas continue to be an import export crop, and the destruction caused to the industry by **Hurricane Mitch** in 1998 had a significant economic impact on Honduras. Further, while recently coffee production has begun to outpace banana production, the companies serve as a reminder of the corruption and economic dependence of years past.

Battalion 3-16

Battalion 3-16, a battalion of the Honduran military, functioned as a death squad charged with subduing and silencing Hondurans thought to be members of **guerrilla groups** during the early 1980s. The group's repression was effective in preventing the spread of leftist guerrilla activity, and political violence in Honduras was less widespread than in other countries in the region. The actions and virtual impunity of Battalion 3-16 demonstrated the extraordinary power and influence enjoyed by the Honduran military in the 1980s.

During the tenure of Gustavo Adolfo **Alvarez Martínez** as head of the military in the early 1980s, more than 140 political disappearances were attributed to Battalion 3-16. Paramilitary death squad activity continued throughout the decade, though it was much less prevalent during the latter half. In the late 1980s two Honduran defectors and former members of Battalion 3-16 living in exile spoke out about their experiences on the death squad and the atrocities they witnessed, admitting that the group's violence usually involved innocent victims, and asserting that the United States aided the group in planning and executing its work.

Early in the administration of Carlos Roberto **Reina Idiáques** (1994–1998) ten arrest warrants were issued for senior military officials associated with disappearances that occurred in 1982, and additional warrants were issued in 1996. Nonetheless, the armed forces refused to accept responsibility for the disappearances. The military continued to protect (and pay) the charged officers, who went into hiding; corrupt courts and death threats to judges made prosecution even more difficult.

Callejas Romero, Rafael Leonardo (1943–   )

Rafael Leonardo Callejas Romero (1990–1994) implemented unpopular neoliberal economic policies, and ac-

cusations of corruption and scandal plagued his administration. Nonetheless, the Callejas administration was one of the first civilian governments to assert itself against the Honduran military.

Born in Tegucigalpa and a graduate of the University of Mississippi in agronomy, Callejas served as minister of natural resources in the early 1970s and was treasurer of the **Honduran National Party** (Partido Nacional Hondureño, PNH) from 1980 to 1982. He lost the 1985 presidential election despite winning more popular votes than José Simón **Azcona Hoya** (1986–1990) due to the stipulations of a new electoral law, but was elected president in 1989. As chief executive, Callejas pursued neoliberal economic reforms. He also initiated land redistribution (though some claimed that the land parceled out was consolidated in the hands of foreign companies) and ended the country's tradition of fixing the exchange rate at two *lempiras* per dollar in 1990 (which resulted in high inflation and even greater economic hardship for the Honduran people). Honduras had received a great deal of military and economic aid from the United States during the 1980s in return for Honduran assistance and complicity in U.S. efforts to quell the civil unrest in neighboring countries, and the decrease in that assistance following the achievement of peace in the region made attaining economic stability in Honduras even more difficult in the 1990s.

A human rights commission formed in 1993 reported that military and civilian leaders were responsible for over 300 political murders as well as the torture of prisoners during the 1979–1990 period. Callejas resisted two coup attempts by the military, in January 1991 and February 1993, the second of which was in response to his administration's efforts to begin human rights abuse proceedings against members of the military, including former officers of **Battalion 3–16** and other special army units that had been led by generals Gustavo Adolfo **Alvarez Martínez** and Discua Elvir.

By 1992 Callejas began to draw increased criticism from a wide range of interests, including trade unions, peasants, indigenous groups, the Catholic Church, and the private sector. At issue were his administration's economic policies and their harsh results, as well as what appeared to be the regime's rampant corruption. Due to popular discontent, voters switched their political allegiance to the opposition **Honduran Liberal Party** (Partido Liberal Hondureño, PLH), which won the next two presidential elections in 1993 and 1997.

Carías Andino, Tiburcio (1876–1969)

Tiburcio Carías Andino ruled Honduras from 1933 to 1948, using repression to maintain his hold on power.

Carías was born in Tegucigalpa in 1876, where he studied law. He joined the **Honduran Liberal Party** (Partido Liberal Hondureño, PLH) and participated in the civil war that removed General Domingo Vázquez

Tiburcio Carías Andino ruled Honduras between 1933 and 1948. *Columbus Memorial Library, General Secretariat of the Organization of American States. Reproduced with permission of the Organization of American States.*

(1893–1894) and the Conservatives from office in 1894. He was forced to leave Honduras in 1904 after opposing a coup against Manuel Bonilla (1903–1907, 1912–1913), whom Carías had supported in the 1902 elections. He lived temporarily in El Salvador and later returned to Honduras. In 1919 he supported unsuccessful presidential candidate Alberto Membreño (1915–1916) of the conservative **Honduran National Party** (Partido Nacional Hondureño, PNH), and soon withdrew from the PLH. While there were multiple reasons for his departure, the fact that his presidential aspirations were constrained by other figures in the party played an important role. Carías ran on the ticket of the PNH in the 1924 presidential election and defeated the two Liberal candidates; however, since he did not achieve the absolute majority required by the constitution, and since the PLH-dominated Congress would not declare him the winner, President Rafael López Gutiérrez (1920–1924) retained office. This led to civil war in 1924, and to eventual U.S. mediation of the conflict, López Gutiérrez's removal, and the election of Vicente Tosta (1924–1925) as interim president. Carías became Tosta's minister of the interior. Carías lost the 1928 presidential election to PLH candidate Vicente Mejía Colindres (1929–1933), but was finally elected in 1932 on the PNH ticket.

Carías consolidated his personal rule by strengthening his relationship with the military, and by winning the favor of the powerful banana companies (see **banana industry**) by repressing labor uprisings. He garnered international support by continuing to pay debts even at the height of the Great Depression. He controlled political opposition by outlawing the Communist Party shortly after taking office, and later by restricting the political activities of the opposition PLH and limiting freedom of the press in 1935. Carías rewrote the constitution in 1936 to allow for his reelection for six more years. When opponents tried to force him from office in 1936 and 1937, he imprisoned or exiled them, and by the end of the decade, the PNH was the only political party of any significance. In 1940 the constitution was again amended to allow Carías to remain in power until January 1, 1949. Though popular pressure forced him to call for elections in 1948 and prevented him from running as a candidate, he maintained his grip on the country by selecting Juan Manuel Gálvez (1949–1954) to run as the (ultimately victorious) PNH candidate. While Carías continued to be extremely influential in governing the country, Gálvez implemented many of his own policies as well.

Flores Facussé, Carlos (1950–)

Carlos Flores Facussé (1998–2002) of the **Honduran Liberal Party** (Partido Liberal Hondureño, PLH) helped Honduras to recover after a hurricane devastated the nation in October 1998.

Born in Tegucigalpa in 1950, Flores earned a degree in industrial engineering and a graduate degree in international economics from Louisiana State University. He advanced quickly in Honduran politics, aided by the fact that he owned and edited *La Tribuna*, one of the country's most important newspapers. He was an important aide in the administration of Roberto **Suazo Córdova** (1982–1986) and also served as a congressman in the 1980s. He lost the 1989 presidential election to Rafael Leonardo **Callejas Romero** (1990–1994), the candidate of the **Honduran National Party** (Partido Nacional Hondureño, PNH), and later served as president of the Honduran Congress from 1994 to 1997.

Flores, elected to the presidency in November 1997, had held the nation's highest office only nine months before **Hurricane Mitch** hit in October 1998. His subsequent efforts were directed at revitalizing the country's battered infrastructure and devastated economy, reconstructing roads, bridges, houses, and other structures and services damaged or interrupted by the hurricane, and soliciting international aid to help repair the destruction. Additionally, early in Flores' administration, tensions rose between Nicaragua and Honduras over ocean territory off the coast of Nicaragua thought to contain large petroleum reserves. Honduras ratified a treaty with Colombia that recognized Colombia's right to this area of the continental shelf, angering Nicaragua. In spite of these challenges, the Flores administration enjoyed widespread support. Flores yielded the presidency to Ricardo Maduro Joest (2002–) of the PNH in early 2002.

Guerrilla Groups

Various leftist guerrilla groups became active in Honduras in the early 1980s and carried out violent acts throughout the decade and into the early 1990s. Most Honduran guerrilla groups were extremely small, numbering less than 100 members. The largest, the Cinchonero Popular Liberation Movement (Movimiento Popular de Liberación Cinchonero, MPLC), included no more than 300 members. Another group, the Morazanist Front (Frente Morazanista), was founded in 1980 and named after Honduran national hero Francisco **Morazán** (1827–1828, 1829, 1830), who tried to maintain a united Central America after the area gained independence from Spain and Mexico (see **United Provinces of Central America**, Appendix 1). The Lorenzo Zelaya Popular Revolutionary Forces (Fuerzas Revolucionarias Populares de Lorenzo Zelaya), also founded in 1980, were named in honor of a communist peasant leader murdered in 1965. The Honduran Revolutionary Party of Central American Workers (Partido Revolucionario Hondureño de Trabajadores de Centroamérica) formed in 1976, but was virtually eliminated in 1983 when the armed forces attacked about 100 members in the town of Olancho in perhaps the largest confrontation between the military and armed guerrilla groups.

The Honduran military's overall response to these groups was swift and brutal. Aware that guerrilla activity and government retaliation had evolved into full-scale civil war in neighboring Nicaragua, El Salvador, and Guatemala, the Honduran armed forces were intent on preventing the escalation of armed resistance in Honduras. Despite the military's strong repression, these groups successfully took hostages, bombed U.S. soldiers stationed in Honduras, and even bombed the U.S. Peace Corps office in Tegucigalpa in 1989. Among the political assassinations they carried out was that of General Gustavo **Alvarez Martínez** in January 1989.

In general, however, guerrilla activity in Honduras was on a much smaller scale than in neighboring Central American republics; Honduran guerrilla groups never gained the degree of popular support that similar groups in those neighboring republics enjoyed, and as a result were never of great significance in Honduras and never threatened the governing elite for control of the country. By the end of the 1990s, the extreme military repression of the 1980s, the restoration of democracy with greater political incorporation, and the end of neighboring countries' conflicts reduced Honduran leftist groups to virtual inactivity.

Honduran Liberal Party (Partido Liberal Hondureño, PLH)

The Honduran Liberal Party (Partido Liberal Hondureño, PLH), officially founded in 1891 by Policarpo Bonilla (1894–1899), emerged from the modernizing, anticlerical nineteenth-century liberalism embodied in Honduras by Marco Aurelio Soto (1876–1883). The PLH and the **Honduran National Party** (Partido Nacional Hondureño, PNH) have traditionally been Honduras' two dominant political parties. The PLH has historically had a broad base of support composed of landowners, small farmers, the rural middle class, urban professionals, and businessmen. The party originally advocated checks on the strength of the armed forces and greater government intervention in the economy through limited land reform, public investment, and the provision of social services. These traditions ended in the 1980s as PLH governments presided over a military buildup and implemented economic austerity packages mandated by the International Monetary Fund (IMF). Since then, progressive elements have had less of a voice within the party. Nonetheless, since Honduras's transition to democracy in 1982, the PLH has consistently been an important political force. Since 1990, the party held the presidency from 1994 to 2002. It also held a majority in the National Assembly from 1994 to 1998 and a plurality from 1998 to 2002. The party again fielded a broad array of candidates in the legislative elections of November 2001.

Honduran National Party (Partido Nacional Hondureño, PNH)

The Honduran National Party (Partido Nacional Hondureño, PNH) evolved from the Conservative Party. It emerged under the second administration of President Ponciano Leiva (1873–1876, 1891–1893) to become the principal opposition to the **Honduran Liberal Party** (Partido Liberal Hondureño, PLH); the Liberals had dominated Honduran politics since the 1870s. While the PNH is to the right of the PLH on the political spectrum, the PNH is not strongly ideological, and in fact, the parties' ideologies have traditionally been similar. Even with the political opening and growth of political parties in the 1980s and 1990s, the PLH and the PNH continue to be the leading political parties in Honduras.

Originally made up of disenchanted Liberals (who subsequently left the party in 1902) and traditional nineteenth-century Conservatives, the PNH became a more cohesive organization when Tiburcio **Carías Andino** (1933–1948) became its leader in the 1920s. The party was tightly linked to the landowning elite, and though initially committed to nationalism, became closely allied to the U.S.-owned United Fruit Company. During the 1950s the party developed very strong ties to the Honduran army, and the modern PNH is supported by the conservative sectors of the business class and large sectors of the peasantry.

With the return of democracy to the country in 1982, the PNH was penalized for its close association with the military, and was defeated in successive elections in

1982 and 1985. In 1989 PNH candidate Rafael Leonardo **Callejas Romero** (1990–1994) finally won the presidency; however, the Callejas administration was rife with corruption, and its neoliberal economic reforms cost Callejas and the PNH popularity. The PNH became much more independent of the armed forces in the 1990s, and though it still lost the presidential elections of 1993 and 1997, it regained control of the nation's highest office in 2002 following the November 2001 election of PNH candidate Ricardo Maduro Joest (2002–   ).

Hurricane Mitch (1998)

Hurricane Mitch struck Central America in October 1998 and had a particularly devastating effect on Honduras, one of the subregion's poorest countries. Reminiscent of violent Hurricane Fifi in 1974, which resulted in 10,000 deaths and the destruction of many banana plantations (see **banana industry**), Mitch produced torrential rains for over a week, causing flooding that took an estimated 6,000 Honduran lives and left thousands homeless. The hurricane also negatively impacted Honduras' economy as agriculture, one of the country's most significant production sectors, was particularly hard hit: the banana plantations lost an entire year's harvest, and other agricultural sectors were devastated as well, leading some to estimate crop damage at between 50 and 70 percent. While Honduras had achieved economic growth in the years preceding Hurricane Mitch, growth was reduced to −2.2 percent in 1999. In addition, much of Honduras' limited infrastructure of roads and bridges was washed away, leaving many towns and villages completely isolated from the rest of the country. Some analysts estimated that the storm set the country's physical infrastructure back by years or perhaps decades, and in 2000 vast amounts of infrastructure were still awaiting repair. The international aid response was strong and helped to mitigate some of the storm's tragic effects, as did the debt cancellation offered by many countries to assist in the recovery and reconstruction efforts. The storm brought increased poverty, threatened to reverse decades of economic development, and heightened the country's potential for political instability.

López Arellano, Oswaldo (1919–   )

Oswaldo López Arellano was president of Honduras from 1963 to 1971, and served as military junta leader from 1972 to 1975. As the country's leader, he focused on improving infrastructure, and resolved the conflict with El Salvador that came to be known as the **Soccer War** (see Appendix 1).

Born in the southern town of Danlí in 1919, López Arellano joined the air force and eventually rose to the rank of brigadier general. In 1963, the military, concerned about what it perceived as the increasing influence of leftists, staged a coup to avoid the election of

the candidate of the **Honduran Liberal Party** (Partido Liberal Hondureño, PLH), Modesto Rodas Alvarado, and installed López Arellano. He aggressively pursued policies to weaken the left. A secret government organization attacked leftists and leaders of the PLH, while the ties between the conservative **Honduran National Party** (Partido Nacional Hondureño, PNH) and the military grew stronger. López Arellano depleted the resources of the National Agrarian Institute (Instituto Nacional Agrario, INA), crippling land reform efforts. Peasant groups were intimidated as well.

López Arellano soon faced increasing popular discontent. Simultaneously, tensions escalated between Honduras and El Salvador over migration and trade issues. The international conflict offered the government a diversion and an external enemy to unite the country, and the Soccer War was fought in 1969. In January 1971, López Arellano announced that the two dominant political parties, the PLH and the PNH, had signed a Political Convention of National Unity. The armed forces, the Honduran Confederation of Workers (Confederación de Trabajadores de Honduras, CTH), and the Superior Council of Private Businesses (Consejo Superior de la Empresa Privada, CSEP) all gave their support to the unity pact.

On March 28, 1971, presidential elections were held. Though López Arellano was a candidate, the 1969 war had damaged his reputation, and PNH candidate Ramón Ernesto Cruz (1971–1972) won the contest. However, support for Cruz soon faded, and the military returned López Arellano to power in 1972. He served as the leader of Honduras until 1975, when he and his ministers of finance and commerce were implicated in a scam in which the government accepted a bribe from the United Fruit Company in exchange for canceling a recently imposed banana tax. Colonel Juan Alberto Melgar Castro (1975–1978) quickly replaced López Arellano as head of state. López Arellano went on to be involved in several businesses, including TAN-SAHSA Airlines and the Central American Financial Bank (Banco Financiero Centroamericano).

Morazán, Francisco (1799–1842)

Born in Tegucigalpa, Francisco Morazán served as head of the province of Honduras (then part of the **United Provinces of Central America**; see Appendix 1) from 1827 to 1828, in 1829, and again in 1830. However, he is most remembered for his leadership of the Central American union.

Civil war gripped the union between 1826 and 1829, and Morazán led the revolutionary army that overthrew the regime of Manuel José Arce in 1829, and proclaimed himself president of the Central American Federation in 1830. Though fellow Honduran José Cecilio del **Valle** defeated him in the 1834 election for president of the union, Valle died before taking office, and Morazán continued in the presidency.

During his second term as head of the United Provinces of Central America, Morazán faced widespread apathy and increasing opposition from Conservatives. Morazán could not hold the union together, and on May 30, 1838, the dissension was so great that the Central American Congress removed Morazán from the presidency and allowed the states to create their own governments. He briefly hung onto control of El Salvador until 1839, and then made an unsuccessful attempt to recapture Guatemala from José Rafael **Carrera** (see Guatemala). He went into voluntary exile in 1840, but was recalled in 1842 by Costa Rica and proclaimed president of that republic. Again he attempted to restore Central American unity, but was betrayed and assassinated in September 1842 by his own partisans. Today he is considered a Central American hero for his efforts to create a Central American federation. The department in which the Honduran capital, Tegucigalpa, is located bears his name, and in the 1980s the leftist revolutionary Morazanist Front (Frente Morazanista) named itself in his honor.

La Mosquitia

The Honduran government had long been supportive of the United States' policies and its intervention in Latin America, and Honduras was sometimes used as a staging area for attacks on neighboring regimes, most notably in 1954, when Carlos **Castillo Armas** (see Guatemala) led U.S.-backed rebels to overthrow Jacobo **Arbenz Guzmán** (see Guatemala) in Guatemala. Further, during the civil war that engulfed Nicaragua in the 1980s, the **counterrevolutionaries** (contrarevolucionarios, contras; see Nicaragua), fought to regain control of their country from the **Sandinista National Liberation Front** (Frente Sandinista de Liberación Nacional, FSLN; see Nicaragua), which had taken hold of the nation's government in 1979. Reluctant to train in Sandinista-controlled Nicaragua, the contras trained and organized (with the support of the U.S. military) in the sparsely populated eastern region of Honduras known as La Mosquitia. In order to support the contras (as well as anticommunist fighters in El Salvador), the United States rotated several thousand troops through the Coto Sano Air Base (previously known as Pamerola Air Base) located in the Comayagua Valley of Honduras. This was unpopular with local Hondurans, who objected to the U.S. stationing troops in the country and thought that the land on which the air base sat should be used for agriculture or for a commercial airport. Additionally, the behavior of soldiers off the base while on leave often left a bad impression. Anti-U.S. sentiment heightened and culminated with the bombing of the United States Peace Corps office in April 1989.

Reina Idiáques, Carlos Roberto (1926–)

Carlos Roberto Reina Idiáques served as president from 1994 to 1998 and made partially successful efforts to bring the military under civilian rule, limit its extrademocratic role, and strengthen democracy.

Born in the town of Comayaguela in 1926, Reina was educated in international law. He and his brother Jorge Arturo Reina Idiáques led a progressive wing of the **Honduran Liberal Party** (Partido Liberal Hondureño, PLH) known as the Liberal Alliance of the People (Alianza Liberal Popular, ALIPO). Reina served as president of the Inter-American Court of Human Rights (an autonomous juridical institution of the **Organization of American States** [OAS]; see Appendix 2) in 1983, and was elected president of Honduras a decade later on the PLH ticket with 52 percent of the vote.

He immediately initiated efforts to address corruption and human rights issues and attempted to limit the role and power of the military. He replaced the military's ill-reputed National Division of Investigation with a civilian-run Directorate of Criminal Investigations in early 1995, and tried to initiate legal prosecution of those who had been involved in the human rights abuses of the 1980s (see **Battalion 3–16**). Though unsuccessful in the human rights violation cases, Reina announced that the next commander-in-chief of the armed forces for the 1996–1999 term would be a civilian, the minister of defense. Legislation was also passed in 1996 to place the police force under civilian authority after decades of military control.

In addition, the Reina administration investigated the extensive corruption of the previous administration of Rafael Leonardo **Callejas Romero** (1990–1994), particularly in relation to *el chinazo*, a scandal in which Honduran passports were illegally sold to Chinese immigrants to help them enter the United States. Though a new anticorruption unit formed in 1995 summoned Callejas to answer questions about improper sales of government equipment during his presidency, Callejas and his colleagues, who were still serving as publicly elected officials at the time, evaded prosecution due to the immunity associated with those posts.

Soccer War (1969). See Appendix 1

Suazo Córdova, Roberto (1927–)

The administration of Robert Suazo Córdova (1982–1986), a member of the conservative wing of the **Honduran Liberal Party** (Partido Liberal Hondureño, PLH), was characterized by deference to the interests of the armed forces and the United States.

Born in 1927 and trained as a doctor in Guatemala, Suazo served as a representative in Congress numerous times from the 1950s to the 1980s, rising to the head of the Rodista faction of the PLH in 1979. In 1981 the military relinquished direct control of the Honduran government and fairly open elections were held, which Suazo Córdova won with 54 percent of the vote. As president, Suazo Córdova was unable to effectively address the grave economic challenges that his country faced, and instead used patronage to reward his supporters. He reversed many progressive economic reforms and implemented austere neoliberal policies, many of them required by the United States and the international financial community in exchange for foreign assistance. Corruption was also widespread. The funding of a $1.5 million soccer stadium in Suazo Córdova's hometown of La Paz, which had only 10,000 citizens—and no soccer team—was indicative of his governing style.

While Suazo Córdova's charge was to move the country toward democracy, in the context of the leftist uprisings in neighboring El Salvador, Nicaragua, and Guatemala, he welcomed an enlarged U.S. military presence in Honduras and willingly cooperated with U.S. efforts against leftists throughout Central America. The military, under the command of General Gustavo Adolfo **Alvarez Martínez** from 1982 to 1984, exerted a very strong influence over politics during Suazo's presidency: army repression reached a new peak and human rights violations increased. Although Suazo Córdova made extraconstitutional attempts to continue his rule, his rival in the PLH, José Simón **Azcona Hoyo** (1986–1990), attained the party's support and successfully ran as the PLH candidate in the presidential election of 1985.

Valle, José Cecilio del (1776–1834)

José Cecilio del Valle was an important Central American statesman, born in the Honduran town of Choluteca. An outstanding scholar, he was educated at the University of San Carlos in Guatemala City, Guatemala. He was active in local politics in the early nineteenth century and became mayor of Guatemala City in 1820. When independence from Spain was achieved the following year, Valle helped guide Central America into the newly formed Mexican Empire. He represented the province of Tegucigalpa at the Mexican Congress in 1822 and became secretary of foreign affairs in the government of Agustín de **Iturbide** (see Mexico). Iturbide's Mexican Empire dissolved in 1823, and Valle returned to Guatemala and in 1824 ran for the presidency of the newly formed **United Provinces of Central America** (see Appendix 1). Although he lacked only one vote for an absolute majority among the candidates, the Central American Congress denied him the office. He ran for the presidency and won a decade later, but died before taking office.

HEADS OF STATE

Dionisio de Herrera	1824–1827
Francisco Morazán	1827–1828
Diego Vijil	1828–1829
Francisco Morazán	1829
Juan Ángel Arias	1829–1830
Francisco Morazán	1830
José Santos del Valle	1830–1831
José Antonio Márquez	1831–1832
Francisco Milla	1832–1833
Joaquín Rivera	1833
Francisco Ferrera	1833–1834
José María Bustillo	1834
Joaquín Rivera	1834–1836
José María Martínez	1837
Justo José Herrera	1837–1838
José María Martínez	1838
Lino Matute	1838–1839
Juan Francisco de Molina	1839
Felipe Neri Medina	1839
Juan José Alvarado	1839
José María Guerrero	1839
José María Bustillo	1839
Francisco Zelaya Ayes	1839–1840
Francisco Ferrera	1841–1844
Coronado Chávez	1845–1847
Juan Lindo	1848–1852
Francisco Gómez	1852
José Trinidad Cabañas	1852–1855
Santiago Bueso	1855
Francisco Aguilar	1856–1862
J. Santos Guardiola	1862
Francisco Montes	1862
José María Medina	1862
Victoriano Castellanos	1862
Francisco Montes	1862
José María Medina	1863–1872
Céleo Arias	1872–1873
Ponciano Leiva	1873–1876
Marco Aurelio Soto	1876–1883
Luis Bográn Barahona	1883–1891
Ponciano Leiva	1891–1893
Domingo Vázquez	1893–1894
Policarpo Bonilla	1894–1899
Terencio Sierra	1899–1903
Juan Ángel Arias	1903
Manuel Bonilla	1903–1907
Miguel R. Dávila	1907–1911
Francisco Beltrán	1911–1912
Manuel Bonilla	1912–1913
Francisco Bertrand	1913–1915
Alberto Membreño	1915–1916
Francisco Bertrand	1916–1919
Rafael López Gutiérrez	1920–1924
Fausto Dávila	1924

Vicente Tosta	1924–1925
Miguel Paz Barahona	1925–1929
Vicente Mejía Colindres	1929–1933
Tiburcio Carías Andino	1933–1948
Juan Manuel Gálvez	1949–1954
Julio Lozano Díaz	1954–1957
Ramón Villeda Morales	1957–1963
Oswaldo López Arellano	1963–1971
Ramón Ernesto Cruz	1971–1972
Oswaldo López Arellano	1972–1975
Juan Alberto Melgar Castro	1975–1978
Policarpo Paz García	1978–1982
Roberto Suazo Córdova	1982–1986
José Simón Azcona Hoyo	1986–1990
Rafael Leonardo Callejas Romero	1990–1994
Carlos Roberto Reina Idiáques	1994–1998
Carlos Roberto Flores Facussé	1998–2002
Ricardo Maduro Joest	2002–

Sources: Honduras.com. www.honduras.com/history/presidents.html; Thomas Skidmore and Peter H. Smith, *Modern Latin America*, 4th ed. (New York: Oxford University Press, 1997.)

BIBLIOGRAPHY

Print Resources

Acker, Alison. *Honduras: The Making of a Banana Republic.* Boston: South End Press, 1988.

Amnesty International. *Honduras: Civilian Authority, Military Power: Human Rights Violations in the 1980s.* London: Amnesty International Publications, 1988.

Anderson, Thomas P. *The War of the Dispossessed: Honduras and El Salvador, 1969.* Lincoln: University of Nebraska Press, 1982.

Barry, Tom, and Kent Norsworthy. *Honduras: A Country Guide.* Albuquerque, NM: Interhemispheric, 1990.

———. *Inside Honduras.* 2nd ed. Albuquerque, NM: Interhemispheric, 1994.

Chamberlain, Robert S. *The Conquest and Colonization of Honduras, 1502–1550.* Washington, DC: Carnegie Institution of Washington, 1953.

Euraque, Dario A. *Reinterpreting the Banana Republic: Region and State in Honduras, 1870–1972.* Chapel Hill: University of North Carolina Press, 1996.

Lapper, Richard, and James Painter. *Honduras: State for Sale.* London: Latin American Bureau, 1989.

MacCameron, Robert. *Bananas, Labor, and Politics in Honduras, 1954–1963.* Syracuse, NY: Maxwell School of Citizenship and Public Affairs, Syracuse University, 1983.

Morris, James A. *Honduras: Caudillo Politics and Military Rulers.* Boulder: Westview Press, 1984.

Peckenham, Nancy, and Annie Street, eds. *Honduras: Portrait of a Captive Nation.* New York: Praeger, 1985.

Schulz, Donald E. *The United States, Honduras, and the Crisis in Central America: A Study of Relations Between Honduras and the United States since 1980.* Boulder: Westview Press, 1994.

Electronic Resources

Honduras This Week Online
http://www.marrder.com/htw/
Online magazine with features on politics, economics, and culture of Central America, with a particular focus on Honduras. (In English)

Latin American Network Information Center (LANIC): Honduras
http://lanic.utexas.edu/la/ca/honduras/
Honduras section of this extensive Web site contains hundreds of links to research resources, cultural centers, economic and business institutions, government agencies, historical sources, magazines and other periodicals, nongovernmental organizations, and grassroots groups, as well as many other subjects. (In English)

Political Database of the Americas: Honduras
http://www.georgetown.edu/pdba/Countries/honduras.html
Comprehensive database run as a joint project of Georgetown University and the Organization of American States. Section on Honduras contains information on and links to the executive, legislative, and judicial branches of the Honduran government; electoral laws and election results; and other political data. (In English, Spanish, Portuguese, and French)

Political Resources.net: Honduras
http://www.politicalresources.net/honduras.htm
Honduras section of a Web site containing a wealth of links to sources of information about national politics. Includes information on political parties, legislative and executive institutions, laws and legislation, and elections, as well as a link to the constitution. (In English)

Tiempo Digital
http://www.tiempo.hn/
The Web version of one of Honduras' main daily newspapers. Offers comprehensive national political, economic, and cultural coverage. (In Spanish)

Wilfried Derksen's Elections Around the World: Honduras
http://www.agora.it/elections/honduras.htm
Honduras section of a comprehensive database of results from elections around the world. Contains results from recent national executive and legislative elections, as well as explanations of and links to political parties and institutions. (In English)

MEXICO

COUNTRY PROFILE

Official name	Estados Unidos Mexicanos
Capital	Ciudad de México (also Distrito Federal)
Type/structure of government	Federal republic with centralized government (presidential system)
Executive	President elected to six-year term (*sexenio*); no reelection; executive branch (president in particular) wields extraordinary influence.
Legislative	Bicameral; Senate (128 members serve six-year terms) and Chamber of Deputies (500 members serve three-year terms); members of Congress can serve only one consecutive term.
Judicial	Highest court is the Supreme Court; justices serve one 15-year term as of the judicial reform of 1995.
Major political parties	**Institutional Revolutionary Party** (Partido Revolucionario Institucional, PRI), **Democratic Revolutionary Party** (Partido de la Revolución Democrática, PRD), **National Action Party** (Partido Acción Nacional, PAN).
Constitution in effect	1917
Location/geography	North America, bordering the United States (to the north), Guatemala and Belize (to the south), the Pacific Ocean (to the west), and the Caribbean Sea and the Gulf of Mexico (to the east). Contains desert, jungle, and mountains.
Geographic area	1,972,550 sq. km.
Population	100,294,036 (1999 est.)
Ethnic groups	Mestizo 60%; indigenous 30%; white (of European descent) 9%; other 1%
Religions	Roman Catholic 89%; Protestant 6%; other 5%
Literacy rate	89% (1999 est.)
Infant mortality rate	24.62 deaths per 1,000 live births (1999 est.)
Life expectancy	72 years (1999 est.)
Monetary unit	Nuevo peso
Exchange rate	1 U.S. dollar = 9.16 nuevos pesos (August 2000)*
Major exports	Oil, coffee, silver, engines, motor vehicles, cotton, consumer electronics
Major imports	Metal-working machines, steel mill products, agricultural machinery, electrical equipment, automotive parts, repair parts for motor vehicles, aircraft, and aircraft parts
GDP	$815 billion (1998)
GDP growth rate	4.8% (1998)
GDP per capita	$8,300 (1998)

*Latin American Weekly Report. August 22, 2000 (WR-00-33), p. 394.

Source: CIA World Fact Book. 1999. http://www.odci.gov/cia/publications/factbook/mx.html#people; U.S. Department of State. Background Notes. http://www.state.gov/www/background_notes/mexico_0899_bgn.html

OVERVIEW

Summary

Mexico is the most populous Spanish-speaking country in the world, with a population exceeding 100 million. It is also the only Latin American country to share a land border with the United States. Mexico's capital, Mexico City, known by the Aztecs as Tenochtitlán prior to the Spanish conquest, is one of the largest cities in the world. While Mexico's political system is generally considered "democratic" when regional political regimes are categorized, some of the political practices that became traditional between 1929 and 2000 suggest that through the twentieth century, the Mexican system was in fact more authoritarian in character. Until the landmark victory of opposition **National Action Party** (Partido Acción Nacional, PAN) candidate Vicente **Fox Quesada** (2000–) in the July 2000 presidential election, the **Institutional Revolutionary Party** (Partido Revolucionario Institucional, PRI) had held the Mexican presidency continuously for over seventy years (1929–2000). In addition, many of the administrations that ruled Mexico over the last decades were rife with corruption.

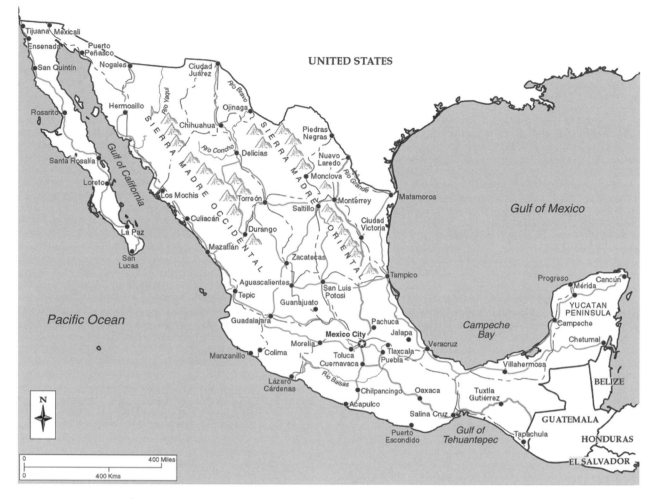

Mexico. © 1998 The Moschovitis Group, Inc.

History

Mexico's early cultures were advanced in many areas, including transportation, irrigation, and art. The Olmecs, the region's earliest occupants, inhabited the area beginning in approximately 1100 B.C. When the Spanish arrived in 1519, indigenous cultures, including the Olmecs, the Teotihuacans, the Maya, the Mixtecs, the Zapotecs, the Tarascans, and the Aztecs, were thriving. Moctezuma II, the ruler of the Aztecs at the time of the Spanish arrival in Veracruz, initially welcomed Spanish conqueror Hernán Cortés, believing that this mysterious foreigner was Quetzalcoatl, the white god of the Aztecs. This misperception, and Cortés' ability to ally with some indigenous peoples against the Aztecs, led to the rapid collapse of the Aztec Empire; Emperor Cuauhtémoc surrendered to the Spanish in August 1521.

Mexico City soon became the Spanish capital of the New World. Over time, missionaries were sent by the Catholic Church to convert the indigenous population that had survived colonization and the scourge of new diseases brought by the Spanish. Gradually, as the colonizers and indigenous peoples mixed, a new generation of Mexicans emerged, mestizos, who mainly occupied the lower to middle classes of Mexican society, while the indigenous peoples were increasingly marginalized. In September 1810 in the town of Dolores, Father Miguel **Hidalgo y Castilla** proclaimed the *Grito de Dolores* (Cry of Freedom), which officially began Mexico's struggle for independence from the Spanish crown. Mexico finally gained independence in 1821.

Despite the belief that independence would bring political and economic stability to Mexico, through the nineteenth century the country experienced a series of internal battles for power between Liberals and Conservatives, as well as with the United States, and France. Texas declared its independence in 1836, and in the **War of 1846** Mexico lost nearly half of its territory to the United States. While stability characterized the beginning of the first presidency of Benito **Juárez** (1858, 1861–1863, 1867–1872), the calm was soon interrupted when the French installed Austrian archduke Ferdinand **Maximilian Von Hapsburg** (1864–1867) as emperor of Mexico in 1864. Following Napoleon Bonaparte III's decision to recall French troops from Mexico in 1867, Maximilian was executed, and Juárez regained power, which he held until his death in 1872. Porfirio **Díaz**, who ruled for thirty-one years (1876–

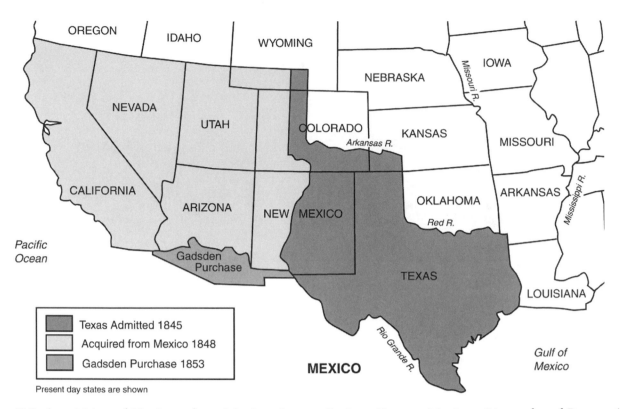

U.S. Acquisition of Territory from Mexico. *Source:* Enrique Krauze, *Mexico—Biography of Power: A History of Modern Mexico, 1810–1996* (New York: HarperCollins, 1997). Reprinted by permission of Enrique Krauze.

1880, 1884–1911), brought stability and economic growth to Mexico at the expense of democracy.

By the first decade of the twentieth century, strong factions began to rise up in opposition to Díaz, each occupying a different geographic section of Mexico. Two of the most famous leaders were Francisco (Pancho) **Villa** in the North and Emiliano **Zapata** in the middle of the country. Opposition turned into violence, and in 1910–1911 a series of revolts marked the start of the **Mexican Revolution** (1910–1929). Although several factions competed for power, they shared the goals that were at the core of the Mexican Revolution: social justice, land reform, and a nationalism that celebrated Mexico's indigenous ancestry. In 1917 the current constitution was promulgated under the administration of Venustiano **Carranza** (1914, 1915–1920). Power struggles between revolutionary leaders continued through the 1920s.

In 1929 former president Plutarco Elías **Calles** (1924–1928) was instrumental in the formation of the National Revolutionary Party (Partido Nacional Revolucionario, PNR), which eventually evolved into the PRI. In 1938 president Lázaro **Cárdenas** (1934–1940), one of the PNR's key leaders, expropriated U.S. and British-owned oil companies and created a state oil company, Mexican Petroleum (Petróleos Mexicanos, PEMEX). Designed to strengthen and consolidate Mexico's oil production, PEMEX proved extremely influ-

ential in the nation's economic development and history. Cárdenas also pursued land reform during his term in office, redistributing almost 4.5 million acres of agricultural land expropriated from large estates to 800,000 peasants to farm collectively.

The further consolidation of and centralization of power in the PRI after 1946 transformed it into a powerful force that would dominate Mexican politics for the remainder of the twentieth century. One of the main keys to the party's success was its corporatist structure, which implied that each of the party's more than 5 million members was associated with a certain sector, such as labor or the peasantry. Despite its traditional strength, the PRI began to face serious challenges during the latter part of the century. The massacre of an unknown number of students in the Plaza de Tres Culturas in the Tlatelolco section of Mexico City in October 1968 (see **Events of 1968, Tlatelolco**) eroded the legitimacy of President Gustavo Díaz Ordaz (1964–1970) and of the PRI, both domestically and internationally. Further, by the late 1970s the country was plagued with debt and inflation due mainly to economic mismanagement, and by the early 1980s the Mexican government was besieged by economic problems. In 1982 President José **López Portillo y Pacheco** (1976–1982) declared a debt moratorium, initiating the chain of events that would lead to the regionwide debt crisis of the 1980s. Finally, a massive earthquake rocked the country in

1985, and the PRI was widely criticized for its response to the devastating disaster.

Proximity to the United States has profoundly influenced Mexican politics. The traditionally complex and sometimes contentious bilateral relationship changed dramatically in the 1980s, culminating in the administration of Carlos **Salinas de Gortari** (1988–1994) initiating the negotiation of the **North American Free Trade Agreement** (NAFTA) in 1991. Soon after the agreement was signed in 1994, the Mexican economy suffered another scare, the **peso crisis of 1995**, during which Mexican currency plummeted in value and capital rapidly began to leave the country. Simultaneously, in the southern state of Chiapas, the **Zapatista National Liberation Army** (Ejército Zapatista de Liberación Nacional, EZLN), a guerrilla movement, gained international attention as it instigated armed uprisings against the government.

In the 1990s the strength of opposition parties from the left and the right continued to gradually increase on the national, state, and local levels. By late in the decade, opposition parties had won various state governorships, and in the July 1997 midterm elections, opposition political parties captured a majority of the seats in the lower house of Congress, the Chamber of Deputies. Cuauhtémoc **Cárdenas** led the **Democratic Revolutionary Party** (Partido de la Revolución Democrática, PRD), the leftist opposition party, to victory in the 1997 contest for the mayorship of Mexico City, marking the first time an opposition party member would fill that post. As the July 2000 presidential election approached, it was clear that the contest would not be the formality and simple endorsement of PRI rule that it had been in previous decades. In the event, Vicente Fox Quesada, the candidate of the conservative opposition party, the PAN, won a historic victory, ending the reign of the world's longest-ruling political party and, many hoped, heralding the birth of a new kind of government in Mexico.

ENTRIES

Acteal Massacre (1997). See **Zapatista National Liberation Army** (Ejército Zapatista de Liberación Nacional, EZLN)

Alemán Valdés, Miguel (1903–1983)

Miguel Alemán Valdés was president of Mexico from 1946 to 1952. The first civilian president of the **Institutional Revolutionary Party** (Partido Revolucionario Institucional, PRI), he guided the party's reorganization.

Alemán, whose father served as a general in the **Mexican Revolution** (1910–1929), earned a law degree at the National University (Universidad Nacional Autónoma de México, UNAM) and soon became involved in politics, quickly attaining posts of increasing importance. He served as governor of the state of Veracruz from 1936 to 1939, directed the successful presidential campaign of Manuel Avila Camacho (1940–1946), and served in Avila Camacho's cabinet.

Alemán won the 1946 presidential election on the ticket of the PRI, becoming the party's first civilian president. Once in office, he reorganized the PRI, allowing the middle and business classes more influence in party politics, and guiding the party toward recruiting politicians from UNAM instead of from the military (from which the PRI had traditionally recruited politicians). Alemán also strengthened Mexico's ties to the United States and liberalized Mexico's stance on foreign investment, a move that brought him some criticism. Despite these actions, the majority of Alemán's policies were notably conservative; while he invested in infrastructure for industry, primarily in and around Mexico City, he spent relatively less money on social programs to help Mexico's lower classes. After leaving office in 1952, Alemán became the leader of the conservative faction of the PRI, and later headed the Mexican Board of Tourism.

Calles, Plutarco Elías (1877–1945)

Plutarco Elías Calles served as president of Mexico from 1924 to 1928, and Mexico's Central Bank was founded under Calles in 1925. Calles continued to be influential in presidential politics well after his time in office, and was instrumental in the 1929 formation of the National Revolutionary Party (Partido Nacional Revolucionario, PNR), a predecessor of the **Institutional Revolutionary Party** (Partido Revolucionario Institucional, PRI).

Born into a farming and cattle ranching family in northern Mexico, Calles spent his early years as an educator, and later became involved in farming and agriculture in Sonora. During the **Mexican Revolution** (1910–1929), Calles led the Sonoran resistance against the dictatorship of Victoriano **Huerta** (1913–1914), and subsequently headed Venustiano **Carranza**'s (1914, 1915–1920) forces. Later, as governor of Sonora, Calles expelled the Catholic priests from that state, as he believed that the church's influence and power could undermine the momentum of the revolution.

Calles subsequently broke his ties with Carranza, allying instead with Álvaro **Obregón** (1920–1924), who became Carranza's main rival. In 1920 Calles and other revolutionary leaders from the north issued the ultimately successful *Plan de Agua Prieta*, which called for the overthrow of President Carranza. Calles served as minister of the interior under Obregón, who succeeded Carranza, establishing important political alliances that would help Calles win the presidency in 1924. As president, Calles confronted the Catholic Church, which began to mobilize in 1925 in opposition to several anticlerical articles of the Constitution of 1917 promulgated under Carranza. The confrontation climaxed in the **Cristero Rebellion**, which disrupted the western and central parts of Mexico from 1926 to 1929.

After leaving office in 1928, Calles, whom politicians and the press referred to as the *jefe máximo* (big boss) of the revolution, formed and led the PNR, and continued to orchestrate politics from behind the scenes. He was exiled in 1936 by Lázaro **Cárdenas** (1934–1940), but returned to Mexico in 1941 at the invitation of President Manuel Avila Camacho (1940–1946). Calles died in Mexico City in October 1945.

Cárdenas, Cuauhtémoc (1934–)

Cuauhtémoc Cárdenas founded the **Democratic Revolutionary Party** (Partido de la Revolución Democrática, PRD) in the 1980s, and ran for president in 1988, 1994, and 2000. He also served as mayor of Mexico City from 1997 to 1999.

The only son of Lázaro **Cárdenas** (1934–1940), Cuauhtémoc Cárdenas was born into political life. Cárdenas founded the Movement for National Liberation (Movimiento de Liberación Nacional, MLN) in 1961 to show support for the **Cuban Revolution of 1959** (see Cuba), and developed his political career through participation in that movement. The MLN eventually disbanded, and by the late 1960s Cárdenas had joined the **Institutional Revolutionary Party** (Partido Revolucionario Institucional, PRI), though, like his father, he leaned farther left than many party members. Cárdenas easily won the governorship of the state of Michoacán on the PRI ticket in 1979, and was a popular governor during the period of economic crisis that Mexico experienced in the early 1980s (see **López Portillo y Pacheco**, José).

Cárdenas became increasingly critical of President Miguel de la **Madrid Hurtado**'s (1982–1988) fiscal policies; his vocal opposition to PRI policy was a rarity in Mexican politics. Cárdenas called for reform of the presidential nomination process, but despite pressure from Cárdenas and others, the PRI continued its tradition of the *dedazo* (the direct designation, rather than nomination by convention, member vote, or primary, of the PRI candidate for president). In protest of the PRI's direct designation of Carlos **Salinas de Gortari** (1988–1994) as the PRI candidate in the 1988 presidential election, Cárdenas left the PRI and sought the nomination from other political parties. He eventually contested the 1988 election on the ticket of the National Democratic Front (Frente Democrático Nacional, FDN). While PRI candidate Salinas was declared the winner of the election, there were widespread accusations of electoral fraud; many observers believe that Cárdenas actually won the election, and that the mysterious crashing of the computer tabulation system while votes were being counted afforded the PRI the opportunity to tamper with the results.

After the election, Cárdenas founded the PRD and continued his campaign to reform Mexican politics. He contested the 2000 presidential election, but was defeated by both Vicente **Fox Quesada** (2000–), the candidate from the center-right **National Action Party** (Partido Acción Nacional, PAN), and by Francisco Labastida Ochoa, the PRI candidate.

Cárdenas, Lázaro (1895–1970)

General Lázaro Cárdenas' (1934–1940) involvement in politics began in 1913 when he joined the armed forces, fighting under both Álvaro **Obregón** (1920–1924) and Plutarco Elías **Calles** (1924–1928) during the **Mexican Revolution** (1910–1929). In the 1920s and 1930s he served as governor of his home state of Michoacán and president of the newly formed National Revolutionary Party (Partido Nacional Revolucionario, PNR), an antecedent of the **Institutional Revolutionary Party** (Partido Revolucionario Institucional, PRI). Following his 1934 presidential election, Cárdenas clearly demonstrated his liberal leanings. He was a major supporter and facilitator of the workers' union, the **Confederation of Mexican Workers** (Confederación de Trabajadores de México, CTM), and when laborers claimed that foreign energy companies were not meeting wage standards, Cárdenas expropriated U.S. and British-owned oil companies in 1938. His government created a state oil company, Mexican Petroleum (Petróleos Mexicanos, PEMEX), which was designed to strengthen and consolidate Mexico's oil production. While land distribution occurred in waves throughout Mexican history, it peaked under Cárdenas; he redistributed almost 4.5 million acres of arable land taken from large estates to 800,000 peasants to farm collectively. In 1938 Cárdenas created the Party of the Mexican Revolution (Partido de la Revolución Mexicana, PRM), a restructured version of the PNR (and another PRI predecessor) that included four major factions: labor, peasantry, popular groups, and the military.

Carranza, Venustiano (1859–1920)

Carranza was a key figure in the **Mexican Revolution** (1910–1929). He served as president of Mexico in 1914, and again from 1915 until his assassination in 1920. From the 1914 ouster of Victoriano **Huerta** (1913–1914) through 1917, Carranza competed for power with Emiliano **Zapata** and Francisco (Pancho) **Villa**.

Born into a military family, Carranza grew up in the state of Coahuila, of which President Francisco **Madero** (1911–1913) later appointed him provisional governor. Carranza was involved in the cultivation of the Mexican Revolution, and eventually emerged as one of the strongmen competing to control Mexico. He gathered together northern Mexicans who opposed Huerta's assumption of the presidency in 1913, and called a convention of revolutionary leaders to elect an interim leader following Huerta's removal from office in 1914.

Though Carranza assumed he would be elected, he was passed over; he consequently went to Veracruz, established his own government, and proclaimed himself president.

From Veracruz, in 1915, Carranza introduced *ejidos*, land grants given by the Mexican government to rural populations. He also pushed for a constitutional convention, which was finally convened in late 1916, and which produced the Constitution of 1917, which is still in effect today. The constitution reflected the primary goals of the Mexican Revolution (including the institutionalization of the policy of providing the peasantry with *ejidos*), and demonstrated that Mexicans were dedicated to achieving social change. The 1917 charter also gave the president more autonomy from the legislature, eliminated the office of vice president, and included an innovative bill of rights that highlighted both industrial and agricultural labor. The constitution had several articles that were considered to be anticlerical and heightened state-church tensions (see **Cristero Rebellion; Calles**, Plutarco Elías).

Carranza was formally elected president in 1917. He took a strong stance against the policies of the United States, speaking out against foreign intervention in Latin America. Carranza's dedication to social reforms waned through his time in office, disappointing Mexicans who had supported him because of his ambitious reform plans. While many thought that Carranza would designate Álvaro **Obregón** (1920–1924) as his successor, he chose a little known politician to succeed him instead. Obregón invaded the capital in 1920, and Carranza fled to Veracruz, where he was soon assassinated by an Obregón supporter.

Colosio, Donaldo. See **Zedillo Ponce de León, Ernesto**

Confederation of Mexican Workers (Confederación de Trabajadores de México, CTM)

The Confederation of Mexican Workers (Confederación de Trabajadores de México, CTM), created in 1936, evolved from another union, the National Committee of Proletarian Defense (Comité Nacional de Defensa Proletaria, CNDP), formed during the presidency of Lázaro **Cárdenas** (1934–1940). Since its inception, the CTM has been the nation's most prominent labor union, wielding significant influence on Mexico's political and economic policy. "Don Fidel" Velázquez, the CTM's patriarch and one of its founders, headed the organization from the mid-1940s until his death in 1997.

In 1935 former president Plutarco Elías **Calles** (1924–1928) criticized workers' strikes as "unjustified" and damaging to the government. Concerned about their rights, unions quickly banded together and formed the CNDP. Early in 1936 the CNDP held its first congress (attended by representatives of Mexican labor from all over the country) and changed its name to the CTM.

While this meeting appeared to demonstrate the unity of the Mexican labor force, in reality there were significant divisions within the community. Not until its fourth congress (1947) would the CTM reach a consensus as to its future course, to "struggle for the economic and social development of Mexico."

After 1947 the CTM worked closely with the **Institutional Revolutionary Party** (Partido Revolucionario Institucional, PRI). In 1952 the PRI revised its own statutes so that the importance of the CTM to the nation's economy and politics was recognized. While the CTM played a prominent role in domestic politics for the next few decades, dissident labor movements grew stronger in the wake of the 1982 economic collapse (see **López Portillo y Pacheco**, José), and began to criticize the CTM and the cozy relationship it maintained with the PRI.

Constitution of 1917. See **Carranza, Venustiano**

Cristero Rebellion (1926–1929)

The Cristero Rebellion was a series of violent uprisings in central and western Mexico between 1926 and 1929.

The Constitution of 1917 included provisions that were meant to minimize the Catholic Church's influence in politics and to separate church and state. The constitution denied the Catholic Church legal standing, prohibited religious education, denied the clergy the right to vote and freedom of speech, and restricted political parties from including any religious references in their name. Revolutionary leaders involved in the creation of the constitution, including President Venustiano **Carranza** (1914, 1915–1920), were concerned that if the church were active in politics it could effectively oppose the **Mexican Revolution** (1910–1929).

Local authorities lacked the power to enforce the constitution's church-related provisions until the implementing legislation was signed by President Plutarco Elías **Calles** (1924–1928) in July 1926. Soon thereafter, in reaction to federal authorities' seizure of churches, sporadic and disorganized uprisings by groups calling for religious freedom and questioning the new role of the state began. By 1927 the movement was unified, and the National League for the Defense of Religious Liberty (Liga Nacional para la Defensa de las Libertades Religiosas, LNDLR) called for a mass insurrection to challenge and overthrow the Calles administration. By late 1927 movement members, dubbed Cristeros, were carrying out larger-scale attacks, and by the end of 1928 they had begun to pose a threat to the military. Meanwhile, the Mexican church and government had initiated negotiations with U.S. ambassador Dwight W. Morrow as the mediator. The death in 1929 of Enrique Gorostieta, who had been leading the rebels, and an agreement signed by President Emilio Portes Gil (1928–

1930) and the church on June 29, 1929 finally led to the end of the rebellion.

Debt Crisis. See **López Portillo y Pacheco, José**

Democratic Revolutionary Party (Partido de la Revolución Democrática, PRD)

The Democratic Revolutionary Party (Partido de la Revolución Democrática, PRD) was created by Cuauhtémoc **Cárdenas** and other liberal leaders in 1989 to give a clearer and more consolidated identity to the Mexican left. Originally supported by a coalition of parties, the PRD's agenda for Mexico included the democratization of politics, particularly the electoral system, economic independence from foreign powers, and the maintenance of state-owned industries in the energy sector. The electoral success of the traditionally conservative opposition party, the **National Action Party** (Partido Acción Nacional, PAN) and the more progressive PRD ended the **Institutional Revolutionary Party's** (Partido Revolucionario Institucional, PRI) long-standing majority in the Chamber of Deputies in 1997. That same year, Cárdenas was elected mayor of Mexico City, putting the Mexican capital under opposition control for the first time since the creation of the PRI in the 1920s. The PRD has had an acrimonious relationship with the state and the PRI, and party members have contested the results of gubernatorial and state-level legislative elections. Cárdenas ran unsuccessfully as the PRD's candidate in the 1994 and 2000 presidential elections.

Díaz, Porfirio (1830–1915)

General Porfirio Díaz served as president from 1876 to 1880 and again from 1884 to 1911, the period known as the *Porfiriato*. Popular dissatisfaction with his policies and the start of the **Mexican Revolution** (1910–1929) drove Díaz from office and Mexico in 1911.

Born in Oaxaca, Díaz became involved in the military early in life, fighting against U.S. forces in the **War of 1846**. He soon became engaged in politics, participating in the 1850s reform movement known as *la Reforma* (see **Juárez, Benito**). Díaz supported President Juárez (1858, 1861–1863, 1867–1872) in his fight against the French (1864–1867; see **Maximilian Von Hapsburg, Ferdinand**), and was appointed to a military post in 1867. From that position, he posed a serious challenge to the Juárez government while developing his own campaign to rule Mexico. Díaz won the presidential election of 1876, and led the nation with an iron fist, consolidating most decision making in the federal government, in the presidency in particular, and taking action against regional leaders whom he believed did not subscribe to his political thinking. Díaz did not run for office in 1880, though he chose his successor and remained prominent in the political sphere. He reassumed the presidency in 1884 and remained in power until 1911.

Díaz's political agenda was guided by the philosophy of Positivism, which called for the establishment of absolute "order," organized from the top down, with the upper classes guiding the nation's future, while the lower classes provided the necessary labor for economic growth. The main objective of the second Díaz administration was to modernize Mexico with the help of aid and investment from foreign countries, and it was successful. During the *Porfiriato*, infrastructure and education were improved, and the country advanced economically. Nonetheless, by the early 1900s many believed that Mexico's growth and democracy were being stifled by Díaz's omnipresence and his overcentralized government.

While serious opposition began to organize in 1910, Díaz contested and won that year's presidential election (which many believed was fraudulent), defeating Francisco **Madero** (1911–1913). From prison in San Luís Potosí, Madero soon called on the people to revolt, and Díaz fled the country in 1911 as the Mexican Revolution erupted.

Echeverría Alvarez, Luis (1922–)

Luis Echeverría Alvarez served as president of Mexico from 1970 to 1976 during a period of mounting disunity within the **Institutional Revolutionary Party** (Partido Revolucionario Institucional, PRI).

Born in Mexico City, Echeverría studied at the National University (Universidad Nacional Autónoma de México, UNAM) and in Chile. He was minister of the interior under President Gustavo Díaz Ordaz (1964–1970), and was believed by some to have been responsible for ordering the massacre of students at the Plaza de Tres Culturas in the Tlatelolco section of Mexico City in October 1968 (see **Events of 1968, Tlatelolco**). Echeverría was elected president in 1970, and his administration faced serious challenges as the economic boom turned to bust. Inflation increased significantly at the end of his tenure, and partly due to his mismanagement of public finances, Mexico's external debt rose over 500 percent in the six years that he held office. Echeverría lost support from within his own party due to these failures, and his provocation of the business community through increased state intervention in the economy.

Nonetheless, he also had a number of popular policies: he implemented extensive land reform (through innovative *ejido*, or land grant, programs) to stimulate the agricultural sector, supported Latin American socialist regimes, and openly opposed U.S. intervention in the region.

Events of 1968, Tlatelolco

Mexico was the first Latin American country to host the Olympics. Pressures on the government related to the beginning of the games in the fall of 1968, political tensions, and student uprisings led to a violent episode in Mexican history.

In preparation for the games, the government launched a public relations campaign to improve Mexico's international image. Implicit in that campaign was the containment of any domestic unrest, which would tarnish the image the country was trying to project. The government kept a close eye on students, as discontent with the **Institutional Revolutionary Party** (Partido Revolucionario Institucional, PRI) had filtered onto college campuses in the 1960s. As the beginning of the games approached, tensions grew and police repression increased. Students organized demonstrations on various university campuses to protest escalating police control. Government tanks were brought in to disband an August 1968 antigovernment rally attended by almost half a million people, and in the turmoil one student died. In September of that year, President Gustavo Díaz Ordaz (1964–1970) ordered the military to seize the National University (Universidad Nacional Autónoma de México, UNAM), creating uproar and resulting in the arrest of hundreds of demonstrators.

On October 2, 1968, approximately 5,000 students gathered peacefully in the Plaza de Tres Culturas in the Tlatelolco section of Mexico City to protest the government's lack of response to their demands, and the police and army soon arrived on the scene. While the violent incident that followed is often remembered as a student massacre, the sequence of events and the exact number of people who died have never been clear. The incident, and the cloudy circumstances surrounding it, eroded the legitimacy of President Díaz Ordaz and the PRI domestically and internationally.

Fox Quesada, Vicente (1942–)

Vicente Fox Quesada, elected in July 2000, was the first president since 1929 who was not a member of the **Institutional Revolutionary Party** (Partido Revolucionario Institucional, PRI).

Fox was born in Mexico City in 1942 to a farming family from the state of Guanajuato. He studied Business Administration at the Universidad Iberoamericana and took a management course at Harvard University. He began his business career working for the Coca-Cola Company as a route supervisor, eventually ascending to president of Coca-Cola for Mexico, and later for Latin America. He joined the **National Action Party** (Partido Acción Nacional, PAN) in the 1980s and was elected to the national Congress on the party's ticket in 1988. He ran unsuccessfully for governor of Guanajuato in 1991 in a contest wrought with allegations of electoral fraud by the ruling PRI; he ran again in 1995 and won. The dynamic Fox began campaigning for the PAN's presidential nomination years before he was awarded the nomination, and his victory in the July 2000 presidential election was a landmark event in Mexican politics.

Fox took office in December 2000 promising dramatic changes, including expanding indigenous rights, strengthening the rule of law, supporting federalism, and implementing fiscal, education, labor and state reform. Fox invited members of other political parties, including the PRI and the **Democratic Revolutionary Party** (Partido de la Revolución Democrática, PRD) to participate in his government and assembled a diverse cabinet. One of Fox's first legislative initiatives was to submit an indigenous rights bill to Congress in order to bring the rebels of the **Zapatista National Liberation Army** (Ejército Zapatista de Liberación Nacional, EZLN) back to the negotiating table. The bill eventually passed, but the final weakened version, the result of heated negotiations between the three main political parties in the divided Congress, did not satisfy the EZLN, who called the bill inadequate. Fox received newly elected U.S. President George W. Bush on Bush's first foreign trip, and set the tone for Mexico's dealings with Washington by articulating his vision for a European Union-style North America; he also put immigration reform high on the bilateral agenda.

Fuentes, Carlos (1928–)

Carlos Fuentes is a world-renowned Mexican writer who focused much of his work on *lo mexicano* or what it means to be Mexican, analyzing many themes, including the struggles of the **Mexican Revolution** (1910–1929) and Mexican foreign relations.

The son of a Mexican career diplomat, Fuentes spent parts of his childhood and a good deal of his adult life abroad. He first began publishing in Chile, where his work was heavily influenced by the Chilean political climate as well as by prominent Chilean writers such as Pablo **Neruda** (see Chile). In the 1950s Fuentes published several books that, together with the work of Octavio Paz (who wrote such pieces as *El laberinto de la soledad* [*Labyrinth of Solitude*], which addresses Mexican life and customs, and struggles to define the Mexican identity), are said to define modern Mexican literature. Perhaps the most notable of Fuentes' works is *La muerte de Artemio Cruz* (*The Death of Artemio Cruz*), which tells the story of the last twelve hours of a Mexican political strongman's life. Fuentes' later work expanded beyond Mexico to try to define a Latin American identity.

Fuentes became more outspoken politically later in life. While he initially supported the **Cuban Revolution of 1959** (see Cuba), in 1965 Fuentes broke his ties with the revolution and began to criticize Soviet domination. Fuentes established close ties with the administration of Luis **Echeverría Álvarez** (1970–1976) and was named ambassador to France in 1975. He resigned two years later in protest of the Mexican government's nomination of former president Gustavo Díaz Ordaz (1964–1970) as the first ambassador to Spain since Mexican independence; Fuentes took exception to the nomination due to Díaz Ordaz's involvement in the massacre at Tlatelolco (see **Events of 1968, Tlatelolco**). In the past two decades, Fuentes has continued to weave political themes into his writing in an attempt to encourage the deepening of democracy in Mexico.

Grito de Dolores. See **Hidalgo y Castilla, Miguel**

Hidalgo y Castilla, Miguel (1753–1811)

Father Miguel Hidalgo y Castilla was heavily involved in a movement to overthrow the Spanish colonial government in the early 1800s.

Born into a wealthy creole family, Hidalgo attended two prestigious educational institutions in Mexico and then committed to the church as his vocation. He entered the priesthood in 1778 and began teaching theology. Soon his interests expanded beyond education, and he became a minister in rural parishes. Hidalgo participated in the evolving plot to overthrow the Spanish government and confiscate all the Mexican lands owned by Spaniards. In September 1810 he released and armed a number of prisoners in the town of Dolores to fight in support of the independence movement. Referred to as the *Grito de Dolores* (Cry of Freedom), this event symbolized the beginning of the Mexican fight for independence.

Hidalgo was expelled from the Catholic Church due to his actions, but he carried on with the campaign for independence, gathering together men from different social classes and various parts of Mexico to expand and strengthen the insurgent army, establishing a provisional government, and distributing materials to inspire and organize the troops. In 1811 the Spanish forced Hidalgo to surrender his position, and soon took him prisoner and executed him. Hidalgo's actions contributed to Mexico's ultimate achievement of independence from Spain in 1821.

Huerta, Victoriano (1854–1916)

Victoriano Huerta led Mexico from 1913, following the assassination of Francisco **Madero** (1911–1913) during the **Mexican Revolution** (1910–1929), until 1914, when supporters of Venustiano **Carranza** (1914, 1915–1920) forced him from power.

Huerta became an officer in the armed forces at an early age, and was promoted to general by President Porfirio **Díaz** (1876–1880, 1884–1911) after he defeated revolts in the state of Guerrero. He remained active in the military under the subsequent Madero administration, and in 1913 he arrested Madero, had him assassinated, and took control of the country. Later that year, other opposition leaders banded together to oppose Huerta's policies, and soon troops led by Francisco (Pancho) **Villa** and Emiliano **Zapata** began to pose realistic challenges to Huerta. Nonetheless, Huerta redeployed troops from domestic battles to confront the U.S. Marines that had been sent to occupy Veracruz;

this diversion of military forces weakened Huerta's position, and in the end he was unable to defend himself simultaneously on multiple fronts. In July 1914 he resigned the presidency and fled the country. He traveled to the United States to plot his return to power in Mexico, but was arrested by U.S. authorities. He died in 1916 under the care of a U.S. doctor.

Institutional Revolutionary Party (Partido Revolucionario Institucional, PRI)

The party initially formed in 1929 as the National Revolutionary Party (Partido Nacional Revolucionario, PNR) changed its name to the Party of the Mexican Revolution (Partido de la Revolución Mexicana, PRM) in 1938, and consolidated power after its 1946 convention, at which it changed its name to the Institutional Revolutionary Party (Partido Revolucionario Institucional, PRI), thus "institutionalizing" the ideals of the **Mexican Revolution** (1910–1929).

The PRI dominated Mexican politics through the second half of the twentieth century. Other than Vicente **Fox Quesada** (2000–) of the **National Action Party** (Partido Acción Nacional, PAN), who was elected in July 2000, every Mexican president after 1946 was a member of the PRI, and until 1997 the PRI held a majority in both houses of Congress. One key to the party's success has been its corporatist structure: each of its more than 5 million members is associated with a certain sector, such as labor or peasantry, and the PRI maintains close relationships with sectoral organizations such as the **Confederation of Mexican Workers** (Confederación de Trabajadores de México, CTM). Many criticized the PRI's dominance in Mexican politics and the party's undemocratic operating style, pointing to traditional practices such as the *dedazo*, the direct designation, rather than nomination by convention, member vote, or primary, of the PRI candidate for president (a tradition symbolically disavowed by President Ernesto **Zedillo Ponce de León** [1994–2000] in 1999).

The line separating the PRI and the state has historically been hazy. While the blurred distinction increased the PRI's control and lent it additional legitimacy, it also resulted in the public's association of the PRI with the problems Mexico experienced in the last two decades of the twentieth century. Severe economic hardship (see **López Portillo y Pacheco**, José; **Peso Crisis of 1995**), mounting divisions within the party, corruption scandals, and guerrilla uprisings (see **Zapatista National Liberation Army** [Ejército Zapatista de Liberación Nacional, EZLN]) brought into question the PRI's ability to manage the state. In addition, the two most important opposition parties, the **Democratic Revolutionary Party** (Partido de la Revolución Democrática, PRD) and the PAN, began to challenge PRI dominance. Further, while campaigning for the 1994 elections, PRI presidential candidate Donaldo Colosio and the secretary general of the PRI were assassinated; rumors of the involvement of Raúl Salinas, brother of outgoing president Carlos **Salinas de Gortari** (1988–1994) in planning the second assassination seriously threatened the PRI's legitimacy.

In the 1990s the PRI made efforts to democratize and to address increasing pressures to modernize. The party held its first presidential primary in 1999, in which Francisco Labastida Ochoa was chosen to run on the PRI ticket in the July 2000 presidential elections. Some believe that the victory of PAN candidate Fox over the PRI's Labastida in that contest, and the PRI's subsequent infighting, will bring the era of absolute PRI domination of Mexican politics to a close. The PRI also lost its majority in the Senate in the 2000 elections; for the first time in the party's history, in 2001, it held a plurality rather than a majority in that legislative body.

Iturbide, Agustín Cosme Damian de (1783–1824)

Agustín Cosme Damian de Iturbide was the unifying force behind the push for Mexican independence from Spain in the early nineteenth century.

Iturbide's upper-class family was openly supportive of the Spanish viceroyalty. At the age of fourteen, Iturbide joined the Spanish forces in Mexico and, after the *Grito de Dolores* (Cry of Freedom) of 1810 (see **Hidalgo y Castilla**, Miguel), he fought actively against the rebels. Iturbide rose quickly in the military ranks, and by 1813 he was a regional commander. However, Iturbide soon became embittered by Spanish rule, as his ambitions for promotion were frustrated by Spanish domination. Differences mounted and Iturbide eventually left the Spanish armed services around 1816. The revolt against the Spanish continued until 1821, when Iturbide, still ostensibly supporting the Spanish, masterminded a three-point compromise peace plan (the *Plan de Iguala*): Mexico would be an independent constitutional monarchy (the crown would be offered to the king of Spain, or another representative), Catholicism would be the national religion, and there would be equality for Spaniards and mestizos.

Almost all the rebel movements supported Iturbide's plan, which they saw as a sure way to Mexican independence. However, once he had used the compromise to unite the independence movement, Iturbide turned against the Spanish, and by the end of 1821 effectively controlled Mexico. In May 1822 the Congress voted Iturbide emperor of Mexico, although voting took place under obvious threats from the armed forces. The area that is today Central America joined Mexico in declaring its independence from Spain in 1821, and shortly after rising to power, Iturbide annexed it. (The area declared independence from Mexico shortly thereafter; see **United Provinces of Central America**, Appendix 1.) As emperor, Iturbide's authoritarian style quickly disappointed the Mexican people. When resistance arose in the Congress, he dissolved the body and appointed a junta. Facing armed opposition from General Santa Anna, Iturbide fled Mexico in 1823. He returned briefly in 1824 and was captured and executed.

Juárez, Benito (1806–1872)

Benito Juárez, a strong proponent of Liberal causes and the first indigenous leader to achieve great political success, served as provisional president of Mexico briefly in 1858, and as president from 1861 to 1863 and 1867 to 1872.

Born in Oaxaca, Juárez was a full-blooded Zapotec Indian. Initially a lawyer, Juárez became a deputy in the state congress in 1833. During the period in the 1850s known as *la Reforma*, Juárez and other political leaders initiated a series of reforms that stripped power from the army and the church, and sought to increase the involvement of mestizos and the indigenous population in Mexican political life. A new constitution, written in 1857, contained a bill of rights including freedom of speech, religion, petition, assembly, education, and the press.

Juárez became president of the Supreme Court in 1857, and the following year he was appointed provisional president when President Ignacio Comonfort (1855–1858) was removed in a revolt led by Conservative elements. Juárez was forced to flee the national capital, Mexico City, soon afterward, and he established a new seat of government at Veracruz. From there, he initiated a number of sweeping reforms, including the reduction of the civil power of the Roman Catholic Church. He defeated the Conservative forces in 1860; in 1861 he reestablished his government in Mexico City and was constitutionally elected president.

Meanwhile, Mexico was facing severe financial difficulties. Struggling to shore up domestic finance, Juárez suspended payments on all external debts for two years. In response, the country's foreign debtors, Great Britain, France, and Spain (with the encouragement of the conservative faction), sent forces to Mexico to guarantee repayment. Their intervention eventually evolved into a full-fledged armed invasion by the French (see **Maximilian Von Hapsburg**, Ferdinand) that drove Juárez and the liberals into exile in 1863. After many battles and the execution of Maximilian, the Liberals finally defeated the French in 1867 and Juárez was reelected to the presidency that same year. However, his election caused a split among his supporters, and his administration was threatened by future dictator Porfirio **Díaz** (1876–1880, 1884–1911), who had risen to military prominence during the French intervention. Juárez died in office in 1872.

López Portillo y Pacheco, José (1920–)

During his presidency (1976–1982), José López Portillo y Pacheco benefited from the boom in the Mexican oil industry and helped to initiate the chain of events that would lead to the regionwide debt crisis of the 1980s.

Oil had a significant impact on Mexican economics

and politics in the second half of the twentieth century, as it provided the country with income and gained Mexico recognition and prestige within the international community. In the 1970s the Middle East oil embargo shifted international attention toward Mexico, and the state-owned oil company, Mexican Petroleum (Petróleos Mexicanos, PEMEX), increased production. By 1981 Mexico was the world's fourth largest oil producer, producing close to 2.5 million barrels a day. Mexico also received many large foreign loans during the 1970s, as lenders were confident that oil provided Mexico with enough collateral to insure repayment. With funds pouring in, President López Portillo invested millions in infrastructure, social programs, and government subsidies.

The López Portillo administration also took an active role in regional affairs. Mexico supported the **Sandinista National Liberation Front** (Frente Sandinista de Liberación Nacional, FSLN; see Nicaragua) in Nicaragua, and in 1981 joined with France in supporting the leftist insurgents in El Salvador's internal power struggle (see **Farabundo Martí National Liberation Front** [Frente Farabundo Martí para la Liberación Nacional, FMLN], El Salvador). In 1980 Mexico and Venezuela created the Economic Cooperation Program for Central America and Caribbean Countries through the San José Accords, which allowed for the provision of subsidized Mexican and Venezuelan oil to other countries included in the pact, effectively increasing Mexico's clout in the region.

However, by the early 1980s an oil glut caused prices to plunge. Confidence in the Mexican economy decreased with oil prices, and in light of massive capital flight, the administration devalued the peso in February 1982. Later that year, the government declared that Mexico would be unable to pay back its external debts, setting off the debt crisis that unfolded in various stages throughout Latin America in the 1980s and damaging Mexico's prestige. López Portillo was accused of economic mismanagement, and when he left office in 1982 Mexico was facing the worst economic crisis in its history.

Madero, Francisco (1873–1913)

Francisco Madero assumed the presidency in 1911, but failed to consolidate power and was assassinated in 1913.

Madero studied in Paris and the University of California, then returned to Mexico to work on his family's farms. He strongly believed that Mexico needed a more liberal democracy, and entered the 1910 race for the presidency as a representative of the Anti-Reelectionist Party, whose main goal was to block the reelection of Porfirio **Díaz** (1876–1880, 1884–1911). Madero's presidential bid was unsuccessful, and Díaz arrested him along with 5,000 other people who had criticized the dictator and his policies. Nonetheless, political tensions

were increasing throughout Mexico, and for the first time in decades, Díaz had serious opposition. From jail in 1910, Madero issued the *Plan de San Luis Potosí,* which called for armed resistance to Díaz. Madero's supporters and other groups began to carry out his plan, and the resultant rebellions evolved into the **Mexican Revolution** (1910–1929). Díaz fled the country in 1911; Madero assumed the presidency, and was elected legitimately in May 1912. Political turmoil increased as groups from around the country began to demand land reform and radical changes in the political system. In 1913 Madero was killed by his military chief of staff, Victoriano **Huerta**. His death is considered by many to have been a catalyst for the Mexican Revolution.

de la Madrid Hurtado, Miguel (1934–)

Miguel de la Madrid Hurtado served as president of Mexico from 1982 to 1988 during a period of severe financial crisis in the country and throughout Latin America.

Born into a wealthy family in Colima, de la Madrid attended law school in Mexico City, obtained a master's degree at Harvard, and later taught law. He entered government service in the Treasury Department, served as minister of budget and planning under President José **López Portillo y Pacheco** (1976–1982), was selected by López Portillo to run for president on the ticket of the **Institutional Revolutionary Party** (Partido Revolucionario Institucional, PRI) in 1982, and won the presidency.

While de la Madrid represented a new generation of the PRI, technocrats willing to experiment with economic policies and public management, he was limited in the actions that he could take by the severe economic crisis and serious external debt that he inherited from López Portillo. By the time he was sworn into office in December 1982, Mexico had fallen into full-scale economic depression, and many of de la Madrid's decisions were guided by economic programs imposed by the International Monetary Fund (IMF) in hopes of pulling Mexico out of the financial abyss.

U.S.-Mexican relations were also tense during de la Madrid's administration, complicated by the migration of Mexican citizens to the United States due to Mexico's economic problems. Relations were made even more difficult by the increase in severity and visibility of drug trafficking and the murder of a U.S. Drug Enforcement Agency (DEA) agent in 1985 in Mexico. Further, although de la Madrid needed U.S. support during these difficult financial times, he disagreed with U.S. president Ronald Reagan's Central America policies (see **Reagan Doctrine**, Appendix 2).

Although tumultuous, de la Madrid's administration ended solidly, with the government continuing to promote trade, with the Mexican economy back on track, and with the country following strict monetary policies.

Maximilian Von Hapsburg, Ferdinand (1832–1867)

Ferdinand Maximilian Von Hapsburg of Austria, known in Mexico simply as Maximilian, ruled Mexico as emperor from 1864 to 1867.

By the early 1860s, Mexico was facing severe financial difficulties, leading President Benito **Juárez** (1858, 1861–1863, 1867–1872) to suspend payment on all external debt for two years. In response, the country's foreign debtors sent forces to Mexico to guarantee repayment, an intervention that eventually evolved into a full-fledged armed invasion by the French. Juárez and the Liberals went into exile in 1863, and in 1864 French emperor Napoleon Bonaparte III installed Maximilian as emperor of Mexico to restore order, hoping that, since Austria had not been involved in the intervention, the imposition of Maximilian would not be interpreted as an attempt to colonize Mexico. Maximilian had agreed to accept the assignment provided that the Mexican people were behind his appointment and that France pledged its support. Napoleon agreed to keep 25,000 French troops in Mexico until Maximilian felt comfortable.

Fighting between the Liberals and Conservatives continued after his arrival, and though he attempted to restore stability and pursue reform, he soon proved ineffectual in both. He faced strong opposition from the Liberals from the start, and his policies soon proved too liberal for the Conservatives, the minority of the population that initially supported him. In 1866 the French minimized their presence, further debilitating Maximilian's weak hold on the government. The Liberals defeated the French and conquered Mexico City in March 1867; Maximilian surrendered, and was executed.

Mexican Revolution (1910–1929)

The political tensions that would develop into the Mexican Revolution emerged in the late nineteenth century during the presidency of Porfirio **Díaz** (1876–1880, 1884–1911). Though Díaz was able to encourage economic growth and significant development in industry, these benefits were overshadowed by the political and economic inequalities plaguing Mexico. A majority of the Mexican population was landless and frustrated with the government's indifference to their cries for agrarian reform.

In 1909 tensions became political struggles as Emiliano **Zapata** led peasants in southern Mexico in reclaiming their ancestral lands from large sugar haciendas. Though Díaz faced viable political opposition in the presidential election of 1910 for the first time in almost forty years, his opponent, Francisco **Madero** (1911–1913), lost the (perhaps fraudulent) election and was jailed. From prison, Madero issued the *Plan de San Luis Potosí*, which called for an uprising against Díaz. Rebellions sparked by the plan evolved into the Mexican Revolution.

Groups from different sectors worked together to defeat Díaz, who finally resigned and fled the country in 1911, but cooperation subsequently dissolved as different leaders began to publicly articulate their visions of the new Mexico. Madero assumed the presidency in 1911 and was officially elected in 1912, but was overthrown and killed by his military advisor, General Victoriano **Huerta** (1913–1914), in 1913. Huerta assumed the presidency, and revolutionary leaders fought against him and each other to gain control. In the South, Zapata spoke out vehemently in favor of agrarian reform and social justice, as did Francisco (Pancho) **Villa** in the North. Generals Venustiano **Carranza** (1914, 1915–1920) and Álvaro **Obregón** (1920–1924) also gained significant support in the North.

Huerta resigned and fled the country in 1914, and Carranza assumed the presidency. By 1917, he had quelled the forces of Villa and Zapata. His administration promulgated a constitution in 1917 that expressed the desires of Villa, Zapata, Carranza, and Obregón: social change, agrarian reform, and an acknowledgment and celebration of Mexico's indigenous heritage. At least partially as a result of the victory that this powerful document seemed to symbolize, fighting declined significantly by 1920. Estimates suggest that more than a million people were killed between 1910 and 1920. Power struggles between revolutionary leaders continued through the 1920s, and a final series of violent uprisings in central and western Mexico (see **Cristero Rebellion**) rocked the nation between 1926 and 1929. In the latter year, one of the most lasting legacies of the revolution, the party that professed to embody its values, the National Revolutionary Party (Partido Nacional Revolucionario, PNR), later known as the **Institutional Revolutionary Party** (Partido Revolucionario Institucional, PRI), formed.

National Action Party (Partido Acción Nacional, PAN)

The National Action Party (Partido Acción Nacional, PAN) was founded by Manuel Gómez Morín in 1939 as an eclectic party created primarily to oppose the policies of President Lázaro **Cárdenas** (1934–1940). While the party's original members included Catholics, academics, and businessmen, it has traditionally served as a vehicle for a diversity of political interests not represented by the **Institutional Revolutionary Party** (Partido Revolucionario Institucional, PRI), and has challenged the PRI and its policies since its inception. Considered conservative, the PAN advocates smaller government and less government control.

In the 1980s the party began to pose a more serious challenge to the PRI in the political arena. In 1988 the PAN forged a pragmatic relationship with President Carlos **Salinas de Gortari** (1988–1994) as he attempted to respond to accusations that the results of the 1988 presidential election were fraudulent. Beginning in 1989, the PAN won several governorships, and subsequently continued to maintain its position in key north-

José Clemente Orozco's 24-panel mural, *The Epic of American Civilization*, depicts the history of Mexico from the migration of the Aztecs to the modernization of the country in the twentieth century. Shown here is Panel 16 (entitled "Hispano-America"), which shows an idealized peasant revolutionary standing between Mexico's modern military-industrial society and a foreigner struggling to hold onto the country's wealth. *Commissioned by the Trustees of Dartmouth College, Hanover, New Hampshire.* © Orozco Valladores Family/Licensed by VAGA, New York, NY.

ern states. PRI president Ernesto **Zedillo Ponce de León** (1994–2000) named a prominent PAN politician as attorney general in 1997.

In the 1997 legislative elections, the PAN, along with the other main opposition party, the **Democratic Revolutionary Party** (Partido de la Revolución Democrática, PRD), and smaller parties, garnered enough electoral support to prevent the PRI from winning a majority in the Chamber of Deputies for the first time in five decades. In the July 2000 presidential contest, PAN candidate Vicente **Fox Quesada** (2000–) won a landmark victory over PRI candidate Francisco Labastida Ochoa, beginning a new era in Mexican politics. In the concurrent legislative elections, the PAN and the PRD successfully kept the PRI from obtaining a major-

ity in the Senate for the first time in the PRI's history. Fox began his administration by distancing himself from the PAN and inviting PRD and PRI members (as well as members of the PAN) to join his cabinet. Early on, Fox began to confront the realities of what many consider Mexico's transition to democracy as his legislative initiatives found opposition from a newly independent Congress eager to assert its will.

National Confederation of Peasants (Confederación Nacional Campesina, CNC)

Land reform has been an issue in Mexican politics since the country's independence, and was one of the most important goals of the **Mexican Revolution** (1910–1929). Due to President Lázaro **Cárdenas'** (1934–1940) belief that a united peasantry could be an important political force and could pose a legitimate challenge to the landholding elite, in 1938 Cárdenas restructured the National Revolutionary Party (Partido Nacional Revolucionario, PNR), a precursor of the **Institutional Revolutionary Party** (Partido Revolucionario Institucional, PRI) so that the National Confederation of Peasants (Confederación Nacional Campesina, CNC) became one of the three sectors of the population represented by the party.

The CNC's close relationship with the party allowed it to act as mediator between the peasants and the government as they negotiated agrarian reform, and facilitated its rise to become the country's most prominent peasant union. However, that close relationship also caused the CNC to struggle for legitimacy among the peasant population, inspired the growth of other more independent peasant organizations, and inhibited the CNC from exerting much pressure on the government.

President Luis **Echeverría Alvarez** (1970–1976) implemented significant land reform and created a new ministry, the Ministry of Agrarian Reform (Secretaría de Reforma Agraria, SRA), which worked in conjunction with the CNC to respond to peasant demands. In the 1990s the CNC suffered a series of internal political struggles as it tried to decide if it should break with Mexico's corporatist tradition, become a more independent body, and advocate a moderate market-oriented course for Mexican agriculture.

National Revolutionary Party (Partido Nacional Revolucionario, PNR). See Institutional Revolutionary Party (Partido Revolucionario Institucional, PRI)

North American Free Trade Agreement (NAFTA)
First discussed in the early 1990s, the North American Free Trade Agreement (NAFTA) was signed in 1992 and went into effect on January 1, 1994. The treaty calls for the elimination of all tariffs between the United States, Canada, and Mexico over fifteen years (1994–2009). NAFTA's architects hope that the phased elimination of tariffs (according to industry and specific product) will allow participating countries' economies sufficient time to adjust to the resultant changes in competition and prices. Complete elimination of tariffs among the three states will establish a free trade area that encompasses all of North America, creating the largest market in the world, with one-third of the world's gross domestic product.

The agreement initially faced serious opposition in the United States. While many predicted that NAFTA would encourage investment and promote fair competition, others in the United States were concerned about the effect that abolishing trade barriers among the three nations might have on the U.S. economy. Environmental groups were concerned that U.S. companies would

relocate most of their manufacturing to Mexico to take advantage of looser environmental regulations there, and labor unions in the United States were concerned that U.S. jobs would be lost to Mexico, where the standard wage is much lower. Concerns about physical mistreatment and poor management of the Mexican labor force were highlighted in both countries. To address these concerns, the final accord included side agreements that addressed environmental and labor issues and established commissions to ensure that regulations were enforced.

The agreement was a turning point for Mexican politics, the Mexican economy, and U.S.-Mexican relations. Initially, NAFTA was embraced in Mexico, as many considered it an important step toward Mexico becoming a major player in the international trade arena. However, the day that the agreement went into effect also marked the emergence of the **Zapatista National Liberation Army** (Ejército Zapatista de Liberación Nacional, EZLN) and the beginning of serious strife between the EZLN and the Mexican government. Nonetheless, the agreement has solidified a U.S.-Mexican relationship based on cooperation rather than conflict, and provided a framework for the resolution of trade disputes.

Obregón, Álvaro (1880–1928)
Álvaro Obregón served as president of Mexico from 1920 to 1924; he was reelected in 1928 but was assassinated before beginning his second presidential term.

Obregón's political career began with his active support of Francisco **Madero** (1911–1913) in his successful challenge to President Porfirio **Díaz** (1876–1880, 1884–1911). Madero took office in 1911, but was assassinated in 1913 by General Venustiano **Huerta** (1913–1914), who subsequently assumed the presidency. Obregón used his political acumen to campaign against Huerta, and used his military skill to rise to prominence. Obregón joined with Venustiano **Carranza** (1914, 1915–1920) in 1914 and led their combined forces to defeat Francisco (Pancho) **Villa** in a bloody battle in 1915.

Carranza was voted into the presidency in 1917, and Obregón appeared to retire. However, his retirement was only a façade to distance himself from Carranza so that he could launch his own political career. Obregón went to the United States to seek the support of U.S. president Woodrow Wilson, and formally announced his candidacy for president of Mexico in 1919. His supporters used the political tensions in Mexico City to call for the ousting of Carranza, and in 1920 Obregón invaded Mexico City accompanied by his own supporters and those of the late Emiliano **Zapata**. Carranza fled the city and was killed in Veracruz, and in December 1920 Obregón was sworn into office.

During Obregón's presidency, Mexican politics calmed significantly, as he focused efforts on eliminating any activists who were planning rebellions or unrest. The labor movement grew stronger during his time in office, as did political parties. The biggest challenge of Obregón's presidency was gaining recognition from the United States, which he finally received in 1923. Obregón was elected again in 1928, but was assassinated a few weeks before he was to take office.

Oil in Mexican Politics. See Cárdenas, Lázaro; López Portillo y Pacheco, José

Paz, Octavio. See Fuentes, Carlos

Peso Crisis of 1995

The peso crisis, which occurred only shortly after Mexico had recovered from the grave economic problems it experienced in the 1980s (see **López Portillo y Pacheco,** José), refers to a period during which Mexico faced severe economic problems due to hasty economic decisions and political turmoil in 1994.

For most of the early 1990s Mexico's economy prospered. International investor interest in Mexico peaked with the negotiations for the **North American Free Trade Agreement** (NAFTA), and international trade with Mexico blossomed in the early 1990s. However, due to unsettling events including the January 1, 1994 uprising in Chiapas by the **Zapatista National Liberation Army** (Ejército Zapatista de Liberación Nacional, EZLN) and the turbulence surrounding the August 1994 presidential elections, investors became wary of Mexico once again. In order to prevent massive capital flight, the government tried to avoid policies that had the potential to spark inflation. To maintain the support of the business community, the government was also hesitant to devalue the peso.

With the transition to the administration of Ernesto **Zedillo Ponce de León** (1994–2000) on December 1, 1994, economic volatility increased. By the time the Mexican government tried to correct the value of the peso in late December 1994, international reserves had already been severely reduced. The markets were unsteady for a number of weeks, while the Mexican government considered its options. In March 1995, with the help of the International Monetary Fund (IMF), Mexico introduced a strict program that included major economic reforms designed to prevent recurring problems, such as currency overvaluation and public sector deficits.

Although the crisis was the most serious economic recession Mexico had experienced since the Great Depression, the government, with a U.S. assistance package, was able to pull out of it and reestablish its creditworthiness.

La Reforma (mid-1850s). See **Juárez, Benito**

Salinas de Gortari, Carlos (1948–)

Carlos Salinas de Gortari served as president of Mexico from 1988 to 1994, implementing key political, social, and economic reforms. His tenure was controversial and marked by revelations of illegal personal enrichment and the involvement of his family in political scandals.

Born into a political family, Salinas pursued graduate studies at Harvard and returned to Mexico in the late 1970s to become a bureaucrat in the Finance Ministry. He served as minister of budget and planning under President Miguel **de la Madrid Hurtado** (1982–1988), who tapped Salinas to be the candidate for the **Institutional Revolutionary Party** (Partido Revolucionario Institucional, PRI) in the 1988 presidential election. Many PRI members worried that Salinas might not effectively lead them as they faced their most serious challenge ever from opposition parties. While the computer system tabulating votes shut down for three days during the 1988 election, Salinas was eventually declared victorious over Cuauhtémoc **Cárdenas,** who contested the election on the ticket of the National Democratic Front (Frente Democrático Nacional, FDN). Many believe that the PRI fixed the election results during the faked outage, and the election is considered one of the most fraudulent in Mexican history.

Once in office, Salinas made sweeping changes, proving himself a legitimate leader with a serious agenda. His administration addressed corruption, and privatized nationalized companies to stimulate the economy. Salinas funneled money into social programs, increasing his popularity, and championed the negotiation and final signing of the **North American Free Trade Agreement** (NAFTA), dramatically improving Mexico's relations with the United States. Nonetheless, problems began to mount as Salinas was leaving office. The murder of the designated PRI candidate for the 1994 presidential election, Luis Donaldo Colosio, on the campaign trail was just the first in a series of assassinations and kidnappings assumed by most to be tied to intra-PRI battles and tensions. In addition, the **Zapatista National Liberation Army** (Ejército Zapatista de Liberación Nacional, EZLN) gained national attention in 1994 when it instigated a rebellion on the day that NAFTA went into effect, and later challenged Salinas' dedication to the Mexican people and accused him of involvement in paramilitary violence. Salinas was succeeded as president by Ermesto **Zedillo Ponce de León** (1994–2000). In 1995, Salinas' brother and close advisor Raúl Salinas de Gortari was accused of (and was later jailed for) having plotted the 1994 assassination of a high-ranking PRI official; Salinas was humiliated, and his popularity, both domestically and internationally, plummeted.

Tlatelolco. See Events of 1968, Tlatelolco

Treaty of Guadalupe Hidalgo. See War of 1846

Villa, Francisco (Pancho) (1878–1923)

Francisco (Pancho) Villa led the revolutionary Conventionist forces that were defeated by the revolutionary Constitutionalist force led by Álvaro **Obregón** (1920–1924) and Venustiano **Carranza** (1914, 1915–1920) during the **Mexican Revolution** (1910–1929).

At the onset of the revolution, Villa worked with Francisco **Madero** (1911–1913) to defeat Porfirio **Díaz** (1876–1880, 1884–1911). Madero assumed the presidency in 1911, but soon called on Villa to defend his government when various counterrevolutionary groups rose up in opposition to Madero. Villa might have joined forces with General Victoriano **Huerta** (1913–1914), who appeared to be working for Madero as well, but Huerta quickly turned on Villa and had him arrested; Huerta overthrew the Madero government in 1913, killing Madero and taking control of the country.

Villa fought against Huerta, defeating the Federal army in the state of Chihuahua and subsequently being named governor of the state by the revolutionary fighting forces. As governor, Villa clearly articulated his vision of the revolution's goals: land reform and more investment in social programs. Huerta left power in 1914, and Villa's troops continued to fight against those that had supported Huerta, inching closer to Mexico City. As Villa's army approached the capital in 1914, Carranza, who led the revolutionary forces approaching Mexico City from the North, asked Villa to turn around and let his forces take the lead. Tensions rose and the revolutionary forces were split into two sides, the Constitutionalists, led by Carranza and Obregón, and the Conventionists, led by Villa and Emiliano **Zapata**.

Villa was brutally defeated by Carranza in 1915. In 1916 Villa wrote to Zapata and urged him to take on the next battlefront, which would pit Zapata's troops against the United States troops that were occupying Veracruz. Meanwhile, Villa and his significantly weakened army attacked a town in New Mexico, leaving seventeen civilians dead. Although the United States tried unfailingly to find him, Villa successfully hid. When Carranza was assassinated in 1920, Villa reached a peace agreement with the new president, Adolfo de la Huerta (1920), and soon removed himself from political life. He was killed in 1923.

War of 1846 (also U.S.-Mexican War) (1846–1848)

In the beginning of the 1800s, what is today Texas was a desolate part of northern Mexico, occupied by a few thousand residents. Prior to Mexican independence, Spain had agreed to let 300 U.S. families migrate to the area to expedite colonization, and following Mexican independence, thousands of U.S. citizens migrated there. By the 1830s, U.S. immigrants living in the area far outnumbered Mexicans, and residents began clamoring for reform and voicing their desire to become a separate state. Mexican politics were far from stable, and the federal government was unable to control either the continual immigration of U.S. citizens into the area or the demands of those living there.

By 1835 there was significant support for the area's independence from Mexico. Mexican general Santa Anna took troops there to quell the independence movement, and on March 2, 1836, Santa Anna was victorious in the infamous Battle of the Alamo. In a show of force, Santa Anna executed all 300 soldiers whom he had been taken prisoner in the battle. This ruthless action angered those pushing for independence, and six weeks later Santa Anna was taken prisoner by members of the independence movement. Fearing for his life, he negotiated and agreed to treaties that granted the area independence; to Mexico's frustration, the United States annexed Texas in 1845.

Border disputes broke out as the United States pushed to get more and more Mexican territory. Once the Mexicans realized that it would be impossible for them to retain the land the United States desired, negotiations over the price at which the United States could purchase the area began. Amid criticism from Mexican nationalists and escalating border disputes, the negotiations fell apart, U.S. soldiers marched on Mexico, and the war began in 1846. Mexico was immediately vulnerable to the United States and its well-organized battle plans, and after bloody defeats in Veracruz and Monterrey, the Mexicans agreed to settle the dispute.

Through the Treaty of Guadalupe Hidalgo, signed in 1848, Mexico lost about one-half of its original territory, including all or parts of what are now the U.S. States of Arizona, California, Colorado, Nevada, New Mexico, and Utah. While the Mexican Congress was humiliated by the defeat, the lost territory was sparsely populated, and most found the loss of land preferable to a prolonged occupation by the United States. The United States bought even more Mexican territory in the 1853 Gadsden Purchase. The war formed the basis of Mexican suspicion of its northern neighbor and lingering tensions in the bilateral relationship.

Zapata, Emiliano (1879–1919)

Emiliano Zapata was an important leader of the **Mexican Revolution** (1910–1929). He called for land reform, and together with Francisco (Pancho) **Villa**, his Conventionist forces battled Venustiano **Carranza** (1914, 1915–1920) and Álvaro **Obregón** (1920–1924) and the Constitutionalist forces.

Zapata was born into a middle-class family. Beginning in 1909, he led peasants in southern Mexico to reclaim their ancestral lands from large sugar estates, and soon became a supporter of Francisco **Madero** (1911–1913) and his efforts to overthrow Porfirio **Díaz** (1876–1880, 1884–1911). Zapata brought together a force of men known as the Zapatistas that contributed to the defeat of Díaz in 1911. That same year, Zapata and his followers released the *Plan de Ayala*, which demanded that land and other resources be returned to the people of Mexico and not monopolized by the Mexican elite. The plan's ideas spread throughout southern Mexico, significantly increasing Zapata's support base. Once Madero came to power, Zapata tried to convince him that agrarian reform throughout Mexico should be an immediate priority. Putting political stability first, Madero asked Zapata to disband his troops; when Zapata did not execute that order swiftly, Madero sent federal troops to disband the Zapatistas. In response, Zapata broke ties with Madero, who was soon overthrown and killed by the forces of General Victoriano **Huerta** (1913–1914).

Zapata did not immediately align himself with the anti-Huerta Constitutionalists of the North, led by Carranza, because he was not certain that they were dedicated to agrarian reform. Nonetheless, Huerta was defeated in 1914. That same year Zapata made a pact with Villa, and by November 1914 they had captured Mexico City and were continuing north. Nonetheless, a series of assassinations soon strained relations between the two leaders, and in 1915, Zapata returned to southern Mexico, where land reform had already begun. Zapata's leadership began to wane as Carranza continued to gather support throughout Mexico and advanced his troops, defending and promoting the Constitution of 1917. In 1919 Zapata sought an alliance with an old ally of Carranza, Jesús Guajardo. Zapata went to his hacienda for a consultation and was ambushed as he rode through the gates.

Even following Zapata's death, many in southern Mexico still campaigned for his beliefs, mainly land reform. The profound effect that he had on the region is reflected in the **Zapatista National Liberation Army** (Ejército Zapatista de Liberación Nacional, EZLN), a rebel group that challenges the government to provide more rights and protections for the indigenous citizenry of Mexico.

Zapatista National Liberation Army (Ejército Zapatista de Liberación Nacional, EZLN)

The Zapatista National Liberation Army (Ejército Zapatista de Liberación Nacional, EZLN) is named for Emiliano **Zapata**, who championed the causes of the landless and impoverished during the **Mexican Revolution** (1910–1929). The EZLN seeks to protect and defend the rights of the indigenous population of Mexico.

The EZLN first emerged on the national and international scene on January 1, 1994, when rebel forces seized the southern town of San Cristóbal de las Casas in the state of Chiapas and proclaimed a revolution, calling the government of President Carlos **Salinas de Gortari** (1988–1994) an illegal dictatorship and accusing it of severely neglecting the needs of the Mexican peasantry and indigenous population. The symbolic attack occurred on the very day on which the **North**

American Free Trade Agreement (NAFTA) went into effect.

The Mexican government moved quickly to ameliorate the situation, as 1994 was an election year and international attention was already focused on Mexico due to the inauguration of NAFTA. After two weeks of fighting a cease-fire was called and peace talks between the government and the rebels began. However, the negotiations soon fell apart as other political events distracted the government and public support for the movement waned. The EZLN called on international human rights organizations to vocalize its concerns and rally support for its cause. The leader of the EZLN, *subcomandante* Marcos, though not a member of the indigenous population, clearly articulated the needs of the indigenous people, and many believe that it was his leadership that won the group its large following.

President Ernesto **Zedillo Ponce de León** (1994–2000) unsuccessfully attempted to arrest the movement's leadership in 1996, aggravating tensions between the government and the Zapatistas. Talks resumed in 1998 after the 1997 massacre of forty-five members of the indigenous population of the town of Acteal, in Chiapas. That incident brought international attention and scrutiny to Zedillo's administration, as human rights organizations reported that state police had helped the attackers obtain weapons, paid little heed to rumors that a massive attack was about to occur, and obstructed a proper investigation of the evidence. After much criticism, the Zedillo administration cracked down on both sides, arresting and prosecuting over a hundred people, disbanding radical pro-government groups, and asking foreigners who had been working with the EZLN to leave Mexico. For the first time, the government seemed serious about implementing legislation that would expand indigenous rights and freedoms. Many interpreted the government's apparent willingness to discuss and implement change as a reflection of its new-found dedication to reforming the Mexican political system. Further, the first legislative initiative of President Vicente **Fox Quesada** (2000–   ) was to submit a bill to expand indigenous rights. The bill passed in 2001, but controversy over changes made by Congress may have undermined its effect.

Zedillo Ponce de Leon, Ernesto (1951–   )

Ernesto Zedillo Ponce de Leon served as president of Mexico from 1994 to 2000 and worked for democratization, decentralization, and reform of the **Institutional Revolutionary Party** (Partido Revolucionario Institucional, PRI).

Zedillo completed his doctoral degree at Yale University and began his career working for the Bank of Mexico, in Mexico City. From that position, Zedillo was appointed undersecretary in the Secretariat of Budget and Planning in the administration of President

Miguel **de la Madrid Hurtado** (1982–1988), where he forged a relationship with Carlos **Salinas de Gortari** (1988–1994), under whose administration he initially served as secretary of budget and planning. In 1992 Zedillo was shifted to minister of education; although still prominent in the cabinet, Zedillo was no longer seen as a likely successor to Salinas. Salinas chose Luis Donaldo Colosio to run for the presidency for the PRI in 1994, but Colosio was assassinated only five months before the election. Salinas and other PRI leaders scrambled to find a replacement, and Zedillo was selected. With only a few months to prepare his candidacy, the election was one of the most difficult that the PRI had faced. Opposition parties were gaining popularity in Mexico, and the PRI had to struggle to explain Colosio's assassination, the 1994 uprising led by the **Zapatista National Liberation Army** (Ejército Zapatista de Liberación Nacional, EZLN), and other political instabilities.

Zedillo won the election, defeating Cuauhtémoc **Cárdenas** of the **Democratic Revolutionary Party** (Partido de la Revolución Democrática, PRD) by a good margin, but soon faced new challenges. The Mexican economy took a turn for the worse with the **peso crisis of 1995**, and the EZLN reappeared on the political scene; Zedillo's unsuccessful attempt (1996) to arrest the group's leaders only heightened tensions between indigenous groups and the state. In spite of these obstacles to progress, Zedillo made significant strides to decentralize the Mexican government and give more autonomy to the states, and to cede more power to the opposition parties. For the first time since 1929, a member of the **National Action Party** (Partido Acción Nacional, PAN) was appointed to the presidential cabinet. Zedillo also broke the tradition of designating the PRI candidate to run in the subsequent presidential election, and in November 1999 the PRI held its first ever primary election. Francisco Labastida Ochoa was chosen to run on the PRI ticket in the July 2000 contest. Zedillo's actions, which seemed to be attempts to further democratize Mexico and reform the PRI itself, had unanticipated results: PAN candidate Vicente **Fox Quesada** (2000–   ) won a landmark victory in the July 2000 presidential election, opening what many hoped would be a new era in Mexican politics.

HEADS OF STATE

Emperor Agustín Cosme Damian de Iturbide	1822–1823
Guadalupe Victoria	1824–1829
Vicente Guerrero	1829
José María Bocanegra (interim)	1829
Pedro Vélez, Luis Quintanar, and Lucas Alamán	1829
Anastasio Bustamente	1830–1832
Melchor Múzquiz (interim)	1832
Manuel Gómez Pedraza	1833
Antonio López de Santa Anna (held office various times)	1833–1855
Valentín Gómez Farías	1833–1834
Miguel Barragán	1835–1836
José Justo Corro	1836–1837
Anastasio Bustamente	1837–1839
Nicolás Bravo (held office various times)	1839–1846
Javier Echeverría	1841
Anastasio Bustamente	1842
Valentín Canalizo	1844
José Joaquín Herrera (interim)	1844, 1845
Mariano Paredes Arrillaga	1846
Mariano Salas	1846
Valentín Gómez Farías	1847
Pedro María Anaya	1847 and 1848
Manuel de la Peña y Peña	1847 and 1848
José Joaquín Herrera	1848–1851
Mariano Arista	1851–1853
Juan Bautista Ceballos (interim)	1853
Manuel María Lombardini	1853–1855
Martín Carrera (interim)	1855
Rómulo Díaz de la Vega	1855
Juan Alvarez	1855
Ignacio Comonfort	1855–1858
Félix Zuloaga	1858
Manuel Robles Pezuela	1858
Benito Juárez (provisional)	1858
Miguel Miramón	1859–1860
Ignacio Pavón	1860
Benito Juárez	1861–1863
Emperor Ferdinand Maximilian Von Hapsburg	1864–1867
Benito Juárez	1867–1872
Sebastián Lerdo de Tejada	1872–1876
Juan N. Méndez	1876
Porfirio Díaz	1876–1880
Manuel González	1880–1884
Porfirio Díaz	1884–1911
Francisco León de la Barra (interim)	1911
Francisco Madero	1911–1913
Pedro Lascuraín (interim)	1913
Victoriano Huerta (interim)	1913–1914
Francisco Carbajal (interim)	1914
Venustiano Carranza	1914
Eulalio Gutiérrez (interim)	1914
Roque González Garza	1914
Francisco Lagos Cházaro	1915

Venustiano Carranza	1915–1920
Adolfo de la Huerta (interim)	1920
Álvaro Obregón	1920–1924
Plutarco Elías Calles	1924–1928
Emilio Portes Gil (interim)	1928–1930
Pascual Ortíz Rubio	1930–1932
Abelardo Rodríguez (interim)	1932–1934
Lázaro Cárdenas	1934–1940
Manuel Avila Camacho	1940–1946
Miguel Alemán Valdés	1946–1952
Adolfo Ruíz Cortines	1952–1958
Adolfo López Mateos	1958–1964
Gustavo Díaz Ordaz	1964–1970
Luis Echeverría Alvarez	1970–1976
José López Portillo y Pacheco	1976–1982
Miguel de la Madrid Hurtado	1982–1988
Carlos Salinas de Gortari	1988–1994
Ernesto Zedillo Ponce de León	1994–2000
Vicente Fox Quesada	2000–

Source: Michael C. Meyer and William L. Sherman, *The Course of Mexican History* (New York: Oxford University Press, 1995), appendix, pp. III–IV.

BIBLIOGRAPHY

Print Resources

Aguilar Camin, Hector, and Lorenzo Meyer. *In the Shadow of the Mexican Revolution: Contemporary Mexican History, 1910–1989*. Austin: University of Texas Press, 1993.

Beals, Carlton. *Porfirio Díaz: Dictator of Mexico*. Philadelphia: Lippincott, 1932.

Camp, Roderic Ai. *Politics in Mexico*. New York: Oxford University Press, 1993.

Castañeda, Jorge. *The Mexican Shock: Its Meaning for the U.S.* New York: The New Press, 1995.

Cothran, Daniel A. *Political Stability and Democracy in Mexico: The Perfect Dictatorship*. Westport, CT: Praeger, 1994.

Krauze, Enrique. *Mexico—Biography of Power: A History of Modern Mexico, 1810–1996*. New York: HarperCollins, 1997.

Lustig, Nora. *Mexico: The Remaking of an Economy*. Washington, DC: Brookings Institution, 1996.

Meyer, Michael C., and William L. Sherman. *The Course of Mexican History*. New York: Oxford University Press, 1995.

Tutino, John. *From Insurrection to Revolution in Mexico: Social Bases of Agrarian Violence, 1750–1940*. Princeton: Princeton University Press, 1986.

Womack, John. *Zapata and the Mexican Revolution*. New York: Knopf, 1968.

Electronic Resources

Center of Research for Development (CIDAC)
http://www.cidac.com.mx

CIDAC is one of Mexico's leading think tanks. This site contains political and economic analysis. (In English and Spanish)

Documents on Mexican Politics
http://www.cs.unb.ca/~alopez-o/polind.html
Comprehensive database of articles, reports, and primary documents about all facets of Mexican local, national, and international politics. Also includes links to a variety of Mexican political institutions and organizations. (In English)

Government of Mexico
www.presidencia.gob.mx
Contains information, press release, and up-to-date speeches and activities of the president. (In English and Spanish)

Latin American Network Information Center (LANIC): Mexico
http://lanic.utexas.edu/la/mexico/
Mexico section of this extensive Web site contains hundreds of links to research resources, cultural centers, economic and business institutions, government agencies, historical sources, magazines and other periodicals, nongovernmental organizations, and grassroots groups, as well as many other subjects. (In English)

Latin Focus: Mexico
http://www.latin-focus.com/countries/mexico.htm
Contains an overview and description of Mexico's government institutions and political environment, economic and financial information and statistics, and links to government ministries and agencies. (In English)

Mexico Online
http://www.mexonline.com/mexagncy.htm
Web site with extensive links to government agencies, political documents, speeches and official papers, and relevant multilateral and international institutions. (In English)

Political Database of the Americas: Mexico
http://www.georgetown.edu/pdba/Countries/mexico.html
Comprehensive database run as a joint project of Georgetown University and the Organization of American States. Section on Mexico contains information on and links to the executive, legislative, and judicial branches of the Mexican government; electoral laws and election results; and other political data. (In English, Spanish, Portuguese, and French)

Political Resources.net: Mexico
http://www.politicalresources.net/mx.htm
Mexico section of a Web site containing a wealth of links to sources of information about national politics. Includes information on political parties, legislative and executive institutions, laws and legislation, and elections, as well as a link to the constitution. (In English)

Reforma
http://www.reforma.com/
The Web version of one of Mexico's premier daily newspapers. Offers comprehensive national and international coverage, with a particularly strong emphasis on national politics and the Mexican economy. (In Spanish)

United States–Mexico Chamber of Commerce
http://www.usmcoc.org
Contains information on business, the economy, the North American Free Trade Agreement, and trade, as well as links to other related sites. (In English)

El Universal
http://www.el-universal.com.mx
The Web version of an important Mexican newspaper. This site is a good source for political news, at both the national and state level, and also has detailed coverage of political parties and Congress, justice and narcotics, government, and foreign relations. (In Spanish)

Wilfried Derksen's Elections Around the World: Mexico
http://www.agora.it/elections/mexico.htm
Mexico section of a comprehensive database of results from elections around the world. Contains results from recent national executive and legislative elections, as well as explanations of and links to political parties and institutions. (In English)

World Policy Institute: Americas Project Mexico Page
http://worldpolicy.org/americas/mexindex.html
Web project of an international relations think tank. Explores democracy and human rights in Mexico through a variety of articles, news pieces, and links to other Web sites. (In English)

NICARAGUA

COUNTRY PROFILE

Official name	República de Nicaragua
Capital	Managua
Type/structure of government	Democratic republic
Executive	President and vice president elected to five-year nonrenewable terms
Legislative	Unicameral National Assembly (93 elected members serve five-year terms).
Judicial	Highest court is Supreme Court; includes twelve members elected to seven-year terms by the National Assembly.
Supreme Electoral Council	Supreme Electoral Council oversees election procedures.
Major political parties	Splinter parties of the **Liberal Party** (Partido Liberal, PL) and **Nicaraguan Conservative Party** (Partido Conservador de Nicaragua, PCN); **Sandinista National Liberation Front** (Frente Sandinista de Liberación Nacional, FSLN).
Constitution in effect	1987
Location/geography	Central America, bordering Costa Rica to the south and Honduras to the north; Pacific Ocean to the west and Caribbean Sea to the east; extremely mountainous and volcanic; features largest body of water in the region (Lake Nicaragua).
Geographic area	118,358 sq. km.
Population	4,807,000 (1998)**
Ethnic groups	Mestizo 69%; white (of European descent) 17%; black (of African descent) 9%; indigenous 5%*
Religions	Roman Catholic 95%; Protestant 5%*
Literacy rate	63.4% (1997)**
Infant mortality rate	43.0 deaths per 1,000 live births (1997)**
Life expectancy	68.1 years (1997)**
Monetary unit	Córdoba
Exchange rate (month, year)	1 U.S. dollar = 11.65 córdobas (August 2000)***
Major exports	Bananas and agricultural goods; lobster and fish products
Major imports	Capital and consumer goods
GDP	$2.2 billion (1998)**
GDP growth rate	4.0% (1998)*
GDP per capita	$2,700 (2000 est.)****

*CIA World Fact Book, 2000. http://www.cia.gov/cia/publiciations/factbook/nu.html

**Inter-American Development Bank. Statistics and Quantitative Analysis Unit Integration and Regional Programs Department. http://www.iadb.org/int/sta/ENGLISH/brpt net/english/nicbrpt.htm

***Latin American Weekly Report. August 22, 2000 (WR-00-33), p. 394.

****CIA World Fact Book. 2001. http://www.cia.gov/cia/publiciations/factbook

OVERVIEW

Summary

Nicaragua is the largest country in Central America, and one whose history has been marked by violent political change and severe economic underdevelopment. Following independence from the Spanish in 1821, Nicaragua experienced a period of political instability and U.S. intervention as local elites from Conservative and Liberal factions sought control. Chronic economic strife and mass poverty combined with violent oppression under the Somoza family dynasty: Anastasio **Somoza García** led the country from 1937 to 1956, his elder son Luis **Somoza Debayle** from 1956 to 1967 and his younger son Anastasio **Somoza Debayle** from 1967 to 1979. The result was the revolution led by the **Sandinista National Liberation Front** (Frente Sandinista de Liberación Nacional, FSLN), which triumphed in 1979. While the drastic change in leadership allowed common people to become part of the political process for the first time, further violence and political maneuvering unseated the FSLN in 1990 and brought democracy to the country. Nicaragua continues to strive to overcome its poverty and its violent past.

History

Prior to the Spanish conquest the area now known as Nicaragua was inhabited by a number of indigenous groups. When the Spanish arrived in the early 1500s adventurer Gil González Dávila was welcomed by a

Nicaragua. © 1998 The Moschovitis Group, Inc.

calm group of Indians, led by the legendary Chief Nicarao. The area was subsequently colonized, and its indigenous population decimated by the Spaniards. The British also occupied the zone, mainly on the Caribbean Coast, from the seventeenth through the nineteenth centuries. The area of Meso-America (current-day Mexico and Central America) declared independence from Spain in September 1821, and while Mexico soon annexed Central America, the **United Provinces of Central America** (see Appendix 1) broke away from Mexico in 1823. Battles between the Liberal and Conservative Parties led to the dissolution of the union and the independence of Nicaragua in 1838.

In Nicaragua the fighting between the **Liberal Party** (Partido Liberal, PL) and the **Nicaraguan Conservative Party** (Partido Conservador de Nicaragua, PCN) dominated the next two decades. It was not until the PL invited United States citizen William **Walker** (1856–1857) and his rebel militia into the country to help them battle the PCN that the PL was able to dominate Nicaraguan politics. Walker unexpectedly took over the leadership of Nicaragua in 1856, but was ousted by neighboring Central American countries the following year. The PL was discredited politically by its support of Walker, and the PCN ruled until 1893. Though Nicaragua's bid to have the Central American canal built in Nicaragua was unsuccessful, the Nicaraguans built railroads during this time that transported gold from mines, coffee from the mountains in the north, and bananas from the Caribbean Coast; foreign investment in these industries fuelled economic growth.

PL leader José Santos **Zelaya** (1893–1909) came to power in 1893 through a coup that unseated PCN president Roberto Sacasa (1889–1893). The repressive Zelaya helped modernize the political administration of the country, pursued improvements in education, and in 1904 forced the British to cede their claim to the **Mosquito Coast**. Conservative opposition to Zelaya escalated, and he was ousted in 1909 with U.S. support. Tenuous control of the government by the PCN brought the U.S. Marines into the country in 1912 to protect U.S. investments and maintain order. The Marines created and trained the Nicaraguan **National Guard**, and appointed Anastasio Somoza García to oversee the group upon the withdrawal of the U.S. The Marines withdrew in 1925, but returned in 1926 and stayed until 1933. Throughout the U.S. occupation, a rebellious Liberal named Augusto César **Sandino Calderón** led a militia force attempting to drive the Marines out. Sandino stood for anti-imperialism, nationalism, and concern for the well-being of the poor, sentiments that resonated with many Nicaraguans. His movement continued even after he was assassinated by the National Guard in 1934, and decades later rebel leaders adopted his name as part of their movement's moniker (see FSLN).

Somoza García, whose extensive military training was complemented by success in business and a distinguished place among the social elite, soon took control of Nicaraguan politics. Officially elected president in 1936, he ruled Nicaragua until 1956 (at times through puppet presidents), using the National Guard to ensure his will. He placated the United States by favoring U.S. investors and helping them with their political objectives in the region. His elder son, Luis Somoza Debayle, took control of the country following Somoza García's assassination in 1956. Luis Somoza Debayle, considered more liberal-minded and less tyrannical than his father, used political rather than military means to accomplish his goals. Luis Somoza Debayle stepped down when his term expired in 1963, though he continued to supervise the country's governance. His younger brother Anastasio Somoza Debayle, who led the National Guard, continued to vie for power, and took control of the country upon Luis Somoza Debayle's death in 1967. Anastasio Somoza Debayle turned to the military to control the country, using brute force to suppress groups that opposed his family's domination and wealth.

The FSLN began to organize in the 1960s to challenge the Somozas. By 1967 the group had grown to a significant size and attained strong popular backing, prompting Anastasio Somoza Debayle to initiate a campaign of violence against the rebels and any Nicaraguans who were suspected of sympathizing with them. Several events in the 1970s, including the earthquake of 1972, which illuminated the corruption and graft of the Somoza administration, and the 1978 assassination of Pedro Joaquín Chamorro Cardenal, a wealthy newspaper publisher and politically active member of the opposition, pushed moderate members of Nicaraguan society to oppose the Somozas. The FSLN's final campaign was a multipronged assault that involved the cooperation and participation of many sectors of Nicaraguan society. That effort, combined with the withdrawal of U.S. support for the Somoza regime and the imposition of an economic embargo, caused the government to begin to cave in by 1979. Anastasio Somoza Debayle fled the country on July 17, 1979, and two days later the FSLN paraded victoriously into downtown Managua and declared themselves the legitimate government of the country.

Later that year, the rebels established the **Governing Junta of National Reconstruction** (Junta de Gobierno de Reconstrucción Nacional, JGRN) to supervise and rebuild their newly liberated country. The JGRN completely replaced the government structures that had existed under the Somozas with more popularly inclusive ones. However, infighting and ideological disagreements led members to join and leave the politically eclectic group in subsequent years. Two long-time members of the JGRN, Daniel José **Ortega Saavedra** (1985–1990) and Sergio **Ramírez Mercado**, were elected president and vice president, respectively in 1984, signaling the FSLN's desire to rule in accordance with democratic principles. They faced opposition from domestic groups such as business leaders and landholders, as well as from international forces led by the United States that feared the growth of socialism and Soviet influence. The most serious challenge came from the **counterrevolutionaries** (contrarevolucionarios, contras), resistance groups funded and armed by the United States that fought the FSLN through the 1980s.

By the 1990 presidential election, the Nicaraguan economy had seriously deteriorated, with inflation spiraling upward, and the revolutionary project had also suffered significantly in the war against the contras. While the FSLN again fielded Ortega for president and Ramírez for vice president, the now larger and better-organized opposition created the **United National Opposition** (Unión Nacional Opositora, UNO), a coalition of fourteen parties. Their presidential candidate, Violeta **Barrios de Chamorro** (1990–1997), was victorious. As president, Chamorro pursued policies of reconciliation and reconstruction, working in conjunction with other opposition factions and the FSLN. Her immediate goals were to stabilize the economy with market-based reforms backed by the International Monetary Fund (IMF) and the World Bank, and to disarm both the FSLN and contra fighters while scaling back the military to less than half its previous size. The country slowly stabilized, but remained poor and politically divided. Serious issues, such as property ownership, remained unresolved.

In the 1996 presidential election, Arnoldo **Alemán Lacayo** (1997–2002), a member of the Liberal Constitutional Party (Partido Liberal Constitucionalista, PLC) and the candidate of the Liberal Alliance (Alianza Liberal, AL) coalition, defeated FSLN presidential candidate Ortega on a reform platform including deepening market-based economic reforms, ending legal protection for unions, and restoring to their original owners lands that had been confiscated by the FSLN. Once in office, Alemán faced severe opposition from the FSLN congressional representatives, who still occupied over one-third of the legislative seats. Though he successfully led the country to overcome the damage wrought by Hurricane Mitch in 1998, he struggled to maintain a political balance between his supporters and the still popular Sandinistas. Elections were held in November 2001. Ortega again contested the presidential election on the FSLN ticket, but Enrique Bolaños Geyer (2002–   ) of the PLC won the election with a majority of the popular vote. The PLC also won a majority in the concurrent National Assembly elections, though the FSLN increased its congressional representation to 42 percent.

ENTRIES

Alemán Lacayo, Arnoldo (1946–   )

Arnoldo Alemán Lacayo, elected president in 1996 on the ticket of the Liberal Alliance (Alianza Liberal, AL), an electoral coalition formed in 1996, held office from 1997 to 2002.

Born in Managua on January 23, 1946, Alemán graduated with a law degree from the National Autonomous University in León in 1967, and then worked as a lawyer in Managua, representing important business interests. He opposed the Sandinista government that triumphed in 1979 (see **Sandinista National Liberation Front** [Frente Sandinista de Liberación Nacional, FSLN]; **Governing Junta of National Reconstruction** [Junta de Gobierno de Reconstrucción Nacional, JGRN]), and was elected mayor of Managua as a candidate of the opposition Liberal Constitutional Party (Partido Liberal Constitucional, PLC) in 1990. As mayor, Alemán dismantled key aspects of FSLN programs in Managua before resigning to run for the presidency in 1996.

There were more than twenty candidates in the 1996 presidential contest, including former Sandinista president Daniel José **Ortega Saavedra** (1985–1990). Alemán was not declared the winner until a month after the voting took place, following intense controversy over lost ballot boxes in the largest department; he was finally inaugurated in January 1997. Alemán's government was immediately at odds with the strong FSLN representation in Congress, and its first few months were marked by conflict and confrontations with FSLN politicians and unions. Nonetheless, Alemán soon came to an agreement with the FSLN congressional membership, enabling him to undertake economic and social reforms, including reorienting the economy along free market lines and borrowing from international lenders such as the International Monetary Fund (IMF) and the **Inter-American Development Bank** (IDB; see Appendix 2). Alemán oversaw Nicaragua's humanitarian efforts when Hurricane Mitch struck the country in 1998, causing millions of dollars in damage and killing thousands of people. He also actively sought to alter legal codes so that land confiscated and distributed under the FSLN could be returned to its original owners, and undertook programs to reorganize the public health and education systems.

Barrios de Chamorro, Violeta (1929–)

Violeta Barrios de Chamorro served as president of Nicaragua from 1990 to 1997. She is considered a symbol of motherhood, traditional religious values, and moderate politics.

Chamorro was born in the Rivas department of Nicaragua on October 18, 1929, into one of the wealthiest and most prominent families in the country. In 1950 she married Pedro Joaquín Chamorro Cardenal, who led part of the moderate opposition to the dictatorships of Luis **Somoza Debayle** (1956–1967) and Anastasio **Somoza Debayle** (1967–1979) and ran the well-known newspaper *La Prensa*. Chamorro Cardenal's assassination in 1978 helped the revolutionary **Sandinista National Liberation Front** (Frente Sandinista de Liberación Nacional, FSLN) gain support, and the group deposed Anastasio Somoza Debayle in July of the following year.

Violeta Chamorro became a member of the **Governing Junta of National Reconstruction** (Junta de Gobierno de Reconstrucción Nacional, JGRN) that ruled Nicaragua from 1979 to 1985 following the FSLN's revolutionary victory but resigned after less than one year due to conflicts with the extreme leftist factions of the FSLN. In the years that followed, Chamorro became a vocal critic of the Sandinista government (later led by Daniel José **Ortega Saavedra**, 1985–1990) and the limitations the regime placed on civil rights (including freedom of the press, with which she had firsthand experience, as she had continued to run her husband's newspaper after his death). Through the 1980s, Chamorro became increasingly supportive of the **counterrevolutionaries** (contrarevolucionarios, contras), the guerrilla groups that waged persistent warfare through that decade in an effort to unseat the ruling Sandinista regime.

Chamorro ran for president in the 1990 contest as a candidate of the **United National Opposition** (Unión Nacional Opositora, UNO). Her campaign focused on a peaceful transition from Sandinista rule, an end to the civil war, and economic recovery. She won with 55 percent of the vote. She immediately began to scale back the army, negotiate disarmament with the contras, and implement an economic stabilization program. By the end of her term peace had returned to most parts of the war-torn country, the economy was slowly improving,

and Nicaragua had reestablished ties with the United States after years of political and economic embargoes. Due to constitutional term limits, Chamorro could not stand as a candidate in the 1996 presidential elections, and Arnoldo **Alemán Lacayo** (1997–2002) of the Liberal Constitutional Party (Partido Liberal Constitucionalista, PLC) was elected president on the ticket of the Liberal Alliance (Alianza Liberal, AL) coalition. Following her term as president, Chamorro drastically decreased her involvement in political activities, turning instead to family responsibilities.

Counterrevolutionaries (Contrarevolucionarios, Contras)

The counterrevolutionaries (contrarevolucionarios, contras) fought to undermine and depose the revolutionary government of the **Sandinista National Liberation Front** (Frente Sandinista de Liberación Nacional, FSLN) throughout the 1980s.

Initial opposition to the FSLN government stemmed from surviving factions of the **National Guard**, the military force that the Somoza dynasty (see **Somoza Debayle**, Anastasio; **Somoza Debayle**, Luis; **Somoza García**, Anastasio) had used to control Nicaragua during its reign from 1937 to 1979. By 1981 opposition to the FSLN had formally organized into the right-wing guerrilla forces known as the contras, which were trained and supported by the U.S. military. Though the U.S. Congress officially voted to end economic support for the rebels in 1984, based on accusations that they had committed human rights abuses, the **Iran-Contra Affair** would subsequently reveal that the U.S. government had continued to funnel money to the contras illegally for an additional two years.

The contras were able to pose a serious threat to the Sandinista government through guerrilla tactics, including strategic attacks on roads, bridges, and educational and health facilities, as well as political organizing. Though they only managed to control certain sections of the country (especially near the northern border with Honduras) for brief periods of time, the destruction they caused to infrastructure, as well as their success in recruiting members and support from various parts of Nicaraguan society, made them a serious threat to the Sandinista government. In response, President Daniel José **Ortega Saavedra** (1985–1990) made the Sandinista Popular Army (which replaced the National Guard) the largest in Central America, and made military service mandatory for young men.

By the late 1980s both the contras and the Sandinista government were in financial ruin, and popular support for the Ortega regime had dwindled. This, combined with increased U.S. political pressure, facilitated the election of Violeta **Barrios de Chamorro** (1990–1997) of the **United National Opposition** (Unión Nacional Opositora, UNO) coalition to the presidency in 1990. Though the contras were legally disbanded in 1990 under agreements made with the Chamorro administration, certain factions, called re-contras, continued to train in remote areas of Nicaragua.

Darío, Rubén (1867–1916)

Renowned poet, diplomat, and national hero Rubén Darío was born Félix Rubén García Sarmiento in Metapa on January 18, 1867. He took his grandparents' surname in order to inherit the prestige in social and business circles that their wealth and prominence brought. Darío showed an affinity for arts and reading from a very young age (beginning a career as a journalist by age fifteen), and he later attended prestigious national institutes in Nicaragua and El Salvador. Searching for a more structured intellectual atmosphere, Darío moved to Chile in 1886, and his first and perhaps most memorable book, *Azul* (*Blue*), was published there in 1888. The style that this work defined, which reflected the influence of French literature, became known as modernism, and established an entire period of Spanish-language literature. Later, his work would include social and political themes.

Darío returned to Nicaragua in 1889 and began a second career as a diplomat, subsequently representing the Nicaraguan government in Costa Rica and Spain. He eventually returned to journalism and writing full time. Some of his other significant works include *Prosas profanas y otros poemas* (*Profane Prose and Other Poems*) (1896) and *Cantos de vida y esperanza* (*Chants of Life and Hope*) (1905). Darío is considered the most important literary figure in Nicaraguan history.

Esquipulas Accords (1987). See Appendix 1

Fonseca Amador, Carlos (1936–1976)

Carlos Fonseca Amador was a revolutionary leader and a founder of the **Sandinista National Liberation Front** (Frente Sandinista de Liberación Nacional, FSLN).

Fonseca was born in Matagalpa on June 23, 1936, the son of a high-level employee of Anastasio **Somoza García** (1937–1956). He studied law at the National Autonomous University in León and became very active in politics. He had already been a member of several political parties, including the Socialist Party, by the time he co-founded the FSLN in 1961. Strongly influenced by the **Cuban Revolution of 1959** (see Cuba) and Marxism, and drawing on the philosophy and goals of late compatriot Augusto César **Sandino Calderón**, Fonseca provided the ideological underpinning to the FSLN: a strong anti-imperialist and anti-U.S. stance, and a desire to redistribute land to peasants.

As a leader of the FSLN, he promoted guerrilla tactics and encouraged the participation of peasants, students, and industrial workers in the struggle. Though Fonseca was arrested in Costa Rica on charges of bank robbery in 1969, he was freed in exchange for hostages taken when the FSLN hijacked a Costa Rican airplane. Fonseca was killed by the **National Guard** in the mountains in northern Nicaragua in November 1976.

Governing Junta of National Reconstruction (Junta de Gobierno de Reconstrucción Nacional, JGRN)

The Governing Junta of National Reconstruction (Junta de Gobierno de Reconstrucción Nacional, JGRN) governed Nicaragua from the July 19, 1979, victory of the **Sandinista National Liberation Front** (Frente Sandinista de Liberación Nacional, FSLN) over the Somoza dynasty (see **Somoza Debayle**, Anastasio; **Somoza Debayle**, Luis; **Somoza García**, Anastasio) until the inauguration of Daniel José **Ortega Saavedra** (1985–1990) as president.

The JGRN was established to supervise and rebuild the newly liberated country after over a decade of civil war had devastated its infrastructure, economy, and morale. While Sandinista leadership was central to the JGRN, many of the eclectic group's members represented key social and economic interests in the country, including peasants, urban workers, business interests, and the military and armed groups. The first JGRN, established in 1979, included Violeta **Barrios de Chamorro** (1990–1997), Moisés Hassan Morales, Ortega, Sergio **Ramírez Mercado,** and Alfonso Robelo Callejas. After the first year, the junta began to disintegrate due to internal ideological differences and continuing political unrest following the revolution. Shuffling continued through 1981, with conservative interests leaving the group and more FSLN representation joining. From 1981 through 1985, junta membership included Ortega, Ramírez, and Rafael Córdova Rivas.

In the early 1980s, the group established a mixed economy that brought together private property as well as cooperatives (which occupied confiscated lands or factories) and pursued a policy of international neutrality, overtly favoring neither the United States nor the Soviet Union. Among the junta's greatest accomplishments were the major social reforms it implemented, including investment in public health and education, and massive literacy campaigns that raised literacy rates by over 40 percent in only one year. The JGRN also completely replaced the government structures that had existed under the Somozas with more popularly inclusive structures, and mobilized people and groups (such as women's groups, church groups, and various technical and agrarian unions) that had previously been marginalized from the country's political life. The JGRN disbanded in 1985 when Ortega and Ramírez were elected president and vice president (respectively) of Nicaragua.

Iran-Contra Affair (1986)

The **counterrevolutionaries** (contrarevolucionarios, contras), funded by the U.S. government, fought to undermine and depose the revolutionary government of the **Sandinista National Liberation Front** (Frente Sandinista de Liberación Nacional, FSLN) throughout the 1980s. Although the U.S. Congress voted to stop military aid to the contras in 1984, the U.S. government illegally funneled money it had generated by selling weapons to Iran to the group for two more years.

This illegal exchange was discovered in 1986 when a U.S. military plane delivering supplies to the contras was shot down over Nicaragua and a crewmember was taken into custody by the Sandinista military. Though U.S. president Ronald Reagan denied having any knowledge of the country's continued involvement in the contra war, fourteen Reagan administration officials were convicted of crimes in conjunction with the diversion of funds, including Lieutenant Colonel Oliver North of the National Security Council, who was implicated as the mastermind of the affair. The charges against most of those convicted, including Lieutenant Colonel North, were reversed after appeals, and U.S. president George Bush pardoned others involved in the scandal. Personnel from the U.S. Central Intelligence Agency (CIA) and the State Department were also incriminated in the final investigation.

The Iran-Contra Affair highlighted U.S. government concern about the security threat posed by the Sandinista government, raised the issue of the sovereignty of Latin American republics, and called into question the goals and methods of U.S. involvement in the countries and governments of Central America.

Liberal Party (Partido Liberal, PL)

The Liberal Party (Partido Liberal, PL) and the **Nicaraguan Conservative Party** (Partido Conservador de Nicaragua, PCN), the two major political groups throughout Nicaragua's postindependence history, battled furiously against each other for control of the country in the early independence period. In 1854 the PL, which favored a split between the church and the state, invited U.S. adventurer William **Walker** (1856–1857), famous for his attempts to declare his own republic in parts of Mexico, to come to Nicaragua and help them force the PCN from power. Walker not only helped the PL to defeat the PCN, but went on to take control of the country. His dictatorial rule discredited the Liberals, leading to years of Conservative rule. Following the U.S. Marine occupation of Nicaragua from 1912 to 1933, Anastasio **Somoza García** (1937–1956) reasserted the power and control of the PL. Several factions of this historic party still exist today within the liberal movement in Nicaragua, including the Independent Liberal Party (Partido Liberal Independiente, PLI) and the Liberal Constitutional Party (Partido Liberal Constitucionalista, PLC), the party of presidents Arnoldo **Alemán Lacayo** (1997–2002), and Enrique Bolaños Geyer (2002–   ).

Mosquito Coast

The Mosquito Coast is a region approximately 60 km wide (though it has never been exactly delimited) on the Caribbean Coast of Nicaragua and Honduras (see **La Mosquitia**, Honduras), geographically separated from the central regions of those countries by a vast tropical rain forest. Different forces have fought for control of the area, including Britain and Spain during the colonial era. In 1904 Nicaraguan President José Santos **Zelaya** (1893–1909) (with some support from the United States) forced the British to sign an agreement ceding their claim to the region and granting Nicaragua complete control of it. In the late 1970s, when the **Sandinista National Liberation Front** (Frente Sandinista de Liberación Nacional, FSLN) battled the regime of Anastasio **Somoza Debayle** (1967–1979), the fact that the isolated population of the Mosquito Coast had suffered less oppression than the rest of the nation under the Somoza dynasty (see also **Somoza Debayle, Luis; Somoza García**, Anastasio), combined with the area's historic marginalization, made it difficult for the FSLN to mobilize support among the region's inhabitants. Following the triumph of the Sandinista revolution in 1979, when the Sandinistas attempted to bring the Mosquito region into their national reconstruction effort without serious regard for its cultural and ethnic differences, the inhabitants' distrust turned into opposition and they began to ally with the **counterrevolutionaries** (contrarevolucionarios, contras). In response, the Sandinistas forcefully moved thousands of Miskito, Suma, and Rama communities to relocation camps. Subsequent complaints of substandard living conditions and limits on personal freedoms created a problem for the Sandinistas, who were facing accusations of human rights violations throughout the country. The relocated population eventually returned to their homes in the late 1980s.

National Guard

The U.S. Marines occupied Nicaragua from 1912 to 1925, and again from 1926 to 1933 in an attempt to stabilize the country after years of fighting between Liberal and Conservative factions. To provide for military security following their withdrawal, the U.S. forces organized the National Guard in 1927 and placed Anastasio **Somoza García** (1937–1956), a trusted pro-U.S. member of the Nicaraguan wealthy elite, in charge of the newly formed security force. The U.S. Marines stayed to supervise the 1932 election, in which Juan Bautista Sacasa (1933–1936) was elected president, and then withdrew in 1933. Somoza García gradually turned the National Guard into his own personal police force and used it to suppress political opposition during his dictatorship. Following his death, his eldest son Luis **Somoza Debayle** (1956–1967) took office, and reduced the role of the National Guard in politics. However, Somoza Garcia's younger son Anastasio **Somoza Debayle** (1967–1979), who succeeded Luis Somoza Debayle as the country's leader, reaffirmed the role of the force during his reign. The **Sandinista National Liber-**

This 1979 photo shows members of the National Guard advancing against Sandinista National Liberation Front guerrilla positions. *Columbus Memorial Library, General Secretariat of the Organization of American States. Reproduced with permission of the Organization of American States.*

ation Front (Frente Sandinista de Liberación Nacional, FSLN) fought the National Guard in the 1960s and 1970s, finally overpowering it in 1979. The National Guard continued to fight the FSLN after the triumph of the Sandinista revolution, and many National Guard members joined the armed opposition led by the **counterrevolutionaries** (contrarevolucionarios, contras) that battled the Sandinista regime through the 1980s.

Nicaraguan Conservative Party (Partido Conservador de Nicaragua, PCN)

The Nicaraguan Conservative Party (Partido Conservador de Nicaragua, PCN) and the **Liberal Party** (Partido Liberal, PL) have been the two major political groups in Nicaragua throughout the country's postindependence history. Conservative and Liberal elites vied for control of the **United Provinces of Central America** (see Appendix 1), and the PCN emerged from the domestic divisions that remained once Nicaragua gained complete independence in 1838. Based around the colonial city of Granada, the party favored business interests and sought to maintain the power of the Catholic Church in society and in politics. The PCN ruled Nicaragua from 1857 to 1893 without interruption, but was overthrown in 1893 by liberal José Santos **Zelaya** (1893–1909). The PCN continued to participate in politics, and eventually splintered into several parties that are still active today. Some of these groups, such as the Conservative Popular Alliance (Alianza Popular Conservadora, APC), fielded candidates in the 1990 and 1996 presidential elections. Candidates ran under the PCN banner in the presidential and legislative elections

of 2001 but garnered very small percentages of the vote in each.

Obando y Bravo, Miguel (1926–)

Nicaragua's Roman Catholic Cardinal Miguel Obando y Bravo was named archbishop of Managua in 1970. After an earthquake in 1972 destroyed parts of Nicaragua and the government of Anastasio **Somoza Debayle** (1967–1979) pillaged large amounts of the relief funds sent to Nicaragua, Obando y Bravo aligned with the moderate, upper-class opposition to the Somoza regime. He successfully negotiated between the **Sandinista National Liberation Front** (Frente Sandinista de Liberación Nacional, FSLN) and the Somoza government on several occasions. A hesitant supporter of the Sandinista regimes that ruled the country through the 1980s, he also served as mediator during the civil war between the FSLN government and the U.S.-supported **counterrevolutionaries** (contrarevolucionarios, contras) that was fought throughout most of that decade and during the negotiation of the peace accords that ended the civil war in 1990. He maintained close ties with Presidents Violeta **Barrios de Chamorro** (1990–1997) and Arnoldo **Alemán Lacayo** (1997–2002). Many associate Obando y Bravo with conservative elements in the Roman Catholic Church; he symbolizes the important role that the church plays in Nicaraguan society and politics.

Ortega Saavedra, Daniel José (1945–)

Daniel José Ortega Saavedra was a revolutionary leader of the **Sandinista National Liberation Front** (Frente Sandinista de Liberación Nacional, FSLN). He led the Gov-

Daniel José Ortega Saavedra (with microphone), who served as Nicaragua's president from 1985 to 1990, addresses a public meeting in 1983. *Columbus Memorial Library, General Secretariat of the Organization of American States. Reproduced with permission of the Organization of American States.*

erning Junta of National Reconstruction (Junta de Gobierno de Reconstrucción Nacional, JGRN) that ruled Nicaragua from 1979 to 1985, and served as president of the country from 1985 to 1990. Ortega symbolizes the Sandinista Revolution.

Ortega was born in La Libertad on November 11, 1945, to parents who were part of the opposition to the Somoza dynasty (see **Somoza Debayle**, Anastasio; **Somoza Debayle**, Luis; **Somoza García**, Anastasio) that ruled the nation from 1937 to 1979. He attended a Catholic seminary in El Salvador, but before finishing his studies there, returned to Nicaragua to attend law school at the University of Central America in Managua. Active in youth and student movements that opposed the Somoza regimes, in 1963 Ortega joined the FSLN and became the head of its urban resistance section in 1967. Following his implication in the assassination of a **National Guard** officer and a bank robbery in 1967, Ortega was taken prisoner by the National Guard and severely tortured. The FSLN fought for his freedom and in 1974 kidnapped a powerful Nicaraguan and arranged to exchange that person's safe return for the release of several prisoners, including Ortega. In 1975 Ortega became a member of the National Directorate, the governing body of the FSLN.

Despite internal divisions, the FSLN united to mount a powerful offensive against the Somozas and the National Guard in early 1979, and that same year, the JGRN took control of the fractured, politically and economically underdeveloped country with Ortega as its leader. Ortega pursued a strategy that combined socialist economic and social policy with free markets and international neutrality. Despite internal divisions, the JGRN was able to make significant strides in the areas of literacy, education, public health, and reorganization of agricultural and industrial ownership and production between 1979 and 1984. Ortega easily won the presidential election of 1984, capturing 67 percent of the popular vote. However, Ortega's government was soon forced to confront the **counterrevolutionaries** (contrarevolucionarios, contras); isolated incidents soon climaxed in a civil war, which cost the country thousands of lives and caused another decade of destruction. The economy eventually began to falter due to lack of production and international isolation, and inflation soared.

Ortega lost the 1990 presidential election to Violeta **Barrios de Chamorro** (1990–1997), lost the 1996 presidential contest to Arnoldo **Alemán Lacayo** (1997–2002), and lost the 2001 contest to Enrique Bolaños Geyer (2002–). Nonetheless, Ortega remained active in the FSLN leadership and Nicaraguan politics.

Ortega Saavedra, Humberto (1942–)

Humberto Ortega Saavedra, the older brother of Daniel **Ortega Saavedra** (1985–1990), was born in the Chontales area in 1942. Active in the movement that formed in opposition to the Somoza dynasty (see **Somoza Debayle**, Anastasio; **Somoza Debayle**, Luis; **Somoza García**, Anastasio) that ruled the country from 1937 to 1979, Ortega led the Nicaraguan Patriotic Youth Organization, and later joined the **Sandinista National Liberation Front** (Frente Sandinista de Liberación Nacional, FSLN). When the FSLN suffered a serious defeat at Pancasán in 1967, Ortega fled to Cuba, where he worked with Fidel **Castro Ruz**'s (see Cuba) anti-U.S. forces, strengthened his commitment to the revolution, and improved his guerrilla warfare tactics. He returned clandestinely to Nicaragua two years later and continued to work in the FSLN leadership and to organize urban revolutionary activities through the 1970s. His contributions as a guerrilla soldier and military tactician were important to the success of the Sandinista Revolution in July 1979. Following that victory and the FSLN's assumption of power, he was appointed defense minister and head of the Sandinista Popular Army that replaced the army of the previous regime, the **National Guard**. Ortega strengthened and enlarged the force so that it could more effectively combat the **counterrevolutionaries** (contrarevolucionarios, contras) that sought to undermine the FSLN government through the 1980s, and the Sandinista Popular Army soon grew to be the largest standing army in Central America. While Ortega continued to command the armed forces under the subsequent administration of Violeta **Barrios de Chamorro** (1990–1997), Chamorro significantly decreased the size of the army and canceled mandatory military service for Nicaraguan men. Ortega left his post in 1994, but remained very active in politics and the FSLN leadership.

Ramírez Mercado, Sergio (1942–)

Sergio Ramírez Mercado was a notable revolutionary leader in the **Sandinista National Liberation Front** (Frente Sandinista de Liberación Nacional, FSLN) and served as vice president of Nicaragua from 1985 to 1990. He is also an accomplished writer recognized in national and international circles.

Ramírez Mercado was born in Masatepe on August 5, 1942. His family was aligned with the regime of Anastasio **Somoza García** (1937–1956), and at a young age he supported the regime through his academic and journalistic writing. He completed a law degree at the National Autonomous University in León in 1964. He eventually became involved in armed opposition through the Student Revolutionary Front, briefly pursued a journalistic and literary career, then joined the FSLN in 1975. Ramírez, Humberto **Ortega Saavedra**, and Daniel **Ortega Saavedra** (1985–1990) were involved in the faction that eventually triumphed in determining the direction of the Sandinista Revolution,

and Ramírez was particularly important in recruiting FSLN support from the middle and upper classes. After the 1979 victory of the revolution, he and Daniel Ortega led the **Governing Junta of National Reconstruction** (Junta de Gobierno de Reconstrucción Nacional, JGRN), and in 1984 the two were elected vice president and president of Nicaragua, respectively.

While the duo was defeated in the presidential election of 1990, Ramírez remained active in the FSLN and led the party's representation in Congress until 1994. He founded the journal *Semanario* in Managua in 1990, and a new political party, the Renovated Sandinista Movement (Movimiento Renovador Sandinista, MRS), which included intellectuals and academics, in 1995. He ran on that party's ticket in the 1996 presidential election, but lost. He continued to write and lecture on political and literary topics in the late 1990s. He has also published several books of note, including *Margarita, está linda la mar* (*Margaret, the Ocean is Beautiful*), *El Pensamiento Vivo de Sandino* (*The Living Thought of Sandino*) (1975), and *Castigo Divino* (*Divine Punishment*) (1988).

Sandinista National Liberation Front (Frente Sandinista de Liberación Nacional, FSLN)

The Sandinista National Liberation Front (Frente Sandinista de Liberación Nacional, FSLN) was a revolutionary guerrilla movement that ousted Anastasio **Somoza Debayle** (1967–1979) in 1979. The FSLN, often referred to as the Sandinistas, ruled Nicaragua from 1979 to 1990, first through the Governing Junta of National Reconstruction (Junta de Gobierno de Reconstrucción Nacional, JGRN) from 1979 to 1985, and then through the presidency of Daniel José **Ortega Saavedra** (1985–1990). The group takes its name from the legendary hero Augusto César **Sandino Calderón** who fought against the U.S. Marines who occupied the country between 1912 and 1933.

Carlos **Fonseca Amador**, Silvio Mayorga, and Tomás Borge had been organizing student and militant groups in opposition to the Somoza dynasty (see also **Somoza Debayle**, Luis; **Somoza García**, Anastasio) that led Nicaragua between 1937 and 1979 for over ten years before they officially organized the FSLN guerrilla movement in 1961. Throughout the 1960s the group grew in number, uniting Marxists, nationalists, university students, poor peasants, and middle-class Nicaraguans to battle the tyrannical rule of the Somozas and their security force, the **National Guard**, through bombings, kidnappings, and guerrilla fighting. They trained and carried out limited attacks in the country's mountainous regions and in cities, and though the National Guard arrested, tortured, and exiled many members of the group, the others found creative ways to free their comrades from prison, including kidnapping officials, hijacking planes, and arranging prisoner-hostage swaps. While in exile, FSLN members often trained with other revolutionary or Marxist groups, including groups in the Soviet Union, Mexico, and Cuba.

By combining many different strategies and a wide variety of participants, the FSLN gained ground in the 1970s, continuing to organize in both urban and rural areas of Nicaragua. The group attacked National Guard facilities, kidnapped and killed high-ranking officers, and attempted to destabilize the armed forces as well as the political support network of the Somoza-dominated **Liberal Party** (Partido Liberal, PL). However, the group's eclectic composition eventually led to strategic and ideological divisions that threatened to weaken and fractionalize it. Some members believed that a violent peasant revolution was the only way to achieve real political change. Others wanted to link with and effect change through political movements within the middle class and students in urban areas, and still others sought alternative methods. Brothers Daniel Ortega and Humberto **Ortega Saavedra** led a faction within the FSLN that favored urban insurrections in conjunction with agrarian rebellion.

Several events in the 1970s pushed some moderate members of Nicaraguan society to support the opposition and the FSLN. The response by the government of Anastasio Somoza Debayle to the 1972 earthquake brought to light the corruption and graft of his administration, and the 1978 assassination, presumably at the hands of the National Guard, of Pedro Joaquín Chamorro Cardenal, a wealthy newspaper publisher and politically active member of the opposition, engendered further animosity toward the regime. The FSLN managed to occupy the National Palace in 1978, disgracing the military forces and demonstrating the movement's strength. Further, while the United States had long supported the Somoza regimes, it began to withdraw support in the 1970s when the dictatorship's human rights abuses against the civilian population became more blatant. U.S. president Jimmy Carter enacted an economic embargo against the regime, and by 1979 the government began to cave in. That same year the FSLN initiated its final multipronged campaign against the government, which combined urban guerrilla attacks with the participation of many societal sectors including high school students, homemakers, traditional peasants, and industrial and service workers. On July 17, 1979, after a final offensive brought Sandinista fighters within miles of Managua, Anastasio Somoza Debayle fled the country. On July 19, the FSLN paraded victoriously into downtown Managua, declaring itself the legitimate government in the company of tens of thousands of supportive citizens.

The FSLN slowly transformed into a political entity, though it continued to embody revolutionary ideals and to press for the institutionalization of such ideals. FSLN candidates Daniel Ortega and Sergio **Ramírez Mercado** were elected president and vice president, respectively, in 1984. While the duo lost the 1990 contest, and Ortega also lost the 1996 and 2001 presidential elections, the FSLN remained active in Nicaraguan politics into the twenty-first century, winning 42 percent of the seats in the National Assembly in the 2001 legislative elections.

Sandinista Revolution. See Sandinista National Liberation Front (Frente Sandinista de Liberación Nacional, FSLN)

Sandino Calderón, Augusto César (1895–1934)
Augusto César Sandino Calderón was a rebel leader who fought the U.S. Marines who occupied Nicaragua from 1912 to 1933.

Sandino was born in Niquinohomo to the wealthy owner of a large estate and a peasant worker. Sandino left his hometown at an early age and journeyed to Nicaragua's Caribbean Coast, Honduras, and Mexico, working in various capacities and developing a complex set of beliefs about social justice (an ideology that later became known as *sandinismo*). Sandino joined the Liberals in their armed opposition to Conservative rule when he returned to Nicaragua in 1926, and fought on the Caribbean Coast alongside Liberal leader José María Moncada (1929–1933). While the U.S. Marines had withdrawn from Nicaragua after a 13-year occupation in 1925, they returned in 1926 to help resolve the conflict and restore order, and Moncada reached a truce with the Conservatives in 1927. Sandino, adamant that Nicaragua should be free to govern itself without the presence of foreign military leaders, fled to the northern mountains to continue his struggle.

In the mountains, Sandino trained a band of rebels and attacked military installations. His ability to disappear into the forested mountains and suddenly reappear, ready to attack, was legendary, and he was highly sought after by the U.S. Marines and the **National Guard**, the Nicaraguan security force formed by the U.S. Marines in 1927. The Marines withdrew in 1933, and by 1934, after years of fighting, Sandino was ready to make a truce with the government. He and other rebel leaders met with newly elected Liberal president Juan Bautista Sacasa (1933–1936) in Managua in February 1934. While they arrived at a truce, the rebels were abducted by the National Guard upon emerging from the meeting, and were soon killed. Sandino's spirit of rebellion did not die, however, and the anti-U.S., nationalist, communal notion that had come to be known as *sandinismo* was revived in the 1960s when Carlos **Fonseca Amador** and others fled to the northern mountains and formed the **Sandinista National Liberation Front** (Frente Sandinista de Liberación Nacional, FSLN) to fight against the tyrannical Somoza dynasty (see **Somoza Debayle**, Anastasio; **Somoza Debayle**, Luis; **Somoza García**, Anastasio) that ruled Nicaragua from 1937 to 1979. Eventually victorious, the Sandinistas took control of the country on July 19, 1979.

Anastasio Somoza Debayle led Nicaragua from 1967 to 1979. *Columbus Memorial Library, General Secretariat of the Organization of American States. Reproduced with permission of the Organization of American States.*

Somoza Debayle, Anastasio (1925–1980)

Anastasio "Tachito" Somoza Debayle controlled Nicaragua from 1967 to 1979 (as president or through puppet presidents). He ruled in a repressive manner, in the mode of his father, Anastasio **Somoza García** (1937–1956).

Somoza Debayle was born in December 1925. He received military training in the United States (graduating from the United States Military Academy at West Point in 1948) and was appointed commander-in-chief of the Nicaraguan **National Guard** by his father. He used the military to control the country, repress opposition, and protect his family's many commercial and political interests. He became president in 1967 through elections that were generally considered to be fraudulent. Once in power, he employed his father's authoritarian and oppressive tactics, unlike his brother Luis **Somoza Debayle** (1956–1967), whose policies had been more lenient. One of Anastasio Somoza Debayle's most notorious acts came in the wake of the December 1972 earthquake that devastated Managua: when relief funds began to pour into the country from foreign governments and international organizations, corrupt administration officials stole some of the money, and contracts for reconstruction (using those international donors' funds) were awarded to Somoza supporters, who neglected to fulfill the contracts or profited from the reconstruction of buildings and roads. Somoza also

continued the family tradition of maintaining a close relationship with the United States.

While the **Sandinista National Liberation Front** (Frente Sandinista de Liberación Nacional, FSLN) challenged Somoza's regime from the very beginning, over time more opposition groups began to appear in response to Somoza's blatant abuse of power and the violent tactics used by the National Guard against the civilian population. Somoza's response included massive military action and intimidation of peasants and other possible opposition sympathizers. When Pedro Joaquín Chamorro Cardenal, a prominent member of the opposition and the editor of the newspaper *La Prensa*, was assassinated in 1978, Somoza and the National Guard were blamed, fueling further support for the opposition.

The administration of U.S. president Jimmy Carter took a hard line against human rights abuses committed by the Somoza regime, eventually imposing an economic embargo on the country; this opposition was a major departure from previous U.S. policy toward the Somoza dynasty. This withdrawal of U.S. support, in combination with the FSLN's military and political assault, finally forced Somoza to abandon the presidency and leave Nicaragua on July 17, 1979. The FSLN marched victoriously into Managua two days later. Somoza Debayle was killed by a car bomb in Asunción, Paraguay, on September 17, 1980.

Somoza Debayle, Luis (1922–1967)

Luis Somoza Debayle was the leading political figure in Nicaragua from 1956 to 1967 (either serving as president or controlling the nation through puppet presidents). His was the least repressive of the three Somoza dictatorships that ruled Nicaragua between 1937 and 1979.

The first son of Nicaraguan dictator Anastasio **Somoza García** (1937–1956), Somoza Debayle was born on November 18, 1922. He attended schools in Nicaragua and the University of Southern California (where he majored in engineering). Prioritizing politics over military affairs, Somoza served as president of the **Liberal Party** (Partido Liberal, PL) while his father was president; he was also a member, and later president, of Congress. When Somoza García was assassinated in 1956, Somoza Debayle took over as president of Nicaragua.

His policies were less repressive than those of his father or those of his younger brother, Anastasio **Somoza Debayle**, who would succeed him (1967–1979). The elder Somoza Debayle did not rule through the military, but rather tried to strengthen economic and political institutions. His outlook and policies were somewhat liberal; he favored university autonomy, stronger political (rather than military) leadership, and more expansive government-sponsored social support networks. He attempted to improve Nicaragua's diplomatic relations with other Central American countries, and maintained the close relationship his father had established with the government of the United States. While he did seek to retain his family's prominent position in Nicaraguan politics and society, he tried to achieve that goal through control of the PL and through established legal frameworks.

Somoza stepped down when his term ended in 1963, allowing René Schick Gutiérrez (1963–1966), a close political ally, and subsequently Lorenzo Guerrero Gutiérrez (1966–1967) to take over the presidency. However, he maintained close supervision of the office of the presidency and the political situation in general until his death from a heart attack on April 13, 1967.

Somoza García, Anastasio (1896–1956)

Anastasio "Tacho" Somoza García was the first member of the Somoza dynasty to lead Nicaragua, ruling as dictator from 1937 through 1956. His sons Luis **Somoza Debayle** (1956–1967) and Anastasio **Somoza Debayle** (1967–1979) ruled the country for twenty-three years after his death. The Somoza regimes were some of the most violently repressive in Central American history.

Born in Carazo, Somoza took advantage of his family's social position and wealth to attend school in the United States, which improved his command of English and increased his familiarity with U.S. customs and values. This experience became valuable as he advanced his military career in Nicaragua, and Somoza reported directly to the U.S. Marines who occupied Nicaragua from 1926 to 1933. The United States identified Somoza as a skilled leader who would effectively represent their interests, and when the U.S. Marines withdrew in 1933 after overseeing the 1932 election of Juan Bautista Sacasa (1933–1936), they left Somoza as commander of the **National Guard** (the security force they had created in 1927). Somoza soon became the central political figure in Nicaragua, and used the National Guard to maintain order and assert his own political agenda in the country for the subsequent twenty-three years.

Though Somoza had strong ties to the **Liberal Party** (Partido Liberal, PL), he forced Sacasa to step down in 1936, and was elected president in December 1936 in what many considered a fraudulent contest. While he allowed Leonardo Argüello (1947), Benjamín Lacayo Sacasa (1947), and Víctor Manuel Román y Reyes (1947–1950) to assume the presidency, Somoza remained in firm control of politics and the military, ruling the country from behind the scenes. He was officially reelected (again in fraudulent elections) in 1950, and retained the presidency until his death in 1956. During his two decades in power, Somoza monopolized the political and military arenas, maintaining control through buying out his competition and the opposition, and, when he faced serious challenges, through violence and repression. Though Nicaragua grew economically

during his tenure and Somoza secured a steadily increasing family fortune, the majority of poor Nicaraguans saw no signs of economic progress. He also maintained a close and dependent relationship with the United States. Somoza García was killed on September 21, 1956, by poet Rigoberto López Pérez.

United National Opposition (Unión Nacional Opositoria, UNO)

The United National Opposition (Unión Nacional Opositora, UNO) was a coalition of fourteen political parties and organizations with varied interests and ideologies that allied to defeat the **Sandinista National Liberation Front** (Frente Sandinista de Liberación Nacional, FSLN) in the 1990 elections.

Formed in 1987, the eclectic alliance included the large Independent Liberal Party (Partido Liberal Independiente, PLI) and many small parties including factions of the **Liberal Party** (Partido Liberal, PL) and the **Nicaraguan Conservative Party** (Partido Conservador de Nicaragua, PCN), Social Christians, Communists, Socialists, and Social Democrats. The coalition was able to achieve electoral success by uniting the opposition to the Sandinistas and thus amassing the opposition vote. The group also received major funding from the United States, which sought to prevent the continuation of Sandinista rule. Nonetheless, the large ideological gap among the parties of the coalition made it difficult for the alliance to agree on policy, strategy, and representation in government offices once its candidates were elected.

In 1990, the first presidential election in which the coalition fielded a candidate, Violeta **Barrios de Chamorro** (1990–1997) and Virgilio Godoy Reyes were elected president and vice president, respectively, with 54.7 percent of the vote. Soon after their election, the coalition began to disband due to disagreements over policies and political appointments. While the UNO also ran a candidate in the 1996 presidential election, the coalition had shrunk and its candidate received few votes.

United States Occupation (1912–1925, 1926–1933). See **National Guard**

Walker, William (1824–1860)

William Walker was an adventurer from the United States who assisted the **Liberal Party** (Partido Liberal, PL) in overpowering and deposing the government of the **Nicaraguan Conservative Party** (Partido Conservador de Nicaragua, PCN) in Nicaragua in 1855. He ruled the country through a puppet president, and then directly, from 1855 to 1857.

Born on May 8, 1824, in Tennessee, Walker studied medicine and pursued careers in law and journalism before beginning his political career. In 1853, accompanied by a small band of rebels, Walker set off for Baja

California to take over parts of Mexico and establish his own republic. He and his conspirators were quickly defeated by Mexican outlaws in 1854 and forced to return to the United States. Meanwhile, in Nicaragua, the PL and the PCN had long been vying for power, and the PL invited Walker to help it end the PCN's domination of politics. Walker and over 300 troops known as "the Immortals" traveled to Nicaragua in 1855 and helped the PL to take control; in return Walker and his men were awarded large plots of land and other political and military incentives. In an unexpected move, Walker assumed control of the military, ruling Nicaragua through a puppet president, Patricio Rivas (1855–1856), and subsequently assuming the presidency himself. He declared English the official language, legalized slavery, and enacted other measures that caused alarm throughout Central America and upset diplomatic relations between the United States and the region. Even Walker's longtime financial backer Cornelius Vanderbilt withdrew his support.

Walker was defeated by a united Central American army and surrendered to U.S. naval commander Charles H. Davis on May 1, 1857. He returned to the United States, but continued to formulate a plot to rule Nicaragua. In a final attempt, he embarked for Central America in 1860, this time landing in Honduras. He was met by angry resistance and was quickly forced to surrender to British naval commander Norvell Salmon. Salmon turned him over to Honduran officials, who executed him by firing squad on September 12, 1860, in Trujillo, Honduras.

Zelaya, José Santos (1853–1919)

Liberal politician José Santos Zelaya served as president of Nicaragua from 1893 to 1909.

Zelaya rose through the ranks of the **Liberal Party** (Partido Liberal, PL) during a time in which the **Nicaraguan Conservative Party** (Partido Conservador de Nicaragua, PCN) dominated politics, though it was challenged by the PL at all levels of government. In 1893 he led a coup that overthrew Conservative Roberto Sacasa (1889–1893) and took over the presidency. Zelaya immediately began to institutionalize his Liberal ideas. He wrote a new constitution in December 1893 that diminished the powers of the Catholic Church and separated church and state. The new charter also allowed for increased trade, which Zelaya facilitated by improving roads, railroads, and other significant infrastructure throughout the country, as well as strengthening the education system. Another of his important accomplishments was the official annexation from the British of the **Mosquito Coast** regions, which were consequently named Zelaya in his honor until the Sandinistas (see **Sandinista National Liberation Front** [Frente Sandinista de Liberación Nacional, FSLN]) restructured the geographic departments in the 1980s.

Zelaya was accused of being a tyrant and a dictator, and often resorted to violence to quiet domestic opposition. While Zelaya was cooperative with many of Nicaragua's neighbors, even exploring the option of uniting with some of them in a united Central American state, serious border disputes arose with Honduras and Costa Rica near the end of his rule. Zelaya competed with Panama over possible canal routes, courting French, British, and U.S. companies to select a Nicaraguan route. When the United States eventually gave up on a Nicaraguan canal, relations between the two countries deteriorated. A serious event in which two U.S. citizens were executed in Nicaragua in 1909 led to open diplomatic hostility between Nicaragua and the United States. Fearing a U.S.-supported coup, Zelaya left office in December 1909. He continued to comment on Nicaraguan politics and U.S. intervention in the country's national affairs.

HEADS OF STATE

Patricio Rivas	1855–1856
William Walker	1856–1857
Máximo Jérez	1857–1859
Tomás Martínez	1859–1867
Fernando Guzmán	1867–1871
Vicente Cuadra	1871–1875
Pedro Joaquín Chamorro Bolaños	1875–1879
Joaquín Zavala	1879–1883
Adán Cárdenas	1883–1887
Evaristo Carazo	1887–1889
Roberto Sacasa	1889–1893
José Santos Zelaya	1893–1909
José Madriz	1909–1910
Juan José Estrada	1910–1911
Adolfo Díaz	1911–1917*
Emiliano Chamorro Vargas	1917–1919*
Diego Manuel Chamorro	1919–1923*
Bartolomeo Martínez	1923–1925*
Carlos Solorzano	1925–1926*
Emiliano Chamorro Vargas	1926
Adolfo Díaz	1926–1929*
José María Moncada	1929–1933*
Juan Bautista Sacasa	1933–1936
Carlos Brenes Jarquín	1936–1937
Anastasio Somoza García	1937–1947
Leonardo Argüello	1947
Benjamín Lacayo Sacasa	1947
Victor Manuel Román y Reyes	1947–1950
Anastasio Somoza García	1950–1956
Luis Somoza Debayle	1956–1963

René Schick Gutiérrez	1963–1966
Lorenzo Guerrero Gutiérrez	1966–1967
Anastasio Somoza Debayle	1967–1972
Governing Junta for Somoza Family	1972–1974
Anastasio Somoza Debayle	1974–1979
Junta de Gobierno de Reconstrucción Nacional (JGRN)	1979–1985
Daniel José Ortega Saavedra	1985–1990
Violeta Barrios de Chamorro	1990–1997
Arnoldo Alemán Lacayo	1997–2002
Enrique Bolaños Geyer	2002–

*U.S. Occupation

Sources: Dieter Nohlen, *Enciclopedia Electoral Latinoamericano y del Caribe* (San José, Costa Rica: Instituto Interamericano de Derechos Humanos, 1933); Thomas E. Skidmore and Peter H. Smith, *Modern Latin America* (New York: Oxford University Press, 1997).

BIBLIOGRAPHY

Print Resources

Booth, John A. *The End and the Beginning: The Nicaraguan Revolution.* Boulder: Westview Press, 1985.

Booth, John A., and Thomas W. Walker, eds. *Understanding Central America.* Boulder: Westview Press, 1999.

Diederich, Bernard. *Somoza and the Legacy of U.S. Involvement in Central America.* New York: Dutton, 1981.

Merrill, Tim, ed. *Nicaragua: A Country Study.* Washington, DC: U.S. GPO, 1994.

Meyer, Harvey Kessler. *Historical Dictionary of Nicaragua.* Metuchen, NJ: Scarecrow Press, 1972.

Millett, Richard. *Guardians of a Dynasty.* Maryknoll, NY: Orbis Books, 1977.

Ramírez, Sergio, ed. *Sandino: The Testimony of a Nicaraguan Patriot, 1921–1934.* Princeton: Princeton University Press, 1990.

Walker, Thomas W., ed. *Revolution and Counterrevolution in Nicaragua.* Boulder: Westview Press, 1991.

———. *Nicaragua Without Illusions: Regime Transition and Structural Adjustment in the 1990s.* Wilmington, DE: SR Books, 1997.

Wall, James T. *Manifest Destiny Denied: America's First Intervention in Nicaragua.* Washington, DC: University Press of America, 1981.

Electronic Resources

Latin American Network Information Center (LANIC): Nicaragua
http://lanic.utexas.edu/la/ca/nicaragua/
Nicaragua section of this extensive Web site contains hundreds of links to research resources, cultural centers, economic and business institutions, government agencies, historical sources, magazines and other periodicals, nongovernmental organizations, and grassroots groups, as well as many other subjects. (In English)

Nicaragua News
http://www.nicaraguanews.com/
Frequently updated Web site containing a wealth of news and information on Nicaraguan politics, economics, business, and cultural events. Also contains a variety of links to other sites with information on Nicaragua. (In English)

Political Database of the Americas: Nicaragua
http://www.georgetown.edu/pdba/Countries/nica.html
Comprehensive database run as a joint project of Georgetown University and the Organization of American States. Section on Nicaragua contains information on and links to the executive, legislative, and judicial branches of the Nicaraguan government; electoral laws and election results; and other political data. (In English, Spanish, Portuguese, and French)

Political Resources.net: Nicaragua
http://www.politicalresources.net/nicaragua.htm
Nicaragua section of a Web site containing a wealth of links to sources of information about national politics. Includes information on political parties, legislative and executive institutions, laws and legislation, and elections, as well as a link to the constitution. (In English)

La Prensa Digital
http://www.laprensa.com.ni/
The Web version of one of Nicaragua's major daily newspapers. Offers comprehensive national political and economic coverage and analysis. (In Spanish)

Wilfried Derksen's Elections Around the World: Nicaragua
http://www.agora.it/elections/nicaragua.htm
Nicaragua section of a comprehensive database of results from elections around the world. Contains results from recent national executive and legislative elections, as well as explanations of and links to political parties and institutions. (In English)

PANAMA

COUNTRY PROFILE

Official name	República de Panamá
Capital	Panama City
Type/structure of government	Presidential republic; constitutional democracy
Executive	Consists of a president and two vice presidents that are popularly elected every five years and may not be elected to two consecutive terms.
Legislative	The Legislative Assembly is a unicameral body of 72 popularly elected members who serve five-year terms.
Judicial	The highest court is the Supreme Court, whose nine members are appointed by the president to ten-year terms.
Major political parties	**Antimilitarist Opposition Democratic Alliance** (Alianza Democrática de Oposición Civilista, ADOC), which is a coalition of the Nationalist Republican Liberal Movement (Movimiento Liberal Republicano Nacionalista, MOLIRENA), the Arnulfista Party (Partido Arnulfista, PA), and the Authentic Liberal Party (Partido Liberal Auténtico, PLA); **Democratic Revolutionary Party** (Partido Revolucionario Democrático, PRD).
Constitution in effect	1972, significantly amended in 1978, 1983, and 1994
Location/geography	Southernmost portion of the Central American Isthmus Bordering Costa Rica (to the northwest) and Colombia (to the southeast); Pacific Ocean to the south and Caribbean Sea to the north. Dense tropical forest spans the south-central part of the country; Panama Canal bisects the country, connecting the Pacific Ocean and Caribbean Sea.
Geographic area	77,082 sq. km**
Population	2,770,000 (1998)**
Ethnic groups	Mestizo 70%; white (of European descent) 10%; indigenous 6%; West Indian 14%*
Religions	Roman Catholic 85%; Protestant 15%*
Literacy rate	91.1% (1997)**
Infant mortality rate	21 deaths per 1,000 live births (1997)**
Life expectancy	74 years (1997)**
Monetary unit	Balboa
Exchange rate	1 U.S. dollar = 1 Balboa (linked to U.S. dollar)
Major exports	Bananas, shrimp, sugar
Major imports	Capital and consumer goods
GDP	$7.74 billion (1998)**
GDP growth rate	2.7% (1998)*
GDP per capita	$2,796 (1998)**

*CIA World Factbook. 1999. http://www.cia.gov/cia/publications/factbook/pm.html

**Statistics and Quantitative Analysis Unit, Integration and Regional Programs Department, Inter-American Development Bank. http://www.iadb.org/int/sta/ENGLISH/brptnet/english/panbrpt.htm

OVERVIEW

Summary

Panama's most distinctive feature is its geography. A thin stretch of land dividing the Caribbean Sea and the Pacific Ocean, the area that is today Panama was identified as having the potential to aid trade and commerce in the region soon after it was settled, an attribute that significantly affected the area's development and growth and led to repeated foreign intervention. The idea of building a canal across the Central American isthmus first surfaced in the sixteenth century, but the project only came to fruition in the twentieth century after the Colombian province of Panama achieved independence from Colombia and became an autonomous republic with the assistance of the United States. In the latter half of the twentieth century, Panamanian politics were marked by corruption and volatility.

History

The Colombian province of Panama was used as a crossing area to transport goods from the Pacific Coast of Latin America to the Caribbean Sea from the early sixteenth century, leading foreign powers to take an in-

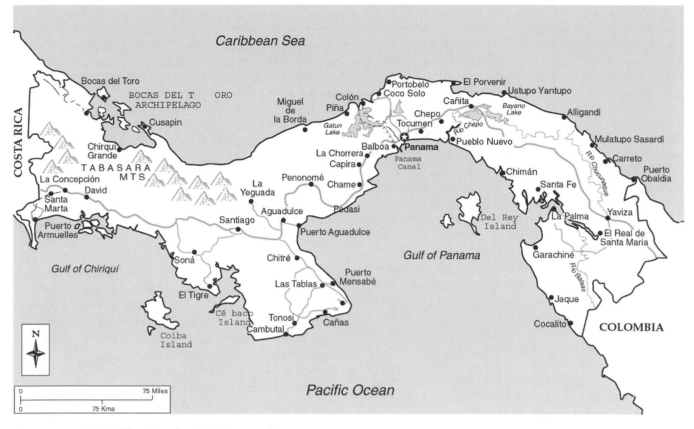

Panama. © 1998 The Moschovitis Group, Inc.

terest in building quick modes of transport across the isthmus. The Spanish first considered a canal in the early 1500s, and the French pursued the idea in the latter half of the nineteenth century (see **Panama Canal**). The French project, enthusiastically begun in 1879, fell apart ten years later due to a series of problems, including design flaws, disease, and a shortage of money. Residents of the Colombian province of Panama feared that, if they remained part of Colombia, the Colombian government would hoard the profits from a canal, and they would reap no benefits. As a result, provincial leaders tried on several occasions to proclaim **independence from Colombia** but were defeated each time by the Colombian army.

As interest in building a canal increased, the United States struck a deal with Panama: if Panama broke free from Colombia and allowed the United States to construct the canal, the United States would protect the newly independent nation and keep the peace. In 1903 Panama successfully seceded from Colombia (with U.S. assistance), and soon thereafter, one of the premier advocates of the canal, Frenchman Philippe Jean **Bunau-Varilla**, went to Washington to negotiate a deal for the construction of the canal. The resultant **Hay–Bunau-Varilla Treaty** (1903) granted the United States the rights to use the existing French construction, to build and operate the canal, and to govern the Canal Zone (the canal itself plus five miles on either side). Thousands flocked to Panama to help in the construc-

tion of the canal, which began in 1904 and was completed in 1915, hoping to later benefit from the commerce it would facilitate. The Panamanian government pushed for the construction of schools, roads, and other elements of infrastructure to help modernize the country, and business and agriculture began to flourish.

In the 1920s many Panamanians began to speak out against the U.S. presence, fearing they were being exploited, and feeling neglected by the Panamanian government. The situation worsened as Panama was hit especially hard by the Great Depression. In 1931 brothers Harmodio **Arias Madrid** (1931, 1932–1936) and Arnulfo **Arias Madrid** (1940–1941, 1949–1951, 1968), populist advocates of equitable growth and Panamanian nationalism, led a group to overthrow the government of Florencio Harmodio Arosemena (1928–1931). Harmodio Arias assumed the presidency, and in 1936 signed a new treaty with Washington that raised the percentage of canal revenues that Panama received.

World War II provided a boost for the Panamanian economy, and while many expected a new constitution passed in 1946 to lead to economic growth and political stability, instead the political situation became more tumultuous. The national police stepped in to act as a political mediator, and initially denied Arnulfo Arias the presidency to which he was rightfully elected in 1948 (though he did take office in 1949). His actions as president only increased political unrest, leading the head of the national police, José Antonio Remón Cantera (1952–1955), to remove him from office in 1951. Remón was elected the next year, and as president, promoted economic development and signed a new treaty with the United States that again increased Panama's share of the revenue from the canal.

Growing popular frustration with U.S. involvement in the country and U.S. control of the canal dominated Panamanian politics in the 1960s. Several student-led riots occurred (see **Flag Riots** [1964]), and for the first time the elite classes did not attempt to quell those protests, which the government saw as a mechanism for diplomatic leverage. Though new canal treaties were negotiated, many Panamanians were displeased that these treaties did not allow for complete Panamanian control of the canal, leading to a postponement of the negotiations and increasing domestic unrest. Arnulfo Arias was reelected in 1968, but held office for only eleven days before being overthrown by the military, led by Colonel Omar **Torrijos Herrera** (1968–1978), who ruled Panama as dictator for the next decade. While the United States did not fully recognize the legitimacy of Torrijos' presidency, it engaged in talks with him regarding the canal. Torrijos and U.S. president Jimmy Carter signed the **Carter-Torrijos Treaty** in 1977, which granted Panama administrative control of the canal and required the United States to cede its military bases in the canal zone as of December 31, 1999. The treaty was not implemented until 1979.

When Torrijos died in a plane crash in 1981, Panamanians were hopeful that democracy would return to the country. However, General Manuel **Noriega** (de facto head of state, 1981–1989), the leader of the National Guard, emerged as Panama's next strongman. Noriega installed several puppet presidents while he ran the country and participated in various illegal activities, including illicit sales of drugs and weapons. In 1988 the United States finally cracked down on Noriega's unlawful pursuits and issued sanctions against Panama. Although tensions rose between the two countries and within Panama, Noriega would not surrender. In May 1989 Guillermo **Endara Galimany** (1989–1994) was elected president, but Noriega refused to recognize the elections and installed another puppet president. Finally, in December 1989, U.S. president George Bush sent troops into Panama to capture Noriega (see **United States Invasion of 1989**), who was taken to Miami, convicted on various charges, and sentenced to forty years in prison. The United States subsequently pledged $1 billion in aid to Panama to ensure the return of democracy, and installed Endara as president.

Endara's administration was weak, as he lacked popular support; even his two vice presidents maneuvered to control the political arena. In 1994 Ernesto **Pérez Balladares** (1994–1999) won the presidential elections with just over one-third of the vote. Although initially he was well regarded, Pérez Balladares' popularity plummeted as the Panamanian economy weakened, and unemployment and the national debt soared. In 1999 Panama elected its first female president, Mireya **Moscoso** (1999–   ), the widow of former president Arnulfo Arias. In December 1999 Moscoso oversaw the transfer of the Panama Canal from the United States to Panama, which gave Panama complete control of its national territory and the administration of the canal for the first time in the country's history.

ENTRIES

Amador Guerrero, Manuel (1833–1909)

Manuel Amador Guerrero (1904–1908) served as Panama's first elected president. Born in Colombia in June 1833 into a wealthy family, Amador Guerrero studied medicine and had an active political career in the **Colombian Conservative Party** (Partido Conservador Colombiano, PCC; see Colombia). He eventually became a major supporter of **independence from Colombia** for the Colombian province of Panama, and conspiring with Philippe Jean **Bunau-Varilla** and the United States, led the battle to win that independence in 1903. He was elected president by a national convention (not by direct popular vote) and held office from 1904 through 1908. He is remembered for his strong commitment to social welfare and specifically for his administration's efforts to improve public health through the eradication of mosquito-borne illnesses such as malaria and yellow fever. During his administration and in the following years Panamanian politics were greatly impacted by U.S. policy, and Panamanian governments relied heavily on the advice and support of the U.S. administration in Washington and its military outpost in the Canal Zone (see **Panama Canal**).

Antimilitarist Opposition Democratic Alliance (Alianza Democrática de Oposición Civilista, ADOC)

This coalition of three political parties, the Nationalist Republican Liberal Movement (Movimiento Liberal Republicano Nacionalista, MOLIRENA), the Arnulfista Party (Partido Arnulfista, PA, a small conservative group named for president Arnulfo **Arias Madrid** [1940–1941, 1949–1951, 1968]), and the Authentic Liberal Party (Partido Liberal Auténtico, PLA, formed and led by Guillermo **Endara Galimany** [1989–1994]) was founded in 1989 to back Endara's presidential bid in that year's election.

Though the ADOC proclaimed victory over Duque Jaen, the candidate supported by General Manuel **Noriega** (de facto head of state, 1981–1989) directly following the elections, Noriega annulled the election results, prompting political protests throughout the country. Following Noriega's removal in the **United States invasion of 1989**, the ADOC was able to claim victory, and Endara was installed in the presidency.

However, the alliance subsequently struggled to gain a majority in the legislature. By 1994 it held only twenty seats, and in the 1999 election the alliance won only fifteen seats. Another alliance evolving from the ADOC was formed in 1999 in order to secure a majority in the legislature to support newly elected PA president Mireya **Moscoso** (1999–   ) and her platform.

Arias Madrid, Arnulfo (1901–1988)

Controversial populist politician Arnulfo Arias Madrid, who strongly advocated Panamanian control of the **Panama Canal**, served as president from 1940 to 1941, from 1949 to 1951, and in 1968.

Arias Madrid, the younger brother of Harmodio **Arias Madrid** (1931, 1932–1936), was born in August 1901. The brothers were central in the political upheaval that deposed Florencio Harmodio Arosemena (1928–1931) in 1931 and ushered in a new period in nationalistic and populist politics in Panama. The younger Arias Madrid was first elected president in 1940, defeating noted diplomat and politician Ricardo Joaquín Alfaro (1931–1932) in a contest marred by violence. In the period leading up to the 1940 election, Arias Madrid developed his philosophy of *panameñismo*, which called for less U.S. involvement in the canal and the country's politics, and a government for and by Panamanians; he would continue to trumpet those ideals in subsequent electoral campaigns. Arias Madrid was well known for his fondness for Adolf Hitler and his dislike of immigrants, some of whom he stripped of citizenship. Though he was overthrown in 1941 by the military, he regained the presidency in 1949 and rekindled his populist and anti-U.S. policies. However, he enraged fellow politicians when he announced that he would suspend the constitution, and he was impeached in 1951. He was reelected in 1968 but served for only twelve days before the National Guard, led by Omar **Torrijos Herrera** (1968–1978), overthrew him.

He remained active in politics until his death in 1988. Soon after, his followers formed the Arnulfista Party (Partido Arnulfista, PA), which continued to use Arias Madrid's populist tactics and advocate for his causes, including Panamanian control of the canal. The party was able to assert political control following the **United States invasion of 1989** that removed strongman Manuel **Noriega** (de facto head of state, 1981–1989), and in 1999 PA candidate (and widow of Arias Madrid) Mireya **Moscoso** (1999–   ) was elected to the presidency.

Arias Madrid, Harmodio (1886–1962)

Harmodio Arias Madrid, older brother of Arnulfo **Arias Madrid** (1940–1941, 1949–1951, 1968), served as president in 1931, and from 1932 to 1936, negotiating an important treaty to impede further U.S. intervention in Panama.

Born in July 1886, Arias Madrid received a doctorate in law and political science in London, England. President Belisario **Porras** (1912–1916, 1918–1920, 1920–1924) charged him with writing a new legal code. He quickly grew tired of the corruption and graft that he discovered in government, and he staunchly opposed the right of the United States to intervene in Panamanian politics, preferring more authentic Panamanian sovereignty. He formed a revolutionary movement to change the political system, **Community Action** (Acción Comunal), and, together with his brother, led that group in the overthrow of the government of Florencio Harmodio Arosemena (1928–1931) in 1931. Arias Madrid briefly held the presidency after the coup, and was elected president in 1932 following the interim presidency of Ricardo Joaquín Alfaro (1931–1932).

Arias Madrid founded the University of Panama in 1935, and in 1936 the Arias Madrid administration negotiated an important treaty through which the United States forfeited the right to intervene in Panamanian affairs, though it continued its commitment to guarantee Panamanian independence. Arias Madrid remained active in political affairs after leaving office at the end of his term in 1936.

Arnulfista Party (Partido Arnulfista, PA). See Antimilitarist Opposition Democratic Alliance (Alianza Democrática de Oposición Civilista, ADOC); Arias Madrid, Arnulfo

Authentic Liberal Party (Partido Liberal Auténtico, PLA). See Antimilitarist Opposition Democratic Alliance (Alianza Democrática de Oposición Civilista, ADOC)

Bunau-Varilla, Philippe Jean (1859–1940)

Philippe Jean Bunau-Varilla was a French engineer who promoted the construction of the **Panama Canal** in the 1880s. Trained in engineering at the École Polytechnique in France, Bunau-Varilla went to the Colombian province of Panama in 1884 to work on the construction of the canal, which the French company Compagnie Nouvelle du Canal de Panama had begun to build in 1879. When the French project failed due to monetary problems and major casualties among workers and Colombia rejected subsequent U.S. attempts to negotiate the rights to continue building the canal, Bunau-Varilla convinced the United States to support Panamanian independence from Colombia. The Frenchman subsequently helped the U.S. government arrange an agreement with the French and the Panamanians that laid out the conditions for the United States to take over the canal's construction. He also served as the Panamanian representative to the negotiations of the **Hay–Bunau-Varilla Treaty** (1903), which was signed only two weeks after Panama declared **independence from Colombia** in 1903.

Omar Torrijos Herrera, who led Panama from 1968 to 1978, signs the 1977 Carter-Torrijos Treaty while U.S. President Jimmy Carter (second from left) looks on. *Columbus Memorial Library, General Secretariat of the Organization of American States. Reproduced with permission of the Organization of American States.*

Carter-Torrijos Treaty (1977)

The Carter-Torrijos Treaty, signed in 1977 by the U.S. and Panamanian governments, implemented a plan to gradually transfer the administration and control of the **Panama Canal** from the United States to the government of Panama.

During the seventy years following the signing of the **Hay–Bunau-Varilla Treaty** (1903), a series of amendments were added that significantly changed the way that Panama and the United States administered and benefited from the Panama Canal. However, many Panamanians remained frustrated by U.S. control of the canal (especially the U.S. military presence in and control of the Canal Zone) and resentful of the political and economic influence the United States wielded on Panamanian affairs under the agreement. This resentment manifested itself in many ways, including fervent nationalism and even violence (see **Flag Riots**). Panamanian leader Omar **Torrijos Herrera** (1968–1978) and U.S. president Jimmy Carter began to negotiate a new set of agreements in 1977 with the help of the **Organization of American States** (OAS; see Appendix 2). The new treaty, signed on September 7, 1977, in Washington, D.C., abrogated the Hay–Bunau-Varilla Treaty and all other agreements regarding the canal.

The new treaty called for the gradual withdrawal of

U.S. troops from the Canal Zone and the transition of control of the canal from U.S. to Panamanian administrators, and set December 31, 1999, as the date on which complete military and administrative change of power would take place. To facilitate the transition several new governing bodies were created, including the Panama Canal Commission; while originally the majority of the commission's nine members were from the United States, between 1978 and 1999 Panamanians assumed a controlling majority, eventually fully staffing the commission. The treaty also created the Combined Board, a group of military leaders charged with overseeing the protection of the canal. Another document, the Treaty Concerning the Permanent Neutrality and Operation of the Panama Canal, was also signed along with the Carter-Torrijos Treaty. In this document both countries pledged to allow the canal to be used by any country regardless of international affiliations or political alliances, ensuring the neutrality of the canal in times of war and peace. The treaty went into effect in 1979.

While the signing of the treaties was a long sought after change that resulted in increased Panamanian control of the canal, many in Panama were concerned that the United States still retained the right to intervene militarily in Panama's internal affairs. To clarify this situation, Torrijos made official modifications to the documents before they were ratified by the Panamanian legislature. The full transition of the canal to Panamanian control was completed, as scheduled, on December 31, 1999.

Community Action (Acción Comunal)

Community Action (Acción Comunal), a revolutionary movement led by Harmodio **Arias Madrid** (1931, 1932–1936) with the help of his brother Arnulfo **Arias Madrid** (1940–1941, 1949–1951, 1968) and others, stood for more equitable politics in Panama, and opposed U.S. interference in Panama's domestic governance and U.S. control of the **Panama Canal**. The group also believed that the political arena was unfairly dominated by the wealthy, and hoped to give the lower and middle classes a more decisive voice in political affairs. Harmodio Arias Madrid led Acción Comunal in overthrowing President Florencio Harmodio Arosemena (1928–1931) in 1931 and briefly assumed the presidency. The group subsequently appointed Ricardo Joaquín Alfaro (1931–1932) as president, and Harmodio Arias Madrid won the presidential election of 1932, holding office through 1936.

Democratic Revolutionary Party (Partido Revolucionario Democrático, PRD)

The Democratic Revolutionary Party (Partido Revolucionario Democrático, PRD) was the political party of Omar **Torrijos Herrera** (1968–1978) and Manuel **Noriega** (de facto head of state, 1981–1989), the military strongmen who dominated Panamanian politics in the 1970s and 1980s. The PRD was created in the 1970s as a vehicle for the Torrijos government to reach out to voters and hear their concerns. While the party's close relationship with the government prevented it from developing an independent platform of policies (it always espoused the policies of the current president), and while its members' diversity complicated the party's creation of a unique identity, the PRD scored electoral victories in the legislature and at the local level through the 1970s and 1980s.

After the **United States invasion of 1989** and the removal of Noriega, the party's reputation was severely damaged. A few years later, however, the PRD regenerated itself and rallied popular support by challenging the government of President Guillermo **Endara Galimany** (1989–1994) and projecting itself as the people's advocate against the new administration. In the 1994 election the PRD won a majority of seats in the legislature, and PRD presidential candidate Ernesto **Pérez Balladares** (1994–1999) was also victorious. In the 1999 presidential election, PRD candidate Martín Torrijos, son of the former president, was narrowly defeated by Mireya **Moscoso** (1999–) of the Arnulfista Party (Partido Arnulfista, PA). Despite the multitude of candidates and parties that have participated in recent elections, the PRD continues to garner significant electoral support and to play a central role in Panamanian politics.

Endara Galimany, Guillermo (1937–)

Guillermo Endara Galimany (1989–1994) won the 1989 presidential election, but was prevented from taking office until the **United States invasion of 1989**, which resulted in the removal of strongman Manuel **Noriega** (de facto head of state, 1981–1989). Endara sought to rebuild Panama but was distracted and derailed by accusations of corruption.

Endara was a professor of law before becoming a politician. He first entered politics as an aide to President Arnulfo **Arias Madrid** (1940–1941, 1949–1951, 1968) and was a member of Arias' cabinet during his brief third term. Endara disappeared from the national political scene for most of the 1970s and 1980s, resurfacing in May 1989 as the **Antimilitarist Opposition Democratic Alliance** (Alianza Democrática de Oposición Civilista, ADOC) candidate for the presidency in that year's election. Endara soundly defeated Duque Jaen (Noriega's puppet candidate), a victory that clearly signaled that the populace sought an end to the Noriega era. However, Noriega refused to relinquish power and used force to prevent Endara from taking office.

In a December 1989 rally held to protest Noriega's stranglehold on the government, violence broke out and Endara and his vice president were severely beaten. Soon after, the United States invaded Panama to force the exit of Noriega, and subsequently helped secure the installation of Endara as president. Endara was initially quite popular, pledging to rebuild Panama after the U.S. invasion and the Noriega era. A year into his presidency, however, several of his cabinet members resigned when rumors spread that Endara was supporting a domestic spy ring that included former colleagues of Noriega in order to control dissidents. Endara left office in 1994 and was succeeded by Ernesto **Pérez Balladares** (1994–1999) of the **Democratic Revolutionary Party** (Partido Revolucionario Democrático, PRD).

Flag Riots (1964)

In 1962 President Roberto Francisco Chiari Remón (1949, 1960–1964) and U.S. president John F. Kennedy agreed that the Panamanian flag should fly in the U.S.-controlled Canal Zone (see **Panama Canal**) alongside the U.S. flag. In 1963 a joint statement to that effect was released. In January 1964 a group of students attempted to post Panamanian flags at a high school in the Canal Zone. The flags were torn down and the students were attacked, setting off a series of riots in which 21 people were killed, more than 300 wounded, and more than 500 arrested. The riots, which mainly involved the participation of Panamanians who opposed U.S. control of the Panama Canal and U.S. influence in Panamanian affairs, even led to the temporary severing of diplomatic relations between the United States and Panama. Though the Panamanian National Guard and U.S. troops were brought in to restore order, tensions remained, and periodic protests and unrest, opposition to U.S. control, and calls for Panamanian sovereignty continued over the next several years, eventually prompting negotiations between the U.S. and Panamanian governments. These resulted in U.S. president Jimmy Carter and Panamanian president Omar **Torrijos Herrera** (1968–1978) signing the 1977 **Carter-Torrijos Treaty**, which called for the delivery of administrative and military control of the canal to Panama by December 1999.

Hay–Bunau-Varilla Treaty (1903)

In 1903, U.S. secretary of state John Hay and Tomás Herrán, the Colombian representative to the United States, attempted to negotiate an agreement between the Colombian and U.S. governments that would have authorized the United States to construct a canal through the Panama province of Colombia. However, the Colombian Congress did not ratify the treaty, fearful that the agreement would allow the United States to dominate the politics and economics of the area and would thus compromise Colombian sovereignty. With the support and assistance of the United States, Panama declared its **independence from Colombia** in November 1903, and Hay and Frenchman Philippe Jean **Bunau-Varilla** negotiated and signed the Hay–Bunau-Varilla Treaty in Washington two weeks later.

The treaty, which allowed the United States to take over the project of building a 51-mile canal through Panama (see **Panama Canal**), included several provisions. Given that the French had initiated the project of building a canal across the isthmus in the late 1800s (though their efforts proved unsuccessful), the treaty called for the French to receive $10 million from the United States in return for the right to use the existing French construction as a basis for the U.S. canal. Further, treaty provisions called for the United States to pay $250,000 to Panama annually for the right to operate the canal. Finally, the treaty stipulated that the canal itself plus five miles on either side of the structure would be known as the Canal Zone, and that the United States would govern the Canal Zone as part of U.S. territory. The treaty was revised several times over the years to increase the amount paid by the United States to Panama, and that figure eventually reached more than $2 million annually. Through the 1960s, Panamanian opposition to the U.S. military presence escalated. As a result, in 1977 U.S. president Jimmy Carter and Panamanian president Omar **Torrijos Herrera** (1968–1978) signed a new treaty, the **Carter-Torrijos Treaty** (1977), which abrogated the Hay-Bunau-Varilla Treaty, called for the United States to transfer control of the canal to Panama on December 31, 1999, and created several institutions to oversee the canal.

Hay-Herrán Treaty (1903). See Hay-Bunau-Varilla Treaty

Independence from Colombia (1903)

The Colombian province of Panama won independence from Colombia in 1903 with significant political and military support from the United States.

The issue of Panama's independence from Colombia had been debated since the area's independence from Spain in 1819. Over the subsequent decades, many residents of Panama, especially those living in Panama City, had grown increasingly frustrated with rule from the Colombian capital of Bogotá. In 1840 Panama took advantage of the Colombian government's distraction with the civil war being fought between adherents of the **Colombian Conservative Party (Partido Conservador Colombiano, PCC) and Liberal Party (Partido Liberal, PL)** (see Colombia) and declared its independence. However, the province was reincorporated into Colombia in 1842. Panama subsequently enjoyed a great degree of autonomy under some Colombian presidents, especially those from the PL, and in 1855 a new constitution allowed the province much more autonomy. However, in the late 1880s Colombian president Rafael Wencesclao **Núñez** (see Colombia) of the PCC sought to bring the area under close control from Bogotá. The Liberals in Panama were the primary promoters of independence, and many fought in the Colombian **War of a Thousand Days** (1899–1902; see Colombia) between Colombian Liberals and Conservatives. Nonetheless, the Liberals were eventually defeated.

Meanwhile, Compagnie Nouvelle du Canal de Panama, the French company that had been unsuccessfully trying to build a canal in the Panama province since 1879, had declared bankruptcy in 1889 (see **Panama Canal**). The United States attempted to negotiate with the Colombian government for the rights to resume building the canal, but the Colombians rejected U.S. plans to continue the project. In response, many leaders within the canal project pushed for Panama's independence from Colombia. Key in the effort were Frenchman Philippe Jean **Bunau-Varilla**, who negotiated support from Washington for a military fight for Panamanian independence from Colombia, and military leader Manuel **Amador Guerrero** (1904–1908), who led the battle against the Colombian government. For its part, the United States stationed gunboats in the area to prevent the Colombians from sending reinforcements to their troops.

Panama declared independence on November 3, 1903, the United States granted recognition to the government on November 6, and two weeks later the **Hay–Bunau-Varilla Treaty** was signed in Washington, D.C., granting the United States the rights to take over the project of building the canal. A provisional government ruled Panama until 1904, when Amador Guerrero became the new nation's first president. While Liberals who had long supported the idea of independence from Colombia were gratified that autonomy had finally been obtained, they were concerned about the intense influence they anticipated the United States would wield in Panama's national affairs and opposed the idea of independence if it meant dependence on the United States for financial and military support.

Moscoso, Mireya (1947–)

Mireya Moscoso (1999–), the widow of three-time president Arnulfo **Arias Madrid** (1940–1941, 1949–1951, 1968), is Panama's first female president. During Moscoso's first year in office, the United States transferred control of the **Panama Canal** to Panama.

Moscoso's involvement in politics stemmed from her marriage to Arias Madrid, whom she wed in the United States during his forced exile following his overthrow in 1968. When Arias Madrid died in 1988, Moscoso was encouraged by his supporters to continue his political work. While she initially rejected those appeals, focusing instead on running Arias Madrid's coffee businesses, in 1990 Moscoso helped form the Arnulfista Party (Partido Arnulfista, PA). A year later she was elected president of that party. She made her first run for president of Panama in 1994, but was defeated by Ernesto **Pérez Balladares** (1994–1999) of the **Democratic Revolutionary Party** (Partido Revolucionario Democrático, PRD). In the 1999 election campaign Moscoso pledged to address the issue of poverty and to pursue economic reforms, such as the privatization of state-owned companies. Her win in 1999 was not only a triumph for her party, but also a groundbreaking event for women in Panama.

However, Moscoso faced challenges even before occupying office. Pérez Balladares attempted to complicate the transition from his government to hers by appointing his colleagues to civil posts prior to his departure and refusing to have any transition meetings with Moscoso or her staff. Her support in the legislature was also weak, as the PA and its allies won only a minority of the seats, and while just days before her inauguration an alliance was forged so that the new president was backed by a majority of congressmen, critics called that alliance and her leadership fragile. On December 31, 1999, the Panama Canal was transferred from the United States to Panama, marking the first time in its history that Panama had control over all of its national territory.

Nationalist Republican Liberal Movement (Movimiento Liberal Republicano Nacionalista, MOLIRENA). See Antimilitarist Opposition Democratic Alliance (Alianza Democrática de Oposición Civilista, ADOC)

Noriega, Manuel (1936–)

Strongman Manuel Noriega ruled Panama from behind the scenes from 1981 through 1989 as leader of the National Guard (the national military police created in 1955), preventing the country from experiencing true democracy, while supporting its economic development and promoting policies in favor of the urban poor. The United States invaded Panama to rid the country of Noriega in 1989 (see **United States Invasion of 1989**).

Born in a poor neighborhood in Panama City, Noriega graduated from a Peruvian military academy, entered the National Guard, and began his rise to power through military service. As an officer he became the protégé of Omar **Torrijos Herrera** (1968–1978), participating in the military coup led by Torrijos in 1968 that overthrew President Arnulfo **Arias Madrid** (1940–1941, 1949–1951, 1968). When Torrijos took control of the government following the coup, Noriega was a close advisor. Noriega was subsequently appointed head of intelligence and placed in charge of quelling dissent. He developed strong ties with foreign intelligence agencies, and some contend that Noriega worked for an array of foreign governments, many of which had conflicting interests in Panama.

When Torrijos died in a plane crash in 1981, a power struggle ensued. While Noriega emerged the victor, he did not assume the presidency. Instead, he became the leader of the National Guard and controlled the country's politics from behind the scenes, choosing and removing presidents at will. His activity in international affairs was closely scrutinized through the 1980s; he helped the Soviet Union get materials that most Western Hemisphere countries would not provide (such as weaponry) and also facilitated several Central American guerrilla movements' acquisition of weapons by allowing them to trade arms through Panama.

The United States grew impatient with Noriega as a result of these activities, especially as they gathered evidence that he was helping Colombian cartels traffic in **drugs** (see Colombia), and in 1987 the United States withdrew support from Noriega. Panamanians also began to grow weary of the government's instability and of Noriega's behind-the-scenes domination. Presidential elections held in May 1989 were contested by numerous anti-Noriega candidates. While Guillermo **Endara Galimany** (1989–1994) won the election with an overwhelming majority, Noriega annulled the results and began a new phase of political repression.

In December 1989 U.S. president George Bush ordered an invasion of Panama with the goal of reestablishing democracy in the country. Noriega went into hiding, but surrendered after ten days. Already indicted in Miami on drug and racketeering charges, Noriega was brought to the United States as a war criminal. In 1992 he was sentenced to forty years in prison, and began to serve that term in a Florida penitentiary. Soon after the U.S. invasion, Endara assumed the presidency, and the United States temporarily maintained a presence in Panama in order to ensure a smooth return to democracy.

A large cargo ship passes through the Panama Canal. *Columbus Memorial Library, General Secretariat of the Organization of American States. Reproduced with permission of the Organization of American States.*

Panama Canal

Construction of the Panama Canal began in 1879, and was completed between 1904 and 1914. The Panama Canal runs across the Central American isthmus to connect the Caribbean Sea and the Pacific Ocean. The canal created a valuable trade and travel route and resulted in great foreign interest in Panama.

The area that today is Panama served as a crossroads from the time the Spanish colonized the Americas, as goods and people moved between the Pacific and the Caribbean coasts of the narrow isthmus by foot, using beasts of burden, and finally on trains. A waterway connecting the coasts was sought since the beginning of the colonial period, and while possible river connections in the Colombian province of Panama, and later in Nicaragua, were explored, no easy route was found. The French, British, and United States governments, which were all interested in dominating the region and benefiting economically from control of a crossing, fought for the right to build in the region. The United States finished the first railway to cross the isthmus in 1855, at the peak of the California Gold Rush.

It was not until over twenty years later that the first efforts to dig a canal began. The French, led by Ferdinand de Lesseps, builder of the Suez Canal, spearheaded the project in 1879. Lesseps chose to initiate the project in the Colombian province of Panama rather than in Nicaragua because Colombia was more politically stable and less prone to earthquakes and volcanic activity. His efforts in Colombia were complicated by difficult geographical features and by the sickness (mainly malaria and yellow fever) and fatalities suffered by his

crew. His attempt ended ten years later, when his company, the Compagnie Nouvelle du Canal de Panama, declared bankruptcy.

The United States then stepped in and began negotiations with the Colombian government to buy out the French company and resume construction of a canal. In 1903 the governments of the United States and Colombia negotiated the Hay-Herrán Treaty, but the Colombian Senate refused to ratify the treaty, fearing that U.S. involvement in the region would compromise Colombian sovereignty. Frenchman Philippe Jean **Bunau-Varilla**, who represented the interests of Lesseps' company, eventually convinced the United States to support Panamanian independence from Colombia and prompted revolutionaries, including Manuel **Amador Guerrero** (1904–1908), to fight for Panamanian independence. The independent republic of Panama was declared on November 3, 1903, and the United States quickly recognized the new country. Two weeks later the United States and Panama signed the **Hay–Bunau-Varilla Treaty**, which allowed the United States to take over the project of building the canal, assigned the United States control of the Canal Zone (the canal itself plus five miles on either side), and established the sum the United States would pay Panama annually for the right to operate the canal.

In 1904 the United States began construction of the canal. Though they encountered the same problems the French had faced, research by Cuban physician Carlos Finlay and U.S. citizen Walter Reed on the role of the mosquito in transmitting yellow fever helped control the disease that affected many of the hundreds of thousands of canal workers, over half of whom were immigrants from as far away as Asia and Africa. The canal was completed in 1914. The total cost of construction was nearly $400 million. The 51-mile long canal, which reaches from Panama City at the Pacific coast to Colón at the Caribbean includes a series of sophisticated locks that lower and raise the water level as ships pass through, allowing the canal to change depth.

The Hay–Bunau-Varilla Treaty was amended in 1936 and 1955 to alter the way in which the United States and Panama administered, controlled and maintained the canal, and to adjust the political and military role of the United States in Panama. Nonetheless, Panamanian nationalists continually pushed for Panamanian authority and control of the Canal Zone, and the **Flag Riots** that took place in Panama in 1964 prompted the governments to consider the issues once again. U.S. president Jimmy Carter and Panamanian leader Omar **Torrijos Herrera** (1968–1978) signed the **Carter-Torrijos Treaty** in 1977, which allowed for a gradual phaseout of U.S. control of the Canal Zone, and on December 31, 1999, the United States fully relinquished control.

Pérez Balladares, Ernesto (1946–)

As president of Panama from 1994 to 1999, Ernesto Pérez Balladares attempted to restore the image of the **Democratic Revolutionary Party** (Partido Revolucionario Democrático, PRD) and worked to reform and develop the Panamanian economy.

Educated in the United States at the University of Notre Dame and then at the University of Pennsylvania, Pérez Balladares was initially a successful businessman. He held various cabinet posts under Omar **Torrijos Herrera** (1968–1978), worked closely with him to form the PRD in the 1970s, and aided him in negotiating the 1977 **Carter-Torrijos Treaty** with the United States. After an absence from politics, Pérez Balladares became active in the PRD again in the early 1990s, trying to give the party a new identity and revive its image, which had been discredited by its association with jailed strongman Manuel **Noriega** (de facto head of state, 1981–1989). Pérez Balladares served as the secretary general of the PRD, and won the 1994 presidential election on the PRD ticket.

As president, Pérez Balladares used his experience in business to attempt to strengthen the Panamanian economy, selling several state-owned industries and engaging in sweeping economic reforms. While he was initially popular, that popularity dissolved during his last year in office for three reasons: he campaigned to amend the constitution so that he could run for president again, his economic policies resulted in high unemployment rates, and only months before the end of his term, he was accused of participating in a scandal in which visas were sold illegally to Chinese immigrants. He chose not to run in the May 1999 presidential election (which was won by Mireya **Moscoso** [1999–   ] of the Arnulfista Party [Partido Arnulfista, PA]), and went to great lengths to ensure that the transition would not be easy for the incoming president, appointing many of his political allies to civil posts and refusing to hold any transition meetings.

Porras, Belisario (1856–1942)

Belisario Porras served as president of Panama from 1912 to 1916, from 1918 to 1920, and from 1920 to 1924.

Porras was born in Las Tablas in 1856, and enjoyed a successful career in the Liberal Party. He was a supporter of Panamanian secession from Colombia, but opposed U.S. control of the country following independence in 1903. He served as the first president of the republic from the Liberal Party, from 1912 to 1916, served as vice president to President Ramón Maximiliano Valdés (1916–1918), and assumed the presidency upon Valdés' death in 1918. Through the first two decades of the twentieth century, the United States used its right to intervene in Panamanian politics in order to stabilize the country's political situation, which was becoming increasingly violent and corrupt. Porras served as president until 1920, resigned, and was subsequently reelected in 1920, serving until 1924. The major contributions of his political career included organizing the country's first legal system, establishing Panama's first political institutions, and representing Panama in a serious border dispute with Costa Rica over the Coto region.

Torrijos Herrera, Omar (1929–1981)

Military and political strongman Omar Torrijos Herrera led Panama from 1968 to 1978 and also served as commander-in-chief of the National Guard. He helped Panama move toward economic independence from the United States.

Born in Santiago de Veraguas, Torrijos began his military career at an early age, joining the National Guard and receiving training at a military academy in El Salvador. In October 1968 he and a group of other officers deposed Arnulfo **Arias Madrid** (1940–1941, 1949–1951, 1968), who had just begun his third term as Panama's president. Initially, Colonel José María Pinilla Fabrega led the junta that took control of the country, but Torrijos soon assumed leadership. The junta dissolved political parties, arrested politicians, professors, and students who opposed them, and also censored the media.

Once Torrijos was in firm control he fought for workers' and peasants' rights (establishing a new legal code for workers' rights), extended citizenship and voting rights, ended segregation, and enacted major land reform. Torrijos also reformed the economy, changing legal codes to benefit companies and financial institutions, allowing Panama to become more important in international banking. He worked to attract investments in infrastructure that facilitated the growing service sector necessitated by the thriving **Panama Canal** business community. While he found opposition within his own ranks, and especially among the elite and wealthy in Panama, he was supported by groups that had not previously been active or powerful in politics or society, including immigrants, black Panamanians, indigenous peoples, and those of mixed racial heritage. He strengthened the National Guard in order to control opposition.

On the international scene Torrijos was interested in asserting Panamanian independence from the United States and attaining complete sovereignty. He developed alliances with many countries that had poor relations with the United States, including Cuba. During his tenure, Panama even joined the Non-Aligned Movement, a group of countries that attempted to avoid alliances with either the United States or the Soviet Union during the Cold War. Perhaps his most striking and notable accomplishment was his negotiation of a new treaty with the United States regarding the Panama Canal. The **Carter-Torrijos Treaty**, which was signed in September 1977 and went into effect in 1979, required that the United States gradually withdraw military forces from Panama and turn over operation of the canal to the Panamanians by December 31, 1999. The treaty not only restored Panamanians' national pride, but also brought them greater financial control of the canal, which had previously mainly benefited the United States economically. Torrijos died in July 1981 in an unexplained plane crash. He is remembered as a nationalist hero by some, and as a tyrant and dictator by others.

United States Invasion of 1989 (Operation Just Cause)

During the final years of General Manuel **Noriega's** reign as de facto head of state (1981–1989), the United States spoke out vehemently against the leader and his politics. In December 1989, U.S. president George Bush sent troops into Panama to capture Noriega and restore democracy in Panama.

The United States tried on several occasions to engage Noriega in negotiations that would decrease the strongman's political involvement. While the United States was optimistic that Noriega might cooperate given the countries' shared interest in the **Panama Canal**, negotiations proved ineffective. In 1987, for example, the United States attempted to encourage Noriega to allow legitimate elections in 1989, seeking support from those close to him. However, few were willing to cooperate, the talks soon broke down, and Noriega lashed out against those who supported the United States. In February 1988 the U.S. government tried another strategy, filing a number of criminal indictments against Noriega

in U.S. courts, specifically charging him with participating in the illicit drug trade. Soon after, the U.S. government cut off all payments to Panama for the Panama Canal and decertified the country, making it ineligible to receive foreign aid. Negotiations between Noriega and the U.S. government began again in May 1988, and despite initial progress, Noriega pulled out of the talks.

Following the victory of Guillermo **Endara Galimany** (1989–1994) in the May 1989 presidential election, Noriega nullified the results and installed his own puppet president, Francisco Rodríguez. This disregard for democratic procedures and growing evidence that Noriega was involved in illegal arms and drug trafficking finally forced the United States into more definitive action. U.S. president George Bush broke diplomatic relations with Panama, and U.S. operatives in the region began to support attempts to overthrow Noriega. While Noriega was captured in an October 1989 coup attempt, those loyal to the strongman were able to free him. After this failure, U.S. leaders began to draw up plans for a foolproof invasion that would lead to Noriega's surrender. On December 20, 1989, U.S. troops descended upon several Panamanian army bases and took control of Panama City, displacing the National Guard and police forces. Damage to the city was substantial, widespread looting occurred, and many residents sustained injuries and were evacuated.

Despite intense U.S. efforts, Noriega initially eluded capture, and the United States immediately put a bounty on his head. For the next four days, U.S. troops fought against those loyal to Noriega and searched for him. Noriega sought refuge in the Vatican Embassy on December 24, and nine days later he surrendered to the United States and was flown to Miami. The United States remained in Panama briefly to ensure that no uprisings occurred and to oversee the transfer of power to Endara.

HEADS OF STATE

Manuel Amador Guerrero	1904–1908
José Domingo de Obaldía	1908–1910
Carlos Antonio Mendoza	1910
Federico Boyd	1910
Pablo Arosemena	1910–1912
Rodolfo F. Chiari	1912
Pablo Arosemena	1912
Belisario Porras	1912–1916
Ramón Maximiliamo Valdés	1916–1918
Ciro Luis Urriola	1918
Pedro Antonio Díaz	1918
Belisario Porras	1918–1920
Ernesto Fido Tisdel Lefevre	1920

Belisario Porras	1920–1924
Rodolfo F. Chiari	1924–1928
Florencio Harmodio Arosemena	1928–1931
Harmodio Arias Madrid	1931
Ricardo Joaquín Alfaro	1931–1932
Harmodio Arias Madrid	1932–1936
Juan Demostenes Arosemena Díaz	1936–1939
Augusto Samuel Boyd	1939
Arnulfo Arias Madrid	1940–1941
Ernesto Jaen Guardia	1941
Ricardo Adolfo de la Guardia	1941–1945
Enrique Adolfo Jiménez	1945–1948
Domingo Díaz Arosemena	1948–1949
Daniel Chanis Pinzón	1949
Roberto Francisco Chiari Remón	1949
Arnulfo Arias Madrid	1949–1951
Alcibíades Arosemena	1951–1952
José Antonio Remón Cantera	1952–1955
José Ramón Guizado	1955
Ricardo Manuel Arias Espinosa	1955–1956
Ernesto de la Guardia Navarro	1956–1960
Roberto Francisco Chiari Remón	1960–1964
Marco Aurelio Robles	1964–1968
Arnulfo Arias Madrid	1968
Omar Torrijos Herrera	1968–1978
Aristides Royo Sánchez	1978–1982
Manuel Noriega (de facto head of state)	1981–1989
Ricardo de la Espriella	1982–1984
Jorge Illueca	1984
Nicolás Ardito Barletta Vallarino	1984
Eric Arturo Delvalle Henríquez	1985–1988
Manuel Solís Palma	1988–1989
Francisco Rodríguez	1989
Guillermo Endara Galimany	1989–1994
Ernesto Pérez Balladares	1994–1999
Mireya Moscoso	1999–

Source: Thomas E. Skidmore and Peter H. Smith, *Modern Latin America*, 4th ed. (New York: Oxford University Press, 1997).

BIBLIOGRAPHY

Print Resources

Arias Madrid, Harmodio. *The Panama Canal: A Study in International Law and Diplomacy*. London: King and Son, 1911.

Conniff, Michael L. *Panama and the United States: The Forced Alliance*. Athens: University of Georgia Press, 1992.

Hedrick, Basil C., and Anne K. Hedrick. *Historical Dictionary of Panama*. Metuchen, NJ: Scarecrow Press, 1970.

Koster, R. M., and Guillermo Sánchez. *In the Time of the Tyrants: Panama, 1968–1989*. New York: W. W. Norton, 1990.

McCullough, David. *The Path Between the Mountain and the Seas: The Creation of the Panama Canal, 1870–1914*. New York: Simon and Schuster, 1977.

Meditz, Sandra W., and Dennis M. Hanratty. *Panama, a Country Study*. Washington, DC: U.S. GPO, 1989.

Phillipps Collazos, Sharon. *Labor and Politics in Panama: The Torrijos Years*. Boulder: Westview Press, 1991.

Ropp, Steve C. *Panamanian Politics: From Guarded Nation to National Guard*. New York: Praeger, 1982.

Sibert, William L., and John F. Stevens. *The Construction of the Panama Canal*. New York: Appleton, 1915.

Zimbalist, Andrew, and John Weeks. *Panama at the Crossroads: Economic Development and Political Change in the Twentieth Century*. Berkeley: University of California Press, 1991.

Electronic Resources

Latin American Network Information Center (LANIC): Panama
http://lanic.utexas.edu/la/ca/panama/
Panama section of this extensive Web site contains hundreds of links to research resources, cultural centers, economic and business institutions, government agencies, historical sources, magazines and other periodicals, nongovernmental organizations, and grassroots groups, as well as many other subjects. (In English)

PANNet Government Page
http://www.pa/gobierno.html
Government section of a Web site jointly run by a nongovernmental organization and an academic institution contains numerous links to official ministries, agencies, and other governmental organizations. (In Spanish)

Political Database of the Americas: Panama
http://www.georgetown.edu/pdba/Countries/panama.html
Comprehensive database run as a joint project of Georgetown University and the Organization of American States. Section on Panama contains information on and links to the executive, legislative, and judicial branches of the Panamanian government; electoral laws and election results; and other political data. (In English, Spanish, Portuguese, and French)

Political Resources.net: Panama
http://www.politicalresources.net/panama.htm
Panama section of a Web site containing a wealth of links to sources of information about national politics. Includes information on political parties, legislative and executive institutions, laws and legislation, and elections, as well as a link to the constitution. (In English)

La Prensa Web
http://www.sinfo.net/prensa/hoy/portada.shtml
The Web version of one of Panama's most prominent daily newspapers. Offers comprehensive national and international coverage, while emphasizing national politics and the Panamanian economy. (In Spanish)

Wilfried Derksen's Elections Around the World: Panama
http://www.agora.it/elections/panama.htm
Panama section of a comprehensive database of results from elections around the world. Contains results from recent national executive and legislative elections, as well as explanations of and links to political parties and institutions. (In English)

PARAGUAY

COUNTRY PROFILE

Official name	República del Paraguay
Capital	Asunción
Type/structure of government	Constitutional republic
Executive	President popularly elected to a five-year nonrenewable term; cabinet appointed by the president.
Legislative	Popularly elected bicameral Congress comprising a 45-member Senate and an 80-member Chamber of Deputies; legislators are elected to serve five-year terms.
Judicial	Highest court is the Supreme Court; nine members selected by the Senate and the executive serve five-year terms.
Major political parties	**Colorado Party** (Partido Colorado, PC); **Liberal Party** (Partido Liberal, PL)
Constitution in effect	1992
Location/geography	In South America, bordering Argentina, Bolivia, and Brazil; mostly lush and fertile, landlocked; the western half of the country is sparsely populated.
Geographic area	406,750 sq. km.
Population	5,434,095 (1999)
Ethnic groups	Mestizo 95%; white (of European descent) and indigenous 5%
Religions	Catholic 90%; Mennonite and other Protestant denominations 10%
Literacy rate	92.1% (1995)
Infant mortality rate	36.35 deaths per 1,000 live births (1999)
Life expectancy	72.43 (1999)
Monetary unit	Guaraní
Exchange rate	1 U.S. dollar = 3,512 guaranís (August 2000)*
Major exports	Cotton, soybeans, timber, vegetable oils, meat products, coffee, tung oil
Major imports	Capital goods, consumer goods, foodstuffs, raw materials, fuels
GDP	$19.8 billion (1998 est.)
GDP growth rate	−0.5% (1998 est.)
GDP per capita	$3,700 (1998, purchasing power parity)

Latin American Weekly Report. August 22, 2000 (WR-00-33), p. 394.

Source: CIA World Factbook, unless noted. http://www.cia.gov/cia/publications/factbook/pa

OVERVIEW

Summary

Paraguay and Bolivia are the only two landlocked countries in Latin America. Paraguay is known for the variety of agricultural products it produces as well as for its homogeneous population: 95 percent is of mixed Spanish and Guaraní descent. (The Guaraní were the indigenous population that inhabited Paraguay prior to the arrival of the Spanish.) Although little of the Guaraní culture remains, 90 percent of the Paraguayan population still speaks the native language. The country does not have a strong democratic tradition, and Paraguayan politics are renowned for being unstable and divisive, punctuated by long dictatorships. Economically, Paraguay has only recently become an international actor, as its landlocked status prevented effective trade prior to its involvement in the **Southern Cone Common Market** (Mercado Común del Cono Sur, MERCOSUR; see Appendix 1). In 2000 the nation had just begun to focus on export industries, breaking its traditional economic reliance on agriculture.

History

Prior to Spanish colonization, Paraguay was populated by an indigenous group (numbering 300,000) that was later named Guaraní by the Spaniards. Though the Guaraní defended their lands valiantly when the Spanish first arrived in Paraguay, by 1537 the Guaraní had retreated. Spaniard Juan de Salazar Espinosa subsequently founded the city of Asunción, initiating the colonization of Paraguay. During colonization, the Guaraní were forced into slave labor. To gain favor

Paraguay. © 1998 The Moschovitis Group, Inc.

with the Spanish, the Guaraní often sold their young female children to their colonizers. These young girls eventually became the wives of the invaders and the mothers of their children, the first generation of the mestizo population of Paraguay. In this early period the economy revolved around agricultural production. As the area that would become Paraguay was landlocked, access to the Paraná, Paraguay, and Pilcomayo Rivers was essential to international trade; it would remain so throughout Paraguay's history.

Paraguay's history as a nation-state began in 1811 when it fended off an Argentine invasion, deposed its colonial governor, and declared itself independent from Spain and Argentina. Paraguay drafted its first constitution in 1813 under José Gaspar **Rodríguez de Francia** (1811–1814 as part of a junta; 1814–1840), whose administration attempted to develop Paraguay's economy and integrate modern technology into the agricultural sector. Carlos Antonio **López** (1841–1844 co-governed; 1844–1862) rewrote the constitution to establish three separate branches of government and worked to improve transportation and communication within the country, raising taxes in order to do so. Upon López's death, his son, Mariscal Francisco **Solano López** (1862–1870), was elected president; he would lead Paraguay into the famous **War of the Triple Alliance** (1865–1870; see Appendix 1), which pitted Paraguay against the combined forces of Uruguay, Brazil, and Argentina. Paraguay's defeat in that conflict had an adverse affect on Paraguayan politics and economics that would resonate for decades.

Paraguay's two main political parties, the **Colorado Party** (Partido Colorado, PC) and the **Liberal Party**

(Partido Liberal, PL), were both founded in the 1880s. Both parties were supporters of free trade and laissez-faire economics, and the main dividing line between them was more personal than ideological, reflecting the different factions that had developed during the War of the Triple Alliance. Political rivalry between the two parties arose immediately after they were founded, and that rivalry would shape Paraguayan politics for the next century. Between 1904 and 1936, twenty-four different presidential administrations ruled Paraguay, with the overwhelming majority of presidents being members of the PL. However, toward the end of this period, the population became disenchanted with the PL platform and began to coalesce around the PC.

In 1932 the Paraguayan army entered into battle with Bolivia over a key piece of land known as the Chaco, dragging the country into the gruesome **Chaco War** (1932–1935; see Appendix 1). By 1935 Paraguay had won most of the Chaco and Bolivian troops were exhausted, both physically and in sheer numbers. The victory boosted the nation's morale, unified Paraguayans, and increased the army's popularity. The military consequently developed into a more significant force in Paraguayan politics, marking an important turning point. The army supported the PC and, as the party's influence grew, the PC posed an increasingly serious threat to the PL. Other more radical groups began to emerge on both sides of the political spectrum, and in 1947 a full-fledged civil war broke out, known as the **Revolution of 1947**, during which the army worked to suppress the more radical factions, particularly those in opposition to the PC. The military's increasing influence and the fact that the PC was successful in putting down the 1947 revolt implied the beginning of the PL's eclipse as the dominant political force in Paraguay.

The prominence of the PC was solidified in 1954 when General Alfredo **Stroessner** (1954–1989) led an uprising and assumed control of the nation. While few predicted that Stroessner would remain in office for thirty-five years or that he would turn Paraguay into a dictatorship, Stroessner restricted political opposition and sent many citizens into exile. Although advances were made economically under Stroessner, he maintained tight political control over the country. Showing signs of senility in the late 1980s, he was removed from office by a coup led by his former colleague, Andrés **Rodríguez** (1989–1993). To the surprise of many, Rodríguez lived up to many of his promises to revive democratic politics in Paraguay; further, it was under Rodríguez that Paraguay joined MERCOSUR in 1991 and promulgated a new constitution (see **Constitution of 1992**) in 1992.

The PC retained power in 1993 with the election of Juan Carlos **Wasmosy** (1993–1998), the first civilian president in over fifty years. Wasmosy initiated an opening of the political system, freeing political prisoners, legalizing political parties, and allowing freedom

This illustration depicts fighting during the War of the Triple Alliance in the 1860s. *Columbus Memorial Library, General Secretariat of the Organization of American States. Reproduced with permission of the Organization of American States.*

of the press, and continued to encourage the country's involvement in international trade. In April 1996, General Lino César Oviedo Silva, a member of the PC, head of the armed forces, and a staunch critic of Wasmosy's policies (especially those that limited the power of the military), unsuccessfully attempted to overthrow Wasmosy. In response, Wasmosy asked for Oviedo's resignation as the head of the armed forces, sparking an important internal rift within the PC. Oviedo was registered as the PC candidate for the presidential election scheduled for March 1998. However, when Oviedo was sentenced to ten years in jail on charges of contempt of the presidency just days before the election, his running mate, Raúl **Cubas Grau** (1998–1999), became the PC's candidate. Cubas won the election and assumed the presidency.

Cubas immediately cleared Oviedo of all charges, sparking even more controversy; the pardon was called unconstitutional by opposition parties and the Supreme Court. Vice President Luis María **Argaña Ferraro**, who spoke out against Cubas for this action and for his economic policy, was assassinated in March 1999. Argaña supporters accused Cubas and Oviedo of being "moral instigators" of the murder. Consequently, Cubas resigned, and both Cubas and Oviedo went into exile. The president of the Senate, Luis Angel **González Macchi** (1999–   ), was sworn into office to serve the remainder of Cubas' term. Through the beginning of his presidency, González Macchi worked to further democratize the nation's politics, and continued the opening

of the traditionally isolated country to trade. Nonetheless, Paraguay's economic woes continued: by late 2000 unemployment was close to 17 percent and Paraguay's foreign debt had risen to 37 percent. Further, for the first time in more than fifty years, in August 2000, the PC lost in a national election: Julio César Franco of the PL was elected vice president in a special contest held to replace the slain Argaña. The contest marked the first time in Paraguay's history that a vice president had been chosen outside a presidential election.

ENTRIES

Argaña Ferraro, Luis María (1932–1999)

As vice president under Raúl **Cubas Grau** (1998–1999), Luis María Argaña Ferraro sought to carry a on party-centered government reminiscent of the regime of Alfredo **Stroessner** (1954–1989) despite the opposition of Cubas. Argaña's assassination in March 1999 damaged the legitimacy of Paraguay's democracy and the country's prospects for democratic consolidation.

Born in Asunción, Argaña graduated from the Universidad Nacional de Asunción in 1958. He served as president of the Supreme Court from 1983 to 1988, as ambassador to the United Nations from 1983 to 1989, and as minister of foreign relations from 1989 to 1993. Representing those still in favor of the old Stroessner regime, Argaña competed with Juan Carlos **Wasmosy**

A commission travels through the countryside of Paraguay following a revolution in 1908. *Columbus Memorial Library, General Secretariat of the Organization of American States. Reproduced with permission of the Organization of American States.*

(1993–1998) for the **Colorado Party** (Partido Colorado, PC) presidential nomination for the 1993 election. Though Wasmosy was favored by President Andrés **Rodríguez** (1989–1993) for the candidacy, Argaña won the party's nomination with 48 percent of the vote. Wasmosy's supporters claimed Argaña had used fraud to win the nomination, however, and the results were reversed; Wasmosy was awarded the candidacy, and was victorious in the election. During Wasmosy's presidency, Argaña began to speak out against the PC.

Lino César Oviedo Silva was registered as the PC candidate for the presidential election scheduled for March 1998. However, when Oviedo was sentenced to ten years in jail on charges of contempt of the presidency (due to his attempted coup against Wasmosy in 1996) shortly before the election, Cubas became the PC's candidate, and chose Argaña as his running mate. By representing two factions of the PC, the ticket easily gained enough support to win the election. As vice president, Argaña continued to speak out against Cubas and others in the PC; when Cubas pardoned Oviedo and released him from jail, Argaña accused the president of acting unconstitutionally and of being a puppet of Oviedo. Argaña was assassinated in March 1999; his supporters accused Cubas and Oviedo of being "moral instigators" of the assassination. Cubas resigned, and both he and Oviedo were forced to leave the country. Following the established succession process, the head of the Senate, Luis Angel **González Macchi** (1999–   ), was sworn in as president.

Chaco War (1932–1935). See Appendix 1

Colorado Party (Partido Colorado, PC)

The highly centralized and corporatist Colorado Party (Partido Colorado, PC) dominated Paraguayan politics for most of the second half of the twentieth century.

The PC was founded in 1880 by General Bernardino Caballero (1880–1886). While the party was initially dedicated to the ideals of equality and nationalism embodied by the nation's first president, José Gaspar **Rodríguez de Francia** (1811–1814 as part of a junta; 1814–1840), it did not actively pursue these ideals due to a lack of economic resources. Instead, the PC became an apparatus to choose the nation's presidents, distribute wealth, and undertake economic development. In an effort to repay the external debt Paraguay had incurred through the **War of the Triple Alliance** (1865–1870; see Appendix 1), for example, the PC replaced Paraguay's unique state-dominated land tenure system, selling state holdings. The policy, which displaced peasant squatters, forcing many to emigrate, was quite unpopular; consequently, in 1904 the **Liberal Party** (Partido Liberal, PL) took control of Paraguayan politics. Nonetheless, the PC was victorious in the **Revolution of 1947**, and PC candidate Juan Natalicio González (1948–1949) ran unopposed in the presidential election of 1947.

The PC underwent an enormous reorganization during the dictatorship of General Alfredo **Stroessner** (1954–1989), building an impressive organizational network that reached an array of societal sectors, from the elite and the army to the rural poor, garnering support through the sponsorship of rallies and control of the media. Ideology took a back seat in the PC, as the lines between the state and the party blurred and the PC became a vehicle to facilitate Stroessner's retention of power. The PC oversaw staffing in the public and semipublic sectors, which allowed the party to co-opt potential opponents by offering them jobs or important posts. In the mid-1980s, the National Committee of the PC began to develop a split between the militants (*militantes*) who favored Stroessner's regime and traditionalists (*tradicionalistas*) who proposed transition to a less authoritarian political system emphasizing the original Colorado ideology. Even these factions became subdivided, creating what is today an extremely fragmented party.

Constitution of 1870

Following its devastating defeat in the **War of the Triple Alliance** (1865–1870; see Appendix 1), Paraguay was on the verge of disintegration in 1870. Paraguay's opponents in the war, Brazil, Argentina, and Uruguay (known as the allies), occupied Asunción in 1869, taking control of Paraguayan affairs. Following their departure, survivors of the Paraguayan Legion (a group of exiles that had fought for the allies during the war) formed a provisional government in 1869, signed the 1870 peace accords (which guaranteed Paraguay's independence and free river navigation), and officially came to power in 1870 under the Constitution of 1870, bringing with them democratic ideals. The document would stand as Paraguay's constitution for seventy years.

While the two constitutions that preceded the Constitution of 1870 essentially awarded the president unlimited power over the nation, the new constitution, inspired by the Argentine Constitution of 1854, was based on principles of popular sovereignty and the separation of powers. The charter created a bicameral congress with a thirteen-member Senate and a twenty-six-member Chamber of Deputies. Though more democratic than the two previous charters, the Constitution of 1870 still awarded the president extensive control over the government and society. Despite the promulgation of the document, political leaders often ignored its fundamental principles and continued to govern in a centralized, nondemocratic way, thus perpetuating authoritarian rule. In 1939 President José Félix **Estigarribia** (1939–1940) responded to a political stalemate by dissolving Congress, declaring himself absolute dictator, and promulgating a new constitution.

Constitution of 1992

After the dictatorship of Alfredo **Stroessner** (1954–1989), international pressure to democratize as well as a will to decentralize on the part of domestic political forces, even within the **Colorado Party** (Partido Colorado, PC), produced pressure for a democratic constitution. (The extant Constitution of 1967 had been promulgated under Stroessner and was considered by most to be less than fully democratic.) The Constitution of 1992, the sixth in Paraguayan history and widely considered the most democratic, was written under the direction of Andrés **Rodríguez** (1989–1993), who led the 1989 coup that ousted Stroessner from the presidency. Based on the principle of the decentralization of power, the new charter weakened the presidency and limited presidents to only one term (in hopes of preventing extended rule by another dictator) while strengthening the Congress (which was given partial responsibility for naming the Supreme Court) and the courts; it also awarded more power to regional and departmental governments. Although the Constitution of 1992 represented significant change, a fuller decentralization and deeper democratization have proven elusive.

Cubas Grau, Raúl (1944–)

Raúl Cubas Grau served as president from August 1998 to March 1999. His actions soon after assuming the presidency led to his quick impeachment.

The son of a bureaucrat, Cubas was not immediately interested in politics. Trained as an engineer, he was heavily involved in the planning and execution of hydroelectric projects in Paraguay. In the mid-1990s, Cubas was appointed to the head of the Planning Secretariat of the **Colorado Party** (Partido Colorado, PC). His fiscal discipline gained him respect and popularity within the party, and in 1997 General Lino César Oviedo Silva (who hoped to gain the PC nomination for the presidential election of 1998) chose Cubas as his running mate. Despite the efforts of President Juan Carlos **Wasmosy** (1993–1998) and the outspoken opposition of Luís María **Argaña Ferraro**, the leader of the PC, Oviedo won the PC nomination. Nonetheless, Oviedo was soon arrested for his participation in the failed coup attempt against Wasmosy in April 1996, and was subsequently sentenced to ten years in prison. Cubas became the PC's presidential candidate and Argaña was nominated to be the vice presidential candidate.

Despite this turmoil, as Cubas and Argaña belonged to different factions of the PC, the Cubas/Argaña ticket united the party's support, and Cubas won the 1998 presidential race with 53 percent of the popular vote. He was inaugurated in August 1998. However, he quickly pardoned Oviedo, outraging Argaña and other political leaders, who accused Cubas of abusing presidential power. Argaña led a campaign to impeach Cubas, and by early 1999 the impeachment process had begun. Unexpectedly, on March 23, 1999, Vice President Argaña was assassinated. Supporters of the vice president immediately called for the resignation or the impeachment of Cubas, as they believed he was to blame for the assassination. Cubas was impeached on March 24, and on March 28 he resigned and requested exile in Brazil. Senate leader Luis Angel **González Macchi** (1999–) assumed the presidency.

Estigarribia, José Félix (1888–1940)

A new Liberal constitution was drafted during the administration of José Félix Estigarribia (1939–1940), who was noted for his heroism in the **Chaco War** (1932–1935; see Appendix 1).

Estigarribia was born in the countryside of Paraguay into a military family. Though he began to study agriculture, Paraguay's turn-of-the-century revolutions pulled him into military service. He received military training in Chile and through the 1920s in France, and in 1927 was named chief of the General Staff of the Army. He soon found himself leading 15,000 Paraguayan troops in the Chaco War. Infamous throughout Paraguay, his troops outmaneuvered the Bolivians, despite being outnumbered by them and in spite of the inhospitable terrain in which the war was fought. Estigarribia's leadership was seen as the primary reason for Paraguayan success in the war, and when the peace treaty was signed in 1935, he was hailed a hero.

After the war, Estigarribia served as ambassador to the United States, and was subsequently elected president of Paraguay in 1939 as the candidate of the **Liberal Party** (Partido Liberal, PL). Soon after taking office, he faced serious opposition from radicals demanding a more active leftist agenda. He implemented a land reform program, which afforded a plot of land to every Paraguayan family, reopened the university, balanced the budget, financed the public debt, increased the capital of the Central Bank, implemented monetary and municipal reforms, and made plans to improve infrastructure and public works. Faced with political stalemate, Estigarribia soon dissolved Congress, declared himself absolute dictator, and promulgated a new constitution that gave the executive branch more power, facilitating the president's implementation of social and economic reform.

Estigarribia was not completely comfortable with his status as dictator, but died in a plane accident in 1940 prior to modifying it. The cabinet named war minister Higínio **Morinigo** (1940–1948) president, marking the beginning of a harsh dictatorship.

González Macchi, Luis Angel (1947–   )

Luis Angel González Macchi (1999–   ) assumed the presidency in 1999 after the March 1999 assassination of Vice President Luis María **Argaña Ferraro** and the subsequent resignation of President Raúl **Cubas Grau** (1998–1999) as a result of his alleged involvement as a "moral instigator" of the murder.

González Macchi was born in 1947 into a political family; his father had been minister of justice and labor under Alfredo **Stroessner** (1954–1989). He became a professional basketball player, then joined the **Colorado Party** (Partido Colorado, PC) in 1966 and later studied labor law at Universidad Nacional de Asunción. In the 1970s and 1980s, he served in various posts in the Ministries of Justice and Labor. In 1993 he was elected to the Chamber of Deputies, serving as its vice president from 1993 to 1994. In 1998 he was elected to the Senate and became its president. He was appointed president of the nation by the legislature following Cubas' 1999 resignation, and the Supreme Court subsequently ruled that he would serve the rest of Cubas' term in office (until 2003) despite concerns about González Macchi's legitimacy as president.

At the beginning of his presidency, González Macchi's government, which enjoyed the support of the military, began to remove supporters of General Lino César Oviedo Silva (who was also implicated in Argaña's murder) from the armed forces and police, and worked to extradite Cubas and Oviedo (both of whom had left the country following Cubas' resignation). González Macchi also tried to encourage greater tolerance of opposition, even incorporating members of other parties such as the Authentic Radical Liberal Party (Partido Liberal Radical Auténtico, PLRA) and the National Encounter Party (Partido Encuentro Nacional, PEN) in his government. He also attempted to further open Paraguay to international trade but had little success strengthening the country's economy: by late 2000, both unemployment and Paraguay's foreign debt remained at very high levels.

Liberal Party (Partido Liberal, PL)

Founded in the 1880s, the Liberal Party (Partido Liberal, PL) and its rival, the **Colorado Party** (Partido Colorado, PC), have dominated Paraguayan politics for more than a century. The PL promoted a laissez-faire approach to economic policy in contrast to the nostalgic Enlightenment ideology of equality and nationalism promoted by the PC. However, the party was never as popular as the PC, and had little opportunity to pursue its platform. With the exception of holding the presidency from 1890 to 1894 and enjoying a brief period of dominance in the early 1900s, the PL was generally seen as the opposition party; it held the presidency only one time later in the twentieth century, from 1939 to 1940. During the PL's first term in power, the party's laissez-faire policy allowed an almost feudal relationship to develop in the countryside, creating a great disparity between the socioeconomic situation of *hacendados* (landowners) and that of peasants; this dynamic diminished the party's popularity. Like other parties in Paraguay, the PL now lacks the organization, finances, and human resources to oppose the PC.

López, Carlos Antonio (1787–1862)

Born in Asunción, Carlos Antonio López (1841–1844 co-governed; 1844–1862) started his professional career teaching arts and theology, and later practiced law. When the death of President José Gaspar **Rodríguez de Francia** (1811–1814 as part of a junta; 1814–1840) in 1840 created a power vacuum, López became involved in politics. He co-governed Paraguay as joint consul with Mariano Roque Alonso from 1841 to 1844, and was subsequently elected by the National Congress to a ten-year term as president.

During his presidency, which was marked by personalism, López implemented certain Liberal reforms, tackling the slavery issue and improving the public education system. He also opened Paraguay's economy to foreign investment, while continuing heavy state intervention in the economy with the goal of achieving economic and social development. All major export industries became state monopolies, and in 1854 López outlawed any foreign purchase of land. Paraguay's economic success during López's administrations was initially stunted by its strained relations with neighboring Argentina: Argentine dictator Juan Manuel de **Rosas** (see Argentina) refused to recognize Paraguay, prohibiting the country from using the Plata River to gain access to the Atlantic Ocean. However, when Rosas was overthrown 1852, relations between the two countries stabilized, facilitating Paraguay's economic development. López's son, Mariscal Francisco **Solano López** (1862–1870), succeeded him as president following Lopez's death in 1862.

Morinigo, Higínio (1897–1983)

Higínio Morinigo served as president of Paraguay from 1940 to 1948, during the **Revolution of 1947**. He established a tradition of military involvement in the government.

Born into a poor family, Morinigo graduated from the Colegio Militar de Asunción and quickly climbed the ranks of the military. An avid nationalist who openly opposed the **Liberal Party** (Partido Liberal, PL), Morinigo was appointed defense minister by President José Félix **Estigarribia** (1939–1940) in 1940, and following Estigarribia's sudden death that same year, Morinigo assumed the presidency. Morinigo's rule quickly became authoritarian, as he took advantage of the recently ratified constitution that increased the power of the executive branch of government. He limited union activities, censored the press, and banned most political parties, including the PL and the Febrerista Party; he tolerated the existence of the **Colorado Party** (Partido Colorado, PC), as he sympathized with its nationalist ideals. He also awarded the armed forces a role in politics, beginning a tradition that would continue for most of the twentieth century.

After 1945 Morinigo faced strong pressure to amend his policies and democratize Paraguayan politics. In June 1946 he reinstated the PL, and the political vacuum his authoritarian policies had created was soon filled with tumultuous political activity. Morinigo's power was reduced significantly when he allowed the formation of a PC-Febrerista coalition government. However, in January 1947 the Febreristas were pushed from the governing coalition by the PC. The conflict severely divided the political arena, and by March 1947 a civil war between a coalition of Paraguayan civilians and members of the military, and the PC, had begun. Morinigo remained in power during the conflict, which the PC quickly won. The military faction of the PC, concerned that Morinigo would not vacate office, ousted him in June 1948. Morinigo went into exile and did not return to Paraguay for almost twenty-five years.

Oviedo Silva, Lino César. See Wasmosy, Juan Carlos

Revolution of 1947 (also Civil War of 1947 or Revolution of Concepción) (1947)

In the wake of World War II, President Higínio **Morinigo** (1940–1948) faced strong pressure to democratize Paraguayan politics. In 1946 the **Colorado Party** (Partido Colorado, PC) and the Febrerista Party formed a coalition government. (The Febrerista Party drew its name from the February 1936 rebellion that unseated Liberal Party [Partido Liberal, PL] President Eusebio Ayala [1932–1936]). However, in January 1947 the Febreristas were ejected from the coalition by the PC, leaving the right wing of the PC in complete control of the government. Frustrated with the PC for using such a tactic to gain control, opposition parties began to rise up in rebellion. The military, which also feared that the ruling right-wing faction of the PC would limit the armed forces' role in Paraguayan politics, supported the civilian opposition. The resulting domestic conflict, the Revolution of 1947, was the longest and bloodiest civil war in Paraguayan history. Over its six-month duration, 50,000 people died, and there was mass immigration to neighboring Argentina; some estimates suggest that up to 300,000 people left Paraguay, fleeing the prospect of living under the rule of the PC and frightened by the PC's stated commitment to exact political revenge from those who had attempted to weaken its grip on the nation. The PC's eventual victory in the conflict strengthened the party's dominance in Paraguayan politics.

Rodríguez, Andrés (1923–1997)

Andrés Rodríguez (1989–1993) came to power through a coup that overthrew longtime Paraguayan dictator General Alfredo **Stroessner** (1954–1989). Rodríguez promoted democracy but kept tight control of the economy.

Rodríguez became involved in politics through the military. He served in the **Revolution of 1947**, during which he forged a close relationship with Stroessner. When Stroessner assumed the presidency in 1954, Rodríguez began to ascend the ranks of the armed forces and soon was one of Stroessner's close advisors. Rodríguez took advantage of his position, accumulating a small fortune in different business ventures that benefited from Stroessner's economic policies. By the late 1980s, Stroessner and his administration were beginning to weaken, causing Rodríguez and other **Colorado**

Party (Partido Colorado, PC) leaders concern regarding the future of the party.

As the party began to debate a replacement for Stroessner, Rodríguez rallied his supporters in the military and staged a coup on February 2, 1989 that unseated the aging dictator. Although the move was sudden, it was welcomed by many, especially as Rodríguez pledged to reintroduce democratic practices into Paraguayan politics. Rodríguez ran in the presidential election in May 1989 and won, gaining 78 percent of the vote. Rodríguez did promote democracy as president, promulgating and promising to uphold the new **Constitution of 1992** and allowing a smooth transition between his regime and that of his successor, Juan Carlos **Wasmosy** (1993–1998). However, Rodríguez faced criticism when he decided to give the army more autonomy and when he vetoed a congressional request to investigate human rights violations that had been committed under Stroessner. He retained tight control over the economy, but supported Paraguay's accession to the **Southern Cone Common Market** (Mercado Común del Cono Sur, MERCOSUR; see Appendix 1) in 1991.

Rodríguez de Francia, José Gaspar (1766–1840)

José Gaspar Rodríguez de Francia led Paraguay as part of a junta from 1811 to 1814, and subsequently ruled the nation as dictator from 1814 to 1840. He implemented nationalist policies that helped Paraguay make the transition from a colony to an independent nation with a burgeoning economy.

Rodríguez de Francia was originally drawn to theology as a profession, but was dismissed from teaching because of his liberal ideas. He subsequently became interested in law, and then served on several municipal councils in the beginning of the 1800s, using his legal expertise to help assemble the revolutionary junta that would lead Paraguay to independence from Spain. Rodríguez de Francia soon became a champion of Paraguayan independence. He authored the country's first constitution in 1813, was elected supreme dictator by the national congress in 1814, and led Paraguay as it evolved into an independent nation over the next two decades.

In the early years of his rule Rodríguez de Francia implemented strongly nationalist policies and worked to eliminate all remnants of Spanish colonization. He diminished the power of the church, converted state lands into small farms that peasants could rent and use to produce goods for local markets, encouraged improved transportation within the country, thus enhancing the possibilities for internal trade, and integrated modern technology into the agricultural sector. At the same time, he tightly monitored external trade and immigration by militarizing Paraguay's borders, and strengthened the role of the military in Paraguayan politics and economics. Upon Rodríguez de Francia's death

in 1840, a three-man junta stepped into the power vacuum, but was quickly overthrown. Chaos continued until Mariano Roque Alonso and Carlos Antonio **López** (1841–1844 co-governed; 1844–1862) assumed power.

Solano López, Mariscal Francisco (1826–1870)

Mariscal Francisco Solano López (1862–1870) led Paraguay in the bloody **War of the Triple Alliance** (1865–1870; see Appendix 1).

The son of President Carlos Antonio **López** (1841–1844 co-governed; 1844–1862), Solano López served as minister of war at the beginning of his father's regime, and was sent to Europe in the early 1850s as part of a Paraguayan effort to establish more open foreign relations, and to gather information about the industrial revolution so that Paraguay could learn from the advances being made in other countries. Upon his return to Paraguay in 1855, he was appointed head of the armed forces. After his father's death in 1862, the National Congress elected Solano López to a ten-year presidential term.

Solano López continued many of his father's economic policies, and in addition began promoting Paraguay's role in the prosperous Plata River region, to which the country had recently gained access following the overthrow of Argentine dictator Juan Manuel de **Rosas** (see Argentina) in 1852. Solano López's campaign to assert Paraguay's presence in that area led to the War of the Triple Alliance, a bloody confrontation that pitted Paraguay against an alliance that included Argentina, Uruguay, and Brazil. Solano López was determined that Paraguay would win the war; however, he was killed in battle in 1870, and the war ended soon after with Paraguay's defeat. Solano López, the only leader from the Americas to have died in a formal battle while still in office, was considered a national hero by many. However, he received criticism from others for involving Paraguay in the conflict, as its defeat severely weakened the country both politically and economically, and encouraged its domination by the larger countries surrounding it.

Stroessner, Alfredo (1912–   )

Alfredo Stroessner was president and dictator of Paraguay from 1954 to 1989, creating a corrupt, party-centered government that favored the rich, failed to address economic problems, and isolated Paraguay from the rest of the world.

Born to an immigrant father and a Paraguayan mother, Stroessner entered military life as a teen. While he was attending a military academy, the **Chaco War** (1932–1935; see Appendix 1) erupted, and Stroessner was sent into battle. He proved to be a dedicated and loyal soldier, and his performance won him awards and facilitated his ascension within the military. During the **Revolution of 1947**, Stroessner remained loyal to the government, gaining the respect and recognition of the

Colorado Party (Partido Colorado, PC). As the war came to an end he was one of the few officers left, and consequently gained a prominent position in the subsequent PC-led regime. He aided in the ouster of President Higínio **Morinigo** (1940–1948) in 1948, and subsequently supported the overthrow of a succession of leaders in order to advance his own political interests. In 1954 Stroessner himself led a successful coup, deposing President Federico **Cháves** (1949–1954), whose administration had been troubled by internal divisions within the PC, and assumed control of the nation.

Stroessner quickly purged his opponents in the military and in the PC, creating solid, unified support for his administration. With his party's internal problems resolved, Stroessner used his political acumen to create an extensive network of political/party-centered organizations, successfully coopting almost every sector of Paraguayan society. He outlawed the opposition, dominated the army, and set strong limits on freedom of expression and on the media. His regime was frequently criticized domestically and internationally for the human rights violations its security forces committed. His economic policies favored the rich, and corruption was rampant throughout his administration.

Many factors contributed to Stroessner's demise. One important cause was the economic trouble that Paraguay began to suffer in the 1980s. In addition, by 1989 Stroessner began to show signs of old age, and was unable to keep the PC unified behind him. When the PC began to debate who would succeed him, two factions emerged within the party: the militants (*militantes*), who held that Stroessner's son should take power, and the traditionalists (*tradicionalistas*), who saw Stroessner's imminent departure from office as an opportunity to revert to more traditional PC ideology and practice. However, just as discussions began in earnest, Stroessner was ousted by his former advisor, General Andrés **Rodríguez** (1989–1993). Stroessner went into forced exile in Brazil, where he remains under threat of extradition.

War of the Triple Alliance (1865–1870). See Appendix 1

Wasmosy, Juan Carlos (1938–   )
Juan Carlos Wasmosy (1993–1998) was Paraguay's first civilian president following fifty years of dictatorial rule. He led the nation during a period of economic hardship and division within his party, the **Colorado Party** (Partido Colorado, PC).

Educated as an engineer, Wasmosy was one of a handful of Paraguayans who profited from the development of the hydroelectric plant at Itapu Dam (at the border of Paraguay and Brazil), making him one of Paraguay's richest citizens. Wasmosy became involved in politics during the dam's construction in the 1970s. He

later joined the PC, campaigned for Paraguay's participation in the **Southern Cone Common Market** (Mercado Común del Cono Sur, MERCOSUR; see Appendix 1) (to which the country acceded in 1991), and served as a cabinet minister during the presidency of Andrés **Rodríguez** (1989–1993).

In 1993 Wasmosy ran for president, winning the three-way race with 40 percent of the vote. He took office in August 1993 and immediately implemented reforms, declaring freedom of the press, repealing repressive laws, legalizing political parties, freeing political prisoners, and ratifying human rights treaties. However, Wasmosy's presidency was immediately plagued with economic problems. Although the country benefited from membership in MERCOSUR, the economy struggled with privatization measures, and labor unions held massive strikes. In addition, General Lino César Oviedo Silva, head of the armed forces and a fellow member of the PC, but a staunch critic of Wasmosy's policies (especially those that limited the power of the military), soon emerged as a threat. In April 1996, Oviedo attempted to overthrow Wasmosy, but was defeated. Wasmosy subsequently asked for Oviedo's resignation as the head of the armed forces. This tension marked the beginning of a precarious divide within the PC.

In 1998 Wasmosy supported the nomination of Luís María **Argaña Ferraro** as the PC presidential candidate. However, Oviedo won the nomination. Just days before the election, Wasmosy had Oviedo arrested for his involvement in the 1996 attempted coup (thus interrupting, though constitutionally, the flow of the democratic election), and the PC's vice presidential candidate, Raul **Cubas Grau** (1998–1999) took over as the PC candidate for president, winning the subsequent election.

HEADS OF STATE

Bernardo de Velazco y Huidobro, Juan Valeriano de Zevallos, José Gaspar Rodríguez de Francia	1811
Fulgencio Yegros, José Gaspar Rodríguez de Francia, Pedro Juan Caballero, Francisco Javier Bogarín, Fernando de la Mora	1811–1813
Fulgencio Yegros, José Gaspar Rodríguez de Francia	1813–1814
José Gaspar Rodríguez de Francia	1814–1840
Manuel Antonio Ortíz, Agustín Cakete, Pablo Ferreira, Miguel Maldonado, Gabino Arroyo	1840–1841
Juan José Medina, José Gregorio Benítez, José Domingo Campos	1841
Mariano Roque Alonso, Carlos Antonio López	1841–1844
Carlos Antonio López	1844–1862
Mariscal Francisco Solano López	1862–1870

Carlos Loizaga, Cirilo Antonio Rivarola, José Díaz de Bedoya	1870
Cirilo Antonio Rivarola	1870–1871
Salvador Jovellanos	1871–1874
Juan Bautista Gill	1874–1877
Higínio Uriarte	1877–1878
Cendido Bareiro	1878–1880
Bernardino Caballero	1880–1886
Patricio Escobar	1886–1890
Juan G. González	1890–1894
Marcos Morinigo	1894
Juan Bautista Egusquiza	1894–1898
Emilio Aceval	1898–1902
Andrés Héctor Carballo	1902
Juan Antonio Escurra	1902–1904
Juan Bautista Gaona	1904–1905
Cecilio Báez	1905–1906
Benigno Ferreira	1906–1908
Emiliano González Navero	1908–1910
Manuel Gondra	1910–1911
Albino Jara	1911
Liberato Marcial Rojas	1911–1912
Pedro Pablo Peña	1912
Emiliano González Navero	1912
Eduardo Schaerer	1912–1916
Manuel Franco	1916–1919
José Pedro Montero	1919–1920
Manuel Gondra	1920–1921
Félix Paiva	1921
Eusebio Ayala	1921–1923
Eligio Ayala	1923–1924
Luis Alberto Riart	1924
Eligio Ayala	1924–1928
José Patricio Guggiari	1928–1931
Emiliano González Navero	1931–1932
José Patricio Guggiari	1932
Eusebio Ayala	1932–1936
Rafael Franco	1936–1937
Félix Paiva	1937–1939
José Félix Estigarribia	1939–1940
Higínio Morinigo	1940–1948
Juan Manuel Frutos	1948
Juan Natalicio González	1948–1949
Raimundo Rolón	1949
Felipe Molas López	1949
Federico Cháves	1949–1954
Tomás Romero Pereira	1954
Alfredo Stroessner	1954–1989
Andrés Rodríguez	1989–1993
Juan Carlos Wasmosy	1993–1998
Raúl Cubas Grau	1998–1999
Luis Angel González Macchi	1999–

Source: Charles J. Kolinski, *Historical Dictionary of Paraguay* (Metuchen, NJ: Scarecrow Press, 1973).

BIBLIOGRAPHY

Print Resources

Gatti Cardozo, Gustavo. *El papel político de los militares en el Paraguay, 1870–1990*. Asunción: Universidad Católica Nuestra Señora de la Asunción, 1990.

Lambert, Peter, and Andrew Nickson, eds. *The Transition to Democracy in Paraguay*. London: Macmillan, 1997.

Lewis, Paul H. *Political Parties and Generations in Paraguay's Liberal Era, 1869–1940*. Chapel Hill: University of North Carolina Press, 1993.

———. *Socialism, Liberalism, and Dictatorship in Paraguay*. New York: Praeger, 1982.

Miranda, Carlos R. *The Stroessner Era: Authoritarian Rule in Paraguay*. Boulder: Westview Press, 1990.

Prieto Yegros, Leandro. *Lectura política del Paraguay contemporáneo*. Asunción: Editorial Cuadernos Republicanos, 1997.

Roett, Riordan, and Richard Scott Sacks. *Paraguay: The Personalist Legacy*. Boulder: Westview Press, 1991.

Sondrol, Paul C. *Power Play in Paraguay: The Rise and Fall of General Stroessner*. Washington, DC: Institute for the Study of Diplomacy, School of Foreign Service, Georgetown University, 1996.

Warren, Harris G. *Paraguay: An Informal History*. Norman: University of Oklahoma Press, 1949.

———. *Paraguay and the Triple Alliance: The Postwar Decade, 1869–1878*. Austin: Institute of Latin American Studies, University of Texas at Austin, 1978.

Wisner, Francisco. *El dictador del Paraguay José Gaspar Rodríguez de Francia*. Buenos Aires: Editorial Ayacucho, 1957.

Electronic Resources

About Paraguay
http://www.emulateme.com/paraguay.htm
This Web site is a comprehensive resource for political, economic, and cultural information about Paraguay. Also contains maps and demographic data. (In English)

Diario ABC Color Digital
http://www.una.py/sitios/abc/
The Web version of one of Paraguay's major newspapers. Offers national economic and political coverage. (In Spanish)

Latin American Network Information Center (LANIC): Paraguay
http://lanic.utexas.edu/la/sa/paraguay/
Paraguay section of this extensive Web site contains hundreds of links to research resources, cultural centers, economic and business institutions, government agencies, historical sources, magazines and other periodicals, nongovernmental organiza-

tions, and grassroots groups, as well as many other subjects. (In English)

Political Database of the Americas: Paraguay
http://www.georgetown.edu/pdba/Countries/paraguay.html
Comprehensive database run as a joint project of Georgetown University and the Organization of American States. Section on Paraguay contains information on and links to the executive, legislative, and judicial branches of the Paraguayan government; electoral laws and election results; and other political data. (In English, Spanish, Portuguese, and French)

Political Resources.net: Paraguay
http://www.politicalresources.net/paraguay.htm

Paraguay section of a Web site containing a wealth of links to sources of information about national politics. Includes information on political parties, legislative and executive institutions, laws and legislation, and elections, as well as a link to the constitution. (In English)

Wilfried Derksen's Elections Around the World: Paraguay
http://www.agora.it/elections/paraguay.htm
Paraguay section of a comprehensive database of results from elections around the world. Contains results from recent national executive and legislative elections, as well as explanations of and links to political parties and institutions. (In English)

PERU

COUNTRY PROFILE

Official name	República del Perú
Capital	Lima
Type/structure of government	Democratic constitutional republic
Executive	Consists of a president elected by popular vote to a five-year term who may serve two consecutive terms; two popularly elected vice presidents; prime minister; Council of Ministers (appointed by the president).
Legislative	120-member unicameral Congress; members are elected to five-year terms by national popular vote; Congress can be dissolved only once during a presidential term.
Judicial	Highest court is Supreme Court of Justice, which includes sixteen judges appointed by National Council of the Judiciary.
Major political parties	**Perú 2000**, Union for Peru (Unión por el Perú, UPP), **American Revolutionary Popular Alliance** (Alianza Popular Revolucionaria Americana, APRA), Perú Posible, **Popular Action** (Acción Popular, AP).
Constitution in effect	1993
Location/geography	Western coast of South America; borders Ecuador and Colombia to the north, Brazil to the east, Bolivia and Chile to the south, Pacific Ocean to the west; topographical regions are the coastal plain, the Andean highlands, and the jungle.
Geographic area	1,285,216 sq. km.
Population	25.2 million (1999)*
Ethnic groups	Indigenous (Quechua, Aymara, Ashaninka) 45%; Mestizo 37%; white (of European descent) 15%; black (of African descent), Japanese, Chinese, other 3%***
Religions	Roman Catholic 90%; Protestant, Evangelist, Jewish 10%***
Literacy rate	93% (1998)***
Infant mortality rate	39 deaths per 1,000 live births (1998)**
Life expectancy	70 years (1998)***
Monetary unit	Nuevo sol (Ns)
Exchange rate	1 U.S. dollar = 3.46 Ns (August 2000)****
Major exports	Gold, copper, fish and fish products, textiles, zinc
Major imports	Machinery, chemicals, food, electrical and electronic equipment, road vehicles and tractors
GDP	$56.7 billion (1999)*
GDP growth rate	3% (1999)*
GDP per capita	$2,518 (1998)**

*The Economist Intelligence Unit. *Country Report, First Quarter 2000*. London: Economist Intelligence Unit, 2000, p. 300.

**CIA *World Factbook 1999*. http://www.cia.gov/cia/publications/factbook/geos/pe.html

***Peruvian Embassy Web site. www.peruemb.org

****Latin American Weekly Report. August 22, 2000 (WR-00–33). pg. 394.

OVERVIEW

Summary

The Incan Empire, which once occupied the area that is today Peru, achieved a cultural sophistication that rivaled and surpassed many of the great empires in world history. In modern Peru the ancient Quechua and Aymara languages, customs, and folklore persist in the highlands and the jungle, and since the 1960s have been more and more present in the capital. The faces of the masses, a mix of Asian, African, Indian, and Caucasian, reflect the country's complex political history, in which the indigenous, mestizo, and Afro-Peruvian multitudes and Hispanic elites have struggled for power and inclusion in the country's political process. Peru suffers perpetual poverty: one-half of Lima's 7 million residents lives in shantytowns, and more than one-third of the country's population is classified as living in or near poverty. Peru is a major grower of coca (used in the production of cocaine), which has led to the proliferation of drug trafficking activity (see **drugs/drug trafficking**).

History

One of the most advanced civilizations in the Western Hemisphere, with a complex social and political system,

Peru. © 1998 The Moschovitis Group, Inc.

the Incan Empire once spanned one-third of the South American continent, including parts of current-day Peru, Argentina, Chile, Bolivia, and Ecuador. When the Spanish colonizers arrived in the early 1500s, the Inca were in the midst of a process of social and political reordering and had been weakened by divided loyalties and years of fighting. Spanish explorer Francisco Pizarro and his men capitalized on the discord within the Incan leadership, allowing the Indians to fight a war of attrition among themselves. Despite continuing indigenous revolts, the Spanish crown, recognizing the extreme wealth available in the area, soon forged ahead with colonization. By the end of the sixteenth century, the Spaniards had gained control of the entire empire, which became the seat of the Spanish colonies in South America and rivaled Mexico as the more important outpost in the New World.

The colonial economy grew and changed through the 1600s. Centers of textile production emerged, as did new agricultural products. Maintaining control of the colonies and the wealth they generated became an increasingly difficult task for the Spanish crown, as foreign powers and local elites threatened their rule. New Granada was separated from the Peruvian viceroyalty in 1717, and as a result of the Bourbon Reforms of the late eighteenth century, the Rio de la Plata viceroyalty was split in 1776. Both divisions weakened the power of Lima, and Peru experienced severe economic and political decline. When Napoleon Bonaparte's French forces overtook the Spanish crown in 1808 the Peruvian elite were divided between those who desired complete independence and those who favored maintaining allegiance to the deposed Spanish king, Ferdinand VII. While Peru was one of the few remaining loyal colonies when Ferdinand VII returned to the Spanish throne, dis-

parate forces continued to fight against the crown. Troops led by Argentine José de **San Martín** (see Argentina) and Simón Antonio de la Santísima Trinidad **Bolívar y Palacios** (see Colombia) and supported by Peruvian forces under Antonio José de Sucre were finally victorious over the Spanish in December 1824 in the Battle of Ayacucho.

Independence brought further instability. The divided elites were hardly prepared to rule the new country, and conflicts between Liberals, desirous of more religious freedom, and Conservatives, who wanted to maintain the power of the Catholic Church, finally led to virtual civil war. The indigenous peoples, who had long rebelled in the name of self-rule, found themselves no closer to that goal than they had been under the Spanish. In 1836 Bolivian leader Andrés de **Santa Cruz** (see Bolivia) took control of the area, creating an alliance that was destroyed over the subsequent three years in the **War of the Peru-Bolivia Confederation** (1836–1839; see Appendix 1). Though **guano** sales boosted the economy and helped propel the country's elite out of postrevolutionary turmoil and into the international economy, prosperity did not reach the majority of the population. Stark differences between rich and poor were exacerbated by Peru's defeat in the **War of the Pacific** (1879–1884; see Appendix 1), which resulted in the destruction of the navy, the decimation of many ports and cities, and the loss of a significant amount of southern territory, including the nitrate-rich area of the Atacama Desert. This, plus the end of the guano boom in the 1870s and significant international debt, severely complicated Peru's economic situation.

Several nonmilitary presidents from the **Civilista Party** led Peru in the early twentieth century, hoping to consolidate civilian rule and engender peace. The economy grew and was increasingly dependent on industrial exports under these leaders, and the new influx of workers to the cities changed the political landscape as laborers began to demand rights and take stands against the ruling elite's defense of their own vested interests. Augusto Bernardino **Leguía** (1908–1912, 1919–1930) undertook major projects to modernize the country and the economy but failed to contain the labor movement and new leftist forces that were gaining strength in Peruvian society. José Carlos **Mariátegui** and Víctor Raúl **Haya de la Torre** soon emerged as important figures in the fight for labor and indigenous rights; each led powerful mass-based movements. Peruvian politics from the 1930s through the 1950s were marked by escalating tensions between the armed forces and the left, by competition between economic models (the orthodox, free-market, export-oriented model vs. the model that involved state intervention in the economy) and by periodic episodes of military rule.

Following Fernando **Belaúnde Terry**'s (1963–1968, 1980–1985) unsuccessful attempt to reform social services, land ownership, and industrial management during his first presidential term, the military initiated its "po-

An Indian woman sells her wares in Huancayo in 1966. *Columbus Memorial Library, General Secretariat of the Organization of American States. Reproduced with permission of the Organization of American States.*

pulist experiment" in 1968. The administration of General Juan **Velasco Alvarado** (1968–1975) enacted land reform and nationalized large agricultural holdings and industries, hoping to rid the economy of international capitalist control and stimulate growth. While these programs won him the support of the left and popular sectors, they further alienated the elite, strained foreign relations, and resulted in economic stagnation. Velasco was replaced by Francisco **Morales Bermúdez Cerrutti** (1975–1980), another military leader. Revolutionary guerrilla movements that had begun to form in the 1960s grew under military rule, and by the mid-1980s the **Shining Path** (Sendero Luminoso) and the **Tupac Amaru Revolutionary Movement** (Movimiento Revolucionario Tupac Amaru, MRTA) had developed into violent insurgencies. Drug trafficking and guerrilla and revolutionary activities significantly affected Peruvian politics in subsequent decades.

Morales Bermúdez allowed for the election of a constituent assembly that produced a new constitution in 1979, presidential elections were announced for 1980, and Belaúnde Terry was reelected. During his second presidency, Belaúnde attempted to address Peru's economic problems by refocusing the economy on exports and foreign investment, and used force to try to quell the threat posed by the leftist insurgencies. Unable to stem the country's economic and social instability, Belaúnde left office with little public support, and was succeeded by Alan **García Pérez** (1985–1990), the first **American Revolutionary Popular Alliance** (Alianza Popular Revolucionaria Americana, APRA) president. García was quickly overwhelmed by the daunting challenges facing his administration, including regaining domestic peace, stopping drug trafficking, and stimulating the economy. By the late 1980s his administration was under fire for the staggering hyperinflation that gripped

A campesino marches in a communist rally in the Plaza San Martín in Lima. *Columbus Memorial Library, General Secretariat of the Organization of American States. Reproduced with permission of the Organization of American States.*

the nation, the human rights abuses it perpetrated, and García's personal enrichment from government coffers. Alberto **Fujimori Fujimori** (1990–2000) was elected in 1990.

Though Fujimori campaigned against free-market economic policies, once in office he implemented a harsh austerity plan that removed price controls, froze public sector wages, and cut social spending. He also befriended the military in an attempt to stamp out the guerrillas, who virtually controlled over one-third of the national territory and had begun aggressive campaigns in Lima and other urban areas. As his lack of a majority in Congress frustrated his attempts to pass many of his controversial policies, in 1992, with the support of the armed forces, Fujimori declared a state of emergency and shut down Congress and the judiciary. He guided the rewriting of the constitution in 1993, which strengthened the executive, reduced the role of the state, and called for new elections. Fujimori's connection with the people and an economic boom in 1994–1995 paved the way for his 1995 reelection, and for his party to gain a majority in Congress in the concurrent legislative elections. As the April 2000 presidential elections approached, general dissatisfaction with the last half of Fujimori's second term gave hope to members of the weak and divided opposition for success at the polls. Though Fujimori won more votes than any other candidate in the first round of the election, he garnered less than 51 percent of the vote forcing a runoff election in May 2000. Fujimori was victorious in that contest. (Opposition candidate Alejandro **Toledo** [2001–] of the Perú Posible Party withdrew his candidacy prior to the second round of voting, protesting that Fujimori had fixed the election.) Widespread allegations of electoral irregularities sparked a series of large-scale popular protests in Lima and condemnation from the international community. In mid-September 2000, Fujimori announced that he would call a new general election in which he would not run. Following subsequent revelations of corruption within the Fujimori administration, the president left for Asia on the pretense of meetings on November 13, and on November 21, 2000 the Peruvian Congress received Fujimori's resignation.

Congress responded by declaring Fujimori "permanently morally unfit" for office, and elected its own speaker, Valentín Paniagua (2000–2001), as a caretaker president. The interim government, with the heavy involvement of the **Organization of American States** (OAS, see Appendix 2), organized a new general election and a series of reforms to restore democracy in Peru. Former president Alan García returned from exile to run as the APRA candidate in the April 2001 presidential contest, and Toledo again ran on the Perú Posible ticket. As neither candidate won a majority of the vote in the first round, a runoff was held in June 2001, resulting in a long-awaited victory for Toledo.

ENTRIES

American Revolutionary Popular Alliance (Alianza Popular Revolucionaria Americana, APRA)

The American Revolutionary Popular Alliance (Alianza Popular Revolucionaria Americana, APRA) is a left-leaning political party representing the working class and union interests. Peru's most enduring party and one of the most notable populist parties in twentieth-century Latin America, APRA has most often served as a vocal and sometimes violent opposition force.

APRA was founded by Víctor Raúl **Haya de la Torre** in 1924 during his forced exile in Mexico (a result of his strong activism) as a continent-wide youth movement based on socialist principles that favored Latin American political unity and the solidarity of all oppressed and exploited peoples and classes of the world. However, Haya de la Torre later rejected orthodox Marxism in favor of anti-imperialism and nationalism, and sought to create a revolutionary alliance to organize and lead Latin America's new middle and working classes, which became dislocated and radicalized in the 1930s by the Great Depression. APRA was repressed

for the first twenty years of its existence, in response to its revolutionary rhetoric and violent uprisings.

Despite this prolonged repression and its outlawing under General Manuel Apolinario **Odría** (1948–1950 as part of a junta, 1950–1956), APRA became a major political party, representing the working class and union interests and serving at times as a radical opposition force against various popularly elected governments and military regimes. Haya de la Torre, who remained at the helm of the party until his death in 1979, ran unsuccessfully for president on the APRA ticket in 1931, 1962, and 1963. The party finally delivered a winning presidential candidate in 1985. Though Alan **García Pérez's** (1985–1990) term was marked by the growth of guerrilla violence, economic mismanagement, hyperinflation, and corruption, at the turn of the century, he remained APRA's dominant personality. García was APRA's candidate in the April 2001 presidential election, in which he earned a surprising 25.8 percent of the first-round vote and a place in the June 2001 runoff against Alejandro **Toledo** (2001–) of the Perú Posible Party. García narrowly lost the second round to Toledo, who earned 51.3 percent of the vote to García's 46.9 percent.

Belaúnde Terry, Fernando (1912–)

Fernando Belaúnde Terry founded **Popular Action** (Acción Popular, AP). A moderate populist president, he held office from 1963 to 1968 and from 1980 to 1985.

Born in October 1912 in Lima, Belaúnde graduated with a degree in architecture from the University of Texas at Austin. In the 1930s he became active in politics, helping to turn the Catholic University in Lima into an important center for the political right as the Catholic Church became increasingly involved in politics. In 1945 he was elected to Congress, and in 1956 founded AP; the new party's platform was based on the social teachings of the church and advocated a system of social democracy governed by a corporative state. Though he lost the presidential election of 1956, he was elected in 1963, defeating Víctor Raúl **Haya de la Torre** of the **American Revolutionary Popular Alliance** (Alianza Popular Revolucionaria Americana, APRA) and General Manuel Apolinario **Odría** (1948–1950 as part of a junta, 1950–1956).

Belaúnde was viewed as a reformer with a strategy for addressing the growing unrest in the depressed highlands. During his first term in office, his priorities were modest agrarian reform, expansion of university education, colonization projects in the jungle, and the construction of the north-south Jungle Border Highway. The dramatic expansion of the fishmeal industry in the later 1960s made possible a variety of infrastructure projects, such as irrigation, transportation, and housing to benefit the urban middle classes. However, economic problems persisted, public discontent grew, and Belaúnde was ousted by the military in 1968.

Belaúnde went into exile following the coup, but returned to Peru in 1980 to contest the presidential election that had been called for in the new Constitution of 1979. He won, his victory facilitated by the fact that APRA was in decline following the death of its leader, Haya de la Torre. Terrorism plagued Belaúnde's second term in office, and widespread flooding in 1982–1983, severe droughts, and depleted coastal fish (a key natural resource) worsened Peru's already precarious economic situation. The rural situation grew increasingly complex as the cultivation of illicit coca increased, and the **Shining Path** (Sendero Luminoso) and the **Tupac Amaru Revolutionary Movement** (Movimiento Revolucionario Tupac Amaru, MRTA) insurgencies formed alliances with narcotraffickers (see **drugs/drug trafficking**). Though Belaúnde declared a state of emergency in 1982 and placed the department of Ayacucho under complete military control, by 1985 guerrilla groups virtually controlled certain sections of the country. Belaúnde's popularity had greatly decreased by 1985, when he yielded power to political rival Alan **García Pérez** (1985–1990), who had won the presidential election of 1985 on the APRA ticket. Nonetheless, Belaúnde continues to be AP's most notable leader.

Benavides, Oscar Raimundo (1876–1945)

The 1914 military uprising engineered by strongman Oscar Raimundo Benavides began a long tradition of military intervention in Peruvian politics. Benavides served as president from 1914 to 1915 and from 1933 to 1939.

Born in Lima to one of Peru's most influential families, Benavides graduated from the Peruvian Military School, studied at several international schools and universities, and quickly climbed through the military ranks. In 1914 Benavides led military forces in a coup to oust President Guillermo Billinghurst (1912–1914), whose populist policies, support for labor, and cuts in military spending had alarmed and angered important members of the oligarchy, the business community, and the army. Benavides briefly led the country but stepped down when José Pardo y Barreda (1904–1908, 1915–1919) was reelected. While Benavides was exiled to Costa Rica during the subsequent regime of Augusto Bernardino **Leguía** (1908–1912, 1919–1930), he returned to participate in the coup that deposed Leguía in 1930. Benavides served as an ambassador and then as the head of the country's armed forces under Colonel Luis Miguel **Sánchez Cerro** (1930–1933), and when a member of the leftist **American Revolutionary Popular Alliance** (Alianza Popular Revolucionaria Americana, APRA) assassinated Sánchez Cerro in 1933, Congress appointed Benavides president for the remainder of his term.

Benavides established a moderately conservative government. Tensions between the armed forces and APRA continued to run high, and like his military predeces-

sors, Benavides repressed APRA while catering to popular groups such as labor. He established an extensive public works program, created a welfare ministry, and promoted export-led growth; the success of the country's diverse range of exports helped Peru weather the worldwide depression of the 1930s. Benavides annulled the 1936 presidential elections when it appeared that the APRA candidate would win, and extended his term until 1939. In the resultant tense political atmosphere, Benavides disbanded Congress and assumed dictatorial powers for the remainder of his time in office. The economy continued to improve, and Benavides raised taxes, further increased social spending, and purchased new weapons and equipment for the military. He stepped down following the 1939 election of his political ally Manuel **Prado y Ugarteche** (1939–1945, 1956–1962), and served as ambassador to Argentina in Prado's first administration. Benavides returned to Peru to run in the 1945 presidential election but retired from the race to support a civilian candidate. His health deteriorated and he died later that year.

Billinghurst, Guillermo. See Benavides, Oscar Raimundo

Bustamante y Rivero, José Luis (1894–1989)

José Luis Bustamante y Rivero served as president from 1945 to 1948. Bustamante sought to end the pattern of alternating oligarchical-military rule by promoting democratization and social reform.

Born in Arequipa, Bustamante was an educated member of the elite class. A prominent legal scholar, he served in Peru's diplomatic corps and as Peru's ambassador to Bolivia in 1942. He won the 1945 presidential election representing the left-leaning National Democratic Front (Frente Democrático Nacional, FDN), a coalition of the Communist, Socialist, and **American Revolutionary Popular Alliance** (Alianza Popular Revolucionaria Americana, APRA) Parties. Bustamante's main goals as president were to reduce Peru's economic dependence on exports and to redistribute wealth, which he accomplished by intervening in the economy to control prices, exchange rates, and wage levels. He responded to increasing pressure from the APRA-dominated Congress and militant organized labor by expanding social spending on public health and food subsidies programs. As the state budget ballooned and the balance of trade deteriorated, inflation surged, squeezing economic growth. By 1947 most had lost faith in Bustamante's ability to govern, and the military ousted him from power in 1948, installing General Manuel Apolinario **Odría** (1948–1950 as part of a junta, 1950–1956) in office.

Bustamante went into exile, but returned to Peru in 1956. He served as a judge on the International Court of Justice from 1960 to 1969, assisted in the mediation of a conflict between Honduras and El Salvador in

1980, and subsequently served as an honorary senator until his death.

Cáceres, Andrés Avelino (1836–1923)

As president from 1886 to 1890 and from 1894 to 1895 and de facto leader from 1890 to 1894, Andrés Avelino Cáceres was the dominant political figure in Peruvian politics during the decade of national reconstruction that followed Peru's debilitating defeat in the **War of the Pacific** (1879–1884; see Appendix 1).

Cáceres joined the military at a young age. He fought in General Ramón **Castilla's** (1845–1851, 1855–1862) revolt against the government of José Rufino Echenique (1851–1855), and helped defeat an attempt by the Spanish to recapture the **guano**-rich islands off the coast of Peru (1866) before serving as one of the most important Peruvian military leaders in the War of the Pacific. Peru's devastating defeat in that war resulted in a loss of territory, the destruction of the country's financial system, and immense foreign debt, and led to a period characterized by intense civil strife and political chaos.

Following his 1886 election to the presidency, Cáceres was faced with the daunting tasks of restoring domestic peace and rebuilding the nation. Cáceres restructured the financial system, stabilizing the value of paper currency, and turned over the control of railroad construction to international creditors for sixty-six years. In return Peru was granted some debt forgiveness and offered access to international credit; the railroad was repaired and extended by its foreign owners, becoming an important factor in the revival of silver mining and export and the initial stages of economic recovery. Cáceres used repression and authoritarianism to maintain law and order and to quash revolts against his rule.

At the end of his term, Cáceres orchestrated the transfer of power to his political ally Remigio Morales Bermúdez (1890–1894), but actually continued to control the country himself; when Morales Bermúdez died unexpectedly in 1894, Cáceres engineered a coup that allowed him to finish out Bermúdez's term. Though Cáceres hoped to be reelected in 1895, before elections could take place Nicolás de **Piérola** (1879–1881, 1895–1899) returned from exile and took over the national palace in a bloody coup. Cáceres was exiled until his death in 1923.

Castilla, Ramón (1796–1867)

Ramón Castilla, one of the most adept soldier-politicians in Peru's history, led Peru from 1845 to 1851 and from 1855 to 1862. Skilled at building political consensus, Castilla established order by moving political contests from the *caudillo's* countryside to the halls of Congress.

Castilla, a first-generation mestizo born in Tarapacá, trained with and served in the Spanish military forces before joining the independence movement. Castilla fought in the **War of the Peru-Bolivia Confederation** (1836–1839; see Appendix 1), served as minister of the exchequer in the second administration of President Agustín Gamarra (1829–1833, 1839–1841), and was elected president in 1845. As president he began to create a national state with a functioning congress, legal statutes, and a budget. He also modernized and enlarged the military, enabling the central state to put down the frequent political revolutions stirred up by local *caudillos*. Through revenues from the **guano** boom, Castilla retired internal and external debt. For the first time in Peru's history, a stable political order on sound financial footing began to emerge. In 1851 Castilla relinquished power to his ally General José Rufino Echenique (1851–1855), the first time in Peruvian history that a presidential election brought about a peaceful transition of power.

Echenique proved to be an inept leader, however, and soon charges of corruption were causing turmoil. Fearing that his successor would disrupt the political and economic stability Peru had achieved under his rule, Castilla started a rebellion against Echenique in 1854. That year, amid the struggle for power, Castilla abolished slavery and native tribute, which broadened his social base and motivated many freed Indian slaves to enlist with his forces, which succeeded in ousting Echenique in 1855. During his second term, Castilla oversaw the drafting of the Constitution of 1860, a conservative charter that restored a strong chief executive and central state. General Miguel de San Román (1862–1863), Castilla's minister of war, easily won the 1862 presidential election.

Castilla subsequently served as senator from Callao. He planned to lead a revolution against Juan Antonio Pezet (1863–1865) due to what he perceived as Pezet's mishandling of Spain's claim to the guano-rich Chincha Islands, but before he could initiate the rebellion, Pezet exiled Castilla to Chile. Nonetheless, Colonel Mariano Ignacio **Prado** (1865–1868, 1876–1879) deposed Pezet and installed himself in the national palace as Peru's de facto dictator. Castilla returned to Peru planning to incite revolution against Prado, but died in 1867 before reaching Lima.

Change 90 (Cambio 90, C90). See Perú 2000

Civilista Party

Manuel **Pardo y Lavalle** (1872–1876) founded the Civilista Party, the first organized political party in Peru, in the early 1870s. The party grew out of opposition to the military governments that ruled Peru following independence, and to the conservative traditions of the old landholding class that had long dominated political life. Civilista Party members, who hoped to facilitate the advancement of a new export bourgeoisie, advocated the democratization of the political system and the modernization of the economy through economic liberalism, capitalism, and export-led development.

Pardo y Lavalle, the party's first presidential candidate, won a resounding victory in 1872 on a platform that advocated channeling substantial government revenues from **guano** into diversified, sustainable development for Peru. Once in office, he implemented public works programs, reduced the size of the armed forces, and reorganized and expanded the educational system. By the close of Pardo y Lavalle's term, however, civil-military unrest had grown, and Peru had suffered deep economic decline due to the world depression of 1873. Civilistas consequently abandoned the call for civilian rule and supported successful presidential candidate Colonel Mariano Ignacio **Prado** (1865–1868, 1876–1879) in the 1876 election. The party represented the oligarchy during the twenty-year Aristocratic Period that begain in the mid-1890s following Peru's defeat in the **War of the Pacific** (1879–1884; see Appendix 1).

With the exception of a brief period prior to World War I, the Civilista Party retained control of the presidency through the early twentieth century until 1919 through political maneuvering, and through an agreement with the Democratic Party (the other leading civilian party) to create a climate that would encourage investment, and to enforce social control of the masses. The Civilista program for economic modernization led to the diversification of Peru's export sector; while this allowed the country to recover quickly from a decline in any one sector in the international marketplace, it also increased foreign control of key industries and the repatriation of profits, decreasing reinvestment in the Peruvian economy.

Through the 1920s the Civilista Party grew weak and divided. The party suffered repression under President Augusto Bernardino **Leguía** (1908–1912, 1919–1930), and simultaneously the public began to demand a change from oligarchical rule, which it considered ill-equipped to deal with the economic and social challenges following World War I. The rise of fascism in the 1930s divided the old Civilista oligarchy into various right-wing political factions, rendering the party obsolete.

Democratic Front (Frente Democrático, FREDEMO). See Vargas Llosa, Mario

Drugs/Drug Trafficking

Coca has long been used by indigenous societies for ritualistic purposes as well as to alleviate the ill effects of life in high altitudes. When United States demand for cocaine (the illicit drug produced with the coca leaf) increased dramatically in the late 1970s, Colombian narcotraffickers (see **drugs**, Colombia), taking advantage of the acute poverty in the Peruvian highlands, began to offer low-interest loans to the farmers of Peru's jungle region to fund the cultivation of coca. Unable to

feed their families with the fruits of their traditional crops, impoverished farmers in the highlands began planting coca and selling the leaves to Colombian narcotraffickers. Alliances formed between drug traffickers and terrorists, who protected these farmers while capitalizing on the rise in the value of the coca leaf to fund their insurgency efforts against the Peruvian government.

Coca leaf fields expanded through the 1980s, and by late in that decade (when coca production in Peru reached its high point), cultivation had risen to over 100,000 hectares, on which many hundreds of millions of dollars worth of coca were grown annually, providing enough raw material to produce over 750 tons of cocaine a year. After 1980 police operations against drug traffickers were carried out alongside military battles to subdue the country's guerrilla movements, often leading to abuses against farmers and the local population. These excesses deepened the public's distrust of state authority and strengthened the guerrillas' influence over the region, and brutality against the peasantry perpetrated by the insurgents, combined with violence on the part of the narcotraffickers, left the peasantry powerless and torn.

The complex interplay of forces in the highlands severely hampered antinarcotics efforts through the 1980s and 1990s. United States antidrug assistance to Peru was formalized by a bilateral agreement signed in 1991 that included an economic package to help Peru balance its budget and meet international debt payments, deemphasized development programs to promote crop substitution, and provided for security assistance for counternarcotics programs. As a result of the efforts of the administration of President Alberto **Fujimori Fujimori** (1990–2000), through the 1990s insurgent movements were largely contained, and coca production decreased.

Fujimori Fujimori, Alberto (1938–)

Autocratic leader Alberto Fujimori Fujimori (1990–2000), the first Latin American president of Japanese descent, led Peru in overcoming the joint economic and terrorist crises the country faced in the early 1990s. Despite these successes, his presidency ended abruptly in 2000 when he resigned amid accusations of electoral tampering and rampant corruption.

Fujimori was born in Lima in July 1938 to Japanese immigrant parents. He graduated with a degree in agricultural engineering from the National Agrarian University in 1960, pursued further graduate studies in the United States and France, and served as the rector of the National Agrarian University from 1984 to 1989. Political newcomer Fujimori ran for president in 1990 on the ticket of Change 90 (Cambio 90, C90; see **Perú 2000**). His vague platform of "honesty, technology, and work" and his populist campaign attracted conservative evangelicals, poor shantytown dwellers, rural peasants,

Secretary General of the Organization of American States (OAS) César Gaviria Trujillo and President Alberto Fujimori Fujimori (1990–2000) (first and second from the left, respectively, at table) at a meeting of the OAS during the hostage crisis at the Japanese embassy in Lima in February 1997. *Columbus Memorial Library, General Secretariat of the Organization of American States. Reproduced with permission of the Organization of American States.*

and small business owners. The electoral atmosphere was tense, challenged by increasing terrorist threats from the **Shining Path** (Sendero Luminoso) and marked by economic decline occasioned by the failed presidency of Alan **García Pérez** (1985–1990). While no candidate won a majority in the first round of voting in April 1990 (Fujimori won 24.6 percent of the vote, placing second to internationally acclaimed novelist Mario **Vargas Llosa**), Fujimori won 56.5 percent of the vote in the June 1990 runoff, emerging victorious.

Though Fujimori had opposed Vargas Llosa's campaign proposals to revamp the economy through massive free market reforms, once in office Fujimori implemented an austerity program (which included removing price controls, freezing public sector wages, and cutting social spending), privatized national industries, and restructured the economy for export-oriented, free market growth. While these policies attacked the hyperinflation that plagued the economy, they also exacerbated the extreme poverty in which the majority of Peruvians live. Fujimori consolidated control over the military, the main institutional foundation of his regime, by legitimating and expanding the armed forces' counterinsurgency efforts. Despite his economic policies, authoritarian style, and continual clashes with Congress, Fujimori remained popular by identifying with the common people operating in the large informal

sector, and paying frequent visits to shantytowns and rural areas.

Tensions between Congress and the executive continued to escalate, and on April 5, 1992, Fujimori staged a "self-coup" (*auto-golpe*), suspending the constitution and closing Congress. With the support of the military, he took over the judiciary, declared a state of emergency, and announced that he would rule by decree. International organizations condemned Fujimori, and a month later the president unveiled plans to restructure the government to increase its efficacy, and promised to hold elections within one year for a Constituent Assembly that would rewrite the constitution. Fujimori's popularity soared when Sendero Luminoso leader Abimael **Guzmán Reinoso** was captured in September 1992, striking a major blow to the terrorist movement. Constituent Assembly elections were held in November 1992, and the new charter was written and approved by referendum in 1993. It included significant judiciary reform, and called for elections for a unicameral congress. The new charter also expanded the power of the executive and allowed presidents to run for immediate reelection (instituting a two-term limit) thus offering Fujimori the opportunity to run in the 1995 presidential election.

Fujimori was reelected in the first round of voting in 1995, affirming his enormous popularity; congressional elections held concurrently gave Fujimori supporters a congressional majority, which made it easier for Fujimori to get his new policies approved. During his second term, he successfully opened up the country to international trade and investment, reduced tariffs, and privatized many state-held corporations. Growth resumed at a healthy pace, in sharp contrast to the previous decade. Continuing his autocratic style, in 1996 Fujimori passed a law allowing him to run for a third term; when that law was overruled by three constitutional judges, they were sacked and replaced. Fujimori's popularity decreased in the last half of his second term due to his constitutional manipulations, a downturn in the economy, and allegations of corruption. His opponents charged him with single-handedly controlling the judiciary and the legislature and ignoring the democratic process.

Nonetheless, in 1999 Fujimori announced that he would stand for reelection in 2000 with the approval of the electoral council, basing his eligibility on the fact that the presidential term to which he hoped to be elected in 2000 would only be his second under the Constitution of 1993 (which had imposed a two-term limit). The opposition remained weak and divided, and Fujimori placed first over Perú Posible candidate Alejandro Toledo (2001–   ) in the first round of voting in April 2000, garnering 49.9 percent of the vote in the "official" tally to Toledo's 40.2 percent. As no candidate won a majority, a runoff had to be held. However, critics accused Fujimori of controlling the election process, and Toledo officially withdrew his candidacy from the runoff in protest. Fujimori ran in the May 2000 runoff unopposed, winning it with 74 percent of the vote.

The shadiness of the 2000 elections sparked a series of protests among Peruvians and international observers. Protestors filled the streets of Lima around the time of Fujimori's inauguration in late July, and several governments and international organizations demanded that he implement democratic reforms. Amid this controversy, Fujimori announced in September 2000 that he would call a general election as soon as possible in which he would not run. He also promised to "deactivate" his powerful and shadowy intelligence chief, Vladimiro Montesinos, who two days earlier had appeared on a leaked videotape apparently offering a $15,000 bribe to an opposition congressman. Montesinos fled the country in late September but returned (though he remained in hiding) in October. After a dubious "manhunt" for Montesinos, Fujimori left Peru on November 13 on the pretense of attending meetings in Asia. On November 21, 2000, from Japan, Fujimori resigned from the presidency by fax; shortly thereafter, the Peruvian Congress declared him "permanently morally unfit" for the office.

Fujimori remained in self-imposed exile in Japan while a caretaker government initiated a series of investigations into his presidency and engineered a new general election. These investigations revealed thousands of additional videotapes documenting the corruption ring run by Montesinos and involving congressmen, judges, and other powerful political figures. Montesinos was apprehended in Venezuela and extradited to Peru in June 2001, where he faces over fifty charges of human rights abuses, money laundering, drug trafficking, and other offenses. Toledo, who won the second round of presidential elections in June 2001 and assumed office in July 2001, immediately called for Fujimori's extradition from Japan to face charges of corruption.

García Pérez, Alan (1949–   )

Alan García Pérez (1985–1990), the youngest president in Peruvian history, was the first president from the populist American Revolutionary Popular Alliance (Alianza Popular Revolucionaria Americana, APRA).

García was born in Lima in May 1949 to parents who had been active in the APRA movement. He studied law at the Catholic University and the University of San Marcos. A charismatic and active leader of student politics for APRA, García soon earned the respect of APRA founder Víctor Raúl Haya de la Torre. He was elected to the Constituent Assembly that was convened in 1978 to rewrite the nation's constitution, and was elected secretary general of APRA in 1982. In 1985 he ran for president on the APRA ticket, promising to address the concerns of the peasantry and the informal sector through job creation, redistribution measures, and social assistance and appealing to the middle class by representing APRA as a social democratic party that emphasized pragmatism, technical capacity, and a social conscience. He also vowed to facilitate economic recovery by replacing the failed neoliberal economic policies of his predecessor, Fernando Belaúnde Terry (1963–1968, 1980–1985) with greater state involvement. García won the presidency with what was, at the time, the largest percentage of the popular vote ever recorded in a Peruvian election.

García's administration practiced selective state intervention in the economy, imposed wage and price controls, created a system of public works programs to boost employment, and restricted the country's payment of its foreign debt to 10 percent of the value of its exports. When declining government income from the country's ineffective tax collection system and the loss of foreign credit due to García's tough stance on debt repayment began to severely restrict government spending, discontent grew among poorly paid public workers and the increasing numbers of unemployed. Hoping to inject new life into his presidency, in 1987 García proposed the nationalization of the banking system; however, when this proposition provoked a strong negative reaction, induced hyperinflation, and hastened the overall deterioration of the country's economic sit-

This 1932 photo of guano harvesting in the Chincha Islands shows flatbed trolley cars loaded with bags of guano being readied for shipment to the mainland. *Columbus Memorial Library, General Secretariat of the Organization of American States. Reproduced with permission of the Organization of American States.*

uation, García withdrew it. The president was also unsuccessful in the war against terrorism: the strength of the **Shining Path** (Sendero Luminoso) peaked during García's administration, and the group moved its campaign to Lima, effecting citywide blackouts, bombings, and assassinations. García's attempts to control guerrilla activity by using extreme violence against the insurgents often caught innocent civilians in the crossfire.

By the end of his term, García's approval ratings had plummeted, and he fled the country for Paris in 1992 amid charges of graft and personal enrichment during his presidency. After spending nine years in voluntary exile, García returned to Peru to run on the APRA ticket in the April 2001 presidential election. Although many Peruvians swore that they would never vote for him again after his disastrous term in the 1980s, Garcia won 25.8 percent of the first-round vote, earning him a place in the runoff against Alejandro **Toledo** (2001–) of the Perú Posible Party. Although García's oratorical skills and promises of job programs and lower tariffs earned him 46.9 percent of the vote in the June 2001 runoff, Toledo was victorious with 53.1 percent of the vote; Toledo assumed the presidency a month later.

Guano

The sale and trade on the world market of guano, a natural fertilizer made from the excrement of aquatic birds that inhabit the Chincha Islands off the Pacific Coast of Peru, peaked between the 1840s and the 1870s

due to the commercial agricultural revolution taking place in Europe and North America. Guano-led economic growth averaged 9 percent a year starting in 1840, and the enormous flow of revenue, which amounted to nearly $750 million over the period, provided the basis for the consolidation of the Peruvian state. By the time guano deposits were exhausted in the 1870s, Peru had exported 12 million tons of the fertilizer and the value of the country's exports had ballooned from 6 million pesos to almost 32 million. With funds from guano exports, President Ramón **Castilla** (1845–1851, 1855–1862) repaid Peru's internal and external debt, greatly improving the country's international credit rating, and reduced political instability by modernizing the army and centralizing state power at the expense of local *caudillos*.

Nonetheless, the liberal export model based on this natural resource did not extract the country from its postindependence economic stagnation; the government did not use the enormous influx of money to address historical inequalities in wealth, nor to diversify the economy, which would have facilitated long-term economic development. Instead the coastal plutocracy amassed great fortunes, and the government acquired foreign loans that it used to embark on an ambitious railroad- and road-building enterprise. The rise of the guano-based mercantile aristocracy corresponded with the decline of the artisan/retailer middle sectors, whose entrepreneurial potential was stifled by massive imports from abroad. Further, through the 1860s, Peru entered into expensive military conflict first with Ecuador (see **Peru/Ecuador Border Conflict**, Appendix 1) and later with Spain when it attempted to seize control of the Chincha Islands. Peru was successful in both of these wars, but by 1870 the country was poised for financial breakdown.

Guzmán Reinoso, Abimael (also Presidente Gonzalo) (1934–)

Abimael Guzmán Reinoso was the leader of the **Shining Path** (Sendero Luminoso) revolutionary organization and one of the most sought-after terrorists in Peruvian history.

Born in Arequipa in December 1934, Guzmán joined the Communist Party as a teenager. He earned a doctorate in philosophy, and in 1962 joined the faculty of the provincial National University of San Cristobal de Huamanga in Ayacucho, where he developed a cult following among the student body, mainly Indian peasants from the countryside. His teachings were strongly influenced by Mao Tse-tung, Karl Marx, and José Carlos **Mariátegui**, and through the 1960s he traveled twice to China, which was in the midst of its Cultural Revolution, to delve more deeply into Maoist doctrine and learn subversive tactics. In 1970 he formed the Communist Party in the Shining Path of Mariátegui (Partido Comunista del Sendero Luminoso de Mariátegui, known as the Shining Path, Sendero Luminoso), using the university to recruit, educate, organize, and subsidize his organization.

While many former leftist revolutionaries collaborated with the populist military experiment in politics of Juan **Velasco Alvarado** (1968–1975), Guzmán grew frustrated by the government's unsuccessful reform project. He sought to wage a "people's war" that would wrest power from the government, elite, and military forces, and establish a communist state based on Maoist principles that would liberate Indian peasants from their traditional domination and inferior social position. In 1975 Guzmán resigned from his teaching position and moved with his followers into the countryside, where he planned to indoctrinate the peasants of the Andes, and then conquer the cities and eventually the state itself. Guzmán organized his followers into revolutionary teams and hierarchical cells, and used them to spread the revolutionary message to the marginalized and mainly indigenous population in the rural highlands.

Emerging publicly in 1980, the movement embarked on a highly organized campaign of selective assassinations and attacks on civilian and military establishments in the highlands, eventually expanding its activities to Lima in 1985. While neither the second administration of Fernando **Belaúnde Terry** (1963–1968, 1980–1985) nor the government led by Alan **García Pérez** (1985–1990) could control the group's violence, which soon spun out of control in both the countryside and the cities, President Alberto **Fujimori Fujimori** (1990–2000) finally succeeded in crippling the insurgency. Guzmán was captured by Fujimori's forces in September 1992, tried in a military court, convicted of aggravated terrorism, issued a life sentence, and jailed in a maximum security prison. Guzmán's arrest severely weakened the Sendero Luminoso movement, though some members of the insurgency continued to fight.

Haya de la Torre, Víctor Raúl (1895–1979)

Víctor Raúl Haya de la Torre was a pivotal figure in Peruvian politics and a founder of the **American Revolutionary Popular Alliance** (Alianza Popular Revolucionaria Americana, APRA) party. His most significant written work is *Anti-Imperialism and the APRA* (1936).

Haya was born in Trujillo in 1895 to an upper-middle-class family. He studied law in Trujillo and at the University of San Marcos, where he was an active leader in student politics, eventually serving as president of the Student Federation. He supported movements to ensure workers' rights and soon connected with José Carlos **Mariátegui**, an aspiring leftist politician and activist. Dictator Augusto Bernardino **Leguía** (1908–1912, 1919–1930) exiled Haya to Mexico in 1924, where Haya found intellectual camaraderie with members of the Mexican postrevolutionary government, and formed APRA in 1924. In 1928 Haya broke intellectually from Mariátegui when they disagreed about the correct revolutionary course for Peru, with Haya rejecting orthodox Marxism in favor of anti-imperialism and nationalism.

Haya returned to Peru in 1930 and established APRA in September of that year. He ran for president in 1931 but was defeated by Luís Miguel **Sánchez Cerro** (1930–1933), and was subsequently imprisoned on several occasions, living in refuge in the Colombian Embassy in Lima from 1949 to 1954. Though APRA was prevented from participating in politics under the regime of General Manuel Apolinario **Odría** (1948–1950, as part of a junta, 1950–1956), the party was subsequently legalized under President Manuel **Prado y Ugarteche** (1939–1945, 1956–1962). Haya ran in the 1962 presidential election, and though he won a slight plurality of the vote, he was prevented from taking office by staunch military and right-wing opposition. A junta took charge of the country in 1962, and another presidential election was held in 1963, in which Haya competed and was defeated. He served as president of the Constituent Assembly called in 1978 to write a new constitution as part of the transition to democracy engineered by General Francisco **Morales Bermúdez Cerrutti** (1975–1980), and died the following year.

Leguía, Augusto Bernardino (1863–1932)

Augusto Bernardino Leguía served as president from 1908 to 1912, and led the country as dictator from

1919 to 1930, the eleven-year period referred to as the *oncenio*.

Leguía was born in Lambayeque in 1863 to a modest but well-connected middle-class family, and was educated in Chile. Skilled at business as well as politics, Leguía worked with British and U.S. multinational corporations and managed his own life insurance and **guano** marketing companies. He served as minister of finance during the first presidency of José Pardo y Barreda (1904–1908, 1915–1919) of the **Civilista Party**, and won the presidency in 1908 with Pardo's support.

As president, Leguía favored state intervention in the economy, and under his direction guano use was increased on the coastal estates, enabling sugar and cotton to become the basic products of the Peruvian economy. This break with the traditional Civilista liberal economic model caused Leguía to split from the party after only one year in office. Leguía then boldly interfered in the 1911 congressional elections to assure the victory of his sympathizers. Thanks to this manipulation, plus the revelation of his plot to cancel the 1912 presidential elections, Leguía was defeated in the 1912 contest by Guillermo Billinghurst (1912–1914). He was then exiled to New York and London during Pardo's second presidential term.

Leguía returned to Peru in 1919, and ran successfully in that year's presidential election as an independent on a reform platform that attracted the support of the emerging middle and working classes. During the *oncenio*, Leguía initially focused on democratic reform, the incorporation of indigenous communities into the political process, and major public works programs (which benefited Leguía's political base, expanded the government bureaucracy, and also resulted in extensive foreign debt). Despite his espousal of economic, political, and social reform, he forcefully repressed his opponents to retain power; under Leguía the Civilista Party was effectively dismantled. Further the clientelist political networks into which his government was organized encouraged rampant graft and economic mismanagement.

Leguía arranged for his own reelection in 1924 and responded to growing political opposition with increased repression and authoritarianism. This, coupled with economic decline induced by the Great Depression, soon depleted Leguía's authority. Colonel Luis **Sánchez Cerro** (1930–1933) led a military coup that deposed Leguía in August 1930, and Leguía died in prison in 1932.

Mariátegui, José Carlos (1894–1930)

José Carlos Mariátegui, one of Peru's most notable intellectual and political activists, founded Peru's first communist party in 1928. His major intellectual work, *Seven Interpretive Essays on Peruvian Reality*, was published that same year.

Mariátegui was born into a poor family in June 1894 in Lima, and was never educated beyond the primary level. In his late teens he worked as a reporter for *La Prensa*, a Peruvian newspaper, and in the early 1920s he lived in France and Italy, where he studied Marxist thought. When he returned to Peru in 1923, his frail health relegated him to a wheelchair; he dedicated himself to writing and expressed his views of the correct revolutionary course for Peru through the journal that he edited, *Amauta*.

Mariátegui's evaluation of the political and social situation in Peru was influenced by *indigenismo*, a denouncement by members of Lima's provincial lower middle class of the arrogant and exploitative class that dominated indigenous towns in the countryside. Mariátegui advocated the incorporation of the largely indigenous Quechua- and Aymara-speaking population, the working class, and other exploited groups in Peru and believed that Marxism would alleviate the exploitation of all such groups. This confidence in Marxism brought an end to Mariátegui's collaboration with fellow leftist Víctor Raúl **Haya de la Torre**, who was not convinced of the applicability of Marxist theory to leftist organizing in Latin America. Mariátegui founded the Communist Party in 1928 in hopes of organizing and leading Peru's middle and working classes, but his health failed him in 1930, and he died at the age of thirty-six.

Mariátegui's philosophy and goals long outlived him; the **Shining Path** (Sendero Luminoso) terrorist group, which formed in 1970, was named for and originally inspired by Mariátegui's philosophies before turning to Maoist ideology and strategy.

Military Experiment (also Military Revolution). See Morales Bermúdez Cerrutti, Francisco; Velasco Alvarado, Juan

Montesinos, Vladimiro. See Fujimori Fujimori, Alberto

Morales Bermúdez Cerrutti, Francisco (1921–)

Francisco Morales Bermúdez Cerrutti (1975–1980), the second of two presidents who led the military's populist experiment, allowed for political opening, oversaw the writing of a new constitution, and called for presidential elections in 1980.

Born in Lima into a prominent and wealthy family, Morales Bermúdez studied at the Military School of Peru and graduated from the Superior Military War school. In the 1960s and early 1970s, he served as minister of finance in the cabinet of Presidents Fernando **Belaúnde Terry** (1963–1968, 1980–1985) and Juan **Velasco Alvarado** (1968–1975). In August 1975 the military removed Velasco and installed Morales Bermúdez as president. Though Morales Bermúdez initially emulated Velasco's military populist governing style, the country's worsening economic situation and pressure from international lending organizations and foreign creditors forced Morales Bermúdez to implement more austere economic measures (including cutting public spending in an attempt to control spiraling inflation), significantly reduce the role of the state, and move toward a market economy.

Public opinion increasingly turned against military rule, which the populace blamed for the country's economic problems in view of perceived widespread corruption and mismanagement of state enterprises. Though right-wing generals called for swift repression and authoritarian rule to quell domestic unrest, Morales Bermúdez favored a transition to civilian rule. A new constitution that limited the military's role in society and politics, allowed for the continuation of the agrarian reform initiated under Velasco and established universal suffrage and a five-year presidential term with no reelection was promulgated in 1979. A presidential election was held in 1980, and following the victory of former president Belaúnde, Morales Bermúdez and the military stepped aside, bringing the military experiment in Peruvian politics to a close.

New Majority (Nueva Mayoría, NM). See Perú 2000

Odría, Manuel Apolinario (1897–1974)

Military strongman Manuel Apolinario Odría seized power from José Luis **Bustamante y Rivero** (1945–1948) in 1948, was popularly elected in 1950, and served as president until 1956.

Born in Tarma in November 1897, Odría studied at the finest military schools in the country and was a member of a conservative elite class of officers that ardently opposed the **American Revolutionary Popular Alliance** (Alianza Popular Revolucionaria Americana, APRA). Odría served as minister of government and later as commander of the military under Bustamante, but became increasingly frustrated with the president's failure to control terrorism inspired by members of APRA, and with the country's deteriorating economic situation. In 1948 Odría led a military coup that overthrew Bustamante and took charge of the junta that assumed power.

Odría immediately outlawed APRA, driving founder Víctor Raúl **Haya de la Torre** into hiding; during his first two years as the country's leader he also repressed the left, abandoned free-market orthodoxy, expanded social security, instituted pay hikes, and increased the military budget. Victorious in the 1950 presidential election, Odría instituted a program of military populism directed at the urban poor: he improved access to land for the most disadvantaged sectors by encouraging the formation of squatter settlements around Lima, and pacified labor with pay increases (though he responded to increasing labor unrest during the recession of 1953–1954 by suspending civil liberties). In 1956 he allowed for orderly elections, which were won by Manuel **Prado y Ugarteche** (1939–1945, 1956–1962).

Odría ran in the 1963 presidential election against Fernando **Belaúnde Terry** (1963–1968, 1980–1985) and Haya de la Torre of APRA, losing narrowly to Belaúnde. Following the election, Odría's party (the National Odriísta Union [Unión Nacional Odriísta]) and APRA allied to create a majority coalition in Congress that they used to oppose and block many of Belaúnde's initiatives throughout his first administration.

Pardo y Lavalle, Manuel (1834–1878)

Manuel Pardo y Lavalle (1872–1876), the first civilian president of Peru, founded its first civilian-based political party, the **Civilista Party**, in the 1870s.

Born in August 1834 in Lima, Pardo was educated in Chile, Peru, Spain, and France. He returned to Peru in 1853, became a prominent businessman and banker, and formed part of the new elite enriched by the lucrative **guano** trade. In 1860 he founded the influential antimilitarist journal, *Revista de Lima*, which advocated democratization and economic liberalism. These ideas, dubbed *civilismo*, which reflected the political stance of the new oligarchy, constituted the platform of the Civilista Party. Pardo served briefly as minister of the treasury in the first administration of Mariano Ignacio **Prado** (1865–1868, 1876–1879), and as mayor of Lima from 1869 to 1870. Pardo won the 1872 presidential election on the Civilista ticket, advocating immigration, foreign investment, and public works to facilitate production, commerce, and exports. He also pledged to reduce the role of the armed forces in Peruvian political life and implement a development agenda based on an extensive railway into the Andes Mountains.

Once in office Pardo undertook various social services initiatives, including secularizing and extending education to the popular classes (including the Indian masses). As Peru faced deep economic decline due to the world depression of 1873, he implemented unpopular austerity measures, cutting the military budget and raising taxes. During Pardo's term civil and military unrest increased, as did political antagonism between the Civilistas and supporters of Nicolás de **Piérola** (1879–1881, 1895–1899), a defender of the church and traditional landholding elites. Consequently, the Civilistas chose former president Prado as their candidate in the 1876 presidential election, and Prado was reelected. Pardo served as a leader in Congress until his assassination, allegedly by Piérola supporters, in 1878. Pardo is remembered as one of Peru's great statesmen.

Pérez de Cuéllar, Javier (1920–)

Well-respected diplomat Javier Pérez de Cuéllar was born in January 1920. He graduated from the Catholic University with a law degree, and joined the Peruvian foreign ministry in 1940 and the Peruvian diplomatic service in 1944, serving in the embassies of France, the United Kingdom, Bolivia, Brazil, and Switzerland. He held the post of minister of foreign affairs from 1961 to 1964 and from 1966 to 1969, and then served as Peru's first ambassador to the Soviet Union from 1969 to 1971. He became Peru's permanent representative to the United Nations (UN) in 1971, and served two consecutive terms as secretary general of the UN, holding the post from 1982 to 1991. His leadership in that post was instrumental in negotiating a cease-fire that ended the hostilities in the Iran-Iraq War (1980–1988) and the internal conflict in El Salvador (see **Farabundo Martí National Liberation Front** [Frente Farabundo Martí para la Liberación Nacional, FMLN], El Salvador). He ran in the 1995 Peruvian presidential election but lost to Alberto **Fujimori Fujimori** (1990–2000).

Perú 2000

Perú 2000 was the third of three political movements formed by Alberto **Fujimori Fujimori** (1990–2000). Rather than formal political parties or institutionalized organizations, these movements were electoral vehicles based on personalism that existed just for, and dissolved quickly after, the electoral moment for which they were created.

The first movement, Change 90 (Cambio 90, C90), created in 1989, ran a populist campaign in the presidential and congressional elections of 1990. Espousing no particular ideology, the party presented a platform of ending corruption, stabilizing the economy, and repressing terrorist insurgents around the country. While Fujimori emerged victorious in the 1990 presidential contest, C90 failed to win a majority in Congress. Congressional and presidential elections were slated for 1995, and Fujimori soon formed a new pro-Fujimori organization, New Majority (Nueva Mayoría, NM), in hopes of attracting professionals and technocrats who were reluctant to affiliate with C90 due to a falling out that had occurred between the movement and Fujimori. The slate of candidates presented by NM won a majority in Congress in the 1995 contest, and Fujimori was reelected by an overwhelming majority on the NM ticket. In the presidential election of 2000, Fujimori ran on the ticket of Perú 2000, an electoral alliance of progovernment political organizations. Though Fujimori was declared the winner in the second round of voting, many had serious concerns about the legitimacy of the election, and within months of his inauguration Fujimori resigned amid a major corruption scandal.

Peru-Bolivia Confederation. See **War of the Peru-Bolivia Confederation**, Appendix 1

Perú Posible. See **Toledo, Alejandro**

Piérola, Nicolás de (1839–1913)

Nicolás de Piérola served two terms as president (1879–1881, 1895–1899). His second term, a period of economic progress and political stability, initiated the Aristocratic Republic, a twenty-year period of autocratic, paternalistic, undemocratic elite civilian rule characterized by relative political harmony and rapid economic growth and modernization.

Piérola was born into an aristocratic family in Arequipa in January 1839 and educated at the prestigious San Toribio Seminary in Lima. His social and political alliances gained him the support of the conservative elite. Piérola served briefly as minister of finance under President José Balta (1868–1872), engineering a major reorganization of the **guano** contract system. He outspokenly defended the church against the anticlericalism advocated by the **Civilista Party**, and endeavored to protect the traditional, landholding elite against the economic encroachment of the new export plutocracy that had expanded under the Civilista administrations of Manuel **Pardo y Lavalle** (1872–1876) and Mariano Ignacio **Prado** (1865–1868, 1876–1879). When Prado exited the presidency and Peru in 1879 at the onset of the **War of the Pacific** (1879–1884; see Appendix 1), Piérola took over the government and declared himself president. When the Peruvian armed forces were unable to repel a Chilean invasion, Piérola dissolved his government and went into exile in Europe in 1881; the Chilean military eventually overpowered the Peruvian forces, resulting in Peru's loss of land and prestige.

Piérola returned to Peru in 1895, enlisted the military's support to oust President Andrés Avelino **Cáceres** (1886–1890, 1894–1895), and took control of the country. By that point, Peru was experiencing severe economic decline and social dislocation, and the military, despite its defeat in the war, continued to be active in the political arena. Piérola established an administration that was firm yet tolerant of dissenters; he also strengthened civilian control over politics, hiring French military advisors to help him train, educate, and professionalize military officers. In addition, the president embarked on a campaign of modernization: he encouraged economic diversification and expansion (to establish the basis for a self-sustaining national economy), created a ministry of development to foster close cooperation between the state and civil society, reorganized the tax system, and centralized and streamlined the state. After leaving office in 1899, Piérola ran unsuccessfully for the presidency in 1904, and remained active in opposition politics until his death.

Popular Action (Acción Popular, AP)

Popular Action (Acción Popular, AP) was founded in 1956 by Fernando **Belaúnde Terry** (1963–1968, 1980–1985), its most notable leader. AP's original platform was populist, reformist, and more conservative than that of its main rival, the **American Revolutionary Popular Alliance** (Alianza Popular Revolucionaria Americana, APRA).

As Belaúnde prepared to run in the 1962 presidential election, he fully developed AP's nationalistic, technocratic, moderate, democratic plan for reform, development, and modernization, which involved an activist government, civic action programs for the military, agrarian reform, greater autonomy for local governments, and nationwide housing development and highway construction. Though Victor Raúl **Haya de la Torre** of APRA won a slight plurality in the 1962 contest (defeating Belaúnde), in order to prevent Haya from taking office, the military ousted Manuel **Prado y Ugarteche** (1939–1945, 1956–1962) and took over the presidency, delaying new elections until 1963. Belaúnde ran in the 1963 contest on the AP ticket and won with overwhelming support from the middle and professional classes that had emerged during the period of industrialization, urbanization, and economic growth following World War II.

Though the influence of AP surged again in the early 1980s when Belaúnde was reelected, the party's authority soon declined as it grew progressively more conservative in an increasingly leftist political environment. AP joined the coalition of conservative parties that supported the unsuccessful candidacy of Mario **Vargas Llosa** and the Democratic Front (Frente Democrático, FREDEMO) in the 1990 presidential elections and subsequently voiced strong opposition to the dictatorial style of President Alberto **Fujimori Fujimori** (1990–2000).

Prado, Mariano Ignacio (1826–1901)

As president from 1865 to 1868 and from 1876 to 1879, Colonel Mariano Ignacio Prado repelled a Spanish incursion in 1866 and brought Peru into the **War of the Pacific** (1879–1884; see Appendix 1).

In 1865 Prado ousted General Juan Antonio Pezet (1863–1865) from the presidency for capitulating to Spanish demands on the **guano**-rich Chincha Islands off Peru's coast, and took control of the country. Prado's early popularity, stemming from his success in resisting a Spanish attack on the port of Callao in May 1866 and gaining Spain's recognition of Peruvian independence, was overshadowed by the outbreak of civil war following the promulgation of an unpopular Liberal constitution in 1867, and he soon resigned. General José Balta (1868–1872) took office and reinstituted the Conservative 1860 constitution. With the unlikely support of outgoing president Manuel **Pardo y Lavalle** (1872–1876) of the **Civilista Party**, whose administration had endeavored to limit the role of the military in politics, Prado easily won the 1876 election.

Peru's financial system had already been overextended with guano-backed foreign loans when the world depression of 1873 caused a sharp decline in the country's exports, and Prado inherited an extremely unstable Peruvian economy. He renegotiated the country's foreign debt with the Council of Foreign Bondholders in London and benefited from a rise in the price of sugar exports, which eased the foreign exchange crisis. He also quashed several revolutionary attempts by Nicolás

de **Piérola** (1879–1881, 1895–1899). Peru entered the War of the Pacific in 1879, and in an apparent effort to secure foreign loans to finance his country's struggling war effort, Prado sailed for Europe in 1879, leaving the presidency open. Piérola took over the government later that same year. Financial mismanagement by the Peruvian government, a loss of naval power due to military cutbacks that had occurred under the Pardo administration, and internal political turmoil all contributed to the rapid defeat of the Peruvian military by the Chileans in the war.

Prado y Ugarteche, Manuel (1889–1967)

Serving as president from 1939 to 1945 and from 1956 to 1962, modernizer Manuel Prado y Ugarteche is remembered for his successful public works programs and protection of political and civil rights.

Prado was born in April 1889 into a political family (see **Prado**, Mariano Ignacio). He achieved success as a banker, and became the leading member of the moderately conservative faction of the oligarchy. He served in the cabinet of President Oscar Raimundo **Benavides** (1914–1915, 1933–1939), in 1939, and contested that year's presidential election on a moderate antifascist platform advocating greater state expenditures, capital investment in industry, and political liberalization. The backing of the outlawed **American Revolutionary Popular Alliance** (Alianza Popular Revolucionaria Americana, APRA) helped guarantee his victory. Showing tolerance for political opposition, Prado officially recognized organized labor groups that had been repressed under military rule, released many APRA leaders from prison, and allowed the party to resume political activities. Peru developed both economically and socially under Prado primarily through fiscal expansion. Though the outbreak of World War II negatively affected the Peruvian economy, which depended heavily on exports to foreign markets, Prado initiated a rapprochement with the United States, an important buyer of Peruvian commodities. In 1941 Peru fought a brief war with Ecuador (see **Peru/Ecuador Border Conflict**, Appendix 1) and was awarded most of the disputed territory by peace accords signed in 1942.

At the close of his first term, Prado oversaw a presidential election won by José Luis **Bustamante y Rivero** (1945–1948). Dictator Manuel Apolinario **Odría** (1948–1950 as part of a junta, 1950–1956) stepped down to allow for orderly elections in 1956, and Prado was reelected, again backed by APRA. During his second administration, Prado continued his quest for political liberalization, legalizing APRA, which had been proscribed again under the Odría dictatorship, and allowing for unprecedented press freedom. Booms in the fishmeal industry and the manufacturing sector following World War II boosted the economy and allowed for the financing of further public works projects, but failed to benefit the severely impoverished sectors of the population who wanted land reform. The military refused to accept the victory of APRA candidate Víctor Raúl **Haya de la Torre** in the 1962 presidential elections, and Prado was deposed ten days before the end of his term and exiled to Paris. He was succeeded by a military junta.

Sánchez Cerro, Luis Miguel (1889–1933)

Military strongman Luis Miguel Sánchez Cerro deposed dictator Augusto Bernardino **Leguía** (1908–1912, 1919–1930) in 1930 and led Peru until 1933.

Born in Piura to a modest family, Sánchez Cerro joined the army as a young man and participated in the military uprising that removed President Guillermo Billinghurst (1912–1914), and in an attempted coup during the first term of President Oscar Raimundo **Benavides** (1914–1915, 1933–1939). Though he was exiled to Europe after engineering two unsuccessful coup attempts against Leguía, Sánchez Cerro returned to Peru in 1929 and finally took the presidential palace in 1930. Sánchez Cerro put Leguía and his followers in prison, initiated a regime of conservative populism, and called elections for the next year.

The bitter presidential election of 1931 pitted Sánchez Cerro against Víctor Raúl **Haya de la Torre**, founder of the **American Revolutionary Popular Alliance** (Alianza Popular Revolucionaria Americana, APRA), showcasing the fierce rivalry that had developed between APRA and the military as well as the polarization of the Peruvian political arena. Sánchez Cerro, supported by upper-middle-class right-wing nationalists and campaigning on a platform that promised restored political order, proved victorious. He then faced the daunting task of managing Peru's severe economic crisis in the context of the worldwide Great Depression. He tried to decrease the country's large national debt through economic reorganization, and imposed an orthodox deflationary economic program; nonetheless, Peru was shut out of international lending markets when Sánchez Cerro declared a moratorium on the repayment of loans in 1931. He also instituted a program of social security, gave full citizenship to the indigenous population, and implemented modest land reform. He reinforced the tension between the military and APRA by using repressive force to quell violent uprisings by the latter, and in April 1933 a member of the APRA movement assassinated him. Congress voted to install former President Benavides to finish out Sánchez Cerro's presidential term.

Shining Path (Sendero Luminoso)

Formally named the Communist Party in the Shining Path of Mariátegui (Partido Comunista del Sendero Luminoso de Mariátegui) after communist leader José Carlos **Mariátegui**, the Shining Path (Sendero Luminoso) was Peru's largest and most powerful revolutionary guerrilla movement. Abimael **Guzmán Reinoso** formed the group in 1970 with the goal of waging a "people's war" that would wrest power from the elite and military forces, violently destroy the state, and establish a communist state based on Maoist principles, liberating Indian peasants from their traditional domination.

Guzmán used the provincial National University of San Cristobal de Huamanga in Ayacucho, where he taught, to recruit, educate, organize, and subsidize his organization, and he and his followers soon moved into the countryside. They organized their ranks into hierarchical cells to spread the revolutionary philosophy to the marginalized and mainly indigenous population in the rural highlands, who had been neglected by the state and dominated by authoritarian local leaders. During the 1980 elections, in its first public act, Sendero Luminoso burned ballot boxes in the small town of Chushi and hung dead dogs from lampposts. Subsequently, the movement embarked on a highly organized campaign of selective, public, and gruesome assassinations of officials, priests, and civic leaders, and attacks on civilian and military establishments in the highlands. In 1985 the group extended its violent activities to Lima.

During the second administration of Fernando **Belaúnde Terry** (1963–1968, 1980–1985) and under President Alan **García Pérez** (1985–1990), the movement grew in size and strength due to the continued recruitment of highland peasants who were growing increasingly impoverished as the nation's economic situation worsened. In 1982, after Sendero Luminoso guerrillas attacked the main prison in Ayacucho and freed dozens of their jailed comrades, President Belaúnde declared a state of emergency in the department of Ayacucho and placed it under complete military control. The military battled the insurgency's violence with harsh repression, often catching the civilian population in the crossfire; through the 1980s, tens of thousands of people died in the fight to subdue the movement.

After the 1990 election of Alberto **Fujimori Fujimori** (1990–2000), military and police offensives against the insurgency intensified. Guzmán's September 1992 capture in Lima by a special unit of the Peruvian police struck a major blow to the organization due to its top-down power structure. Though small groups continued to operate in the Upper Huallaga Valley and to some extent in urban areas, direct urban attacks decreased in frequency after the loss of the movement's key leadership. Also, by the mid-1990s Sendero Luminoso's indiscriminate violence and inflexible tactics had begun to alienate the powerless peasantry in the highlands, and the military had helped peasants organize patrols to defend themselves against the movement. Fujimori's relentlessness in the war against terrorism, in combination with his promise to grant amnesty to Sendero Luminoso members who surrendered to the government, resulted in the containment of the movement by the close of the 1990s.

Toledo, Alejandro (1946–)

Alejandro Toledo (2001–), Peru's first democratically elected president of Andean Indian descent, was elected in a second-round runoff in June 2001, defeating former president Alan **García Pérez** (1985–1990), of the **American Revolutionary Popular Alliance** (Alianza Popular Revolucionaria Americana, APRA).

Toledo was born to an impoverished indigenous family in the village of Cabana in 1946. He grew up in Chimbote, where he worked as a shoeshine boy. In his late teens, he earned a one-year scholarship to attend the University of San Francisco, where he later earned a partial soccer scholarship and continued his education. He subsequently won a scholarship to Stanford University and eventually became an economic adviser to the World Bank.

Toledo established himself as a well-known political figure in 2000 when he became the strongest challenger to Alberto **Fujimori Fujimori**'s (1990–2000) bid for a third presidential term. His relentless attacks on the corruption of the Fujimori regime and his appeals to Peru's poor attracted hordes of disenchanted voters, and in the April 2000 election, Toledo and his Perú Posible Party garnered 40.2 percent of the vote, to Fujimori's 49.9 percent. His second-place finish and Fujimori's failure to earn 51 percent of the vote qualified Toledo to contest the runoff election to be held in May 2000, but Toledo withdrew his candidacy, claiming that Fujimori had fixed the election. Even though Toledo's charges attracted widespread attention within Peru and in the international community, Fujimori was reelected. Domestic and international protest, in combination with revelations of corruption within the Fujimori administration, eventually led to Fujimori's resignation in November 2000. Interim president Valentín Paniagua called for elections in April 2001, and Toledo quickly emerged as the front-runner.

Toledo campaigned on a center-left platform criticizing the corruption of the Fujimori regime and the economic disasters of the previous administration of his opponent, García. He also used traditional Andean symbolism to attract support in the Peruvian highlands where the majority of the people are of indigenous descent. Although accusations of cocaine abuse and an extramarital affair marred his campaign, Toledo came in first in the presidential election in April 2001, winning 36.5 percent of the vote; challengers García and Lourdes Flores finished second and third with 25.8 percent and 24.3 percent of the vote, respectively. A second round was held in June 2001 in which Toledo was victorious, garnering approximately 53 percent of the vote to García's 46.9 percent. Thanks to the support of other political parties, including **Popular Action** (Acción Popular, AP), Toledo began his term as president on July 28, 2001 with a majority in Congress. While Toledo promised to bring unity to Peru and to build a broad-based government, he faced many challenges including recasting democratic institutions in the aftermath of the Fujimori regime, rooting out widespread corruption in the Peruvian government, and overseeing continued economic reform.

Túpac Amaru II (also José Gabriel Condoracanqui). See Tupac Amaru Revolutionary Movement (Movimiento Revolucionario Tupac Amaru, MRTA)

Tupac Amaru Revolutionary Movement (Movimiento Revolucionario Tupac Amaru, MRTA)

The Tupac Amaru Revolutionary Movement (Movimiento Revolucionario Tupac Amaru, MRTA), a leftist insurgency based on Marxist-Leninist principles, was formally founded in 1984 by urban middle-class intellectuals. Smaller, less ruthless, and more political than the **Shining Path** (Sendero Luminoso), the MRTA carried out spectacular acts in the name of broader justice. The group is named for Túpac Amaru II (actual name José Gabriel Condoracanqui), a member of elite society in the late 1700s who, outraged by the abusive treatment of the indigenous peoples by the Spanish colonizers, led an army of tens of thousands of Indians in an unsuccessful revolt against the Spanish ruling forces in 1780.

The MRTA had its origins in several Peruvian guerrilla groups that had formed in the 1960s, inspired by the **Cuban Revolution of 1959** (see Cuba), but had been subdued by military forces well trained in counterinsurgency efforts. These included the Movement of the Revolutionary Left (Movimiento de Izquierda Revolucionaria, MIR, an extreme left-wing faction of the **American Revolutionary Popular Alliance** [Alianza Popular Revolucionaria Americana, APRA] that set up guerrilla operations in the Andes Mountains in 1965), and the National Liberation Army (Ejército de Liberación Nacional, ELN). The MRTA hoped to revive their violent tradition, rid Peru of its imperialist influence, and establish a Marxist regime.

Though the group's members were mainly middle-class youth from the cities, it enjoyed the support of peasants in the rural areas, and was estimated to have 3,000 guerrillas in the field in the mid-1980s. The movement encouraged voters to boycott elections (which it felt only reinforced the strength of the corrupt and elite-dominated oligarchy) and often bombed U.S. symbols such as the American Embassy, U.S. banks, and fast food chains. In the late 1980s the group began kidnapping government officials and businessmen in order to raise funds.

The second administration of Fernando **Belaúnde Terry** (1963–1968, 1980–1985) carried out extensive counterinsurgency efforts aimed at weakening the MRTA and Sendero Luminoso. The MRTA's strength was further undermined when security forces captured an MRTA information center and arrested the group's

Juan Velasco Alvarado (standing at table) addresses the country shortly after seizing power in Peru in 1968. *Columbus Memorial Library, General Secretariat of the Organization of American States. Reproduced with permission of the Organization of American States.*

leader, Miguel Rincón Rincón, in 1995. In December 1996 a small group of MRTA members occupied the home of the Japanese ambassador, holding over seventy hostages, many of whom were high-ranking officials. The standoff lasted until April 22, 1997, when Peruvian military forces under the direction of President Alberto **Fujimori Fujimori** (1990–2000) raided the residence, killing all fourteen guerrillas, including the group's leader, Nestor Cerpa Cartolini. This successful raid practically eliminated the movement.

Vargas Llosa, Mario (1936–   )

Internationally acclaimed novelist Mario Vargas Llosa was born in 1936 to a middle-class family in Arequipa. He studied in Lima at the Leonardo Prado Military School and the San Marcos University and pursued doctoral work at the University of Madrid. Vargas Llosa later worked as a journalist in Paris and wrote novels, and by the 1970s he had written prize-winning works such as *La Casa Verde* (*The Green House*, 1966) and *Conversación en la Catedral* (*Conversation in the Cathedral*, 1969). Though originally convinced of the merits of socialism, at this point Vargas Llosa began to move toward the political right.

Vargas Llosa headed the official investigation into the massacre of eight journalists near Ayacucho in 1983. In 1987 he publicly denounced President Alan **García Perez**'s (1985–1990) proposed nationalization of the banking system, and that same year, he organized the

center-right Liberty Movement (Movimiento Libertad). In 1989 he was chosen by the Democratic Front (Frente Democrático, FREDEMO), a conservative alliance between **Popular Action** (Acción Popular, AP) and the Popular Christian Party, as its presidential candidate for the 1990 election. Though Vargas Llosa received the most votes in the first round, his economic austerity plan and conservative aristocratic image cost him support, and he was defeated in the second round by Alberto **Fujimori Fujimori** (1990–2000).

Velasco Alvarado, Juan (1910–1977)

Juan Velasco Alvarado led Peru from 1968 to 1975 during the first phase of the military experiment in politics. His reformist and populist administration was unique among modern Latin American military regimes.

Velasco was born in 1910 in Castilla. He enlisted in the army in 1929, graduated from the Chorrillos Military School with high honors, and by 1968 was the commander-in-chief of the army. The failure of the first administration of Fernando **Belaúnde Terry** (1963–1968, 1980–1985) to implement its program of reform and development prompted Velasco to lead a military coup in 1968. The military attributed Belaúnde's failure to flaws in the democratic political system that had enabled the opposition to block and stalemate reform initiatives in Congress, and Velasco moved to create a strong authoritarian government, devoid of party politics. Following a nationalist philosophy that posited that underdevelopment was caused by dependence on foreign capital and the domination of the Peruvian oligarchy, Velasco began to dismantle the liberal model of export-led development, replacing it with import-substitution industrialization; he also implemented the most extensive agrarian reform program in Latin America and nationalized foreign holdings. By 1975 state enterprises accounted for more than half of mining output, two-thirds of the banking system, a fifth of industrial production, and half of total productive investment. Velasco also implemented a series of social measures designed to protect workers and redistribute income in order to expand the domestic market.

In 1973 Velasco developed an abdominal aneurism that resulted in the amputation of his right leg. As his health deteriorated over the next year he gradually lost touch with his government and the public, and his behavior became erratic. Economic problems in 1974 due to the OPEC oil embargo sparked an increase in labor unrest, and conservative civilian and military opposition to Velasco's regime intensified. Francisco **Morales Bermúdez Cerrutti** (1975–1980), Velasco's finance minister and premier, led the coup that deposed Velasco in 1975.

War of the Pacific (1879–1884). See Appendix 1

War of the Peru-Bolivia Confederation (1836–1839). See Appendix 1

HEADS OF STATE

José de San Martín	1821–1822
Junta (José de la Mar, Manuel Salazar y Baquijano, Felipe A. Alvarado)	1822–1823
José de la Riva-Aguero	1823
José Bernardo de Torre Tagle	1823–1824
Simón Antonio de la Santísima Trinidad Bolívar y Palacios, Antonio José de Sucre	1824–1826
Andrés de Santa Cruz	1826–1827
José de la Mar	1827–1829
Agustín Gamarra	1829–1833
Pedro Pablo Bermúdez	1834
Luis José de Orbegoso	1834–1835
Felipe Santiago Salaverry	1835–1836
Andrés de Santa Cruz (Peru-Bolivia Confederation)	1836–1839
Agustín Gamarra	1839–1841
Francisco Vidal, Juan Crisóstomo Torrico	1842–1843
Domingo Elías, Domingo Nieto	1843–1844
Justo Figuerola	1844
Ramón Castilla	1845–1851
José Rufino Echenique	1851–1855
Ramón Castilla	1855–1862
Miguel de San Román	1862–1863
Juan Antonio Pezet	1863–1865
Mariano Ignacio Prado	1865–1868
Pedro Diez Canseco (provisional)	1868
José Balta	1868–1872
Manuel Pardo y Lavalle	1872–1876
Mariano Ignacio Prado	1876–1879
Nicolás de Piérola	1879–1881
Francisco García Calderón	1881
Lizardo Montero	1881–1883
Miguel Iglesias	1883–1886
Andrés Avelino Cáceres	1886–1890
Remigio Morales Bermúdez	1890–1894
Justiniano Borgoño	1894
Andrés Avelino Cáceres	1894–1895
Manuel Eduardo Candamo (Junta)	1895
Nicolás de Piérola	1895–1899
Eduardo López de Romaña	1899–1903
Manuel Eduardo Candamo	1903–1904
Serapio Calderón	1904
José Pardo y Barreda	1904–1908
Augusto Bernardino Leguía	1908–1912
Guillermo Billinghurst	1912–1914
Oscar Raimundo Benavides	1914–1915
José Pardo y Barreda	1915–1919
Augusto Bernardino Leguía	1919–1930
Luis Miguel Sánchez Cerro	1930–1933
Oscar Raimundo Benavides	1933–1939
Manuel Prado y Ugarteche	1939–1945
José Luis Bustamante y Rivero	1945–1948
Manuel Apolinario Odría (Junta)	1948–1950
Manuel Apolinario Odría	1950–1956
Manuel Prado y Ugarteche	1956–1962
Ricardo Pérez Godoy, Nicolás Lindey López	1962–1963
Fernando Belaúnde Terry	1963–1968
Juan Velasco Alvarado	1968–1975
Francisco Morales Bermúdez Cerrutti	1975–1980
Fernando Belaúnde Terry	1980–1985
Alan García Pérez	1985–1990
Alberto Fujimori Fujimori	1990–2000
Valentín Paniagua [interim]	2000–2001
Alejandro Toledo	2001–

Source: Peter Klaren, *Peru: Society & Nationhood in the Andes* (London: Oxford University Press, 2000).

BIBLIOGRAPHY

Print Resources

Cameron, Maxwell A., and Philip Mauceri, eds. *The Peruvian Labyrinth: Polity, Society, Economy.* University Park: Pennsylvania State University Press, 1997.

Garay Seminario, Martín. *Perfiles Humanos: Los hombres que hacen historia en el Perú.* Lima: Editorial Atlantida, 1985.

Hudson, Rex A., ed. *Peru: A Country Study.* Washington, DC: Department of the Army, 1993.

Klaren, Peter. *Peru: Society and Nationhood in the Andes.* London: Oxford University Press, 2000.

Markham, Clements R. *A History of Peru.* Westport, CT: Greenwood Press, 1968.

McClintock, Cynthia, and Abraham F. Lowenthal, eds. *The Peruvian Experiment Reconsidered.* Princeton: Princeton University Press, 1983.

Palmer, David Scott. *Peru: The Authoritarian Tradition.* New York: Praeger, 1980.

———, ed. *Shining Path of Peru.* New York: St. Martin's Press, 1994.

Pike, Frederick B. *The Modern History of Peru.* New York: Praeger, 1967.

Prescott, William H. *History of the Conquest of Peru.* Philadelphia: J. B. Lippincott, 1905.

Starn, Orin, Carlos Iván Degregori, and Robin Kirk, eds. *The Peru Reader: History, Culture, Politics.* Durham, NC: Duke University Press, 1995.

Electronic Resources

Asociación Civil Transparencia
www.transparencia.org.pe
Contains Peruvian electoral statistics and election legislation documents. Also contains the text of reports published by the association. A reading room contains links to the constitutions of various Latin American countries, their electoral organizations, and electoral laws. (In Spanish)

El Comercio Peru
www.elcomercioperu.com.pe
Web version of an important Peruvian newspaper focusing on economic trends and political events. (In Spanish)

Expreso
www.expreso.com.pe
Web version of an important Peruvian newspaper focusing on topics relating to Peru's society, economy, and politics. (In Spanish)

Latin American Network Information Center (LANIC): Peru
http://lanic.utexas.edu/la/peru/
Peru section of this extensive Web site contains hundreds of links to research resources, cultural centers, economic and business institutions, government agencies, historical sources, magazines and other periodicals, nongovernmental organizations, and grassroots groups, as well as many other subjects. (In English)

Latin Focus: Peru
http://www.latin-focus.com/countries/peru.htm
Contains an overview and description of Peru's government institutions and political environment, economic and financial information and statistics, and links to government ministries and agencies. (In English)

Peru Links: Government and Politics
http://www.perulinks.com/pages/english/Government_and_Politics/
Web page with extensive links to a variety of Internet sites of government institutions and agencies, nongovernmental organizations, political parties, and other political actors and institutions. (In English)

Peru News
http://www.limapost.com/
Comprehensive and constantly updated source for political and economic news stories about Peru from wire services and major newspaper reports. Also contains regional news and analysis. (In English)

Peru.com
www.peru.com
Site contains links to Peruvian national, political, and economic news updated constantly, links to Peruvian radio stations, and links to Peruvian government ministries, the armed forces, political parties, embassies, regional governments, and government institutions. (In Spanish)

Peruvian Government's National Office of Electoral Processes
www.onpe.gob.pe
Contains documentation of the Peruvian electoral system in Peruvian law, a complete list of Peruvian leaders from 1821 to 2000, and the presidential candidates in Peru from 1931 to 2000. (In Spanish)

Political Database of the Americas: Peru
http://www.georgetown.edu/pdba/Countries/peru.html
Comprehensive database run as a joint project of Georgetown University and the Organization of American States. Section on Peru contains information on and links to the executive, legislative, and judicial branches of the Peruvian government; electoral laws and election results; and other political data. (In English, Spanish, Portuguese, and French)

Political Resources.net: Peru
http://www.politicalresources.net/peru.htm
Peru section of a Web site containing a wealth of links to sources of information about national politics. Includes information on political parties, legislative and executive institutions, laws and legislation, and elections, as well as a link to the constitution. (In English)

La República
www.larepublica.com.pe/diario/home.htm
The Web version of one of Peru's most widely read daily newspapers. Offers comprehensive national and international

coverage, with a particularly strong emphasis on national politics and the Peruvian economy. (In Spanish)

Wilfried Derksen's Elections Around the World: Peru
http://www.agora.it/elections/peru.htm

Peru section of a comprehensive database of results from elections around the world. Contains results from recent national executive and legislative elections, as well as explanations of and links to political parties and institutions. (In English)

PUERTO RICO

COMMONWEALTH PROFILE

Official name	Commonwealth of Puerto Rico
Capital	San Juan
Type/structure of government	Commonwealth of the United States
Executive	Governor elected to four-year renewable term; chief of state is the president of the United States.
Legislative	Bicameral; Senate (currently 28 members), House of Representatives (54 members); all members of the legislature are elected by popular vote and serve four-year terms.
Representation in U.S. government	Resident commissioner is popularly elected to a four-year term and officially represents Puerto Rico before the United States House of Representatives (but possesses voting privileges only within House committees).
Judicial	Highest court is Supreme Court (justices appointed by the governor with the consent of the Senate); U.S. federal courts antecede Puerto Rican courts in all federal and constitutional matters.
Major political parties	**Popular Democratic Party** (Partido Popular Democrático, PPD); **New Progressive Party** (Partido Nuevo Progresista, PNP); **Puerto Rican Independence Party** (Partido Independentista Puertorriqueño, PIP).
Constitution in effect	1952
Location/geography	Caribbean island located between the Caribbean Sea and the North Atlantic Ocean, east of the Dominican Republic; mostly mountains with coastal plain belt in north and south; mountains extend to the sea on the east and west coasts.
Geographic area	9,104 sq. km.
Population	3,887,652 (1999 estimate)
Ethnic groups	Mestizo 98%; other 2%
Religions	Roman Catholic 85%; Protestant denominations and other 15%
Literacy rate	93% (1998 estimate)
Infant mortality rate	10.79 deaths per 1,000 live births (1999 estimate)
Life expectancy	75.06 years (1999 estimate)
Monetary unit	U.S. dollar
Exchange rate	NA
Major exports	Pharmaceuticals, electronics, apparel, canned tuna, rum, beverage concentrates, medical equipment
Major imports	Chemicals, machinery and equipment, clothing, food, fish, petroleum products
GDP	$34.7 billion (1998 estimate)
GDP growth rate	3.1% (1998 estimate)
GDP per capita	$9,000 (1998 estimate)

Sources: Puerto Rico Planning Board. http://www.jp.gov.pr
Puerto Rico Labor Department. http://www.ocalarh.com.
CIA World Factbook 2000. http://www.cia.gov/cia/publications/factbook/geos/rq.htlm/

OVERVIEW

Summary

Since its colonization by Spain, Puerto Rico has never known autonomy as defined by international conventions. Today the island is designated a commonwealth (or nonincorporated) territory of the United States. Persons born in Puerto Rico are U.S. citizens by disposition of the U.S. Congress since 1917. Puerto Ricans remain divided over what political relationship the island should establish with the United States. The three most debated possibilities are **independence**, statehood, or a continued form of commonwealth status. These three options and their possible consequences form the basis of Puerto Rico's political debates, and stance on the **status issue** in large part defines the island's political parties, typically overshadowing substantive policy issues.

History

Christopher Columbus arrived on the island of Puerto Rico on November 19, 1493, and claimed it for the Castilian monarchy. Columbus soon changed the name of the island from Boriquén (the name used by the native inhabitants, the Taíno Indians) to San Juan Bautista

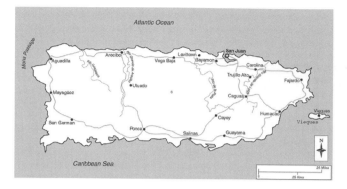

Puerto Rico. © 1998 The Moschovitis Group, Inc.

del Puerto Rico ("rich port" in English). Attracted to the island by its strategic location and stories that it was filled with gold, Spanish explorer Juan Ponce de León founded the settlement of Caparra and began to mine for riches. He served as the Spanish governor from 1510 to 1512, and in 1511 changed the name of the territory to Puerto Rico. By 1540 the gold supply was exhausted and the Indian population had been devastated by European diseases and social disruption brought by forced labor and revolts. Agriculture became the main legal means to generate revenue on the island, and, given its labor-intensive character, this led to increased importation of African slaves to substitute for the disappearing native labor. There is evidence that slaves were first brought to the island in 1509, though they were officially introduced into Puerto Rico in 1513 through a Spanish royal decree.

By 1550 Puerto Rico had fallen into deep economic neglect. Spain never tried to develop the economic potential of the island, focusing only on protecting the strategic port of San Juan from outside forces. The island suffered attacks by French, Dutch, and English forces during the subsequent 250 years. Contraband with other Caribbean islands thrived, as did pirating in areas where surviving Indians, escaped slaves, or retired soldiers created their own communities, separate from the crown. A report to the Spanish monarchy by Spanish emissary Alejandro de O'Reilly in 1765 explained that only 5 or 6 percent of usable land on the island was cultivated and that the booming segment of the economy was contraband. This report motivated the Spaniards to rebuild Puerto Rico and attract a new population with the promise of land. All along Puerto Rico remained an administrative province within the "Capitanía General" of Cuba, with which it always maintained close contact.

Through the nineteenth century, as increasing numbers of slaves were imported to work Puerto Rico's sugar plantations, the battle to end slavery brewed in both Puerto Rico and Cuba. Spain resisted any ideas of emancipation, and even mandated a system of forced labor for the free population because of the general scarcity of workers. The island's inhabitants' anger at such unfair treatment, coupled with a desire for independence (fueled from Cuba), led to a revolutionary uprising (*el Grito de Lares*) on September 23, 1868. While the Spanish quickly put down the rebellion, dissatisfaction and unrest continued over the next decades as Puerto Rican patriots continued the fight for autonomy. Toward the end of the **Spanish-American War** (1895–1898; see Appendix 1) in July 1898, U.S. soldiers landed at Guánica (Puerto Rico) and soon defeated the Spanish. The Treaty of Paris, signed on December 10, 1898, separated Puerto Rico from Cuba and officially ceded Puerto Rico to the United States.

Since that time, the issue of Puerto Rico's political relationship with the United States has been a complicated and contentious one. The **Foraker Act** of April 1900 made Puerto Rico the first "unincorporated" territory (a label used to refer to regions that are not on the way to statehood) in the history of the United States. The act ended military rule on the island and granted Puerto Rico a civilian government with an appointed governor, an appointed executive council (upper legislative body) with veto power over an elected house of delegates (lower legislative body), and an elected but powerless resident commissioner to the U.S. House of Representatives. Early stirring of discontent with the island's relationship with the United States had already begun when U.S. president Woodrow Wilson signed the **Jones Act** in 1917. The act granted blanket U.S. citizenship to the Puerto Rican population, established a bicameral Puerto Rican legislature with a nineteen-member senate and a thirty-nine-member house of representatives, and gave the U.S. president veto authority over legislation passed by the Puerto Rican legislature and on the island's selection of its governor.

Politics on the island have revolved around the issue of Puerto Rico's status vis-à-vis the United States since early in the twentieth century. From the end of the Spanish American War until the mid-1900s, the most influential Puerto Rican political parties advocated self-determination and the right of Puerto Ricans to define their options. However, the United States refused to recognize Puerto Rico's right of self-determination.

In the second half of the century, Puerto Rican political parties began to lock themselves into particular definitions and formulae for the island's status, instead of advocating for the right of the people to define and decide the issue. Luis **Muñoz Marín** (1949–1965), founder of the **Popular Democratic Party** (Partido Popular Democrático, PPD) and Puerto Rico's first elected governor, lobbied for the status of the island to be changed from unincorporated territory to Commonwealth or Free Associated State (Estado Libre Asociado). While the island's status did officially change to U.S. Commonwealth in 1952, the change was really in name only. The PPD, which subsequently supported the island's enhanced commonwealth status, the **New Pro-**

gressive Party (Partido Nuevo Progresista, PNP), which favors statehood for Puerto Rico, and the **Puerto Rican Independence Party** (Partido Independentista Puertorriqueño, PIP), which strives for Puerto Rico's political independence from the United States, shared power through the rest of the twentieth century. There is considerable consensus among Puerto Ricans on three points: that the island have (1) a national identity, (2) access to the United States, and (3) the power to self-govern. However, none of the solutions presented by the three main political parties addresses all three items of consensus. Thus, they confabulate with Congress in a "policy" of deadlock.

Today, the movement for greater autonomy remains undefined as the U.S. Congress debates the island's status and Puerto Rico continues to hold referenda in hopes that a clear consensus will emerge. While political status is an important issue, it is certainly not the only concern of Puerto Rican voters. Puerto Rico has problems with drugs, unemployment, urbanization, corruption, crime, and AIDS, all of which affect electoral outcomes. Further, in 1995 the U.S. Congress began a process that will phase out federal tax exemptions for American businesses operating in Puerto Rico over ten years. That move could have a large negative impact on the economic development of Puerto Rico, as tax incentives are an important inducement for U.S. manufacturers to maintain operations and untaxed deposits in Puerto Rico; in 1996, U.S. corporations had more than $10 billion in Puerto Rican banks.

Gubernatorial elections held in November 2000 were won by PPD candidate Sila María Calderón (2001–   ), Puerto Rico's first female governor, whose electoral platform included an anticorruption strategy and opposition to the U.S. military's use of the island of Vieques as a training ground for bombing exercises.

ENTRIES

Albizu Campos, Pedro (1891–1965)
Pedro Albizu Campos was a leader in the Puerto Rican fight for **independence**, promoting the legal and illegal, violent and nonviolent overthrow of U.S. authority on the island. He remains an important symbol for the independence movement.

Born in Ponce, Albizu was educated in Puerto Rico and at the University of Vermont, and received bachelor's and law degrees from Harvard University. He began his political involvement in Puerto Rico with the centrist Union Party and later joined the **Nationalist Party** (Partido Nacionalista, PN). While he initially advocated peaceful means of achieving independence, he became frustrated as it began to appear that the United States did not consider independence an option for the island.

Albizu was elected president of the PN in 1930, and under his influential leadership, party membership reached almost 12,000. Albizu created an atmosphere of militancy and violence in the PN, outspokenly voicing his pro-Hispanic views and his conviction that the one obligation of all those born in Puerto Rico was to strive for their island's independence. Following the murder by the police of two PN members in 1935, Albizu made a public statement advocating retaliation; when the chief of police was assassinated in San Juan in February 1936, Albizu was convicted of conspiracy and sent to prison for ten years. In his absence, PN activists continued their demonstrations, some of which led to violence; the most notorious incident occurred in Ponce in 1937 when a peaceful march of unarmed Cadets of the Republic (the military force associated with the PN) ended with the massacre of twenty-one people at the hands of the local police.

Following his release from prison, Albizu led the **Nationalist Revolution of 1950**. As a result of his involvement in the insurrection, Albizu was found guilty of murder, illegal use of arms, and subversion, and jailed again. Although he was pardoned in 1953 by Governor Luis **Muñoz Marín** (1949–1965), he refused to leave prison in protest of the continued incarceration of two other PN prisoners; he was eventually forcibly removed. He was imprisoned for a third time following his implication in the Nationalist attack on the U.S. Congress (see Independence) in March 1954. Albizu was eventually transferred to a hospital due to his failing health, and died a prisoner in 1965.

Armed Forces of National Liberation (Fuerzas Armadas de Liberación Nacional, FALN). See Independence

Berríos Martínez, Rubén (1939–   )
Since 1970 Rubén Berríos Martínez has served as president of the **Puerto Rican Independence Party** (Partido Independentista Puertorriqueño, PIP). A steadfast opponent of U.S. control of Puerto Rico, Berríos embraces ideas of democratic socialism and maintains ties with the international social democratic movement. He has served in the Puerto Rican Senate and run unsuccessfully for governor of Puerto Rico.

Berríos holds a bachelor's degree from Georgetown University and a law degree from Yale. Berríos and the PIP do not advocate the use of violence to carry out their mission, and they have been unwilling to take an active role in the movement to free imprisoned members of the Armed Forces of National Liberation (Fuerzas Armadas de Liberación Nacional, FALN; see **Independence**) or *los Macheteros*. Berríos believes that Puerto Ricans constitute a distinct nationality with a unique language and culture, and should thus have the opportunity to be a free nation. He holds that independence is supported by only a small percentage of Puerto Ricans because they have been discouraged from supporting independence by a 1948 law that prohibited seditious speech and resulted in the arrest of hundreds of people who recited patriotic poetry and unfurled the Puerto Rican flag.

In 1971 Berríos led a nonviolent demonstration on the island of **Vieques** to protest the U.S. Navy's use of the island as a practice bombing site for its trainees; he was subsequently jailed for three months. In April 1999 a civilian was killed on Vieques when one of the navy bombs missed its target; Berríos again organized a nonviolent sit-in on the beaches of Vieques, where demonstrators successfully prevented U.S. bombing for the subsequent year before they were forcibly but peacefully removed in May 2000.

Cerro Maravilla. See Independence

Commonwealth of Puerto Rico. See Status Issue

Ferré Aguayo, Luis (1904–)
Luis Ferré Aguayo is a noted Puerto Rican industrialist, philanthropist, politician, and businessman. He served as governor of Puerto Rico from 1969 to 1973.

Born in Ponce, Ferré graduated in 1924 from the Massachusetts Institute of Technology with a bachelor's and a master's degree in engineering. He returned to Puerto Rico and worked in his family's industrial businesses. He began to focus on politics in the 1940s, running unsuccessfully for mayor of Ponce and for resident commissioner (see **Foraker Act**). He was elected to the Constitutional Convention of the Free Associated State of Puerto Rico in 1951 (which produced the Constitution of 1952, under which Puerto Rico was still governed in 2002), and then served in the Puerto Rican House of Representatives from 1953 to 1957. As a member of the Statehood Republican Party (Partido Estadista Republicano, PER), Ferré ran unsuccessfully for governor of Puerto Rico in 1956, 1960, and 1964. In spite of these losses, he maintained a mass following.

Ferré founded the **New Progressive Party** (Partido Nuevo Progresista, PNP) in 1967 and was elected the first pro-statehood governor of Puerto Rico in 1968, ending the domination of the **Popular Democratic Party** (Partido Popular Democrático, PPD). As governor, Ferré lobbied the administration of U.S. president Richard Nixon for more financial support for Puerto Rico from the U.S. government. He also successfully pushed the United States to create a place for Puerto Rico within the U.S. federal structure. Ferré lost the gubernatorial election in 1972 but remained active in politics. He was president of the Puerto Rican Senate from 1977 to 1981, and in November 1991 received the Medal of Freedom from U.S. president George Bush.

Foraker Act (also **First Organic Act**) (1900–1917)
The Foraker Act was ratified by the U.S. Congress on April 12, 1900, following the two years of U.S. military

Luis Ferré Aguayo, Governor of Puerto Rico from 1969 to 1973. *Library of Congress, U9-20438-35.*

occupation of Puerto Rico (1898–1900) subsequent to the end of the **Spanish American War** (1895–1898; see Appendix 1). It set forth the provisions of the first civil government of Puerto Rico under U.S. control.

The act's stipulations included the formation of an Executive Council (eleven members appointed by the U.S. president, five of whom had to be Puerto Rican), and the popularly elected House of Delegates (the lower house of the legislature including thirty-five delegates). The Foraker Act established the office of the governor appointed by the U.S. president and made the U.S. Supreme Court the ultimate decision-making body in the Puerto Rican legal system. It also established the office and created the role of the resident commissioner, the elected official who still represents Puerto Rico before the United States House of Representatives today. The resident commissioner did not originally possess voting privileges, although he was granted the right to vote within House committees in the 1970s.

Economically, the act integrated Puerto Rico into the United States in some ways, making the U.S. dollar the legal currency on the island and implementing a system of tariffs. The tariff system caused hardship as Puerto Ricans struggled to afford basic necessities. Even given the significant degree of control the United States exerted over the island, the people of Puerto Rico were considered citizens of Puerto Rico, and not of the United States. The Foraker Act remained in effect until 1917 when the U.S. Congress passed the **Jones Act,** which granted Puerto Ricans full U.S. citizenship and replaced the Executive Council with an elected Senate. (See also **Status Issue.**)

Free Associated State (Estado Libre Asociado, ELA). See Status Issue

Hernández Colón, Rafael (1936–)

Rafael Hernández Colón is a prominent and highly respected politician who served three terms as governor of Puerto Rico (1973–1977, 1985–1989, 1989–1993).

Born in Ponce, Hernández earned a bachelor's degree from Johns Hopkins University and a law degree from the University of Puerto Rico. He published the classic law text *Procedimiento Civil* in 1968. Hernández served as the island's secretary of justice and as president of the Senate before being elected governor. As governor, he led public and private efforts to restore cities such as Ponce and San Germán to their original beauty. Hernández also attempted to increase the autonomy and political power of the commonwealth. His earliest and most overt efforts were blocked by tenets of the U.S. Constitution or rulings of the U.S. Senate. His later, more subtle efforts included trying to negotiate with Japan independently of the United States, excluding the U.S. flag and national anthem from public ceremonies, and (unsuccessfully) encouraging the U.S. Congress to allow Puerto Rico to hold a plebiscite on the island's relationship with the United States that would be binding on the U.S. Congress (see **Independence**).

Suspecting that Puerto Ricans were not completely receptive to his ideas, he decided not to run for governor in 1992. He subsequently founded the RHC Library Foundation and currently lives in Ponce and teaches at the Pontifical Catholic University.

Independence

While Puerto Rico's status has been a contentious issue on the island for the last five centuries, the debate became even more heated in the 1900s. There is consensus that Puerto Rico's current relationship with the United States is unsatisfactory (it is a commonwealth or Free Associated State [Estado Libre Asociado]); many feel it harkens back to the colonial relationship the island had with Spain from the 1500s through the 1800s. However, there is less agreement on what type of relationship *should* exist with the United States. Some favor complete independence from the United States (though since 1948 this view has received less support, as many fear that Puerto Rico would be unable to survive economically without the support of the United States). Others believe that Puerto Rico should become a state

of the United States, and still others would prefer that the island remain a commonwealth of the United States (though with enhanced sovereignty and independent administrative and political control) (see **status issue**). What most residents *do* want is self-determination: the ability to control their laws, their constitution, and their economy, and the right to choose for themselves what is best for the island.

Puerto Ricans have voted on their desired relationship with the United States three times in the past four decades, in plebiscites held in 1967, 1993, and 1998. (These plebiscites are nonbinding: while the United States takes the votes under consideration, it does not recognize any changes in Puerto Rico's status on the basis of the outcome of the plebiscites.) In 1967 the results were commonwealth 60.4 percent, statehood 39.0 percent, independence 0.6 percent. The 1993 results were commonwealth 48.6 percent, statehood 46.3 percent, independence 4.4 percent. In the 1998 plebiscite, two new options were presented by the United States (which defined the status alternatives on which Puerto Ricans voted): "none of the above" and "free association" (which implied the establishment of a bilateral treaty between the United States and Puerto Rico as two sovereign nations). The 1998 results were: none of the above, 50.2 percent, statehood 46.5 percent, independence 2.5 percent, free association 0.3 percent and commonwealth 0.1 percent. Some interpreted the outcome as an expression of Puerto Rican discontent with the options defined and presented by the United States, while others held that the results indicated that Puerto Ricans remained indecisive about what they want for the island.

The debate and the struggle for greater independence have sparked numerous events, some of them violent. In February 1936, for instance, members of the **Nationalist Party** (Partido Nacionalista, PN) assassinated the chief of police. Subsequently, members of the PN instigated the **Nationalist Revolution of 1950,** a failed attempt to overthrow U.S. control of the island and delay or prevent the approval of a referendum to change Puerto Rico's status to Free Associated State. On March 1, 1954, outraged by the United Nations' removal of Puerto Rico from its list of non–self-governing territories, four PN members entered the U.S. House of Representatives and shot and wounded five congressmen; the attackers were incarcerated in federal prisons for twenty-five years. In addition, two members of the more violent sector of the pro-independence movement (*independentistas*) were killed at Cerro Maravilla in July 1978; while the police insisted that they were killed because they resisted arrest, some believe they were murdered, and that Puerto Rican and U.S. officials attempted to cover up the controversial incident.

Several revolutionary groups have also appeared in the late twentieth century, including *los Macheteros* and the Armed Forces of National Liberation (Fuerzas Armadas de Liberación Nacional, FALN). The FALN assumed responsibility for 120 bombings (claiming a total of five lives) of corporate and government buildings in the United States between 1974 and 1981. For FALN members, who blame the economic and educational problems of Puerto Ricans living in the United States on the destructive colonial relationship that the United States maintains with the island, these targets represented the U.S. exploitation of Puerto Rico and U.S. infringement of Puerto Rican independence. More than a dozen members of the group were tried and convicted of treason, and sentenced to an average of seventy years in prison.

Jones Act (also Organic Act or Second Organic Act) (1917)

The Jones Act, the successor to the **Foraker Act** (1900), was ratified by the U.S. Congress in March 1917.

For fifteen years following the passage of the Foraker Act, the dominant Puerto Rican party, the Union Party, spoke out against what it perceived as an absence of basic democratic rights on the island. In February 1914 talks began in the U.S. House of Representatives regarding granting U.S. citizenship to the people of Puerto Rico. In response, in March 1914, the Puerto Rican House of Delegates approved a resolution in opposition to U.S. citizenship because they did not want to be citizens within a colony. This opposition halted the hearings, but the bill to grant U.S. citizenship to Puerto Ricans resurfaced in 1916.

U.S. president Woodrow Wilson signed the Jones Act (now called the Federal Relations Act) in March 1917. The act granted Puerto Ricans U.S. citizenship (making them eligible for military draft) and established a bicameral Puerto Rican legislature with a nineteen-member popularly elected Senate (which replaced the Executive Council established under the Foraker Act as the higher legislative body) and a thirty-nine-member popularly elected House of Representatives (the lower legislative body). The Jones Act also gave the U.S. president veto authority over legislation passed by the Puerto Rican legislature as well as over the island's selection of its governor, and awarded the U.S. president the ability to appoint an auditor who had the final word on government expenditures in Puerto Rico.

While the bill enjoyed broad popular support on the island, some worried that its stipulations would diminish the possibility of achieving **independence** in the future. The Union Party opposed the act, claiming that it actually disregarded the will of the Puerto Rican people and gave more power to the United States. Many felt that the act left the island in a state of undefined limbo: under the tenets of the act, Puerto Rico was neither a part of the United States nor a completely independent nation. (See also **Status Issue**.)

Los Macheteros (also Boricua Popular Army [Ejército Popular Boricua])

Founded by Filiberto Ojeda Ríos, this Puerto Rican revolutionary group's principal goal is to encourage the Puerto Rican people to challenge what some interpret as continued colonization of the island by the United States. The symbol of *los Macheteros*, the machete used by cane cutters, represents their identification with the Puerto Rican masses exploited under Spanish and (what they see as) U.S. colonialism. The group was most active from 1978 to 1985, and at its peak had an estimated membership of 300. The eclectic organization includes both uneducated and well-educated Puerto Ricans, nationalists, communists, women, men, young, and old. Inspired by Ramón Emeterio Betances, a nineteenth-century Puerto Rican revolutionary, and Pedro **Albizu Campos**, *los Macheteros* advocate revolution, convinced that violence is both a necessary and legal means to end colonial rule.

In 1979 *los Macheteros* killed a group of American marines, and in 1981 they staged attacks on a National Guard post in Isla Verde and detonated several war planes at the Muñoz Airport. Subsequent to these attacks, group members went on television to state their message—that as a united people, Puerto Rico could defeat the United States. In 1983 members of the group robbed $7.1 million from a Wells Fargo Bank in West Hartford, Connecticut. The Puerto Rican people have never openly expressed strong opinions about the group, though it is considered a terrorist organization by some.

Moscoso, Teodoro. See Operation Bootstrap

Muñoz Marín, Luis (1898–1980)

Luis Muñoz Marín (1949–1965), a noted poet and journalist, is most remembered for his leadership as governor of Puerto Rico. He was honored throughout his life, receiving the United States Medal of Freedom, the French Legion of Honor, honorary doctorates from Harvard and Rutgers Universities, and the Peruvian *Orden del Sol*.

Muñoz Marín's father, Luis Muñoz Rivera, was a prominent figure in early Puerto Rican politics and an outspoken critic of the Republican forces that he felt corrupted the island's 1902 elections. Muñoz Rivera moved his family to the United States in 1902, where Muñoz Marín was raised. He graduated from Georgetown University, and later returned to Puerto Rico and affiliated with the Socialist Party (Partido Socialista, PS). He switched his allegiance to his father's Liberal Party (Partido Liberal, PL) during the 1930s. The 1930s brought difficult economic times to Puerto Rico, and Muñoz Marín supported maintaining strong ties with the United States in the interest of receiving economic assistance to fund reconstruction of the island. Through

Puerto Rican Governor Luis Muñoz Marín (1949–1965) (right) with U.S. President Dwight D. Eisenhower in the early 1950s. *Library of Congress, U9-3901.*

the 1930s and 1940s, Muñoz Marín met with numerous officials from the administration of U.S. president Franklin D. Roosevelt, and actively supported Roosevelt's New Deal, as well as the Chardón Plan for reforming the sugar industry; that plan was the model for **Operation Bootstrap**, a later economic initiative to promote industrial development on the island.

Always an advocate for the people of Puerto Rico, Muñoz Marín was concerned throughout his life with improving work conditions on the island. In pursuit of this goal, and in a clash with the liberals, who refused to recognize his "radical leadership," Muñoz Marín founded the **Popular Democratic Party** (Partido Popular Democrático, PPD) in 1938. The party initially focused on improving the economic situation of the people of Puerto Rico, winning a great deal of popular support. Muñoz Marín became the island's first popularly elected governor in 1949. As Puerto Rico's leader, he carried out many social and economic reforms and was the key proponent of the island's acquiring and adopting Commonwealth (or Free Associated State) status in 1952. He also led Operation Bootstrap.

Because the acquisition of Free Associated State status did not fundamentally alter the relationship between Puerto Rico and the United States, and because Muñoz Marín was unsuccessful in expanding Puerto Rico's sovereignty under the new status, he began to lose the support of the Puerto Rican populace. Sensitive to criticisms of his one-man rule, he delegated the PPD candidacy for governor in the 1964 contest to his close supporter Roberto Sánchez Vilella (1965–1969) and ran instead for the Senate. Both men were elected, but the PPD lost the 1968 gubernatorial race to the **New Progressive Party** (Partido Nuevo Progresista, PNP) after a rift between Muñoz Marín and Sánchez Vilella divided the PPD vote in half. Muñoz Marín retired from politics and moved to Italy to write his memoirs. He remained a leading inspiration in Puerto Rican political affairs until his death in 1980.

Nationalist Attack on Congress (1954). See **Independence**

Nationalist Party (Partido Nacionalista, PN)

Founded in 1922, the Nationalist Party (Partido Nacionalista, PN) long advocated revolutionary change for the island. The party was most active from 1930 to the mid-1950s, when Pedro **Albizu Campos** was its president. During that time, members of the PN created a military force called the Cadets of the Republic and encouraged every form of resistance against what they considered to be foreign colonialism. The party also developed an economic plan that involved redirecting sugar and tobacco profits from absent U.S. landowners to workers. The PN hoped to revive native industries and end shipping laws that raised costs on exports and imports, and also strove to promote pride in the island's Spanish heritage. The party is most known for the **Nationalist Revolution of 1950**, an armed attempt to end U.S. control of Puerto Rico. While the strength of the party diminished for a time following the insurrection as a result of the arrest of many of its leaders, there was renewed interest in the party in the 1990s on the part of Puerto Ricans from all party affiliations.

Nationalist Revolution of 1950

The Nationalist Revolution of 1950, an insurrection carried out both in the continental United States and in Puerto Rico, was a failed attempt by the **Nationalist Party** (Partido Nacionalista, PN) to end U.S. control of Puerto Rico and delay or prevent the passage of Public Law 600, the legislation through which Puerto Rican status in relation to the United States was changed to that of Commonwealth (or Free Associated State). Despite the uprising, the law was passed in 1952 (see **status issue**).

On October 27, 1950, police stopped a car carrying Pedro **Albizu Campos** and found guns, ammunition, and bombs. Leaders of the PN, cognizant that this discovery would spark suspicion and might prompt the arrest of party members across the island, took action immediately. At the end of October 1950, the group issued a declaration of independence, and small bands of PN activists attacked police stations and the Puerto Rican governor's residence in La Fortaleza, and took control of the town of Jayuya for a short time, burning federal buildings. In addition, on October 31, PN members attacked Blair House in Washington, D.C., where U.S. president Harry S. Truman was temporarily living.

Despite these efforts, the island's National Guard and U.S. forces extinguished the rebellion within days. About 164 PN revolutionaries were convicted of various crimes in the wake of the uprising. Few Puerto Ricans approved of the use of violence to achieve **independence**, though they were sympathetic to the viewpoint and goals of the PN. People from all political affiliations called for unconditional amnesty for Albizu

Campos (who, together with several other PN members, had been incarcerated after the uprising), and he was pardoned in September 1953. On November 23, 1972, Governor Luís Ferré Aguayo (1969–1973) pardoned the four remaining prisoners in Puerto Rico.

New Progressive Party (Partido Nuevo Progresista, PNP)

The New Progressive Party (Partido Nuevo Progresista, PNP), one of the two most popular political parties in Puerto Rico, supports statehood, working toward its goal both on the island and in the Untied States.

The PNP emerged in 1967 from a rift between Luis Ferré Aguayo (1969–1973) and the Statehood Republican Party (Partido Estadista Republicano, PER) when the PER refused to participate in the 1967 plebiscite on Puerto Rico's status vis-à-vis the United States (see **independence**). Ferré led the group pushing for statehood in the plebiscite, and later took the statehood symbol used in the plebiscite (the palm tree) as the symbol of what became the PNP. The PER then emptied into the PNP.

Convinced that Puerto Rico's commonwealth status only perpetuates the island's unequal relationship with the United States, the PNP has on several occasions tried to hold referenda on the issue of Puerto Rico's political status. Party supporters see many benefits to statehood: they believe the state of Puerto Rico could be a powerful one, and predict that as a state, Puerto Rico would be eligible for approximately $3–4 billion more in federal aid than it currently receives ($8 billion). Many credit the support for and success of the PNP to the popularity and leadership of Carlos **Romero Barceló** (1977–1985) who helped found the party, and later served as its president. During the time that he led the PNP, party rhetoric emphasized the economic benefits that statehood would bring. Between the party's formation in 1967 and 2000, PNP gubernatorial candidates have been victorious in five out of eight elections: 1968 (Ferré), 1976 and 1980 (Barceló), and 1992 and 1996 (Pedro Rosselló González).

Operation Bootstrap (Operación Manos de Obra) (1945–1964)

This economic initiative, carried out between 1945 and 1964, was an effort to industrialize Puerto Rico.

Operation Bootstrap was the eventual successor of the Chardón Plan, a strategy to revitalize the Puerto Rican economy that was initiated during the Great Depression. The Chardón Plan included measures to encourage the development of labor-intensive industries, revitalize the sugar industry, establish tax credits to draw investors to the island, and initiate land reform. The plan's critics argued that it relied too much on the United States for its completion, and that the revitalized sugar industry anticipated in the plan would have no room for growth due to quotas established by the ad-ministration of U.S. president Franklin D. Roosevelt limiting the amount of sugar that could be produced in Puerto Rico. Due to resistance from both Puerto Rican and U.S. owners of land on which sugar was harvested, the Chardón Plan was never implemented. Puerto Rican political leaders continued to lobby Washington unsuccessfully for land redistribution in hopes of facilitating agricultural development until the early 1940s, but were consistently opposed by U.S. sugar interests. The island's leaders subsequently began to deemphasize agriculture, and to focus on stimulating Puerto Rico's economic growth by encouraging the development of industry.

Proudly stating that Puerto Ricans were trying to lift themselves up by their bootstraps, in 1945 influential Puerto Rican politician Teodoro Moscoso proposed and initiated Operation Bootstrap. The program, inspired by the ideology of the **Popular Democratic Party** (Partido Popular Democrático, PPD) and supported by Governors Luís **Muñoz Marín** (1949–1965) and Rexford G. Tugwell (1941–1946), was implemented in Puerto Rico from the mid-1940s to the mid 1960s. The plan led to the approval by the Puerto Rican legislature (May 1948) of Act No. 184 granting full exemption from payment of income, property, excise, and municipal taxes to new industries established on Puerto Rico for ten years, and granting partial exemption for an additional three years. This, in combination with the lack of tariff barriers on trade between Puerto Rico and the United States, served as a catalyst to investment in the island, and contributed significantly to its successful industrialization.

The initiative also established the Puerto Rican Economic Development Administration (FOMENTO), which implemented a host of local government programs. FOMENTO's subsidiary, the Puerto Rican Industrial Development Company (Compañía de Fomento Industrial, CFI) initially owned five industrial operations designed to promote private and public investments through forward and backward linkages. However, all five suffered from inexpert management and were subsequently privatized. CFI then focused on providing government-owned plant sites to private ventures promoted by FOMENTO. Thus, while Operation Bootstrap emphasized the development of industry via government-owned firms from 1948 to 1956, in the late 1950s the plants were privatized, and the initiative became a plan to bring U.S. firms to Puerto Rico.

The plan successfully facilitated economic development: Puerto Rico's industrial base evolved from labor-intensive textiles to petrochemicals and later to electronics and pharmaceuticals, and between 1952 and 1961, U.S. firms invested millions in the island's economy. Further, Operation Bootstrap helped Puerto Rico to create one of the best-educated labor forces in Latin America. However, the initiative did not turn out to be the comprehensive, enduring development plan that many had hoped and anticipated. High rates of economic growth were unable to dent high levels of unemployment, as the plan did not lead to the development of a Puerto Rican entrepreneurial class able to create enough businesses to absorb unemployment. Further, by the early 1970s, Puerto Rico was emphasizing petrochemicals and had several refineries in place and more in the pipeline; when the oil crisis of 1973 hit, Puerto Rico was devastated, and unemployment was officially tagged at over 20 percent. Finally, U.S. tax reforms in 1982 and 1993 reduced the relative attractiveness of the incentives offered to those investing on the island.

Puerto Ricans are still searching for a new path to economic development and are presently at a loss for a strategy. While funding is not an issue, as Puerto Ricans have access to U.S. capital markets, the island generates few new businesses. In addition, many islanders doubt that Puerto Rico has the independent political power necessary to achieve self-sustaining economic growth.

Popular Democratic Party (Partido Popular Democrático, PPD)

Founded in 1938 by Luís **Muñoz Marín** (1949–1965), the Popular Democratic Party (Partido Popular Democrático, PPD) is one of the two leading political parties in Puerto Rico. The party supports the continuation and enhancement of Puerto Rico's current commonwealth status (see **status issue**).

While the island acquired its status as a commonwealth (Free Associated State) in 1952 under the leadership of party founder Muñoz Marín, the PPD initially focused on improving the economic situation of the people of Puerto Rico. This emphasis gained the party popular support, and PPD candidates won various elections in the 1940s. The PPD is also credited with introducing **Operation Bootstrap** (a socioeconomic plan to industrialize the island) in the mid-1940s. A major push of the party during the 1950s and 1960s was to convince the U.S. government to grant additional powers to Puerto Rico. Specifically, the party hoped to attain domestic control of U.S. federal funds as well as the authority to negotiate international trade agreements.

The PPD controlled Puerto Rico from 1949 to 1965 under Governor Muñoz Marín, and from 1973 to 1977 and 1985 to 1993 under Governor Rafael **Hernández Colón**; PPD candidate Sila María Calderón was elected governor in November 2000. The party has shared popularity and power with the **New Progressive Party** (Partido Nuevo Progresista, PNP) since the 1970s.

Puerto Rican Independence Party (Partido Independentista Puertorriqueño, PIP)

Founded in 1946 by Gilberto Concepción de Gracia, the Puerto Rican Independence Party (Partido Independentista Puertorriqueño, PIP) advocates Puerto Rican political **independence** from the United States through a negotiated settlement with the U.S. government.

The party evolved when **Popular Democratic Party** (Partido Popular Democrático, PPD) leader Luis **Muñoz Marín** (1949–1965) and other party members attempted to remove Puerto Rican independence from the PPD's platform, choosing instead to support Puerto Rico's commonwealth status (see **status issue**). In response, other PPD members organized *El Congreso Pro-Independencia*, and the PIP subsequently was formed to offer political representation to those in favor of the island's independence. The party ardently believes that Puerto Ricans constitute a distinct nationality with a language and culture separate from that of the United States and that Puerto Rico should therefore have the opportunity to be a free nation. The party's moderate leftist ideology emphasizes working within the established political system to achieve its goals. Since 1948 the PIP has participated in every election, and from that year through 1956, the PIP was the second strongest political force in Puerto Rico. The PIP presently retains the support of approximately 5 percent of the electorate. The party's current leader, Rubén **Berríos Martínez**, has served as PIP president since 1970.

Resident Commissioner. See Foraker Act

Romero Barceló, Carlos (1932–   )

Carlos Romero Barceló served as mayor of San Juan in 1968 and as governor of Puerto Rico from 1977 to 1985. He was Puerto Rico's resident commissioner (the elected official who represents Puerto Rico before the United States House of Representatives; see **Foraker Act**) from 1993 to 2001.

Born in Santurce, Romero Barceló earned his B.A. from Yale University and his law degree from the University of Puerto Rico. Active in Puerto Rican politics throughout his life, Romero Barceló, together with Luís **Ferré Aguayo** (1969–1973), founded the **New Progressive Party** (Partido Nuevo Progresista, PNP) in 1967. An advocate of statehood for Puerto Rico, Romero Barceló wrote a book called *Statehood Is for the Poor* (1978), in which he maintains that if Puerto Rico remains a commonwealth or gains independence, the inevitable result will be the loss of a significant amount of U.S. federal aid for which the island would be eligible as a state (see **status issue**). He has, at times, been at the center of controversy: the murder of two members of the more violent sector of the pro-independence movement (*independentistas*) at Cerro Maravilla (see **independence**) in 1978 occurred during his first term as governor, and many in Puerto Rico still believe that Romero Barceló lied during the investigation of the murders. He is also known to have been at odds with members of his own party during the 1990s. His second term as resident commissioner ended in 2001, when Aníbal Acevedo-Vilá of the **Popular Democratic Party** (Partido Popular Democrático, PPD) took over the post.

Spanish American War (1895–1898). See Appendix 1; see also **Status Issue**

Status Issue

The contentious and complicated issue of Puerto Rico's political status in relation to the United States dates back to the Treaty of Paris, which officially ended the **Spanish American War** (1895–1898; see Appendix 1). Under that treaty, signed by the United States and Spain in December 1898 and formally ratified in 1899, Spain withdrew from Cuba, Puerto Rico, the Philippine Islands, and other islands in the Pacific and West Indies. Puerto Rico became a possession of the United States in May 1899.

Early opponents of Puerto Rico's status as a possession of the United States claimed that the U.S. constitution did not authorize the federal government to acquire and keep permanent colonies. (Pointedly, Puerto Rico was not incorporated as a territory, a label, as defined by the U.S. Constitution, given to areas for which statehood is anticipated.) Some U.S. legislators initially refused to support the treaty, prompting U.S. president William McKinley to offer them incentives such as patronage appointments and choice committee assignments. The constitutional question was not (and has never been) resolved, and the U.S. Congress' eventual endorsement of the treaty left Puerto Ricans in a situation that many felt was worse than being a colony of Spain; they interpreted Puerto Rico's situation as one in which the rights of the island's inhabitants were under the control of the U.S. Congress, and the island's status was unilaterally decided by the United States.

A military administration governed Puerto Rico from 1898 to 1900. In April 1900, the U.S. Congress ratified the **Foraker Act**, which set forth the provisions of the first civil government of Puerto Rico under U.S. control. The successor to the Foraker Act, the **Jones Act**, passed in March 1917 in the context of World War I and aggressive German incursions in the Caribbean and Central America, granted Puerto Ricans U.S. citizenship, established a bicameral Puerto Rican legislature, and gave the U.S. president wide authority over Puerto Rican decisions. In 1936, amid clamor by liberals and nationalists, the U.S. Congress presented the Tydings Bill, which offered the island independence within an unrealistic four-year time period; the bill never came to a vote. In August 1947, the U.S. Congress and U.S. president Harry S. Truman signed into law the Crawford Project, which allowed Puerto Ricans to elect their own governor (who had previously been appointed by the United States). In 1950 the U.S. Congress passed Public Law 600 which changed the island's political status to commonwealth (or Free Associated State) of the United States, allowed islanders to vote for local officials (mak-ing Puerto Ricans as self-governing in local affairs as citizens of a state of the United States), and authorized the drafting of a constitution (akin to a U.S. state constitution within the federal framework). A constitution was soon drafted which was overwhelmingly approved by the Puerto Rican people in a 1952 referendum, and was formally inaugurated on July 25, 1952.

Puerto Ricans voted on whether they want to continue to be a Commonwealth of the United States or would prefer to be a state or an independent country three times in the past four decades, in 1967, 1993, and 1998 (see **independence**). Today, the island remains a commonwealth. Puerto Ricans are U.S. citizens; while Puerto Ricans living on the island cannot vote in U.S. presidential elections, Puerto Ricans living in the United States have the same voting rights as any other U.S. citizen. Puerto Rican males are eligible for military draft, and the island is subject to all U.S. federal laws except federal taxation. Puerto Ricans are represented in the U.S. House of Representatives by a resident commissioner (see Foraker Act) who possesses voting privileges only on House committees.

Treaty of Paris (1898). See **Status Issue**; see also **Spanish American War** (1895–1898), Appendix 1

Vieques

The island of Vieques is one of Puerto Rico's seventy-eight municipalities and is home to approximately 9,400 people. Vieques hosts the U.S. Naval Munitions Center, located on the western third of the island, and the U.S. Atlantic Fleet Weapons Training Center and Live Impact Range, located on the eastern third. The United States began using Vieques for training exercises in 1941.

The relationship between the U.S. outposts and the residents of the island and other Puerto Ricans has traditionally been an uneasy one. Protests against the U.S. naval presence first occurred in 1971. When an accident in October 1999 during bombing maneuvers at the Live Impact Range resulted in the death of a civilian Vieques resident, Rubén **Berríos Martínez** and other **Puerto Rican Independence Party** (Partido Independentista Puertorriqueño, PIP) supporters began to camp on the beaches on Vieques, preventing the U.S. Navy from continuing its bombing maneuvers. The demonstrators hoped to convince the navy to permanently cease all bombing maneuvers and to transfer use of the island's land to the government of Puerto Rico. In January 2000, Governor Pedro Rosselló González (1993–2001) and U.S. president Bill Clinton reached an agreement that allowed the U.S. Navy to resume limited training on the island and called for the Puerto Rican government to hold a referendum in which residents of Vieques would vote on whether to allow the U.S. Navy to resume use of the range on its own terms or require the Navy to cease all training by May 3, 2003. In May

2001, U.S. Federal Bureau of Investigations (FBI) agents and U.S. marshals forcibly removed protesters from the beaches in a peaceful raid, and U.S. Navy exercises resumed later in May using dummy bombs. Protests at the training facility continued as the bombing exercises resumed, and several dozen protesters were arrested. The political pressure contributed to a decision by the administration of U.S. president George W. Bush in June 2001 to end the bombing exercises in May 2003; that pledge represented a significant victory for newly elected governor Sila María Calderón (2001–). The referendum called for in the January 2000 agreement was held on July 29, 2001 nonetheless, and close to 70 percent of those Vieques residents who voted chose the option that stipulated that the U.S. Navy stop the bombing of the island immediately and permanently and return the island to its people. U.S. president Bush and the Pentagon responded to the referendum by noting that they would hold to the schedule established in the January 2000 agreement.

HEADS OF STATE (GOVERNORS)

John R. Brooke	1898
Guy V. Henry	1898–1899
George W. Davis	1899–1900
Charles Allen	1900–1901
William T. Hunt	1901–1904
Beeckman Winthrop	1904–1907
Regis H. Post	1907–1909
George R. Colton	1909–1913
Arthur Yager	1913–1921
José E. Benedicto (acting)	1921
Emmet Montgomery Reilly	1921–1923
Horace M. Towner	1923–1929
Theodore Roosevelt	1929–1932
James R. Beverly	1932–1933
Robert H. Gore	1933–1934
Blanton Winship	1934–1939
William D. Leahy	1939–1940
Guy J. Swope	1941
Rexford G. Tugwell	1941–1946
Jesús T. Piñero Jiménez (1st Puerto Rican Governor)	1946–1949
Luis Muñoz Marín (1st elected governor)	1949–1965
Roberto Sánchez Vilella	1965–1969
Luis Ferré Aguayo	1969–1973
Rafael Hernández Colón	1973–1977
Carlos Romero Barceló	1977–1985
Rafael Hernández Colón	1985–1993
Pedro Rosselló González	1993–2001
Sila María Calderón	2001–

Sources: Gail Cueto, Ronald Fernández, and Serafín Méndez Méndez, *Puerto Rico Past and Present: An Encyclopedia* (Westport, CT: Greenwood Press, 1998); Kenneth R. Farr, *Historical Dictionary of Puerto Rico and the U.S. Virgin Islands* (Metuchen, NJ: Scarecrow Press, 1973).

BIBLIOGRAPHY

Print Resources

Báez, Vicente, ed. *La Gran Enciclopedia de Puerto Rico*. 15 vols. Madrid: Ediciones R., 1976.

Berríos, Rubén. *Independencia de Puerto Rico: Razón y lucha*. Mexico D.F.: Editorial Línea, 1983.

Cabán, Pedro A. *Constructing a Colonial People: Puerto Rico and the United States, 1898–1932*. Boulder: Westview Press, 1999.

Cueto, Gail, Ronald Fernández, and Serafín Méndez Méndez. *Puerto Rico Past and Present: An Encyclopedia*. Westport, CT: Greenwood Press, 1998.

Farr, Kenneth R. *Historical Dictionary of Puerto Rico and the U.S. Virgin Islands*. Metuchen, NJ: Scarecrow Press, 1973.

Maldonado, A.W. *Teodoro Moscoso and Puerto Rico's Operation Bootstrap*. Miami: University Press of Florida, 1997.

Maldonado-Denis, Manuel. *Puerto Rico: A Socio-Historic Interpretation*. New York: Random House, 1972.

Morales Carrión, Arturo. *Puerto Rico: A Political and Cultural History*. New York: Norton, 1983.

———. *Puerto Rico and the United States: The Quest for a New Encounter*. San Juan: Editorial Académica, 1990.

Muñoz Marín, Luis. *Historia del Partido Popular Democrático*. San Juan: Editorial El Batey, 1984.

Romero Barceló, Carlos. *Statehood Is for the Poor*. San Juan: Romero-Barceló, 1978.

Trías Monge, José. *Puerto Rico: The Trials of the Oldest Colony in the World*. New Haven: Yale University Press, 1997.

Electronic Resources

Elections
http://ElectionsPuertoRico.org/
Database of Puerto Rico's electoral results. (In English and Spanish)

Government of Puerto Rico
http://fortaleza.govpr.org/
The official Web site of the government of Puerto Rico. (In Spanish)

Latin American Network Information Center (LANIC): Puerto Rico
http//lanic.utexas.edu/la/cb/other/pr/
Puerto Rico section of this extensive Web site contains hundreds of links to research resources, cultural centers, economic and business institutions, government agencies, historical sources, magazines and other periodicals, nongovernmental

organizations, and grassroots groups, as well as many other subjects. (In English)

New Progressive Party
http://www.pnp.org/
The official Web site of the New Progressive Party (Partido Nuevo Progresista, PNP). (In Spanish)

El Nuevo Día Interactivo
http://endi.zonai.com/
The Web version of one of Puerto Rico's major Spanish-language daily newspapers. Offers comprehensive coverage of local and U.S. politics and business. (In Spanish)

Political Resources.net: Puerto Rico
http://www.politicalresources.net/puertorico.htm
Puerto Rico section of a Web sites containing a wealth of links to sources of information about national politics. Includes information on political parties, legislative and executive institutions, laws, and legislation. (In English)

Puerto Rican Independence Party
http://www.pip.org.pr/

The official Web site of the Puerto Rican Independence Party (Partido Independentista Puertoriqueño PIP). (In Spanish)

Puerto Rico en breve (PReb)
http://www.PReb.com/
Site containing information on Puerto Rico's current affairs, politics, history, and culture. (In Spanish)

Puerto Rico Statehood
http://www.puertorico51.org/
A Web site dedicated to exploring the issue of, and lobbying for, statehood for Puerto Rico. Contains news, documents, and editorial opinions on the issue of statehood. (In English)

Wilfried Derksen's Elections Around the World: Puerto Rico
http://www.agora.it/elections/puertorico.htm
Puerto Rico section of a comprehensive database of results from elections around the world. Contains results from recent national executive and legislative elections, as well as explanations of and links to political parties and institutions. (In English)

URUGUAY

COUNTRY PROFILE

Official name	República Oriental del Uruguay
Capital	Montevideo
Type/structure of government	Democratic republic (presidential democracy)
Executive	President (chief of state and head of government) and vice president elected by popular vote to five-year renewable terms (president may not serve two consecutive terms); Council of Ministers appointed by the president with parliamentary approval.
Legislative	Bicameral General Assembly consists of Chamber of Senators (30 members elected by popular vote to serve five-year terms) and Chamber of Representatives (99 members elected by popular vote to serve five-year terms).
Judicial	Highest court is the Supreme Court; judges are nominated by the president and elected to ten-year terms by the General Assembly.
Major political parties	**National Party** (Partido Nacional, Blanco Party) **Colorado Party** (Partido Colorado, PC); **Frente Amplio** (Broad Front) coalition.
Constitution in effect	1967, reformed in 1989 and 1997
Location/geography	Southern South America, bordering the South Atlantic Ocean to the east and south, Argentina to the west and Brazil to the north. Mostly rolling plains and low hills; fertile coastal lowland.
Geographic area	176,220 sq. km.
Population	3,308,523 (July 1999 est.)
Ethnic groups	White (of European descent) 88%; mestizo 8%; black (of African descent) 4%; indigenous practically nonexistent
Religions	Roman Catholic 66%; Protestant 2%; Jewish 2%; nonprofessing or other 30%
Literacy rate	97.3% (1995 est.)
Infant mortality rate	13.49 deaths per 1,000 live births (1999 est.)
Life expectancy	75.83 years (1998)
Monetary unit	Nuevo peso
Exchange rate	1 U.S. dollar = 11.6 nuevos pesos (August 2000)*
Major exports	Wool and textile manufactures; beef and other animal products; rice; fish and shellfish
Major imports	Chemicals, machinery and equipment, minerals, plastics, oil, vehicles
GDP	$28.4 billion (1998)
GDP growth rate	3% (1998 est.)
GDP per capita	$3,437 (1997)

*Latin American Weekly Report. August 22, 2000 (WR-00-33), p. 394.

Source: Inter-American Development Bank, Integration and Regional Programs Department, Statistics and Quantitative Analysis Unit. http://www.iadb.org/int/ENGLISH/StaWeb

OVERVIEW

Summary

Uruguay was once known as the "Switzerland of South America" because it enjoyed Swiss-like attributes: it was a peaceful, conservative country with a bountiful, livestock-based economy. South America's first social democracy, Uruguay had a cradle-to-grave welfare system and a largely urban, homogeneous, and relatively well-educated population. Unfortunately, like many other Latin American nations, Uruguay confronted significant economic crisis during the last half of the twentieth century, and also suffered a dark period of military rule from 1973 to 1985.

History

The Spanish arrived in the region now known as Uruguay in 1516. They named the area Banda Oriental (Eastern Bank) and settled there mainly due to the high quality of the grasslands and the area's natural port on the Plata River. As both the Spanish and the Portuguese laid claim to the territory, both crowns struggled to settle towns and cities wherever they could to establish permanent foundations. When the Europeans arrived, modern Uruguay was populated by only a few thousand

Uruguay. © 1998 The Moschovitis Group, Inc.

indigenous people, whose demography, natural environment, and customs the Europeans soon altered; it is estimated that by 1831, the indigenous population had virtually disappeared from the area.

The country gained its independence from Spain in several stages. Between 1811 and 1814, the *orientales*, led by José **Gervasio Artigas**, fought against Spain for Montevideo and Buenos Aires. Though Gervasio Artigas' army won an important victory against Spain in May 1811, Buenos Aires attacked Montevideo in June 1814, prompting Gervasio Artigas and the *orientales* to declare war on Buenos Aires. By 1815 Gervasio Artigas' forces had repelled the forces from Buenos Aires. However, an invasion of Portuguese forces from Brazil (1816–1820) ended in defeat for Gervasio Artigas and resulted in the annexation of the Banda Oriental to Brazil as its southmost province. The second stage of the area's fight for independence began in 1825 when a group of insurgents in the Banda Oriental, with the aid of Buenos Aires, declared the territory's independence from Brazil and its incorporation into the United Provinces of the Plata River. Brazil instantly declared war on them. With British mediation, Brazil and Argentina finally signed the Treaty of Montevideo at Rio de Janeiro on August 27, 1828, renouncing their claims to the area. In 1830 an elected assembly approved the constitution of the Estado Oriental del Uruguay, officially creating the new country.

At the time of independence, Uruguay had an estimated population of fewer than 75,000. Less than 20 percent of the populace resided in Montevideo; most people were scattered throughout the countryside where *caudillos* held political power, attracting followers through their power, bravery, or wealth. Consequently, politics developed along very personalistic lines. The **Colorado Party** (Partido Colorado, PC) and the **National Party** (Partido Nacional, Blanco Party), both of which would become extremely important in Uruguayan politics, sprang from and perpetuated civil wars over control of territory. The PC would dominate national politics through the nineteenth and much of the twentieth centuries.

Under José **Batlle y Ordóñez** (1903–1907, 1911–1915), one of the PC's important leaders, the state played a large role in addressing social and economic issues. Batlle y Ordóñez promoted development and social welfare policies, and also proposed the creation of a *colegiado* (multimember executive branch), inspired by the Swiss executive model. In 1917, during the administration of Feliciano Viera (1915–1919), a new constitution was promulgated that partially enacted the *colegiado* concept. While the new system contributed to fractionalization of the PC, which soon divided between Batlle y Ordóñez's followers (called *Batlistas*) and other more conservative factions, the *colegiado* remained intact for the subsequent fourteen years, a peaceful time

Uruguay's Declaration of Independence. *Columbus Memorial Library, General Secretariat of the Organization of American States. Reproduced with permission of the Organization of American States.*

during which Uruguay enjoyed stable democracy. However, beginning in the 1930s Uruguay experienced economic and political crisis.

In March 1933, President Gabriel Terra (1931–1938) staged a "self-coup," eliminating the *colegiado* system and organizing an authoritarian, repressive government that combined the conservative branches of the PC and the Blanco Party and repressed the opposition. A new constitution was promulgated in 1934 that concentrated executive power in the presidency and excluded members of the Blanco Party and *Batllistas* from the political scene. In 1942 the legislature was dissolved (in what was known as the *golpe bueno* or good coup) and replaced by the Council of State, composed mainly of *Batllistas* and other Colorados. The constitution was amended in November 1942 to allow all political groups to operate unrestricted and to reestablish the General Assembly. The election of Luis **Batlle Berres** (1947–1951, 1955–1956) heralded the era of neo-Batllism and strong nationalism in Uruguay. Echoing the policies of his uncle (Batlle Ordóñez), Batlle Berres enacted social security legislation and pension plans,

protected workers' rights, and promoted national industry and national self-sufficiency.

Andrés Martínez Trueba (1951–1955) finally realized Batlle y Ordóñez's dream of a full *colegiado* system. A constitutional amendment approved by plebiscite in 1951 replaced the office of president with a National Council of Government (Consejo Nacional de Gobierno, CNG) consisting of nine members, six from the majority party and three from the minority party; the presidency rotated each year among the six members of the majority party. Though the PC continued to dominate politics for most of the 1950s, the Blancos won a majority in Congress in the elections of 1958 and 1962. Once in power, the Blancos instituted liberal economic policies that proved to be inefficient, and Uruguay endured extreme economic and social difficulties. In 1962 inflation was running at a historical high of 35 percent, and an inefficient financial system and high speculation had also produced a significant banking problem. By the late 1960s, both traditional parties began to perceive the *colegiado* as ineffective and the source of Uruguay's continual economic crises. In 1967 a new constitution was adopted that eliminated the CNG and reestablished the office of the president (granting increased power to the president, and increasing the presidential term to five years), thus bringing the second *colegiado* period to an end.

President Jorge **Pacheco Areco** (1967–1972) banned the Socialist Party and other leftist groups as economic crisis continued, with inflation reaching 183 percent in 1972 and real wages dropping to the lowest level in a decade. Pacheco Areco's presidency also witnessed the rise of revolutionary groups such as the **Tupamaros**. Due to the increase in crime, including robberies, kidnapping, and murders, and the growing strength of the Tupamaros, Pacheco Areco increased the power of the military, expanding its role, budget, and autonomy to facilitate its battle against guerrilla activity. In 1973 President Juan María **Bordaberry Arocena** (1972–1976) allowed his authority to be countermanded by the military. He dissolved Congress, but kept his position as a figurehead under military control until 1976.

Under the subsequent series of military dictators (1976–1985), human rights violations were rampant, and all left-wing parties and groups and their members were repressed. The military planned to restructure all major government institutions (including political parties), and called for a new constitution that would confer all major political powers on the military. The military was handed a significant defeat when in 1980 the proposed constitution was voted down 57 to 43 percent in a national plebiscite. Slowly, opposition to the regime grew and became more public; internal party primaries showed that 77 percent of voters supported opposition party factions. Talks between the military and civilian leaders began slowly in 1982, culminating in 1983 with the Naval Club Pact, which set the terms

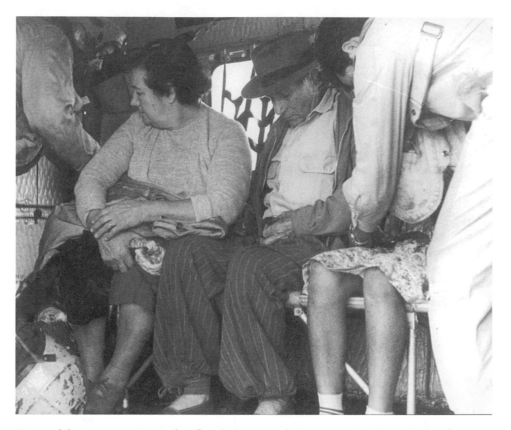

Pictured here are victims of a flood that struck Uruguay in 1959. *Columbus Memorial Library, General Secretariat of the Organization of American States. Reproduced with permission of the Organization of American States.*

of the transition to civilian rule and reinstated the 1967 constitution. In March 1985, Julio María **Sanguinetti** (1985–1990, 1995–2000) was inaugurated as the first democratic president since 1972.

Sanguinetti's first administration faced two immediate challenges: to placate the military and to revive the economy. Questions arose immediately about amnesty for those who had committed human rights violations during the military regime, and the military was amnestied in a 1986 law. Blanco president Luis Alberto Lacalle de Herrera (1990–1995) initiated an accelerated economic liberalization program that included Uruguayan accession to the **Southern Cone Common Market** (Mercado Común del Cono Sur, MERCOSUR; see Appendix 1) and was successful in reducing deficit spending, downsizing government, and lowering inflation. Despite these economic successes, social problems and austerity measures combined to foster increasing popular discontent and political polarization by 1992. During his second administration, Sanguinetti actively pursued the liberalization programs begun by the previous administration. As the candidate of the governing party in the 1999 presidential election, Jorge **Batlle Ibáñez** (2000–   ) promised to pursue a vigorous foreign policy that would open markets for Uruguay's dairy and wool products, and improve educational opportunities by broadly expanding computer and Internet ac-

cess. He was victorious in the November 1999 election. While economic recession plagued the early years of his presidency, Batlle Ibáñez was able to assemble a commission to investigate human rights abuses perpetrated under the military dictatorship, and he remained popular in 2001.

ENTRIES

Batlle Berres, Luis (1897–1964)

Luis Batlle Berres (1947–1951, 1955–1956) was noted for his support of the presidential system and for the labor union politics of his administration.

Batlle Berres entered politics in the 1920s as a deputy representing Montevideo in Congress. He was elected vice president in 1946, and became president in 1947 after the death of Tomás Berreta (1947). Though the Batlle Berres administration practiced urban labor-oriented politics, unlike other political leaders of his era, Batlle Berres rejected both communist and populist-authoritarian political ideologies. His main concerns were to address the great economic inequalities created by the country's socioeconomic structure and to safeguard social peace. He was a strong supporter of the import-substitution industrialization development strategy, and of agricultural expansion, and strongly opposed the austerity plans advocated by international financial institutions such as the International Monetary Fund (IMF).

Though Batlle Berres was the nephew of the great leader of the **Colorado Party** (Partido Colorado, PC), José **Batlle y Ordóñez** (1903–1907, 1911–1915), he felt constrained by the traditional views of the PC faction led by José Batlle's sons, Lorenzo and César Batlle Pacheco. Batlle Berres' first break with that faction came in 1948 when he started the newspaper *Acción*, which competed with *El Día*, the PC newspaper run by the Batlle Pacheco brothers. Before long, he became the leader of a new faction of the PC. This faction, commonly referred to as Unity and Reform (Unidad y Reforma) or "List 15" (because of the list number under which it participated in subsequent elections), became the dominant political movement within the party in 1950.

Batlle Berres advocated the continuation of the presidential system in Uruguay even though those faithful to *Batllismo* (the ideology inspired by Batlle y Ordóñez) advocated the creation of a multimember executive system (see *colegiado*). Concerned by Batlle Berres' success and popularity, and by the growing strength of his coalition, Luis Alberto de Herrera, the leader of the **National Party** (Partido Nacional, Blanco Party), joined with Lorenzo and César Batlle Pacheco to create a coalition in support of establishing a *colegiado*. Batlle Berres eventually supported the 1951 plebiscite granting Uruguay a *colegiado* system, which was institutionalized in the 1952 Constitution. Though Batlle Berres' presidential term ended in 1951, "List 15" continued to control PC voting, and in turn, Uruguayan politics through the 1950s. Batlle Berres led the nation again as president of the National Council of Government (Consejo Nacional de Gobierno, CNG), the body that constituted the *colegiado* from 1955 to 1956. After his death in 1964, his son, Jorge **Batlle Ibáñez** (2000–) assumed the leadership of "List 15."

Batlle Ibáñez, Jorge (1927–)

Jorge Batlle Ibáñez (2000–) is a member of Uruguay's most influential political dynasty (see **Batlle Berres**, Luis [1947–1951, 1955–1956]; **Batlle y Ordóñez**, José [1903–1907, 1911–1915]). In open defiance to his family legacy and the instincts of the **Colorado Party** (Partido Colorado, PC), of which he is a member, Batlle Ibáñez was an early advocate of free-market policies. In 1971, during his second unsuccessful attempt to win the presidency, Batlle Ibáñez ran on an overtly liberal economic platform, with policies that both baffled and terrified voters. He continued in the same vein during his 1999 campaign as the PC's presidential candidate, promising to strengthen Uruguay's international economic ties, advocating that Uruguay join the **North American Free Trade Agreement** (NAFTA; see **Mexico**),

and lambasting the agricultural protectionism he suggested was shutting Uruguay out of world markets. Batlle Ibáñez won the presidency of Uruguay in the second round of elections in November 1999, receiving 54.1 percent of the vote. He faced various challenges upon assuming the presidency, including decreasing state involvement in the economy (the state still controls the energy sector, basic telephony, and much of the construction industry). Further, his party lacked a majority in Congress, which suggested that, in order to pass legislation successfully, Batlle Ibáñez would have to collaborate closely with the other center-right political party, the **National Party** (Partido Nacional, Blanco Party). Economic recession plagued his early years as president; Uruguay's unemployment rate rose to 15 percent, and its public debt increased to 45 percent of the country's GDP. However, Batlle Ibáñez successfully created a multiparty commission to investigate the "disappearances" during the country's years of dictatorship (1973–1985), and he maintained his popularity early into his term.

Batlle y Ordóñez, José (1856–1929)

President José Batlle y Ordóñez (1903–1907, 1911–1915) proposed a multimember executive system (see *colegiado*), which sought to reduce the authoritarian power of the president, encourage social reform, and promote democracy. Batlle y Ordóñez's statist political agenda helped convert Uruguay into one of Latin America's most aggressive welfare states.

Born on May 21, 1856, into a prominent **Colorado Party** (Partido Colorado, PC) family, Batlle y Ordóñez began to play an active role in politics in 1876. He stood against the military dictatorship of Lorenzo Latorre (1876–1880), and participated in the 1886 Quebracho Revolution that unseated dictator Máximo Santos (1882–1886) and marked the beginning of Uruguay's transition to civilian rule. In 1886 Batlle y Ordóñez founded *El Día*, the newspaper of the PC, which was to become the foremost newspaper in Uruguay, and in 1887 President Máximo Tajes (1886–1890) appointed him the political chief of the Department of Mines. Batlle y Ordóñez, who worked tirelessly to form a popular faction within the PC, was elected to the Chamber of Deputies in 1893 and to the Senate in 1896. While he was eventually elected president of the Senate, he later lost that position as a result of criticizing the **National Party** (Partido Nacional, Blanco Party) too strongly.

Batlle y Ordóñez was elected president of the republic by the General Assembly in March 1903. Confronted with pressure from the Blanco Party, Batlle y Ordóñez structured a political system based on co-participation, which implied the incorporation of the Blanco Party in government decisions and administrative control. In 1907 Batlle y Ordóñez participated in the Second International Peace Conference at The Hague, taking advantage of his time in Europe to study European social conflict and to formulate reform ideas that he would propose in his second term as president of Uruguay. He returned to Uruguay in 1911 and was elected president by an overwhelming majority in the General Assembly.

During his second, more progressive administration, Batlle y Ordóñez focused on economic, social, rural, fiscal, moral, and political reform. The basic tenets of the program that would come to be known as *Batllismo* were social equity, state intervention (to regulate inequalities and better distribute wealth), national economic development, and a plural executive system; *Batllismo* also deemed political participation and the electoral process vital to the functioning of a modern state. Batlle y Ordóñez was not successful in enacting the full *Batllista* program, due to opposition from special interest groups, and from within his own party. Nonetheless, several reforms were enacted during Batlle y Ordóñez's second presidential term including the abolition of the death penalty, the legalization of divorce, the establishment of an eight-hour workday, the separation of church and state, and educational reform.

In 1913 Batlle y Ordóñez proposed his most controversial reform, the formation of a multimember executive branch of government. He believed a nine-member *colegiado* would guard against dictatorship and increase democracy. This idea caused a split in the PC and provided an issue around which the Blanco Party could unite in opposition to Batlle y Ordóñez. Nevertheless, a hybrid *colegiado* system was adopted in 1919 in which executive power was shared by a president and a nine-member *colegiado* (the National Council of Administration [Consejo Nacional de Administración, CNA]). Batlle y Ordóñez's successor, Feliciano Viera (1915–1919), initiated a process through which Batlle y Ordóñez's reformist policies would be overturned, a reflection of the decreasing strength of *Batllismo*.

Following his second presidency, Batlle y Ordóñez continued to be politically active. He served as president of the CNA (in 1921 and 1927), fought to maintain unity among the factions of the PC, and continued with his grassroots work.

Blanco Party. See **National Party (Partido Nacional)**

Bordaberry Arocena, Juan María (1928–)
Juan María Bordaberry Arocena (1972–1976), a conservative rancher, first entered politics as the minister of agriculture. Though initially a member of Benito Nardone's (1960–1961) populist *ruralista* movement, which was influential in the 1958 electoral victory of the **National Party** (Partido Nacional, Blanco Party), Bordaberry later became allied to the **Colorado Party** (Partido Colorado, PC) under the leadership of Jorge **Pacheco Areco** (1967–1972). He was elected to the Uruguayan Senate, where he served from 1969 to 1971, and subsequently defeated Blanco candidate Wilson

Ferreira Aldunate in the controversial presidential election of 1971. Difficulties at the beginning of his term with the leftist **Tupamaros** urban guerrilla movement and with the military resulted in a *golpe blando* or soft coup in February 1973. By June 1973, Congress had been dissolved, and Bordaberry became head of a military regime that ruled by decree until 1976. He established the Council of State (Consejo de Estado), which substituted for the Congress, and his regime carried out intense persecution of all popular protest movements, shut down all media with opposing views, and suspended all trade union activity. He was forced to resign in 1976 after he submitted a proposal to the military calling for the elimination of political parties and the creation of a permanent dictatorship with himself as president.

Colegiado (Multimember Executive System)

Colegiado refers to a form of executive system in which there is not one chief executive, but rather an executive governing body. Uruguay experimented with two different *colegiado* systems in the twentieth century.

The idea of a collective executive was proposed during the second presidential term of José **Batlle y Ordóñez** (1903–1907, 1911–1915). The system visualized an executive branch based on collaboration and participation between the major political parties, which Batlle y Ordóñez saw as a solution to the instability and abuse of power he perceived in the presidency and as a medium for eliminating the historical "zero-sum game" of Uruguayan politics. Batlle y Ordóñez's ideal plan abolished the presidency and called for a group of nine members to form a governing body. Due to opposition from within Batlle's **Colorado Party** (Partido Colorado, PC) and from the rival **National Party** (Partido Nacional, Blanco Party), under the first *colegiado* the office of the president of the republic was not eliminated, though its responsibility was limited to foreign affairs and the maintenance of international order and external security while the nine-member National Council of Administration (Consejo Nacional de Administración, CNA) was charged with all other functions of the state.

The first *colegiado* was institutionalized in the 1917 Constitution and lasted fourteen years, including the presidencies of Baltásar Brum (1919–1923), José Serrato (1923–1927), and Juan Campísteguy (1927–1931). Soon after assuming the presidency, Gabriel Terra (1931–1938), a member of the *Batllista* faction of the PC, became dissatisfied with the CNA. Amid the economic turmoil brought on by the Great Depression, Terra aligned himself with Blanco Party leader Luis Alberto de Herrera, and the two staged a nonviolent coup on March 13, 1933. Congress was dissolved and the CNA disbanded, and Terra acted as dictator. A Constituent Assembly was formed with supporters of Terra and Herrera, and a new constitution was promulgated in 1934 returning Uruguay to a full presidential system.

The second *colegiado* governed Uruguay from 1952 to 1966. In contrast to the first system, under the second *colegiado*, the office of president of the republic was abolished and executive power was completely remanded to the nine-member National Council of Government (Consejo Nacional de Gobierno, CNG). The CNG included six members from the majority party and three from the minority party, with the presidency rotating each year among the six members of the majority party. However, a lack of collaboration and cooperation within the *colegiado* soon diminished its legitimacy, prompting Oscar Diego Gestido (1967) (a prominent member of the PC) and others to call for a renewal of the presidency. In 1967 the country adopted a new constitution that returned Uruguay to a presidential system.

Colorado Party (Partido Colorado, PC)

Founded in the nineteenth century, the Colorado Party (Partido Colorado, PC), originally the party of urban middle-class liberals, and the more conservative **National Party** (Partido Nacional, Blanco Party), which had more rural support, are the two oldest political parties in Uruguay. Though the PC has dominated politics and the presidency almost without interruption since Uruguay gained independence from Spain, each PC administration has compromised with and made concessions to the Blancos in the interest of maintaining order and effectively governing the nation.

Through the nineteenth century, the parties struggled and warred. The PC began to truly take shape under the organization and leadership of José **Batlle y Ordóñez** (1903–1907, 1911–1915). As president of the nation, Batlle y Ordóñez introduced many sociopolitical reforms and strove to strengthen Uruguay's nascent democratic political system. Differing opinions regarding Batlle y Ordóñez's reforms caused divisions to emerge within the PC, and his death in 1929 resulted in the further separation of the factions. Nonetheless, given the economic prosperity Uruguay enjoyed from 1919 to 1933, the Colorados had little trouble leading the country. From the 1940s to the present, the two main factions within the party have been "List 14" (which includes those in support of the *colegiado* system) and "List 15" (composed of those in favor of a powerful president).

In 1984, following eleven years of authoritarian rule, the PC, the **Frente Amplio** (Broad Front) coalition, and the Civic Union (Unión Cívica, UC) signed the Naval Club Pact that called for national elections that same year. With new leadership and effective use of the media, the PC was able to win 41 percent of the vote in the November 1984 presidential election, and in March 1985, Julio María **Sanguinetti** (1985–1990, 1995–2000) was inaugurated. The party retained control of the presidency into the new millennium.

Communist Party of Uruguay (Partido Comunista del Uruguay, PCU)

Founded in April 1921 when a majority faction of the **Socialist Party** (Partido Socialista, PS) led by Eugenio Gómez and others split from the PS, the Communist Party of Uruguay (Partido Comunista del Uruguay, PCU) operated freely from its inception, though it was not until the 1960s that it gained strength and became more effective.

Gómez led the party as its general secretary from 1921 to 1955. Under his leadership, the PCU was quite radical, becoming an avid promoter of Uruguayan solidarity with the Spanish Republic and with the Anti-Nazi Action organization in its early years. In the late 1920s, the party adopted Stalinism. The PCU was most successful in the elections of 1946, and by 1955 PCU membership totaled about 5,000. Gómez was expelled from the party in 1955 and replaced by Rodney Arismendi, and the group subsequently decided to participate to a greater degree in Uruguayan politics by creating popular fronts to appeal to the electorate and gain support. The first such front, created in the 1960s, never received a majority of electoral votes, and in 1971 the PCU and other parties formed the **Frente Amplio** (Broad Front) coalition. Though the PCU originally supported the 1973 coup staged by Juan María **Bordaberry Arocena** (1972–1976), it soon withdrew its backing due to the conservative and authoritarian nature of the military regime that took power.

While the PCU suffered persecution during Uruguay's authoritarian interlude from 1973 to 1984, with the return of democracy, the PCU was relegalized. The party achieved its best electoral results in 1989, but subsequently split into two factions in a crisis of ideology between the renovators (which included all the legislators elected in 1989) who held a less radical political perspective, and the traditionalists, who maintained a more conservative political stand. Support for the PCU has greatly decreased as leftist groups have banded together in the Frente Amplio coalition.

Ferreira Aldunate, Wilson (1919–1988)

Wilson Ferreira Aldunate was a charismatic political leader and a modern *caudillo* of the **National Party** (Partido Nacional, Blanco Party).

Ferreira Aldunate was born into a ranching family in Uruguay. In 1963 he entered political life as minister of agriculture, later serving in the Chamber of Deputies, and then in the Senate from 1967 to 1972. Ferreira Aldunate ran for president in 1971, and though he received more votes than any other candidate, due to the mechanics of the electoral system (which awarded the presidency to the candidate of the party that received the most votes) a **Colorado Party** (Partido Colorado, PC) candidate was elected. Ferreira Aldunate went into exile after the military coup in 1973. An outspoken critic of the military regime, he vociferously opposed the military's constitutional project, and the project's defeat in a plebiscite in 1980 strengthened his popularity. Ferreira Aldunate's faction of the Blanco Party was successful in the internal party elections allowed by the dictatorship in 1982, and by 1984 it was clear that if presidential elections were held, Ferreira would win.

The 1984 Naval Club Pact, an agreement signed by the PC, the Civic Union (Unión Cívica) party, and the **Frente Amplio** (Broad Front) coalition, called for presidential elections in 1984 and signified the start of the redemocratization of Uruguay. Ferreira Aldunate traveled to Argentina (from exile in London) in June 1984, but was soon arrested and jailed until several days after the elections. Though he was a strong advocate for holding the military accountable for the human rights violations it committed during its years in power, when increasing pressure for judicial proceedings appeared to have the potential to lead to a return to military rule, Ferreira Aldunate eventually supported amnesty for the military. Ferreira Aldunate was diagnosed with cancer in 1987, and died the following year.

Frente Amplio (Broad Front) Coalition

The leftist coalition known as the Frente Amplio (Broad Front), formed in March 1971, includes the country's traditional left, the **Communist Party of Uruguay** (Partido Comunista del Uruguay, PCU) and the **Socialist Party** (Partido Socialista, PS), the new radical left, and individuals from traditional parties such as the **Colorado Party** (Partido Colorado, PC) and the **National Party** (Partido Nacional, Blanco Party).

The Frente Amplio emerged during a tumultuous period in Uruguay when the traditional parties lacked political leadership, left-wing radicalism was growing in the unions, and an urban guerrilla movement was emerging (see **Tupamaros**). The coalition formed in an effort to construct a political force that could compete with the traditional political parties, aspiring to recreate the **Popular Unity** (Unidad Popular, UP; see Chile) electoral coalition that brought Salvador **Allende Gossens** (see Chile) to power in 1970. However, the Frente Amplio won only 18.3 percent of the vote in 1971.

Following the coup led by Juan María **Bordaberry Arocena** (1972–1976) in 1973, the Frente Amplio was outlawed, and its leaders persecuted, jailed, and sent into exile. However, its activity continued in secret and outside Uruguay. The coalition organized a general strike against the Bordaberry government in June 1973, and by the end of the military dictatorship (1985), the Frente Amplio had become an important actor in the process of redemocratization; it eventually became a political unit with its own unique identity and purpose, in spite of being a coalition of many groups. As a legalized coalition, the Frente Amplio obtained 21.3 percent of the vote in the 1984 presidential election, and in 1989 it found victory when socialist Tabaré Vázquez, running on the Frente Amplio ticket, was elected mayor of Mon-

A statue of José Gervasio Artigas, a hero of Uruguay's fight for independence. *Columbus Memorial Library, General Secretariat of the Organization of American States. Reproduced with permission of the Organization of American States.*

tevideo. The coalition also had a strong showing in that year's presidential contest, winning 21.2 percent of the overall vote. Support for the Frente Amplio increased through the 1990s; in the presidential election of November 1999, coalition candidate Tabaré Vázquez received 44 percent of the vote.

Gervasio Artigas, José (1764–1850)

José Gervasio Artigas was born in Montevideo to a landowning family. While he was involved in smuggling early in his life, in 1799 he began service in the military as an official of the Blandengues, a regiment in Montevideo that protected the rural settlers against Indian raids and intercepted smuggling activities in the area that is modern day Brazil. Following the overthrow of the Spanish viceroy in charge of what is today southern South America in 1810 (one of modern day Uruguay's first moves toward independence), Gervasio Artigas became head of a rural militia, the *Orientales*, which fought against Spain for Montevideo and Buenos Aires over the next ten years. He also attempted to repel advances by the Portuguese in the east. The Portuguese occupied Montevideo in January 1817, and fighting continued for another three years, eventually ending in

Gervasio Artigas' defeat and Brazil's annexation of the area that is today Uruguay. Gervasio Artigas was exiled to Paraguay, where he lived in obscurity and died thirty years later. Though opinions of Gervasio Artigas vary, he has been referred to as the "Father of Uruguay," "Protector of the Free Peoples," and "Chief of the *Orientales.*"

National Liberation Movement (Movimiento de Liberación Nacional, MLN). See Tupamaros

National Party (Partido Nacional, also Blanco Party)

Founded in the nineteenth century during the presidency of Manuel Oribe (1835–1838), the conservative National Party (Partido Nacional, Blanco Party) originated as a federalist party of landowners, merchants, and senior clergy that enjoyed rural support. The Blanco Party and the more liberal **Colorado Party** (Partido Colorado, PC) are the two oldest parties in Uruguay. The initial tension and rivalry between them led to several civil wars in the nineteenth century, but evolved into campaigning and political debates in the twentieth. The PC enjoyed greater electoral success through the nineteenth and most of the twentieth centuries.

During José **Batlle y Ordóñez's** (1903–1907, 1911–1915) first presidency, the country was divided, as the PC controlled thirteen regional departments and the Blancos controlled six. The six areas held by the Blanco Party acted independently and distrusted the PC, and it was difficult for the new president to control the disintegrated nation. The country experienced an eight-month civil war in 1904, after which a new electoral system was implemented that transferred the departments previously under Blanco domination to the PC, leaving the PC in control of the country. After this defeat, the Blanco Party was determined to evolve into a modern political party and emphasize its ideological differences from the PC. Nonetheless, the party remained divided internally between conservative *Herreristas* (named for party leader Luis Alberto de Herrera) and more progressive groups like the Blanco Democratic Union (Unión Blanco Democrática).

The Blancos scored their first national-level victories in the party's history in the general elections of 1958 and 1962 (see *colegiado*), ending PC-dominated governance. Blanco's success resulted from popular dissatisfaction with various aspects of Uruguayan reality in the late 1950s and early 1960s, including the country's economic problems, the **Tupamaros** guerrilla movement, rumors of corruption in the PC administration, and the PC's internal strife. However, the Blancos were not able to establish the necessary economic policies to revive Uruguay's economy, and the party suffered decreasing support in the late twentieth century. While in 2000 the Blanco Party remained one of the nation's most popular parties, its dominance has been challenged, most significantly by the rise of the **Frente Amplio** (Broad Front) leftist coalition.

Pacheco Areco, Jorge (1920–1998)

Jorge Pacheco Areco served as president of Uruguay from 1967 to 1972.

A member of the **Colorado Party** (Partido Colorado, PC), Pacheco served as vice president to President Oscar Diego Gestido (1967). During his presidency, Gestido worked to unify the various arms of the PC, halted rising inflation, and handled the communist-led labor unions strictly and constitutionally. When Gestido died suddenly in 1967, Pacheco ascended to the presidency. Despite Gestido's good work, Pacheco found himself leading a country that was coping with social unrest, inflation, strikes, and an emerging guerrilla movement (see **Tupamaros**). As a result, Pacheco invoked a limited state of siege that he did not revoke for most of his presidency. He relied heavily on the military to squelch the Tupamaros, leading to bloody struggle and the general infringement of civil liberties, dynamics that brought him congressional criticism.

In 1971 Pacheco tried to succeed himself through a change in the constitution. Though he was unsuccessful, he was able to select the next president and chose rural rancher Juan María **Bordaberry Arocena** (1972–1976). After 1972, Pacheco served as ambassador to Spain, the United States, and Switzerland. Strong support from his faction within the PC, the Colorado and *Batllista* Union, helped the PC win the presidential election of 1984. Pacheco ran for president of Uruguay in 1989 on his faction's ticket, but lost. Nonetheless, through the 1990s until his death in 1998, his following was still large among the urban poor in Montevideo, who respected him as a politician focused on law and order.

Sanguinetti, Julio María (1936–)

Julio María Sanguinetti, the first civilian president following Uruguay's period of military rule (1973–1985), served as president of Uruguay from 1985 to 1990, and from 1995 to 2000. During his first term, he tried to help Uruguay heal its internal wounds, and battled recession, and later, economic stagnation. During his second term, Sanguinetti secured important reforms aimed at improving the electoral system, education, social security, and public safety.

A lawyer by profession, Sanguinetti became involved with the **Colorado Party** (Partido Colorado, PC) at the age of nineteen, and was elected to the Chamber of Deputies in 1962, 1966, and 1971. He served as minister of education and culture under President Juan María **Bordaberry Arocena** (1972–1976) in 1972, but resigned in 1973 in protest of the military's increased involvement in the government. Known for his speaking and negotiating skills, Sanguinetti was the general secretary of the PC during the talks in 1983 and 1984 that led to the Naval Club Pact, which brought a negotiated end to military rule. Sanguinetti won the 1984 presidential election with 41 percent of the vote.

Recession and a country traumatized by the repressive regime that had ruled it for the previous twelve years greeted Sanguinetti as he assumed the presidency in 1985. He moved toward reforming the country's trade policy, and Uruguay experienced economic growth in 1986 and 1987. He also freed all political prisoners. While political controversy flared over a law approved by the legislature in December 1986 that granted what amounted to amnesty to the military for human rights abuses committed during the previous military regime, the amnesty was ratified in a national referendum in 1989.

A struggle ensued within Sanguinetti's *Batllista* faction of the PC over whom to nominate as a candidate for the 1989 presidential election. Sanguinetti's vice president, Enrique Tarigo, the party's eventual choice, was defeated in the 1989 contest by Luis Alberto Lacalle de Herrera (1990–1995). Sanguinetti won the 1994 presidential election as head of the Colorado faction known as the *Batllista* Forum, and took office in March 1995. He used his second term to consolidate Uruguay's economic reforms and to integrate the country into the **Southern Cone Common Market** (Mercado Común del Cono Sur, MERCOSUR; see Appendix 1), increasing economic growth and reducing inflation.

Sendic Antonaccio, Raúl (1925–1989)

Raúl Sendic Antonaccio helped to form the notorious **Tupamaros** guerrilla movement.

Sendic left law school to join the **Socialist Party** (Partido Socialista, PS) in the late 1950s, and subsequently worked as a legal advisor for rural labor unions in northern Uruguay. He ran for president on the PS ticket twice, losing each time, and subsequently left the party to organize poor sugar workers in their fight for land distribution. Sendic led strikes in 1960 and 1961 but soon became frustrated with the apparent inefficacy of using legal means to achieve social justice. In 1962 Sendic and the Uruguayan left formed the Tupamaros, and a year later, Sendic led the first Tupamaro raid, seizing a gun club in a town about eighty miles from Montevideo. Sendic was captured in 1964, released, and captured again in 1970. Though he escaped from the Punta Carreta Prison in 1971 with approximately 100 other Tupamaro members, he was shot, captured, and again imprisoned in September 1972. The Tupamaros were subsequently completely defeated by the armed forces. During his time in prison, Sendic wrote *Cartas desde la prisión* (Letters from Prison) and *Reflexiones sobre política económica: Apuntes desde la prisión* (Reflections on Political Economy: Notes from Prison).

Sendic and other Tupamaro leaders were granted freedom through the amnesty law implemented during the first administration of Julio María **Sanguinetti** (1985–1990, 1995–2000) after Uruguay's transition to democracy in 1984. Sendic continued to serve as leader of the Tupamaros after being released from prison, and the group later reentered politics on peaceful and legal terms. As a result of the torture he experienced while incarcerated, Sendic became sick and died in France in 1989.

Socialist Party (Partido Socialista, PS)

The first guilds and associations with Marxist tendencies began to emerge in Uruguay at the end of the nineteenth century. In 1901, with the help of the Masons, socialists ran in municipal elections but were not successful. In 1904 Emilio Frugoni moved to form a socialist party that would successfully rally the support of the working class. After a failed attempt to organize the socialists in support of *Batllismo* (the philosophy inspired by José **Batlle y Ordóñez** [1903–1907, 1911–1915]), he wrote the socialist manifesto in 1910 (which supported Uruguay's constitutional order rather than promoting politics to cause division), and officially founded the Socialist Party (Partido Socialista, PS) that same year.

As a socialist deputy to Congress, Frugoni was able to work with Batlle y Ordóñez and his **Colorado Party** (Partido Colorado, PC) on socioeconomic reforms for the working class. As a result of this cooperation, the PS never gained a major following, as the PC already respresented the workers. The PS suffered a split in 1921 when a faction left to join the **Communist Party of Uruguay** (Partido Comunista del Uruguay, PCU), and subsequently lost parliamentary representation until 1928. The PS responded by taking a new, more moderate reformist stance. However, by the mid-1950s, a new generation of militants encouraged a redefinition of the PS that radicalized it into a revolutionary and anti-imperialist party that advocated violence and guerrilla warfare.

The radicalization of the party blemished its reputation, and President Jorge **Pacheco Areco** (1967–1972) dissolved the PS in 1968. While the PS was again legalized in 1971, following the 1973 coup, it was outlawed again until 1984. In response to the historical control of politics by the PC and the **National Party** (Partido Nacional, Blanco Party), in the last two decades of the twentieth century the PS formed alliances with other leftist groups in order to create a formidable third option. The resulting coalition, known as the **Frente Amplio** (Broad Front), successfully challenged political control by the traditional parties. In 1989 socialist Tabaré Vázquez was elected mayor of Montevideo on the Frente Amplio ticket, and in the November 1999 presidential elections, Tabaré Vázquez received 44 percent of the vote.

Tupamaros (also National Liberation Movement [Movimiento de Liberación Nacional, MLN])

The National Liberation Movement (Movimiento de Liberación Nacional, MLN), commonly referred to as the Tupamaros, was established in 1962 by Raúl **Sendic Antonaccio** and a breakaway militant faction of the radicalized **Socialist Party** (Partido Socialista, PS). The movement, named for Túpac Amaru, a sixteenth century Inca chieftain who led an unsuccessful rebellion against the Spanish, was created to wreak violent havoc through mass insurrection and to discredit the old political and economic system in order to start a new revolutionary tradition in Uruguay. A movement named for a descendant of Túpac Amaru, Túpac Amaru II, was active in Peru through the 1980s and 1990s (see **Tupac Amaru Revolutionary Movement** [Movimiento Revolucionario Tupac Amaru, MRTA], Peru).

The Tupamaros spent their first few years of existence training, stealing weapons, and organizing. In 1967 the Tupamaros became publicly recognized in Uruguay because of a letter they sent to a newspaper stating that they were willing to use violence to raise political consciousness, and indicating that their ultimate goal was to modify the political and economic structure of the country. Tupamaro propaganda was nationalist, socialist, and revolutionary, but never offered a good economic or political plan for Uruguay. At the height of their popularity, the Tupamaros recruited from the middle class, intellectuals, professionals, and unionized workers. Their initial activities included a series of robberies, the exposure of questionable financial transactions by the government, and distribution of food in poor neighborhoods. The group soon turned to kidnappings and assassinations. In 1972 the military was given complete liberty to eliminate guerrilla activity using any means necessary. The Tupamaros were quickly defeated.

Many in Uruguay considered the Tupamaros an important cause of the 1973 coup, as they increased social conflict and helped bring political power to the military. In truth, the Tupamaros were eliminated prior to the coup, and did not renew activities during the subsequent twelve years of military dictatorship. All Tupamaro prisoners were released and pardoned by President Julio María **Sanguinetti** (1985–1990, 1995–2000), the first popularly elected president following the transition to democracy. Upon acquiring freedom, the Tupamaros announced their desire to organize a peaceful political party, but by the late 1990s, they had only succeeded in publishing a newspaper and managing a radio program.

HEADS OF STATE

Luis Eduardo Pérez (acting)	1830
Fructuoso Rivera	1830–1834
Carlos Anaya (acting)	1834–1835
Manuel Oribe	1835–1838
Gabriel Antonio Pereira (acting)	1838
Fructuoso Rivera	1838–1839
Gabriel Antonio Pereira (acting)	1839
Fructuoso Rivera	1839–1843
Joaquín Suárez del Rondelo (acting)	1843–1852
Bernardo P. Berro	1852
Juan Francisco Giró	1852–1853
Venancio Flores, Juan Antonio Lavalleja	1853–1854
Venancio Flores	1854–1855
Manuel Basilio Bustamente	1855–1856
José María Plá (acting)	1856
Gabriel Antonio Pereira	1856–1860
Bernardo P. Berro	1860–1864
Atanasio Aguirre	1864–1865
Venancio Flores	1865–1868
Lorenzo Batlle	1868–1872
Tomás Gomensoro (acting)	1872–1873
José E. Ellauri	1873–1875
Pedro Varela	1875–1876
Lorenzo Latorre	1876–1880
Francisco Antonio Vidal	1880–1882
Máximo Santos	1882–1886
Francisco Antonio Vidal	1886
Máximo Tajes	1886–1890
Julio Herrera y Obés	1890–1894
Juan Idiarte Borda	1894–1897
Juan Lindolfo Cuestas	1897–1903
José Batlle y Ordóñez	1903–1907
Claudio Williman	1907–1911
José Batlle y Ordóñez	1911–1915
Feliciano Viera	1915–1919
Baltásar Brum	1919–1923
José Serrato	1923–1927
Juan Campísteguy	1927–1931
Gabriel Terra	1931–1938
Alfredo Baldomir	1938–1943
Juan José de Amézaga	1943–1947
Tomás Berreta	1947
Luis Batlle Berres	1947–1951
Andrés Martínez Trueba	1951–1955
Luis Batlle Berres	1955–1956
Alberto Fermín Zubiría	1956–1957
Arturo Lezama	1957–1958
Carlos L. Fischer	1958–1959
Martín R. Echegoyen	1959–1960
Benito Nardone	1960–1961

Eduardo Víctor Haedo	1961–1962
Faustino Harrison	1962–1963
Daniel Fernández Crespo	1963–1964
Luis Giannattasio	1964–1965
Wáshington Beltrán	1965–1966
Alberto Héber Usher	1966–1967
Oscar Diego Gestido	1967
Jorge Pacheco Areco	1967–1972
Juan María Bordaberry Arocena	1972–1976
Alberto Demicheli (acting)	1976
Aparicio Méndez	1976–1981
Gregorio Conrado Álvarez Armelino	1981–1985
Julio María Sanguinetti	1985–1990
Luis Alberto Lacalle de Herrera	1990–1995
Julio María Sanguinetti	1995–2000
Jorge Batlle Ibáñez	2000–

Source: *Geocities*. http://www.geocities.com/Athens/1058/rulu.html

BIBLIOGRAPHY

Print Resources

Calvert, Peter, ed. *Political and Economic Encyclopedia of South America and the Caribbean*. London: Longman Group UK, 1991.

Generals and Tupamaros: The Struggle for Power in Uruguay, 1969–1973. London: Latin America Review of Books, 1974.

González, Luis E. *Political Structures and Democracy in Uruguay*. Notre Dame: Published for the Helen Kellogg Institute for International Studies by University of Notre Dame Press, 1991.

Núñez, Carlos. *The Tupamaros: Urban Guerrillas of Uruguay*. New York: Times Change Press, 1970.

Popkin, Louise B., and Saúl Sosnowski, eds. *Repression, Exile, and Democracy: Uruguayan Culture*. Latin America in Translation/En Traducción/Em Traducao. Durham, NC: Duke University Press, 1992.

Tannebaum, Barbara A. *Latin American History and Culture*. 5 vols. New York: Charles Scribner's Sons, 1996.

Taylor, Philip Bates. *Government and Politics of Uruguay*. New Orleans: Tulane University, 1960.

Weinstein, Martin. *Uruguay: Democracy at the Crossroads*. Boulder: Westview Press, 1988.

Weschler, Lawrence. *A Miracle, a Universe: Settling Accounts with Torturers*. New York: Penguin Books, 1990.

Willis, Jean L. *Historical Dictionary of Uruguay*. Metuchen, NJ: Scarecrow Press, 1974.

Electronic Resources

Latin American Network Information Center (LANIC): Uruguay
http://lanic.utexas.edu/la/uruguay/
Uruguay section of this extensive Web site contains hundreds of links to research resources, cultural centers, economic and business institutions, government agencies, historical sources, magazines and other periodicals, nongovernmental organizations, and grassroots groups, as well as many other subjects. (In English).

El País Edición Digital
http://www3.diarioelpais.com/edicion/
The Web version of one of Uruguay's premier daily newspapers. Offers comprehensive national and international coverage, with a particularly strong emphasis on national politics and the local economy. (In Spanish)

Political Database of the Americas: Uruguay
http://www.georgetown.edu/pdba/Countries/uruguay.html
Comprehensive database run as a joint project of Georgetown University and the Organization of American States. Section on Uruguay contains information on and links to the executive, legislative, and judicial branches of the Uruguayan government; electoral laws and election results; and other political data. (In English, Spanish, Portuguese, and French)

Political Resources.net: Uruguay
http://www.politicalresources.net/uruguay.htm
Uruguay section of a Web site containing a wealth of links to sources of information about national politics. Includes information on political parties, legislative and executive institutions, laws and legislation. (In English)

Uruguay Total.com
http://www.uruguaytotal.com/index.html
Web site devoted to Uruguayan business, culture, economics, politics and society.

Wilfried Derksen's Elections Around the World: Uruguay
http://www.agora.it/elections/uruguay.htm
Uruguay section of a comprehensive database of results from elections around the world. Contains results from recent national executive and legislative elections, as well as explanations of and links to political parties and institutions. (In English)

VENEZUELA

COUNTRY PROFILE

Official name	República Bolivariana de Venezuela (since 1999; previously República de Venezuela)
Capital	Caracas
Type/structure of government	Federal republic
Executive	Consists of the president and Council of Ministers. The president is elected to a six-year term, can be immediately reelected, and can serve no more than two terms. The president may nominate and remove cabinet ministers and dissolve the National Assembly.
Legislative	Consists of the unicameral National Assembly; some deputies are popularly elected from each federal district; other deputies are elected by designated indigenous communities; deputies serve five-year terms, can be reelected, and can serve no more than two consecutive terms.
Judicial	Highest court is the Supreme Tribunal of Justice (El Tribunal Supremo de Justicia); magistrates of the Supreme Tribunal are chosen by the National Assembly to serve for twelve years.
Major political parties	Fifth Republic Movement (Movimiento Quinta República, MVR), **Democratic Action** (Acción Democrática, AD), **Committee of Independent Electoral Political Organization** (Comité de Organización Política Electoral Independiente, COPEI), National Convergence (Convergencia), Radical Cause (La Causa R), and Movement Toward Socialism (Movimiento al Socialismo, MAS).
Constitution in effect	Bolivarian Constitution was written by an elected Constituent Assembly, accepted by Congress, and promulgated in 1999, replacing the Constitution of 1961.
Location/geography	Northern South America on the Caribbean Sea and the North Atlantic Ocean, bordering Colombia to the west, Brazil to the south, and Guyana to the east. Subtropical northwestern and northeastern plateaus, northwestern tropical lowland basin of Lake Maracaibo, upland plains in the southeast.
Geographic area	912,050 sq. km.
Population	23,203,466 (1999)
Ethnic groups	Mestizo 67%; mixed white (of European descent)/Arab 21%; black (of African descent) 10%; indigenous 2%
Religions	Roman Catholic 92.7%; Protestant denominations and other 7.3%
Literacy rate	91.1% (1995)
Infant mortality rate	26.51 deaths per 1,000 live births (1999)
Life expectancy	72.95 years (1999)
Monetary unit	Bolívar
Exchange rate	1 U.S. dollar = 689.22 bolivares (August 2000)*
Major exports	Petroleum, bauxite and aluminum, steel, chemicals, agricultural products
Major imports	Raw materials, machinery and equipment, transport equipment, construction materials
GDP	$194.5 billion (1998)
GDP real growth rate	−0.9% (1998)
GDP per capita	$8,500 (1998)

*Latin American Weekly Report. August 22, 2000 (WR-00-33), p. 394.

Source: CIA World Factbook 1999. http://www.cia.gov/cia/publications/factbook/gros/ve.html; Britannica.com. http://www.britannica.com; U.S. State Department. http://www.state.gov

OVERVIEW

Summary

In the nineteenth century Venezuela's economy was agriculturally based, and its politics were characterized by *caudillo* rule, military privilege, and oligarchic primacy. With the development of a nascent oil industry early in the twentieth century, Venezuela saw the growth of a

Venezuela. © *1998 The Moschovitis Group, Inc.*

substantial state bureaucracy, infrastructure, and a politically active middle class. By the 1980s, however, Venezuela's external debt was escalating, socioeconomic problems festered, and corruption was rampant. Further, since the 1999 election of President Hugo Rafael **Chávez Frías**, the international community has been wary of the quality of Venezuela's democracy under an unpredictable, populist regime. Nonetheless, Venezuela, which has historically served as a model of democratic stability in the region, remains connected to its democratic traditions and dedicated to fulfilling its considerable potential as an economic leader in Latin America.

History

Pre-Columbian Venezuela, unlike other areas, such as (modern day) Mexico and Peru, was not home to large indigenous populations, though scattered groups of mainly Carib and Arawak peoples had established themselves throughout the territory by at least 2000 B.C. Slash-and-burn agriculturalists exploited the vast prairie lands (*llanos*) in Venezuela's interior, while along the coast and river valleys hunting and gathering was the way of life. In 1498, on his third voyage to the New World, Christopher Columbus glimpsed the tropical coast of what is today Venezuela. A year later Spanish explorers in search of precious stones and metals named the newly claimed territory Venezuela, or "Little Venice," after observing that the Indians had built their homes on stilts over the swampy shores of huge Lake Maracaibo.

Early searches for the gold, pearls, and other riches rumored to be plentiful in the area proved fruitless in Venezuela, and as a result it was unattractive to Spanish explorers driven by a hunger for wealth. Consequently, the area remained a relatively low priority for the Span-

ish monarchy and received far less military, bureaucratic, and religious attention than did Mexico and Peru. Nonetheless, permanent European settlement began in 1528, and colonizers were quick to exploit the native people. Slavery, combined with the deadly force of smallpox, contributed to a precipitous decline in the indigenous population, and therefore a labor shortage, leading the Spanish to import large numbers of black slaves from Africa and the Caribbean islands. The result was a society in which a small number of *peninsulares* and creoles owned almost all the land and wealth and thought of themselves as racially and culturally superior, while the majority of Venezuelans (who were black or mestizo) were illiterate, poor, and tied to the plantations on which they worked by debt or servitude.

In the later 1700s, in an effort to reverse Spain's decline in both Europe and America, Spain imposed far-reaching administrative and political reforms which, ironically, set the stage for the independence movements that would soon develop in the New World. In 1813, a revolutionary junta appointed Simón Antonio de la Santísima Trinidad **Bolívar y Palacios** (see Colombia) commander of the Venezuelan forces. That army fought a protracted battle for independence and in 1819, Venezuelan independence was declared. On June 24, 1821, Bolívar defeated the royalist army in the Battle of Carabobo, and on October 9, 1823, the last of the royalist forces surrendered. Bolívar, eager to see the entire continent of South America free of Spanish rule, liberated the viceroyalty of Quito (present-day Ecuador) in 1822, and later that year, Gran Colombia (Venezuela, Quito, and New Granada) was proclaimed. However, as Bolívar's power began to dwindle, Gran Colombia began to break apart, and Venezuela became an independent republic in 1830, with Caracas as its capital.

Venezuela suffered under *caudillismo* for over a century, from 1830 to 1935. The efficient, stable, and economically successful era of Conservative Party domination came to a close in 1848 with the rise of General José Tadeo Monagas (1847–1851, 1855–1858) and his brother General José Gregorio Monagas (1851–1855), whose corruption and incompetence led both the Liberal and Conservative Parties to unite in their overthrow in 1858. The resulting chaos led to the **Federal Wars** (1859–1863), bloody civil wars between the Conservatives and the Liberals. Though the Liberals triumphed in 1863, peace did not follow, as local *caudillos* remained strong and controlled the countryside. Finally, in 1870 there was a break from disorder and economic stagnation as Liberal general Antonio **Guzmán Blanco** (1870–1877, 1878–1884, 1886–1887) assumed power and pacified the country, implementing a wide range of reforms. A long line of traditional and modern *caudillos* followed him, most ruling corruptly and inefficiently.

Following the Restoration Revolution (1899) until

A 1968 view of Caracas, the Venezuelan capital. *Columbus Memorial Library, General Secretariat of the Organization of American States. Reproduced with permission of the Organization of American States.*

1958 (with the exception of 1945–1948, the reformist period know as *El Trienio*), Venezuela was mainly ruled by a succession of military strongmen known as the *Andinos* (as each hailed from the Andean highlands). The oil industry began to develop early in this period, attracting foreign investment, spurring the economy, and enriching the nation's elite, while the vast majority of Venezuelans continued to live in poverty. Though the 1930s and 1940s were marked by political instability and weak democracy, the political system witnessed a gradual opening and the emergence of new parties after 1935. Amid the uncertainty, Venezuela bounced back and forth between military and civilian rule. Brutal dictator Marcos **Pérez Jiménez** (1952–1958) used revenue from the sale of oil from the nation's ever-increasing petroleum reserves to fund extravagant construction projects, and he and others involved in his regime pocketed many millions of dollars of petroleum wealth. Pérez Jiménez was overthrown by military forces supported by a civilian coalition, the Patriotic Junta (Junta Patriótica), in January 1958. This archetypical Latin American dictator was Venezuela's last.

The fall of Pérez Jiménez led to a lasting system of democracy centered on three parties, the **Democratic Republican Union** (Unión Republicana Democrática, URD), **Democratic Action** (Acción Democrática, AD), and the **Committee of Independent Electoral Political Organization** (Comité de Organización Política Electoral Independiente, COPEI). The system rested on the

Pact of **Punto Fijo**, a power-sharing agreement written in 1958 that bound the parties to cooperate after elections. Following the withdrawal of the URD from the pact, the presidency and cabinet positions alternated between AD and COPEI. This political system functioned relatively smoothly through the subsequent decades, though the success of policies and parties was always affected by changes in oil prices and economic difficulties. Thanks to a quadrupling of crude oil prices due to the October 1973 Arab-Israeli War, the first administration of AD leader Carlos Andrés **Pérez Rodríguez** (1974–1979, 1989–1993) began a spending spree whose stated purpose was to spread the oil wealth through the citizenry, but which instead contributed to the development of a privileged economic elite. Corruption in business and government increased, and by the late 1970s international recession had also set in.

The electorate transferred power to COPEI in the December 1978 presidential election. However, Luis **Herrera Campins** (1979–1984) proved an ineffective leader, mismanaging the country's oil wealth and struggling with economic stagnation, unemployment, rising inflation, and dwindling capital and currency reserves. In 1983, 70 percent of Venezuela's external debt came due, forcing the government to stop interest payments and freeze prices to control increasing inflation. The electorate, shaken by economic instability, grew ever wearier of ineffective governance. While President Jaime **Lusinchi** (1984–1989) of AD attempted to avert eco-

This 1920 photo shows the first Venezuelan oil well at Tarra. *Columbus Memorial Library, General Secretariat of the Organization of American States. Reproduced with permission of the Organization of American States.*

Venezuela's growing dependence on petroleum revenues is illustrated by this 1960 photo showing the profusion of oil wells on Lake Maracaibo. *Columbus Memorial Library, General Secretariat of the Organization of American States. Reproduced with permission of the Organization of American States.*

nomic disaster by implementing harsh austerity measures, and policies to lessen Venezuela's economic dependence on oil profits, by 1988 the drastic decline in oil prices had cut government income in half. Debt payment became increasingly difficult and inflation continued to rise, reaching 20 percent during Lusinchi's administration.

In December 1988 the electorate returned former AD president Pérez to office. Pérez achieved a measure of economic stability at the cost of rising poverty levels, and in 1989 riots broke out across the country in reaction to an increase in bus fares, part of Pérez's package of austerity measures. Hundreds of people were killed as military troops were called upon to put down the disturbances. In 1992 disgruntled military officers mounted two unsuccessful coup attempts, calling for an end to corruption and a halt to economic mismanagement. Bringing the chaos to a head, in 1993 Congress impeached President Pérez on corruption charges. A mere 40 percent of the populace voted in the December 1993 general elections, which brought independent candidate Rafael **Caldera Rodríguez** (1969–1974, 1994–1999) to office. President Caldera's options were limited by international and domestic pressures, and social unrest increased, leading to student demonstrations and protests against price increases for previously subsidized public services. Increasing levels of crime, tied to the drug trade centered in Colombia (see **drugs**, Colombia), prompted the administration to send security forces to major urban areas.

As a result of dissatisfaction with the nation's political parties, candidates in the 1998 presidential election ran as independents, or as representatives of new personalistic parties, bringing to an end the long era of two-party rule. Unexpectedly, the leader of the February 1992 coup, Lieutenant Colonel Hugo Chávez, running on a classically populist, antiestablishment platform, won the 1998 election with 57 percent of the vote. While his victory brought hope to poorer Venezuelans, the international community and business interests expressed concern over Chávez's leftist leanings, the populist tendencies that he displayed during his campaign, and the penchant for concentrating power in his own hands that he demonstrated once in office. While through 2001 the president maintained his commitment to semi-democratic politics and economic growth in Venezuela, at the start of the twenty-first century, Venezuela's political and economic situation remained tense.

ENTRIES

Armed Forces of National Liberation (Fuerzas Armadas de Liberación Nacional, FALN)

The Armed Forces of National Liberation (Fuerzas Armadas de Liberación Nacional, FALN) began activities in 1962, in the wake of the **Cuban Revolution of 1959** (see Cuba) when Latin American socialist and communist activity peaked. The group was formally founded in 1963 as a coalition of the Movement of the Revolutionary Left (Movimiento de Izquierda Revolucionaria, MIR), hard-liners from the Communist Party of Venezuela (Partido Comunista de Venezuela, PCV), and leftist student groups. FALN violence climaxed in 1963–1964, and by the end of the decade the group had virtually dissolved.

The plan of the FALN, led by Domingo Alberto Rangel, Moisés Moleiro, and Américo Martín, was to stimulate unrest in the nation, compel the military to install a repressive dictatorship, organize opposition to military rule, and come to power with broad support. The FALN engaged in many forms of violence, including sabotaging oil pipelines and bombing a Sears Roebuck warehouse and the U.S. Embassy in Caracas. The group never gained much of a popular following, and lost what support it had in 1963 when a train derailment it caused resulted in civilian deaths. During the 1963 elections, many communists and MIR congressmen were jailed, though they were eventually pardoned under Rafael **Caldera Rodríguez** (1969–1974, 1994–1999). By 1965 it was apparent that guerrilla warfare had failed in Venezuela. Slowly the FALN, with the support of the PCV and part of the MIR, called for the abandonment of violent tactics and the acceptance of the electoral road to power. By 1969 the PCV and the MIR chose to participate legally in Venezuela's political sphere, encouraged by Caldera's "pacification" policies.

The Red Flag Party (Partido Bandera Roja), a radical MIR splinter group that wanted to continue armed struggle, operated in 1969 in Venezuela and eastern Colombia under the leadership of Gabriel Puerta Aponte and Asdrúbal Cordero, but posed no real threat to the country.

Betancourt, Rómulo (1908–1981)

Politically active from the age of twenty, Rómulo Betancourt was head of the Revolutionary Council of Government (Consejo de Gobierno Revolucionario, CGR) that led Venezuela during the three-year period known as *El Trienio* (1945–1948). He was later democratically elected, serving as president from 1959 to 1964. His second administration achieved economic recovery and industrial development while enacting reforms in education, agriculture, and labor.

Born in Guatire, Betancourt attended the Central University of Venezuela in Caracas. He abandoned his studies and went into exile following the February 1928 student protests against the authoritarian rule of President Juan Vicente **Gómez** (1908–1914, 1915–1929, 1931–1935). While in exile, Betancourt became a member of the Venezuelan Revolutionary Party (Partido Revolucionario Venezolano), participated in the

1929 *Falke* expedition, co-founded the Unionist Alliance of Great Colombia (Alianza Unionista de Gran Colombia) in 1930, and helped found the Revolutionary Group of the Left (Agrupación Revolucionaria de Izquierda, ARDI) in Barranquilla, Colombia. Betancourt also developed the *Plan of Barranquilla*, an analysis of the Venezuelan condition informed by Marxism. He moved to Costa Rica in 1932 and co-founded the Costa Rican **Communist Party** (Partido Comunista, PC; see Costa Rica).

Betancourt returned to Venezuela in 1936 following the 1935 death of President Gómez, and helped found the Venezuelan Organization (Organización Venezolana, ORVE), a movement comprising most of the Generation of 1928 (see **Federation of Students of Venezuela** [Federación de Estudiantes de Venezuela, FEV]). ORVE was almost immediately denied permission to operate legally, and soon joined with other parties to form the National Democratic Party (Partido Democrático Nacional, PDN). The PDN was also declared illegal in the anticommunist climate of 1937, and its leaders, accused of being communists by the government of Eleazar López Contreras (1935–1941), were forced into exile. The PDN continued to operate underground in Venezuela but split in 1939: Betancourt and his followers maintained the PDN in exile, while others formed the Communist Party of Venezuela (Partido Comunista de Venezuela, PCV). In 1940 Betancourt returned to Venezuela and supported Rómulo **Gallegos Freire** (1948) in his unsuccessful presidential bid in 1941. The victor in that presidential election, Isaías **Medina Angarita** (1941–1945), opened the political system and legalized the PDN. The PDN promptly changed its name to **Democratic Action** (Acción Democrática, AD), with Betancourt as its leader.

Betancourt began to organize the party's national platform, and in 1945, AD initiated negotiations with the government of Medina regarding an acceptable candidate for that year's presidential elections. The negotiations were unsuccessful, and AD joined with the military to form the **Patriotic Military Union** (Unión Patriótica Militar, UPM) to overthrow Medina's floundering regime. In October 1945, the CGR, a seven-man junta, took control of the country, naming Betancourt president. During its three years in power, a period known as *El Trienio*, the CGR introduced universal voting and adopted a new constitution. Gallegos took power as the elected president in February 1948, but was overthrown by the military in November 1948. Betancourt once again had to flee Venezuela.

Betancourt returned to the country in February 1958 (following the overthrow of dictator Marcos **Pérez Jiménez** [1952–1958]) as head of AD. He reorganized the party, contested and won the presidential election of 1958, and served as president of Venezuela from 1959 to 1964. As Betancourt attempted to reimplement democratic rule, he faced economic crisis, violent pro-

tests, and guerrilla uprisings. Nonetheless, he successfully stimulated economic and industrial development and enacted education, labor, and agricultural reforms. Following the "Betancourt Doctrine," which stipulated that Venezuela would not recognize any regime that came to power by military force, Betancourt shunned the regime of Fidel **Castro Ruz** (see Cuba).

Raúl **Leoni** (1964–1969), also a member of AD, succeeded Betancourt. Betancourt lived outside of Venezuela for eight years following his presidency, but returned to Venezuela in 1972 to support AD presidential candidate Carlos Andrés **Pérez Rodríguez** (1974–1979, 1989–1993) in the election of 1974. Betancourt remained the honorary president of AD until his death in 1981.

Caldera Rodríguez, Rafael (1916–   )

Rafael Caldera Rodríguez is the founder the **Committee of Independent Electoral Political Organization** (Comité de Organización Política Electoral Independiente, COPEI), one of the two most important Venezuelan parties of the contemporary period. He was the first member of COPEI to become president, serving from 1969 to 1974 and again from 1994 to 1999.

Born in San Felipe, Caldera Rodríguez completed a degree in political science at the Central University of Venezuela in 1939. He formed the National Union of Students (Unión Nacional de Estudiantes, UNE) in May 1936, which separated from the **Federation of Students of Venezuela** (Federación de Estudiantes de Venezuela, FEV) when the latter called for the closing of all religious orders. Caldera served as a deputy in the National Congress from 1941 to 1944, and in January 1946, founded COPEI. This group, with roots in the UNE, combined Catholic religious appeal with moderate social welfare programs for the lower and middle classes.

Caldera ran unsuccessfully for president as the COPEI candidate in 1947, and also lost the fraudulent election of 1953 to Marcos **Pérez Jiménez** (1952–1958). Caldera was subsequently jailed and exiled by the Pérez Jiménez regime, which considered him the principal representative of the opposition. After the fall of Pérez Jiménez in 1958, Caldera returned to Venezuela to represent COPEI in the signing of the **Pact of *Punto Fijo***. Though he also lost the presidential election of 1958 and 1963, Caldera was key to maintaining the pact with **Democratic Action** (Acción Democrática, AD). Caldera was finally elected president in 1968. During his administration, he implemented policies to pacify the **Armed Forces of National Liberation** (Fuerzas Armadas de Liberación Nacional, FALN), and brought the Communist Party of Venezuela (Partido Comunista de Venezuela, PCV), and the Movement of the Revolutionary Left (Movimiento de Izquierda Revolucionaria, MIR) into the legal political sphere. Most notably, he initiated educational reform and nationalized the natural gas industry. He also smoothed relations with

Cuba by replacing the "Betancourt Doctrine" (see **Betancourt, Rómulo**) with the more flexible politics of "pluralistic solidarity" with all Latin American nations, democratic or not. He was named senator for life following the end of his presidential term in 1974.

Caldera taught at the Central University for the next decade, and then ran unsuccessfully for president in 1983. Following his defeat, Caldera split from COPEI, and was elected president in 1993 with the support of a seventeen-party coalition. Though his campaign promises included halting economic austerity measures, his administration furthered free-market reforms, expanding privatization and cutting subsidies. He also failed to fulfill his promise to fight corruption. He was succeeded as president by Hugo **Chávez Frías** (1999–).

Castro, Cipriano (1858–1924)

Cipriano Castro, who served as president from 1899 to 1908, was the first in a long line of *Andino* leaders (rulers who hailed from the Andean highlands). He is known as the most corrupt and inefficient president in Venezuelan history. His reign is considered the beginning of the end of *caudillo* rule, and the start of the modern, centralized Venezuelan state.

Born in Capacho in Táchira, Castro attended the Seminary of Pamplona in Colombia. He began his career in politics in 1878 and held various government posts at the local and national levels. Castro was forced into exile in 1892 as a result of his participation in the Legalistic Revolution, a military campaign to overthrow the government of President Raimundo Andueza Palacio (1890–1892). Castro returned to Venezuela in May 1899 with Juan Vicente **Gómez** (1908–1914, 1915–1929, 1931–1935) to lead the Restoration Revolution (1899), whose goal was to install as president an *Andino* able to transform the Liberal policies of past presidents which the revolution's leaders believed had weakened the political system.

The revolution placed Castro at the head of the government, a post he held from October 1899 to December 1908. His rule was considered corrupt, licentious, reckless, despotic, and inefficient, and he was domestically and internationally unpopular. Regional *caudillos* and international business interests, upset by Castro's modernization and centralization of the state, staged an unsuccessful attempt to overthrow him in the Liberating Revolution (1901–1903). In 1902 Castro suspended payment on Venezuela's internal and external debt, prompting Germany and England to issue ultimata, and subsequently send warships to establish a pacific German-Italian-English blockade of Venezuela. In addition, in 1906 France broke diplomatic ties with Venezuela over the confiscation of Cable Francés (a French-owned company).

The differences between Castro and Gómez, who served as his vice president, increased over time, as Gó-mez grew weary of Castro's inept and chaotic rule. Gómez convinced Castro to go to Europe for medical treatment for his failing health in 1908, seized the government in his absence in December of that year, and ruled the nation for the next twenty-seven years. Castro was prohibited from returning to Venezuela by the United States, France, the Netherlands, and the United Kingdom and was prohibited by the Venezuelan government from ever again serving as president or holding public office. He died in Puerto Rico.

Chávez Frías, Hugo Rafael (1954–)

Hugo Rafael Chávez Frías (1999–), a passionate advocate of social justice self-modeled after the great liberator of South America, Simón Antonio de la Santísima Trinidad **Bolívar y Palacios** (see Colombia), was elected president of Venezuela in December 1998 with 57 percent of the popular vote. His election demonstrated the electorate's frustration with the old two-party system.

Chávez was born in Sabaneta, Barinas. He received a degree in military sciences and arts, graduating as a second lieutenant in July 1975, and later did graduate work in political science at Simón Bolívar University. By 1990 he had risen to the rank of lieutenant colonel. In February 1992, Chávez led a movement of young military officers in an unsuccessful rebellion against the government of Carlos Andrés **Pérez Rodríguez** (1974–1979, 1989–1993), which he considered corrupt and unjust. Chávez was imprisoned, but as a result of demands voiced by the Venezuelan people and echoed by President Rafael **Caldera Rodríguez** (1969–1974, 1994–1999), he was released in 1994.

He immediately reinitiated his struggle, founding the anticorruption and antiestablishment Fifth Republic Movement (Movimiento Quinta República, MVR) with some fellow army officers. This group became Chávez's main populist vehicle, and together with numerous political organizations and a broad array of forces from civil society, gave Chávez the support he needed to eventually win the presidency in 1998. He campaigned across the country, venturing to even the most remote corners of Venezuela, wooing the populace by advocating the universally accepted principles of liberty and justice. His proposal for the creation of a new republic through the supreme democratic option of a National Constituent Assembly resonated with the Venezuelan populace, as did his promises to eliminate corruption, distribute state revenues from petroleum more equitably, and strike a balance between reforms designed to address the structural deformities of the economy and those designed to improve living standards.

Upon assuming office in 1999, Chávez held elections for a Constituent Assembly, which undertook the task of drafting a new constitution. The Constitution of 1999 dismantled the bicameral legislature, creating a unicameral National Assembly, restricted the independence of the state oil company, augmented the autonomy of the military, and increased the power of the presidency, allowing immediate reelection for presidents of the republic. It also guaranteed rights to indigenous communities and minorities. In a general election held on July 30, 2000, the first under the new constitution, Chávez won a second term as president (garnering 59 percent of the vote). His MVR won 92 of the 165 seats in the new single-chamber National Assembly; through alliances, it could command a three-fifths majority. Further, the MVR and the Movement Toward Socialism (Movimiento al Socialismo, MAS) took control of more than half of the twenty-four state governorships. Four months later, in November 2000, Chávez signed his second "enabling law" in less than two years, which authorized him to legislate by decree on issues ranging from the economy to "the organization of the state." In May 2001, in an announcement that confused many, Chávez made public plans to reactivate the Revolutionary Bolivarian Movement (Movimiento Bolivariano Revolucionario, MBR), a military-civilian organization that backed his 1992 attempted coup.

Though Chávez's election offered hope to Venezuela's poorest citizens, many of whose plight was worsened when destructive floods swept the country in early 2000, by 2001 the president's populist tendencies, as well as his motives and aspirations, concerned many. Specifically, the president's critics questioned his commitment to building independent democratic political institutions and worried about the degree to which he was concentrating power in his own hands.

Committee of Independent Electoral Political Organization (Comité de Organización Política Electoral Independiente, COPEI)

Formed in January 1946 by former members of the National Union of Students (Unión Nacional de Estudiantes, UNE), COPEI is a conservative, nationalist Christian Democratic party that emphasizes the dignity of the individual, the social function of property, and the need for cooperation between the Roman Catholic Church and the state. COPEI served as the political rival of **Democratic Action** (Acción Democrática, AD) after the 1958 transition to democracy, though the two parties have traditionally proposed similar economic programs.

COPEI's first presidential candidate was Rafael **Caldera Rodríguez** (1969–1974, 1994–1999), who lost the election of 1947 to AD candidate Rómulo **Gallegos Freire** (1948). COPEI was not involved in the overthrow of Gallegos in November 1948, though it did cooperate with the military juntas that ruled Venezuela until 1952. President Marcos **Pérez Jiménez** (1952–1958) declared political parties illegal, impeding COPEI's activities. When presidential elections were called for in 1958, AD, COPEI, and the **Democratic Republican Union** (Unión Republicana Democrática, URD) jointly picked COPEI's Caldera as their presidential candidate.

However, before he could run, Caldera was jailed and exiled by the regime, and AD candidate Rómulo **Betancourt** (1945–1948 as junta leader, 1959–1964) was elected. In 1958 AD, COPEI, and the URD signed the Pact of *Punto Fijo*, in which each pledged to defend constitutionality, accept and abide by electoral results, and form a coalition government to present a common program to the electorate.

COPEI finally won the presidency in 1968, when fragmentation within AD allowed a political opening and Caldera was elected. Another COPEI candidate, Luis **Herrera Campins** (1979–1984), was victorious in the 1978 presidential contest, closely defeating the AD candidate, who was backed by a strong, reunified AD. The 1978 victory made COPEI the largest political party in Venezuela. Though COPEI was unsuccessful in presidential elections through the rest of the twentieth century due mainly to the population's waning faith in traditional parties, in 2001 it was still active in Venezuelan political life.

Communist Party of Venezuela (Partido Comunista de Venezuela, PCV). See Armed Forces of National Liberation (Fuerzas Armadas de Liberación Nacional, FALN)

Conservative Party. See Federal Wars

Crespo, Joaquín (1841–1898)

Joaquín Crespo led Venezuela during a politically tumultuous period characterized by *caudillo* struggle for power. His first term (1884–1886) is remembered for its poor economic policy. During his second administration, which consisted of a two-year dictatorship (1892–1894) and a four-year term as constitutional president (1894–1898), Crespo incurred a large debt and managed a boundary dispute with British Guyana.

Born in San Francisco de Cara, Crespo began his military career at age seventeen and eventually reached the rank of brigadier general. He served with the Federalists in the **Federal Wars** (1859–1863) and was minister of war under President Francisco Linares Alcántara (1877–1878). Devoted to powerful *caudillo* Antonio **Guzmán Blanco** (1870–1877, 1878–1884, 1886–1887), Crespo became chief of the general staff in the southern states in 1882 and presided over a conflictive military regime from 1884 to 1886. This period is remembered for economic hardship, a locust plague that hindered coffee production, and continuous fighting for political power among regional *caudillos*.

Failing in his drive to become president in 1888, Crespo led an unsuccessful revolution against President Juan Pablo Rojas Pául (1888–1890) and was jailed. He then headed the rebellion that unseated President Raimundo Andueza Palacio (1890–1892) and took control of the country as dictator, dissolving Congress and calling for a new constitution. He was elected president under the new constitution for the 1894–1898 presidential term. During this period, Venezuela incurred a large foreign debt to Germany, and the "First Venezuelan Incident" (a boundary dispute between Venezuela and British Guyana) erupted when gold was discovered along the nations' border. Crespo returned to the military as commander of the army when his presidential term ended and was killed during a revolt in 1898. Ignacio Andrade (1898–1899) succeeded Crespo as president and settled the boundary dispute in 1899, losing practically all the disputed territory to British Guyana.

Delgado Chalbaud, Román (1882–1929)

Born in Mérida, Román Delgado Chalbaud studied at the Naval School in Port Cabello, and became a powerful military and political figure in the first decades of the twentieth century. He held many positions in the administration of President Cipriano **Castro** (1899–1908), including chief of the national army from 1903 to 1906. However, Delgado's military ties with Juan Vicente **Gómez** (1908–1914, 1915–1929, 1931–1935), who served as Castro's vice president, led to his involvement in the December 1908 revolt that replaced Castro with Gómez.

During Gómez's first administration, he and Delgado founded a national shipping company to colonize, exploit, promote, and develop the Amazon Territory, and controlled all water transportation to and from the area. Delgado traveled to Europe in 1911, and returned to Venezuela convinced of the merits of modernization through foreign investment and the creation of a state bank. While Gómez originally advocated the same projects, he later demurred, and as a result, Delgado planned a conspiracy to overthrow Gómez in 1913. Gómez learned of the plot and jailed Delgado for fourteen years. Delgado obtained amnesty, and was released from prison and exiled in 1927. He began to plan another coup against Gómez from abroad, and later joined the National Liberation Council and became involved in the *Falke* **Expedition** of 1929, the most important (though unsuccessful) rebellion against Gómez. Delgado led the land invasion of Cumaná in August 1929, and died in battle. His son, Carlos Román Delgado Chalbaud Gómez (1948–1950), who also participated in the failed invasion, would later assume the presidency.

Democratic Action (Acción Democrática, AD)

Founded in 1941, Democratic Action (Acción Democrática, AD) is the most successful democratic political party in Venezuelan history. AD, a social democratic party with bases among trade unions and labor organizations, has advocated civilian government, freedom of thought and expression, opposition to dictators, state-led economic growth, and protection for workers. Almost none of its original Marxist influences remain evident today.

AD's roots can be traced to three organizations: the Revolutionary Group of the Left (Agrupación Revolucionaria de Izquierda, ARDI), founded in Colombia in March 1931 by exiles opposed to the dictatorship of Juan Vicente **Gómez** (1908–1914, 1915–1929, 1931–1935); the Venezuelan Organization (Organización Venezolano, ORVE), founded in January 1936; and the National Democratic Party (Partido Democrático Nacional, PDN), founded in November 1936. The leaders of the PDN changed their party's name to AD in September 1941, and it quickly became a dominant political force in Venezuela.

AD members cooperated with a group of young military officers (see **Patriotic Military Union** [Unión Patriótica Militar, UPM]) in October 1945 to overthrow the government of Isaías Medina Angarita (1941–1945). They established the Revolutionary Council of Government (Consejo de Gobierno Revolucionario, CGR) consisting of five civilians (four of whom were from AD) and two military officers. Rómulo **Betancourt** (1945–1948 as junta leader, 1959–1964) of AD was named head of the CGR and president of Venezuela. Though this path to power was anathema to AD's political ideals, the AD-controlled junta had many democratic achievements during its three years in power, known as *El Trienio*: it allowed new political parties to form, enacted universal suffrage for adults, promulgated a new constitution in 1947, passed new oil laws, initiated agrarian reform, and reactivated the labor movement through the creation of the Confederation of Workers of Venezuela (Confederación de Trabajadores Venezolanos, CTV) in 1947.

The junta held free elections in 1947, and AD candidate Rómulo **Gallegos Freire** was elected. Gallegos took office in February 1948 and was promptly overthrown by the military in November 1948. Two military juntas, the first led by Carlos Román Delgado Chalbaud Gómez (1948–1950) and the second by Germán Suárez Flamerich (1950–1952) led to the dictatorship of Marcos **Pérez Jiménez** (1952–1958). Pérez Jiménez killed and imprisoned AD leaders, angered by their opposition in the presidential election he arranged in 1953 to legitimate his control, and AD was eventually forced underground. A patriotic junta including AD overthrew Pérez Jiménez in January 1958 and returned AD's Betancourt to the presidency. In 1958, AD, the **Democratic Republican Union** (Unión Republicana Democrática, URD), and the **Committee of Independent Electoral Political Organization** (Comité de Organización Política Electoral Independiente, COPEI) signed the **Pact of *Punto Fijo*** in an effort to assure democratic governance and avoid future dictatorial interludes.

Early in 1960, in the wake of the **Cuban Revolution of 1959** (see Cuba), splinter groups left AD and formed more radical leftist groups. Some of the younger leaders created the Movement of the Revolutionary Left (Movimiento de Izquierda Revolucionaria, MIR; see **Armed Forces of National Liberation** [Fuerzas Armadas de Liberación Nacional, FALN]), and in 1961–1962 the Democratic Action-Opposition (Acción Democrática-Oposición, AD-O) formed. AD experienced its most extreme fragmentation when Jesús Angel Paz Galarraga and Luis Beltrán Prieto Figueroa formed the Electoral Movement of the People (Movimiento Electoral Popular, MEP). This division contributed to AD's loss in the 1968 presidential election. However, AD candidates Carlos Andrés **Pérez Rodríguez** (1974–1979, 1989–1993) and Jaime **Lusinchi** (1984–1989) won the 1973, 1983, and 1988 presidential contests. While AD remained an important party in Venezuela, the general disillusionment of the electorate with the country's traditional parties led to a drastic decline in AD's influence by the end of the 1990s.

Democratic Republican Union (Unión Republicana Democrática, URD)

The Democratic Republican Union (Unión Republicana Democrática, URD), formed in December 1945 by former members of the Venezuelan Democratic Party (Partido Democrático de Venezuela, PDV), was initially led by Elías Toro, Andrés Germán Otero, and Isaac Pardo. By 1947 the original leaders had left the URD, and Jóvito Villalba took up the party's leadership, transforming it into a personalistic vehicle.

The party was officially recognized in February 1947, and immediately denounced the control of the government by **Democratic Action** (Acción Democrática, AD). The URD did not participate in the coup that overthrew Rómulo **Gallegos Freire** (1948) in 1948, but supported the military governments that led the country from 1948 to 1952. However, by the time Marcos **Pérez Jiménez** (1952–1958) took control of the government, the URD had begun to violently oppose military rule. Villalba ran as the URD candidate in the 1953 election that Pérez Jiménez organized to legitimize his rule, and would have won by a wide margin had the corrupt dictator not demanded a ballot recount and fraudulently declared himself the winner. Pérez Jiménez quickly exiled Villalba and other URD leaders.

The URD reorganized, and its presidential candidate in the 1958 election, Wolfgang **Larrazábal Ugueto** (who briefly led the junta that had replaced Pérez Jiménez earlier that year), lost, but received about 30 percent of the vote. Leaders of AD, URD and the **Committee of Independent Electoral Political Organization** (Comité de Organización Política Electoral Independiente, COPEI) soon signed the **Pact of *Punto Fijo*** in an effort to assure democratic governance and avoid future dictatorial interludes. The pact, which institutionalized power-sharing, enabled the URD to gain assignments to the first cabinet of the second administration of Rómulo

Betancourt (1945–1948 as junta leader, 1959–1964). However, the URD left the coalition formed by the pact in 1962 because it opposed AD's firm stance against the regime of Fidel **Castro Ruz** (see Cuba) in Cuba, and subsequently deteriorated in importance.

Villalba ran again for president in 1963 and did poorly. Splinter groups, both radical (such as the Popular Nationalist Vanguard [Vanguardia Nacionalista Popular, VNP]) and democratic (for instance, the Independent Democratic Movement [Movimiento Democrático Independiente, MDI]), began to break with the main body of the URD. In 1968 the weakened party joined a coalition of four parties to support Miguel Angel Burelli Rivas' unsuccessful bid for president. In 1973 URD leaders formed a coalition with the Communist Party of Venezuela (Partido Comunista de Venezuela, PCV) and the Electoral Movement of the People (Movimiento Electoral Popular, MEP), but pulled out when they realized that Villalba was not to be the alliance's candidate in the 1973 presidential election. Villalba still ran for the presidency that year, but received only 3 percent of the vote. In the 1978 and 1983 elections, the URD supported other parties and their candidates in coalitions. While the URD continued to exist, its influence remained minimal.

Falke Expedition (1929)

In 1927 Román **Delgado Chalbaud**, in exile following a fourteen-year prison term, began to plan a rebellion to overthrow ruthless autocrat Juan Vicente **Gómez** (1908–1914, 1915–1929, 1931–1935). That revolt, remembered as the *Falke* expedition, was the most important—albeit unsuccessful—rebellion against the powerful dictator.

The three-pronged plan involved a land attack on Cumaná, a simultaneous assault by sea, and another attack on the state of Táchira. Two separate groups participated: the first group consisted of important political/military actors, and the second group mainly comprised students united by the events of the Student Strike of 1928 (see **Federation of Students of Venezuela** [Federación de Estudiantes de Venezuela, FEV]). In early August 1929, one hundred men (including Delgado's son, future president Carlos Román Delgado Chalbaud Gómez [1948–1950]) departed from Europe on a ship called the *Falke* and crossed the Atlantic Ocean, arriving at Cumaná on August 10. While the land forces did not reach Cumaná as intended, Delgado Chalbaud Gómez proceeded with the attack on Cumaná on August 11. However, Gómez had been informed of the attack, was ready for the rebels' arrival and easily overpowered them. (The residents of Cumaná sided with the invaders but had no weapons with which to join in the struggle.) The land forces, which eventually arrived at Cumaná and attacked on August 13, were defeated as well. The Táchira uprising, which had also commenced on August

10, was also quickly put down by government forces faithful to Gómez.

Federal Wars (also Federal Revolution and Liberal Revolution) (1859–1863)

From 1859 to 1863 Liberal and Conservative regional *caudillos* engaged in a chaotic power struggle known as the Federal Wars because the triumphant Liberals favored federalism. Divisions left over from the wars of independence and the dissolution of Simón Antonio de la Santísima Trinidad **Bolívar y Palacios'** (see Colombia) Gran Colombia were the underlying causes of the conflicts.

The Liberal Party (Venezuela's first party) advocated expansion of suffrage, land reform, public education, and the separation of church and state, as well as decentralization. The Conservative Party generally supported the interests of landowners and commercial elites, the church, and the military. In reality, the Liberal and Conservative Parties of this time differed very little in terms of their political stance and were in essence mechanisms to further the ambitions of *caudillos*.

The wars ended with the signing of the Treaty of Coche in April 1863. The subsequent Liberal administration of Juan Crisóstomo Falcón (1863–1869) changed the constitution to reflect federalist principals, but did little to actually implement those changes, as he spent most of his term putting down revolts led by rival *caudillos*. Nonetheless, the federalist victory led to the decentralization of Venezuela into twenty separate states, which at the end of the wars were all headed by generals, many of whom were illiterate and inept. The wars cost 40,000 lives and brought economic ruin to the nation.

Federation of Students of Venezuela (Federación de Estudiantes de Venezuela, FEV)

In 1926 a tenacious group of students at the Central University in Caracas resurrected the Federation of Students of Venezuela (Federación de Estudiantes de Venezuela, FEV), which had been suppressed by unpopular president Cipriano **Castro** (1899–1908) at the beginning of the twentieth century. The students involved in the federation, who called for democratic government and an end to Venezuela's closed political system, came to be known as the Generation of 1928 (Generación de 1928). Many evolved into important Venezuelan politicians.

Jacinto Fombona Pachano was the first president of the new federation, and Raúl **Leoni** (1964–1969), its second president; membership in 1926 also included such illustrious individuals as Rómulo **Betancourt** (1945–1948 as junta leader, 1959–1964) and Jóvito Villalba (see **Democratic Republican Union** [Unión Republicana Democrática, URD]). Outraged by the lack of cultural activities at the university, the federation organized conferences, founded the review *La Universi-*

dad, and planned the Week of the Student (February 6–12, 1928), which evolved into the Student Strike of 1928.

The activities of the 1928 Week of the Student quickly became politicized. The police invaded, the students reacted against the police, and the government halted the activities and arrested Villalba and others. When the governor of the Federal District refused to honor a student petition requesting the release of those who had been arrested, the FEV sent a telegram to President Juan Vicente **Gómez** (1908–1914, 1915–1929, 1931–1935) challenging him to jail them as well. As a result, 214 students were detained in the city of Puerto Cabello for twelve days. Protests erupted in Venezuela's major cities denouncing the government, and the students were released and hailed as heroes. A few of the more radical students joined a disgruntled group of young military officers and tried to overthrow the Gómez government in April 1928. Despite much public outcry, the students considered to be most volatile were sent to Palenque prison, and the rest were detained in Puerto Cabello until early 1929; most were exiled soon thereafter.

Some of the exiled students continued to fight against the Gómez government, and some participated in the 1929 *Falke* Expedition. A subset established the Revolutionary Group of the Left (Agrupación Revolucionaria de Izquierda, ARDI) and issued the *Plan of Barranquilla* from Barranquilla, Colombia, on March 22, 1931. The declaration called for the traditional, oligarchic system to open and allow the participation of a burgeoning and frustrated middle class. The plan also outlined the reforms the group hoped to institute after achieving control of the presidency of Venezuela, including awarding full civil liberties to the populace; confiscating the property of dictator Gómez, his family, and associates; creating a revolutionary tribunal for addressing damages; promoting literacy; renegotiating oil concessions; nationalizing the economy (to a limited degree); and creating a constitutional assembly to choose a provisional president and draft a constitution. The twelve Venezuelans who signed the document included some of the county's most renowned future leaders, including Betancourt and Leoni. The plan, the first document to structurally analyze Venezuelan history and society and offer a program for change, laid the foundations of what would become the transforming political party **Democratic Action** (Acción Democrática, AD).

After Gómez's death in 1935, the FEV, led by Villalba, organized a general strike in February 1936 to protest censorship. When soldiers fired on the protesters, Villalba led a crowd of 30,000 to the presidential palace. In the face of such pressure, President Eleazar **López Contreras** (1935–1941) lifted press restrictions and removed government leaders who had been part of the Gómez regime. While the FEV eventually disbanded, it is remembered as one of the most active student forces in contemporary Latin American politics.

Gallegos Freire, Rómulo (1884–1969)

Rómulo Gallegos Freire served a brief and unsuccessful stint as president of Venezuela in 1948. He is best known and more fondly remembered for his writing; he received the National Prize for Literature (1957–1958) and became a member of the celebrated Spanish Royal Academy of Language.

Born in Caracas, Gallegos was a novelist, and a secondary school teacher and administrator from 1912 to 1930. Most prolific early in life, he co-edited the weekly *El Arco Iris* (*Rainbow*) in 1903, published many works in *La Alborada* (*Dawn*) after 1909, and was published in *El Cojo Ilustrado* (*The Erudite Cripple*) in 1910 and in *Los Aventureros* (*The Adventurers*) in 1913. In 1920 his first novel, *El Ultimo Solar* (*The Last Ancestral Home*), depicted the social concerns that faced his generation in a destructive natural environment. Another novel, *La Trepadora* (*The Climber*, 1925), postulated the possibilities of a new constructive society. *Doña Bárbara* (*Lady Barbara*, 1929), perhaps his best-known work, described the barbarism in Venezuela that had to be destroyed before the country could be "civilized" and progress into modernization. *Cantaclaro* (*Clearchant*, 1931) was the last of his vital works.

Exiled by Juan Vicente **Gómez** (1908–1914, 1915–1929, 1931–1935) in 1930, Gallegos returned to Venezuela in 1935, and served as minister of public instruction in 1937, as deputy to the National Congress from 1937 to 1940, and as president of the Municipal Council of the Federal District in 1940–1941. He ran unsuccessfully for president in 1941, but was elected in 1947 on the ticket of **Democratic Action** (Acción Democrática, AD).

Gallegos was inaugurated in February 1948 and was overthrown nine months later by military forces (which were threatened by his policies to reduce military power), supported by large landowners (who were alarmed by his agrarian reform measures). A military junta was installed, led by Carlos Román Delgado Chalbaud Gómez (1948–1950). Gallegos went into exile for ten years, returning to Venezuela in 1958.

Generation of 1928 (Generación de 1928). See Federation of Students of Venezuela (Federación de Estudiantes de Venezuela, FEV)

Gómez, Juan Vicente (1857–1935)

Juan Vicente Gómez was a semiliterate *Andino* who rose through the military ranks to become a powerful Venezuelan ruler, leading the country either from the presidency or through puppet presidents from 1908 to 1935. His regime was brutally harsh, but he oversaw the transformation of Venezuela from a rural, *caudillo*-dominated traditional society with an economy based on agriculture to a more modern, urban, and centrally-ruled nation with an industrial economy based on the exploitation of oil reserves.

Born in El Salcedo, Táchira, Gómez became involved in the chaotic *caudillo* politics of the late nineteenth century. In 1892 he supported the government of President Raimundo Andueza Palacio (1890–1892) against the Legalistic Revolution, whose instigators advocated a return to the constitutional legality overturned by Andueza Palacio. Gómez fled to Colombia when the revolution succeeded but returned to Venezuela with Cipriano **Castro** (1899–1908) in the late 1890s to lead a successful counterrevolution, the Restoration Revolution (May 1899), which placed Castro at the head of the Venezuelan government.

Gómez became governor of the Federal District, and later served as governor of the state of Táchira. He became first vice president of the nation in February 1901, and served as commander of the army from 1902 to 1908. As commander of the army, Gómez helped in the suppression of the Liberating Revolution (1901–1903), an attempt to overthrow Castro led by regional *caudillos*. An ambitious politician, Gómez soon grew tired of the endless problems produced by Castro's inept rule; when Castro went to Europe in 1908 for health reasons, Gómez took control of the government in December of that year.

Gómez served as president from 1908 to 1914, 1915 to 1929, and 1931 to 1935, and ruled from behind the scenes in the interim periods. He ruled harshly, eliminating regional, state, and local authorities, abolishing the militia, and building a national army of career officers. While political dissidents were imprisoned and tortured during his years in office, thanks to censorship and propaganda, the outside world viewed Venezuela as peaceful, or at least stable. Gómez did strengthen the economy, welcoming foreign investors, including oil prospectors, into Venezuela. An oil law drafted in 1918 protected national interests and benefited petroleum companies. Gómez also established the first labor laws for Venezuela in the latter years of his presidency.

Gómez governed until his death in December 1935, after which Eleazar **López Contreras** (1935–1941) assumed the powers of the presidency. López Contreras was formally elected in April 1936.

Guzmán Blanco, Antonio (1829–1899)

A military officer, statesman, and diplomat, Antonio Guzmán Blanco served as president of Venezuela from 1870 to 1877, from 1878 to 1884, and from 1886 to 1887, though he controlled Venezuelan politics continuously from 1870 to 1888. His dictatorship established central government authority in Venezuela.

Born in Caracas, Guzmán Blanco earned a bachelor's degree in philosophy and civil rights, a master's degree in civil rights and law, and a doctorate in civil rights. He began his political career in the United States as consul in New York and Philadelphia and as secretary in the Venezuelan Embassy in Washington, D.C., under José Tadeo Monagas (1847–1851, 1855–1858). Guzmán Blanco returned to Venezuela in 1858 and is believed to have been involved with the antigovernmental forces in the **Federal Wars** (1859–1863). Guzmán Blanco served as vice president and minister of foreign relations and the treasury under Juan Crisóstomo Falcón (1863–1869). The Blue Revolution (1867–1868) placed José Ruperto Monagas (1869–1870) in the presidency, and Guzmán Blanco was exiled for his ties to Falcón.

Guzmán Blanco led the April Revolution (1870) that overthrew José Ruperto Monagas, and controlled politics in Venezuela for the next eighteen years. During these years, his administration built roads and railroads, modernized cities, improved ports, restored national credit, mandated education, and modernized the penal system. He oversaw the shortening of the presidential term to two years under the Constitution of 1874 and instituted the selection of presidents by a Federal Council in the Constitution of 1881. He also separated church and state in Venezuela, weakening the church's power. Civil unrest was not uncommon during his rule, and on a trip to Paris in 1888, he heard news of growing discontent in his homeland and decided to stay in France. He died in France in 1899.

Herrera Campins, Luis (1925–)

Luis Herrera Campins wrote about and was involved in politics from a young age. He served in the National Congress in the 1960s and 1970s, and as president from 1979 to 1984.

Born in Acarigua, Portuguesa, Herrera attended the Central University of Venezuela in Caracas and participated in the National Union of Students (Unión Nacional de Estudiantes, UNE). Herrera became one of the youth leaders of the **Committee of Independent Electoral Political Organization** (Comité de Organización Política Electoral Independiente, COPEI), the political party that grew out of the UNE, and from 1946 to 1948 wrote in the daily *El Gráfico* and in the weekly *COPEI*. Herrera served as deputy of the legislative assembly in the state of Portuguesa in the late 1940s, and was imprisoned when a military junta ousted constitutionally elected president Rómulo **Gallegos Freire** (1948) in 1948. Subsequently exiled to Spain, Herrera wrote for an underground publication expressing opposition to the government of Marcos **Pérez Jiménez** (1952–1958).

Herrera returned to Venezuela after the fall of Pérez Jiménez and served as a deputy in Congress from 1959 to 1974. He led the Social Christian faction of COPEI through the 1960s, and soon became the secretary general of the Christian Democratic Organization of Latin America (Organización Demócrata-Cristiana de América Latina, ODCA). He was senator from 1974 to 1977.

Herrera ran in the presidential election of 1978 as the COPEI candidate on a platform to cut public spending, which had grown fiscally irresponsible under the first administration of Carlos Andrés **Pérez Rodríguez** (1974–1979, 1989–1993) of **Democratic Action** (Acción Democrática, AD). Herrera won the election by a narrow margin, and as president, ordered consumer subsidies cut and increased interest rates to encourage savings. When the Iranian Revolution (1979) and the outbreak of the Iran-Iraq War (1980–1988) caused oil prices to skyrocket in 1980, he abandoned his austerity measures and pursued ambitious construction projects, including the building of natural gas plants and a huge steel and coal plant. The expenditures caused the deficit to balloon, and capital flight followed in early 1983; soon thereafter price controls were implemented to control inflation.

The opposition was easily victorious in the December 1983 presidential election, and Herrera relinquished power to AD's Jaime **Lusinchi** (1984–1989). Herrera subsequently served as president of COPEI and became an active political journalist.

Larrazábal Ugueto, Wolfgang (1911–)

Unsuccessful in his attempts to win the presidency via the electoral process, the only experience Wolfgang Larrazábal Ugueto had with national leadership came during his brief stint as head of the five-man military junta that took control of Venezuela in 1958 after the overthrow of Marcos **Pérez Jiménez** (1952–1958). He is remembered for supporting democratic governance at a time when many military leaders preferred to remain in power through undemocratic means.

Born in Carúpano, Larrazábal studied at the Naval School and eventually became commander of the naval base at Puerto Cabello. He served as naval attaché in Washington, D.C. from 1952 to 1955 and rose to commander of the navy in 1957. Larrazábal joined other military and civilian leaders to overthrow Pérez Jiménez in January 1958, and headed the governing junta that assumed control, serving as the nation's provisional president until November 1958, when he resigned from the military to run for the presidency as the candidate of a coalition that included the **Democratic Republican Union** (Unión Republicana Democrática, URD) and the Communist Party of Venezuela (Partido Comunista de Venezuela, PCV). He was defeated by Rómulo **Betancourt** (1945–1948 as junta leader, 1959–1964) of **Democratic Action** (Acción Democrática, AD). Larrazábal held a diplomatic post in Chile from 1959 to 1963 and ran unsuccessfully for president again in 1963. He is well known for encouraging the military to support the transition to democracy and upholding the electoral process.

Larrazábal, who held the honor of senator for life, remained politically active through the 1980s.

Leoni, Raúl (1905–1972)

Raúl Leoni served as a deputy in Congress from 1936 to 1937, as a senator from 1958 to 1962, and as president of Venezuela from 1964 to 1969.

As president of the **Federation of Students of Venezuela** (Federación de Estudiantes de Venezuela, FEV), Leoni was involved in the Student Strike of 1928, a political protest against President Juan Vicente **Gómez** (1908–1914, 1915–1929, 1931–1935). Exiled as a result of his participation, he was involved in the *Falke Expedition* (1929) and co-founded the Revolutionary Group of the Left (Agrupación Revolucionaria de Izquierda, ARDI) with Rómulo **Betancourt** (1945–1948 as junta leader, 1959–1964). He also signed the *Plan of Barranquilla* (1931), a structural analysis of the Venezuelan condition.

After the death of Gómez in 1935, Leoni returned to Venezuela, co-founded the Venezuelan Organization (Organización Venezolana, ORVE) movement in January 1936, and was elected as deputy to Congress later that year. However, he and others were again expelled from the country in March 1937 when Eleazar **López Contreras** (1935–1941) abolished political parties. Leoni secretly returned to Venezuela and participated in the National Democratic Party (Partido Democrático Nacional, PDN) in June 1939, and later became a member of the executive committee of **Democratic Action** (Acción Democrática, AD). Leoni was involved in the overthrow of Isaías **Medina Angarita** (1941–1945) in October 1945, and served as minister of labor during *El Trienio* (1945–1948) and under President Rómulo **Gallegos Freire** (1948).

Leoni was again forced to leave the country in November 1948 when Gallegos was overthrown by the military. He did not return until 1958, when he was elected to the Senate. He subsequently served as its speaker from 1959 to 1962. Running as the AD candidate, Leoni won the presidential contest of 1963; his election marked the first time in Venezuelan history that the presidential sash had passed from one constitutionally elected chief executive to another. During Leoni's term, Venezuela enjoyed stability: economic growth was healthy, reform programs continued, impressive infrastructure projects were completed, and regional integration efforts were advanced. Rafael **Caldera Rodríguez** (1969–1974, 1994–1999) of the **Committee of Independent Electoral Political Organization** (Comité de Organización Política Electoral Independiente, COPEI) succeeded Leoni, who died in 1972.

Liberal Party. See Federal Wars

López Contreras, Eleazar (1883–1973)

Though Eleazar López Contreras had a successful military career, he advocated democracy and a transition to civilian rule during his presidency (1935–1941).

Born in Queniquea, López joined the military when he was sixteen, serving with Cipriano **Castro** (1899–1908) in the Restoration Revolution (1899). López subsequently held civilian posts, but returned to the military in 1914 and began to rise through its ranks, advancing through the Venezuelan air force, becoming chief of staff in 1930, and serving as minister of war and the marines under Juan Vicente **Gomez** (1908–1914, 1915–1929, 1931–1935) from 1931 to 1935.

When Gómez died in December 1935, López assumed the powers of the presidency, and was formally elected in April 1936. As president, López tried to create a national ideology based on reverence for Simón Antonio de la Santísima Trinidad **Bolívar y Palacios** (see Colombia), encouraged the peaceful transition to democracy, reinstituted freedom of the press and other personal freedoms, and legalized political parties. He enacted a three-year program for material, social, and educational improvement in July 1938, and also strove to improve the situation of labor. He requested that the presidency be a term of five years and refused to be reelected, though he personally selected Isaías **Medina Angarita** (1941–1945) as his successor.

López retired after leaving office, but participated in the overthrow of Medina Angarita in October 1945 after Medina Angarita failed to produce a smooth transition to electoral democracy. López was exiled that same year, but returned to Venezuela in 1951 with the privilege to serve as senator for life.

Lusinchi, Jaime (1924–)

Jaime Lusinchi, doctor and politician, is a member of **Democratic Action** (Acción Democrática, AD). His presidency (1984–1989) was plagued by economic crisis.

Born in Clarines, Lusinchi joined the Democratic National Party (Partido Democrático Nacional, PDN), the predecessor of AD, at the age of fifteen. While studying medicine, Lusinchi was the president of the **Federation of Students of Venezuela** (Federación de Estudiantes de Venezuela, FEV) and of the Association of Venezuelan Youth. He began practicing rural medicine in 1947 in Cantaura, was soon elected to the state Assembly, and served as head of the Assembly in 1948. Following the coup that ousted Rómulo **Gallegos Freire** (1948) in 1948, Lusinchi co-edited the publication *Resistencia*, and was arrested many times for political activities against the ruling Military Council. He was exiled in 1952, and spent time in Argentina, Chile, and the United States before returning to Venezuela after the ousting of Marcos **Pérez Jiménez** (1952–1958). He rejoined AD, served four terms as deputy to the National Congress (1958–1978), and then served as senator from 1978 to 1983. Elected president in 1983, Lusinchi led a country plagued by rising inflation and a huge external debt. A fall in oil prices during his tenure further complicated the country's economic situation. Lusinchi was succeeded by AD's Carlos Andrés **Pérez Rodríguez** (1974–1979, 1989–1993).

Medina Angarita, Isaías (1897–1953)

Isaías Medina Angarita served as president of Venezuela from 1941 to 1945, introducing a wide array of political and economic reforms before being overthrown by an impatient pro-democracy coalition of the armed forces (see **Patriotic Military Union** [Unión Patriótica Militar, UPM]) and **Democratic Action** (Acción Democrática, AD).

Medina Angarita became active in the Venezuelan military at a young age, and by 1919 was commander of the military school. He joined the Commission of Military and Naval Regulation in 1930. In April 1941, Medina Angarita was personally selected by outgoing president Eleazar **López Contreras** (1935–1941) to succeed him. As president, Medina Angarita attempted to guide Venezuela toward the democratic opening begun by López Contreras, introducing an eclectic array of reforms: he implemented Venezuela's first income tax system, improved social security, oversaw the new constitution of 1945 that produced the direct election of the Chamber of Deputies, awarded suffrage to women in municipal elections, and passed an agrarian reform law in 1945. During Medina Angarita's tenure, Venezuela also became involved in World War II, declaring war on Germany and Japan in February 1945.

Medina Angarita was overthrown by the armed forces and AD in October 1945, after his plans for a transition to democracy were complicated by factionalization within the military. For the subsequent three years, a period known as *El Trienio*, Venezuela was governed by the Revolutionary Council of Government (Consejo de Gobierno Revolucionario, CGR), with Rómulo **Betancourt** (1945–1948 as junta leader, 1959–1964) at its helm. Medina was exiled to New York in 1945 and returned to Venezuela in 1952, where he died a year later.

Movement of the Revolutionary Left (Movimiento de Izquierda Revolucionaria, MIR). See Armed Forces of National Liberation (Fuerzas Armadas de Liberación Nacional, FALN)

Pact of *Punto Fijo (Pacto de Punto Fijo)* (1958)

On October 31, 1958, following the overthrow of Marcos **Pérez Jiménez** (1952–1958) and the restoration of democracy with the election of Rómulo **Betancourt** (1945–1948 as junta leader, 1959–1964), Venezuela's three key parties agreed to a political pact in an effort to assure democratic governance and avoid future dictatorial interludes. The signatories to the agreement were **Democratic Action** (Acción Democrática, AD), the **Committee of Independent Electoral Political Organization** (Comité de Organización Política Electoral Independiente, COPEI), and the **Democratic Republican Union** (Unión Republicana Democrática, URD).

The parties agreed to act jointly in support of three points: (1) the defense of constitutionality and the discouragement of the use of force to change electoral results; (2) the formation of a coalition government in which none of the three parties had a supreme position in the executive cabinet; and (3) the presentation of a common program to the electorate.

This type of cooperation among rival political parties was very unusual in Venezuela, and very important to the strengthening of democracy in the country. Perhaps as a result of the pact, Betancourt became the first Venezuelan president in the twentieth century to finish out the term to which he had been elected. The URD pulled out of the agreement in 1962, and subsequently operated only as a marginal political party.

Patriotic Military Union (Unión Patriótica Militar, UPM)

The Patriotic Military Union (Unión Patriótica Militar, UPM) began to take shape in 1942, and was officially founded in 1945 by a group of military officers. The UPM, whose membership included Marcos **Pérez Jiménez** (1952–1958), hoped to modernize the military's structure and elevate government service by demanding credentials of honesty and justice from anyone in a leadership position. The group approached **Democratic Action** (Acción Democrática, AD) in June 1945 to propose a collaborative effort to overthrow president Isaías **Medina Angarita** (1941–1945). While the strictly democratic AD initially refused to join a coup coalition, AD finally agreed to work with the UPM. The original plan was to revolt in December 1945, but when Pérez Jiménez was arrested in October 1945, the ouster of Medina occurred later that month instead. During the three years following the coup, a period known as *El Trienio*, Venezuela was governed by the Revolutionary Council of Government (Consejo de Gobierno Revolucionario, CGR) led by Rómulo **Betancourt** (1945–1948 as junta leader, 1959–1964) of AD.

Pérez Jiménez, Marcos (1914–2001)

Marcos Pérez Jiménez took control of Venezuela in 1952 and ruled the country as a ruthless dictator for the next six years. He was forced to resign by the military in 1958 and fled the country, carrying with him much of what remained of the national treasury.

Born in Michelena, Pérez Jiménez began military school in 1934, focusing on artillery and advanced war training in Peru. He was a key organizer of the **Patriotic Military Union** (Unión Patriótica Militar, UPM) and was instrumental in that group's cooperation with **Democratic Action** (Acción Democrática, AD) in the overthrow of Isaías **Medina Angarita** (1941–1945) in October 1945. During the subsequent three-year period known as *El Trienio* (1945–1948; see **Betancourt**, Rómulo), Pérez Jiménez served as chief of staff of the army through July 1946 and as minister of defense until June 1948.

Dissatisfied with the path down which Betancourt's successor, Rómulo **Gallegos Freire** (1948), appeared to be taking the country, Pérez Jiménez led the overthrow of Gallegos in November 1948, and was a member of the military junta that subsequently ruled Venezuela under the leadership of Carlos Román Delgado Chalbaud Gómez (1948–1950). After Delgado Chalbaud's Gómez's assassination in November 1950, Pérez Jiménez helped form and served as a member of the Governing Junta of the United States of Venezuela (Junta de Gobierno de los Estados Unidos de Venezuela), which was led by Germán Suárez Flamerich (1950–1952). In December 1952, Pérez Jiménez halted the legal elections in which he was a losing candidate, seized the government, and sent leaders of AD, the **Committee of Independent Electoral Political Organization** (Comité de Organización Política Electoral Independiente, COPEI), and the **Democratic Republican Union** (Unión Republicana Democrática, URD) into exile. He manipulated the results of the April 1953 presidential election and was fraudulently elected on the ticket of his political party, the Independent Electoral Front (Frente Electoral Independiente, FEI).

As president, Pérez Jiménez monitored his opposition through a spy and police organization that jailed, exiled, tortured, or murdered any competition. He censored the press and closed the Central University in Caracas once it became a center of opposition to his regime. Pérez Jiménez used much of the nation's ever-increasing revenues from the oil industry for extravagant construction projects, ignoring health, education, and other social programs that lacked needed resources. He also accumulated a personal fortune estimated to exceed U.S. $250 million. A fraudulent plebiscite in December 1957 granted Pérez Jiménez an additional presidential term, but a joint civilian-military movement overthrew his government in January 1958. Pérez Jiménez fled to the United States but was eventually extradited to Venezuela to face charges of misuse of governmental funds and embezzlement. He was convicted and sent to prison.

While in prison, Pérez Jiménez formed the personalistic Nationalist Civic Crusade (Cruzada Cívica Nacional, CCN). Though the party never won a presidential election, Pérez Jiménez was elected senator in 1968 on the CCN ticket. The results of his senatorial election were overturned on a technicality, and he never assumed that position. Though Pérez Jiménez hoped to win the presidency again, he was prohibited from running in the 1973 presidential election by a constitutional amendment that barred convicted felons who had served more than three years in prison from holding public office. Pérez Jiménez later resided in Madrid, Spain until his death in 2001.

Pérez Rodríguez, Carlos Andrés (1922–)

Carlos Andrés Pérez Rodríguez, best known as CAP, served as president from 1974 to 1979 and from 1989 to 1993. He was later jailed on embezzlement and corruption charges.

Pérez was educated at the Central University of Venezuela, and soon joined the National Democratic Party (Partido Democrático Nacional, PDN), which became **Democratic Action** (Acción Democrática, AD) in 1941. During *El Trienio* (1945–1948), Pérez served briefly as private secretary to Rómulo **Betancourt** (1945–1948 as junta leader, 1959–1964), the leader of the Revolutionary Council of Government (Consejo de Gobierno Revolucionario, CGR) that ruled Venezuela during that period. He also served as secretary to the Council of Ministers, deputy to the legislative Assembly of Táchira in 1946, and deputy to the National Congress in 1947. After the CGR was overthrown in 1948, Pérez was imprisoned and went into exile in Costa Rica, where he worked as the chief editor of the San José daily *La República* for five years.

When Marcos **Pérez Jiménez** (1952–1958) was overthrown in January 1958, Pérez returned to Venezuela to work for AD in the state of Táchira. In 1968 Pérez became the secretary general of AD and was elected to the presidency of the nation in 1973 with 48.8 percent of the vote. During his first term as president, Pérez nationalized the steel, oil, and iron industries; established a program to send Venezuelan graduate students abroad; broadened territorial sovereignty of waters; aided in the negotiation of the **Carter/Torrijos Treaty** (see Panama) regarding the **Panama Canal** (see Panama); mediated in the Argentina/Chile dispute over the Beagle Channel (see **Videla**, Jorge Rafael, Argentina); and wrote the constitution of the Latin American Economic System (Sistema Económico Latinoamericano, SELA). Luís **Herrera Campins** (1979–1984) succeeded Pérez, who became senator for life, remaining a visible force in the Venezuelan political arena.

Pérez was reelected president in 1988 on the AD ticket and assumed the presidency in 1989, facing a country in political, social, and economic turmoil. Venezuela's role in the international drug trade was growing, and official fiscal irresponsibility had resulted in chronic economic instability. His administration's attempt to implement an economic package assembled by the International Monetary Fund (IMF) spurred massive rioting in major Venezuelan cities, which Pérez ordered be forcefully put down. Pérez never escaped his unpopularity, and weathered two coup attempts in 1992; the leader of one of those coups, Hugo Rafael **Chávez Frías** (1999–), was elected to the presidency in 1998.

In 1993 Pérez was indicted for embezzlement and corruption. He was suspended from office in May 1993, and was permanently removed from office in August 1993. He was jailed without bail in May 1994, and in 1996 was sentenced to two years and four months of house arrest. Pérez was expelled from AD in March 1997 and lost the privilege of senator for life.

Plan of Barranquilla (1931). See Federation of Students of Venezuela (Federación de Estudiantes de Venezuela, FEV)

Revolution of 1945. See Patriotic Military Union (Unión Patriótica Militar, UPM)

Revolutionary Council of Government (Consejo de Gobierno Revolucionario, CGR). See Betancourt, Rómulo; see also Patriotic Military Union (Unión Patriótica Militar, UPM)

Student Strike of 1928. See Federation of Students of Venezuela (Federación de Estudiantes de Venezuela, FEV)

El Trienio. See Betancourt, Rómulo; see also Democratic Action (Acción Democrática, AD)

Velásquez, Ramón José (1916–)

Ramón José Velásquez was a lawyer, politician, historian, and writer. He served as president from 1993 to 1994.

Born in San Juan de Colón, Velásquez began his studies in San Cristóbal and continued his university work in Caracas, receiving a doctorate in political and social sciences in 1942 and a law degree in 1943. Over the next 40 years, Velásquez wrote sporadically for various Venezuelan periodicals including *Ultimas Noticias* (*Latest News*), *El País* (*The Country*), *El Mundo* (*The World*), *El Nacional* (*The National*), and *Signo* (*Symbol*). After the overthrow of Rómulo **Gallegos Freire** (1948), Velásquez was imprisoned until 1950 for his ties to **Democratic Action** (Acción Democrática, AD). In 1953 Velásquez was incarcerated for his involvement in writing the controversial, anti-authoritarian *Libro negro de la dictadura* (*Black Book of the Dictatorship*). He used a pseudonym to write *Elite* (*Elite*) in 1955.

Released from prison in 1956, Velásquez became a senator in 1958. He founded the Historical Archive of Miraflores in 1961, subsequently undertaking the mammoth task of editing and salvaging the written history of the country. Velásquez received the María Moors Cabot Prize in 1967 for his newspaper writing, and in 1973 received the Municipal Prize for Prose for *La caída del liberalismo amarillo* (*The Fall of Yellow Liberalism*), considered by many the best political study of Venezuela. In 1974 Velásquez began a foundation dedicated to restoring and retaining books and works about Venezuela's history.

Between 1984 and 1992, Velásquez served as senator and president of the Presidential Commission for State Reform (Comisión Presidencial por la Reforma del Estado, COPRE), and later participated in the Presidential Commission for Colombian-Venezuelan Border Affairs. From 1992 to 1993, he served as an advisor to President Carlos Andrés **Pérez Rodríguez** (1974–1979, 1989–1993). When Pérez was charged with crimes of corruption in 1993 and impeached, a national election was held, and Velásquez was elected president, despite receiving only 30 percent of the vote. He served as president until 1994, when Rafael **Caldera Rodríguez** (1969–1974, 1994–1999) was reelected.

Villalba, Jóvito. See Democratic Republican Union (Unión Republicana Democrática, URN)

HEADS OF STATE

José Antonio Páez	1830–1835
José María Vargas	1835–1836
Andrés Narvarte, José María Carreño, and Carlos Soublette	1836–1839
José Antonio Páez	1839–1843
Carlos Soublette	1843–1847
José Tadeo Monagas	1847–1851
José Gregorio Monagas	1851–1855
José Tadeo Monagas	1855–1858
Julian Castro	1858–1859
Manuel Felipe Tovar	1859–1861
José Antonio Páez	1861–1863
Juan Crisóstomo Falcón	1863–1869
José Ruperto Monagas	1869–1870
Antonio Guzmán Blanco	1870–1877
Francisco Linares Alcántara	1877–1878
Antonio Guzmán Blanco	1878–1884
Joaquín Crespo	1884–1886
Antonio Guzmán Blanco	1886–1887
Hermogenes López	1887–1888
Juan Pablo Rojas Pául	1888–1890
Raimundo Andueza Palacio	1890–1892
Joaquín Crespo	1892–1898
Ignacio Andrade	1898–1899
Cipriano Castro	1899–1908
Juan Vicente Gómez	1908–1914
Victorino Márquez Bustillos	1914–1915
Juan Vicente Gómez	1915–1929
Juan Bautista Pérez	1929–1931
Juan Vicente Gómez	1931–1935
Eleazar López Contreras	1935–1941
Isaías Medina Angarita	1941–1945
Rómulo Betancourt (leader of Consejo de Gobierno Revolucionario, CGR)	1945–1948
Rómulo Gallegos Freire	1948
Carlos Román Delgado Chalbaud Gómez (leader of junta)	1948–1950

Germán Suárez Flamerich (leader of junta)	1950–1952
Marcos Pérez Jiménez	1952–1958
Wolfgang Larrazábal Ugueto (leader of junta)	1958
Edgard Sanabria Arcia	1958–1959
Rómulo Betancourt	1959–1964
Raúl Leoni	1964–1969
Rafael Caldera Rodríguez	1969–1974
Carlos Andrés Pérez Rodríguez	1974–1979
Luis Herrera Campins	1979–1984
Jaime Lusinchi	1984–1989
Carlos Andrés Pérez Rodríguez	1989–1993
Ramón José Velásquez	1993–1994
Rafael Caldera Rodríguez	1994–1999
Hugo Rafael Chávez Frías	1999–

Source: *The Political Reference Almanac* (*PoliSci.com*). http://www.polisci.com; *Innvista*. http://www.innvista.com

BIBLIOGRAPHY

Print Resources

Calvert, Peter, ed. *Political and Economic Encyclopedia of South America and the Caribbean*. London: Longman Group UK, 1991.

Coronil, Fernando. *The Magical State: Nature, Money, and Modernity in Venezuela*. Chicago: University of Chicago Press, 1997.

Ferry, Robert J. *The Colonial Elite of Early Caracas: Formation and Crisis, 1567–1767*. Berkeley: University of California Press, 1989.

Gross, Liza. *Handbook of Leftist Guerrilla Groups in Latin America and the Caribbean*. Boulder: Westview Press, 1995.

Haggerty, Richard A. *Venezuela: A Country Study*. Washington, DC: Library of Congress, 1993.

Herman, Donald L., ed. *Democracy in Latin America: Colombia and Venezuela*. New York: Praeger, 1988.

Hernández Caballero, Serafín, ed. *Gran Enciclopedia de Venezuela*. 10 vols. Caracas: Editorial Globe, 1998.

McCoy, Jennifer, ed. *Venezuelan Democracy under Stress*. New Brunswick, NJ: Transaction, 1995.

Oviedo y Baños, José de. *The Conquest and Settlement of Venezuela*. Translated by Jeannette Johnson Varner. Berkeley: University of California Press, 1987.

Rossi, Ernest E., and Jack C. Plano. *Latin America: A Political Dictionary*. Santa Barbara CA: ABC-CLIO, 1992.

Rudolph, Donna Keyse, and G. A. Rudolph. *Historical Dictionary of Venezuela*. 2nd ed. Lanham, MD: Scarecrow Press, 1996.

South America, Central America and the Caribbean 1999. London: Europa Publications, 1998.

Tannenbaum, Barbara A. *Encyclopedia of Latin American History and Culture*. 5 vols. New York: Charles Scribner's Sons, 1996.

Electronic Resources

Embassy of Venezuela in the United States
http://www.embavenez-us.org
Contains links to Venezuelan government documents, diplomatic offices, and general information on Venezuelan government, economy, and culture. (In Spanish)

Latin American Network Information Center (LANIC): Venezuela
http://lanic.utexas.edu/la/venezuela/
Venezuela section of this extensive Web site contains hundreds of links to research resources, cultural centers, economic and business institutions, government agencies, historical sources, magazines and other periodicals, nongovernmental organizations, and grassroots groups, as well as many other subjects. (In English)

Latin Focus: Venezuela
http://www.latin-focus.com/countries/venezuela.htm
Contains an overview and description of Venezuela's government institutions and political environment, economic and financial information and statistics, and links to government ministries and agencies. (In English)

Permanent Mission of Venezuela Before the Organization of American States (OAS)
http://www.venezuela-oas.org
Has links to Venezuela's government and diplomatic offices, important documents, and information on Venezuela's activities with the OAS. (In Spanish)

Political Database of the Americas: Venezuela
http://www.georgetown.edu/pdba/Countries/venezuela.html
Comprehensive database run as a joint project of Georgetown University and the Organization of American States. Section on Venezuela contains information on and links to the executive, legislative, and judicial branches of the Venezuelan government; electoral laws and election results; and other political data. (In English, Spanish, Portuguese, and French)

Political Resources.net: Venezuela
http://www.politicalresources.net/venez.htm
Venezuela section of a Web site containing a wealth of links to sources of information about national politics. Includes information on political parties, legislative and executive institutions, laws and legislation, and elections, as well as a link to the constitution. (In English)

El Universal.com
http://www.el-universal.com/
The Web version of one of Venezuela's most widely read daily newspapers. Offers national and international coverage, with a focus on national politics and the Venezuelan economy. (In Spanish)

Wilfried Derksen's Elections Around the World: Venezuela
http://www.agora.it/elections/venezuela.htm
Venezuela section of a comprehensive database of results from elections around the world. Contains results from recent national executive and legislative elections, as well as explanations of and links to political parties and institutions. (In English)

Appendix 1: Multilateral Agreements, Groupings, Organizations, and Wars

As the chapters in this volume illustrate, Latin America is far from a homogeneous entity. Each country in the region has a distinct history and culture, and a unique set of relations with and policies toward the other countries of the region and the international community in general. Further, those relations and policies have varied over time. In short, there are few patterns to which we can point; any attempt to make generalizations about the relationships among the countries of the region or about Latin American policy toward other nations and areas of the world would necessarily oversimplify regional affairs to the point of inaccuracy. The entries in this appendix, which focus on intra–Latin American dynamics and include some of the many agreements, conflicts, groupings, meetings and organizations that have existed among the countries of the region over the past two centuries, illustrate the variability, across space and time, of relations within the Latin American region.

Andean Group (Grupo Andino)

In May 1969 Colombia, Ecuador, Peru, Bolivia, and Chile signed the Andean Pact (the Agreement of Cartagena), forming the Andean Group and pledging to (1) eliminate all trade barriers among them, creating a common market; (2) establish a common external tariff on imports from outside the subregion; (3) develop a mechanism to coordinate investment and encourage specialization rather than duplication of industry; and (4) institute a common foreign (non-Andean) investment code. Venezuela joined the group in 1973, Chile withdrew from the pact in 1976, and a common external tariff was instituted by 1976. After 1976 Andean Group members substantially modified the original pact. While internal tariffs were eliminated by 1982, additional progress toward full integration was halting through the 1980s. More advancement occurred in the 1990s however. In 1991, Colombia, Venezuela, Ecuador, and Bo-

livia began reducing trade barriers and in 1993 all tariffs among them were eliminated, establishing the four countries as a free trade area. In 1995, Colombia, Ecuador, and Venezuela established a common external tariff.

Central American Common Market (CACM; Mercado Común Centroamericano, MCCA)

A series of treaties signed between 1958 and 1960 finally led to the creation of the Central American Common Market (CACM) in 1960 with the signing of the General Treaty of Central American Economic Integration (which provided for the gradual establishment of a Central American customs union and projected a series of coordinated policies) and the Convention Chartering the Central American Bank for Economic Integration. By 1963 CACM members included Costa Rica, El Salvador, Guatemala, Honduras, and Nicaragua. While the CACM was successful during its early years, increasing trade and foreign investment within the area, the grouping soon faced internal economic disagreements and serious conflict among its members. This, in addition to political conflict throughout Central America in the 1980s, ended most common market activities, and by the end of the decade, the organization had virtually dissolved.

Chaco War (1932–1935)

In the Chaco War, the only major war between Latin American states in the twentieth century, Paraguay and Bolivia fought over ownership of the Chaco Boreal, a desolate area of Paraguay near the Paraguay/Bolivia border to which both countries had made claims for centuries. Border disputes flared periodically beginning in 1927, and when rumors of vast oil deposits in the area began to circulate in 1932, full-scale war broke out. While Bolivia's population was much larger than Paraguay's, its army was mainly composed of members of the indigenous community who were not accustomed to the tropical heat of the Chaco and were not invested in the conflict. By contrast, Paraguayan soldiers were more comfortable in the climate and considered the fight a defense of their homeland. The war dragged on for three years. By the time a cease-fire was declared in 1935, Paraguay had won most of the Chaco, both countries had lost tens of thousands of soldiers, had poured significant resources into the war, and were suffering economically. Paraguay was awarded most of the disputed Chaco through the peace treaty signed in 1938.

Conference of Latin American Bishops (Conferencia Episcopal Latinoamericana, CELAM)

Latin American bishops established the Conference of Latin American Bishops (Conferencia Episcopal Latinoamericana, CELAM) in 1953. CELAM increased intraregional religious cooperation and became an important forum for debate and communication. The organization searches for common positions among bishops, issues policy statements, and offers guidance to national church officials. CELAM has held four major conferences, in Rio de Janeiro, Brazil, in 1955, in Medellín, Colombia, in 1968, in Puebla, Mexico, in 1979, and in Santo Domingo, Dominican Republic, in 1992. The church was most active in Latin American politics through the 1980s, professing its most progressive ideas, those involving liberation theology, at the Medellín and Puebla CELAM conferences.

Contadora Process (1983–1985)

Mexico, Venezuela, Colombia, and Panama established the Contadora Group in January 1983 to design a formula for a negotiated settlement of the Central American conflict; Argentina, Brazil, Peru, and Uruguay later joined in a Contadora support group. Despite U.S. opposition, in September 1983 the twenty-one–point Contadora peace plan was unveiled, and by the end of the year, five Central American nations (Costa Rica, El Salvador, Guatemala, Honduras, and Nicaragua) signed a document establishing as objectives the prohibition of support for regional insurgencies and foreign military bases, the phasing-out of foreign military advisors, the limiting of conventional military forces, and the encouragement of reconciliation among conflicting groups within each nation. While the Central American nations were poised to sign a treaty concretizing these objectives in September 1984, U.S. pressure forced a few of the nations to declare the treaty unacceptable, and the Contadora process never came to fruition. (See **Esquipulas Accords.**)

Economic Commission of Latin America and the Caribbean (ECLAC; Comisión Económica para América Latina, CEPAL)

The Economic Commission of Latin America and the Caribbean (ECLAC, or ECLA, as it is sometimes called), headquartered in Santiago, Chile, is a United Nations regional agency created in 1948 to examine Latin America's regional and country-specific economic problems. Originally led by Argentine economist Raúl Prebisch (one of the originators of dependency theory), ECLAC soon became an aggressive participant in the analysis of Latin America's relationship to the world economy. One of its most important early messages, the Prebisch-ECLA thesis, held that the world economy since 1880 had been working systematically to the disadvantage of countries that relied on the export of primary products (as most Latin American nations either had at one point, or still did). Through the early 1980s, ECLAC proposed various strategies for Latin American economic development, including import substitution industrialization (ISI) and regional integration.

Esquipulas Accords

Following the failure of the **Contadora Process** (1983–1985), the presidents of Costa Rica, El Salvador, Guatemala, Honduras, and Nicaragua, led by Costa Rican president Oscar **Arias Sánchez** (see Costa Rica), met in Esquipulas, Guatemala, in May 1986 to discuss regional problems. This meeting generated the Esquipulas Declaration (Esquipulas I), signed by all five presidents, in which they stated their intention to formalize and institutionalize the peace process and reaffirmed their commitment to that process. Arias subsequently proposed a multilateral peace plan that served as the basis for the conflict resolution effort. In August 1987 the same five Central American presidents met in Guatemala City and signed the Esquipulas Accords (Esquipulas II), more formally known as the Procedure for the Establishment of a Firm and Lasting Peace in Central America. Through that agreement, which was similar to the plan proposed through the Contadora Process, the presidents pledged to establish pluralist democratic political systems with free elections and respect for human rights, and also promised to strive for a cease-fire and national reconciliation through political dialogue in those countries experiencing armed conflict. The ambitious plan helped bring a measure of peace to the region and also won Arias the Nobel Peace Prize.

Free Trade Area of the Americas (FTAA)

The effort to unite the economies of the Western Hemisphere into a single free trade arrangement was initiated at the first **Summit of the Americas** in 1994, when the heads of state of the thirty-four democracies in the hemisphere agreed to construct a Free Trade Area of the Americas, or FTAA. Specifically, the leaders made a commitment to achieve substantial progress toward building the FTAA by 2000, and to complete negotiations for the agreement by 2005. The hemisphere's trade ministers met in June 1995 in Denver, Colorado, in March 1996 in Cartagena, Colombia, in May 1997 in Belo Horizonte, Brazil, and in March 1998 in San

José, Costa Rica, to formulate and execute a work plan for the FTAA. In March 1998 regional trade ministers agreed to the San José Declaration, which served as the basis for the launch of hemispheric trade negotiations at the Second Summit of the Americas in Santiago, Chile, in April 1998. The trade ministers met again to further negotiations in Toronto, Canada in November 1999 in advance of the third Summit of the Americas in Quebec City, Canada, in April 2001.

Gran Colombia. See **Bolívar y Palacios, Simón Antonio de la Santísima Trinidad** (Colombia)

Peru-Bolivia Confederation. See **War of the Peru-Bolivia Confederation**

Peru/Ecuador Border Conflict

Tensions and periodic open conflict between Peru and Ecuador over disputed territory in the Amazon began in the early 1800s. While the García-Herrera Treaty of 1890 divided the disputed land evenly between the struggling nations, this treaty was never ratified. In 1924 the countries appealed to the United States to arbitrate, and while a protocol was accepted in 1936, talks ended in 1938. In 1941 Peru invaded Ecuador. Ecuador's army was greatly outnumbered, and with few other options, Ecuador requested peace talks. An agreement endorsed and mediated by the United States, Brazil, Argentina, and Chile was signed in 1942. That accord, the Rio Protocol, awarded most of the disputed Amazonian territory to Peru; Ecuador was forced to give up its claim to about 80,000 square miles of land, as well as its access to the Amazon River, concessions that the nation resisted but that it was pressured to accept by the international mediators. Public outcry against the agreement in Ecuador was strong, and in 1960 Ecuador declared the treaty void. Conflict broke out again in 1995 (motivated at least in part by a desire on the part of Ecuador and Peru to divert attention from their internal political problems). Both countries mobilized troops, and it appeared that a full-fledged war might begin. However, in May 1999 the two nations finally signed an agreement clearly defining the border and bringing an end to the historical struggle.

Rio Treaty (Inter-American Treaty of Reciprocal Assistance) (1947)

Regional foreign ministers met in Rio de Janeiro in September 1947, and that conference produced the Rio Treaty, the primary source of mutual security principles and procedures in the hemisphere. Treaty signatories agreed to consider an armed attack by any country against an American nation an attack on all American nations, and pledged to collectively defend any signatory in the event of such an attack.

Soccer War (1969)

While relations between El Salvador and Honduras have historically been discordant, matters came to a head in the 1960s. Through that decade, Honduras was running large trade deficits with El Salvador under the **Central American Common Market** (CACM), and tens of thousands of Salvadorans had migrated to Honduras in search of jobs and land. However, land that could support agricultural production in Honduras was already scarce, and the increased population pressure due to the immigration of Salvadorans exacerbated that problem. Consequently, in 1968 the Honduran government issued a decree that prevented Salvadorans from gaining title to Honduran land. With these disparities and tensions as a backdrop, violence erupted in both capitals in June 1969 when the soccer teams of the two countries were engaged in a three-game elimination round in the World Cup competition. Disturbances broke out during the first game in Tegucigalpa, and violence continued to mount, sending Salvadorans streaming back to El Salvador. Honduras broke diplomatic relations with El Salvador on June 27, 1969, and early on the morning of July 14, 1969, concerted military action began with Salvadoran attacks on Honduras. The next day, the **Organization of American States** (OAS; see Appendix 2) called for an immediate cease-fire and a withdrawal of El Salvador's forces from Honduras. El Salvador resisted the OAS pressures for several days, demanding that Honduras first agree to pay reparations for the attacks on Salvadoran citizens and guarantee the safety of Salvadorans remaining in Honduras. A cease-fire was arranged on the night of July 18 and took full effect on July 20, though a peace treaty was not signed until 1980. That treaty did not resolve the conflict, however, and a border dispute continued to fester for decades. As a result of the war, between 60,000 and 130,000 Salvadorans were forcibly expelled or fled from Honduras, up to 2,000 people (the majority Honduran civilians) were killed, and thousands of Hondurans in the border area lost their homes.

Southern Cone Common Market (Mercado Común del Cono Sur, MERCOSUR)

Under the Treaty of Asunción, signed in March 1991, Argentina, Brazil, Paraguay, and Uruguay committed themselves to construct, by December 1994, a customs union with a common external tariff, and to establish a full-fledged common market in subsequent years. Through the agreement, the Southern Cone Common Market (Mercado Común del Cono Sur, MERCOSUR) nations sought to increase their competitiveness in the international economy, as well as to solidify democratic initiatives and foster regional peace. The member nations account for nearly one-half of Latin America's gross domestic product, more than 40 percent of its total population, and about one-third of its foreign trade. By the late 1990s, MERCOSUR had emerged as the largest and most successful example of regional economic cooperation in the world.

Spanish American War (1895–1898)

The Spanish American War actually began in Cuba in 1895, when José Julian **Martí y Pérez** (see Cuba) and Cuban rebels renewed their efforts to win Cuban independence from Spain, inciting a brutal rebellion. While U.S. president William McKinley did not wish to involve the United States in the conflict, the unexplained explosion of a U.S. battleship (the *Maine*) in Havana harbor in February 1898 increased tensions, and the U.S. Congress declared war against Spain in April 1898. Following initial battles in the Philippines, fighting moved to Cuba in June 1898, where a combination of land victories by Cuban and U.S. forces and a July victory over the Spanish naval fleet resulted in Spain's final surrender in August 1898. The Treaty of Paris, signed in December 1898, officially ended the Spanish American War and effectively discontinued the reign of the Spanish Empire in the Western Hemisphere by calling for Spain's withdrawal from Cuba, Puerto Rico, the Philippine Islands, and other islands in the Pacific and West Indies. The treaty placed Cuba under the trusteeship of the United States; full Cuban independence did not come until May 1902, when the United States gave control of the island to the first elected president. Puerto Rico became a possession of the United States in May 1899 and remains a commonwealth territory today. (See **Independence**, Puerto Rico; **Status issue**, Puerto Rico.)

Summits of the Americas

The leaders of the nations of the Americas have met at various times in the past half-century to forward hemispheric cooperation. Meetings of American chiefs of state occurred in Panama City, Panama, in 1956, and in Punta del Este, Uruguay, in 1967. The first Summit of the Americas was held in Miami, Florida, in December 1994. This meeting, and the 1996, 1998, and 2001 summits, were attended by the heads of state of the thirty-four democracies of the hemisphere; Cuba's Fidel **Castro Ruz** (see Cuba) did not attend. While the goal of the Miami Summit was to forge a hemispheric plan for the twenty-first century, the agenda eventually came to focus on a **Free Trade Area of the Americas** (FTAA). A Summit of the Americas on Sustainable Development took place in Santa Cruz de la Sierra, Bolivia, in December 1996, and a second Summit of the Americas took place in Santiago, Chile, in April 1998. This second summit again focused heavily on free trade, and also stressed the necessity of strengthening democracy, engaging in political dialogue, promoting economic stability, and expediting progress toward social justice. The Third Summit of the Americas was held in Quebec City, Canada, in April 2001. At that meeting, the heads of state of the Americas reaffirmed their commitment to hemispheric economic integration and issued a Plan of Action enumerating eighteen goals, including consolidating democracy in the hemisphere, developing and implementing judicial and law enforcement reforms, and strengthening civil society.

United Provinces of Central America

The area that is today Central America (with the exception of Panama) joined Mexico in declaring its independence from Spain in September 1821. Mexico emerged as an empire under Agustín Cosme Damian de **Iturbide** (see Mexico) and annexed Central America. However, in 1823 the Central American provinces held a congress at which they established the United Provinces of Central America (independent of Mexico), and in 1824 they promulgated their own constitution. Conflict among the provinces of the union soon broke out, and civil wars ensued. General Francisco **Morazán**'s (see Honduras) Liberal forces defeated Conservative federal forces in 1829, and Morazán established a dictatorship and declared himself president of the Central American Federation (another name for the same five provinces) in 1830. The violence of party politics (Liberals vs. Conservatives) coupled with localism and emerging nationalism resulted in the continuation of popular uprisings in, and civil wars among, the provinces. By 1837 Conservative forces led by José Rafael **Carrera** (see Guatemala) began to take control of the area, and in 1838 the federation Congress declared each of the member states to be sovereign, dissolving the federation and establishing five separate countries, Costa Rica, El Salvador, Guatemala, Honduras, and Nicaragua.

War of the Pacific (1879–1884)

The **War of the Triple Alliance** (1865–1870) and the War of the Pacific were the two most serious nineteenth-century international conflicts in Latin America. The War of the Pacific had its roots in the Chilean discovery, in 1866, of vast deposits of nitrates in the barren Atacama Desert, mainly in the Bolivian coastal region. The discovery turned the area into a valuable resource, and by 1870 Chileans, Bolivians, and Peruvians were all investing in operations to extract resources from the desert. (Bolivian investors lacked the capacity to effectively execute the extraction project alone.) By 1878, with Bolivia's dictator plundering the national treasury for funds to maintain his rule and the nation's fiscal situation becoming increasingly dire, the regime looked to the coastal region for new sources of funds, levying a new tax on nitrate exports. When Chilean investors, fully supported by the Chilean government, refused to pay the new tax, the Bolivian government announced that it would begin seizing property. The Chilean government responded by invading the Bolivian desert regions in February 1879, and Peru soon entered the war on the side of Bolivia (allied by an 1873 treaty). Though the Chilean military forces were outnumbered by a large margin, their naval campaign against the Peruvians was eventually successful. A series of miscalculations and poor strategy on the part of the Bolivian forces led to massive desertions from their military ranks, and their exclusion from most of the fighting by 1880. Chileans pushed the lone Peruvian forces northward and eventually sacked and occupied Lima. Following unsuccessful U.S. and European attempts at mediation, Chile finally defeated the Bolivia-Peruvian alliance. The Ancón Treaty, signed in October 1883 by Chile and Peru, called for Peru's permanent ceding of the province of Tarapacá to Chile and allowed Chile to occupy the Peruvian provinces of Tacna and Arica for ten years. (The dispute over these areas was finally resolved in 1929 when Chile annexed Arica and returned Tacna to Peru.) A truce signed between Chile and Bolivia in April 1884 provided for an indefinite armistice and for Chilean occupation of the Bolivian portion of the Atacama. A treaty formally ending the war was signed in October 1904, through which Bolivia lost that land, and thus its coastline and access to the sea. As a result of the war, Chilean territory was substantially expanded, and its nitrate revenues significantly increased.

War of the Peru-Bolivia Confederation (1836–1839)

After an attempt by Peruvian leader Agustín Gamarra to intervene in Bolivian affairs, Bolivian general Andrés de **Santa Cruz** (see Bolivia) invaded Peru, which was engulfed in a civil war, and annexed it to Bolivia, establishing the Peru-Bolivia Confederation (Confederación Perú-Boliviana) in 1835. He quickly enacted reforms in the new territory similar to those he had successfully implemented in Bolivia. Both Argentina and Chile opposed the alliance, as it represented a concentration of power that posed an economic and military threat to their continued independence. Chile declared war against the confederation in 1836, and Argentina did the same the following year (though the Argentines played a minor military role). The Chilean military invaded Peru in 1838 and, though it was initially over-powered by Bolivian troops in Peru, eventually defeated the combined Peru-Bolivian army in 1839, bringing an end to the confederation.

War of the Triple Alliance (Paraguayan War) (1865–1870)

The War of the Triple Alliance and the **War of the Pacific** were the two most important international conflicts in Latin America in the nineteenth century. The War of the Triple Alliance grew out of internal conflict in Uruguay between the Colorados (see **Colorado Party** [Partido Colorado, PC], Uruguay) and the Blancos (see **National Party** [Partido Nacional, Blanco Party], Uruguay). By the late 1850s, Brazilians had gained a financial and commercial foothold in Uruguay, and on several occasions Brazilian troops participated in domestic Uruguayan battles on the side of the Colorados. However, despite Brazilian and later Argentine backing, the Colorados lost control in Uruguay, and the victorious Blancos turned to Paraguayan leader Mariscal Francisco **Solano López** (see Paraguay) for support. Solano López, who needed greater land and population resources in order to maintain his military state, aided the Blancos, intending simultaneously to gain control of the upper Paraná River and parts of Brazil. Increasing foreign involvement in Uruguay soon led to direct military confrontation between Brazil and Paraguay: Solano López invaded both Argentina and Brazil in 1865, pushing Argentines, Brazilians and the Uruguayan Colorados into a triple alliance. The Paraguayan army proved to be well-trained, extremely disciplined, and courageous, and it took five years for the three-nation alliance to overpower the Paraguayan-Uruguayan Blanco partnership. Paraguay eventually conceded defeat after the death of Solano López, and in June 1870, Brazil, Argentina, and Paraguay signed an accord that ended the conflict. The war had important consequences: access to the Plata River network was guaranteed, Argentina and Brazil consolidated strong relations, Brazil cemented its position (economic and political) in Uruguay, and Paraguay was left in ruins, having lost a significant percentage of its population and portions of its territory.

Appendix 2: U.S. Policy in Latin America and U.S.-Based Inter-American Organizations

U.S. policy toward Latin America has passed through a number of distinct phases, from the paternalistic period of the early 1800s, marked by policies such as the **Monroe Doctrine** (1823), to the Pan American Movement of the mid-1800s, to the interventionist period of the late 1800s and early 1900s, to the era of the **Good Neighbor Policy** in the mid-1900s, to the United States' Cold War–influenced involvement in the region following World War II, to its more strategic and issue-based participation in regional affairs in the late twentieth century. U.S.-Latin American relations have in fact been characterized by a pattern: long periods of equanimity punctuated by brief, intense intervals of U.S. involvement in the domestic affairs of the countries of the Americas—periodic shifts from cooperation to conflict. The U.S. government has traditionally emphasized that its policy toward the region represented (and represents) an attempt to promote democracy. However, others have interpreted U.S. policy as an effort to influence the internal affairs of the countries of the region in the interest of maintaining political stability in, and preventing the spread of foreign influence through, the Americas. Regardless of how one evaluates U.S. policy toward the region, as described in the entries in this appendix and throughout this volume, it is indisputable that the United States has historically played a major role in Latin American politics.

Alliance for Progress (1960s)

U.S. president John F. Kennedy (1961–1963) announced the Alliance for Progress, a plan to revitalize economic, social, and political development in Latin America over a ten-year period, in March 1961. The plan was, in large part, a response to the success of the **Cuban Revolution of 1959** (see Cuba), and the shift in Soviet policy in the mid-1950s toward increasing economic aid to the underdeveloped world and in particular to revolutionary movements. The Alliance was made multilateral when U.S. and Latin American leaders met at Punta del Este, Uruguay in August 1961 and approved a declaration of ninety-four specific economic and social objectives. The United States agreed to contribute (principally in public funds) a major part of the minimum $20 billion needed to execute the plan. Despite the investment of much money and effort, the program accomplished far less than its founders had hoped, and by 1970 excitement over the Alliance in the United States and Latin America had greatly diminished.

Baker Plan (1985)

Named for U.S. secretary of the treasury James Baker (during the second administration of U.S. president Ronald Reagan, 1981–1985, 1985–1989), this plan was introduced to address Latin America's economic problems. The plan proposed that private lending institutions give the countries of the region the necessary funds to get back on track and to stimulate economic growth. However, as the region's continuing economic crisis had made clear, Latin American economies had to be fundamentally restructured in order to prevent the recurrence of similar problems. Private banks consequently rejected the plan, as it lacked any explicit requirement for reform. (See **Brady Plan.**)

Benign Neglect (1969–1977)

Benign neglect generally refers to U.S. policy toward Latin America under U.S. presidents Richard Nixon (1969–1974) and Gerald Ford (1974–1977), though the term also accurately describes U.S. policy toward the region at various other points during the nineteenth and twentieth centuries. Nixon sought to lower the profile and reduce the presence of the United States in Latin America by establishing a "mature partnership" through which the United States responded to Latin American assertiveness by cutting back U.S. programs and toning down U.S. rhetoric. The 1973 Arab oil embargo refocused Washington's attention on the developing world, and prompted the Ford administration to call for a "new dialogue" with Latin America; nonetheless, top officials in the U.S. government still paid little sustained attention to the region through the mid-1970s, apparently believing, as officials under Nixon had seemed to, that Latin America counted for little in the context of superpower geopolitics generated by the Cold War.

Brady Plan (1989)

The Brady Plan, named for U.S. secretary of the treasury Nicholas Brady (under U.S. president George Bush, 1989–1993), was a program to address Latin America's economic crisis. Through the plan, commercial banks reduced by 20 to 35 percent the commercial debt owed by some Latin American debtor countries; the issuing of "Brady Bonds" provided banks with the guarantees of governments and international financial institutions on the remaining debt. In return, participating Latin American countries were required to implement economic reform, under the tutelage of international financial institutions like the International Monetary Fund (IMF) and according to a market-oriented policy framework that came to be known as the **Washington Consensus**. Latin American countries with relatively large commercial debt took advantage of the Brady Plan, including Argentina, Brazil, Costa Rica, the Dominican Republic, Ecuador, Mexico, Nicaragua, Panama, Peru and Uruguay. The plan enjoyed gradual success as reforms deepened. (See also **Baker Plan**.)

Caribbean Basin Initiative (CBI) (1983)

In 1981 U.S. president Ronald Reagan (1981–1989) offered a model economic development program for Central America and the Caribbean, the Caribbean Basin Initiative (CBI), a one-way free trade agreement that permitted the nations of the Caribbean Basin to export some products duty-free to the United States. The program reflected the administration's belief that economic development was a key tool in fighting the spread of communism. Reagan announced the CBI before the **Organization of American States** (OAS) in February 1982, but the program received a cool reception, as many considered its policies were too weak to bring the Caribbean economies out of their deep doldrums. The U.S. Congress also failed to support the program, as U.S. business and labor groups had the power to block trade preferences and tax incentives for foreign investment abroad. The version of the CBI that Congress finally passed in December 1983 had little impact on the region.

Carter Doctrine (1977–1981)

Emphasis on the protection of human rights was the cornerstone of U.S. president Jimmy Carter's (1977–1981) Latin American policy. Carter threatened to cut foreign aid to any country that continued to abuse its citizens and stopped military aid to El Salvador, Guatemala, and Nicaragua. The Carter administration hoped to define a new relationship with Latin America, based on the recommendations of two reports issued by the Commission on U.S.–Latin American Relations (a private, bipartisan group established in 1974), which emphasized the world's increasing interdependence and Latin America's desire for independence. Carter's foreign policy toward the region deemphasized paternalism, and sought to pursue pro-democratic and anti-interventionist goals rather than anticommunist ones. (Contrast with **intervention; Reagan Doctrine**.)

Cuban Missile Crisis (1962). See Cuba

Dollar Diplomacy (1909–1913)

Dollar diplomacy refers to the foreign policy toward Latin America employed by the administration of U.S. president William Howard Taft (1909–1913). Taft aggressively sought to spread U.S. influence and ensure economic and political stability in Latin America by promoting, expanding, and protecting U.S. investments and financial, banking, and business interests in the region. Under this policy, which led to a pattern of **intervention**, businessmen joined militia commanders and civilian politicians in promoting U.S. foreign policy and solidifying the U.S. hold on the hemisphere. (See, for instance, **National Guard**, Nicaragua.)

Drugs (1980s and 1990s)

During most of the 1980s, U.S. policymakers viewed drug trafficking and drug usage as primarily criminal and health issues, and the majority of Latin American and Caribbean leaders either neglected the questions or saw them as U.S. problems that should be resolved by U.S. officials. By 1990, however, many U.S. and Latin American leaders had begun to consider drug production, smuggling, and abuse as significant threats to national security and societal well-being throughout the hemisphere. Today, narcotrafficking is one of the most significant issues in U.S.–Latin American relations. While the issue is two-sided (it includes both the consumption and production of drugs), U.S. efforts have centered on the "supply" side rather than on the "demand" side. Those efforts, which have infrequently attempted real cooperation with the nations of Latin America or the Caribbean, have been largely ineffective in stemming the production in South America, the trafficking through Central America, the Caribbean, and Mexico, or the consumption in the United States of illegal narcotics. (See **Drug Trade**, Bolivia; **Drugs**, Colombia; **Drugs/Drug Trafficking**, Peru.)

Enterprise for the Americas Initiative (EAI) (1990s)

Announced by U.S. president George Bush (1989–1993) in June 1990, the Enterprise for the Americas Initiative

(EAI) was the centerpiece of the Bush administration's new approach to Latin America. Labeled "a new partnership for trade, investment and growth" by the White House, the initiative was seen by many as emblematic of U.S. interest in forging a more cooperative, constructive, and mutually beneficial relationship with Latin America. The initiative included three main projects: it expanded on the **Brady Plan** by advocating the reduction/restructuring of debt owed to the U.S. government by the countries of Latin America; promised those countries that successfully liberalized their economies unprecedented access to the U.S. market and a significant comparative advantage in attracting needed investment capital; and proposed free trade with Latin America through the establishment of a hemispheric free trade zone (see **Free Trade Area of the Americas**, Appendix 1).

Good Neighbor Policy (1933–1945)

The Good Neighbor Policy refers to U.S. foreign policy toward Latin America during the administration of U.S. president Franklin D. Roosevelt (1933–1945). The cornerstone of the policy, which brought a new spirit of cooperation to hemispheric relations, was U.S. nonintervention in the internal political affairs of other American republics (even for the promotion of democracy). In fact, Roosevelt's first two administrations were marked by what appeared to be a withdrawal of U.S. interest from the region. World War II forced the United States to take a more active stance however, and it began to openly cooperate with all stable regimes in Latin America, dictatorships and democracies, that opposed the Axis powers (see **Inter-American Defense Board**). (Contrast with **Dollar Diplomacy; intervention; Missionary Diplomacy; Roosevelt Corollary to the Monroe Doctrine**.)

Gunboat Diplomacy (1913–1921). See Missionary Diplomacy

Inter-American Defense Board (Washington, D.C.)

In view of the expanding geographical reach of World War II, in January 1942 the United States called for a consultative meeting of the foreign ministers of Latin America and the Caribbean in Rio de Janeiro, Brazil to encourage hemispheric solidarity. The United States won the cooperation of all of the attending nations (with the exception of Chile and Argentina), and various resolutions were passed through which Latin America pledged its support for the United States. One such resolution provided for military cooperation for the defense of the hemisphere, and to this end, the Inter-American Defense Board was established in Washington in March 1942 under U.S. auspices. While the actual military contribution made by Latin America to the Allied war effort was limited, wartime cooperation between the United States and Latin America helped to improve subsequent hemispheric relations.

Inter-American Development Bank (IDB; Banco Interamericano de Desarrollo, BID)

The Inter-American Development Bank (IDB) was established in April 1959 with $1 billion in capital, of which the United States supplied 45 percent and the nations of Latin America 55 percent. The original mandate of the organization, headquartered in Washington, D.C., was to act as a lending institution providing low-interest loans for modernization projects in Latin America. Through the 1970s, loans and advice from the IDB and the World Bank gradually came to supplant U.S. aid, and those multilateral lending institutions became the principal vehicles for the external promotion of development in Latin America. This change permitted a gradual reorientation of U.S.–Latin American relations toward hemispheric cooperation. Nonetheless, albeit to a lesser degree, the United States continued to use its aid, and its influence over multilateral lending institutions such as the IDB, to pursue its own interests in the region.

Intervention (nineteenth and twentieth centuries)

Intervention is defined as interference in the domestic affairs of a country for the purpose of altering the conditions in that country. The United States has intervened in the nations of Latin America and the Caribbean in direct and indirect ways, generally with the stated purpose of promoting stability and democracy in the region, on many occasions. The United States has used a variety of methods to influence politics in the region, including military occupations, applying economic sanctions, awarding and withholding aid and investment, providing arms and military funding, and granting and denying diplomatic recognition, among others. U.S. intervention in the region, and the region's rejection of U.S. intervention and continued reverence for the principle of nonintervention, have been the axis around which U.S.–Latin American relations have revolved for most of the twentieth century. (See, for example, **Bay of Pigs Invasion**, Cuba; **U.S. Intervention**, Haiti; **Arbenz Guzmán**, Jacobo, Guatemala; **Counterrevolutionaries** [contrarevolucionarios, contras], Nicaragua; **United States Occupation**, Dominican Republic.)

Missionary Diplomacy (1913–1921)

U.S. president Woodrow Wilson (1913–1921) saw the promotion of democracy in the hemisphere as a moral duty of the dominant power (the United States) and of "good men" in Latin America. Believing that Latin Americans could be "civilized" through democracy, and in a quest to "teach the South Americans to elect good men," in 1913 Wilson announced that he would withdraw or refuse to award U.S. diplomatic recognition to unconstitutional and/or revolutionary governments in Latin America. In reality, this "Wilson Doctrine" was employed selectively. The United States intervened in Latin America, primarily in the Caribbean Basin, on many occasions under Wilson, earning the president's policy in the region the nickname "gunboat diplomacy." In many cases, U.S. **intervention** did more to solidify dictatorial regimes than to encourage the practice of constitutional governance. (See, for example, **U.S. Intervention**, Haiti; **United States Occupation**, Dominican Republic; **Sandino Calderón**, Augusto César, Nicaragua.)

Monroe Doctrine (1823)
Enunciated by U.S. president James Monroe (1817–1825) in December 1823, the Monroe Doctrine issued a warning against any new colonial incursions in the Western Hemisphere and served notice that any threat to the new republics of Latin America would be viewed as a threat to the United States. The Monroe Doctrine, which introduced the United States into the mainstream of international power politics, formed the basis for much subsequent U.S. policy in the region, and is viewed by many as the most basic statement of U.S.-Latin American relations.

Organization of American States (OAS; Organización de Estados Americanos, OEA)
Capitalizing on improved hemispheric cooperation brought about by World War II (see **Inter-American Defense Board**), regional foreign ministers agreed, at a 1945 meeting in Mexico City, Mexico, to redesign the Pan-American system. The first step was the approval of the **Rio Treaty** for collective security (see Appendix 1) in 1947. The second step was the creation of the Organization of American States (OAS) in Bogotá, Colombia, in March 1948. The statutes of the organization, headquartered in Washington, D.C., include a legal charter stipulating that a council to deal with day-to-day business would be formed, that inter-American conferences would be held every five years, and that foreign ministers' consultative meetings would be called on an ad hoc basis to handle threats to the hemisphere. Member states committed themselves to continental solidarity and absolute nonintervention, as well as democracy, economic cooperation, social justice, and human rights. The record of the OAS in terms of resolving regional issues in the past half-century has been mixed, and many criticize the organization as overly bureaucratized and ineffective.

Platt Amendment (1901–1934). See Cuba

Reagan Doctrine (1981–1989)
In the 1980s U.S. president Ronald Reagan (1981–1989) moved U.S. foreign policy initiatives away from an emphasis on human rights (see **Carter Doctrine**) and

back toward assuring stability and containing communism in the Western Hemisphere. Reagan believed that U.S. security interests were directly threatened by communists operating in Central America with the support of Cuba and the Soviet Union. In an attempt to prevent communist rebels from gaining power, the United States strengthened its presence in the region and supplied large amounts of economic and military aid to its allies in Central America (see **counterrevolutionaries** [contrarevolucionarios, contras], Nicaragua; **Duarte Fuentes**, José Napoleon, El Salvador). In addition, in the early 1980s the Reagan administration rebuilt diplomatic and military ties with the military governments of Argentina, Brazil, and Chile, though Reagan also offered diplomatic support to the new democratic governments that began to emerge in South America later in the decade.

Roosevelt Corollary to the Monroe Doctrine (1904)
Faced with the possibility of European intervention in Latin America, in 1904 U.S. president Theodore Roosevelt (1901–1909) enunciated a policy that reflected both the new realities of U.S. power and the president's own belief that the United States should wield a "big stick" in foreign policy. The Roosevelt Corollary surpassed the mainly defensive Monroe Doctrine (1823), asserting the responsibility of the United States to bring political and financial order to the hemisphere, and maintaining that in some instances the United States might serve as an international policing agent in the Western Hemisphere. This corollary, which was used to justify many U.S. **interventions** in the Caribbean and Central America, remained the backbone of U.S. policy in Latin America until the implementation of U.S. president Franklin D. Roosevelt's (1933–1945) **Good Neighbor Policy**.

School of the Americas
The Latin American Training Center—Ground Division was established in 1946 in the Panama Canal Zone (see **Panama Canal**, Panama). It was renamed the U.S. Army School of the Americas in July 1963. Under the provisions of the 1977 **Carter-Torrijos Treaty** (see Panama) regarding the Panama Canal, the school was relocated to Fort Benning, Georgia, in October 1984 and designated an official U.S. Army training and doctrine command school. This U.S.-operated and -financed institution trains military forces from Latin America in combat, human rights awareness, marksmanship, civilized interrogation techniques, counterinsurgency, and counter-narcotics. The school is controversial: its critics cite evidence that its graduates or attendees have been heavily involved in human rights abuses upon their return to their home countries, while the school itself insists that since its inception, it has promoted the professionalization of the armed forces in Latin America, including military subordination to civil authority.

Washington Consensus (1990s)

The Washington Consensus refers to a list of ten policy recommendations for economic reform compiled and articulated by U.S. economist John Williamson in 1989. The ten policies are (1) increasing fiscal discipline; (2) redirecting public expenditure; (3) implementing tax reform; (4) implementing financial liberalization; (5) adopting a single, competitive exchange rate; (6) implementing trade liberalization; (7) eliminating barriers to foreign direct investment; (8) privatizing state-owned enterprises; (9) deregulating market entry and competition; and (10) ensuring secure property rights. The general philosophy behind the Consensus is that once governments effectively deal with these issues, private markets will allocate resources efficiently and generate growth. The policies suggested by the Consensus formed the basis for many of the economic reform strategies designed and encouraged by multilateral lending organizations, and implemented in Latin America, during the 1990s.

Glossary

Agrarian reform. The traditional inequitable distribution of land in Latin America has engendered continual popular frustration, which some Latin American governments have attempted to diffuse (with varying degrees of success) through implementing agrarian reform. This process entails a change in land ownership, often accomplished through government seizure of large portions of land from the privately held estates of the traditional land-owning classes for redistribution to the peasantry.

Audiencia. In the early colonial period, it quickly proved impossible for the viceroys in the New World appointed by the Spanish royalty to single-handedly lead the two vast areas into which Spanish America was initially divided (the viceroyalty of New Spain and the viceroyalty of Peru). Consequently in the 1500s the Spanish government (in Spain) created a series of councils, called *audiencias.* These bodies assisted and advised the viceroys, helped them to carry their authority far from the two viceregal capitals of the time, and also functioned as regional courts of appeal.

Bourbon Reforms. The Bourbon monarchs of Spain, seeking to reverse Spain's decline and strengthen New World defenses against rival European powers while increasing revenues for the crown, imposed far-reaching administrative and political reforms in the mid- to late 1700s. These included the creation of new viceroyalties, the appointment of intendants (local governors directly responsible to the crown), the tightening of royal control of the Catholic Church, the establishment of colonial militias, and the opening of trade among the twenty-four ports of Spanish America, and from any of those ports directly with any port in Spain. While these policies led to more efficient colonial administration, improved defense, and a flourishing colonial economy, they also threatened the status and influence of creoles in Spanish America, hastening independence movements in the New World.

Bureaucratic authoritarianism. Argentine political scientist Guillermo O'Donnell first described the governing strategy of the military regimes that ruled Argentina, Brazil, Chile, and Uruguay in the 1970s as bureaucratic author-itarianism. These regimes were politically exclusionary and brutally repressive. They adopted a monetarist approach to economic policy, and integrated their national economies into the international economic system with the goal of fostering economic development. The proponents of bureaucratic authoritarianism (technocrats allied with the military) considered military rule a long-term alternative to civilian rule, rather than a temporary intervention to restore stability.

Caudillismo. While the term *caudillo* simply means "chief" or "leader," it often applies specifically to the strongmen who led the newly formed nations of Spanish America, or particular areas of those new nations, immediately after independence. *Caudillos* combined personalism and force to gain and retain power. Although the "typical" *caudillo* is depicted as a repressive dictator of rural origin who based his power on the control of informal military force, in fact the *caudillos* who ruled Spanish America in the early nineteenth century differed significantly from each other in terms of their origins and the way in which they exercised power.

Christian Base Communities (Comunidades Eclesiales de Base, CEBs). The "crisis of development" that Latin America experienced in the 1960s and 1970s and the subsequent emergence in some countries of authoritarian regimes led to the flourishing of Christian Base Communities (Comunidades Eclesiales de Base, CEBs) in the 1970s and 1980s. While CEBs originated in and maintained some linkage to the institutional church, they were created by Christians without prior action by the church hierarchy. These small groups, usually homogeneous in social composition (based on class and neighborhood or village), gathered regularly to read and comment on the Bible. A minority of CEBs were seedbeds of a new, democratic culture and social order and advocated norms that legitimated equality and the promotion of justice; these CEBs played an important role in religious and political change in Latin America.

Civil society. The set of intermediate associations that are neither the state nor the family. Civil society includes voluntary associations (interest groups, social movements, community groups), firms, and other corporate bodies through which citizens can obtain the benefits of democracy and hold government accountable for its obligation to the people. An engaged and active civil society is considered by many to be fundamental to democracy.

Cold War (1945–1991). Refers to the period of intense conflict between the United States and the Soviet Union after World War II. Following World War II, the United States and the Soviet Union emerged as the world's two leading powers, with the Soviet Union promoting communism (its political and economic system) and the United States promoting capitalism and democracy. Each superpower had a sphere of influence: the Soviet Union retained influence in the countries of Eastern Europe, while Western Europe and Latin America fell into the camp of the United States. By 1987 the two superpowers had moved decisively back toward cooperation, and by 1991 the Soviet Union—and communism—had collapsed. The war is referred to as "cold" because it involved no direct military battles between the United States and the Soviet Union.

Communism. A process of social class conflict and revolutionary struggle resulting in the victory of the proletariat (a class of wage earners in a capitalist society that lives solely by its labor power and which, unlike the bourgeoisie, neither profits from capital nor owns the means of production) and the establishment of a classless, socialist society in which private ownership has been abolished and the means of production and subsistence belong to the community.

Coronelismo. *Coronelismo* in Brazil (similar to *caudillismo* in Spanish America) refers to the tradition of influential politicians using rural political bosses to control townspeople and peasants. In return for the local population's obedience, the *coronel* was responsible for that population's well-being. Some set up small armies, or hired backland outlaws (*cangeçeiros*) to protect them. After the overthrow of the monarchy (1889), *coronéis* (plural of *coronel*) ensured votes for politicians in return for favors. The power of the *coronéis* in north and northeastern Brazil remained strong from the mid-1800s to about 1940, when wide-scale urbanization and government centralization undermined their power.

Corporatism. A system of interest intermediation vertically linking producer interests (at the base) and the state (at the top) in which explicitly recognized interest organizations (such as labor unions or peasant associations) are incorporated into the policy-making process, both in terms of the negotiation of policy and of securing compliance from their members with the agreed upon policy. Corporatism stresses the hierarchical organization of modern institutions and top-down control.

Coup (*coup d'etat*). See *Golpe de estado.*

Creoles (*criollos*). Spaniards born in the New World.

Debt crisis. In 1982 the administration of Mexican president José **López Portillo y Pacheco** (see Mexico) declared that Mexico was unable to pay back its external debts. This declaration contributed to the initiation of the debt crisis that unfolded throughout Latin America in the 1980s.

During that time, known as the region's "lost decade," many Latin American nations struggled with severe economic strife, high inflation and hyperinflation, devalued currencies, and limited external financing. The United States introduced the **Baker Plan** (1985; see Appendix 2) and the **Brady Plan** (1989; see Appendix 2) to help address Latin America's economic problems. The crisis was relieved and Latin American economies stabilized only after debt forgiveness, economic restructuring, and the implementation of strict economic plans. (See **Washington Consensus**, Appendix 2.)

Decentralization. The dispersion or distribution of the functions and powers of government from the national (federal) level to regional and/or local authorities. (See also **Federalism.**)

Dependency theory. An explanation of Latin American underdevelopment that emerged in the 1960s. Dependency theory proposed that the distribution of power and status in national and international arenas was ultimately determined by economic relationships, that underdevelopment was caused by the pattern of economic relations between the world's more developed and less developed economies, and that the uncontrolled forces of the marketplace tended to exacerbate existing inequalities. Most of the theory's proponents believed that only by breaking out of the international capitalist system and establishing socialist regimes could the nations of Latin America expand the options available to them and achieve economic growth and development.

Los desaparecidos (**the disappeared**). The name given to those who suddenly "disappeared" in some Latin American countries during the 1960s, 1970s, and 1980s as a result of military or paramilitary actions designed to destroy leftist forces that were perceived to be a threat to the state. The term eventually came to refer to anyone who had disappeared and who it was assumed had died at the hands of the military dictatorships that ruled many nations of the region during that time period. (See, for example, Argentina, Brazil, Chile.)

Dollarization. An economic measure through which a country's national currency is replaced with the U.S. dollar. (See, for example, **Noboa Bajarano**, Gustavo, Ecuador.)

Drug trade. See **Narcotrafficking**

Encomienda **system.** The system whereby indigenous people were "distributed" among Spanish colonists and required to work or supply a tribute in goods or cash, in return for protection and education regarding Christianity and the Spanish way of life. In practice, few Spaniards fulfilled their part of the bargain, and the *encomienda* ("entrustment") system often became an oppressive means of forcing the indigenous population to work for the colonists. As a labor institution, the *encomienda* system was significant chiefly during the sixteenth century (the first century of Spain's colonial rule).

Extradition. The surrender of an alleged criminal (usually under the provisions of a treaty or statute) by one country, state, or other authority to another having jurisdiction to try the charge against the alleged criminal.

Federalism. A method of arranging government and accommodating national and sub-national (regional, provincial, or state) interests by combining all those interests within a complex web of checks and balances between a federal (national) government and a multiplicity of sub-national governments. Countries employing federalism hope to avoid both the perceived overcentralization of unitary systems and the extreme decentralization of confederation.

Golpe de estado (*coup d'état*). Usually carried out by the armed forces or some faction of the military, a *golpe de estado* is the sudden, forcible, and illegal removal of one government, and often the installation of another that may or may not be military, and may or may not count on some degree of civilian collaboration. Such rapid political change is generally preceded by widespread and prolonged unrest, and precipitated by more immediate grievances bearing directly on the military. *Golpes de estado* generally focus on the amelioration of a specific or immediate issue, and rarely contribute to the resolution of long-term social and economic problems. (For an exceptional case, see **Pinochet Ugarte**, Augusto, Chile.)

Gross domestic product (GDP). The value (at market price) of all final goods and services produced within a country.

Gross national product (GNP). The value (at market price) of all final goods and services produced by domestically owned factors of production, either domestically or abroad, within a given period. *Nominal GNP* measures the value of output in a given period in the prices of that period (or in "current dollars"). *Real GNP* measures the value of output in any given period in "constant dollars" (presently in the prices of 1992 or 1996).

Guerrilla movements. Through the 1960s and 1970s, guerrilla movements emerged and grew in several Latin American countries. Some were inspired by Marxist ideologies and spawned by communist or socialist movements, and others formed after splitting from populist movements. Most active in the countryside, these movements waged armed struggle (characterized by sporadic violent engagements with national armies rather than by clearly defined battles), demanding sociopolitical transformation and generally aiming to discredit and challenge the power of the state rather than defeat the government and take power themselves. Guerrilla movements persist in several Latin American countries. (See, for instance, **Shining Path** [Sendero Luminoso], Peru; **Farabundo Martí National Liberation Front** [Frente Farabundo Martí para la Liberación Nacíonal, FMLN], El Salvador; **Sandinista National Liberation Front** [Frente Sandinista de Liberación Nacional, FSLN], Nicaragua.)

Hacienda system. The most striking single change in the economic system of the Spanish colonies in Latin America was the change from the *encomienda* system to the hacienda system, or from estates based formally on tribute and labor rights to estates based formally on land ownership. The hacienda (or large landed estate) began to be the dominant form of agricultural enterprise through the seventeenth and eighteenth centuries, and the system expanded and consolidated during the nineteenth century. The hacienda, both a capitalist and feudal enterprise, was a self-contained social, economic, political, and religious unit, with its tenants and peasants caught in a system of peonage that differed little from earlier slavery.

Hyperinflation. Hyperinflation refers to a rapid increase in prices on the domestic market that usually leads households to abstain from making purchases. A country is generally considered to be experiencing hyperinflation when its inflation rate tops 50 percent per month or 1,000 percent per annum, as it did in many Latin American countries in the 1980s. In the Latin American context, hyperinflation has most often been caused by a combination of factors, including countries' inability to pay back foreign debt (which has frequently led to high rates of money creation), decreases in export prices (leading to a large fall in real income and government revenues), and capital flight due to political instability.

Import-substitution industrialization (ISI). The Great Depression had a crushing effect on the economies of Latin America, leading some countries to implement an economic development model called import-substitution industrialization (ISI) during the subsequent decades. ISI entailed producing domestic goods previously imported from the United States and Europe (thus decreasing Latin American countries' economic dependence on the developed world, and creating jobs for the Latin American working classes), and increasing regional economic integration and self-sufficiency to make the economies of the countries of Latin America less vulnerable to external shocks. The model failed in most Latin American nations: domestic demand for the goods produced through ISI was restricted, ISI produced a limited number of jobs for workers, and ISI only altered (not decreased) the dependency of Latin American economies on industrialized nations.

Indigenous population. Refers to both the native populations of Latin America encountered by the Spanish and Portuguese colonizers in the late 1400s and 1500s and to the descendants of those populations, who still live in the region today. These people are also referred to as Indians.

International Monetary Fund (IMF). The Bretton Woods agreement, a pact signed by forty-four countries in July 1944 toward the end of World War II, established an international monetary and payments system. It was agreed that primary responsibility for the regulation of monetary relationships among national economies, of private financial flows, and of balance of payments adjustment should rest in the hands of public multilateral institutions and national governments with a view to underpinning a cooperative international economic order. The IMF and its sister institution, the International Bank for Reconstruction and Development (IBRD or World Bank) were the multilateral institutions anticipated by the agreement. The IMF played a major role in Latin America in the 1980s during the region's debt crisis, and today continues to be important in promoting economic stability and development in the region.

Junta. Though this Spanish term literally means "council," it usually refers to a council, often made up of members of the military, that rules a country following a *golpe de estado* (*coup d'etat*) before constitutional rule is restored. In Latin America, juntas are often formed by the chiefs of the army, air force, and navy.

Labor movements. Labor movements, comprising organized groups such as unions, have played an influential role in politics in many Latin American nations by voicing the concerns of the working class through protesting, and pressuring political parties. In some instances, political parties have attempted to ally with strong and inclusive labor movements in an attempt to gain favor with and advocate for members of that movement. (See, for instance, **Justicialist Party** [Partido Justicialista, PJ, also Peronist Party], Argentina; **Workers Party** [Partido dos Trabalhadores, PT] Brazil.)

Latifundio. In Latin America, the land that was distributed by the crown immediately after the Spanish conquest was used to produce goods for domestic and foreign markets, and was also a foundation for social control by a privileged class. The nineteenth century witnessed the expansion of cultivation for export, and the consequent growth in size, importance, and power of *latifundios*, huge (and often inefficient) landed estates that generally produced for the export market and that grew at the expense of the indigenous communities, peasants, and small landowners. *Latifundio* owners often used only a fraction of their extensive land holdings, keeping large amounts of acreage under their domination in order to control labor.

Liberation theology. The Latin American Catholic Church changed significantly in the late twentieth century, influenced by papal encyclicals, the tone of and documents produced during the Second Vatican Council (1963–1965), and the conferences of Latin American bishops held in Colombia (1968) and Mexico (1979) (see **Conference of Latin American Bishops** [Conferencia Episcopal Latinoamericana, CELAM], Appendix 1). Liberation theology, one of the major (and controversial) developments in the history of the Catholic Church in Latin America, emerged in the early 1960s. This theology, which stresses the equality of all believers (lay people as well as clerics and bishops), holds that the church is of and for this world and should take a stance against repression and violence, particularly "institutionalized violence" (the life-demeaning and -threatening violence experienced by the poor), and encourages the poor to lift themselves out of the destitution in which man, not God, has placed them. The theology was embraced by clerics to varying degrees across and within the countries of the region.

Mercantilism. An economic conception held by many Spanish and Portuguese colonists in the Americas through the colonial period that the colonies in the New World existed to enrich Spain and Portugal. As a result of this conception, much of Latin America's wealth was drained away through Spain and Portugal to Europe, where it helped to stimulate the rise of capitalism.

Mestizo. An individual of mixed Spanish and indigenous descent.

Mita. A term used in the Andean region of Latin America to describe the indigenous system of draft rotary labor that was adopted and adapted by the area's Spanish conquerors to carry out public works or to work the lands of the landowner. While the *mita* system used by the Inca (one of the indigenous civilizations living in the area prior to the Spanish conquest) was built on the idea of reciprocity (workers were compensated for their labor), under the Spanish, workers were virtually slaves. (This labor-tribute obligation was referred to as the *repartimiento* in other areas of Spanish America.)

Mulatto. An individual of mixed European and African descent.

Narcotrafficking. Also known as drug trafficking, narcotrafficking became increasingly prevalent in Latin America, and involved increasing numbers of Latin Americans, in the late twentieth century. Cocaine production and trafficking in Latin America is particularly significant. Cocaine production involves various steps: in general, coca is grown on small peasant farms by poor farmers (mainly in Colombia, Peru, and Bolivia) for traders who process it (usually in Colombia) into its illegal drug form (cocaine), pack it, and export it through smuggling networks in Mexico and the islands of the Caribbean for sale on the streets of U.S. and European cities. Drug trafficking has evolved into an extremely lucrative and violent activity in many countries of the region, and Latin American and U.S. efforts to curb it have most often been unsuccessful. The issue is complicated by the fact that coca is an ideal cash crop for many in the Andean region, as it is easy to grow, produces a number of harvests a year, and is highly profitable. Further, the coca leaf is a beneficial product that has played an integral role in traditional Andean culture; it has been used for centuries in rituals, to combat the effects of high altitude, and to stave off hunger and fatigue during long periods of work. (See **Drugs**, Colombia; **Drugs/Drug Trafficking**, Peru; **Drugs**, Appendix 2.)

Nationalism. Nationalism is a fundamental force in Latin American domestic politics and foreign policy. It is usually defined as a group consciousness in which individuals identify themselves with and give supreme loyalty to the abstraction of the nation, which reinforces the state as the ultimate source of authority and legitimacy. Those espousing nationalism may use it to attempt to attain control of the state and its authority, claiming to speak for the nation in order to gain political advantage. Nationalism in Latin American countries is complex and may assume multiple ideologies and loyalties even within individual nations.

Nationalization. The process by which private assets are transferred to public ownership; that is, the process by which control or ownership (often of large corporations) is transferred from the private sector and invested in the national government of a country. (Contrast with **Privatization**.)

Neoliberalism. The philosophy behind a specific type of economic restructuring and reform employed in many countries of Latin America beginning in the late 1980s to bring them out of their "lost decade" of economic crisis. Neoliberalism involves the introduction of economic stabilization measures and structural reforms, in short, the "marketization" of economic decision making: stabilization of the currency (through removing most exchange rate controls), trade liberalization and the reorientation of production toward the world market, deregulation of private activity, privatization of state enterprises, downsizing of the state and the elimination of subsidies and price controls, and fiscal austerity. (See **Washington Consensus**, Appendix 2.)

Organization of Petroleum Exporting Countries (OPEC). Originally the inspiration of Venezuela and Iran, the Organization of Petroleum Exporting Countries (OPEC) is an intergovernmental organization created in 1960 in reaction to the pricing and production policies of the big oil companies in 1959 and 1960. OPEC comprises Algeria, Gabon, Indonesia, Iran, Iraq, Kuwait, Libya, Nigeria, Qatar, Saudi Arabia, United Arab Emirates, and Venezuela. While member countries attempt to set oil prices and determine production and sales policies through coordination, the organization has yet to develop an effective formula for cooperation among its members.

Peninsulares. Europeans born in Spain or Portugal living in the New World; often colonial officials.

Populism. Latin American populism first emerged during the 1930s and 1940s in the larger Latin American nations, drawing its support from an urban constituency in the midst of early industrialization. Populism is an exercise in charismatic and personalistic leadership heavily dependent on a single person (rather than on sophisticated political party organizations) for cohesion. It is generally manipulative in style, nationalist in sentiment, and massive in appeal. The goal of some of the populists who came to power in Latin America in the 1940s, like some who followed them, was economic gain for themselves and for the groups that supported them (in the 1940s, urban entrepreneurs and workers). (Two prototypical populists are Juan Domingo **Perón** [see Argentina] and Getúlio **Vargas** [see Brazil].)

Privatization. The process by which public assets are transferred to the private sector by sale or contracting out; that is, the process by which control or ownership (often of large corporations) is transferred from the national government of a country and invested in private hands. (Contrast with **Nationalization**.)

Purchasing power parity (PPP). The theory of purchasing power parity (PPP) holds that the same goods should sell for the same relative price in different countries when measured in a common currency. PPP is a method of measuring the relative purchasing power of different countries' currencies over the same types of goods and services with the goal of producing accurate comparisons of price levels and real income standards of living across countries. It is calculated by converting different countries' currencies into a common currency. (While PPP estimates use price comparisons of comparable items, since not all items can be matched exactly across countries and time, the estimates are not always completely accurate.)

Repartimiento. Utilized in Latin America during the colonial period, the *repartimiento* followed (and was similar to) the *encomienda* system. The *repartimiento* divided the indigenous labor force in an ad hoc manner, for short periods of time, among Spanish entrepreneurs in the Americas in rough proportion to the needs of those entrepreneurs; these entrepreneurs then exploited that Indian labor force in profit-making enterprises such as construction, mining, ranching, and, later, textiles. (This forced labor system was referred to as the *mita* in the Andean region.)

Social movements. Social movements aimed at restoring, broadening, and deepening democracy were important throughout Latin America in the 1980s and 1990s as many nations of the region transitioned to and tried to consolidate democracy. Social movements form when diverse organizations such as political parties, trade unions, employers' associations, students, and or a host of other groups coalesce in loosely organized efforts to pressure political regimes and to lobby, for example, for respect for citizenship and civil rights. Following transitions to democracy, in many Latin American countries, social movements remained active to push for social reform measures, or policies that would increase economic equality and popular participation in the political process.

Socialism. A political and economic theory or system of social organization based on collective or state ownership of the means of production, distribution, and exchange. Like capitalism, socialism takes many and diverse forms and is a continually developing concept.

Viceroyalties. The regions into which the New World was separated by the Spanish crown in the sixteenth through eighteenth centuries. The initial two vice royalties (with their capitals in Mexico City and Lima) were eventually further divided. Viceroys were appointed by the crown to govern these areas.

World Bank (International Bank for Reconstruction and Development). The Washington-based World Bank group of institutions comprises the International Bank for Reconstruction and Development (established in 1945) and its affiliates, the International Development Association (established in 1960), the International Finance Corporation (established in 1956), and the Multilateral Investment Guarantee Agency (established in 1988). Funded through their member countries, the common objective of these organizations is to help raise living standards in developing countries by channeling financial resources to them from developed countries. Between 1946 and 1990, international development banks loaned more than $100 billion to Latin American and the Caribbean, with the World Bank accounting for roughly 60 percent and the **Inter-American Development Bank** (IDB, see Appendix 2) 40 percent.

World Trade Organization (WTO). The Uruguay Round of multilateral trade negotiations under the auspices of the General Agreement on Tariffs and Trade (GATT) established the World Trade Organization (WTO) in 1995; the WTO replaced GATT as the global multilateral trade organization. The WTO aims to regulate international trade through an elaborate set of rules and regulations, and also includes a judicial branch that can hear and judge trade disputes. The organization is headquartered in Geneva, Switzerland.

Index

Contributors

EDITORIAL STAFF

DIANA KAPISZEWSKI, Editor
Diana holds a bachelor's degree in Spanish from Dartmouth College (1988), a master's degree in Spanish from Middlebury College (1991), a master's degree in Latin American Studies from Georgetown University (1994) and a master's degree in Political Science from U.C. Berkeley (2001). She served as Director for Academic Programs at Georgetown University's Center for Latin American Studies from August 1996 through May 2000, and is currently a doctoral student in the Department of Political Science at U.C. Berkeley.

ALEXANDER KAZAN, Assistant Editor
Alex holds a bachelor's degree in international relations from the University of California, Davis, and a master's degree in Latin American Studies from Georgetown University. He has worked at the Inter-American Development Bank and for the Political Database of the Americas, a project of the Organization of American States and Georgetown University. He is currently the Latin America analyst for the G-7 Group. He is a contributing author to *Social Protection for Equity and Growth* (Johns Hopkins/Inter-American Development Bank, 2000).

RACHEL HARVEY, Formatting Assistant
Rachel holds a Bachelor of Science in Foreign Service from Georgetown University and is currently a Juris Doctor candidate in the Levin College of Law at the University of Florida.

CONTRIBUTORS

JOANNA BONARRIVA (Contributing author, chapter on Peru) Analyst, International Trade Commission, U.S. Government

INGRID CARLSON (Contributing author, chapter on Venezuela) Consultant, Public Policy Management and Transportation Network, Regional Policy Dialogue, Inter-American Development Bank

OSCAR CRUZ (Contributing author, chapter on Uruguay) Latin American Programs Coordinator, International Programs, Center for Civic Education

AMANDA CURTIS (Contributing author, chapter on Cuba) Presidential Management Intern, Office of Caribbean Affairs, Bureau of Western Hemisphere Affairs, U.S. Department of State

AMY EINSPAHR (Contributing author, chapter on Costa Rica) Master's candidate, Center for Latin American Studies, Georgetown University

RACHEL HARVEY (Contributing author, chapters on Dominican Republic, Ecuador, and Paraguay) See above.

KIM HEALEY (Contributing author, chapter on Mexico) Analyst, U.S. Government

MARISABEL IRIZARRY (Contributing author, chapter on Puerto Rico) Office Manager, Center for the Support of Native Lands

ALEXANDER KAZAN (Contributing author, chapters on Bolivia and Chile; contributing editor, chapters on Costa Rica, El Salvador, Guatemala, Honduras, Nicaragua, and Panama) See above.

AMY MCKEE (Author, chapter on Nicaragua; contributing author, chapter on Panama) Human Rights Analyst, U.S. Government

MARYELLEN MCQUADE (Contributing author, chapters on Colombia, Costa Rica, Mexico, Panama, and Paraguay) Independent consultant

SHARON PHILBLAD (Contributing author, chapters on Guatemala, Puerto Rico, Uruguay, and Venezuela) Analyst, Department of Defense, U.S. Government

MATTHEW ROBIDA (Contributing author, chapter on Argentina) Managing Consultant, Blueframe Group, LLC

HILLEL SOIFER (Contributing author, chapter on Colombia) Doctoral student, Department of Government, Harvard University

JEFFREY TAGGART (Contributing author, chapters on Argentina, Dominican Republic, and Honduras; author, Introduction) Program Manager for Latin American Programs, National Association of Homebuilders Research Center

CAROLINE TIMBERS (Author, chapters on Brazil and Haiti; contributing author, chapters on Bolivia and El Salvador) Director of Archives, Fundação Internacional de Capoeira Angola

ELIZABETH VICENS (Contributing author, chapter on Guatemala) Consultant, New York-based consulting firm

ACADEMIC ADVISORY BOARD

JOHN BAILEY, Professor of Government, Georgetown University

MARC CHERNICK, Adjunct Professor of Government, Georgetown University

GILLIAN GUNN CLISSOLD, Director, Caribbean Project, Center for Latin American Studies, Georgetown University

RAMÓN DAUBON, Associate, Kettering Foundation; Executive Director, Caribbean Environment and Development Institute (San Juan, Puerto Rico)

ERICK LANGER, Associate Professor of History, Georgetown University

MICHAEL SHIFTER, Adjunct Professor of Latin American Studies, Georgetown University, Senior Fellow, Inter-American Dialogue

PETER SIAVELIS, Assistant Professor of Politics, Wake Forest University

Special thanks to Christopher Cardona (Doctoral student, Department of Political Science, U.C. Berkeley) and Sally Roever (Doctoral student, Department of Political Science, U.C. Berkeley).